1

HORROR FILMS
OF THE 1970S

HORROR FILMS OF THE 1970s

John Kenneth Muir

Volume 1
*(Acknowledgments; Introduction; Part I;
Part II: 1970–1975)*

McFarland & Company, Inc., Publishers
Jefferson, North Carolina, and London

The present work is a reprint of the illustrated casebound edition of Horror Films of the 1970s, *first published in 2002 by McFarland.*

Volume 1

LIBRARY OF CONGRESS CATALOGUING-IN-PUBLICATION DATA

Muir, John Kenneth, 1969–
Horror films of the 1970s / John Kenneth Muir.
p.   cm.
Includes bibliographical references and index.

2 volume set—
ISBN-13: 978-0-7864-3104-5
softcover : 50# alkaline paper ∞

1. Horror films— United States— History and criticism.
I. Title.
PN1995.9.H6M85   2008   791.43'614 — dc21   2002006759

British Library cataloguing data are available

On the cover: *It's Alive* (1973)

Manufactured in the United States of America

*McFarland & Company, Inc., Publishers
Box 611, Jefferson, North Carolina 28640
www.mcfarlandpub.com*

For Ken and Loretta,
who took me to the drive-in to see *Boggy Creek*
and have encouraged me always.

Acknowledgments

This author wishes to thank the following people for their assistance and support in the shaping and development of this text: Kathryn Muir, Bill Latham, Johnny Byrne, Teddy Tenenbaum, Steve Hockensmith, Mateo Latosa, Robert, Tom, and Greg. Thanks, folks!

Contents

1975

• Volume 2 •

1976

1977

1978

1979

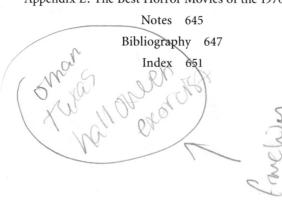

Introduction

We've all heard the axiom that "art imitates life," and most of us have a pretty good idea what it signifies. *Art does not exist in a vacuum.* Instead, it is inexorably bound to the time period from which it sprang. Sometimes an insight into a social or historical context in a work of art is entirely coincidental, arising from a set of understandings unknown even to the artist who rendered it. But more often than not there is *intent* in art to reflect, compare, reveal, contrast or echo some important element of the creator's universe.

Another truism, one hoisted from the darker side of the aesthetic shelf, might offer an ancillary proclamation. Specifically, horror films have always mirrored the fears and anxieties of their "real life" epochs.

In the 1930s, protean genre films such as *Dracula* (1931) and *King Kong* (1933) represented a form of "escapism" for adventure-hungry and romance-starved audiences seeking to forget the daily drags and vicissitudes of the Great Depression. Likewise, 1950s era horror gems such as *Them!* (1955), which concerned radiation-spawned giant ants, played on the not-so-hidden fears of the American audience that its own government had opened up a deadly Pandora's box by splitting the atom. In the same era, *Invasion of the Body Snatchers* (1956) was viewed by many prominent critics as a thinly veiled indictment of Communism, a particularly timely target considering the pitch of the Cold War with America's competitor, the Soviet Union, and the rampant paranoia of the McCarthy age.

Not surprisingly, the same paradigm proves true for yet another decade of the turbulent twentieth century: the "free-wheeling" 1970s. The myriad horror films of the disco era likewise represent a catalog of that time's mortal dreads and anxieties. Perhaps the only real significant difference between the 1930s or 1950s and the 1970s, however, is the sheer number of fears and apprehensions being evinced by the horror films of the period. Bluntly expressed, there was a lot more to be afraid about in the seventies.

Consider that the decade found people, and especially Americans, anxious about virtually every aspect of contemporary life. What was to be a woman's role in American society during the post-hippie, women's lib, bicentennial world? *The Stepford Wives* (1975) offered one nightmarish answer. What was to be the up-shot of all the random violence in the streets, and the worst crime rates in recorded American history? Stanley Kubrick's *A Clockwork Orange* (1971) had a few thoughts about that subject. Could the average citizen's inadvertent exposure to microwave ovens, industrial pollution, X-rays, a weakening ozone layer, or contaminated water alter the fundamental shape and evolution of human life? Larry Cohen's *It's Alive* (1973) explored that frightening notion.

Similarly, Robert Wise's *The Andromeda Strain* (1971) and Michael Crichton's *Westworld* (1972) fretted that man's escalating reliance on machines might prove his undoing. At the same time, *Frogs* (1972), *Night of the Lepus* (1972), *Squirm* (1976), *Day of the Animals* (1977), *Kingdom of the Spiders* (1977), *Empire of the Ants* (1977), *The Swarm* (1978), *Prophecy* (1979) and other '70s horror films about rampaging animals traded on different fears. Beneath the hokey special effects, these films reflected genuine audience trepidation that Mother Nature would not stand for man's continued pillaging and pollution of the Earth. These "eco-horrors" envisioned environmental apocalypse caused by humankind's own shortsightedness.

Even the innocence of the old *King Kong* was flipped on its head in the mid–1970s. The big-budget (and much loathed) 1976 remake of the 1930s classic found an American oil corporation (a surrogate for Exxon) exploiting Kong, like some natural resource, on a mission not of unbridled adventure and awesome exploration, but of imperialism and cynicism. Kong's new bride in the 1970s version was no innocent, either, but a struggling, opportunistic actress looking to find her fifteen minutes of fame.

And it didn't stop there.

The Watergate scandal and President Nixon's impeachment erupted in the early 1970s, and so the long-standing American pillar of "trust in government" soon crumbled to dust too. Consequently, horror films began to posit "evil" conspiracies at all levels of governmental bureaucracy. The town elders of Amity kept the beaches open in *Jaws* (1975) even though they knew a killer shark was prowling the waters off their coast. The doctors and politicos of *Coma* (1978) were responsible for a vast conspiracy exploiting the weak and rewarding only the rich and powerful. The presidential candidate of *The Clonus Horror* (1979) utilized living human clones as a bank of replacement body parts, and organized a cover-up to keep it under wraps ... all the while playing the public role of "populist." Ron Rosenbaum succinctly described the national mood in *Harpers Magazine* in September of 1979:

> Horror is here with us again. Even the White House has been haunted, as witness the rhetoric of Watergate; Alexander Haig's "sinister outside force," John Mitchell's "White House horrors," Howard Hunt's night-stalking "spooks," a secret list of illegal campaign contributions maintained by the President's secretary and known as "Rosemary's Baby"; a cover-up, of course, is a premature burial, impeachment an exorcism [1].

If political machinations were a major concern in the 1970s, then the widening divide between races was another. Accordingly "old," silver screen menaces such as Dracula and the Frankenstein monster were re-imagined during this decade as relevant "ethnic" ghouls in films with titles like *Blacula* (1972), *Scream Blacula Scream* (1973), *Blood Couple* (1973) *Blackenstein* (1973), *Black Werewolf* (1974), and *J.D.'s Revenge* (1976). The trend was quickly dubbed "blaxploitation," an unholy integration of the words "black" and "exploitation," and the sub-genre could not have been more aptly named. At the same time that white America was recognizing the economic potential of the black community at the box office, it also was selling the same community films that cast men of color as "monsters." And —*to gain the community's sympathy (and ticket money)*— Hollywood depicted these "villains" as being manipulated by a malevolent force known simply as the "Man." Hence heroic (and black) Rosey Grier became a misshapen monster when white Ray Milland's head was attached to his body in *The Thing with Two Heads* (1972), and so forth.

A deep-seated fear of "ethnicism" on the part of white America also played out in other major horror films, such as *The Possession of Joel Delaney* (1971), which saw Shirley MacLaine and her lily-white family implicitly "threatened" by the tenets of Puerto Rican faith and community.

The list of 1970s pre-occupations could go on for pages. Environmental, technological, sexual, governmental and ethnic fears all resulted in a slew of horror "mini-trends" in the 1970s. For instance, *Deliverance* (1972) and *Straw Dogs* (1971) orbited about a fundamental question: what does it mean to be "a man" in the eighth decade of the twentieth century? Remember, the 1970s were the dawn of Alan Alda, and the new age of "sensitive men," and these films might be viewed as a response to the developing expectation that men eschew "machismo" and "express" their emotions instead.

Seventies films such as *Frenzy* (1972), *The Last House on the Left* (1972), *The Texas Chainsaw Massacre* (1973), *The Hills Have Eyes* (1977), and *I Spit on Your Grave* (1978) were also more explicit, and far more intense, than previous horror productions had been. This was the result of the "new freedom" in cinema to freely depict graphic violence and bloodletting, and a shift to the paradigm of existential "realism" over the romantic "supernatural." These films are representative of what horror historians term "savage cinema," and they are wholly unique to the 1970s.

And what was to be the cumulative effect of so much intense questioning and fear about so many important topics, as well as such straight-faced glimpses of random violence (influenced, no doubt, by TV news footage of the Vietnam conflict)? Well, the fear shaped a decade filled with President Bush's (Sr.) so-called "malaise days." The president was referring specifically to the economy and American confidence when he coined that memorable phrase, but he might as well have been talking about the general anxiety that swept the nation before the dawning of the "Don't Worry, Be Happy," yuppified 1980s.

One direct result of the anxiety-ridden 1970s was a retreat from the issues. After the sexual and drug revolutions of the late '60s and early '70s, many Americans were left feeling empty, de-valued and bereft of the moral values that had comforted previous generations. Accordingly, some people retreated to religion, to the Christian values that had guided life in the United States for generations. But this was, lest we forget, the 1970s, not the 1950s. Many well-educated American citizens found they simply couldn't go home again; that the old ideas of good and evil, black and white, and absolutes simply didn't stand up to scrutiny in the wake of new discoveries about evolution, genetics and history. Religion was no longer the shelter some imagined.

Seizing on this spiritual doubt and vulnerability was another blockbuster movie trend of the 1970s, the religious horror film. *The Exorcist* (1973), *Beyond the Door* (1975), *The Omen* (1976), *The Sentinel* (1977), *Damien— Omen II* (1978) and many, many more found stark terror in the concept that the Devil was real, and that mankind's eternal soul was in jeopardy from demonic possession and the Antichrist, among other iconic bogeyman. Religious authorities should have been delighted that Hollywood was re-opening the debate about good versus evil, but most evangelicals were appalled by these films because they suggested that the Church was corrupt, and the Devil unbeatable. *The Blood on Satan's Claw* (1970), *Asylum of Satan* (1971), *The Brotherhood of Satan* (1971), *Daughters of Satan* (1972), *The Devil's Rain* (1975), *A Touch of Satan* (1973), *Race with the Devil* (1975), *Lisa and the Devil* (1975), *The Omen* (1976), *Damien — Omen II* (1978) and other "Devil" films culminated in stalemates, or with evil forces out and out victorious. That result —*in the eyes of some*— was akin to heresy.

Billy Graham, for one, railed against *The Exorcist*, claiming that William Friedkin's film was responsible for real-life instances of demonic possession, and Paul Leggett wrote the following in *Christianity Today*:

> The devil, it seems is upon us. That is, if the mass media is to be believed…. While we should criticize the current excesses of the Gothic film, we should also heed its warnings. These films may only be reflecting our present moral climate. Why has the triumph of evil apparently become a resounding symbol of our time?… Part of the answer lies with the incessant accounts of war, corruption, and torture that seem to be destined to dominate the news for the remainder of this century [2].

In other words, a godless people — or even a questioning people — get the godless films they deserve. Art imitates life. Again.

Interestingly, all the debating and doubting about spirituality had another side-effect on '70s horror cinema. Those who could no longer find adequate comfort in a Catholic structure to the universe were treated to another sub-genre of horror flicks: the non-explanation genre picture. Peter Weir's *Picnic at Hanging Rock* (1975) highlighted a wondrous mystery, a disappearance of several schoolgirls in the rugged Australian wilderness, which could

never be solved in satisfactory "human" terms. In this case, law enforcement, science, and even reason could not solve the mystery, let alone explain it.

Similarly John Carpenter's *Halloween* (1978) showcased a villain, Michael Myers, who could not be diagnosed, contained, stopped, killed or likewise explained or understood. It seems fair to argue, then, that in the seventies, people were so frightened about the future that they began to sense that there were *no answers* out there in the universe to be had at all. Hence this brand of horror film.

Why were people so worried in the 1970s that their horror films reflected not one or two, but this whole multitude of uncertainties? The answers are many. Some writers, including the Irish poet Johnny Byrne, have called the 1970s the "wake-up" after the hippie dream. Look at how David Frum, author of *How We Got Here: The 70's — The Decade That Brought You Modern Life (For Better or Worse)*, described the time:

> They were strange feverish years, the 1970s. They were a time of unease and despair, punctuated by disaster. The murder of athletes at the 1972 Olympic games. Desert emirates cutting off America's oil. Military humiliation in Indochina. Criminals taking control of America's streets. The dollar plunging in value. Marriages collapsing. Drugs for sale in every high school. A president toppled from office. The worst economic slump since the great Depression, followed four years later by the second-worst slump since the Depression. The U.S. Government baffled as its diplomats are taken hostage. And in the background loomed still wilder and stranger alarms and panics. The ice age was returning. Killer bees were swarming up across the Rio Grande. The world was running out of natural resources. Kahoutek's comet was hurtling toward the planet. Epidemic swine flu would carry off millions of elderly people… [3].

That's quite a list of bugaboos, and it is important to remember that Frum is a cultural warrior as well as a historian, a Reagan revolutionary and ardent conservative of the highest stripe. Still, his reading of the time period is not so skewed (though he fails to mention the good aspects of the decade).

In fact, if one were looking objectively at the time, one might be tempted to write of the 1970s as the best of times *and* the worst of times. Though America celebrated its bicentennial birthday and flew high with the Apollo space program, it also faced the many deep-seated concerns listed above. The Vietnam War, the energy crisis, double-digit inflation, and the hostage situation in Iran were just a few of the disturbing news stories.

Importantly, the decade also began with a dearth (and the deaths) of principled leadership, following the assassinations of Robert Kennedy and Martin Luther King, Jr. These figures of greatness seemed to be replaced, strangely enough, by "celebrity" monsters like mad-dog Charles Manson, the insane Son of Sam, the thuggish Gordon Liddy, and powerful corruption personified, Richard Nixon. It was a decade of controversy about everything from a woman's role in American society (remember the E.R.A.?) to her right to control her own body. This was the decade, after all, that *Roe vs. Wade* became, in the words of Attorney General John Ashcroft, "the settled law of the land." All of these events played out in the horror films of the day. Again and again, we can see cause and effect; life influencing art; art reflecting life.

Basically, the world just looked a lot less certain in the 1970s than it had in the idealistic '60s, when many young Americans in college felt they could make a difference in the process, and genuinely contribute to a climate of "world peace." At home, Johnson's "Great Society" promised

an end to poverty and civil inequalities ... but welfare didn't seem to help, and poverty didn't go away either. So the seventies were the end of many great dreams, a time of deep questioning and uncertainties, before America moved on to something else (the accumulation of wealth and the dependence again on traditional religious values in the Reagan '80s). The seventies were a decade of pause, of introspection. At least that is one good thing that can be said of the seventies, that these issues were being explored, not repressed or swept under the carpet. People were afraid of change, yes, but they were introspective too, willing to look into themselves and to the facts of life that seemed so scary. Horror directors, especially, took advantage of this time of doubt. As director of the documentary *The American Nightmare*, Adam Simon, has noted of horror's capacity to comment on society:

> Horror as a genre, when it's done honestly, when it's done with serious intent, will naturally be open to the traumas of the world in ways that other genres aren't and can't be. Somehow by being focused on what disturbs us, especially if it's being done by somebody who's sort of determined to search their own soul for what's disturbing ... then it will naturally convey truths— universal ones, or at least national ones [4].

Looking back at those years between 1970 and 1979, one can detect it is the extended moment between utter idealism (the '60s) and utter conservative retrenchment (the '80s) in American history, the moment between the Peace Corps mentality and the yuppie mentality. As a nation, American went from being a country that wanted to help the world to a country whose populace wanted better stock options. The seventies are the bridge between those disparate mind-states, and the decade's many clever horror films capitalized

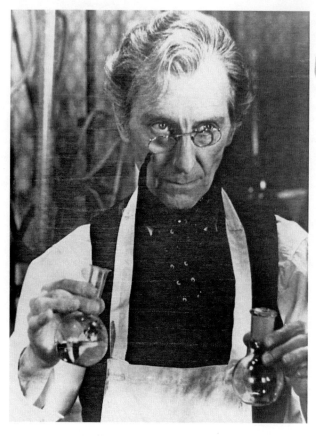

Horror movies of the 1970s can be divided into two categories: those that starred Peter Cushing (pictured here in *Curse of Frankenstein* [1957]), and those that didn't.

dignity and restraint, two factors not always found in the horror genre. As much as Nixon, the Devil and Vietnam are responsible for the look and feel of horror cinema, so, perhaps, is Peter Cushing, a true icon of the genre. Whether the villainous Dr. Frankenstein or the heroic vampire killer, Van Helsing, Cushing left an indelible mark on a genre he helped to redefine.

But beyond the joke about the ubiquitous Peter Cushing, this text is designed to categorize and review, often at length, many of the most interesting, meaningful and bizarre horror films that were produced in the 1970s, and note why they are special to their time period. Though the focus is generally on American films, this text also charts representative horror films from other countries, especially those that found favor in theaters on U.S. shores. In this regard, England is surely the undisputed champion of horror production in the 1970s, and Hammer Studios and Amicus both contributed many fine genre works during this, their twilight decade. In Italy, artists like Mario Bava and Dario Argento were toiling to re-invent the look and feel of horror (usually with a lot of the red stuff...), and in Australia directors such as Peter Weir and Richard Franklin were adopting the same mission. Canada, the home of David Cronenberg, is represented here as well, as are some unique works from Spain and Germany.

on the looming sense of transition to highlight the national and universal truths Simon writes about. The old notions of patriotism, trust in government, trust in science, trust in technology, and trust in law enforcement, were evaporating ... and that left audiences disturbed and unsettled. Their entertainment looked much the same way, at least in the horror genre (and particularly pre–*Star Wars* [1977]).

In much less high-minded terms, horror films of the 1970s can be split into distinct categories: those that star British Peter Cushing (1913–1994) and those that don't. Seriously, this gentlemanly actor was in more horror films than any man in history ... and the world is probably better for it, since his screen presence is one of

There will no doubt be some readers who flip through the pages of this book and ask why every single horror movie in the world made between 1970 and 1979 is not included. The problem is, simply, that some seventies horrors films have never been released on the home video market, are not currently available, or have disappeared from the face of the Earth all together. The author has endeavored to be as complete as possible in tracking down "signature" horror films of the 1970s, but there are no doubt other genre jewels out there in video store clearance bins, just waiting to be re-discovered and re-evaluated. This book is a beginning point for researchers, but no doubt the last word on the subject has yet to be written.

So let's boogie…

I

The History of the Decade (in Brief...)

What a decade it was! Unlike the paranoid 1950s, or the conformist 1980s (a decade in which a new slasher movie seemed to arrive in theaters every week), the 1970s represented a truly eclectic time in the annals of horror cinema. This was a reflection, perhaps, of how life was growing more complex in the '70s, with competing problems tugging audiences towards different dreads.

Some horror pictures of the 1970s were revolutionary, based on the fresh precepts of a freer, more personal cinema (which also gave rise to films like *Easy Rider* [1969]). Other horrors were merely old hat: toothless resurrections and variations on monsters who had appeared on the silver screen, in one form or another, since the 1930s and 1940s. What a decade, and what a mixed bag of tricks and treats.

Hammer Time

England's Hammer Studios had been in operation since 1935 (founded by Enrique Carreras and Will "Hammer" Hinds), but its reputation as a horror studio of the highest caliber wasn't cemented until the late 1950s. *The Curse of Frankenstein* (1957), starring Peter Cushing, and *The Horror of Dracula,* starring Christopher Lee, became unexpected hits in England and abroad as the Eisenhower era wound down. Shepherded by Sir James Carreras (1909–1990), Hammer Studios' "niche" in the horror market was soon pinpointed: colorful period horror films drenched in garish red blood and populated by scantily clad, buxom women. The studio's films also countenanced top-quality production values, so it was no surprise when Hammer quickly became a world leader in the genre and remained perched there throughout the 1960s. Good sets, pioneering special effects, likable actors, gorgeous women and technicolor blood made for fun, chilling viewing.

Throughout the late fifties and early '60s, Hammer Studios unveiled a barrage of sequels to its popular *Dracula* and *Frankenstein* films. Titles included *Revenge of Frankenstein* (1958), *Brides of Dracula* (1960), *Dracula — Prince of Darkness* (1966), *Frankenstein Created Woman* (1966), *Dracula*

Has Risen from the Grave (1968) and *Taste the Blood of Dracula* (1969). But, as is so often the case when sequels are involved, this was an instance of genre franchises going to the well once (or several times…) too often.

By the advent of the 1970s, the British Hammer films were showing the warning signs of age, and some serious quality slippage. James Carreras retired from the entertainment industry in 1972, and Michael Carreras, grandson of Enrique, reigned as studio head. By now, the *Dracula* and *Frankenstein* series were growing long in the tooth, well over a dozen years old. The recipe for continued profitability? *New blood.*

To re-invigorate their profitable "monster" lines, Hammer went to extraordinary lengths to "re-vamp" them, particularly its leading franchise, *Dracula. Dracula A.D. 1972* (1972) brought the vampire (once again portrayed by imposing Christopher Lee) into the swinging seventies to menace a group of "mod" teenagers. The film, directed by Alan Gibson, had some fine moments of comedy and wit, but never overcame the big disappointment that Dracula didn't get to interact with his new locale (and time period). Though surrounded by beauties like Caroline Munro, the vampire never escaped a ruined church to find himself in "hip" London, surely a grave miscalculation in the screenplay. Still, the film was not without merit, and Peter Cushing was back as a descendant of Van Helsing, while his granddaughter was portrayed by fetching Stephanie Beacham.

The next entry in the franchise was probably the worst of the long-lived saga. *The Satanic Rites of Dracula* (1973) transformed the Transylvanian count into the corporate head of a 20th century business venture. Dracula's plan for apocalypse involved the unleashing of a new bubonic plague on mankind. The film, again directed by Gibson, broke from Hammer tradition by introducing a "speaking" Dracula. In previous entries Lee had remained a hulking, hissing, but mostly silent, presence of darkness.

Neither of these '70s *Dracula* films were well-regarded by series fans, or particularly successful at the box office, and a dissatisfied Christopher Lee retired from the role that had made him a celebrity. The last Hammer *Dracula* film of the decade, *The Legend of 7 Golden Vampires* (1974), recast Dracula as the less-than-charismatic John Forbes-Robinson. And, taking the franchise further from its horror roots, the movie was a Chinese co-production, a "martial arts" vampire film packed with wall-to-wall karate moves and kung-fu fighting. Peter Cushing returned as Van Helsing (a welcome constant in the series…), and the film was quite an entertaining one, an improvement over *Satanic Rites.* Unfortunately, *Legend* was cut badly for distribution in the United States and received only limited release on this side of the Atlantic. It was even re-titled as *The Seven Brothers Meet Dracula.*

Hammer's *Dracula* series, horror trendsetter in the late '50s and the '60s, had come to smack of desperation in the seventies. The central conceit of *Dracula A.D. 1972* (vampire dwelling in contemporary society) had already been done in the States as *Count Yorga, Vampire* (1970). *The Satanic Rites of Dracula* smelled like a bad James Bond film, or an episode of the British television series *The Avengers* (1961–68), and *Legend of 7 Golden Vampires* hopped willy-nilly on the kung-fu bandwagon popularized by star Bruce Lee. All the abrupt format shifts represented an inauspicious close to a franchise that had once seemed immortal.

Hammer's *Frankenstein* series showed far fewer overt signs of stress and slippage in the 1970s. Rather than casting aimlessly about for new formats to co-opt and popular film trends to emulate, the series remained faithful to its source material, while endlessly recycling the same plot. Invariably, mad Dr. Frankenstein (usually Peter Cushing) created a monster (either through stitching body parts, or in the case of *Frankenstein Must Be Destroyed* [1970], through brain transplants...). The monster then wreaked havoc, was consequently destroyed, and Frankenstein himself was killed ... only to pop up again in yet another sequel. As the decade wore on, the plots of the *Frankenstein* films grew increasingly farfetched and repetitive even though Cushing's performances never lost their luster. In *Frankenstein Must Be Destroyed*, the good doctor added rape to his list of atrocities, but beyond that kinky addition to the mix, this was another once-proud Hammer franchise in dire need of life-support.

Thanks to more intense horror films such as George A. Romero's *Night of the Living Dead* (1968), Roman Polanski's *Rosemary's Baby* (1968) and Tobe Hooper's *The Texas Chainsaw Massacre* (1974), the stately, even dignified films of Hammer Studios began to look old and out of date as the decade developed. Audiences of the 1970s hungered for something new and different, something that would more accurately echo their turbulent times, and Hammer was clearly in a rut. How many times could Dracula and Frankenstein be killed, and then revived? The resurrections were growing increasingly ludicrous, along with the narratives. In *Scars of Dracula* (1970), for instance, a bat swooped into the Transylvania castle and, with pinpoint precision, dripped blood onto Dracula's ashes to revive the ghoul ... a strangely convenient and contrived opening. The climaxes too, began to suffer from creative fatigue. By the time of Lee's final Hammer Drac film (*Satanic Rites*), Dracula had been electrocuted, impaled, killed by running water, destroyed by the sun, and (in the most silly climax of all), chased into a thorny

thicket(!?). Many of these bizarre sequences were beautifully orchestrated by British special effects magician Les Bowie, but the situations themselves were completely ludicrous.

In search of things new and different, Hammer Studios soon seized on a brilliant and timely notion: greater titillation. In the late '60s and early '70s, films of all genres were revealing increased glimpses of frontal nudity. Hammer thus subtracted the flowing diaphanous gowns from its formula and added some tasteful, implied lesbianism to go with the ramped-up nudity. In 1970, Hammer spawned a new horror franchise based on Sheridan Le Fanu's (1814–1873) novella *Carmilla*, which had originally been published in 1872. This story of a female vampire had been lensed on film before (Roger Vadim's *Blood and Roses* [1960]), but Hammer played up the lesbian and nudity angles, and in the process made a star of its lead vampire, the luscious Ingrid Pitt. After Pitt's entry in the series, *The Vampire Lovers* (1970), less charismatic leading ladies (like the cross-eyed Yutte Stensgaard) appeared in the *Carmilla* follow-ups *Lust for a Vampire* (1970) and *Twins of Evil* (1971). Invariably set at girls' schools with plenty of healthy female pulchritude abounding, these films recycled the vampire lore of the Dracula pictures while simultaneously offering plenty of opportunities for sensual massages, skinny-dipping and the like. Not that there's anything wrong with that...

On a far less prurient level, Hammer also began to experiment in the 1970s with some more adult, serious horror. *Demons of the Mind* (1972) and *Hands of the Ripper* (1971) were more gritty horror films about "monstrous" family legacies. In the former, an aristocratic family was cursed with madness and incest by a depraved patriarch, and in the latter, Jack the Ripper's daughter inherited her father's penchant for spilling blood. Both of these films played up psychology rather than blood and guts, and took a distinctly less romantic approach to the horrific material. Other films of the decade, including the psychological thriller *Fear in the Night* (1973) with Judy Geeson and Joan Collins, and *To the Devil a Daughter* (1976) starring Richard Widmark, failed to revitalize Hammer Studios. Coupled with the problems of the British film industry, and country-wide power outages, the studio collapsed into ruin before being resurrected in the 1980s as a purveyor of terror television.

Today, Hammer films boast a large cult following, and are generally very highly regarded among the genre faithful. Rumors have been flying about for years that remakes of Hammer's great horrors are on the way, though as of this writing, none have yet appeared. At the risk of alienating a very large and very vocal fan base, it seems fair to state that Hammer's best days were in the late '50s and early '60s, and that some of its 1970s productions feel like rehashes from the Studio's glory days. By the same token, Hammer's desperation in the '70s resulted in some fine experimentation, and the Carmilla films are light, fun and erotic ones, while *Demons of the Mind* and *The Hands of the Ripper* are exceedingly interesting and valuable works that probably deserve greater recognition than the *Frankenstein* and *Dracula* sequels of the '70s.

Amicus Briefs

If Hammer faced a challenge cornering the largest share of the horror market in the early 1970s, it was no doubt because competition was springing up everywhere, on both sides of the Atlantic. In America, AIP (American International Pictures) and Samuel J. Arkoff were cranking out horror films left and right, and in Great Britain, Hammer found itself vying for superiority with Amicus, a studio formed by two American producers, Milton Subotsky (1921–1991) and Max J. Rosenberg, in the mid 1960s. Adding insult to injury, Amicus conscripted some of Hammer's biggest talent, including the ubiquitous Peter Cushing, for their adventures in the macabre.

Differentiating itself from Hammer, Amicus concentrated (in the '70s) on a series of droll horror anthologies. *Tales from the Crypt* (1972) and its sequel *Vault of Horror* (1973) were based on the popular American comic books published by Bill Gaines and E.C. comics, and the films adapted several stories straight from that source. In *Tales from the Crypt*, Joan Collins faced a diabolical Santa Claus in "And All Through The House," but the standout "episode" of the film was its climax, "Blind Alleys," which saw a cruel administrator forced to navigate a narrow corridor lined with razor blades. After viewing the HBO series of *Tales from the Crypt* in the late '80s and early '90s, with its animated puppet Cryptkeeper, it's something of a shock to look back at Amicus's *Crypt*, which puts dignified Ralph Richardson in the role of the decaying "creep."

Asylum (1972) was another Amicus anthology, this time of stories penned by horror legend Robert "*Psycho*" Bloch. Herbert Lom, Barry Morse, Britt Ekland, Peter Cushing (again!) and Barbara Parkins were among the inmates who had gruesome — and horrifying — stories to recount. The anthology *From Beyond the Grave* (1973), directed by Kevin Connor, featured more ghoulish "shorts," this time revolving around a devilish antique store run by, *guess who* — Peter Cushing. Before Amicus was done, Donald Pleasence, Ian Hendry, Joan Collins, Herbert Lom, Jon Pertwee, Ingrid Pitt, and other genre veterans populated their films, which were inevitably of good humor, and somewhat lighter than the dour Hammer offerings.

In the non-anthology category, Amicus also had (in a venture with AIP) what

Britain's Amicus Films released a number of horror anthologies in the 1970s, including *The House That Dripped Blood* (1972), starring Jon Pertwee (pictured).

was probably the coup of the decade. It cast Peter Cushing, Vincent Price and Christopher Lee in *Scream and Scream Again* (1970), a macabre film about body part replacements and strange surgeries. Though the film was somewhat muddled and the three actors never actually shared a scene together, having these three popular horror stars in one film was a major marquee attraction of the decade.

By the mid 1970s, Amicus had sidestepped out of horror with adaptations of Edgar Rice Burroughs' adventures (*The Land That Time Forgot* [1974], *At the Earth's Core* [1976]), and *The People That Time Forgot* [1977], all directed by Kevin Connor). Though these films were quite successful in America, Amicus folded in late 1977 when producers Rosenberg and Subotsky parted company. Subotsky con-

tinued to be a voice in American horror films in the 1980s, but his name may forever be associated with Amicus (and with the two AARU *Doctor Who* feature films he produced in the late '60s).

Frankenstein and Dracula (Unbound)

In the 1970s, Hammer wasn't the only studio attempting to breathe life into the old monsters that had proven so successful at scaring audiences in the 1930s and 1940s. American International Pictures and Samuel Z. Arkoff were also intent on seeing these legends re-born, and milking their potential for box office. To that end, AIP released a plethora of horror films that reinterpreted the monsters of yesteryear with new, sometimes quite odd, twists.

Blacula (1972) was part of the seventies trend of "blaxploitation," the re-casting of famous "white" ghouls as black icons instead. Starring William Marshall, *Blacula* was the tale of a regal African prince "enslaved" by Count Dracula during a diplomatic visit to Transylvania (designed, incidentally, to curb the slave trade...). After centuries locked away in his coffin, the vampirized Blacula was awakened in the twentieth century by two gay antique dealers. Unlike Dracula, Blacula was only mildly villainous, and his purpose in our world was to reunite with the reincarnation of his beloved princess. By the climax of *Blacula*, most audience members were cheering for him to defeat the police authorities (whites, it goes without saying...) and other enemies. The final moments of the film were actually touching, as Blacula chose a dignified death — suicide by sunlight — rather than eternal life without his beloved.

In the sequel, *Scream Blacula Scream* (1973), Blacula was, again, concerned primarily with lifting the curse that made him a servant of evil. To this end, he recruited voodoo priestess Pam Grier. Again, Blacula was depicted as a vampire anti-hero, and audiences loved him.

Far less successful thematically and financially was AIP's one hundredth film (1), a re-casting of *Frankenstein* in the blaxploitation mold. *Blackenstein: The Black Frankenstein* (1973), as it was named, was the story of a Vietnam veteran and amputee who was given surgical replacements by the white "Dr. Stein." In a twist, it was an African-America lab assistant who sabotaged the experiment, turning the vet into a monster. Crippled by a low-budget, weak acting, and an indifferent screenplay (which just seemed to stop mid-way through the film), *Blackenstein* turned out to be something of a bomb.

More interesting, and much more unusual was Bill Gunn's artful updating of the vampire myth in general, *Blood Couple* (1973), which starred *Night of the Living Dead*'s Duane Jones as a wealthy black man who became a vampire, and in the process, started to "feed" on the black community. A highly symbolic film filled with Christian and non–Christian imagery, Gunn's picture was known in some circles as *Ganja and Hess*, and it drew a very clear metaphor between vampirism and drug addiction. The film was a challenging one that received less coverage than it deserved, though it has been re-evaluated today.

The vampire myth was also "resurrected" under the AIP banner in *Count Yorga, Vampire* (1970) and its sequel *The Return of Count Yorga* (1972), two films starring Robert Quarry as a modern-day vampire dwelling in trendy California. Quarry portrayed a particularly down-to-earth creature of the night in each franchise entry, and interestingly the first film had begun production as a low-budget ($64,000) soft-core porno movie (2)! That inauspicious beginning may have resulted in the final film's fascinating sleazy quality. In Los Angeles of the 1970s, Yorga was just another strange "creature of the night," and Quarry played him as a combination of a playboy, sugar daddy, and cult leader. In the second film, his primary task was to seduce a young Mariette Hartley.

The sexual side of the old movie monsters was not slighted in other 1970s films, either. Andy Warhol, the unusual pop artist celebrated in the late '60s and early '70s, produced two low-budget features *Andy Warhol's Dracula* (1974) and *Andy Warhol's Frankenstein* (1974), both directed by Paul Morrissey. These films featured screenplays that appeared to be improvised, and were envisioned as sex romps as much as horror films. Udo Kier starred as Dracula in the former and Dr. Frankenstein in the latter picture (shot in 3-D), and became a cult figure for his impenetrable (and often humorous) accent. In both films, Kier was opposed by the hunky but dim Joe Dallesandro, and surrounded by a bevy of scantily clad ladies who had no inhibitions about baring it all for the project.

In *Andy Warhol's Dracula,* Kier portrayed a crippled Count searching for Italian virgins to "drink from," and in *Frankenstein,* he was a craven mad-doctor seeking to assemble perfect bodies. The biggest stumbling block for Kier's Dr. Frankenstein was that he had an unfortunate habit of cutting open his cadavers and making love to their innards...

As the decade rolled on, even more controversial versions of the Dracula legend continued to appear. In 1970, prolific European filmmaker Jess Franco (1930–) undertook a difficult task. His *El Conde Dracula* promised to be a faithful version of Bram Stoker's novel, but offered mostly boredom, despite a powerful performance by Christopher Lee. Herbert Lom portrayed Van Helsing, and Klaus Kinski was Renfield, but Franco just didn't possess the directing chops (or the budget) to make the film fly. In one of the film's crazier sequences, a group of stuffed (and mounted) animal carcasses come to life, but the special effects are amateurish, and Franco generates no chills by continuously zooming in and out on the inanimate critters. The scene, like many in the film, goes on at embarrassing length.

In 1979, John Badham, the director of *Saturday Night Fever* (1977), re-imagined the famous vampire Count yet again in yet another adaptation of *Dracula.* This time Dracula was portrayed as a dashing, perfectly coiffed romantic hero with an open shirt and a hairy chest. Frank Langella played the title role with enthusiasm, accenting the character's sexual appeal over the more horrific aspects of life as a vampire. Laurence Olivier played his nemesis,

Van Helsing, and Kate Nelligan his intended.

Werner Herzog also resurrected Dracula, in slightly different fashion, in *Nosferatu* (1979), an artsy re-make of the 1922 silent film by Murnau. Klaus Kinski portrayed the rat-like vampire, and Isabelle Adjani (*Diabolique* [1995]) was his prey. The film had a fine sense of place and time, and used hundreds of rats to signal the vampire's (and death's...) arrival in Lucy's world.

The Price Is Right

The popularity of vampires and new franchise films (*Yorgas, Blaculas, Andy Warhols* and two *Dark Shadows*) in the early 1970s encouraged producers' notions that horror films could meet with great financial success when fronted by a particularly charismatic star or genre "icon." In the 1970s, Vincent Price (1911–1993) rose to this coveted spot, competing with Christopher Lee and Peter Cushing as the most popular horror star of the decade. In 1971 and 1972 respectively, he portrayed a deranged mad scientist named "Dr. Phibes" in *The Abominable Dr. Phibes* and *Dr. Phibes Rises Again.* Directed by Robert Fuest, the films were inventive, humorous, roller coaster rides that existed primarily to showcase grotesque death-scenes and incredible set-designs. Price seemingly relished the role of a deformed scientist twisted by his need for revenge, and earned kudos for his tongue-in-cheek portrayal of a new "screen monster." In *The Abominable Dr. Phibes,* Price visited ten curses on the medical professionals he deemed responsible for his wife's death, and in the sequel vied with co-star Robert Quarry to find the magical River of Life which could revive his beloved. Before the *Phibes* films were done, victims were killed by rats, hail, frogs, bats, locusts, scorpions, and even a giant vise.

Price played a similar role in 1973's *Theatre of Blood*. As Edwin Lionheart, he was a "great" (though hammy) actor dissed by London's haughty critical elite. With his hero-worshiping daughter (Diana Rigg) at his side, Lionheart set about murdering the critics by creatively (and violently...) re-enacting dramatic scenes from the plays of Shakespeare. Like the *Phibes* films, *Theatre of Blood* was well received for its potent combination of gore and humor.

There Is Still Only One...

Remakes proved to be incredibly popular in the 1970s, as the seemingly infinite variations of *Dracula* and *Frankenstein* soon proved. But in 1976 along lumbered the decade's most controversial remake: Dino De Laurentiis' monster epic *King Kong* (1976). At first, Universal Studios and De Laurentiis had gone to war (and to court) over which party had the right to produce a remake of the 1930s giant ape story. Universal desired to offer a faithful black-and-white remake of the 1933 original with Barbra Streisand in the Fay Wray role and Peter Falk as Carl Denham. It would be lensed in the then-popular mode of "sensurround," which shook and jostled audiences at appropriate times during the picture.

By contrast, De Laurentiis wanted to update the legend, and offer a full-color, special effects extravaganza. He even promised that the big-budget film could be shot in a year, in time for a Christmas 1976 release. Unexpectedly, De Laurentiis won the rights to produce the remake (with Universal grabbing a piece of the profits), but then had to live up to his own bluster. John Guillermin, director of *The Towering Inferno* (1974), signed on to orchestrate the suddenly fast-track project, which would star Jeff Bridges and Charles Grodin.

No expense was spared to make the new *Kong* a spectacular blockbuster. The native wall that would block Kong from the native population of Skull Island, for instance, was 47 feet high, 500 feet long, made of eucalyptus tree trunks and 126,000 yards of grapevine. Alone, it cost one million dollars (3). But that wouldn't be the only excess, as time would reveal.

With a script penned by Lorenzo Semple, Jr., the new *King Kong* was controversial for a number of reasons. The first was that the colorful De Laurentiis claimed in print several times that Kong would be portrayed in his new film by a 50 foot fully articulated robot (built by Italian Carlo Rambaldi). In fact, Kong was portrayed in the film by a man in an ape suit (Rick Baker), a man who lumbered around on miniature sets ... just like in the myriad *Godzilla* films of Toho Studios. The Rambaldi robot was featured in only one sequence, wherein an out-of-sorts Kong breaks out of a cage at the moment of his "debut" in New York society. Also,

"I am not an animal, I am a human being ... in a gorilla costume." The new *King Kong* (1976) bares his teeth.

the giant mechanical "Kong" hand was a disaster for the production team, often malfunctioning and causing several delays.

Similarly, fans of the original *King Kong* did not cotton to Semple's screenplay, which had a strong tongue-in-cheek element to it, and which replaced 1930s icons like the Empire State Building, with '70s kitsch like the World Trade Center. Though the film is notable for introducing Oscar-winner Jessica Lange to Hollywood, it is today remembered as something of a bomb, despite the fact it made a huge profit for De Laurentiis and Paramount Studio. Historically, the film is valuable because it set the stage for the merchandising blitzes of later 1970s films like *Star Wars*. In 1976, for instance, Jim Beam offered a drink called the "King Kong Cocktail," and fans of the film could buy plastic glasses emblazoned with scenes from the film at Seven-Eleven Stores, or pull-out *King Kong* iron-ons from *Family Circle* magazine (4). *King Kong* was one of the first movies as "media events," and as such is worth remembering.

A more critically successful remake of a genre favorite came in 1978. Director Philip Kaufman re-made *Invasion of the Body Snatchers*, based on the famous 1956 film by Don Siegel. It starred Donald Sutherland, Brooke Adams, Leonard Nimoy, Veronica Cartwright and Jeff Goldblum. Shot in scenic San Francisco, the film was lensed over a period of 49 days (5), had a budget reported at 6 million dollars (6), and competed at the box office with *Superman* (1978) and *The Wiz* (1978). Replete with a memorable and disturbing climax, *Invasion of the Body Snatchers*— take two— successfully re-imagined the Communist pod people of the 1950s as the alienated "me generation" of the 1970s. Improved special effects turned the foamy "pods" of the original into veiny, leathery purveyors of true terror, and the alien birthing sequences were a spell-binding showcase of gore. A perfect blend of paranoia and horror, the new *Invasion* took America by storm.

It's Not Nice to Fool with Mother Nature...

At the same time studios were seeking to propagate franchises headed by personalities such as Robert Quarry, William Marshall, Vincent Price, Jonathan Frid and Udo Kier, there was also a dawning realization that scary films could make a profit without a well-known leading man or lady's name above the title. Producers just had to play their cards right. In fact, rampaging animals made for the perfect "bogeymen" in a series of 1970s "revenge of nature" horror films. Most of these motion pictures were based on the idea that mankind, with his science, pollution and technology, had so poisoned the Earth that God's creations (such as frogs, spiders, worms, ants, and rabbits) would revolt wholesale against *Homo sapiens*.

In fairness, the idea of animals suddenly turning nasty and attacking their human superiors was not at all new to the 1970s. Alfred Hitchcock's masterpiece *The Birds* basically defined the genre in 1963. It just took until the 1970s for the next property in the trend to come along and successfully exploit the idea.

That property was *Willard*, the story of an isolated loner (Bruce Davison) who trains an army of rats to attack those who have wronged him. Ernest Borgnine played the film's nasty antagonist, and Elsa Lanchester was Willard's overbearing mother. Based on the novel *Ratman's Notebooks* by Stephen Gilbert, *Willard* cost just under one million dollars to produce, and very quickly grossed more than eight times that amount upon its release in 1971. The film's success was due, in no small part, to the film's fantastic "special effects": the trained rats themselves. In fact, a minimum of visual trickery was used in the film, and most scenes really deposited live rats in close association with the human cast (who had been smeared with peanut butter to make them more appetizing to beasties...). Moe Di Sesso trained the critters, and was acknowledged by many as the real "star" of *Willard*.

After the unexpected success of *Willard*, other filmmakers were so quick to jump on the animal bandwagon that 1972 became known as "the year of the rabbit, not to mention the pig, frog, snake, rabbit, spider and scorpion" (7). Indeed, *Willard* ignited a red-hot "animal" movie trend that lasted throughout the remainder of the decade.

The year 1972 brought along a much-less-fun sequel to *Willard* entitled *Ben*. It featured a title song by Michael Jackson, and made a hero of its titular character, a resourceful black rat who led a rodent revolution in the sewers of Los Angeles. Lee Harcourt Montgomery played Ben's friend in the human community, Joseph Campanella his nemesis, but the film lacked the intelligence of the first picture. Though the closing moments of the movie set up the ground work for a sequel, no third "rat" picture was ever made. At least not yet.

Stanley (1972) was an out-and-out copy of *Willard*, but with a different loner (an orphaned American-Indian, Vietnam veteran played by *General Hospital*'s Chris Robinson). This time, the outsider was training a different breed of animals, snakes, to attack and murder his enemies. Among the victims in this low-budgeter was a stripper who had bitten off the head of a snake onstage. She paid for her crimes dearly. Oh yes.

Then there was the oddball horror film *Night of the Lepus* (1972), starring Janet Leigh and *Star Trek*'s DeForest Kelley, about giant bunnies on the rampage in western prairies. In this case, scientists experimenting with hormones were to blame for the oversized rabbit crisis. The film was a joke for two reasons. Firstly, rabbits are hardly scary. Secondly, the lame special effects consisted primarily of rabbits jumping around on miniature sets in slow-motion photography.

Another famous animal film of '72 was *Frogs*, starring Ray Milland, Joan Van Ark, and Sam Elliott. The plot saw Milland, as the patriarch of a rich Southern family, punished for his polluting ways when frogs, crocodiles, lizards and other local wildlife attacked his exclusive plantation estate. Unlike *Willard*, the "attack" scenes in *Frogs* were poorly staged, with Ray Milland never even in the same shot as the frog army.

Before the decade was through, audiences also witnessed *The Bug* (1975), an adaptation of the Thomas Page novel *The Hephaestus Plague* about intelligent, fire-spewing cockroaches. The film, which was produced by William Castle and starred Bradford Dillman, had the misfortune of opening in American movie houses the same day as *Jaws* (1975)(8). Next on the animal roster was *Squirm* (1976), about worms attacking a small southern community as the result of an electrical accident. *Squirm* was filmed in Port Wentworth, Georgia, and the movie's production team flew in thousands of live sandworms from Wiscosset, Maine; the climax alone featured some 250,000 wriggling critters (9). After that offering came *The Pack* (about rabid dogs), starring Joe Don Baker and R.G. Armstrong.

Schlockmeister Bert I. Gordon (of *The Amazing Colossal Man* [1957]) even got into the animal act in 1976, with *Food of the Gods*, a film about giant rats shot in Vancouver, and the unforgettable Joan Collins vehicle *Empire of the Ants*, which was lensed in Panama (10). Both films utilized primitive special effects to depict their oversized menaces, but have since

When animals attack: Bruce the Shark rears his head in Steven Spielberg's *Jaws* (1975).

become cult classics nonetheless. The bugaboo in *Empire of the Ants* was a shipment of radioactive waste, washed ashore on a "vacation" resort. Enterprising ants ate the radioactive goop, grew to colossal proportions, and then decided that mankind should serve their queen. Humans Pamela Susan Shoop and Robert Lansing had other ideas, but escaping the ants was no picnic.

The turning point in the "when animals attack" genre came in the year 1975 with the release of Steven Spielberg's *Jaws*, an adventure film based on the best-selling novel by Peter Benchley. The beautifully photographed, highly suspenseful movie pitted Roy Scheider, Richard Dreyfuss, Robert Shaw, and a small beach community named Amity against a hungry great white shark. In the first scene of the film, a lovely girl took a midnight swim in the beautiful Amity waters ... only to be ruthlessly devoured by nature's oldest predator. That shocking opening set the tone for the rest of the picture, and changed horror films forever.

Accompanied by an expressive score from composer John Williams, *Jaws* was also buttressed by bloody good special effects (and a mechanical shark named Bruce). It quickly became the highest grossing film of all time, and re-directed the animal craze towards a less-fantastic route. Giant animals were out, and real-life man-eaters were in. Scientific explanations for attacks were a thing of a the past, and biological imperatives replaced them.

The first person out of the gate on this new aspect of the animal movie fad was low-budget filmmaker William Girdler. A veteran of such titles as *Asylum of Satan* (1971) and *Abby* (1974), Girdler armed forest ranger Christopher George against a rampaging grizzly bear in *Grizzly* (1976), the highest-grossing independent film of 1976. It was a ridiculously bad film, one that aped every aspect of *Jaws*, but it resonated with audiences who still wanted to be scared by attacking animals.

Similarly, *Night Creature* (1977) was filmed in Thailand and landed Donald Pleasence in close quarter combat with a big game cat, a black panther. *Orca* (1977) produced by Dino De Laurentiis, was another cockamamie fish story, with star Richard Harris duking it out with a killer whale that he had wronged! And Joe Dante, just 29 years old, directed the delightful *Piranha* (1978) another child of *Jaws*, and one of the most successful features released by its studio, New World Pictures (11). Finally, along flew *Nightwing* (1979), a film its director, Arthur Hiller, dubbed "*Jaws* with wings on an Indian Reservation" (12). Its subject? Vampire bats.

Before Jimmy Carter was out of office, the animal trend in horror films was completely exhausted by a number of exceedingly bad variations on the theme. A swarm of killer bees ravaged Houston (and Michael Caine) in master-of-disaster Irwin Allen's lackluster *The Swarm* (1978), a film which cost a then-staggering 12 million dollars. Holes in the ozone caused lions and tigers and bears (oh my!) to attack Leslie Nielsen in Bill Girdler's follow-up to *Grizzly*, entitled *Day of the Animals* (1977). This Girdler picture didn't emulate *Grizzly's* box office numbers, in no small part because it opened the same day as a popular little 1970s film entitled *Star Wars* (1977).

Another weak link in the animal sweepstakes was *Prophecy* (1979), directed by John Frankenheimer, which explored the notion that mercury poisoning had mutated wild-life in a Maine forest. *Prophecy* was undone by weak special effects, particularly its unconvincing "monster" suit, but Talia Shire did well with a subplot involving her unborn child ... an embryo also threatened by mercury poisoning.

In 1978, there was also the inevitable sequel, *Jaws II*. Roy Scheider was back as Sheriff Brody, again combating a great white shark in Amity waters, but this time Richard Dreyfuss chose not to appear, and a bevy of virtually indistinguishable teenagers had supporting roles. Jeannot Szwarc (director of *The Bug*) replaced another director, John Hancock, early in the Florida shoot, and salvaged the film as much as was possible considering the studio's haste to release the film.

However, the best of all the post–*Jaws* animal attack movies was *Kingdom of the Spiders* (1977), a tense little opus about an organized tarantula attack on a small Arizona community. The cause of this animal revolt was overuse of pesticides in the region, and *Star Trek* veteran William Shatner starred as the appealing veterinarian combating the arachnid plague. As in *Willard*, more than five years before, *Kingdom of the Spiders* benefited from a sense of realism. Its actors (including Shatner) were frequently seen in the same shots as the spiders, and there seemed to be a minimum of post-production trickery.

Oppositely, the worst film about attacking animals also featured spiders. Bill Rebane's *The Giant Spider Invasion* (1975), which re-dressed a Volkswagen bug as a hairy, oversized tarantula, represented the nadir of 1970s animal cinema. Alan Hale—the skipper of *Gilligan's Island*—portrayed a town sheriff combating this particular threat, which had arrived in rural

Wisconsin courtesy of an inconveniently open "black hole."

He's in the Details: Devil Cinema of the 1970s

If *Jaws* proved to be the inspiration for a litter of animal attack movies, then William Friedkin's 1973 blockbuster, *The Exorcist*, must have been the source for at least two dozen or so "devil" themed horror movies in the 1970s. Based on the best-selling novel by William Peter Blatty, which in turn was based on a "real life" case of demonic possession in 1949 Washington, D.C., *The Exorcist* is, perhaps, like *Jaws*, a film which changed horror cinema forever. At the same time that director Friedkin packed his movie with memorable, over-the-top special effects such as projectile green-pea vomit, levitating beds, and spinning heads, he also recounted this riveting story in more starkly realistic terms than any horror film before *The Exorcist*.

In lensing the trauma of a possessed girl, Regan MacNeil (Linda Blair), Friedkin employed documentary-style techniques for the opening "travelogue" portion in Iraq, as well as the latest psychological jargon to explain the inexplicable, and even subliminal imagery to foster terror. Adding to the sense of authenticity, three Catholic priests, Father Thomas V. Bermingham, Father John Nicola and Father William O'Malley, consulted on the project and played priests in the film.

Though *The Exorcist* was badly received by critics at the time of its release, and vehemently denounced by many religious authorities (including the Reverend Billy Graham), it became a top grosser at the box office, earning more than 90 million dollars. Hollywood recognized the film's excellence as well, giving it the nod with 10 Academy Award nominations.

When the film was re-released in the summer of 2000, it was a high earner again, despite 25 years of "improvements" in genre pictures. According to Friedkin, who was interviewed while making the film, *The Exorcist*'s sense of reality is what grants it such power.

> I intend to do it very realistically. It's a realistic story about inexplicable things, and it's all going to take place in cold light, with ordinary people, on ordinary streets [13].

Shot in 85 days, with roughly two thirds of that time spent in New York City and one third on location in Georgetown, *The Exorcist* revolutionized the horror film. As crazy as the subject matter was, the film felt real, and the actors (including Max Von Sydow, Ellen Burstyn and Jason Miller) played it that way. Blatty produced the movie, based on his own script, and reportedly signed a deal reserving him in excess of 20 percent of the film's profits. It was a smart move, and like Friedkin, he had an agenda in shepherding his novel to the screen:

> My primary purpose in the film is to persuade those who do not believe that there is a case to be made for the supernatural and to offer the possibility that there is a supernatural force of evil at work in the universe whose game plan is to convince us that he does not exist [14].

One might even say that Blatty reached his goal too well, because very shortly, *The Exorcist* spawned a number of imitations in the "Devil" cycle of the 1970s. *Beyond the Door* (1975) was an Italian variation on the Friedkin film in which a possessed Juliet Mills was pregnant with the Devil's spawn. William Girdler's *Abby* (1974) saw *The Exorcist* re-hashed as a blaxploitation film, with another demonic possession of a young girl in evidence (and

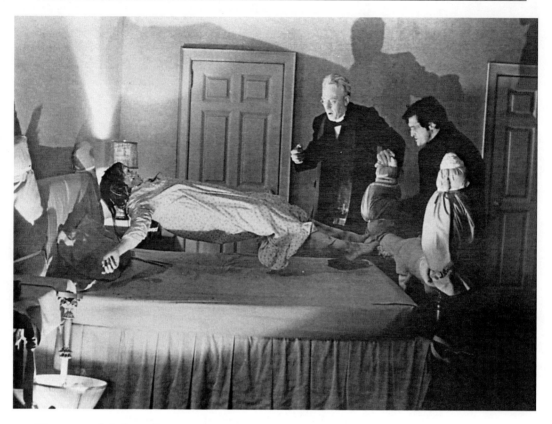

The power of the box office compels them! The final showdown in William Friedkin's *The Exorcist* (1973).

William Marshall of *Blacula* fame as the exorcist on record.)

Nineteen-hundred and seventy five's *The Devil's Rain* cast *Willard*'s heavy, Ernest Borgnine, as Corbis, a satanic priest damning helpless souls (including Ida Lupino, William Shatner, and Tom Skerritt) to Hell with the help of a demonic ledger. *Race with the Devil* (1975) was another strange excursion into devil territory, placing tourists Peter Fonda and Loretta Swit in a road rage situation with pursuing, hot-rodding Satanists (led by R.G. Armstrong). A kind of early, demonic *The Road Warrior* (1981), the film was a high-octane action movie and a horror film to boot.

Then came David Seltzer's *The Omen* (1976), a polished, big budget horror film that concerned the ascent of the Devil's child on Earth, the antichrist. Politics were involved as the young Devil boy, named Damien, infiltrated the powerful Thorn family headed by Gregory Peck. *The Omen* very quickly became famous for its over-the-top gore sequences, particularly the moment when actor David Warner's head appeared to be rather convincingly severed by a sheet of plate glass.

The Sentinel (1977) was yet another devil film, this one highlighting the plight of a fallen woman (Christine Rains) whose fate was to defend the gateway to Hell (in a New York brownstone...) from demons. Burgess Meredith played a ghost, John Carradine an earlier Sentinel (a blind priest), and Michael Sarandon was Rains' unscrupulous boyfriend. Though much of the movie was lackluster and muddled, its final moments—which cast the real-life physically deformed as souls trapped in Hell — were oddly unsettling.

Finally, there was *Damien — Omen II*, Don Taylor's 1978 sequel to *The Omen*. This follow-up to the blockbuster sent the Antichrist off packing to military school (under the tutelage of *Millennium*'s Lance Henriksen…). No matter where audiences went in the 1970s, it seemed they couldn't escape the Devil or his cinematic minions.

In fairness to *The Exorcist*, it didn't actually spawn the devil cycle of the 1970s, though it no doubt popularized the horror sub-genre. In fact, before *The Exorcist*, there was a whole slew of satanic films making the rounds, though most of them were forgettable low-budget films. *Asylum of Satan* (1971) was William Girdler's first film, and it concerned the Devil's attempt to impregnate a virgin with his progeny. Lucifer faced disappointment in an unintentionally funny ending, which established that the virgin was more experienced than the Prince of Darkness had anticipated.

The Brotherhood of Satan (1971) was a disturbing little film in which cult leader Strother Martin attempted to possess the souls of several children in a small town so his coven members could attain virtual immortality. Instead of being hampered by limited resources, director Bernard McEveety staged creepy P.O.V. attacks on the *dramatis personae* in moments that seemed genuinely infused with evil. Maybe it was just the cameraman, but there always seemed to be a dark presence just out of view in this effective horror picture.

A Touch of Satan (1973) and *Daughters of Satan* (1972) followed similar lines, equating witchcraft with Devil worship. *Daughters of Satan* was particularly ludicrous, but is remembered today for introducing the world to its star, Tom Selleck. A bigger-budget entry in the Devil market was *The Mephisto Waltz* (1971), which depicted reporter Alan Alda losing his soul to pianist and Satanist Curt Jurgens. Alda's

wife, Jacqueline Bisset, noted the change, but in an odd-twist found the new soul in her husband's body to be a superior lover…

Interestingly, just as *The Exorcist* had revved up interest in satanic cinema, so did its sequel, *Exorcist II: The Heretic* (1977) dim such interest. Directed by John Boorman and starring a teenage Linda Blair, this sequel failed to live up to its predecessor, and has since earned an honored position among all bad-movie lovers. It has been described as "the greatest commercial disappointment of any film in the 1970s" even though the director has argued that it contains some of his "best work" (15). In fact, the film is a strange journey into the nature of evil, and it lacks many of the notable scary effects that dominated the first film. Richard Burton played a priest and Louise Fletcher a psychologist, but even these fine actors could do little with stilted dialogue, and patently absurd touches (such as a "synch" device which could connect the minds of two individuals through hypnosis).

Psycho— *logy*

Alfred Hitchcock's *The Birds* gave rise to all manner of feral cinematic offspring in the 1970s, but it is the master of suspense's biggest box office success, *Psycho* (1960), that wielded the greatest influence on the horror films of the 1970s. The surprise revelation of *Psycho*'s climax (that Norman Bates *was* his mother); the wordy psychological explanation for his mental condition (recounted in *Psycho*'s exposition-heavy coda); and the shock of a major character dying early in the proceedings (à la Janet Leigh in the shower), very quickly became *de rigueur* elements in the 1970s psycho film trend.

A bicycle trip through rural France became an opportunity for horror when two English girls were stalked by a murderer in Robert Fuest's tautly directed psycho-film, *And Soon the Darkness* (1970). When her traveling companion "disappeared," tourist Pamela Franklin, alone in a foreign land, had to escape a deadly stretch of highway. Was the killer that man she had seen at a café? The strange local constable? A British teacher living in France? Or was the killer that strange, barely glimpsed figure, seen at a distance in the fields far from the road's pavement? The variety of suspects, the language barrier, and the impending nightfall all made this film a tense, effective one.

Play Misty for Me (1971), directed by Clint Eastwood, was another variation of the *Psycho* ethos, as a "hip" California disc jockey (Eastwood) was stalked by a zealous fan he'd once had a fling with. This groupie (Jessica Walter) began the film as a sexy one-night fling, and ended it as a knife-wielding maniac. Replete with a 1970s-style "jazz" montage/interlude, *Play Misty* offered a sometimes vulgar-mouthed assailant who could be sexy and vulnerable one moment, murderous the next. Today, we'd say she is bi-polar, but in 1971 there was no one around to pass out the Prozac, and she was terrifying.

The master himself, Alfred Hitchcock, returned to the terrain of *Psycho* in his 52nd film, *Frenzy* (1972). The film focused on the hijinks of a serial killer in London dubbed the "Necktie Murderer." In reality, the anti-social bloke was a "kindly" grocer who had a thing for strangling women. The film is notorious for one particular sequence, the strangulation of actress Barbara Leigh Hunt, which director Hitchcock lingered on with more than loving attention. The murder sequence culminated in the implication that the killer had been sexually satisfied by his gruesome handiwork, and remains a truly perverse bit of filmmaking. Otherwise, the grocer with the choking fetish was a total

sociopath: a smiling monster who might just live next door. What was surprising about the film was that Hitchcock alternated laughs with suspense, particularly in a sequence that found the killer outsmarting himself in the back of a potato truck.

Cinematic killers had all kinds of bizarre mental hang-ups in the 1970s psycho movies. A boy who despised his shrewish mother for arguing with his father (and for taking away his teddy bear...) grew up to be a homicidal woman-hater (and carnie...) in the low-budget entry filmed on Coney Island *Carnival of Blood* (1971). The same film had the honor of introducing *Rocky*'s (1976) Burt Young to the world.

A playboy with a pathological hatred for brides and weddings set out to destroy beautiful newlyweds in Italian Mario Bava's kinky *Hatchet for a Honeymoon* (1971). A man guilty about committing his daughter to an insane asylum went on an axe-murder spree in a small town with a secret in the completely nutty *Silent Night, Bloody Night* (1973). A politician enmeshed in a political scandal and ashamed about his own impotence staged a series of gory killings in the debauched *Savage Weekend* (1978). A little girl was suspected of committing murder in New Jersey's contribution to "stalk-n-slash" cinema, *Alice, Sweet Alice* (1977), but in fact a woman twisted by Catholicism was to blame for the violence.

By far and away, however, it was the killer with "the splintered psyche" who was most popular in the psycho-films of the 1970s. In Brian DePalma's *Sisters* (1973), a Siamese twin (Margot Kidder) so mourned her deceased twin that she developed a split personality. When she adopted the characteristics of her dead sibling, she also became homicidal. DePalma utilized split screens to reinforce the notion of doubling, and schizophrenia. In *Magic* (1977), the retiring, shy Anthony Hopkins also developed a murderous alternative personality, but this time in a ventriloquist's dummy named Corky rather than an imaginary sibling. In *Schizo* (1976), a schizophrenic young bride (Lynne Frederick) executed a series of terrible murders, though the film's *modus operandi* had audiences believing it was her convicted father-in-law who was the true culprit.

Two interesting psycho films of the decade utilized a modern convenience, the telephone, as an instrument of horror. In 1974's *Black Christmas*, a hidden madman utilized the phone to stalk the comely residents of a Canadian sorority (including Margot Kidder and Olivia Hussey). The ringing of the phone very soon became a prompt for terror, and the film never revealed the identity of its loquacious maniac. Keir Dullea was one of the suspects, and John Saxon played the police officer investigating the crimes.

When a Stranger Calls (1979) was a more coherent genre exercise that made use of the telephone, with a psychopath terrorizing a babysitter (Carol Kane) by pitch of night. In a truly frightening preamble, the film revealed that the psycho — an escaped mental patient — was calling from *inside* the house. Charles Durning was the cop who chased down this madman, but it was the silk-voiced killer, who kept croaking "have you checked the children?" who remained most memorable.

If there was one psycho-on-the-loose film that defined the 1970s, it was director John Carpenter's *Halloween* (1978). Written by producer Debra Hill and Carpenter, *Halloween* began the seemingly unending saga of Michael Myers, one of cinema's most enduring monsters. After escaping from a mental institution (and psychiatrist Donald Pleasence), the masked sociopath returned to his sleepy little hometown, Haddonfield, on All Hallow's Eve, to terrorize three teenagers (Jamie Lee Curtis,

P.J. Soles and Nancy Loomis). Shot in 22 days at a cost of $300,000, *Halloween* became the top grossing independent film of all time (until 1990). A critical favorite, *Halloween* also spawned dozens of imitations in the 1980s (including *Friday the 13th* [1980], *Prom Night* [1980], *Mother's Day* [1981], *My Bloody Valentine* [1981], and *New Year's Evil* [1981] to name but a few).

More interestingly, *Halloween* solidified the horror credentials of its director, John Carpenter, who has since become a major voice in the genre. The film also changed the direction of the psycho-film. Before *Halloween*, the psycho-films, like *Schizo*, *Magic* and *Sisters*, all sought reasonable explanations in psychology. *Halloween* was literally anti–Hitchcockian because it suggested that there was no rational explanation for Myers. Unlike Norman Bates, Myers was pure evil. He was the bogeyman, the "Shape." He was unstoppable, and unkillable. Later films, such as the adventures of Jason Voorhees, adopted the same anti-rational stance, though to a much lesser effect. The indestructible super human that no science could diagnose thus supplanted the "human" monster that was a victim of his own mind.

The multitude of psycho films in the 1970s ran the gamut of themes. Hammer's 1973 film, *Fear in the Night*, re-staged the dynamic of *Les Diaboliques* (1955), with two lovers conspiring to drive a spouse (Judy Geeson) to the deathbed. *Don't Look in the Basement* (1973) revived the old chestnut of an insane asylum run by maniacs, including an axe wielding freak. *The Town That Dreaded Sundown* (1976) was "based on the true story" of a serial killer's rampage in Texarkana in the late 1940s, and had some brutal moments in it. In 1971's *See No Evil* (starring Mia Farrow), a killer was defined only by his telltale cowboy boots. Nothing else was revealed about him (beside his homicidal acts).

Draped in a sheet, Michael Myers approaches his next victim in John Carpenter's *Halloween* (1978).

Taking the opposite route, George A Romero's *Martin* (1976) was a study in psychology. Martin, a lonely outsider twisted by the religious guilt and shame of his conservative upbringing, fancied himself a vampire, and so re-shaped himself into one. With razors, hypodermic needles and other tools of the technological 20th century, he went out into the night and claimed victims as a vampire would — drinking their blood. Filmed for less than $100,000 dollars (16), *Martin* was a low-budget masterpiece, a sensitive horror film starring, like *Psycho* before it, a truly pitiable madman.

The Savage Cinema   *Vietnam*

A woman bites off a man's penis while giving him head. A vacationer is ordered to squeal like a pig while sodomized by an unwashed mountain man. A teenager is impaled on a meat hook by a squealing lunatic who wears human skin. A crazed cannibal bites the head off a parakeet and drinks the bird's life-blood like it's a Budweiser. These things can't be happening, and yet they do happen —*onscreen*— in the high impact films of the 1970s savage cinema. "The New Freedom" in film meant that more graphic violence could be shown in all kinds of films, and horror movie directors such as Wes Craven, Tobe Hooper, Sam Peckinpah, Stanley Kubrick and John Boorman took advantage of the development. In the process they created some of the most perverse, disgusting *and intense* horror films imaginable.

The Vietnam War may have been the catalyst for the 1970s "savage" cycle. After all, that war (and the media) had brought atrocities into American living rooms with stunning news footage. Monks immolated themselves. Soldiers shot innocent civilians in the head. American soldiers burned down villages, and so forth. If that wasn't bad enough, there were the Manson murders to contend with at home. In this real-life horror, ex-hippies ripped out the entrails of their victims, and even killed an expectant mother. How could any fiction compare with these apocalypses, all of which were being gleefully shepherded into suburbia by Walter Cronkite, Dan Rather and their ilk? Accordingly, a primary tenet of the so-called savage cinema is that terrible things happen to good people for no larger purpose or reason.

The Last House on the Left (1972), Wes Craven's first feature film, was a secular retelling of the Ingmar Bergman religious epic *The Virgin Spring* (1958). In it, two nice suburban girls, Mari and Phyllis, are kidnapped, raped and murdered by a gang of escaped convicts. In a bizarre twist, the criminals led by Krug (David Hess), end up at the home of one of their victim's. The parents of the slain Mari then brutally kill the thugs with their bare hands. A suburban housewife bites off the manhood of a sex offender after luring him to the backyard, while a mild general practitioner puts down scalpel for chainsaw and decapitates Krug. It's a vicious descent into violence, and Craven's camera captures it all with brutal efficiency. The song which repeats on the soundtrack, "The Road Leads to Nowhere," reminds audiences that nothing has been gained through the bloody revenge ("the castle stays the same…"), and everything — especially innocence — has been sacrificed.

Though the film was roundly excoriated by critics (but for Roger Ebert), the low-budget production (shot for under $100,000 dollars in Westport, New York) confronted issues of violence in a respectable manner. Yes, *Last House* depicted scenes of sickening behavior and violence, but it also disdained such behavior and showed that ultimately it had no purpose. In other words, *Last House on the Left* was *about* violence, not merely exploiting it for box office potential.

At around the same time, other film artists were on the same page as Craven. Sam Peckinpah's *Straw Dogs* (1971) was also a meditation about the place of violence in society. In this movie, a geeky mathematician (Dustin Hoffman) was driven to brutal murder when locals (led by Ken Hutchison) raped his wife (Susan George) and threatened to kill the village simpleton (David Warner). Some viewers saw the picture as a validation of the macho ethos, as a sort of fascist "rite of passage" film. But the movie was much more than a brutal parable about the nature of man; it was an examination of what happens when a person is simply pushed too far, and his security is threatened. It is about a man who finds that place within himself where violence is the only solution left. The last twenty minutes of *Straw Dogs* were particularly harrowing, and included a siege on Hoffman's farm house involving bear traps, boiling water, and gaping gunshot wounds. It was unremittingly violent, but like *Last House on the Left*, was powerful in its themes and meaning. Both of these films were part of the sub-class of horror films that have come to be known as "rape and revenge."

Deliverance, a story of survival in the wild, very much traded on the same issues, this time pitting four city boys (Burt Reynolds, Jon Voight, Ned Beatty, and Ronny Cox) against a roaring, unforgiving river and two redneck "wild men." John Boorman's film was a legitimate rite of passage picture, a test of resilience and strength in the most traumatic of situations and locations. Some survived the ordeal, some were horribly scarred, and the experience of life and death was as basic as the forest in which it all occurred. *Deliverance* was one part culture-clash, one part natural adventure, and completely hardcore. It put people off of camping for years.

The 1970s savage cinema reached its pinnacle in 1974 with Tobe Hooper's premiere feature film, *The Texas Chainsaw Massacre.* Unlike other entries in this particular horror cycle, *Chainsaw* had no explicit meaning or greater thematic purpose. It was purposefully anti-rational, a plunge into a nightmare world where man was little more than "meat" to a deranged family of cannibals. A retarded human called Leatherface, armed with his saw, would cut up anyone (even invalids...) for ingredients in his family's special barbe-

cue. And there was no reasoning with this particular cook, either. He didn't relate to human beings as such, and wasn't interested even in sex (until the 1987 sequel...). The story of five teens who ran afoul of Leatherface occurred under a hot, and careless, Texas sun; *The Texas Chainsaw Massacre* reeked of random, irrational violence.

Chainsaw's power as a film was that it successfully put viewers into the mindset of a caged, hunted animal about to be cut up for someone's stew. It was chilling, extreme, and totally over-the-top. Though there was little blood seen in the final cut, Hooper's *Chainsaw* is psychologically savage. Like the humming teeth of that chainsaw, the film never stops, and is buttressed by its insane momentum.

The savage cinema took a variety of forms in the 1970s. Stanley Kubrick played rape and brutality as fast-motion, operatic ballet in 1971's notorious (and X-rated) epic, *A Clockwork Orange.* He infuriated his critics because the film suggested it was better to tolerate monsters like "Droogie" Alex (Malcolm McDowell) than to live in a society that repressed individuality. 1979's *I Spit on Your Grave* was also part of the "rape and revenge" sub-genre, depicting how a beautiful female writer wreaks revenge on four rapists (including a retarded grocery delivery boy). In one especially gruesome sequence, the writer castrated the worst of her assailants during a seductive bubble bath, and the tub turned deep red with his blood in seconds. Unlike *Last House on the Left*, there seemed to be little context or meaning in the violence of *I Spit on Your Grave.* Instead it evinced only "eye for an eye" justice, like the worst of the *Death Wish* films.

Cannibalism was an important element of the violent 1970s films, perhaps because it represented the ultimate taboo to be broken, and the '70s were all about breaking taboos. In addition to *The Texas*

Chainsaw Massacre, men ate men in Wes Craven's brutal battle for territorial superiority, *The Hills Have Eyes* (1977). The film waged a bloody war between a "civilized" family (the Carters), and a savage one in the hot Nevada desert. Before long the differentiation between families was lost.

Cannibalism was played with more lightly in the Australian horror satire *Terror at Red Wolf Inn* (1972), at a bed and breakfast with an unusual menu, and for unintentional humor in such non-classics as *Shriek of the Mutilated* (1974) and *Bloodsucking Freaks* (1977).

If unflinching, brutal violence and bloody gore were prime facets of the 1970s trend of "savage" films, then at least two other films deserve mention in this category. George A. Romero's *Dawn of the Dead* (1979) featured more bullets to the head and raw scenes of cannibalism than any film in motion picture history before or since. It went out to theaters unrated and was a smash hit with critics and audiences alike. The sequel to *Night of the Living Dead* (1968), *Dawn* set four human survivors against the zombie plague in a suburban shopping mall. The film saw limbs torn asunder, blood feasted upon, skulls crunched by helicopter blades and other disgusting set-pieces, while balancing that violent mentality with pie-fights and overt satire of the 1970s consumer culture. It was an adroit mix that kept audiences off-balance, and tense. A less elegant sequel, *Day of the Dead* followed Romero's masterpiece in 1985.

Finally, there was *Alien* (1979), directed by Ridley Scott. This $10 million feature (which opened two years to the day after *Star Wars*) might have been termed *Jaws in Space*, as it featured a malevolent extraterrestrial killing off the crew of a commercial spaceship. But there was one scene in *Alien* that catapulted the film to legendary status. About mid-way through the proceedings, an alien "chest burster" unexpectedly wormed its way out of astronaut John Hurt's stomach, leaving the rest of the film's shell-shocked cast covered in blood and guts. This scene alone was indicative of the fact that, by decade's end, there were no boundaries left to be broken. Anything that could be depicted on film, no matter how disgusting and repellant, would be depicted. In the next decade, it would be expected, and gore and violence would no longer seem so savage, but simply, and frighteningly, *routine*.

Science Gone Awry

In 1970s America, it was difficult to see how science had not gone completely wild. The incident at Three Mile Island proved that nuclear power wasn't so safe after all. The Apollo 13 mission nearly tanked, almost killing its crew. The world's first test tube baby was born, and that fact unnerved conservatives who felt that God's master plan was being tampered with. Medicine failed to cure cancer or any other major diseases, and the country (and the world at large) hadn't found a cheap or effective alternative for fossil fuel during the energy crisis either. Military equipment, scientific technology and good old American know-how had failed to get the hostages in Iran released, and so forth. Science — *once the new frontier of human ingenuity* — was more or less responsible for every one of these failures, and people were, not surprisingly, losing faith in it. Earlier successes, such as the trip to the moon in 1969, were even believed to be Watergate-like conspiracies in mainstream adventure films such as *Capricorn One* (1978). The magazine *New West* succinctly described the situation:

> Increasingly, we have handed over our destinies, our bodies, our lives to spe-

cialized experts. The short-term effects have been dazzling in some cases. Over the longer range, however, our dependence on expertise is creating a paralyzing sense of individual helplessness. And the experts have often been wrong. They showed us how to defeat the Vietcong with technology. They concocted deadly pesticides to increase food production. They devised indestructible plastic substances to take the place of metal and wood [17].

It was not a shock, considering the backlash against science, that many horror movies of the 1970s blamed the medical and technological quarters for their innumerable and strange disasters. Remember the giant, malevolent bunnies of *Night of the Lepus* (1972), and the encroaching arachnids in *Kingdom of the Spiders* (1977)? Science had caused these anomalies by experimenting with rabbit hormones and over-spraying dangerous pesticides in spider territory, respectively. But there was more.

The cinema of Canadian director David Cronenberg in the '70s was a virtual paean to the overreaching dangers and errors of the scientific community. A modern, and totally misguided, doctor unwittingly released a "sexual plague" in the contained Starliner Apartment Complex in 1975's *Shivers* (also known as *The Parasite Murders* and *They Came from Within*). The genetically engineered slug-like parasite jumped from person to person in the graphic film, infecting children and adults alike, turning them into strange sex zombies.

Cronenberg's follow-up, *Rabid* (1976), saw another irresponsible doctor (at the Keloid Institute this time) releasing a similar plague into unsuspecting Montreal. This infection commenced with a skin graft on porn star Marilyn Chambers, and proceeded into a strange case of rabies that spread across the community

at lightning-fast speed. Cronenberg's final horror film of the '70s, *The Brood* (1979), dramatized the story of another scientist (a psychologist played by Oliver Reed) who was able to create "living" embodiments of rage in the form of a murderous brood of hooded children.

George A. Romero's 1973 film *The Crazies* (also known as *The Mad People* and *Codename: Trixie*) was in synch with many of Cronenberg's graphic imaginings, revealing how the government, military and scientific establishments had released a biological weapon, "Trixie," into the drinking water of a small Pittsburgh town. The film examined martial law (like *Rabid*), and defined the military and scientific community's mentality as nothing less than insane. Predictably, there was no end in sight to the plague of *The Crazies*...

The films of novelist Michael Crichton also ran with the fear that science had gone dangerously awry. In *The Andromeda Strain*, directed by Robert Wise, another American town (this time in the Southwest) was destroyed by an alien disease carried back from a national space satellite. The military and scientific communities failed to contain the entity, and winds threatened to spread the deadly bacterial agent across the continental United States.

Westworld, directed by Crichton himself, was a futuristic tale about an expensive amusement park where humans could interact with realistic robots in fantasy settings (Roman World, Westworld, and Medieval World). Not surprisingly, the robots, led by Yul Brynner, didn't appreciate being treated as slaves, and turned murderous. Man's very technology, his trusted friend once taken for granted, had turned on him. *The Terminal Man* (1974), directed by Mike Hodges and based on another Crichton novel, also took a swipe at the medical establishment. In this film, doctors surgically implanted a behavior modification chip into the brain of a violent offender (George Segal). But instead of containing the man's violence, the new technology only spurred murderous anti-social behavior. The message, not unlike that in Mary Shelley's *Frankenstein*, was that men of science shouldn't endeavor to play God.

As the decade wore on, science became the scapegoat for all kinds of monstrosities. Ghoulish body transplants were the subject of the British entry *Scream and Scream Again* (1970). Scientist Rock Hudson tampered with fetal growth in the low-budget *Embryo* (1976) and ended up creating a so-called "perfect woman" named Victoria (Barbara Carrera). The only problem was that Hudson's new creation, an adult, sexual being, had no morals and no hesitation in killing. *The Island of Dr. Moreau* (1977) explored how scientist Burt Lancaster had fooled with animal and human DNA to create a race of "humanimals." On his island paradise, actually St. Croix in the Virgin Islands, sixty-three-year-old Lancaster menaced protagonist Michael York and his innocent ward, Barbara Carrera again. By the film's denouement, Moreau had been strung up by his own animal creations for daring to tamper in God's domain.

Another curious scientist interfered in the cycle of life in *The Asphyx* (1972), because he believed he could prevent death. Strother Martin, previously a cult leader in *The Brotherhood of Satan* (1971), played a mad scientist in *Sssssss* (1973), a picture which cost $600,000 dollars and transformed hunky Dirk Benedict (later of *Battlestar Galactica* [1978]) into a snake-man. Cloning was another dread of the decade, and the subject of the 12 million dollar ITC picture *The Boys from Brazil* (1978) and the more low budget *The Clonus Horror* (1979), to name just two.

The atmosphere of fear surrounding medicine grew so paranoid that doctors, along with government bureaucrats, be-

came the villains of a number of medical dramas. Michael Crichton's *Coma* (1978) was a prime example of this trend, as Genevieve Bujold and Michael Douglas learned of a wide-ranging hospital conspiracy to incapacitate patients and then sell their healthy organs to the highest bidders. From the ridiculous (amphibious, genetically engineered Nazi troopers in *Shock Waves* [1970]) and the routine (*Frankenstein Must Be Destroyed* [1970]) to 3-D gimmickry (*Andy Warhol's Frankenstein* [1974]), the villainy of modern science came in all shapes, sizes and colors (*Blackenstein* [1973]). It was a decade of unrest and uncertainty about the shape of things to come.

Women's Studies

A corollary to "science gone awry" was the socially minded horror films of the 1970s, in which women's issues were at stake. Scientific advances (and mistakes) were again to blame for the problems, but the disasters in these films always impacted women, and changed their role in our society.

George Romero's little-seen *Jack's Wife* (1971) was a horror film about a woman who believed society had defined her only as the spouse of a distant, "superior" husband. In dreams, she imagined herself to be her husband's dog, leashed and caged. Then, the woman "discovered" witchcraft and her own individual voice. At first a symbol of her independence, witchcraft ultimately proved to be as much a trap as the shackles of a patriarchal society.

The Stepford Wives (1975) starred Katherine Ross as a "liberated" woman who moved to a small Connecticut town with her family. She very soon learned that the women of Stepford were "different." In fact, the wives of this suburban utopia were robots programmed to "please" husbands. Ross learned of the secret too late, and discovered her husband had arranged for her to be in line for the same treatment. The film, based on the novel by Ira Levin, was horror and satire at the same time, examining the changing role of women in 1970s America. Men still wanted cooking, cleaning, baby machines, and in Stepford, that job description prevailed. A photographer and free-thinker, Ross's character wanted more out of life than to pick up after the baby and her husband, but her needs were not considered by the patriarchal conspiracy. In the amazing conclusion of the film, Ross faced a robotic Doppelgänger ... one with bigger breasts, and the movie's point was made visually.

In *Demon Seed* (1977), another liberated 1970s career woman, this time played by Julie Christie, faced the same brand of personal apocalypse. After deciding not to bear children with her workaholic husband, Christie's character, a psychologist, was kidnapped by her husband's latest creation, a super-advanced computer called Proteus (voiced by Robert Vaughn). The computer locked Christie in her home, raped her, and forced her to conceive his child ... a hybrid of human genetics and artificial intelligence.

Again, the role of the woman in contemporary society was the subject of a horror film, this time one based on a novel by Dean Koontz. Proteus was so intelligent a computer (and so powerful an abuser) that he could force Christie's character to experience an orgasm against her will, and one felt the filmmakers were making a potent point. Some men want to control women's biology, to the point of telling them when and how to experience pleasure.

Larry Cohen's *It's Alive* (1973) and *It Lives Again* (1978) concerned a human issue that has often been written in terms of a woman's right to choose, but in fact,

the double-bill dealt with a universal human issue: reproduction. What would happen if it were learned that many American women were carrying in their wombs mutant babies (a result of environmental contaminants such as microwaves, x-rays and the like)? Would the women choose to abort the babies? Would the government force the women to abort the babies? Would religious groups demand that the babies be allowed to live, even if, as in the films, they turned out to be homicidal monsters? Would the mothers, once they gave birth to the mutant babies, bond with their children? These issues of conception, birth, abortion, bonding, parenthood and reproduction were at the heart of Cohen's tense low-budget films, as were Rick Baker's primitive but efficient "baby" special effects. Few who saw *It's Alive*'s monster babies (puppets, actually), would ever forget the murderous tykes, or the issues they raised about what it means to be a "parent."

Psychic Powers, the Paranormal, and Haunted Houses

Not every horror movie made in the 1970s spoke specifically to the fears of the decade. There were many, many horror films that used the same ideas and settings that had appeared in genre films since the beginning of the medium. Instead of offering new ideas on these well-worn topics, the horror films of the 1970s improved on the special effects wizardry of past efforts, and generally offered more intensity than their predecessors.

Perhaps because science had proven so lousy at handling many of America's problems, audiences turned to more "extreme" possibilities in the 1970s, hence the resurgence of films about psychic powers. *Carrie* (1976), based on the first novel by horrormeister Stephen King, and

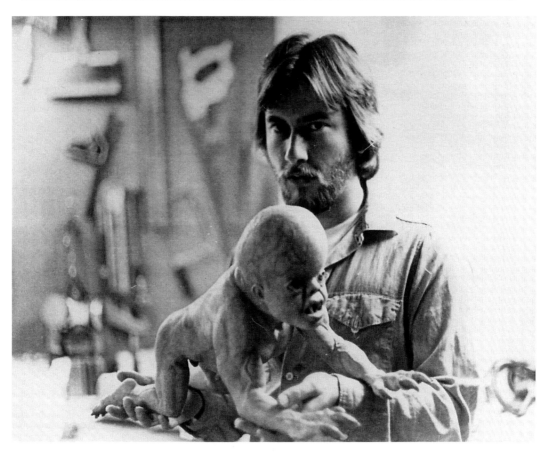

One man and a (mutant) baby: Make-up guru Rick Baker fondles the monstrous child of *It's Alive* (1973).

directed by Brian DePalma, highlighted the travails of a shy girl (Sissy Spacek) who developed telekinetic powers on the eve of her transition to adulthood (signaled by the onset of her period). Once imbued with the power to defend herself, Carrie struck back "psychically" at her Christian fanatic mother (Piper Laurie) as well as the cruel teens at her high school that had victimized her (including Nancy Allen and John Travolta). The picture was so stylishly shot by DePalma, and well acted by Spacek that *Carrie* set off a mini-trend of its own.

Before long, there was *Ruby* (1977), about a girl (again the daughter of Piper Laurie) with strange powers, and *Jennifer* (1978), wherein actress Lisa Pelikan uti-

lized her psychic ability to conjure venomous snakes (?!) to kill those who had tormented her in school. Another interesting variation on *Carrie* and psychic powers came from Australian director Richard Franklin in 1978. *Patrick* was the story of a comatose patient who was capable of directing mental energy at his enemies. Unlike Carrie, however, the sleeping Patrick was a monster through and through, evincing almost no sympathy. The weirdest telekinesis film of the 1970s may have been *Tourist Trap* (1979) which saw a nutty Chuck Connors animating grotesque mannequins with his psychic abilities...

Telekinesis was in evidence in another Brian DePalma film of the 1970s,

The Fury (1978). Here, the government was kidnapping powerful psychics (including Andrew Stevens) and training them as assassins. A side effect of psychic powers, it seemed, was the ability to disrupt the blood flow of other human beings in close proximity. In *The Fury*'s over-the-top finale, psychic Amy Irving focused her mental energy on government operative John Cassavetes and reduced him to bloody smithereens. The incredible special effects, which looked like Cassavetes had been wired with explosives and then detonated, were viewed in several rapid cuts for the unexpected climax. David Cronenberg followed up on many of *The Fury*'s conceits with his 1981 film, *Scanners.*

Telekinesis wasn't the only psychic power to gain film attention in the 1970s. ESP or psychic vision was the subject of *Eyes of Laura Mars* (1978), a thriller in which photographer Faye Dunaway could see through the eyes of a psychotic killer (Tommy Lee Jones). Reincarnation also received a thorough once-over in Robert Wise's thoughtful film on the subject, *Audrey Rose* (1977). But if any occult happening received as much attention as vengeful telekinesis in the 1970s, it was surely spirit possession, a topic made popular by *The Exorcist* in 1973. Though the Friedkin film had involved demonic possession, many filmmakers were taken with the idea that spirits of the dead could also possess the living to right some perceived wrong in a past life.

A dead gangster possessed the living in both the blaxploitation horror film *J.D.'s Revenge* (1976) and the aforementioned Curtis Harrington picture, *Ruby.* The spirit of a powerful Indian medicine man grew out of a tumor (!) on Susan Strasberg's back in the last film directed by cult '70s icon William Girdler, *The Manitou* (1978). A man was possessed by the spirit of his dead ancestor in Dan Curtis's franchise picture, *Night of Dark Shadows*

(1971), and Shirley MacLaine's brother was "taken over" by the spirit of a Puerto Rican serial killer in *The Possession of Joel Delaney* (1971).

Actually, every trope of the occult and paranormal had its day in the 1970s. Alien abductions were the subject of Larry Cohen's bizarre *God Told Me To* (1976), a precursor to *The X-Files* (1993–). Big Foot sightings were the subject of the "documentary"-like low-budgeter by Charlie Pierce, *Legend of Boggy Creek* (1973), an early *Blair Witch Project* type of film.

That old cinematic favorite, the haunted house, dominated such films as *The Legend of Hell House* (1973), *Burnt Offerings* (1976), *The Haunting of Julia* (1976) and the "based on a true story" thriller *The Amityville Horror* (1979). Each of these films was pretty interesting, and oddly, quite different from the rest. *The Legend of Hell House*, starring Roddy McDowall, perfectly staged an intellectual debate comparing science and the paranormal, while *The Amityville Horror*, based on the Jay Anson best-seller, was a more visceral, gut-punching take on haunted houses.

Even witchcraft and other "pagan" religions had their day in variety of seventies horror films. Witches and witchhunters found favor in such films as *The Blood on Satan's Claw* (1970), Ken Russell's *The Devils* (1971), and the incredibly violent Udo Kier vehicle *The Mark of the Devil* (1972).

Genre favorite Dario Argento guided audiences to a dancing school populated by powerful witches in the Italian-made gorefest *Suspiria* (1977), a high-water mark for the director. Australian helmer Peter Weir delved deep into "pagan" aborigine lore in a stunning film about "apocalypse" called *The Last Wave* (1977), his follow-up to the lyrical *Picnic at Hanging Rock* (1975). And then there was *The Wicker Man* (1971), a compelling horror movie about

The truth about Summerisle is revealed in the fiery climax of *The Wicker Man* (1971).

pagan "fertility" rituals on the English island of Summerisle. The film, which starred Christopher Lee, Britt Ekland, and Edward Woodward, culminated in one of the most unexpected (but logical...) climaxes in horror history.

And the Rest

Many horror films of the 1970s defy easy categorization. *Phantasm* (1979), directed by Don Coscarelli, was an unusual effort that seemed to march to the rhythm of its own internal logic. It played out like a nightmare, featured an iconic villain (Angus Scrimm's the Tall Man), and offered grotesque special effects (including a flying silver sphere that could drain the blood of its victims). Was it a dream? An alternate universe? A nightmare come to life? Whatever it was, *Phantasm* was beautifully done, and an affecting horror movie.

The Car (1977) was probably the weirdest *Jaws* rip-off yet imagined, because it pitted a "hellish" organism (like the great white shark in *Jaws*) against a small community and its sheriff (James Brolin). Unlike *Jaws*, however, the threat in *The Car* was clearly a machine, an automobile, and the film also included supernatural resonance. It was a strange hybrid, to be sure.

And speaking of hybrids, there was the unforgettable *The Thing with Two Heads* (1972), an AIP blaxploitation/science gone awry/car chase/comedy which had the audacity to transplant Ray Milland's head onto Rosey Grier's body.

Only in the '70s.

II

The Films (by Year)

The over 225 films reviewed in this section are dated to the time of their American release. For example, some sources list *Frankenstein Must Be Destroyed!* as being produced by Hammer in 1969, but the film didn't hit American shores (or reviewers) until 1970, hence its inclusion in this text. As critics will no doubt note, this is an American-centric text, but it also includes representative "foreign" horror films when they made an impact on the United States market, its directors, or audiences.

The films listed in this section appear alphabetically by year of American release, and most entries include several categories of information. *Critical Reception* is a sampling of '70s and contemporary reviews, *Cast & Crew* highlights the film's personnel, and the *P.O.V.* offers a pithy quotation from a talent pertinent to that film's production. *Critical Reception* and *P.O.V.* sections appear only where pertinent information is available. It is difficult, after all,

to find three reviews of barely remembered films such as *Shriek of the Mutilated* (1974) or *Carnival of Blood* (1971).

The *Synopsis* is a recounting of the film's story, and the *Commentary* is this author's analysis of the film in question. Some especially notable horror films, such as *Halloween* (1978), also feature a section entitled *Legacy,* which looks at the film's position in the horror pantheon beyond the 1970s.

For a handful of films—most of them genre efforts that played at local drive-ins—the Synopsis and Commentary sections have been folded into one short paragraph called *Details*. Because few of these films are available for viewing today, it was not possible to provide full information or commentary.

All the films are rated in the traditional four star system, with four stars (* * * *) being the highest rating and one star (*) the lowest.

(1 9 7 0)

And Soon the Darkness (1970) ✶ ✶ ✶ ½

Critical Reception

"…Everything goes well toward building tensions with understated effects. But eventually, by mere repetition, the understated effects begin to look like poverty of the imagination. Then terror becomes a function of gratuitous camera technique…."— Roger Greenspun, *New York Times*, April 5, 1970, page 44.

Cast & Crew

CAST: Pamela Franklin (Jane); Michele Dotrice (Cathy); Sandor Eles (Paul); John Nettleton (Gendarme); Clare Kelly (Schoolmistress); Hana-Marie Pravda (Madame Lassal); John Franklyn (Old Man); Claude Bertrand (Lassal); Jean Carmet (Renier).

CREW: *Production Supervisor:* Johnny Goodman. *Assistant Directors:* Ken Baker, Alain Bennett. *Continuity:* Mary Spain. *Casting Director:* Robert Lennard. *Director of Photography:* Ian Wilson. *Camera Operator:* Godfrey Godar. *Camera Assistant:* Brian Cole. *Make-up:* Gerry Fletcher. *Hairdresser:* Allan McKeown. *Sets Designed by:* Phillip Harrison. *Assistant Art Director:* Roger Christian, Eric Simon. *Wardrobe:* Roy Ponting. *Construction Manager:* Stan Gale. *Properties:* Rex Hobbs. *Editor:* Ann Chegwidden. *Sound:* Bill Rowe. *Sound Assistant:* Terry Allen. *Dubbing Editor:* Peter Lennard. *Music:* Laurie Johnson. *Original story and screenplay by:* Brian Clemens and Terry Nation. *Produced by:* Albert Fennell and Brian Clemens. *Directed by:* Robert Fuest. Made on location in France and at the Elstree Studios of Associate British Productions Ltd., London, England. *M.P.A.A. rating:* PG. *Running Time:* 94 minutes.

SYNOPSIS: Two beautiful English girls, Cathy and Jane, tour rural France by bicycle. They stop at a cafe and plan their next destination when Cathy makes eyes at a mysterious Frenchman named Paul. They resume their journey and Paul blazes by them on his motor scooter. He parks and waits for them ahead, and they pass him by. When they are gone, Paul visits the grave of a young woman not far from the roadside.

Cathy and Jane stop for a rest. They discuss marriage and life until Jane decides it is time to get going … because it will be dark soon. The girls quarrel because Cathy wants to meet Paul and catch a nap. Subsequently, Jane sets off without Cathy. Then, thinking better of it, Jane stops at the Cafe San Rivo and waits for Cathy to catch up. Madame Lassal, owner of the cafe, warns Jane that the road is "bad." This fact is proven dramatically to Cathy when she awakens from a nap and is observed by a dangerous stranger. Cathy finds her bike sabotaged and is then attacked by the stranger.

The hours pass and Jane grows worried about Cathy. She rides back to the spot off-road where her friend was resting and finds Cathy's camera, but no sign of Cathy. Paul mysteriously arrives at the same time, claiming to be a Parisian detective, and helps Jane search for her friend. Jane backtracks to another road stop and meets a British schoolmistress who warns her that a beautiful tourist was murdered on this very road three years earlier. When Jane meets up with Paul again, he tells her he has found Cathy's bike under a car in a junkyard. Jane grows suspicious of Paul and flees from him when he exposes the film in Cathy's camera, the very film that might have photographed a murderer.

Jane runs to Cafe San Rivo, gets no help, and makes her way to the gendarme's house. There, she meets the gendarme's deaf father, a weird old bird who has been wandering the road and backwoods all day. Jane tells the gendarme her story and he drives his motorcycle to Cafe San Rivo to confirm the story with the owners.

Meanwhile, Paul catches up with Jane at the gendarme's house and begs to be allowed inside. When Paul breaks into the house, Jane flees through the backyard and runs to a junkyard of trailers and derelict cars. Jane hides in a trailer as Paul hunts her down, saying he needs desperately to talk with her. As Jane hides in the closet, Cathy's dead body falls on her! Jane screams and runs from the trailer, Paul in hot pursuit. Jane fights back and strikes Paul in the face with a rock.

Just then, Jane runs into the gendarme. He comforts her for a moment, but then starts to make advances toward her. Jane realizes that the gendarme is the killer, and tries to escape. In the end, a wounded Paul comes to her aid and saves Jane from the gendarme who is also a rapist-murderer.

COMMENTARY: Penned by British fantasy television's most renowned writers Brian Clemens, who created *The Avengers*, and Terry Nation, creator of *Blake's 7* and *Doctor Who*'s popular Daleks, *And Soon the Darkness* is a suspenseful little masterpiece of the psycho-film variety. The film is admirably compact, dealing with only a handful of characters (many serve as red herrings), an isolated setting (a stretch of country road in France…) and a terribly brutal crime: the rape and murder of a beautiful tourist. From this simple template, director Robert Fuest wrings maximum shivers, proving he can accomplish his best work in a quasi–Hitchcockian framework rather than the more campy, though amusing, supernatural horror his name came to be associated with (*The*

Abominable Dr. Phibes, Dr. Phibes Rises Again, and *The Devil's Rain*).

Some horror/suspense films fail by attempting to stretch shallow concepts across a wide canvas when a more personal, more intimate approach seems appropriate. *And Soon the Darkness* is a film that understands this shortcoming and focuses itself on the issue at hand: a tiny stretch of road in rural France. During the course of the picture, the viewer travels this road with protagonist Jane (Pamela Franklin) so many times, back and forth almost endlessly, that even the most rudimentary landmarks (like trees and rocks) become recognizable. Yet, amazingly, the mystery deepens as viewers become more familiar with the terrain. The geography may be plain, but the psychological geography of Cathy's murder (which Paul calls "the most unpredictable of crimes") remains hidden until the closing moments of the picture.

The consequence of traveling this particular road so frequently is that every change, every nuance in the well-explored terrain takes on significance in the mystery. What are the owners of the San Rivo Cafe burning in their garage? What is hidden in the haystack on the curb? What secret is shrouded inside the automobile junkyard behind the gendarme's house? Who is the strange figure that appears periodically (in cryptic long shot) out in the distant fields? All of these questions take on a sense of menace because director Fuest has given the film time to develop its isolated landscape before plunging into the pertinent action. Fuest is especially strong at not revealing his hand too early, and the film builds slowly enough, never pushing the tension, to allow audiences to ponder important questions.

Who is Paul and why does he follow the girls? Is it wise for Cathy and Jane to separate? Why is the gendarme so disliked by locals? How is the British school teacher, who gazes about suspiciously after offering Jane a ride, involved in Cathy's disappearance? To the film's credit, it moves forward purposefully, while hitting each note of suspense on the way to crescendo.

And Soon the Darkness also trades effectively on its conventional horror setting and situation: the road trip gone wrong. A set-up featured in many 1970s horror films, including *The Brotherhood of Satan, The Texas Chainsaw Massacre, Race with the Devil*, and *Tourist Trap*, the "road trip to terror" is usually an effective scenario because the audience comes to sympathize with the fish-out-of-water protagonists. While traveling, after all, everyone is a stranger. When you don't know where you are, when you don't know or understand local customs, when you are in fact, a stranger to everyone nearby, it is difficult to be sure where to go seeking help or who to trust during an emergency. *And Soon the Darkness* plays on the fear of being isolated in a strange land and becomes ever more sinister because the viewer realizes just how much he or she does not know about the locale. Like Jane, the viewer does not know who to fear and who to trust, and director Fuest ruthlessly exploits that sympathetic uncertainty to achieve his effects. The film literally makes one tight-throated with suspense as it goes from murder to trust to mistrust, but never loses focus on its anchor: Franklin's expressive, increasingly fearful face.

And Soon the Darkness earns its suspense stripes in other ways too. The film makes use of the anxiety-provoking knowledge that sundown is inevitably approaching (hence the title), and that it would be terrible, catastrophic even, for Jane to remain in this neck of the woods as night falls. It is also a unique-looking horror film because it is set almost entirely out-of-doors, and even has a psychological complexity in dealing with reflections of the same demented personality. Two law-enforcement officials stalk that stretch of the road: both obsessed; both solitary; both wanting something from Jane. Yet only one of them is a murderer.

In all horror films, there is (consciously or unconsciously), a directorial approach: shock versus suspense. A movie can either "jolt" a viewer with surprise information, or drive a viewer up the wall by making him or her aware of how certain facts might play out. Like the best of its genre, *And Soon the Darkness* incorporates both approaches well, interspersing jolts with an air of uncertainty. The early scene in the woods wherein Cathy is killed is a notable example. The audience is aware that the girls have been followed. It is aware that Cathy and Jane have quarreled and that Jane has elected to continue her bike journey, leaving Cathy alone in a clearing. The audience has also seen the grave of a beautiful blonde girl who died on that very road. All of these facts, taken together, generate a feeling of tension or suspense: a shadowy pursuer, an opportunity to strike, and a history of violence in this place. The suspense becomes palpable when Cathy awakens from a nap and realizes that an intruder is close by, that he has sabotaged her bike and made off with her luggage (including her spare underwear…). She hears a rustling in the woods and then BOOM — the jolt, "the stinger" comes. It is just one very well handled scene in a picture of Hitchcockian purity and dimension.

The last sequence of shots in *And Soon the Darkness* serve the picture particularly well, heightening suspense, providing release, and ultimately issuing a warning to all travelers. After Jane has grappled with her attacker (the gendarme) in high angle (expressing her entrapment), Paul rescues her. Mysteriously, the camera adopts an even higher angle, looking straight down at the action as it withdraws from the scene, the conflict resolved. As Fuest's camera glides away from Jane, now safe, and Paul, now vindicated, it gazes down briefly through the transparent sunroof of a discarded trailer (where Cathy's corpse has been stowed.) The camera glimpses part of her twisted body and the audience is reminded of the preceding horror. But then a cleansing rain falls on the window, obscuring the corpse and letting the audience know that this particular nightmare is over. Yet next, the camera cuts to the road, that same bloody road, and two innocent bikers traverse it playfully, blissfully unaware. Fuest's message is plain: this particular horror may be over, but there are others lying in wait on the road for those who are not careful. It is a stunning finale, and one that understands how camera placement and movement can convey theme and mood.

And Soon the Darkness is a terrifying venture into a foreign land, where foreign secrets threaten to reach out and strangle the innocent. The film never reveals precisely why the gendarme has turned into a homicidal rapist, but nor should it. Were we in Jane or Cathy's place, traveling gleefully on vacation in another country, we wouldn't know the answer either. And that's what makes *And Soon the Darkness* a truly frightening picture. It reminds us that what we don't know can hurt us.

The Blood on Satan's Claw (1970) ✳ ✳ ✳

Critical Reception

"…for the first hour, Piers Haggard keeps his themes and the blood flowing nicely. It begins in style…. Sadly, Haggard lets things slip and the make-up man takes over."— Adrian Turner, *Time Out Film Guide*, Seventh Edition, Penguin Books, 1999, page 789.

"…cinematic diabolism of some style and intelligence … a horror movie of more than routine interest … it contains Lovecraft's perfectly straightfaced acceptance of a universe whose natural order may, at any time, be overturned by supernatural disorder."— Vincent Canby, *New York Times*, April 15, 1971, page 35.

"What makes this British movie about witchcraft … more effective than most period horror pictures is its convincing and dramatic depiction of its historical setting…. The script may fall down in spots, but the well-crafted mood … still manages to carry the ball."— Dr. Cyclops, *Fangoria* #30, October, 1983, page 44.

Cast & Crew

CAST: Patrick Wymark (the Judge); Linda Hayden (Angel Blake); Barry Andrews (Ralph Gower); Michele Dotrice (Margaret); James Hayter (Squire Middleton); Anthony Ainley (Reverend Fallowfield); Howard Goorney (the Doctor); Avice Landon (Isobel Banham); Charlotte Mitchell (Ellen); Wendy Padbury (Cathy Vespers); Tamara Ustinov (Rosalind Barton); Simon Williams (Peter Edmonton); Robin Davies (Mark Vespers).

CREW: Dennis Friedland and Christopher C. Dewey Present a Tigon British/Chilton Film Production. *Music composed and conducted by:* Marc Wilkinson. *Art Director:* Arnold Chapkis. *Editor:* Richard Best. *Production Manager:* Ron Jackson. *Assistant Director:* Stephen Christian. *Camera Operator:* Dudley Lovell. *Sound Mixer:* Tony Dawe. *Sound Editor:* Bill Trent. *Dubbing Mixer:* Ken Barker. *Casting Director:* Weston Drury, Jr. *Set Dresser:* Milly Burns. *Continuity:* Josie Fulford. *Make-up:* Eddie Knight. *Hairdresser:* Olga Angelinetta. *Wardrobe Mistress:* Dulcie Midwinter. *Focus Puller:* Mike Rutter. *Grip:* Peg Hall. *Titles and Opticals:* General Screen Enterprises Ltd. *Processed by:* Rank Film Labs, Denham. *Director of Photography:* Dick Bush. *Executive Producer:* Tony Tenser. *Original Screenplay by:* Robert Wynne-Simmons. *With additional material by:* Piers Haggard. *Produced by:* Peter L. Andrews, Malcolm B. Heyworth. *Directed by:* Piers Haggard. Made at Pinewood Studios, England, and on location. *M.P.A.A. Rating:* R. *Running Time:* 90 minutes.

SYNOPSIS: In 1670, young Ralph Gower is plowing the Edmonton field when he unearths a bizarre, inhuman skull in the mud.

He reports his finding to the Judge, an official visiting from London, but his report is dismissed when the skull mysteriously vanishes. Meanwhile, young Peter Edmonton has brought his fiancée, Rosalind, to the farm. She is to spend the night in an attic room, but once darkness falls, Rosalind goes crazy, terrified of some dark presence in the room. The next morning she is carted off to an insane asylum ... her hand transformed into a hairy, pointed claw. Peter's aunt, scratched by Rosalind's clawed digits, then disappears ... not to be found anywhere.

Peter becomes convinced that evil is free in his small parish, even as the judge returns to London to research the possibility of witchcraft and Satanism in the small rural hamlet. Soon, other villagers are cursed by the claw of Satan. While frolicking in the Edmonton field, beautiful teen Angel Blake also finds a satanic claw ... and becomes possessed with evil. She attempts to seduce the Reverend Fallowfield, but he rejects her advances. Later, she accuses him of raping her, and the town squire believes the charges. This witch hunt gives Angel and her strange satanic cult the time it needs to grow and spread among the youngsters of the parish.

Before long, the virtuous young are becoming minions of evil. Kathy Vespers is raped and killed for bearing the mark of the devil (a hairy tuft on her back), and another boy, Mark, is found murdered at the bottom of a woodpile. Ralph, terrified at the terror his discovery has wrought, seeks to protect Margaret, a girl being hunted as a witch. He finds, to his horror, that she too bears the mark of the devil and asks the local doctor to cut it out. Even with the hairy deformity lopped off, Margaret still confesses her allegiance to the Dark One, and Ralph realizes that she is truly a devil worshiper. Soon, the forests outside town are too dangerous to traverse, and devil rites are held by night with Angel Blake presiding.

Peter visits the judge in London, who declares he is ready to return and defeat the growing evil. He sets out with vicious dogs to hunt the devil and his kindred. Mean-while, the morally upright citizens of town form a mob to burn the witches. Ralph, hoping to stop the evil, visits the Edmonton attic, is confronted by a dark specter ... and is then prepared for a satanic ceremony. Before Ralph can be sacrificed, the witch hunters (led by the judge) interfere in the rite, killing Angel Blake. Satan himself is stabbed by the stalwart judge with a sword, and then hurled into a fire.

COMMENTARY: Piers Haggard's *The Blood on Satan's Claw* transports the viewer to a world without sunlight, and consequently without hope. In this strikingly photographed horror picture, all light is a cold blue, deathly as it were, and every color is distinctly faded ... as if life itself has been bled out of reality. This icy look, coupled with a very accurate, very detailed art design, is the film's greatest advantage. Never for a moment is the viewer required to leave the reality of the historical period for lack of accuracy or believability. For better or worse, the audience inhabits the English parish besieged by evil, and that grounding in a specific place ultimately plays in the film's favor. In keeping with the look of the film, *The Blood on Satan's Claw*'s plot is less than linear, less than coherent even, and the story is muddled and confusing at times. But, in horror the story is not always as paramount as the texture or mood established, and in this regard, *The Blood on Satan's Claw* clearly excels. Its bleak visage is a memorable one, and echoed by the particulars of its story.

A world without hope is the terrain of *The Blood on Satan's Claw*. The sun — a warm, welcoming, bright source of light that casts hopeful yellow illumination — is never seen in this picture. Skies are overcast and slate gray. But the absence of the sun is not the only element in the film that reflects hopelessness and death. As the film opens, young Ralph Gower tends to a field. All around him in that fallow field is overturned mud, earth, and dirt, but importantly no greens, no bright colors whatsoever. Even behind him, the green of the foliage is washed out to a muted gray. Appropriately, the demon skull is found in this spot, which the color palette informs the audience is quite dead. Nothing will grow from that earth except evil.

In the same sequence, young Cathy Vespers greets Ralph, and Haggard's camera adopts a position behind her, amidst the woods. This beautiful young girl (Wendy Padbury — Zoe of *Doctor Who*), is seen through the lifeless branches of dead trees. The lack of leaves, of vegetation, again cements the impression of a cold, dead world (or season) where life does not flourish. In keeping with this motif of pallor and death, Ralph discovers not a bud blooming in the Edmonton field, but the skull of an ancient "fiend." The land has brought up only a flower of death, and soon that death will spread across the rural landscape like ivy, infecting all it touches.

There can be no hope, no future, in a world where the children (the torchbearers in human terms) are lost, and *The Blood on Satan's Claw* continues the metaphor of hope murdered by making it the children (or the young adults, anyway) who are contaminated by evil first. It is no accident that the children are corrupted initially, because their conversion to evil signals the death of the future, hence the death of a better tomorrow, or any tomorrow at all. Virginal Angel Blake is transformed into a lusty whore, forsaking the church to bring down the virtuous (in her attempted seduction of Reverend Fallowfield). The transformation to evil is played out on her very face; it is darkened by overarching black eyebrows, a stark contrast to the sunny blond hair that informs her young beauty. Likewise, Cathy Vespers, a humble servant girl of solid character, is deflowered, robbed of her virtue, and killed in her prime. Even the level-headed Ralph succumbs to the spreading evil, only to be rescued by the judge at the last minute. And those children who do not die outright (such as poor Rosalind) are tainted forever by madness, doomed to fruitless lives of incarceration and mental

illness. Thus Haggard has visually killed hope (with the washed out, lifeless look of the picture) and metaphorically done so to boot, by targeting the future in the form of the next generation. It goes without saying that the adults represent a kind of emptiness. The reverend, a man purportedly representing God, is named "Fallowfield," a synonym for "empty." Adults, and even religious faith, offer nothing but dogma.

The Blood on Satan's Claw is a bizarre, frightening film despite the meandering of its plot, emerging as a creepy, atmospheric nose-dive into the irrational (and anti-rational). Accordingly, some of the scenes in the picture are genuinely frightening. Early in the film, Rosalind sleeps in the dark Edmonton attic, and the film plays on that primal human fear that there is something malevolent waiting for us in the blackness of night. In this case, that fear is well grounded, and the film only hints at the precise appearance and nature of this evil: a flash of dark motion in a dark room, a glimpse of something hairy and animal-like, before the silence at midnight is punctuated by terrified shrieks.

Two other characters, Peter and Ralph, journey to that attic (at night as well, naturally) in due order, and each occasion is similarly terrifying. The monster inhabiting that room seems to exist in barely lit corners, under floorboards, beside the bed ... waiting. To some, this notion of an old evil infecting our reality is representative of a Lovecraftian order, but fear of the dark is a universal dread, one exploited by *The Blood on Satan's Claw*.

Oddly, *The Blood on Satan's Claw* does not unfold in the dogmatic manner of its brethren horror films. As viewers, we have all been conditioned to expect things at certain times, and to feel certain ways when images of terror pop up. This movie defies that training and marches along to its own unusual rhythm. If the plot does not exactly make literal sense that too seems a reflection of its content. In its tale of a diabolical world order inexplicably and irrevocably replacing our own, the film kills reason, rationality and science. Characters change into monsters with no prologue, demons shrouded in hoods prowl the forests, the virtuous become deviant, and there is nary an explanation in sight. The spread of evil seems random and rampant, nonsensical even. Yet what better way to depict a world without hope than to murder those very things which provide man a measure of solace in this mortal coil? The comfort of reasonable scientific explanation, of faith even, is denied the audience.

In its depiction of an anti-rational spread of pure evil, *The Blood on Satan's Claw* generates real psychological discomfort. Why is this outbreak occurring here, now? Why and how are people succumbing so rapidly? The movie denies all impulses to frame answers, and audiences are left with a perplexing, but ultimately rewarding meditation on the fact that it is the essence of the human condition not to have answers. Existence is mysterious, and our physics are but human constructs designed to explain these enigmas. But, in the end, explanations are merely constructs, and oddities and anomalies, like an inhuman skull unearthed in the mud, have a way of popping up and shattering the delusion that we understand our universe.

As a witch hunt movie, *The Blood on Satan's Claw is* quite interesting because it takes a stance opposite from the majority of its brethren (such as *The Devils* [1971], *Mark of the Devil* [1972], and *The Crucible* [1996]). In those instances, there are no witches, and the witch-hunters are depicted as self-righteous opportunists and demagogues out to destroy that which they do not approve. In this film, the judge (Wymark) is heroic, and there truly are witches loose in the woods. Again, this is interesting only in that it is an unconventional take on timeworn material. This movie is not out to make a social comment about paranoia, the mob mentality, politics or the like. Its scope is actually grander. It wants viewers to question their assumptions about reality and reveal a world where sunlight (and reason) don't penetrate.

Though populated by too many bland characters and saddled with far too many irrelevant, seemingly unconnected incidents, as well as weak make-up for the demon (only briefly glimpsed), *The Blood on Satan's Claw* is a film that generates a feeling of unease. Though good is vindicated in the abrupt finale, there is the sense that this evil flower could blossom again, that malevolence has not been stamped out. It is a gray, hopeless, and frightening motion picture, and in that way, quite effective as horror.

Bram Stoker's Count Dracula (*El Conde Dracula*) (1970) ✶ ✶

Critical Reception

"*Count Dracula* … despite claims of being completely faithful, is a complete mess…. Lee makes the most he can of the opportunity, but the shabby production values defeat him in the end…."— Steve Biodrowski, *Cinefantastique* Volume 23, #4: "Dracula The Oft Told Story," December 1992, page 29.

"It was a good idea to attempt an exact filming of Bram Stoker's 1897 novel, but Franco and producer Harry Alan Towers clearly weren't up to the task…. The film proceeds clumsily and looks disgustingly cheap…. Lee's performance is authoritative but loses its edge under the deadpan stare of Manuel Merino's inept camera…."— Tim Lucas, *Fangoria* #78: "The Agony and the Ecstasy of Jess Franco" (Part I); page 18.

"...demonstrates none of the flair and ingenuity of Badham's *Dracula* and none of the unpretentious craft of Fisher's [Hammer] vampire films.... Problems with sound synchronization, dubbing dialogue and inappropriate locations ... often turn this film into unintentionally humorous camp."—Gregory A. Waller, *The Living and the Undead: From Stoker's Dracula to Romero's Dawn of the Dead*, 1986, page 136.

Cast & Crew

CAST: Christopher Lee (Count Dracula); Herbert Lom (Professor Van Helsing); Klaus Kinski (Renfield); Maria Rohm (Mina); Frederick Williams (Jonathan Harker); Soledad Miranda (Lucy); Jack Taylor (Quincy Morris); Paul Muller (Dr. Seward).

CREW: *Photographed by:* Manuel Merino. *Assistant Director:* John Thompson. *Art Director:* George O'Brown. *Production Manager:* Jose Climent. *Editor:* Derek Parsons. *Sound Editor:* Joyce Oxley. *Music:* Bruno Nicolai. *Editor:* Derek Parsons. *Screenplay by:* Peter Weibeck. *Produced by:* Harry Alan Towers. *Directed by:* Jess Franco. A Towers of London Production.

SYNOPSIS: In 1897, a young lawyer from London, Jonathan Harker, boards a train for Transylvania to visit with a new client, Count Dracula. A fellow passenger on the train and the wife of an innkeeper in Transylvania warn Harker not to visit the strange count on St. George's night because it is a bad omen. Harker ignores these warnings and proceeds. In the dark of the night, he is picked up by Dracula's carriage and driven to a magnificent castle. On the way, wolves bay in the woods, and the mysterious carriage driver — Dracula himself — clears them away with a supernatural power.

Jonathan arrives at the castle of Dracula and notes that his host casts no reflection. Ignoring this oddity, Harker gets down to the business at hand: Dracula wants to purchase land in London, specifically Carfax Abbey. Meanwhile, Dracula spies a photograph of Harker's beautiful fiancée, Mina, and her lovely friend Lucy, and his old blood is subsequently stirred to devilish new action. Harker is locked in his room for the evening, and then captured by three brides of Dracula—all vampires. Dracula prevents the women from feeding on his guest, and the women hungrily drink a baby's blood instead.

The next morning, Harker awakens with two puncture marks on his neck and realizes that his escape from the lair of Dracula is a matter of life and death. After discovering Dracula asleep in a coffin, Harker jumps out a window and is carried away to safety on the currents of a river.

Some time later, a demented Jonathan Harker arrives at the private clinic of Professor Van Helsing and Dr. Seward in London, just across the street from Carfax Abbey. Harker is not the only one to rave about the power of Dracula. Another patient, Renfield, has also been driven mad by his encounter with the demonic count. Soon, Mina and Lucy visit the clinic to check on Harker, and decide to remain there until he is well. But by night, Dracula summons Lucy, calling her out onto the grounds of the clinic. Mina follows the mesmerized Lucy and finds her victimized: her neck drained of blood! Learning of Lucy's desperate condition, her fiancé, Quincy Morris, arrives to give his beloved a much-needed blood transfusion.

That night, Dracula strikes again. He steals into Lucy's room and dines on the blood from her sweet neck until Mina interrupts. Meanwhile, Van Helsing tells Quincy Morris and the rapidly recovering Jonathan Harker that poor Renfield's daughter was the victim of a mythological creature known as a vampire. Furthermore, Van Helsing believes Dracula to be that vampire: an undead creature of the night capable of maintaining eternal youth by feeding on the blood of the innocent. He also fears that poor Lucy, dead from Dracula's consumption, will return to life as a vampire herself. This is a more accurate guess than he realizes; Lucy has already risen from her coffin and feasted on the blood of a young girl! That night, Van Helsing, Morris and Harker visit Lucy's mausoleum and drive a stake through her heart to prevent any further resurrection from the grave.

Dracula sets his vampiric sights on Mina, and attacks her at the opera. Aware that Van Helsing and the others are onto him, the Prince of Darkness decides it is time to return to Transylvania, and books passage on a ship bound for Varna. While Van Helsing remains behind to protect Mina from Dracula's deadly attentions, Morris, Seward and Harker race to Transylvania in an attempt to beat the count to his castle. They successfully interrupt his journey and burn Dracula's body while he sleeps peacefully in a coffin. Dracula ages hundreds of years in just seconds, and finally dies.

COMMENTARY: Bram Stoker's novel *Dracula* is to horror films what William Shakespeare's *Hamlet* is to the theatre and film: a great work of art revisited time and again across the decades, always a bit different from previous incarnations, but always the same in important ways too. And, like *Hamlet*, the primary interest in any adaptation of *Dracula* is the portrayal of the lead role. Every new actor who essays either the Prince of Denmark or the Prince of Darkness injects a fresh spin on the familiar material. And, audiences never grow fatigued with the different cadences and nuances in such updatings.

On the silver screen there have been at least three significant Hamlets: Laurence Olivier in 1948, Mel Gibson in 1990 and Kenneth Branagh in 1997. There have been even more Count Draculas (Bela Lugosi in 1931, Lon Chaney, Jr. in 1943, John Carradine in 1944, Christopher Lee in 1958, David Niven in 1973, Udo Kier in 1974, Frank Langella in 1979 and Gary Oldman in 1992). On TV, Jack Palance and Louis Jordan have had the honor of portraying the famous vampire.

If one is of the opinion that both versions of *Nosferatu* (1922 and 1979 respec-

tively) are also variations on the Dracula myth, horror's equivalent of Hamlet has been produced for film a staggering number of times. *Dracula* (1931), *The Horror of Dracula* (1958), *Bram Stoker's Count Dracula* (1970), *Andy Warhol's Dracula* (1974), *Dracula* (1979), and *Bram Stoker's Dracula* (1992) all employ the characters and situations outlined in Stoker's seminal book. If one adds the sequels, spin-offs and such, the appearances of horror's Hamlet increase geometrically. *Dracula's Daughter* (1936), *Son of Dracula* (1943), *House of Dracula* (1944), *Dracula — Prince of Darkness* (1965), *Dracula Has Risen from the Grave* (1968), *Dracula A.D. 1972* (1972), *Dracula's Dog* (1978), and *Dracula's Widow* (1988) are a few such titles.

When one delves further, matters get even more bizarre: the regal count has been a porn star in vehicles such as *Dracula Sucks* (1978) and *Dracula Blows His Cool* (1979) and, in an even less dignified moment, he co-starred in *Abbott and Costello Meet Frankenstein* [1948])! *Blacula* (1972), *Love at First Bite* (1979), and *Dracula: Dead and Loving It!* (1995) represent other twists on the oft-repeated mythos.

Why is Dracula so popular a story to dramatize on film? The answers are numerous. Like Hamlet, Dracula can be interpreted as a tragedy. Dracula, once a great and noble warrior, is doomed to an eternal half-life spent feeding on the living, and his great love always eludes him. Depending on the version, Dracula can be seen primarily not as horror, but a love story which "crosses oceans of time," (*Dracula* [1979], *Bram Stoker's Dracula* [1992]).

Other answers have less to do with literature and romance and more to do with plain old lust. Those who seek to analyze Dracula's popularity inevitably find themselves discussing the "the blood is the life" notion of the novel and its numerous adaptations. Specifically, Dracula steals the bodily fluid of beautiful women, enslaving them to his will. He is a charming seducer, a foreigner, who, inevitably, saves the beautiful Mina (or Lucy, depending on interpretation) at least briefly from a life of domestic boredom with the oh-so-stolid Jonathan Harker. Dracula is the perfect last fling before marriage: a sexual partner who promises great pleasures and then who conveniently dies, thus allowing his lovers to return to more "appropriate" life styles. A tragic love-story and a Victorian sexual adventure, *Dracula* is also about man's quest for immortality, something moviegoers of every generation can relate to.

And, at a basic level *Dracula* is a simple horror story: good versus evil, man versus monster. *Dracula* is also perfect film fodder because it has a powerful central role (the count himself), multiple beautiful women (Mina, Lucy and brides of Dracula), and an opportunity for an abundance of special effects (Dracula can be wolf, bat, man, or fog). What's not to like?

Since *Dracula* has been dramatized so frequently, it is hard to put a new spin on the story. It is difficult, if not impossible, to shock audiences with a story they are already familiar with. And that fact, at long last, brings to mind Jess Franco's 1970 production, *Bram Stoker's Dracula*. As the film opens, a title card reveals that "for the first time" filmmakers are intent on re-telling Bram Stoker's story "exactly as he wrote" it.

In other words, the twist evident here is a high degree of faithfulness to the source material. In *Bram Stoker's Count Dracula* this faithfulness is primarily demonstrated in that the early part of the novel, Harker's adventure at the Castle of Dracula, has been re-inserted. Most Dracula films dispense with this section of Stoker's text, and skip immediately to Victorian England and the Count's arrival there. So, it is a delight to report that *Bram Stoker's Count Dracula* does restore this section of the novel, and in fact, it is the most interesting portion of the film. If Franco's intent is to remain faithful to Stoker, then one can see why certain choices have been made. Christopher Lee's count wears all black and is decked out in a moustache — touches straight from Stoker. And, Lee even gets to mouth authentic dialogue (about Dracula's

lineage in regards to Attila the Hun) from the novel. In a bow to realism, Lee's Count is equipped with pointed fangs at all times. In other words, his vampire teeth are not retractable as in most versions of the story, lowering and appearing only when he comes in for the kill.

So earnest and respectful is director Franco in his attempt to make his *Count Dracula* faithful to Stoker that he presents what could be termed the most restrained version of the story yet. There are no surreal special effects or showy film techniques in the picture, and that might be considered a good thing. Some of the crazy effects and jumpy film techniques orchestrated by Francis Ford Coppola in his 1992 version transformed the story of Dracula into a freak show, so it is nice that such a path is not chosen here.

In addition, histrionics among the cast of *Count Dracula* have been discouraged. All of the actors are mightily restrained, to the degree that even the deranged Renfield is affected by the overarching air of respect and dignity for the material. Most frequently in film, Renfield is depicted as a crazy blabberer, but Kinski's interpretation is that of a silent brooder, a man more sullen than animated with fear. Herbert Lom is so taciturn and restrained as Van Helsing that in one crucial scene it is impossible to tell if he has suffered from a narcoleptic attack, is merely resting his eyes, or (as is actually the case) has suddenly suffered the effects of a debilitating stroke!

Christopher Lee makes for a remarkable Dracula, as usual, but he is not in the picture as much as one would hope. He is almost a guest star, appearing occasionally and then vanishing from the goings-on for interminable stretches. The inevitable result of such a restrained, respectful treatment is that *Count Dracula* becomes totally and utterly lifeless — a bore, in fact.

Once the die has been cast, and Franco has chosen what might be deemed the high road (faithfulness, restraint and respect for the material), he is left with perilously few options. Above all, a horror movie is intended to scare or thrill. Unfolding at a leisurely pace and flattened out by minimalist performances, *Count Dracula* is lacking in thrills, romance and fear. Lucy is played as a zombie who virtually surrenders at the drop of a hat to Dracula, and since there is never a bond formed between Mina and Dracula there is no romance either. Because the performances are so spare, the motivations of the characters seem missing in this version of *Dracula*. The count sees a picture of Mina and Lucy early in the picture and then goes to London to "take them" for reasons known only to him. In other versions of the film, Mina and the count share a timeless kind of love, or at least a powerful, seductive relationship. There is no such eroticism or suggestion of affection here, much to the film's detriment.

The decision to make a "realistic" Dracula without the surreal, and without hint of the Gothic, also results in the most lifeless finale to a vampire film ever put to celluloid. Seward, Morris and Harker catch Dracula sleeping and burn him in his coffin. *The end.* There is no feeling of relief (because no terror or suspense has been generated) and no sense of accomplishment or victory either.

The horror film is a tricky game: too little respect for the genre and its conventions and filmmakers end up with an ugly exploitation that pleases no one; too much respect for old material (as evidenced here) drains the life and inspiration out of a film and renders it stodgy. Jess Franco re-tells *Dracula* as though he, as director, is incidental to what unfolds on screen and Stoker's vision has apparently been substituted for his own creative input. *Count Dracula* may be faithful to a greater degree than many other Dracula films, but the film is so basic, so lacking in inspiration that it advances the Dracula legend not a bit. It could have been made in 1931 or 1958 because no new thought or inspiration (even as far as execution of the standard special effects) has been included. In horror, there are films that push the envelope, look forward to the future, and carry the genre to new edges. In the seventies, such films were *The Exorcist* (1973), *The Texas Chainsaw Massacre* (1974), *Carrie* (1976) and even *The Last House on the Left* (1972). Unfortunately, there are also those horror films that look backward and seem dated almost the moment they are released. If not for the technique *Count Dracula* most frequently deploys (zooms), the movie could have been made (and made better) by Hammer Studios in 1959.

One element of *Count Dracula* that dates it to the 1970s is the pervasive use of the zoom lens. In the seventies, zooms were terribly overused. As a result, most films made today shun the zoom as a laughable technique. The zoom is disliked by many cinematographers and directors because it distorts the edges of the frame as it does its thing, moving in or out. Today, zooms are utilized mostly to generate campy effect. A quick zoom in on somebody's face can generate a scare or a laugh, if done just right. *Count Dracula*, unfortunately, is mired in zooms.

Franco zooms in on wolves, zooms out from the castle, zooms in Dracula's eyes, zooms out from candelabras, zooms in on Lucy's catatonic face, zooms in on bars from Renfield's cell (and gets so close that the bars actually go out of focus then flicker back and forth, in and out of focus), *ad nauseam, ad infinitum.* When used sparingly and suddenly, a zoom can have dramatic and meaningful visual effect: shock! surprise! horror! But in *Count Dracula* Franco most often zooms at the slowest possible velocity, making his shots utterly predictable. The audience understands from the start how the zoom shots will end (either pulling back, or closing in), and thus long passages become waiting games as the camera endlessly zeroes in or backs up.

Often, it is unclear why a zoom is being used at all. A zoom is a useful technique in formalist film because it pinpoints something important to the audience — a detail, a face, a view. When used all the time, the zoom loses its potency because it is pinpointing every detail—often to the bewilderment of viewers.

Franco is not well served by the editing of the picture either. Much of the action of the film occurs in Van Helsing's clinic. One or two exterior shots of the clinic are appropriate. Strangely, the editor shows the same establishing shot of the clinic no less than five times during the duration of the picture, and holds on the familiar view for at least five or six seconds too long on each occurrence.

Another grave miscalculation is the ludicrous scene in which a bevy of stuffed and mounted animals come to life in Carfax Abbey. Not only are there too many blurry zooms in this sequence (a flaw, alas, of the entire film), but it is obvious that a stagehand is moving these lifeless creatures incrementally, just out of camera range. There is no sense that the animals are "animated' by the evil of Dracula, only the clear perception that a hand is twisting these stiff little critters back and forth. On top of all that, there are a multitude of zooms and close-ups, which only succeed in making the sequence last at least a minute too long. An editor cognizant of pace and fluent in the language of shock (which demands that scary things be shown once or twice but not repetitively), would have trimmed this scene.

Another editing blunder finds Lucy in the middle of her bed in one shot and at least seven or eight inches from the center of the bed in the very next. So continuity is not a strong point either. With all of these editing and technical missteps, the only moments that really come alive in *Count Dracula* are the two occasions in which the camera is untethered, and Franco generates an unsteady feeling from the use of a hand-held. Lucy's pursuit of an innocent girl and Dracula's final attack on Lucy both use this technique well.

Oddly, scenes that should be occurring at night are lensed in the daytime and blue skies and clouds are visible overhead. Some Franco defenders would no doubt argue that this is another example of the director's faithfulness to his source. After all, in Stoker, Dracula was not "allergic" to sunlight (that allergy was invented for the 1922 Murnau film *Nosferatu*), and so it is perfectly appropriate for the heroes of this Dracula film to be skulking around the castle by daylight. That answer does not hold up, however, with the details of the individual scenes. When first mesmerized by the count, Lucy awakes from a deep sleep and heads out into the grounds—daylight obvious above her. Was she just napping in the afternoon, or was this scene really supposed to be lensed at night?

Secondly, when Seward, Morris and Harker stalk Dracula, they are carrying a lantern. If the scene is not meant to be happening at night, why bring an artificial light source along?

It has been widely reported that Christopher Lee participated in this film because it was to be a faithful rendering of Bram Stoker's timeless novel. Though the final result is faithful, to a high degree, the audience walks away feeling neither thrilled nor excited by *Count Dracula*, but bored. The cast is excellent (Lom, Lee and Kinski—what a combo!), the musical score is terrific, and Franco's sincere approach is appreciated, but *Count Dracula* is like a Cliffs Notes version of Stoker. It provides all the information one might need to know to pass a test about Dracula, but a successful artistic approach to the classic material is absent.

Count Yorga, Vampire (1970) ⋆ ⋆ ½

Critical Reception

"...the special appeal of *Count Yorga, Vampire* may well be its Los Angeles locale.... *Count Yorga*'s ambience is pure Hollywood and the seamy elegance of Robert Quarry's performance ... exactly compliments [sic] that ambience. Bob Kelljan's direction, often resourceful, does especially well by Quarry's disdainful civility...."— Roger Greenspun, *New York Times*, November 12, 1970, page 49.

"...primitive, but not unimaginative."— Tom Charity, *Time Out Film Guide*, Seventh Edition, Penguin Books, 1999, page 181.

Cast & Crew

CAST: Robert Quarry (Count Yorga); Roger Perry (Dr. Jim Hayes); Michael Murphy (Paul); Michael Macready (Michael); Donna Anders (Donna); Judith Lang (Erica); Edward Walsh (Brudeh); George Macready (Narrator); Julie Connors, Paul Hansen, Sybil Scotford, Marsha Jordan, Deborah Darnell.

CREW: American International Pictures Presents *Count Yorga, Vampire*, an Erica Production. *Production Supervisor:* Robert N. O'Neil. *Camera Assistant:* Pat O'Mara, Jr. *Chief Electrician:* John Murphy. *Wardrobe:* Nancy Stone. *Property Master:* James Stinson. *Animal Owner/Trainer:* Vee Kasegan. *Script Supervisor:* Pat Townsend. *Sound Assistant:* George Garrin. *Set Design:* Bob Wilder. *Make-up:* Mark Rogers, Master Dentalsmith. *Special Effects:* James Tanerbaum. *Sound Recorder:* Robert Dietz, Lowell Brown. *Sound Effects:* Edit International. *Rerecording:* Producers Sound Services, Inc. *Color:* Movielab. *Film Editor:* Tony de Zarraga. *Cinematography:* Arch Achambault. *Music:* William Marx. *Produced by:* Michael Macready. *Written and Directed by:* Bob Kelljan. *M.P.A.A. Rating:* PG. *Running Time:* 92 minutes.

P.O.V.

"I was fighting against the Bela Lugosi image and Christopher Lee's Dracula. Not that there was anything wrong with either of them, but they were unreal in a certain way, and I wanted to give Yorga kind of reality and play him straight" (1).— Robert Quarry discusses his interpretation of the modern vampire in *Count Yorga* (1970).

SYNOPSIS: In contemporary Los Angeles, a group of hip young adults gather for a séance in an attempt to contact the recently deceased mother of Donna, one of their number. Unfortunately, the medium selected on this occasion is none other than Count Yorga, a modern-day vampire living in the City of Angels. While the others watch, Yorga secretly enslaves Donna with his powers of telepathy.

After the séance, Erica and Paul agree to drive Yorga home in their van, while Donna wonders why the count was not present at her mother's funeral, as he insists. After dropping Yorga off at his secluded mansion, Erica and Paul find their VW van trapped in the mud on a dark road. They are forced to spend the night there. They make love in the back of the van, but afterwards, Yorga attacks. Paul is knocked unconscious, without remembering his assailant, and Erica is bitten by the vampire.

The next day, Paul notices the odd puncture marks on Erica's neck and takes her to see Dr. Hayes. Later, when Hayes and Paul find Erica drinking the blood of a kitten, Hayes suggests there is a vampire at work. Understandably, Paul is doubtful such a thing could happen in modern L.A. But that night, the hypnotic Yorga summons Erica.

She awakens, lustful, and he offers her eternal life as one of his vampire brides. When Erica agrees, Yorga takes her back to his castle. In hot pursuit, Paul, Dr. Hayes and Donna's boyfriend, Michael, try to save Erica before it is too late. Paul arrives first and is murdered by Yorga's brutish manservant. When, Dr. Hayes, Michael and Donna arrive at the castle, there is no sign of Paul. Suspecting that Yorga is a vampire, Hayes attempts to keep the vampire awake with polite conversation until daylight. He even asks the count if vampires are real. Yorga's response is chilling. Vampires are real, he concludes, and they are far superior to human beings. When Yorga retires just before the deadly rays of sunrise, Hayes and Michael plot to kill him the following evening.

The next day, Yorga calls to the enslaved Donna, ordering her to his house. When she arrives, Donna suffers a worse indignity than Yorga's domination: Brudeh, the brute manservant, forces himself on her. Later, Michael and Hayes storm the house to rescue her. In the cellar, Hayes and Yorga engage in battle, but Yorga's vampire brides (including the transformed Erica) rise and feed on the good doctor. Desperate and alone, Michael attempts to dispatch Yorga and save his beloved Donna. He kills Brudeh and then finds Hayes, barely alive. Hayes informs him that Donna is locked up safely upstairs, where Yorga has reintroduced her to her dead mother — now a vampire bride.

Taking action, Michael impales the monstrous mother, then Yorga himself. As Michael and Donna attempt to escape, they are confronted by two vampire brides. Just as Michael's escape looks to be assured, he faces a nasty shock: Donna is already a vampire.

COMMENTARY: There are two ways in which one might assess *Count Yorga, Vampire* (actually, onscreen, *Count Iorga Vampire*). By looking at it in 1970 terms, the film would garner a (reservedly) positive review for the manner in which it inches forward

the notion of vampires dwelling in a modern technological society. But studied in Y2K terms, *Yorga* seems distinctly old hat, offering precious few twists and turns on the well-established canon of vampire lore. Of course, one goal in critiquing these films in the year 2001 is to study their accomplishments within their historical context, at the time of release, so perhaps it is not fair to expect *Yorga* to appear innovative after thirty years in circulation.

After all, it is easy to forget that in the year 1970, vampire films were invariably set in Victorian times— or the 1930s at the latest. Hammer's Dracula (Christopher Lee) had not voyaged to the present yet (*Dracula A.D. 1972* would usher in that development) and Kolchak's face-off with Janos Skorzeny in the popular TV movie *The Night Stalker* (1971) was another year off. Contemporary visions like *The Hunger* (1982), *Fright Night* (1985), *The Lost Boys* (1987), *A Vampire in Brooklyn* (1995), *John Carpenter's Vampires* (1998) and *Blade* (1998) were a long, long way off too. So, *Count Yorga's* central plot twist, bringing a vampire to 1970s California was, if not revolutionary, at least ahead of the curve. In fact, *Yorga's* identity as a vampire not Dracula (or one of his brides or many offspring) might even be considered trail-blazing in a way. Before *Yorga,* vampires and Dracula were pretty much synonymous. Yorga's a very different cat.

On the other hand, the best 1970s horror films (*The Texas Chainsaw Massacre, Halloween, The Exorcist, Jaws,* even *Let's Scare Jessica to Death* and *Last House on the Left*) do retain their aura of inspiration and innovation even in the opening days of the 21st century, decades after their release. *Count Yorga* is clearly not in that class. It lacks the directorial flair of a true classic, and substitutes camp humor for chills at its most critical junctures. Though it is fun to hear Quarry's Yorga declare that he'll "have a snack later," or to watch as a VW van, a symbol of the hippie generation, is molded into a vehicle of action, the film skimps on the thrills and charts a bland, ultimately unsatisfying course. It is a cheap film, and one feels that budgetary limitations hampered its ability to thrill on a significant level.

Count Yorga opens in almost amateurish fashion as a narrator describes the arrival of a modern-day vampire in California. As this breathy narrator relates the story, the film's images reveal a crate being lowered onto a pick-up truck, and the truck then heading out on a sprawling American highway. Oddly, the narration is unnecessary, as is the opening sequence: Yorga has obviously been in the States for some time when the plot proper begins, so what does the arrival of his coffin (we presume it is his, anyway) have to do with this story? Why is it necessary to show that Yorga came from Europe, when all the action takes place in the United States? *Blacula* took a different, and more coherent, tack in 1972: revealing the origin of Blacula in Europe and then dramatizing how he came to be re-awakened in the United States. *Yorga*'s opening feels more like an attempt to pad the running time than a legitimate jumping off point for the story.

Still, *Count Yorga* has some fun, effective moments, as though a bunch of artists got together and decided what they would want to see happen in a vampire movie. Thus wooden stakes are fashioned from broken broom handles, a weak vampire sucks on a kitten to gain nourishment, and the film's highpoint is a reasoned, rational conversation between vampire and vampire hunter. All of these moments, particularly the well-acted confrontation between Roger Perry and Robert Quarry, speak to a real creativity on the part of *Yorga*'s production team, but these flashes of inspiration (as well as the groovy 1970s touches) serve an old story that looks back rather than forward.

For instance, when Paul learns of Jim's suspicion that Yorga is a vampire, he is completely dismissive, even though Jim's theory perfectly fits all the facts. This is the movie automatic pilot answer to such a situation, not a genuine one arising out of character. People are being felled by pernicious anemia after showing up sick with puncture marks on their neck, and a blood specialist says they have been drained of blood. And, on top of that, your girlfriend is found sucking the blood of a helpless kitten … with fangs!!? Could it be a vampire? The obvious answer is yes, but *Count Yorga*'s script feels obliged, wrongly, to kowtow to the old movie cliché stating that reasonable characters should disbelieve in vampires (thus allowing the ghouls the opportunity to continue killing…). Yet, here, as in most such stories, the facts happen to fit Jim's thesis.

Ironically, *Count Yorga*'s strengths and weaknesses can be found side by side in one particular scene. Yorga stalks two young people as they make love in their VW van. There are longs pans across the darkness, the noise of crickets on the soundtrack, and the camera adopts the eerie, subjective, P.O.V. angle, closing in on the unaware innocents. The sound of the crickets turns to a loud screech when the camera focuses on Yorga, lit from below, as he stands outside the window, waiting to attack. It is a very effective and suspenseful moment until the actual attack comes. Then it becomes plain that Yorga is garbed in a black suit and a long, flowing cape … a cliché of vampire films that has lost the power to scare.

Somehow, the image of the 19th century vampire is not really scary anymore. The well orchestrated approach to terror, mixing an appropriate camera angle, well-used sound effects and creepy lighting, is finally undercut by an image out of place in modern Los Angeles: an old guy in a cape with pointed teeth. In the '80s and '90s, vampires were reinvented, courtesy of productions like *The Hunger, The Lost Boys, Buffy the Vampire Slayer* and even *John Carpenter's Vampires*. These, and other, films eschewed old traditions like capes and middle–European accents, and in some cases even made fun of such unfashionable affectations. It is strange that *Count Yorga* has the foresight to imagine that a vampire might dwell in contemporary America, but not the smarts to update the vampire's look to go with the modern feel. If a vampire wanted to "blend in" in the late 1960s or early 1970s, shouldn't he wear bell-bottoms and tie-dye shirts? That would have been an innovation.

Though it might accurately be called a bridge between vampire generations, *Count Yorga*'s lasting strength, even today, remains its central performance. Robert Quarry is ideal as the vampire: cunning, slick, smart and with a malicious leer that suggests appetites most unhealthy. He is better than the script, which ends with Yorga's demise and, finally, an easily anticipated "sting."

LEGACY: *Count Yorga, Vampire,* was so popular and well-received that a sequel, *Return of Count Yorga* (1971), followed, and Robert Quarry, for a time, became a cult-horror star, leaping franchises and appearing as Vincent Price's nemesis in *Dr. Phibes Rises Again* (1972).

The Crimson Cult

Cast & Crew

CAST: Boris Karloff (Professor Marsh); Christopher Lee (Marley); Barbara Steele (Lavinia); Michael Gough (Elder); Mark Eden (Robert Manning); Virginia Wetherell (Eve).

CREW: *Directed by:* Vernon Sewell. *Screenplay by:* Mervyn Haisman and Henry Lincoln. *Director of Photography:* Johnny Coquillon. *Music:* Peter Knight. *Produced by:* Louis M. Heyward. American International Pictures.

M.P.A.A. Rating: PG. *Running Time:* 87 minutes.

DETAILS: In an English hamlet, a scholar in the ways of witchcraft (Karloff) faces off against a coven of witches that bears a historical grudge. Long believed to be Karloff's final film, *The Crimson Cult* features an all-star horror cast, including Lee, Gough and Steele.

Cry of the Banshee

Cast & Crew

CAST: Vincent Price (Lord Whitman); Hilary Dwyer (Maureen Whitman); Patrick Mower (Roderick); Elisabeth Bergner (Oona); Essy Perrson (Lady Whitman).

CREW: *Directed and Produced by:* Gordon Hessler. *Screenplay by:* Christopher Wicking and Tim Kelly. *Director of Photography:* John Coquillon. *Music:* Les Baxter. *Film Editor:* Oswald Hafenrichter. *M.P.A.A. Rating:* R. *Running Time:* 90 minutes (approx).

DETAILS: An evil nobleman (Price) goes on a rampage, killing all the witches of the land. One wrathful witch named Oona (Bergner) takes exception to this cause, and summons a banshee to strike back at the lord's family. A cheap "witchhunt" type of movie, though spiced with Price's fine performance and plenty of nudity.

The Dunwich Horror

Cast & Crew

CAST: Sandra Dee (Nancy Walker); Dean Stockwell (Wilbur Whateley); Ed Begley (Dr. Henry Armitage); Sam Jaffe (Grandpa); Lloyd Bachner (Dr. Cory); Donna Baccala (Elizabeth Hamilton).

CREW: *Directed by:* Daniel Haller. *Screenplay by:* Curtis Lee Hanson, Henry Rosenbaum and Ronald Silkosky. *Based on the Story by:* H. P. Lovecraft. *Director of Photography:* Richard C. Glouner. *Music by:* Les Baxter. *Produced by:* James H. Nicholson and Samuel Z. Arkoff. American International Pictures. *M.P.A.A. Rating:* PG. *Running Time:* 90 minutes.

DETAILS: An early screen adaptation of H. P. Lovecraft's terrifying work. When a sacred book is stolen from Miskatonic University, a doorway is opened for a race of evil creatures imprisoned in another dimension. Sandra Dee plays a college student who gets involved in supernatural happenings, and Sam Jaffe, an old man who warns of horrors to come.

Frankenstein Must Be Destroyed! (1970) ✶ ✶

Critical Reception

"…Anthony Nelson Keys and Bert Batt, who wrote the original story for this one, have made a couple of minor, though notable, changes in the recent [Hammer Films] formula."— Vincent Canby, *New York Times*, April 16, 1970, page 54.

Cast & Crew

CAST: Peter Cushing (Baron Frankenstein); Simon Ward (Karl); Veronica Carlson (Anna); Thorley Walters (Inspector Frisch); Freddie Jones (Dr. Richter); Maxine Audley (Ella Brandt); Geoffrey Bayldon (Police Doctor); George Pravda (Doctor Brandt); Colette O'Neil (Mad Woman); Peter Copley (Principal); Frank Middlemass, George Belban, Norman Shelley, Michael Goren (Guests); Jim Collier (Dr. Heidecke); Allan Surtees, Windsor Davies (Police).

CREW: Warner Brothers and Seven Arts Present a Hammer Film Production. Produced at Associate British Studios, Elstree, London, England. Distributed by Warner Brothers— Seven Arts. *Directed by:* Terence Fisher. *Produced by:* Anthony Nelson Keys. *Music Composed by:* James Bernard. *Musical Director:* Philip Martell. *Director of Photography:* Arthur Grant. *Supporting Art Director:* Bernard Robinson. *Editor:* Gordon Hales. *Production Manager:* Christopher Neame. *Assistant Director:* Bert Batt. *Camera Operator:* Neil Binney. *Sound Recordist:* Ben Hawkins. *Sound Editor:* Don Hanasinghe. *Continuity:* Dolcen Dearnaley. *Casting Director:* Irene Lamb. *Make-up:* Eddie Knight. *Hairstylist:* Nat McDermott. *Wardrobe Supervisor:* Rosemary Burrows. *Wardrobe Mistress:* Coffie Slattery. *Construction Manager:* Arthur Hanley. *Screenplay by:* Bert Batt. *From an original story idea by:* Anthony Nelson Keys and Bert Batt. *M.P.A.A. Rating:* PG. *Running Time:* 103 minutes.

P.O.V.

"Freddie Jones plays a man who has his brain transplanted to a new body by Frankenstein. He visits his wife, who fails to recognize

Lucky Peter Cushing gets a grip on buxom Veronica Carlson in a publicity still from *Frankenstein Must Be Destroyed!* (1970).

him, and she rejects him. I love that subject! I thought about that film more than any of the others, because of that one element" (2).—Director Terence Fisher reflects on *Frankenstein Must Be Destroyed!* (1970).

————————

SYNOPSIS: Forced from his homeland and living in hiding in England, the Baron Frankenstein is up to his old ghoulish tricks. He murders a prominent city doctor to possess his head, and the city police investigate the crime, aware they are looking for a dangerous, mad, medical "adventurer." Frankenstein moves into the boarding house of a beautiful girl named Anna. When the Baron learns that Anna and her boyfriend, Dr. Karl Holst of the local insane asylum, are involved in illegal narcotics, he blackmails them into becoming his assistants. Karl helps Frankenstein steal equipment one night and kills a night watchman, getting himself in even deeper with the mad Frankenstein.

The Baron has come to England with a purpose. His compatriot, Dr. Brandt, possessed the knowledge to keep disembodied brains alive for transplant surgery, and Frankenstein needs that information. Unfortunately, Brandt went insane after his dealings with Frankenstein and is now residing in the asylum where Karl works. Frankenstein and Karl break Brandt out of his imprisonment, but he is injured in the process. Frankenstein transplants Brandt's valuable brain into the body of another man, Professor Richter. Meanwhile, the police tighten their search and Brandt's wife, Ella, recognizes Frankenstein on the street. She pursues him to the boarding house and Frankenstein shows her how he has saved her husband's life by transplanting his living brain into the body of Richter. He swears Ella to secrecy, but when she leaves, flees with his patient and Anna and Karl back to his homeland. Ella informs the police.

At Frankenstein's castle, Karl and Anna plot to escape from the madman. Brandt awakens in his new body and realizes what has become of him. Frightened by Brandt, Anna attempts to kill him. Frankenstein kills Anna for her transgression, leaving an angry Karl. Meanwhile, Brandt returns to London, Frankenstein in hot pursuit, and has a tender last meeting with his wife Ella. Then, he decides that all his work pertaining to successful brain transplants must be destroyed. Plotting revenge against Frankenstein, Brandt taunts him with the formula he so desperately desires. But Brandt burns down his own house and carries Frankenstein to a fiery death while Karl watches.

————————

COMMENTARY: The horror films produced by Hammer Studios are beloved by fans around the globe for so many good reasons. When they re-invented and re-introduced the *Frankenstein* and *Dracula* myths in the late 1950s and 1960s, Hammer Studios updated the horror ethos with gore galore (i.e. running blood), garish color (running red blood), and a whole lot of female pulchritude. Fine production values were in evidence, and the films were invariably fronted by Peter Cushing, Christopher Lee, and, praise Heaven, Ingrid Pitt. The stories were familiar for the most part, but solidly scripted and competently directed. Most importantly, the Hammer horrors treated their subject matter with straight-faced respect, not camp humor or jokey irreverence. The thoughtful approach alone was enough to win the films legions of admirers.

But by the 1970s, the light behind Hammer's films was starting to fade. Peter Cushing, Christopher Lee, the gore, the women and the production values were still in the limelight, as was the straight-faced, honest approach to storytelling, but the films no longer felt new or innovative, not after a dozen years (and a dozen films) repeating the same formula. Christopher Lee was bored out of his mind towards the end, the scripts became re-hashes, wit was absent, and the Hammer *Frankenstein* and *Dracula* series suffered the fate of all franchises. Quality declined and so did audience affection. This is not an attack on Hammer, it is merely a fact.

All franchises decline at some point, as witnessed by the fall of *Star Trek* today, or the fading of the James Bond film series in the late '80s before Pierce Brosnan took over. The fact that Hammer's films grew worse in the '70s in no way subtracts from the fact that in the late '50s and all throughout the 1960s Hammer was a pioneer and a producer of fine, memorable pictures. But much of its output in the seventies was plainly inferior to what had come before. In a way, this acknowledgment is another backhanded compliment because, among others, Hammer was clearly competing with itself and its own history of excellence at this point.

Which brings the discussion to *Frankenstein Must Be Destroyed!*, the luridly-titled Frankenstein opus of 1970. It is sad and discomforting to see a pioneer become old hat, but that is exactly what happens here in a subdued, slow-paced film that never reaches the intensity promised by its title. The film opens with melodrama. Two schemers, Karl and Anna, are caught in an illegal narcotic ring by the Baron Frankenstein and consequently forced to serve as his assistants while he attempts to preserve the mind of an insane associate named Brandt. The elaborate plot winds on through drug trafficking, blackmail, murder, prison breakouts and precious little horror or suspense until the absurd true plot is laid bare. Get this: Brandt has learned the secret of successful brain transplants, but he's crazy. So Frankenstein breaks him out of an asylum and cures his insanity so as to get the secret formula of brain transplants. But, Brandt is wounded in the asylum breakout and Frankenstein must transplant his healthy brain into a new body to save him.

Okay, that plot is either absurd or inspired, depending on one's point of view. At the very least, it is workable, though only Frankenstein could see curing insanity as just one more little hurdle to jump. However, at the end of the movie, this plot is revealed to be completely ridiculous when Brandt returns to his home and burns all of his research about brain transplants. Now wait a

minute! If Brandt recorded the all-important secret formula for successful brain transplant surgery in his notes, why didn't Frankenstein simply go to the Brandt home and take the notes, thereby getting the secret he needed? If Brandt's wife had refused Frankenstein access, he could have broken in and stolen the notes. Instead, Frankenstein adheres to his crazy plan: breaking Brandt out of the asylum, transplanting his brain, curing his insanity, and getting the formula straight from the horse's mouth. Personally, this author would have tried for the notes first.

It isn't often that a film renders its own plot idiotic, but *Frankenstein Must Be Destroyed!*'s unbelievable final act does just that. Actually, *Frankenstein Must Be Destroyed!*'s script is shoddy in a number of areas. All through the picture, it cuts back to London police officers as they valiantly attempt to track down Frankenstein and stop his reign of terror. There are at least four scenes of the inspector, the doctor and other officers following the case of what they presume to be a murdering doctor. Yet, amazingly, there is no closure to these sequences, and they ultimately contribute nothing to the film. The police do not solve the case, and do not catch Frankenstein either. They do not even get in a token appearance at the end of the picture. With no punctuation, no closure whatsoever to these scenes, the cop subplot is revealed to be a time-waster; padding that adds nothing to the film on any thematic level.

But *Frankenstein Must Be Destroyed!*'s worst transgression is neither its absurd plot nor its dead-end script structure. Worst of all, the screenplay fails to really understand the character of Brandt, the surrogate Frankenstein monster in this case. Again, it is helpful to review the situation. Brandt is wasting away in an asylum, driven irrevocably insane as the picture starts. His doctor believes this melancholy is incurable, so Brandt is a man with no future. In the course of the story, Frankenstein restores Brandt's sanity and puts his brain in a healthy body when his old one is mortally wounded. There is just one side effect: a long scar on Brandt's forehead.

But is Brandt grateful to have his mind back after beings nuts, alone, and consigned forever after to an insane asylum? Is he glad to be alive and whole and sentient? Of course not, because the great law of movie clichés tells us that Brandt is an abomination against God! Instead of thanking Frankenstein for saving him, Brandt wants revenge against the good doctor. Why should the character possibly feel this way? Without Frankenstein's intervention he was doomed, forsaken, and crazed!

If this is indeed a moral, ethical and religious issue that Frankenstein tampered in "God's domain," then there still should have been a moment in the screenplay when Brandt weighed these factors against his own newfound health. Instead, *Frankenstein Must Be Destroyed!* relies on clichés, flies on autopilot and assumes that Brandt would simply want vengeance for his new shape. Bizarrely, the script makes the same assumption about Brandt's wife, Ella. If your spouse was condemned to insanity wouldn't you rejoice to have him or her back, even in a new, slightly scarred body? If one thinks about it, Frankenstein accomplishes two miracles in this movie (successful brain transplant surgery, and the curing of insanity) but all anybody can do about it is complain!

Despite the numerous script flaws, Peter Cushing, the busiest man in horror in the 1970s, remains a marvel as Frankenstein. Though the character is doomed to be static, never learning from mistakes, always creating death rather than life, Cushing nonethe-less imbues the character with a most compelling brand of obsession. Whether arguing for scientific advances ("without pushing the boundaries of knowledge, we'd still be living in caves!!!" he snaps), or barking orders at his unwilling underlings, Cushing paints a fine portrait of genius-tinged madness. A tribute to his skill is that the most fascinating moment of *Frankenstein Must Be Destroyed!* comes when Cushing's doctor catches a glimpse of the beautiful Anna undressing in her bedroom. A lustful Frankenstein breaks in, and viciously has his way with her, proving he is not all intellect and science after all. If there is anything surprising in the least about this film, Cushing's moment of physical release would certainly qualify. Frankenstein, usually so focused on other matters, succumbs to the desires of the flesh in a flurry of violence ... if only for a moment. Cushing seems to understand here, and throughout the film, what makes this madman tick, right down to his carnal appetites.

Hammer films are much, much more than buxom women in diaphanous nightgowns and torrents of running red blood, but *Frankenstein Must Be Destroyed!* reveals a franchise in serious decline. It looks good and it is well acted, but the script is awful, filled with plot dead-ends and implausibilities that undermine the narrative. An old saying goes: "if it isn't on the page, it won't be on the stage." That truism could have been the motto of *Frankenstein Must Be Destroyed!* It has all the icing of Hammer's best desserts, but the cake underneath is stale.

Horror of Frankenstein

Cast & Crew

CAST: Ralph Bates (Victor Frankenstein); Graham James (Wilhem); Kate O'Mara (Alice); Veronica Carlson (Elizabeth); Dennis Price (Grave Robber); David Prowse (the Monster). **CREW:** *Produced and Directed by:* Jimmy Sangster. *Written by:* Jeremy Sangster and Jeremy Burnham. A Hammer Production. *M.P.A.A. Rating:* R. *Running Time:* 94 minutes.

DETAILS: Yet another entry in Hammer's long standing Frankenstein film franchise, though this one lacks the star presence of Peter Cushing. Ralph Bates is the new Frankenstein, but he's trapped in a familiar story involving murder, a monster, body parts and the doctor's laboratory.

House of Dark Shadows (1970) * *

Critical Reception

"…has no subject except its special effects (which aren't very good) and its … shock sequences. Characters are picked up and dropped with indifference…. And by the end of the movie everybody is either dead or discarded or a vampire…. It is neither fun nor even especially clean."— Roger Greenspun, *New York Times*, October 29, 1970, page 58.

Cast & Crew

CAST: Jonathan Frid (Barnabas Collins); Grayson Hall (Dr. Julia Hoffman); Kathryn Leigh Scott (Maggie Evans); Roger Davis (Jeff Clark); Nancy Barrett (Carolyn Stoddard); John Karlen (Willie Loomis); Thayer David (Professor T. Eliot Stokes); Louis Edmonds (Roger Collins); Donal Biscoe (Todd Jennings); David Henasy (David Collins); Dennis Patrick (Sheriff George Patterson); Joan Bennett (Elizabeth Collins Stoddard); Lisa Richards (Daphne Budd); Jerry Lacy (Minister); Barbara Cason (Mrs. Johnson); Paul Michael (Old Man); Humbert Astredo (Dr. Forbes); Terry Crawford (Todd's Nurse); Michael Stroka (Pallbearer).

CREW: Metro Goldwyn Mayer Presents A Dan Curtis Production, *House of Dark Shadows*. *Film Editor:* Arline Garson. *Camera Operator:* Dick Mingalone. *Sound:* Chris Newman, Jack C. Jacobsen. *Sound Mixer:* Bob Fine. *Titles:* F. Hillsberg Inc. *Special Make-up:* Dick Smith. *Wardrobe Designer:* Ramse Mostoller. *Make-up:* Robert Layden. *Hairdresser:* Verne Caruso. *Set Decoration:* Ken Fitzpatrick. *Casting:* Linda Otto. *Stunt Choreographer:* Alex Stevens. *Filmed in:* Metrocolor. *Production Supervisor:* Hal Schaffel. *Assistant Director:* William Gerrity, Jr. *Music Composed and Conducted by:* Robert Cobert. *Director of Photography:* Arthur Ornitz. *Production Designer/Associate Producer:* Trevor Williams. *Screenplay:* Sam Hall and Gordon Russell. Based upon the ABC-TV Series. *Produced and Directed by:* Dan Curtis. *M.P.A.A. Rating:* R. *Running time:* 90 minutes.

P.O.V.

"Youngsters today are looking for a new morality. And so is Barnabas… He hates what he is and he's in terrible agony. Just like the kids today, he's confused, lost, screwed up and searching for something" (3).— Jonathan Frid ruminates on the popularity of his vampiric alter ego.

SYNOPSIS: Looking for young David Collins, the youngest child of a wealthy New England family, governess Maggie Evans stumbles across drunk Willie Loomis on the family grounds at nightfall. He is searching for the legendary Collins jewels in the estate graveyard, but he uncovers something infinitely more frightening. In the Collins crypt, Loomis opens a sealed casket and frees an ancient evil, the regal vampire Barnabas Collins. Before long, this vampire has sucked dry his first victim, Daphne, leaving two puncture marks on her neck. Meanwhile, Maggie becomes locked in the old Collins estate until her boyfriend Jeff finds her, along with the naughty, mischievous David.

A few nights later, and after more deadly vampire attacks, Barnabas introduces himself to the polite society of Collinsport, passing himself off as a Collins cousin from England. Barnabas immediately charms the relatives and is welcomed to live in the old Collinswood house. Ironically, this is the home he lived in a hundred and eighty years ago, and it has hardly changed in the intervening decades. On the eve of a masquerade ball, Barnabas seduces and bites Carolyn Collins, making her his undead slave. At the party, Barnabas also finds himself interested in Maggie Evans because she is a dead ringer for the love of his life, Josette DuPres. Almost two hundred years ago, Josette jumped to her death from Widow's Hill when she learned that her beloved was an undead monster. Feeling that Josette has returned to him, Barnabas sets out to woo Maggie. A jealous Carolyn attempts to stop these romantic attempts, but Barnabas bites her again, killing her this time.

At the same time, a doctor named Julia Hoffman, who is writing the Collins family history, analyzes some of the blood on Carolyn's corpse and determines that the creature who attacked her suffers from a rare form of a disease — vampirism — that could be curable through advanced medical science.

That night, a living dead Carolyn Collins rises from her grave and attacks young David in the dried-up Collinswood pool house. He escapes and warns his family that Carolyn lives, but the family does not believe his wild story. Carolyn's lover, Todd, is attacked by Carolyn that very night, but an angry Barnabas warns her not to act without his direct authority. Carolyn ignores this warning and makes Todd a full vampire. The police arrive, armed with crucifixes, and put an end to Carolyn's defiance.

Now that Dr. Hoffman knows that Barnabas is a vampire, she offers him a cure. Barnabas eagerly accepts the chance to escape his disease, and soon after the therapy begins, shows signs of improvement, even being able to walk in the sun. However,

Hoffman has secretly fallen in love with Barnabas and is jealous of the affection he showers on Maggie. Hoffman purposefully botches the cure and Barnabas ages hundreds of years in a matter of seconds. An angry Barnabas kills Julia for her betrayal and feeds on Maggie to restore his youth. The Collinsport police and Collins family rally their forces to protect Maggie from the vampire, but Barnabas returns to her, seeking his bride, and takes her to the old house.

Finally, it is up to Maggie's boyfriend David to defeat Barnabas in the old house before a deadly wedding can occur.

COMMENTARY: Adapting a popular TV series into a successful feature film is rarely an easy task. The *Star Trek* franchise has attempted this balancing act nine times (as of this writing) and had, arguably, only two or three successes in translating its video material into original, but faithful, screen gold. Forget about *The Wild Wild West* (1999), *Mission: Impossible 2* (2000) or *Lost in Space* (1998): they did not even attempt to honor their TV material, instead relying only on a well-known franchise name, and big star appeal. But long before any of these TV-to-film ventures came about, *Dark Shadows* producer Dan Curtis was confronting the same problems. How could he translate the success of an afternoon daily soap opera (which aired more than 1,000 episodes!) into a box office success that nonetheless remained true to the ethos of what he and Art Wallace had created for the tube?

What Curtis did, which is evident in *House of Dark Shadows*, was to improve the overall production values, retain the original cast, and telescope a long and familiar story into a short, familiar one. The first two decisions work to the film's advantage to some degree; the third does not. Because the cast is so large, it is ill served in a feature of this length (barely 90 minutes), with only Frid making any impact. And the story, now stripped of the soap's tangential (and often inspired) flourishes, looks more imitative of *Bram Stoker's Dracula* than ever before.

First impressions from *House of Dark Shadows* are rather positive. The film looks good, getting a leg-up on its on-the-cheap TV brother by featuring real exteriors (rather than soundstages), and genuinely impressive sets, as well as more explicit bloodletting. The menacing Frid, a powerful screen presence as the vampire Barnabas, is rightly held back for a time (with the audience catching glimpses only of his ringed fingers and trademark cane), thus building anticipation and making for a grand entrance. And, fostering a sense of nostalgic enjoyment, Curtis's direction employs then-timely camera moves and techniques to flashily serve the story.

But, *House of Dark Shadows* has a weak script in an important regard: there are no introductions to any of the Collins family other than Barnabas, meaning that those who do not follow the show are left rudderless. Who are these people? What are their relationships to one another? *House of Dark Shadows* assumes that the audience already knows all of that material, rightly or wrongly, and the characters (on the movie screen) never translate as individuals. This problem is enhanced by the fact that few of the Collins get separate screen time, let alone meaningful dialogue, unless they are featured in a death sequence … not the best venue in which to get to know someone.

Lacking the extraordinary individuality of the TV characters, as well as the subplots that made their machinations interesting, *House of Dark Shadows* emerges as something that the TV series never was, a bland derivation of Bram Stoker's novel. To wit, Willie Loomis now seems like Renfield, less the opportunist of the TV series and more the vampire stoolie of cliché. The old Collins house where Barnabas takes up residence also smacks of Carfax Abbey without the rich detail of the long-lived soap. Elliott is a dull Van Helsing substitute, and so forth. It is a shame to witness this homogenization of *Dark Shadows* because the TV series really saw things through a skewed, and wonderfully energetic, perspective.

Frid's Barnabas (on TV) was a Byronic vampire worthy of sympathy, an anti-hero who hated what he was, and even became a kind of generational spokesman for disaffected youth of the late '60s and early '70s. Though in the film, Barnabas is still tortured (decrying "how could anyone live like this?"), he is more like the traditional vampire of yore, garbed in cape and fangs, seducing the innocent and drinking their blood. The portions of the film that work best are those that involve Barnabas's belief that he can be cured, and thus redeemed. But those moments, unlike the TV series, are brief.

House of Dark Shadows also depends on what this author often calls "selective stupidity" in its plotting. A clever viewer will ask some pertinent questions. Like, who is the one new person in town, whose very arrival coincides with a rash of vampiric attacks and death? Gee, could it be the caped fellow who just happens to be a dead ringer for a Collins who "mysteriously vanished" 180 years ago? Over the weeks and months on the TV series, issues like this were flattened out through time, barely having impact, but in a sparse 90 minutes, the story of Barnabas is exposed as rather weak. And, sadly, the audience is once again back in that predictable world where vampire bites on the neck are dismissed as animal bites, a factor also in *Count Yorga, Vampire* (1970) and *Blacula* (1972). It is a shame, but *House of Dark Shadows* is a horror film with dumb characters. As it stands, half the Collins family is exterminated by the time anyone realizes something sinister is really happening.

The best way to describe the difference between *Dark Shadows* on TV and *Dark Shadows* as film is that the former is soap opera first and horror second, while the latter is the reverse. What made the low-budget series unique, charming, and long-lived was its concentration on characters and relationships. The film lops out all of that good stuff, all of that interpersonal intrigue, and is left with a hollow shell, the bare bones of its familiar vampire story. No, the movie is not terrible, and Frid is still a great vampire, but in the end, *House of Dark Shadows* is another TV-to-film failure, a movie that fails to understand why *Dark Shadows* was so popular in the first place.

LEGACY: A sequel (sans Jonathan Frid, and the Barnabas connection), was released in 1971, entitled *Night of Long Dark Shadows*. Poorly received, the film landed *Dark Shadows* in cult obscurity until 1991, when Dan Curtis revived the franchise in a short-lived NBC TV series, featuring Ben Cross as Barnabas Collins. Since then, there has been talk of a *Dark Shadows* movie, and a *Dark Shadows* Broadway production. The show remains a staple on The Sci-Fi Channel.

Lust for a Vampire (1970) ✷ ✷ ✷

Critical Reception

> "…it offers an increasingly complicated plot combined with elements of jokiness which together render *Lust for a Vampire* more an example of early 1970s camp, a curious hybrid of romance, comedy and thriller, than a horror film." — Peter Hutchings, *Hammer and Beyond: The British Horror Film*, Manchester University Press, 1993, page 165.

Cast & Crew

CAST: Ralph Bates (Giles Barton); Barbara Jefford (Countess Herritzen); Suzanna Leigh (Janet Playfair); Michael Johnson (Richard Lestrange); Yutte Stensgaard (Mircalla); Helen Christie (Miss Simpson); Pippa Steel (Susan Pelley); David Healy (Raymond Pelley); Harvey Hall (Inspector Heinreich); Mike Raven (Count Karnstein); Michael Brennan (Landlord); Jack Melford (Bishop); Judy Matheson (Amanda); Christopher Neame (Hans); Erik Chitty (Professor Herz); Caryl Little (Isabel); Jonathan Cecil (Biggs); Kirsten Lindholm (Peasant Girl); Luan Peters (Trudi); Nick Brimble (First Villager); David Richardson (Second Villager); Vivienne Chandler, Erica Beale, Melinda Churche, Melita Clarke, Jackie Chapman, Sue Longhurt, Patricia Warner (School Girls).

CREW: A Hammer Production. *Director of Photography:* David Muir. *Art Director:* Don Mingaye. *Editor:* Spencer Reeve. *Music composed by:* Harry Robinson. *"Strange Love" sung by:* Tracy, *Lyrics by:* Frank Godwin. *Musical Supervisor:* Philip Martell. *Production Manager:* Tom Sachs. *Assistant Director:* David Bracknell. *Sound Recordist:* Ron Barron. *Sound Editor:* Terry Poulton. *Camera:* R. Anstisss. *Continuity:* Betty Harley. *Make-up Supervisor:* George Blackler. *Hairdressing Supervisor:* Laura Nightingale. *Construction Manager:* Bill Greene. *Recording Director:* Tony Lumkin. *Dubbing Mixer:* Len Abbott. *Choreographer:* Babbie McManus. *Screenplay:* Tudor Gates. *Based on characters created by:* J. Sheridan Le Fanu. *Produced by:* Harry Fine, Michael Style. *Directed by:* Jimmy Sangster. A Hammer Film Production made at EMI/MGM Elstree Studios, England. Distributed by Anglo-EMI Film Distributors Ltd. *M.P.A.A. Rating:* R. *Running time:* 92 minutes.

SYNOPSIS: In 1830, a peasant girl is abducted in a carriage belonging to Count Karnstein, and transported to the family castle. There, she is killed in a sacrificial homage to Satan and her virginal blood resurrects the beautiful vampire Carmilla (also known as Mircalla).

In the nearby village, playboy and writer Richard Lestrange takes up residence

Yutte Stensgaard portrays the vampire Mircalla/Carmilla, embodying *Lust for a Vampire* (1970).

and is warned about the Karnstein family of vampires. Ignoring the danger, Lestrange visits Karnstein castle and meets a bevy of local schoolgirls who are also visiting the decaying mansion on a field trap. Lestrange returns to the school with the girls and meets the beautiful new student who has just enrolled — actually the vampire Mircalla. At the same time, Lestrange befriends the odd science teacher, Giles Barton.

Before long, Mircalla Karnstein is up to her old vampire ways. She drains the blood of a barmaid at the inn, and then sucks dry a beautiful schoolgirl, Susan Pelley. The pupil is consequently dumped in a well by a secret accomplice. As Mircalla works her way through the tasty schoolgirls, Lestrange finds himself hopelessly in love with her. This does not please Janet Playfair, a fellow teacher who has developed an affection for Richard. Richard also shares his obsession for Mircalla with Giles Barton. One night, Barton arranges to meet secretly with Mircalla at the Karnstein Castle. He tells her that he knows who she is, and that he wants to worship both her and the Devil. Mircalla rejects his offer and kills him. The following morning, Barton's pale, drained body is found on the school grounds.

While investigating the deaths of Susan and Barton, Richard realizes Mircalla's true identity and arranges to meet Mircalla at the castle that night, repeating Barton's mistake. Mircalla reveals that she is a Karnstein, but claims to have changed her name. She also denies being a vampire. Richard demands that she make love to him as proof of her innocence. She acquiesces.

The police and Susan Pelley's father investigate Susan's disappearance and Barton's death. Susan's body is discovered in the well (where Barton hid it to protect Mircalla), but the police inspector comes to an unpleasant end when Count Karstein hurls him down the well too. Meanwhile, Janet Playfair protects herself from the hunger of Mircalla with a crucifix. Susan's father and a pathologist discover vampire bites on Susan's corpse and confer with a visiting Catholic

priest about it. Their forces marshaled, the priest, the villagers and Mr. Pelley storm the castle. They kill the Karnsteins, and burn down the castle. Mircalla is killed when a flaming two-by-four falls from the castle roof and stakes her through the heart. Richard is then released from his lust for a vampire.

––––––––––––––––––––

COMMENTARY: You have to love Hammer. There is very little doubt why this vampire movie (the second in the Karnstein cycle after *The Vampire Lovers*) exists at all. *Breasts.* It's all about breasts. Every element of this picture, from setting to plot incident, is designed solely to reveal breasts in all their glory. Big breasts, little breasts, breasts under nightgowns, exposed breasts in water, heaving breasts, etc. But movies have been made with less noble intentions and *Lust for a Vampire* displays its up-front charms with enough good humor and blood-letting to give one the illusion that the baser human instincts are not being pandered to. But, of course, they are.

Considering the new freedom of 1970s cinema and the loosening of the moral code, perhaps it was only a matter of time before Hammer Studios set a horror film at an all-girl's school. This setting permits for many lascivious moments, all wonderfully lit and filmed. In one notable scene, a bevy of adolescent girls frolic and dance on the school grounds in skimpy dresses that have slits cut all the way up the legs. In another scene, set in a dormitory room, a beautiful student (the luscious Pippa Steel…) thoughtfully massages Mircalla's (the even more luscious Yutte Stensgaard's…) shoulders, and her blouse "inadvertently" (right!) drops to reveal her ample breasts. Then, because there is a God, the same student (Steel) obligingly suggests a midnight visit to the nearby lake … and a skinny dip.

At this point in the film, this reviewer's wife was starting to grow suspicious. As the camera lingered on the two beautiful girls in the water … mostly topless, she pointed out that it still appeared to be daylight. "Midnight is really bright in England, isn't it?" she noted with a hint of irritation. *All the better to see those breasts by, my dear.*

Before long, there have been eight shots of beautiful breasts and three flashbacks of scenes already shown (quite smart, actually, in case attention was diverted from the plot by the visual charms of the female cast). Then, there is the immortal love scene in which Mircalla (the iron-willed queen of evil) is seduced against her will by a randy teacher. Stensgaard's eyes go cross, and then roll back in her head as she makes love: a funny visual cue to her attainment of orgasm. All this happens, humorously, to a wretched pop song entitled "Strange Love." Throughout this sequence and the film itself Stensgaard is unfailingly beautiful and sensual, though perhaps lacking in the gravitas of her predecessor in the role, Ingrid Pitt.

Predictably, all the elements of *Lust for a Vampire* not involving nudity seem rushed and poorly conceived. Mircalla dies when —

get this — a flaming two-by-four from her castle ceiling conveniently stakes her through the heart! Talk about good aim (and bad luck)! And, of course, there is also a sexist double standard at work here. Mircalla clearly enjoys going both ways (seducing men and women), but the audience never sees Christopher Lee, as Dracula, seducing a man, does it? Even more to the point, Mircalla gets seduced herself by that randy professor, not vice versa. Again, Dracula was never so weak as to be the victim of his own prey, was he? Poor Mircalla ... she's got a long way to go, baby.

All in all, *Lust for a Vampire* is a brilliant male fantasy. A man goes to work at an all-girl school and gets to make it with a really hot lesbian vampire. The period detail, the stately acting, the presence of evil ... that's all afterglow here. Stensgaard, Steele, and Leigh (as another teacher) are unfailingly gorgeous (and ample), and they make *Lust for a Vampire* eminently watchable and thoroughly enjoyable.

Next!

Cast & Crew

CAST: Alberto De Mondoza (Neil Ward); Edwise Fenech (Julie Ward); Cristina Airoldi (Carol); George Hilton (George); Ivan Rassimov (Jean).

CREW: *Directed by:* Luciano Martino. *Screenplay by:* Ernesto Gastaldi *with the collaboration of:* Vittorio Caronia. *Original story:* Eduardo M. Brochero. *Director of Photography:* Emilio Foriscat. *Music:* Nora Orlandi. *Produced by:* Sergio Martino and Antonio Crescenzi. *Released by:* Marion Films Limited and Gemini Releasing. *M.P.A.A. Rating:* R. *Running Time:* 81 minutes.

DETAILS: *The New York Times* called this slasher picture "splattery and sloppy" in its August 7, 1970, review of the film. Various sources list it as being of Italian, Spanish or German origination. The ad line was "Heaven Help Whoever is ... *Next!*" The film involves a series of murders in Vienna that are being conducted by a sex-crazed lunatic who strikes with a razor. Released on American video as *Blade of the Ripper.*

Scars of Dracula (1970) * *

Cast & Crew

CAST: Christopher Lee (Dracula); Dennis Waterman (Simon); Jenny Hanley (Sarah); Christopher Matthews (Paul); Patrick Troughton (Klove); Michael Gwynn (Priest); Michael Ripper (Landlord); Wendy Hamilton (Julie); Anouska Hempel (Tania); Delia Lindsay (Alice); Bob Todd (Burgomaster); Toke Townley (Elderly Wagoner); David Leland (First Officer); Richard Durden (Second Officer); Morris Bush (Farmer); Margo Boht (Landlord's Wife); Clive Barker (Fat Young Man).

CREW: EMI Films Productions Ltd. Present a Hammer Production, *Scars of Dracula. Director of Photography:* Moray Grant. *Art Director:* Scott MacGregor. *Editor:* James Needs. *Music Composed by:* James Bernard. *Musical Supervisor:* Philip Martell. *Production Manager:* Tom Sacks. *Assistant Director:* Derek Whitehurst. *Sound Recordist:* Ron Barron. *Sound Editor:* Roy Hyde. *Continuity:* Betty Harley. *Make-up Supervisor:* Wally Schneiderman. *Special Effects:* Roger Dicken. *Dubbing Mixer:* Dennis Whitlock. *Recording Supervisor:* Tony Lumkin. *Screenplay by:* John Elder. *Based on a character created by:* Bram Stoker. *Produced by:* Aida Young. *Color by:* Technicolor. *Directed by:* Roy Ward Baker. A Hammer Production made at EMI/MGM Elstree Studios England. Distributed by Anglo-EMI Film Distribution Ltd. and released through MGM-EMI Film Distribution Ltd. *M.P.A.A. Rating:* PG. *Running Time:* 96 minutes.

SYNOPSIS: The blood of a bat spills on the ashes of Count Dracula and he is resurrected. Before long, he is up to his old vampiric tricks, draining the blood of beautiful local women. A mob, led by a barkeep and a priest, stages an attack on his castle and starts a fire. Dracula survives the attack and goes on the counter-offensive, sending an army of vampire bats to murder all the townswomen as they pray in church.

Elsewhere, a gallant fellow named Paul is chased by the police for his deflowering of the daughter of a local official. He survives a trip on a runaway carriage and ends up in Dracula's woods. After being denied access to the inn, he travels to the still-standing castle. He is welcomed by Dracula, and compelled to stay the night. Paul soon realizes he is a prisoner in the mansion and attempts to escape by climbing out a window. He ends up in Dracula's bedroom … with the sleeping vampire only feet away.

Meanwhile, the police search for Paul and are told he went to the castle. Paul's brother, Simon, and his beautiful betrothed, Sarah, try to find Paul by retracing his steps. They too meet Dracula at his castle. Simon questions Dracula's hulking manservant, Klove, about Paul, and the odd fellow warns Simon to take Sarah away before Dracula has his way with her. Simon and Sarah escape from the castle as night falls.

In the village, the townspeople refuse to help Simon and Sarah, except for the town priest. He takes them to the church, the site of the massacre, and shares the history of Dracula with them while they wait for dawn. When dawn comes, Simon returns to the castle to find Paul, only to learn that the count has murdered his brother. Dracula mesmerizes Simon, and the young hero is unable to stake the vampire. Back in the village, a bat pecks the town priest to death and Sarah is compelled to return to the castle. Simon breaks free of Dracula's power and fights him off with a crucifix as Sarah finds herself in imminent danger. Simon delivers the vampire a final death blow by spearing him with a metal rod. Lightning then reaches down from heaven and electrocutes the vampire.

COMMENTARY: Hammer Studios is back to its old bag of tricks in the lackluster *Scars of Dracula*, a by-the-numbers sequel that amply demonstrates why the studio's audience was shrinking as the 1960s became the

1970s. The film commences with the inevitable fake bat flapping about on wires. Unlike most bats, this fella proves extremely accommodating: it flies into Dracula's castle on a specific trajectory, obligingly spits blood on the vampire's ashes (thus resurrecting him…), and then flaps out on its preordained wire path. In film history, has there ever been a more uninspiring or silly monster resurrection? Well, in fairness, probably so, since a dog's urine (?) brought life back to Freddy Krueger's discarded bones in *A Nightmare on Elm Street IV: The Dream Master* (1989). Still, this ludicrous *deus ex machina* resurrection ranks high (or is it low?), lacking the pomp and dignity that Count Dracula should surely embody.

From that inauspicious start, *Scars of Dracula*, as if on automatic pilot, re-hashes in rote fashion all the popular plot elements of previous *Dracula* films. The audience sees the fearful, superstitious villagers, there is the imprisonment of a stranger in the Count's foreboding castle, there appears a lovely maiden who Dracula takes a liking to, et cetera. In toto, these vampire movie clichés are so old they are brittle. Watching the great Christopher Lee go through the same set of hackneyed paces for the umpteenth time, one is left to wonder some deep questions about the meaning of life. Is Dracula happy to be "alive" yet again, living the same old existence in his lonely castle? The isolation, the dependence on blood, the interference of strangers in his personal affairs—these must seem awfully tiring things for the old count to deal with. If the movie actually dealt with the questions of Dracula's unusual existence (seemingly a bunch of painful deaths separated by intervals of equally painful undead life), it might have actually been interesting. Instead, it is all leftovers from Bram Stoker and previous Drac films.

Making matters even more dire, *Scars of Dracula* puts up no worthy opponent in Dracula's path. Peter Cushing is (wisely) nowhere to be found. The only question this time around is how will the count be offed? In that respect, the film does not disappoint, flashily employing electricity as the mode of the vampire's inevitable (but temporary) destruction.

The films of Hammer Studios are pretty well impervious to criticism since so many people love them so deeply (and in some cases, so blindly). But, it is important to remember that not all Hammer films are created equal. *Scars of Dracula,* like a *Phantom Menace* (1999) or a *Final Frontier* (1989), is a retread of past glories rather than an innovative chapter in a well-established franchise. It is no wonder that after *Scars of Dracula,* Hammer went fishing about madly for new concepts to enliven their moribund vampire series. *Dracula A.D. 1972* brought the count into the twentieth century, *Rites of Dracula* saw him involved in an *Avengers*-like caper to unleash bubonic plague upon an unsuspecting world, and *The Legend of 7 Golden Vampires* depicted Dracula in the form of an ass-kicking, Chinese martial artist/warlord. Any of those unusual (and rather wacky) developments would have been welcome in *Scars of Dracula,* which suffers a terminal case of tired blood.

Scream and Scream Again (1970) ⋆ ⋆

Critical Reception

"*Scream and Scream Again* proceeds to unwind British-style, crisply, puzzlingly and with some restraint … into a good, tight knot, after the director, Gordon Hessler, bears down hard and graphically on a countryside pursuit.…

But ... the picture slouches into standard fare and ends up in still another mad scientist's lair...." — Howard Thompson, *New York Times*, July 9, 1970, page 44.

Cast and Credits

CAST: Vincent Price (Dr. Browning); Christopher Lee (Fremont); Peter Cushing (Major Benedek); Alfred Marks (Detective Superintendent Bellaver); Christopher Matthews (David Sorel); Judy Huxtable (Sylvia); Anthony Newland (Ludwig); Kenneth Benda (Professor Kingsmill); Marshall Jones (Konratz); Rita Lerka (Jane); David Lodge (Detective Inspector Strickland); Peter Sallis (Schweitz); The Amen Corner (Themselves); Michael Gothard (Keith); With: Yutte Stensgaard, Julian Holloway, Judi Bloom, Clifford Earl, Nigel Lambert.

CREW: American International Pictures Presents *Scream and Scream Again*. *Lighting Cameraman:* John Coquillon. *Editor:* Peter Elliott. *Production Manager:* Teresa Bolland. *Art Director:* Don Mingaye. *Make-up:* Jimmie Evans. *Hairdresser:* Betty Sherriff. *Wardrobe:* Evelyn Gibbs. *Dubbing Editor:* Michael Readborn. *Dubbing Mixer:* Hugh Strain. *Sound Mixer:* Bert Ross. *Screenplay:* Christopher Wicking. *From the Press Editorial Services novel* The Disoriented Man *by:* Peter Saxon. *Produced by:* Max J. Rosenberg, Milton Subotsky. *Executive Producer:* Louis M. Heyward. *Directed by:* Gordon Hessler. *Screenplay by:* Christopher Wicking. *Music:* Dave Whittaker (*video release*— Kendall Schmidt). *M.P.A.A. Rating:* PG. *Running Time:* 94 minutes.

P.O.V.

"It was interesting to have them all in the same film, but they should have had the contretemps between them, utilizing all three in one scene in a face-to-face showdown. But there was no way of working it in: We just brought them in to take advantage of the names, for marquee value" (4).—*Scream and Scream Again*'s executive producer, Louis M. Heyward, comments on the horror trifecta of Price, Cushing and Lee.

SYNOPSIS: In London, a man collapses while jogging in the park and is promptly taken to a medical ward for attention. When he awakens there, he finds, to his horror, that a leg has been amputated...

Meanwhile, there have been a series of deaths in London. Recently, a woman, Eileen, was found dead in a park, her throat cut, her body drained of blood. The police, led by Detective Bellaver, question her employer, the mysterious Dr. Browning, but he claims to know nothing of the so-called "Vampire Murders." Not far away, the beleaguered jogger awakens from a deep sleep to find he is missing his other leg...

In another part of the world, a strangely powerful man named Konratz moves up the chain of command in his dictatorship-like government by murdering his superior officers. He has a dark secret, one related to the murders in England, but Major Benedek is killed before he can stop Konratz.

Back in London, Bellaver, teaming up with a young coroner, sets up a sting operation for the vampire killer. Aware that the killer stalks his prey at nightclubs, the police set up a female officer as bait. She is nearly murdered by the killer, a superstrong man, but he escapes. They pursue him to a quarry, and he flees on foot up the side of a treacherous mountain. Even after falling down the hill and being cuffed to the car, the vampire-like killer escapes. This time, he breaks off his own wrist to escape custody!

The police chase leads to Crossways, the home of Dr. Browning. The killer jumps into a trough of acid to escape captivity. With the killer dead, the case is considered closed, but the coroner suspects intrigue, and examines the amputated hand. By night, the jogger's nurse (who has now overseen the amputation of the poor man's arms), steals the hand from the coroner's office!

At the same time, Konratz has traveled

to the U.K. to meet with Fremont, a top government official. Konratz demands all materials relating to the vampire murders in trade for the release of a captured spy plane and pilot. With Fremont's permission, Konratz takes the file, killing Superintendent Bellaver in the process.

Still suspecting foul play, the coroner breaks into Browning's home and finds a high tech laboratory there, as well as a repository of frozen body parts. He is confronted by Browning, who shows him the entire operation. It seems that Browning is part of a special elite of scientists who are building "composite" people: sentient beings assembled from various limbs and body parts. Browning even reveals he is a composite himself, part of what he calls a super race. Unfortunately, Konratz arrives in the laboratory and tells Browning that he and all his kind are expendable. Browning and Konratz then fight, while the coroner and a captive would-be organ bank flee Crossways. Browning kills Konratz, submerging him in a bath of acid, but then Fremont — another composite man — arrives to kill Browning. Fremont tells the coroner that the affair is not over, that it is "just beginning."

COMMENTARY: Gordon Hessler's *Scream and Scream Again* has one nifty and rather ghoulish visual joke in it. A healthy-looking jogger collapses during an afternoon run, and awakens in a hospital to find that one of his legs has been amputated without his knowledge (or permission). Later in the film, the jogger awakens again, to find his other leg missing. When the audience next sees the poor man, he is missing both arms. Scream and scream again, literally! Alas, the rest of this film does not live up to that moment of Grand Guignol humor. Worse, it squanders the once-in-a-lifetime opportunity to witness Peter Cushing, Christopher Lee and Vincent Price interacting on film, making it a missed opportunity rather than the high-water genre mark it aimed to be.

To fully understand a critic's frustration with *Scream and Scream Again*, one must only consider expectations. Price, Cushing and Lee are the great horror icons of the 1960s and 1970s. Price for his Poe roles and *Phibes* films; Cushing for his efforts as Dr. Frankenstein and Van Helsing; and Lee as (arguably) the greatest screen Dracula of all time. What a coup to have signed these three stars for one film! Price's devilish humor, Cushing's genteel determination, Lee's overt physical presence and menace ... just imagine how those qualities might have played out in full-blooded scene after dramatic scene.

Now, keep imagining, because none of those scenes exist in *Scream and Scream Again*. Peter Cushing appears as a Nazi-like officer in only one scene (before being killed by a technique that resembles Mr. Spock's famous Vulcan nerve pinch...), and doesn't get to share the screen with either Price or Lee. Vincent Price appears at the start of the film, and also has a significant presence at the denouement, but is otherwise missing in action. As for Lee, he appears a few times (perhaps four), all in the latter half of the picture, but shares just one (brief) moment with Price. What a disappointment! The icons never work in combination, and a great opportunity is lost. Although it is better to judge a film on what it does, rather than what it fails to do, it is difficult to forgive a movie that makes a blunder like this ... even if the rest of the picture is exemplary (which it isn't).

Foremost among the film's problems is its so-called plot (or rather plots, since there seem to be about four of them...). There are the goings-on in an unidentified eastern European country modeled after Nazi Germany (down to swastika-like symbols on blazing red arm bands), as an officer tortures refugees (Yutte Stensgaard in a cameo), kills his superiors (including Cushing), and plots some kind of military and political upheaval. In addition to being boring and mostly indecipherable, these sequences go nowhere and have little bearing on the remainder of the film. Then there's poor Christopher Lee, laboring through his very dry espionage sub-plot ... mostly sitting behind a desk and answering the phone. Then there is a sub-plot about a serial killer called the "Vampire Murderer," and the police attempts to catch him before he kills again. Then there is Price as Dr. Browning, a suspicious character working up something strange in his laboratory. Then there's the young coroner trying to solve the case. Finally, there is the revelation of a conspiracy of super-intelligent, super-strong supermen sewn from stolen body parts (hence the jogger's unfortunate limb deficiency). *Scream and Scream Again* has an excess of plots, but none of them are handled with much flair. Audiences need a note pad to keep up with all the various threads. The destination is not worth the complexity of the trip.

Scream and Scream Again plays like a James Bond film without James Bond, for there is a plot to rule the world, yet no worthy or interesting hero to step in and fight it. And, like the James Bond films, *Scream and Scream Again* suffers from what Roger Ebert calls the "Fallacy of the Talking Villain." At the end of the picture, mad-scientist Vincent Price confronts the young coroner (a deadly bland Christopher Matthews) and invites him to look over his secret operation. Then, in detail, Price explains everything to the young man, making sure to leave no detail out. Of course, the coroner is able to escape eventually, whereas if Price had just killed the guy before talking, his plan might not have been jeopardized...

Scream and Scream Again also fails to convince in its scientific thesis. The ultimate point of the film is that man should not tamper in God's domain by building supermen out of human spare parts. That is fine, but today it seems a thematic dead end. In 2000, audiences understand that if a super race is created, it will happen courtesy of DNA and genetic engineering, not the sewing together of spare parts. Even in 1970 such a plot does not really hold up well. How does a "new" superman, assembled from spare parts, become a different sentient individual if the brain in use is from another (already living) human being? Would not you merely have another person's brain inside a super powerful new body, rather than a new personality who is consciously part of a master race and its conspiracy? And why no seams? If these folks are sewn together from spare parts like the Frankenstein monster, should not there be physical remnants or traces of the surgical procedure? If not seams, then how about scars? As was stated so eloquently in *Spinal Tap*, there is a fine line between stupid and clever, and *Scream and Scream Again* crosses that line.

Besides an exciting car chase and the extended pursuit of a super being who is difficult to injure, let alone capture, *Scream and Scream Again* is more baffling than intriguing. In some fan circles, the film enjoys a reputation as being quite good, a classic even. One has to wonder how that assessment was reached, as the film is resolutely style-less and lacking in pace. Throw in an ineffective, overly cumbersome plot, a ridiculous scientific resolution to the mystery, and a failure to exploit the presence of three genre greats, and one is left feeling *suspiciously* like that poor jogger ... as if pieces are missing.

Shock Waves (1970) ✶ ✶ ✶

Cast and Crew

CAST: Peter Cushing (S.S. Commandant); Brook Adams (Rose); Fred Buch (Chuck); Jack Davidson (Norman); Luke Halpin (Keith); D.J. Sidney (Beverly); Don Stout (Dobbs); John Carradine (Captain); Clarence Thomas (Fisherman); With: Sammy Graham, Preston

White, Reid Finger, Mike Kennedy, Donahue Guillory, Jay Maeder, Talmadge Scott, Gary Levinson, Robert Miller.

CREW: A Joseph Brenner Associates Inc., Release. *Music:* Richard Einhorn. *Screenplay:* John Harrison, Ken Wiederhorn. *Produced by:* Reuben Trane. *Directed by:* Ken Wiederhorn. *Film Editor:* Norman Gray. *Director of Photography:* Reuben Trane. *Underwater Photography:* Irving Pare. *Production Design:* Jessica Sack. *Make-up Design:* Alan Ormsby. *Assistant to Producer:* Rosanne Hemming. *Assistant Director:* George Berndt. *Production Manager:* Doug Kauffman. *Unit Manager:* Wayne Hood. *Second Assistant Director:* Roger Skelton. *Assistant Editor:* Greg Sheldon. *Assistant Cameraman:* Tom Schroeppel. *Apprentice Editor:* Eva Gardos, Denine Rowan. *Script Supervisor:* Dee Miller. *Continuity:* Jacque Kegeles. *Chief Electrician:* Gerry Rhodes. *Prop Master:* Mykie Metlee. *Sound Recordist:* Stephen Manners. *Boom Man:* Parris Buckner. *Production Assistant*: Daryl Polan. *Grips:* Eric Lacor, Frank Smithers. *Production Assistants:* Jennie Jerome, Gene Picchi, Laurie Latarelli, John O'Gorman, Terry Twyman. *Sound Mix:* Emil Neroda. *M.P.A.A. Rating:* R. *Running Time:* 86 minutes.

SYNOPSIS: Two fishermen rescue a beautiful woman, Rose, out of a lifeboat, and she tells them a bizarre and frightening story.

Rose was on the second day of a diving boat expedition when the ship's motor broke. Rose and her friends heard a rumbling under the ramshackle vessel, and demanded that their cranky captain leave the area. The compass malfunctioned too, and the ship was lost in unknown waters. By night, the diving boat collided with a massive, rusted old ship, and the crew was forced to abandon their vehicle for a small tropical island. The captain did not survive the evacuation.

Disturbed, Rose and her cohorts, Chuck, Keith, Beverly and Norman, moved inland, and discovered a rotted out old hotel in the forest. There was only one inhabitant: a Nazi S.S. commander, a crazed scientist. This old, scarred man allowed the marooned vacationers to bunk down in the ruined hotel

for the night, but had a disturbing secret to share. Many years earlier, during World War II, he had engineered a platoon of Nazi amphibian storm troopers. This S.S. death corps could breathe underwater, and thus function as the perfect soldiers. Unfortunately, the soldiers had become dangerously unpredictable, and were exiled from Germany before they could harm the very people they had been created to protect. Now, the platoon inhabited the deepest regions of the sea, and the rusted old ship that the diving boat collided with. With a taste for murder, these insane soldiers would soon come after the new inhabitants of the island.

At this terrible news, Rose and her friends decided to flee for a lifeboat on the far side of the island. The tourists were hunted through the woods by the inhuman Nazi soldiers and the soldiers even murdered their former commandant! The fleeing vacationers became caught in a patch of mud, and had to drag the boat to open sea. Unfortunately, they were again confronted by the death corps, this time in the surf. When the boat was inadvertently lost, the survivors split up and returned to the island. The Nazis soon killed Norman, the smart-ass of the bunch.

Rose was attacked, but she ripped off her assailant's goggles, and blinded him. Apparently, the Nazi zombies had adapted to the murkiness at the bottom of the sea, and were unable to face clear sunlight. The survivors then held up in the commander's hotel as the Nazi zombies surrounded the building. Rose and the others locked themselves in a massive refrigerator behind a reinforced door as the zombies trashed the hotel. Chuck, a claustrophobic, held Rose and the others at gunpoint and forced his friends to flee the freezer after firing a flare inside it.

The Nazi death troopers seized the next opportunity to kill Chuck. They then drowned Beverly, leaving Keith and Rose the last chance to escape. They managed to get to a life raft from their boat, the *Bonaventure*, and make for the ocean. One last sentry attacked, killing Keith, leaving Rose alone to tell the tale of Nazi evil that still survives at the bottom of a turbulent sea…

———————————

COMMENTARY: If only TV's reality show *Survivor* (2000) had been as gripping as 1970's *Shock Waves*, a nightmarish "zombie" movie in which unsuspecting vacationers are voted off the island (and off the mortal coil…) by a team of automaton-like mutant Nazis…

Sure, this is a low-budget exploitation film with a ludicrous B-movie premise (underwater fascist ghouls…), but director Ken Wiederhorn handily carries the film beyond so silly-sounding a premise, marshalling all of his creative resources to engender feelings of true suspense and danger. Although on the surface this is a movie boasting that favorite '70s horror trope, "science gone awry," it actually generates the same kind of random-feeling terror as *Night of the Living Dead* (1968) by introducing the world to a variation on the idea of faceless, homicidal goons. They're not cannibalistic flesh-eaters, sure, but the effect is not far different. The intense creep factor in *Shock Waves* comes from the evil death corps lurking underwater, undetected, and popping up to strangle unsuspecting humans. Whenever you least suspect it, there's a ghoul waiting to pull you down to the depths … and that's scary stuff. But the other important point is that these Nazis are not at all individualized as people, so there is no identification with them (as one might feel sympathy or empathy for Dracula or the Frankenstein monster). Instead, these pale, emotionless antagonists remain emotionally distant, breaking the glassy water surface to hunt in a pack like *Star Trek*'s popular Borg villains. They have no names, no personalities, and no individuality, but they strike in tandem, and are dedicated to the extermination of the victims. They make for great villains.

And, who can deny that there's something intrinsically terrifying about the water, a realm in which humans naturally feel quite endangered? *Shock Waves*, like *Jaws* (1975), remembers that humans don't have a home field advantage when tromping through rivers or paddling through a vast ocean. Water slows us down, discomforts us, and is a perfect hiding place for predators. Evoking memories of *Creature from the Black Lagoon* (1954), which also traded on such feelings of unease about "what dwells beneath," there is a tantalizing and troubling image in *Shock Waves* as lovely Brook Adams bathes in a black stream, the water looking thick, viscous and wholly mysterious. The scene ends when she swims into a dead body (the cook), but before that crescendo, the film captures the beauty and danger of a remote swimming hole where relaxation may turn to terror.

"The sea spits up what it can't keep down," states one of the characters early in the film, and that's a perfect metaphor for *Shock Waves*' use of water as an arena for terror. Though uniformed, jackbooted, goggled underwater Nazis sound like really stupid antagonists, the film is successful because it co-joins fear of the water with these ridiculous-seeming, but deadly serious villains, and does so with a straight face. Peter Cushing, horror's old friend, lends the film further authenticity by offering (in his own inimitable fashion) tons of exposition about the Nazis, building up the audience's feelings of terror.

It's a perfect recipe for a solid horror movie: a favorite performer (Cushing), a popular threat (zombies), a remote location (a tropical island), and an arena which gives audiences reason to pause (the murky depths of the ocean). Add a beautiful star (Adams), and some suspenseful, frightening murders, and *Shock Waves* represents a great day at the beach for horror fans.

Trog (1970) ⋆ ⋆

Cast & Credits

CAST: Joan Crawford (Dr. Brockton); Michael Gough (Sam Murdock); Bernard Kay (Inspector Greenham); Kim Braden (Anne Brockton); David Griffin (Malcolm Travers); John Hamill (Cliff); Thorley Walters (Magistrate); Jack May (Dr. Selbourne); Geoffrey Case (Bill); Robert Hutton (Dr. Richard Hutton); Simon Lack (Colonel Vickers); David Warbeck (Alan Davis); Chloe Francis (Little Girl); Maurice Good (Reporter); Joe Cornelius (Trog).

CREW: A Herman Cohen Production, *Trog*. *Associate Producer:* Harry Woolveridge. *Art Director:* Geoffrey Tozer. *Film Editor:* Oswald Hafenrichter. *Trog Designed by:* Charles Parker. *Production Manager:* Eddie Dorian. *Camera Operator:* Norman Jones. *Casting:* Maud Spector. *Director of Photography:* Desmond Dickinson. *Music:* John Scott. *Screenplay:* Aben Kandel. *Original Story:* Peter Bryan and John Gilling. *Produced by:* Herman Cohen. *Directed by:* Freddie Francis. *M.P.A.A. Rating:* PG. *Running time:* 91 minutes.

SYNOPSIS: Three amateur prospectors, Cliff, Billy and Malcolm, discover a fissure leading down into an ancient, untouched cavern. After traversing an underground spring, they discover a prehistoric ape-man dwelling inside the deep cave. Terrified by the intrusion of modern man into his solitary world, the apeman kills Billy while Malcolm and Cliff escape.

Malcolm, a student in zoology, takes the injured Cliff to the nearby Brockton Research Center, where the world's foremost anthropologist, Dr. Brockton, is fascinated to hear the story of a creature she believes is the missing link. Brockton returns to the cave with Malcolm and photographs the creature, which she calls a "trog," half-man/half ape. Trog is a cave dweller, maybe thawed out from an age 10 million years earlier.

The police, the press, Brockton and curious locals descend on Trog's cave in an attempt to capture him. Though Trog injures a police diver and wrecks some TV equipment, he finally works his way out of the cave, seeking escape. Brockton uses a hypo-gun to tranquilize the creature, and takes him back to her laboratory for study.

Brockton, Malcolm, and Brockton's daughter, Ann, collaborate with the stuffy Dr. Selbourne to train and domesticate Trog. Brockton believes Trog is the missing link, and that he can be trained to reveal the earliest chapters of human evolution and history. But a closed-minded local, Sam Murdock, doesn't like the attention Trog has received and wants the creature destroyed. Soon, a jealous Dr. Selbourne joins forces with Murdock to discredit Brockton, and a public court of inquiry is convened to determine the disposition of Trog. While the court hears evidence, Dr. Brockton and a team of scientists operate on his vocal cords to grant the apeman the power of speech.

When Brockton gains worldwide respect and admiration for her work with Trog, Murdock takes matters into his own hands. He breaks into the Brockton lab and wrecks it. He then sets Trog free to take the blame for the destruction, but Trog escapes and murders Murdock instead.

Now local authorities have just the excuse they need to execute Trog, and the police hunt him down. Trog goes on a murder spree in the nearby village and kidnaps a little blond girl from a playground. Terrified, Trog retreats to his cave. The police surround the hole, and Brockton steals into the fissure to rescue the child. Brockton secures Trog's release, but once she has escaped from the cave, a demolition squad blasts open a larger entrance. Soldiers descend into the cave in force and open fire on Trog with machine guns. Riddled with bullets, Trog falls to his death in the cave.

COMMENTARY: Joan Crawford's final film, *Trog*, starts with a strong narrative pull. Three amateur prospectors find a cavern, and explore it, only to find a cave man, Trog, dwelling deep below the surface of the Earth. This very premise recalls a more innocent time in film history, when audiences could suspend disbelief enough to believe that it was possible to jump down a cave, explore a new place, and make a great discovery around the next turn. It's evocative of Jules Verne and *Journey to the Center of the Earth*. There's something terribly innocent and charming about this notion of a world-beneath-the-world, and *Trog* benefits from it. It's an innocent sort of film, and its heart is in the right place.

But, sadly, *Trog* is also a terribly naïve, brainless sort of film. For instance, much is made in the film of a deadly serious court of inquiry to determine if *Trog* should live or die. Only in a bad horror film would such a creature's existence even be a point of debate. The eyes of the world would be on this momentous project, and the public (not to mention the scientific community or the national government…) would never permit so valuable a specimen as Trog to be executed. This plot exists in the film simply to raise tension. It's a B-movie gimmick, pure and simple. If the community that found Trog were really that afraid of the beast, he'd be transported to London, or the United States, or to any zoo in the world with a research branch. *Never* would there be discussion of murdering the world's one and only missing link.

In its sincere naïveté and limited understanding of its own premise, this movie skirts the real significance of Trog's existence. This creature, this "missing link," is the proof the world would need that creationism, and thus Christianity, is nothing but bunk, pure mythology. The villainous Murdock makes plenty of comments in the film about "the Lord," and even quotes from scripture (Genesis, specifically), yet *Trog* never shows either the courage or the wit to tackle what Trog's existence truly represents to the 20th century. He represents a bedrock change in knowledge that fundamentalist parties and religious orders would want to destroy because he challenges their authority, power, and hold over so many people. If the film were about that idea — how *Trog* frightens traditionalists and religious zealots — then it would have been a whole lot more interesting, not to mention smarter. As it stands, Murdock is simply a two-dimensional villain who hates Trog because the screenplay demands it of him. He is evil "just because." As Murdock, Gough is a little over the top too. Apparently, he learned nothing from *Konga*…

For a film that depends so heavily on scientific babble, *Trog* also makes some terrible blunders. For instance, it perpetuates that old movie mistake of putting dinosaurs and primitive man into the same prehistoric epoch. Science seems to have proved that these two species never co-existed, so the trippy scene in which Trog has a "flashback" to a dinosaur fight is a factual mistake. It doesn't work from a plot standpoint either. Trog just suddenly "remembers" a fight amongst the dinosaurs, and then the film cuts to a protracted battle between miniature model dinosaurs fighting in really dreadful stop-motion animation. This interlude has nothing whatsoever to do with the rest of the film, and goes on at least two minutes too long. It is rather obvious padding to get the film up to a 90-minute length.

The legendary Joan Crawford does her best with *Trog*'s ludicrous screenplay, but her sincerity and passion in the role of Dr. Brockton ill serves a film that is already way too serious. So many scenes border on camp that Crawford's scene-chewing only makes the film seem sillier. Take for instance the moment that Trog sways breezily to classical music, but then reacts badly to rock-'n'-roll. The cast takes it so seriously, but any sensible viewer is tempted to joke that Trog may just be the world's oldest music critic…

Trog's problems are many. The script introduces Malcolm and Ann Brockton as major characters, and then drops them completely. They don't participate in the climax of the film, and have no valedictory scene. Bernard Kay's Inspector Greenham is a problem too, sometimes seeming reasonable; sometimes seeming to be a hard and fast enemy to Trog. Even Crawford's character is somewhat insufferable. She barks orders at her daughter ("Never show fear, only *trust!*"), has her staff fetch things for her ("bring me my hypo gun, quickly!!!"), and is a dyed-in-the-wool know-it-all. One is tempted to think of *Mommie Dearest*, but let's not go there...

Still, even in its worst moments, *Trog* is oddly affecting. Its very innocence is charming in some way. As fake as the Trog make-up looks, the audience bonds with this innocent creature, and doesn't want to see it hurt or exploited. The film features some oddball tenderness to it in that regard. And horror fans will really dig the gory murder sequence in which Trog hangs a troublesome butcher on his own meat hook (forecasting a similarly gruesome murder in *The Texas Chainsaw Massacre* [1974]).

Ultimately, there's little this critic can state about *Trog* that every critic hasn't already said about the film. In essence, it's a laughable, lowbrow version of *Iceman* (1985). In fact, the outstanding *Iceman* makes *Trog* look like a neanderthal.

The Vampire Lovers (1970) ⋆ ⋆ ⋆

Cast & Credits

CAST: Ingrid Pitt (Mircalla/Carmilla); George Cole (Morton); Kate O'Mara (Governess); Peter Cushing (the General); Ferdy Mayne (Doctor); Douglas Wilmer (Baron Hartog); Madeline Smith (Emma); Dawn Addams (Countess); Jon Finch (Carl Ebhardt); Pippa Steel (Laura); Kirsten Betts (First Vampire); Janet Key (Gretchin); Harvey Hall (Renton); John Forbes Robertson (Man in Black); Charles Farrell (Landlord); Shelagh Wilcocks (Housekeeper); Graham James (First Young Man); Tom Browne (Second Young Man); Joanna Shelley (Woodman's Daughter); Olga James (Village Girl).

CREW: American International Pictures and Hammer Films Present *The Vampire Lovers*. *Based on:* J. Sheridan Le Fanu's story "Carmilla." *Adapted by:* Harry Fine, Tudor Gates, Michael Style. *Director of Photography:* Moray Grant. *Editor:* James Needs. *Art Director:* Scott MacGregor. *Costume Design:* Brian Cox. *Music:* Harry Robinson. *Music Supervisor:* Philip Martell. *Production Manager:* Tom Sachs. *Assistant Director:* Derek Whitehurst. *Sound Recordist:* Claude Hitchcock. *Sound Editor:* Roy Hyde. *Camera Operator:* Neil Binney. *Continuity:* Betty Harley. *Make-up:* Tom Smith.

Screenplay: Tudor Gates. *Produced by:* Harry Fine, Michael Style. *Directed by:* Roy Ward Baker. *M.P.A.A. Rating:* R. *Running Time:* 89 minutes.

SYNOPSIS: Baron Hartog writes in his memoirs of a ferocious battle with the Karnsteins: a family of vampires. Hartog recounts his effort to decapitate a beautiful female vampire, as well as his hope that he has ended the curse for all time.

Years later, a lovely foreign countess arrives at the engagement party of a general's beautiful daughter, Laura. She brings with her the beautiful Mircalla — in truth the Karnstein vampire, Carmilla. Unaware of the danger, the general invites Mircalla to spend the night in his home when her countess is unexpectedly called away to a funeral. He comes to regret that decision when Mircalla drains the beautiful Laura of blood, killing her. After her death, two puncture marks are found above her breasts, and her fiancé, Carl Ebhardt, swears vengeance.

Mircalla moves on, changing her name to Carmilla. She befriends another innocent girl, Emma Morton, and is invited to stay at the Morton house for a time. The same cycle soon repeats, with Carmilla draining Emma of blood over a period of days. As Emma grows weaker, the house butler, Renton, realizes she is the target of a vampire. He arranges for garlic plants to be brought to her room. These stop Carmilla for a time, but she seduces Renton and the Morton governess in an attempt to get to Emma.

Mr. Morton, Emma's father, joins forces with an aged Baron Hartog, Carl Ebhardt, and the general, to stop the Karnstein evil. They visit the Karnstein castle and gain proof that Mircalla/Carmilla is a vampire. While Carl rides back to the Morton house to save Emma, Carmilla strikes again, killing the local doctor. Later, Carmilla decides to bring Emma back to her castle with her. Carl attempts to stop this voyage, and Carmilla is forced to de-materialize. She re-materializes at her coffin in the Karnstein cemetery, and the general, Morton and Hartog await her arrival. The general stakes Carmilla through the heart in the name of his beloved Laura. Then, in one blow, he decapitates Carmilla, ending the vampire curse ... hopefully.

COMMENTARY: What distinguishes one Hammer film above its brethren, since, to one degree or another, all of the studio's output features the same strengths? Think about it: the Hammer films are inevitably buttressed by a lush, high-quality look, and by indoor studio sets that double as exteriors, yet serve effectively in a stylized way. Perhaps more importantly, just about every individual in the Hammer repertory company knows (and understands) his or her terrain. Peter Cushing, Ingrid Pitt, Christopher Lee and the rest know just how long to hold a sideways glance, how to spin a terrible line into something evocative and meaningful, and how to underplay the most "gonzo" of horror scenes, thereby grounding them in reality. But for this author at least, the Hammer films work best when something new is thrown into the predictable formula. *The*

Legend of 7 Golden Vampires (1974) kicks into high gear with martial arts action, and *Dracula A.D. 1972* transports the vampire count to the "mod" early '70s in a droll way.

The Vampire Lovers, the first in the Carmilla/Mircalla cycle (followed by the enjoyable romp, *Lust for a Vampire*) is a notch above typical Hammer product in the '70s for two reasons. Firstly, it makes a star of actress Ingrid Pitt, an actress with not only the beauty and the charisma to play a powerful vampire, but the *gravitas* as well. Secondly, the film has the courage to offer insights about Mircalla's cursed existence rather than rely merely on bloodletting and breasts (though there is plenty of each on hand, as well).

"I want you to love me for all of your life," a jealous Mircalla informs Emma, a beautiful young girl destined to be her victim, in *The Vampire Lovers*. "It's not the same," Emma replies thoughtlessly, comparing her "fraternal" love for Carmilla to her more romantic feelings for a "boyfriend." This conversation highlights *The Vampire Lovers*' interesting decision to confront the sexual preference of its villain, and what it means to her in a society that forbids such "alternative" couplings. For Mircalla genuinely loves Emma and each of the women she seduces and kills. She doesn't want them to die, but she does not want to lose them (to men) either. If they live, they will be "taken" by their boyfriends, never to be hers again. Yet, if Mircalla murders the girls she desires, draining their blood, they are lost to her as well. What a terrible dilemma! Accordingly, there is serious melancholy in this vampire ... she is truly cursed.

In one monologue, Mircalla spells it all out, making it clear that she despises death for the things and people it takes away from her. This awareness of death, of her own role in fostering it, differentiates Mircalla from Hammer's Dracula. He thrives on death, on the seduction, on the corruption of life. By contrast, one feels of Mircalla that she is a woman trapped by her preferences. Her appetites are unacceptable (i.e. lesbian-

Ingrid Pitt (far left) leads a harem of "innocent" schoolgirls in *The Vampire Lovers* (1970).

ism/vampirism) in the Victorian age, but she bows to them out of a sense of biological need, out of a sense of desperation, out of a sense of jealousy. In a strange way, that makes this vampire almost human, understandable. Are not all of us, at one time or another, slaves to desire? For most of us, those desires, those appetites, fall into the norm, and are permitted expression in "normal" society (i.e. heterosexuality). But what of those with "alternative" tastes? Are they to hide their needs in dark and secret, like vampires? That is the argument *The Vampire Lovers* makes, and one it states rather successfully.

It is clear that Mircalla despises herself, and how her appetites force her to hurt the very people she longs to share life with. By facing this duality in Mircalla's nature (she is both killer and lover), *The Vampire Lovers*

offers something that most Hammer films lack: subtext. It is not all period detail, lush forestry, and beautiful woman. There's a point to the violence, to the terror, and that makes it a worthwhile character study, and consequently a worthwhile film.

And, Ingrid Pitt is the perfect actress to present the material. She can be seductress and vampire, or tragic anti-hero, depending on how the audience seeks to view her. Her portrayal has layers, something that cannot be said for the fetching Yutte Stensgaard in *Lust for a Vampire*. In that film, one does not really understand who Mircalla is, or why she is that way. But Pitt is the better actress, a strong central presence that dominates the film in an unusually masculine way. She has the raw power a vampire should embody, but is burdened with the seeds of a conscience as well. Pitt gives it her all, embodying both vampire and lover, and this film is all the stronger for it.

The rest of the movie is, alas, your standard vampire stuff. Peter Cushing is around as an aggrieved father, out for revenge, and there are the requisite shots of Pitt's breasts and pubic zone, but *The Vampire Lovers* works well because it re-captures the core of the vampire ethos: the haunted soul, the eternal torment, the love forever lost. Mircalla is beautiful, powerful, and even evil, but tortured too. *The Vampire Lovers* works best when it remembers that even in monsters, the audience looks for identification, for itself.

(1 9 7 1)

The Abominable Dr. Phibes (1971) ✶ ✶ ✶

Critical Reception

"…the plot, buried under all the iron tinsel, isn't bad. But the tone of steam roller camp flattens the fun. Price finally climbs into his own grave to the tune of 'Over the Rainbow.' Up the creek is more like it."—Howard Thompson, *New York Times*, August 5, 1971, page 25.

"…cult camp horror, with Price in fine fettle…. Often amusing, occasionally sickening, always impressive for the imagination of the Art Deco sets, it's pretty flatly directed."—Geoff Andrew, *Time Out Film Guide*, Seventh Edition, Penguin Books, 1999, page 3.

"…the last great grandstand of perennial ham Vincent Price. It is a delicious camp film about a deformed music genius…. It also features a wonderful parade of Art Deco backgrounds, some imaginative deaths, thefts from a dozen famous films, trivia-wise horror dialogue, and a Busby Berkeley extravaganza at the end … the only horror film that feels like a musical."—Darrell Moore, *The Best, Worst, Most Unusual: Horror Films*, Crowne Publishers, 1983, page 136.

"While never really scary, this is probably the most stylish horror film of the decade, with an evil villain you can't help but love. It's hard to imagine anyone other than Vincent Price in the title role — never was his scenery chewing more appropriate. As a precursor to the *Friday the 13th* series, where the murder scenes *were* the movies, this film showed murder in the hands of an artist, harkening to Nicholson's Joker and Hopkins' Hannibal Lecter to come. Along with *Theatre of Blood* and *Dr. Phibes Rises Again*, this is probably a much more influential film than people realize, particularly in the 1980s…."—Bill Latham, author of *Mary's Monster*, Powys Books.

"Directed flamboyantly by Robert Fuest. Aided by … clever makeup, Price, without any dialogue, manages to be both terrifying and hilarious…. As a parody, the camp film works very well."—Frank Manchel, *An Album of Modern Horror Films*, Franklin Watts Publisher, 1983, page 71.

Cast & Crew

CAST: Vincent Price (Dr. Anton Phibes); Joseph Cotten (Dr. Vesalius); Hugh Griffith (Rabbi); Terry-Thomas (Dr Longstreet); Peter Jeffrey (Trout); Derek Godfrey (Crow); Norman Jones (Schenley); John Cater (Waverley); Aubrey Woods (Goldsmith); John Laurie (Darrow); Maurice Kaufmann (Dr. Whitcombe); Barbara Keogh (Mrs. Fraley); Sean Bury (Lem); Charles Farrell (Chauffeur); Susan Travers (Nurse Alen); David Hutcheson (Dr. Hedgepath); Edward Burnham (Dr. Dunwoody); Alex Scott (Dr. Hargreaves); Peter Gilmore (Dr. Kifaj); Virginia Noth (Vulnavia); Alan Zipson (1st Police Officer); Dallas Adams (2nd Police Officer); James Grout (Sergeant); Alister Williamson, Thomas Heathcoate, Ian Marter, Julian Grant (Police); John Franklyn (Graveyard Attendant); Walter Harsbrugh (Butler).

CREW: American International Pictures and James H. Nicholson and Samuel Z. Arkoff Present *The Abominable Dr. Phibes*. *Production Manager:* Richard Dalton. *Assistant Director:* Frank Ernst. *Continuity:* Gladys Goldsmith. *Casting Director:* Sally Nicholl. *Director of Photography:* Norman Warwick. *Camera Operator:* Godfrey Godar. *Camera Assistant:* Steve Clayton. *Make-up:* Trevor Crole-Rees. *Hairdresser:* Bernadette Ibbetson. *Sets:* Brian Eatwell. *Assistant Art Director:* Christopher Burke. *Wardrobe:* Elsa Fennell. *Special Effects:* Geoerge Blackwell. *Properties:* Rex Hobbs. *Editor:* Tristam Cones. *Sound Recordist:* Denis Whitlock. *Dubbing Editor:* Peter Lennard. *Music Composed and arranged by:* Basil Kirchin *in association with:* Jack Nathan. *Written by:* James Whiton and William Goldstein. *Executive Producers:* Samuel Z. Arkoff, James H. Nicholson. *Produced by:* Louis M. Heyward and Donald S. Dunas. *Directed by:* Robert Fuest. The Producers wish to thank the Big Three Music Company for Permission to Use the Following Songs: "What Can I Say Dear After I Say I'm Sorry," "Dark Town Strutters Ball," "Close Your Eyes," "Elmer's Tune," "All I Do Is Dream of You," "You Stepped Out of a Dream," "Charmaine," "100 Years from Today," "Over the Rainbow." Made on Location and at the EMI-MGM Elstree Studios Boreham Wood, Hertfordshire, England. An American International Picture Release. *M.P.A.A. Rating:* PG. *Running Time:* 95 minutes.

SYNOPSIS: In the 1930s, someone is going to extraordinary lengths to arrange and orchestrate horrible, elaborate deaths for the most prominent surgeons of London. One doctor is stung to death by bees in his library, and another has his face shredded by hungry bats in his bedroom. Then, at a costume ball, a psychiatrist named Hargreaves has his head crushed by a collapsible frog mask. The same dark perpetrator then invades the home of Dr. Longstreet and exsanguinates the good doctor, leaving several bottles of his blood on the mantle. The London police investigate this series of crimes against the medical profession and seek the assistance of Dr. Vesalius, an associate of all the dead medicos.

At the next crime scene, an amulet is found with a Hebrew mark emblazoned on it. This mark signifies "blood" and relates directly to the ten curses visited upon the pharaohs before Exodus. These curses are Blood, Bats, Frogs, Rats, Hail, Beasts, Locusts, Death of a Firstborn, and finally, Darkness. Someone has been murdering members of the medical community by these very curses! As Vesalius puts the pieces together, he realizes that all the doctors had one patient in common: Victoria Regina Phibes, who underwent surgery with nine professionals, but died nonetheless. Her case was a strange one because her husband, Dr. Phibes, died in a horrible car fire on his way to see her. Now Phibes has returned, apparently quite alive, to seek revenge against the surgical team that caused the death of his beloved wife.

Using a portable air conditioning unit, Phibes next arranges a curse of hail on one of the unsuspecting men he deems responsible for Victoria's death. The police and Dr. Vesalius go to the Phibes family tomb to examine the bodies of Phibes and his wife, but they find only ashes in his crypt, and come to suspect that Dr. Phibes did not die in the terrible fire. That Victoria's body is missing from her coffin also seems to confirm their suspicions that Phibes is somehow involved. Before the police can save another endangered medico, Phibes kills him by loading his airplane cockpit with hungry rats! The police next put Dr. Wickham under police custody, but Phibes gets to him easily.

Next up on Dr. Phibes' hit list is a nurse who participated in the surgery of Victoria. The evil doctor gains access to her bedroom and lets a horde of locusts have a go at her face. At this point, Dr. Vesalius, who was the chief surgeon on Victoria's case, realizes he is next line for gruesome treatment. He realizes his curse is to be the death of the first-born son, so he races home, but finds that Phibes has already kidnapped his adolescent boy. Soon, Phibes telephones Vesalius and plays him some ominous organ music before telling him that the nine responsible for his wife's death will soon be dead. He then informs Vesalius to come alone to his house if he wants to see his son alive again. Against the better judgment of the police, Vesalius goes to the Phibes residence. In the art deco mansion, Phibes shows Vesalius his son, who is strapped to a table. Phibes makes the good doctor perform heart surgery to remove a key from the boy's chest that will free him from the operating table. If Vesalius should fail the operation, acid will spill down on the boy's face from an elaborate device suspended above him.

Phibes also reveals his true face to Vesalius: he is horribly mutilated from the car fire and is little more than a monster. His vocal cords were destroyed, but he manages to speak via a device of his own creation that operates on the principles of acoustics, music and sound waves.

Working under intense pressure, Vesalius manages to acquire the key and save his son. When he is attacked by Vulnavia, Phibes' beautiful assistant and co-perpetrator, Vesalius is shocked to see the acid fall down on her face … scorching and killing her.

Considering his job of revenge done, Phibes joins his dead wife on an elaborate bed, replacing his own blood with embalming fluid, all to the strains of "Over the Rainbow."

COMMENTARY: Some horror movies are critic-proof. *The Abominable Dr. Phibes* is one of them. The film's plot consists of nothing but one spectacular murder scene after the other, with the inimitable Vincent Price at the center of it all, playing camp and having fun. Subtext? *Nope.* Deeper meaning? *Not really.* But it is a fun picture, and sometimes, that's enough. No, the movie does not combine editing, pace, or interesting angles to create a frightening meaningful picture in the tradition of *The Exorcist*, or even Fuest's previous picture, *And Soon the Darkness*. It relies instead on inventive horror setpieces, a deranged musical score, and fantastic art deco sets. Welcome everyone, to *Phantom of the Opera* meets Busby Berkeley!

Perhaps more accurately, *The Abominable Dr. Phibes* is the horror equivalent of a James Bond film: a charismatic super character (antagonist Phibes) goes on a visually stunning, action-packed adventure, encountering thrilling locations, and high production values. For those who want nothing more out of a genre flick, this is your movie.

Perhaps the most interesting thing about *Phibes* is its context, the climate in which it was born. In the early 1970s, filmmakers were casting about for a new horror franchise that could supplant the monsters of old. Dracula, the Mummy, the Wolfman, and Frankenstein had worn out their welcome through umpteen Universal and Hammer films, and besides, these familiar icons did not necessarily speak to the concerns of a modern audience. So, something new was needed to stir the blood. Accordingly then, in just the first three years of the '70s, the "new" franchises were born. Most of them didn't survive beyond one sequel, but along they came nonetheless. Transmutations of Dracula came in the form *of Count Yorga, Vampire,* the Mircalla films (*The Vampire Lovers, Lust for a Vampire, Twins of Evil*), *Blacula,* and the *Dark Shadows* motion picture.

Among these attempts to create a new horror villain was *The Abominable Dr. Phibes* and its sequel, *Dr. Phibes Rises Again*. The *Phibes* films exist solely to depict a charismatic star (Price) committing inventive murders against a percentage of the community (doctors, theater critics, competitors) who were perceived to have done the main character wrong. Humor is highlighted as the "bad" people get their just deserts at the hand of the equally bad Price. It's as simple a formula as that.

But just because the equation is a simple one should not rule out *The Abominable Dr. Phibes* as a bad film. To the contrary, one can see its myriad good qualities simply by looking ahead to the following decade, the 1980s. One of the most popular franchises of that era was *Friday the 13th*. Now, there was a film series lacking a charismatic monster (the silent serial killer Jason), any interesting music (beyond the trademark Manfredini theme, *chee chee, hah hah*), and even a varied setting. Film after film featured the same bland monster killing the same group of protagonists (stupid teens), in the same locale (Camp Crystal Lake). So, in just a decade, the *Phibes* formula had degenerated to true blandness. Compared to any *Friday the 13th* film, *Phibes* is indeed high art. In fairness, the *Elm Street* saga of the 1980s had more success aping the *Phibes* equation, featuring a truly imaginative villain (Robert Englund's dream stalker Freddy Krueger), and diverse settings (a plethora of character-driven dreamscapes). Still, *Phibes* has one element that most of the later *Elm Street* movies lack: class! The film looks as though it were made by a director, not a special effects team, and there is an overriding intelligence behind the scenes, one with flashes of wit.

Ironically, *Phibes*, *Blacula*, *Yorga* and the rest of the '70s would-be icons did not survive the decade, primarily because their creators made a serious miscalculation. What was coming to scare audiences in the '70s was random violence (a shark attack, a rape, inexplicable murders in rural Texas), not these larger-than-life super characters that seemed so far away from everyday reality. In a world with *Jaws*, *The Texas Chainsaw Massacre*, *Last House on the Left*, and the rest, vampires, and monsters of *Phibes*' ilk inevitably looked quaint and charming in comparison, even silly sometimes. They lost their power to scare. Today these films are remembered with nostalgia by the generation that grew up with them, but ask anyone without that pre-disposition of nostalgia to watch these horror films, and wait for the response. These films just ain't scary.

What is there to like about *The Abominable Dr. Phibes*? Well, the film cleverly notes that Phibes succeeds on his murderous rampages because of his maniacal precision, his obsession with planning, and by following his own blueprints. It likewise notes that the only way to stop him is to mess up his standards, so he can't continue his plan. That alone is a clever conceit, because it requires the film, like Phibes himself, to have a plan. So many horror films unfold seemingly at random, where anything and everything is possible. *The Abominable Dr. Phibes* visits the ten curses of the pharaohs upon its victims, thus providing an admirable umbrella of consistency.

Once the outline is known, the audience preps itself for the inevitable: the curse of the locusts, the curse of rats, the curse of hail. In hinting to the audience what will come, *Phibes* is actually clever because it then has the opportunity to play with expectations. Anticipating one kind of death, the audience is surprised when things unfold unpredictably, with a different victim, or a "red herring." Perhaps that is not much of a "rave" review, but audiences generally want a roller coaster ride when they see a horror film. They want to be scared, grossed out, surprised, and amused. *Phibes* never manages to be scary, but it is gross, surprising and amusing. Three out of four isn't bad.

LEGACY: *The Abominable Dr. Phibes* was hugely successful with horror fans and critics alike, and the mad Doctor returned to bloody action in *Dr. Phibes Rises Again*

(1972). The notion of Vincent Price essaying a villain who kills his victims in amusing manner was then picked up in another '70s picture, *Theatre of Blood* (1973). More recently, the *Nightmare on Elm Street* films showcased a Phibes-like anti-hero, a tongue-in-cheek murderer (Freddy Krueger) who indulged in murderous, spectacular set-pieces, with tongue planted firmly in cheek. A third *Phibes* film was listed briefly as a possible George Romero project, *Phibes Resurrected,* in the mid–'80s, but it was never produced.

The Andromeda Strain (1971) ✶ ✶ ✶ ✶

Critical Reception

"…spends millions to mask its grade-B origins. Beneath its extravagant collection of computer read-out screens and space lab gadgets beats the heart of a golden oldie it-came-from-outer-space melodrama. Full of the dazzling scientific lingo and simple suspense that makes this genre so endearing…. Director Robert Wise brings the highest professionalism to this adaptation of Michael Crichton's best seller." — Paul D. Zimmerman, *Newsweek*: "The Germonauts," March 29, 1971, page 98.

"…the year's best sci-fier. It could have been better acted, but it could not have been better art-directed (William Tuntke) … several sequences are gripping." — Daphne Norris, *Films in Review*, Volume XXII, Number 4, April 1971.

"Director Robert Wise didn't miss a trick. His actors … are not superstars, but they are solid performers all. His sets are superb and thoroughly convincing, his photography is striking, and the story, based on the bestseller by Michael Crichton, is gripping, intelligent and frightening." — Jeff Rovin, *A Pictorial History of Science Fiction Films*, Citadel Press, 1975, page 193.

"*The Andromeda Strain*'s ending is somewhat anti-climactic … but James Olson, Arthur Hill, David Wayne and Kate Reid deliver controlled performances as scientists who have become dominated by technology itself…. The settings are stark and antiseptic-looking, and the electronic gadgetry is worth the great expense." — Gregory B. Richards, *Great Science Fiction Movies*, Gallery Books, 1984, page 51.

Cast & Crew

CAST: Arthur Hill (Dr. Jeremy Stone); David Wayne (Dr. Charles Dutton); James Olson (Dr. Mark Hall); Kate Reid (Dr. Ruth Leavitt); Paula Kelly (Karen Anson); George Mitchell (Jackson); Ramon Bieri (Major Manchek); Kermit Murdock (Dr. Robertson); Richard O'Brien (Grimes); Peter Hobbs (General Sparks); Eric Christmas (Senator from Vermont); With: Ken Swofford, Michael Pataki.

CREW: A Universal Release of a Robert Wise Production, *The Andromeda Strain. Production Designer:* Boris Leven. *Director of Photography:* Richard B. Kline. *Film Editors:* Stuart Gilmore, John W. Holmes. *Special Photographic Effects:* Douglas Trumball, James Shourt. *Technical Advisors:* Dr. Richard Green, George Hobby, William Koselka. *Scientific Background Support:* Cal Tech, Jet Propulsion Laboratory. *Costumes:* Helen Colvig. *Set Decorator:* Ruby Levitt. *Production Manager:* Ernest B. Wehmeyer. *Assistant Director:* Ridgeway Callow. *Matte Supervisor:* Albert Whitlock. *Script Supervisor:* Marie Kenney. *Music Engineering:* Allan Sohl and Gordon Clark. *Art Director:* William

Tuntke. *Production Illustrator:* Thomas Wright. *Make-up:* Bud Westmore. *Hairstylist:* Larry Germain. *Titles and Opticals:* Universal Title/Attila de Lado. *Filmed in:* Panavision. *Color:* Technicolor. Animal Sequences filmed under the supervision of the A.S.P.C.A, W. M. Blackmore. *Scientific Equipment:* Korad Lasers, Pekin-Elmer Corporation, Central Research Labs, Inc., R.C.A., Concord Electricity Corporation, Du Pont, Van Waters and Rogers Corporation, Technicon Corporation, Honeywell Corporation. *Music:* Gil Melle. *From the novel by:* Michael Crichton. *Screenplay:* Nelson Gidding. *Directed by:* Robert Wise. *M.P.A.A. Rating:* G. *Running time:* 130 minutes.

SYNOPSIS: All the citizens of Piedmont, New Mexico, die after a United States satellite carrying a strange micro-organism crashes in town. An Army recovery team learns of the tragedy and immediately calls up an alert. A team of scientists including leader Jeremy Stone, surgeon Mark Hall, and experts Charlie Dutton and Ruth Leavitt, are rounded up to study the offending organism.

In protective suits, Hall and Stone make a sweep of Piedmont, and study the dead town. They discover hundreds of corpses whose blood has clotted and turned to powder. They also locate two survivors: a baby and an old man named Jackson. With these survivors in tow, Hall and Stone proceed to Nevada, where a secret underground laboratory consisting of five levels has been constructed. During a decontamination process that lasts 16 hours, Stone tells Hall that he is to be "the odd man": the one person in the installation who has the power (and the key) to disarm the nuclear self destruct device in case of emergency.

Leavitt, Dutton, Stone and Hall commence their study of the plague survivors and the satellite in extremely sterile environs, using the latest in technological advances. They soon learn that the lethal organism transmits itself by air, and that it is approximately 2 microns in diameter. They also find an indentation in the satellite collector scoop, thereby locating a green organism that

seems to be growing. Meanwhile, Hall tries to understand the connection between the old man (a sterno drinker) and the baby. Why were they protected from the germ?

In a different study, Ruth Leavitt searches for something that will prevent the growth of the organism and misses an important sample because of a secret condition: epilepsy.

Before long, the space-borne entity is given the code name Andromeda. The team views Andromeda under an electron microscope and determines that it has a crystalline structure; one that is constantly mutating and dividing. It can grow in a vacuum, and is accelerated by exposure to energy. Worse, a super-colony of it has formed over the Pacific Coast, and is growing larger.

With time growing short, Dr. Hall realizes that acidity and blood chemistry play a role in Andromeda's survival. It can only survive within a narrow range of pH levels. Environments too acid or too alkaline destroy it. This fact saves Dutton's life when he is inadvertently exposed to the bug. Another problem surfaces, however, when Andromeda mutates again and melts all the plastic seals in the laboratory. This contamination triggers the self-destruct nuclear machine at the lab's heart. This is an especially big problem because Andromeda would actually thrive and grow in the energy released by a nuclear blast!

Hall battles defensive lasers, stun gas, and other hazards to prevent the installation from triggering the growth of Andromeda. He is successful ... with 8 seconds to spare.

The immediate danger gone, the scientists set out to destroy the Andromeda super-colony by seeding the clouds above it, and forcing the organism into the salty environment of the sea.

COMMENTARY: Readers might fairly wonder why *The Andromeda Strain,* most often viewed as a science fiction film, is reviewed at all in this book about "horror." The answer comes down to motivation and

Death in small-town America: A white-suited scientist surveys the devastation wrought by *The Andromeda Strain* (1971).

intent. This is a movie about (in the words of director Robert Wise) "the first crisis of the space-age." Andromeda is a biological crisis, and one with a frightening impact on the human race. The concept of an alien micro-organism is used in the film not so much to enlighten, illuminate and generate wonder (all hallmarks of science fiction), but to cause deep fear and insecurity about man's place in the universe, and even here on Earth. With its suspense, its grisly town of the dead, and its thesis of a threatened mankind, it is no strain to see *Andromeda* as an incredibly effective horror piece.

The Andromeda Strain sets up a very interesting dynamic. The film loves its science and techno jargon, wallowing in the details of man-made machinery at the expense of natural beauty. At the same time,

the film assesses humans as innately flawed creatures who cannot deal effectively with the perfect tools they have created. It is clear even from the opening sequence that director Wise idolizes the machines and technology his camera captures, and in the film's trailer he pointedly refers to the Wildfire underground laboratory as "the star" of his film. Accordingly, the opening credits depict technology in literally glowing terms, as art even, in an overlapping, colorful montage of images. It is a swirl of vivid contrasting shades and movements, yet the images featured are those of blueprints, schematics, maps, communiqués, top secret documents, graphs and the like. These "soulless" images are superimposed over one another to the tune of Gil Melle's electronic, futuristic score, and the film's thesis shines through.

It's the automation as art; blueprints as beauty. Lump a bunch of dot matrix images of different colors together and you have something more than a Jackson Pollock; you've got computer-generated, artistic composition.

The film's screenplay reflects Wise's love of (and faith in) man's world of technology, and is filled with more techno-jargon than an entire season of *Star Trek: The Next Generation*. The film's characters converse in computer-speak as though it rolls off their tongues. "Order up a 712," Stone barks; the scientists eat "Nutrient 42-5"; and the scientists go to a "Red Kappa Phoenix Status." These phrases are meaningless in human terms, but in the context of a world where technology and science are worshipped at the expense of humanity, they are telling. In fact, the viewer of *The Andromeda Strain* is inundated with such talk. We hear of biological crises, odd man hypotheses, sterile conveyer systems, med-coms, nuclear magnoscanners, and the like. Though the concentration on this science-talk nicely accommodates Wise's predilection for a documentary-style approach, it is also indicative of his thesis that machines are perfect, and that man is flawed.

Many film scholars opine that *The Andromeda Strain* is actually anti-science and pro-human, and these same sources point to one piece of evidence. During the film, a piece of paper jams in a communication device and prevents the scientists from communicating with the outside world (and the military) regarding the dropping of a nuclear bomb. This "mechanical" flaw, these critics insist, reveals the fallacy of depending on technology. Yet, the scene could be read in an entirely different fashion. Had Stone been able to communicate with the military at an earlier date, he would have insisted on a 712 (the dropping of a nuclear weapon on Piedmont). This insistence would have resulted in the geometric expansion of Andromeda over the Pacific ... possibly destroying the human race in the process. The machinery — by failing at the opportune time — actually granted Stone and his team, the human com-

ponent of the film, time to save the human race. So, even in malfunction, computers are worthier than man.

Indeed, all of the setbacks in *The Andromeda Strain* are the result of human failings. The computer accurately finds the component that will cause "no growth" of the deadly alien strain. This information is never found because Dr. Leavitt is an epileptic (a fact she has hidden). She goes into a trance when the computer displays the pertinent information, and her condition nearly threatens the world. Leavitt's personal failings (both the disease and the insecurity to hide it) sabotage the machinery.

Similarly many humans in the film are portrayed as hysterics or worse, cowards. Trained scientists flee in terror when they fear Andromeda has broken loose in the lab, leaving only the machinery (which closes bulkheads, vents air, et cetera) to solve the problem for them. What the film seems to be stating is that mankind may develop computers, thermographic scans, electron microscopes and the like, but the people who man these machines are inherently flawed and prone to self-destruction. In fact, they have created an entire installation geared to self-annihilation! The lab is built around a nuclear device, for God's sake! Though man ostensibly has the final say over the detonation of this device, not technology, Hall barely makes it to the de-activation substation in time (with only seconds to spare). He is heroic, and does his job, but his success is a matter of luck and happenstance ... factors that would not affect a "perfect machine." Machines are never, if ever, at the whim of such forces.

The Andromeda Strain throws man down the ladder of superiority even further. The central bug, the alien organism, is also far more perfect than *Homo sapiens*. Andromeda can live and grow in any environment, including a vacuum. It can reproduce itself, it can adapt, and it doesn't make mistakes. Perhaps the ultimate reason that *The Andromeda Strain* deserves discussion as a horror movie is that it reveals to audiences just how fragile humans are. We could be threatened by a superior life form, and even our perfect technology cannot save us if we misapply it, or let our humanity get in the way. Some may differ with that philosophy, but its all there on-screen.

"What a world we're making. No wonder the kids are dropping out of schools," Dr. Dutton declares at one point. He is not referring to science, but to the human values that allowed the concept of germ warfare to flourish and develop in the first place. Indeed, it was the government's top-secret plan to capture the ultimate biological weapon, Andromeda, which resulted in the satellite's existence at all. Had the satellite not gone to the stars for man's dark purpose, the deadly Andromeda would never have returned to threaten the species! Again, mankind is directly responsible for its own destruction.

The Andromeda Strain works so well as an indictment of man, and as a horror film because Robert Wise is a splendid visual storyteller. Early in the film, there is a striking scene that establishes just how lethal Andromeda is. In their protective suits, Stone and Hall scan the carnage in Piedmont. These towns-people, cut down in mid-stride, are revealed to be dead in shot after disturbing shot. In fact, Wise provides a kind of rapid-fire montage of the carnage, showing corpse after corpse in a series of split screens. The searchers are depicted on the left frame, the dead on the right, and a kind of seer/seen dynamic is established. It is a striking and horrific scene that shows, straight-faced, how a new "bug" or virus could threaten our population.

To Wise's credit, the climax of the film is incredibly suspenseful, with Hall climbing a long ladder to reach a substation that can avert nuclear disaster. If Andromeda's lethal nature had not been so well established, this scene would not be so powerful. As Hall climbs, mechanical obstacles in his way, the clock to destruction ticks down mercilessly. The net effect is that it is hard to sit still as the climax arrives.

It is also interesting to note that *The Andromeda Strain* is ahead of its time. During the film, Nurse Anson shows Dr. Hall how to order tests on a computer called medcom. He touches the screen with a light pen to do so. This was science fiction in 1971, but this very system was being used in major hospitals (such as Presbyterian Hospital in North Carolina) in 1996 and 1997, where it was named SIMON. In fact much of the technology predicted by this film has become standard equipment 30 years later. So not only is technology paramount in this film, it is well researched and prophetic.

Though the actors come second, after the equipment, it should also be noted in any review of *The Andromeda Strain* that Reid, Olson, Wayne and Hill give effective low key performances, augmenting the feeling that this is a documentary. Also lending a "realistic" feel to the story is Wise's insistence on using *X-Files*–like on-screen scrawls to remind audiences where and when the action is occurring. All this groundwork provides for a sense of reality which just makes the terror that much starker. Though the film is not "pure" horror like Wise's *The Haunting* (1960) or *Audrey Rose* (1977), it is nonetheless a smart film that understands the best way to scare an audience is to give 'em the facts.

LEGACY: A forerunner of *Outbreak* (1995), and the TV series *The Burning Zone* (1997), *The Andromeda Strain* depicts the danger of unknown micro-organisms set loose in contemporary America. Though the bug here is extra-terrestrial in nature, there are many similarities in content between this 1970s pioneer and its 1990s brethren. Author Crichton also revised *The Andromeda Strain* in 1998, to reappear as the film *Sphere*. There, a group of scientists (with Dustin Hoffman in the Arthur Hill role) traveled deep beneath the ocean to study not an alien germ, but a spherical alien organism. That film was markedly less effective than *The Andromeda Strain*, which is probably still the best "germ" movie yet made.

Asylum of Satan (1971) ✶ ✶

Cast & Crew

CAST: Charles Kissinger (Dr. Jason Specter/Martine); Carla Borelli (Lucina Martin); Nick Jolley (Chris Duncan); Louis Bandy (Lt. Tom Walshe); Claude Wayne Fulkerson (Head Aide); Jack Peterkin (Dr. Nolan); Sherry Steiner (Blind Girl); Mimi Honce (Cripple); Harry Roehrig (Mate); Pamela Gatz (the Creature); With: Don Dunkle, Gary Morris, Don Cox, Biggs Tabler, Jim Pickett, Ken Jones, Karen Stone, Joan Edwards, Liz Cherry, P.J. Childers, Beth Pearce, Nancy Marshall, Lila Baden, Lynne Kelly.

CREW: Studio I Associates Presents *Asylum of Satan. Story and Screenplay:* William B. Girdler, J. Patrick Kelly, III. *Director of Photography:* William L. Asman. *Produced by:* J. Patrick Kelly III. *Directed by:* William Girdler. *"The Satan Spectrum Theme" and "Lucina's Theme" written by:* William Girdler, *arranged by:* William Girdler and Greg Walker, *and performed by:* Eddy Dee, The Blues Express. *"Red Light Lady" written and arranged by:* William Girdler; *sung by:* Nick Jolley. *Editor:* Gene Ruggiero. *Production Managers:* Pat Kelly, Lee Jones. *Production Secretary:* Charles Bond Pearce. *Script Clerk:* Lois Haynie. *Second Camera:* Henry B. Asman. *Sound Recorder:* Warren Maxey, Dave Portugal. *Assistant Editor:* Eva Ruggiero. *Assistant Director:* Lee Jones. *Special Effects:* Richard Albain, Jr. *Special Make-up:* James C. Pickett. *Make-up Artist:* Glen Lawrence. *Property:* Alice Hay. *Wardrobe Mistress:* Barbara Girdler. *Technical Consultant:* Church of Satan. *Publicity Manager:* Robert E. Lee. *Titles and Opticals:* H & H Color Lab. *Sound Mixer:* MGM Studios. A Studio I Associates Presentation. *M.P.A.A Rating:* R. *Running time:* 85 minutes.

SYNOPSIS: Beautiful pianist Lucina Martin awakens at Pleasant Hill Sanitarium to discover that her regular doctor has transferred her to the care of the strange and mysterious Dr. Specter. Lucina doesn't know why she is in an asylum, or why she was not informed of the transfer. However, she takes an instant dislike to Martine, Dr. Specter's harsh assistant.

When she is escorted to the cafeteria for dinner, Lucina sees that most of the other patients are garbed in white cloaks and hoods. Disturbed, she befriends three "normal" patients: a crippled woman, a blind woman, and a mute. After dinner, Lucina hears the mumblings of a mysterious satanic ritual behind a locked door.

Chris Duncan, Lucina's boyfriend, learns his lover has been transferred, and sets out to release her. He meets Dr. Specter, who tells him that Lucina has suffered a nervous breakdown and cannot receive guests. Angry, Duncan goes to the police, and returns to Pleasant Hill with Detective Walshe. Surprisingly, the asylum is abandoned, and Duncan learns it has not been occupied in years. Worse, Dr. Specter is known to be an old man in his 70s, not the vigorous, bearded fellow Duncan met earlier.

Inside the asylum, Specter kills his crippled patient by exposing her to a room of poisonous gas and deadly spiders. Then he turns his sadistic attention to the mute, and his cloaked minions burn the fellow alive. The blind patient is killed too, released into a pool filled with venomous snakes. Lucina fears she is losing her mind, but is comforted when Specter promises to release her following one special test. That special test turns out to be a satanic ritual! Lucina is strapped to an altar and surrounded by devout Satanists. Specter, who also dresses up as the nasty Martine, plans to sacrifice Lucina, a virgin he believes, so as to attain eternal life from Lucifer.

The other sacrifices were in line with satanic rituals, and Lucina's rape by the devil will be the final act of devotion. The Devil materializes in the flesh but is most disturbed to find that Lucina ain't a virgin after all. Angry, Satan smites Dr. Specter and his hapless followers.

Chris and the police rescue Lucina after Specter has been zapped. As they leave the premises, Chris is possessed by Satan.

COMMENTARY: The most atmospheric of William Girdler's films, *Asylum of Satan* is an effective if artless low-budget horror film. Though the late Girdler usually exploited a specific film (*Grizzly* looks like *Jaws*; *Abby* resembles *The Exorcist*, et al.), the director chose a different route for his first outing. He picks up here on the budding trend of "satanic" movies that were becoming popular in the early '70s like *The Mephisto Waltz, Brotherhood of Satan, Daughters of Satan*, and the rest. That's not a bad template for Girdler to struggle with because he was actually a competent, if uninspired filmmaker, and the low-budget Satan movies of this era sometimes worked in a creepy, off-the-wall way, well outside of considerations of budget limitations. There's no real need for logic, clarity, or situational logic in Satan films: the mood of all-encompassing evil is more vital. Girdler makes the best of that niche, undone only by some weak effects and ineffective acting. In the realm of Satan movies, *Asylum of Satan* is a far better picture than *Daughters of Satan* yet not nearly as discomforting and bizarre as *Brotherhood of Satan*.

The best portions of Girdler's premiere motion picture involve the dueling perspectives of Pleasant Hills asylum. Is it a dilapidated, destroyed edifice now exploited by Satanists, or the new, clean (but emotionally frigid) establishment perceived by Lucina? In various scenes, reality bends, and Girdler handles the transitions well. In an early scene in the sanitarium cafeteria, the camera slowly recedes to reveal a room populated with hooded, cloaked wards—silent and strange … being served eggs (?!). That's the kind of weird touch the film strives for, and often attains. Why does the asylum shift between realities? What does it mean? Who knows, but, it's memorable, and, possibly, Girdler's attempt to dramatize visually how a person's mental state can dictate his per-

ception of his surroundings. Or, that reading could be giving Girdler too much credit. But, considering the quality of *Grizzly* or *Three on a Meathook* (1973), this one could have been a lot worse.

Contrarily, *Asylum of Satan* features some of the lamest visual effects imaginable … often showcasing phoniness with an incomprehensible enthusiasm. Patently fake spiders, pulled along on obvious strings, threaten a patient, as do rubber snakes. But the *coup de grâce* is no doubt the film's depiction of Satan. The Prince of Darkness is revealed with great dramatic flair, but ends up being a stuntman in a malformed mask with ping-pong ball eyes, horns, and a smirking expression. He looks more like a Mardi Gras denizen than the Devil. Worse, when he zaps his impudent followers, it appears as though the Great Deceiver has expelled a fatal pulse of gas. Smoke wafts over his disciples, and the inescapable impression is one of a Lactose-intolerant Dark One. Of course, *Asylum of Satan* is a low budget film without the resources for high-class prosthetics or make-up, but a clever low-budget film (like *Brotherhood of Satan*) would hide Satan in shadows, cloak him in darkness, or not reveal him at all. *Asylum of Satan* is brazen in its phoniness.

Also, Girdler seems not to understand that some of the plot twists in *Asylum of Satan* are funny. That the fearsome Dr. Specter, high satanic priest, routinely doubles in drag as Martine is one of the odder story ideas to come down the pike in a while. Someone who really wants to read into the film could make the claim that Specter/Martine reflects "the doubling" schizophrenic theme of the film, also depicted in the double nature of the asylum. Again, that's probably giving this movie too much credit. The silly Specter may be one of the screen's first transvestite villains (forecasting *The Rocky Horror Picture Show*), but his predilection for women's fashion does little to enhance his menace.

The film's final twist, that Satan permits Lucina to survive because she is no longer a virgin, is another bit of unintentional humor. One can just imagine the Devil's frustration. It was probably hard to find a good virgin in the "sexual revolution" days of the early 70s.

Despite the gaffes, *Asylum of Satan* is representative of an extinct species: the independently produced, regional low-budget horror film. Where have all the William Girdlers gone? Today, a film like this would cost 25 million dollars, star the cast of a popular WB TV series, and feature impeccable sound, editing, and special effects. It would also be boring, predictable and lacking in style. With all its flaws, *Asylum of Satan* is still fun because it represents a bold initiative. Girdler may have made bad films, but at least he did so under his own auspices, and built a career for himself doing it. Though he made terrible movies, he was an *independent* filmmaker when that concept wasn't in vogue. His films bear his personal stamp, even if that imprimatur is "cheese-wiz" all the way.

LEGACY: The low-budget *Asylum of Satan*, all but forgotten today, made enough money to assure director William Girdler a spot as a cult filmmaker. Before his untimely death in 1978, he directed *Three on a Meathook* (1973), *Abby* (1974), a low-budget *Exorcist* knock-off, *Grizzly* (1976), a low-budget *Jaws* knock-off, *Day of the Animals* (1977), and *The Manitou* (1978).

The Beast in the Cellar

Cast and Crew

CAST: Beryl Reid (Ellie Ballantyne); Flora Robson (Joyce Ballantyne); John Hamill (Alan Marlow); Tessa Wyatt (Nurse Sutherland); T. P. McKenna, David Dodimead.

CREW: *Written and Directed by:* James Kelly. *Director of Photography:* Harry Waxman. *Produced by:* Graham Harris and Christopher Neame. *Executive Producer: Tony* Tenser. *Music Conducted and Composed by:* Tony Macauley.

Film Editor: Nicholas Napier-Bell. *M.P.A.A. Rating:* R. *Running Time:* 101 minutes.

DETAILS: A low-budget British horror film about two women who harbor a terrible monstrosity in the basement. The "beast in the cellar" escapes on a murder spree, and the two old biddies have some explaining to do. A rather bare production.

Big Foot

Cast and Crew

CAST: John Carradine (Jasper); Joi Lansing (Joi); Lindsay Crosby (Wheels); James Stellar (Big Foot); Chris Mitchum (Rick); Ken Maynard (Bennett); Tony Cardoza (Fisherman).

CREW: *Directed by:* Robert F. Slatzer. *Written by:* Robert F. Slatzer and James Gordon White. *Produced by:* Tony Cardoza. *Executive Producer:*

Herman Tomlin. *Film Editor:* Hugo Grimaldi. *Music:* Richard Podalar. *Director of Photography:* Wilson Hong. From Ellman Enterprises. *M.P.A.A Rating:* PG. *Running Time:* 95 minutes.

DETAILS: In this low-budget flick, an airplane makes an unscheduled landing in the

Pacific Northwest, and a woman passenger (Lansing) is subsequently captured by a monstrous creature, the Big Foot! A shop owner (Maynard), some hikers, and John Carradine attempt to rescue the damsel in distress before the missing link does something really unpleasant to the poor woman. Though shot in the late '60s, *Big Foot* was released on the unsuspecting public in 1971.

The Brotherhood of Satan (1971) ✶ ✶ ✶

Critical Reception

"...the film displays bold, direct, relatively uncomplicated acceptance of its supernature that seems the essence of fantasy moviemaking and that extends to some wonderfully spooky scenes— in a car, in a family living room — in which nothing quite happens and which are the most terrifying in *The Brotherhood of Satan*."— Roger Greenspun, *New York Times*, August 7, 1970.

"The whole thing has an Ed Woodsian quality of enthusiastic incoherence that's irritating and endearing in about equal measures. Veteran character actor Strother Martin ... attacks the material with gusto."— Mike Mayo, *Videohound's Horror Show*, Visible Ink Press, 1998, page 46.

"A superb example of a small-scale horror movie that packs infinitely more punch than many other more pretentious offerings. Acting, script and direction are all uniformly good."— Alan Frank, *The Horror Film Handbook*, 1982, page 26.

Cast & Crew

CAST: Strother Martin (Doc Duncan); L.Q. Jones (Sheriff); Charles Bateman (Ben); Ahna Capri (Nicky); Charles Robinson (Priest); Alvy Moore (Tobey); Helene Winston (Dame Alice); Joyce Easton (Mildred Meadows); Debi Storm (Billie Joe); Jeff Williams (Stuart); Judy McConnell (Phyllis); Robert Ward (Mike); Geri Reischl (K.T.); Kevin McEveety, Cindy Holden, Sheila McEveety, Grant MacGregor, Brian McEveety, Alyson Moore, Debbie Judith, Scott Aguiar, Jonathan Easley, Robyn Grei, Linda Tiffany (the Children); John Barclay, Patrick Sullivan Burke, Ysabel MacCloskey, Cicily Walper, Phillis Coghlan, Anthony Jochim, Donald Journeaux, Elsie Moore, Lenore Shaenwise, Margaret Wheeler, Gertrude Graner (the Witches).

CREW: Columbia Pictures Presents *The Brotherhood of Satan*. From Four Star Excelsior Releasing Company. *Written by:* William Welch. *From a story idea by:* Sean MacGregor. *Directed by:* Bernard McEveety. An LQ JAF Presentation. *Produced by:* L.Q. Jones and Alvy Moore. *Associate Producer:* Sheila Clague. *Photographed by:* John Arthur Morrill. *Music by:* Jaime Mendoza-Nava. *Film Editor:* Marvin Walowitz. *Production Manager:* Rob Jones. *Sound Effects:* Sonic Editorial Service. *Production Design:* Ray Boyle. *Production Mixer:* Rod Sutton. *Special Effects:* Steve Karkus. *Script Supervisor:* Blair Brooks. *Titles:* Cinefx. *Technical Director:* James Bruner. *Make-up:* Lou Lane. *M.P.A.A. Rating:* PG. *Running Time:* 92 minutes.

SYNOPSIS: In a small southwestern town, a normal American family attempts to escape from an unseen evil. The effort is thwarted, however, when a toy tank becomes "real" and crushes the family car ... killing all inside. As the strange incident occurs, a group of impassive children watch...

Meanwhile, Ben Holden, daughter K.T., and girlfriend Nicky are on a cross-country car trip when they are unexpectedly waylaid in the small southwestern town called Hillsboro. Though they have stopped in the tiny hamlet to report a strange car accident, the police and townspeople inexplicably mob the family. Ben and his family flee the town, stunned. A few minutes later, a child appears mysteriously on the road ahead and Ben crashes the car into a pole to avoid hitting her. Their car wrecked, the family is left with no choice but to return to Hillsboro for assistance … despite Nicky's misgivings about the town.

In Hillsboro, the Meadows family lives in mortal terror. The children are not allowed to play outside because of some strange danger. That night, both parents are killed by their daughter's malevolent doll. Afterwards, the Meadows children join three others and are led away to an isolated house, the location of a demonic coven. Not long afterwards, Ben, Nicky and K.T. arrive at the Meadows home and discover the corpses of the parents. They make a report to the police, who respond quickly. The corpses are then stored in a meat locker, and Ben learns that many of the town's dead have been stored in that manner after some kind of bizarre epidemic of violence.

Elsewhere in town, a satanic cult is being run by the town's seemingly mild-mannered, elderly doctor. Another member of the senior citizen cult, Dame Alice, is shunned by her cohorts for supporting the baptizing of a local child. Judged guilty of treason by the Dark Lord, Alice is beaten to death by her former comrades.

Later, Ben meets with the town's sheriff, the deputy, the priest and the doctor, whose leadership role in the coven is a closely held secret. Indeed, the town authorities are all convinced that a malevolent outside force is isolating the town. Six families have been killed in 72 hours, and all the children are missing. Has something evil cordoned off the town for some terrible purpose? Later in the night, Nicky has a terrifying nightmare and she awakens convinced that the town itself is evil. The next morning, Nicky, Ben and K.T.

attempt to flee in the sheriff's car but on leaving Hillsboro, the car develops a flat tire. Worse, K.T. vanishes out of the back seat and is "returned" to town … to the coven! At the devil's lair, she is forced to attend a birthday party with the other missing children and several black-robed cultists.

Desperate, Ben and Nicky return to town to find K.T. The priest there warns that Ben's innocent child is now in the hands of the coven. The cultists apparently need K.T. for some dark purpose. In fact, it is known that there must be 13 children in the coven, and that K.T. is the twelfth missing child. The sheriff, priest, Nicky and Ben arm themselves and set out to protect a little boy named Joey, who might just be the 13th abductee for the coven. Joey's father tries to protect the boy, but is decapitated by a toy knight that has come to life. Too late to help, Nicky, Ben and the others continue their search.

Now armed with 13 children, the devil cult, led by the doctor, conducts a terrible ritual. The 13 young souls form a bridge between Earth and Hell. As the sheriff and Ben close in on the coven, the 13 children are transformed into vessels for the aging cult members. As the old cultists kill themselves, their souls pass into the helpless children. The adults of Hillsboro break in too late, and find the children all playing in seemingly innocent fashion. Unfortunately, the evil replacement has already been made.

COMMENTARY: *The Brotherhood of Satan* is an energetic small picture that grapples successfully with its frightening imagery. It is a distinctly unsettling movie that understands the core tenet of low-budget moviemaking: limitations should be adopted as strengths. Specifically, the film reveals almost nothing directly, yet nonetheless expresses a real feeling of evil in its frequent satanic attacks. Coupled with a theme of immediate importance (children jeopardized), Bernard McEveety's film understands how scene transitions can serve as both counterpoint and connection. This intelligence in editing, framing and camera movement make for a scary and dark picture, one with an aura of terror that hangs long after the picture is over.

All towns have their secrets, and *The Brotherhood of Satan* adopts that truth as its starting point, and primary structural conceit. Strangers drive into a town where something terrible is happening, something that they do not understand and are not welcome to understand. Accordingly, McEveety's camera frequently stands back and watches many scenes through windows, holes in walls, and doorways. This continuous "looking in" on the townsfolk lands the viewer in the same situation as the "family" of travelers who have arrived and seek to understand the town's unique secret. We are voyeurs, as they are. We all look in, but do not necessarily understand what we witness inside the town's confines.

The satanic "assaults" on the residents of Hillsboro are masterpieces of visual suggestion. The poor victims actually seem to be killed by the camera, since the murders are filmed in the first-person subjective shot. Usually when the P.O.V. perspective is adopted, the viewer eventually learns who or what is doing the attacking. In *Halloween*, the punctuation of the prologue was the discovery that the killer (whose eyes the audience had gazed through) was actually a cute little boy, Michael Myers. Contrarily, in *The Brotherhood of Satan*, the camera simply closes in on victims as shadows cross their faces. Suddenly, the victims seize and die ... as if strangled by an invisible force.

The suggestion is made that the Devil worshipers are bringing toys to life (such as dolls or tanks), but because of the low budget, these items are never seen or register as ambulatory (until the end of the picture, when a toy knight on a horse becomes "real"). When a young father is murdered (ostensibly by a doll) in his living room, the camera simply approaches him ominously, he gurgles up blood and drops dead. It is as though the atmosphere has simply turned poisonous or evil, and, amazingly this tech-

nique works! The camera becomes purveyor of a dark storm cloud of terror, and it is an unsettling and effective use of a well-worn technique. It would have been much less scary to see a fake "doll" strangle a man. That's how the film takes its budgetary limitations as strength. It suggests instead of depicting. The audience sees the doll, understands it is controlled by a malevolent force, and then shows a bizarre attack of "atmosphere." It is a resourceful, visually distinct solution. And, it is creepy.

The Brotherhood of Satan moves from setpiece to setpiece with a confidence and intelligence atypical in horror films of this type. After a family has been attacked, and the children stolen, the camera pans up from the scene of the crime to a wall of pictures that depict the family together in a better, more normal time. Without going into extensive dialogue about "loss" or even showing a funeral, the film establishes in one transition (from violence to fall-out) what has been lost. Later, the film cuts from an illustration in the priest's book of deviltry depicting captured children, to another photograph in the Meadows house, showing the "real" missing children. A nice connection has been forged: myth has become reality. What was imagined has become living terror.

Another expressive scene reveals a terrifying dream, Nicky trapped in an ice house with all the corpses of the town. This dream is a potent combination of disturbing images and angles as Bob, her lover, is shown to be both lover and corpse. At one point in this scene mixing sex, blood and death, Nicky sees her own dead body on an ice block. It is an unsettling image that propels the film towards its conclusion.

There is a lot to admire in *The Brotherhood of Satan*. The Satanists are all cheery senior citizens, their wrinkled faces cracked by smiles that could be interpreted as either senile or purely evil. The Satanist scenes play like cocktail parties, where nasty old folks party and discuss an agenda that just happens to involve the ritual sacrifice of children. And, the theme of a future stolen (seen also in *The Blood on Satan's Claw*) quietly informs the film. The ineffective heroes of the picture (parents, police, doctors, and priests) are unable to stop the spiritual death of the next generation. The Satanists take the children, and the future will suffer for it. This was one of the core themes of the '70s: that contemporary authority was so mismanaging America's fate that the future would be one of emptiness, evil, and destruction. The film starts with murders in typical middle-class homes (representing the disintegration of the family), and then shows how various institutions (police, businesses) face the fall-out from that horror. It all works rather well, so this is a case where thoughtful direction and interesting theme combine to make something more than a standard horror film.

Brotherhood of Satan indicts our establishments (churches and families) and reveals them to be lost before a belief system of true devotion (Satanism — a bizarre inversion of Christianity as depicted here). In the end, the children are lost, and the future goes right into darkness. To reveal this spiritual emptiness, the last shot of *The Brotherhood of Satan* is a slow, long zoom into a dark black hole in a cracked wall. The viewer, who has peered in at living rooms, sheriff's offices, car interiors and the like throughout the film, is suddenly given a final glimpse at something meaningful: nothingness; the abyss. An offscreen voice welcomes evil: "Come in children," it says. Thus the vacuum, the evil, has taken the future, and the visual plunge into the crevice of blackness expresses our "falling" into a bankrupt future. If we don't welcome our children into a world where our values are strong and righteous, then they will fill the black void inside with the values of others. Values we may not agree with.

Though *Brotherhood of Satan* isn't often discussed in popular horror texts, it deserves to be. It's as smart as it is scary, and it exploits an uncertainty about the future that was so rampant in the '70s.

Captain Kronos: Vampire Hunter

Cast and Crew

CAST: Horst Janson (Captain Kronos); Ian Hendry (Kerr); Caroline Munro (Carla); Wanda Ventham (Lady Durwood); Shane Briant (Durwood).

CREW: *Written, Produced and Directed by:* Brian Clemens. *Director of Photography:* Ian Wilson. *Film Editor:* James Needs. *Music:* Laurie Johnson. Hammer Studios. *M.P.A.A. Rating:* R. *Running Time:* 90 minutes.

DETAILS: Hammer takes a twisted new slant on vampires in the satiric *Captain Kronos*, directed by *The Avengers* creator Brian Clemens. It's silly, nasty fun, but the box office was dismal and Hammer abandoned the film's self-referential approach in subsequent horror outings. Worth a look.

Carnival of Blood (1971) *

Cast and Crew

CAST: Earle Edgerton (Tom); Judith Resnick (Laura); Martin Barolsky (Dan); Katy Mills (Fortune Teller); John Harris [Burt Young] (Gimpy); Linda Kurtz (Claire); William Grinell (Harry); Glen Kimberley (Drunken Soldier); Eve Packer (Slut); Gloria Spivak (Fat Lady).

CREW: Art Film International Presents *Carnival of Blood*. *Music:* the Brooks Group. *Electronic Music:* Hekii Brisman. *Songs sung by:* Patrice Sarnett. *Produced, written and directed by:* Leonard Kirtman. *Director of Photography:* David Howe. *Editor:* Harvey Howe. *Camerman:* Leonard Kirtman, David Howe. *Script Girl:* Deborah Howe. *Make-up:* Troy Roberts. *Set Designer:* Deborah Howe. A Kirt Film International Film Presentation. *M.P.A.A. Rating:* R. *Running time:* 90 minutes.

SYNOPSIS: Tom runs the balloon-popping booth at Coney Island with the help of his deformed, simpleton assistant, Gimpy. On one night, Tom and Gimpy watch with aggravation as a couple, Harry and Claire, bicker over the dart-throwing game. Tom gives Claire a prize, a teddy bear, just to be free of her incessant whining. Later that night, Claire is decapitated inside the funhouse.

Meanwhile, Laura and Dan have just become engaged. Dan has been promoted to assistant D.A., and thinks he should investigate the murder at the nearby amusement park. Laura tells Tom, who lives in her apartment building, that she believes this to be a bad idea. Tom tells Laura she and Dan should never fight, and remembers with emotion how his parents always fought. Becoming more agreeable, Laura joins Dan at Coney Island. They follow the trail of Claire and Harry, from fortune-teller to bumper cars, to cotton candy, to Tom and Gimpy's balloon booth. Tom gives Laura a special teddy bear and reminds the couple to always get along. At the same time, a prostitute is murdered after first visiting the fortune-teller and then Tom's booth with a drunken sailor.

There is another murder the next night, following the same pattern. An aggressive, opinionated woman goes to the fortune-teller, enjoys the boardwalk, and angers Gimpy and Tom. She is punished when her eyes are plucked out. Dan drags Laura back to the amusement park, but this time they fight about it, and Laura throws away her engagement ring. While Dan questions the fortune-teller, Laura reveals to Tom that she destroyed the teddy bear he gave her in a fit of anger. Tom calls her a slut, and tells her she is just like all the other girls. He decides to kill her.

Gimpy tries to prevent Tom from hurting Laura, but Tom stabs and kills him. Dan realizes Tom is the killer and goes in search of Laura before it is too late. Tom abducts Laura, taking her first on the skyride across the park, and then on the Ferris wheel. He tries to strangle her, recalling the cruelty and infidelities of his mother, who once withheld his teddy bear from him. Before killing Laura, Tom comes to his senses, and runs off, upset. He crosses a busy road and is struck down by oncoming traffic. Dan and Laura reconcile over his corpse.

COMMENTARY: A latter day version of *The Incredibly Strange Creatures Who Stopped Living and Became Mixed-Up Zombies* (1966) replete with carnival setting and a prominent role for an oily fortune-teller, Leonard Kirtman's *Carnival of Blood* at least has the good sense to abandon its predecessor's fixation with musical numbers and cabaret acts. Other than that bit of good judgment, there is precious little in this film worth lauding or even noting.

The film is ostensibly about Tom, played by an actor who looks and sounds like the living embodiment of *South Park*'s Mr.

Garrison (and who even talks to a teddy bear in *voix haute*, a kind of hirsute Mr. Hat). It seems that Tom was traumatized during his youth by his parents' perpetual bickering. Now he takes his anger out on the women who frequent his boardwalk balloon attraction. Although both parents were cruel to him (denying him his precious plush bears), it is Tom's mom who bears the brunt of his blame. Thus women are Tom's victims, and what women they are!

The first female to die is Claire, a shrew of a wife who second-guesses and contradicts her (idiot) husband at every turn. To reveal Claire's nasty nature, the film show's Claire's disembodied face jabbering endlessly (sans sound) in the right corner of several shots, silently arguing over the backdrop of routine carnival footage. It is an odd, almost avante-garde moment in a film otherwise lacking in filmic style. From that high-point of the absurd, things go right down hill, and the film awkwardly cuts to a blatantly phony prosthetic head (supposed to be Claire's) as it is chopped in two with a knife.

Other women are also depicted as hateful in *Carnival of Blood*. Tom is visited at the carnival by an obnoxious, fat woman in sunglasses. She has flabby arms, sagging breasts, a huge nose, and the most grating voice imaginable. Not surprisingly, she is also killed in short (but not short enough) order, her eyes plucked out of her head. A third victim is a prostitute Tom determines is attempting to steal the cash of a drunken sailor.

In all of these negative female roles, *Carnival of Blood* seems to be defining the parameters of a bizarre social order in which women want, and demand, gift teddy bears from carnival attractions, as if a teddy bear is the most valuable status symbol imaginable in modern society. Men are judged purely on the basis of whether or not they can adequately provide the women these stuffed animals, but are otherwise held 100 percent blameless for domestic strife.

As is plain from even the most cursory viewing, *Carnival of Blood* was made cheaply, with inexperienced actors and crew, so it is not really nice to criticize the picture as unprofessional. That established, the film evidences all the problems typical of an amateur production. The camera is shaky and indeterminate, and focus is a perpetual stumbling block — blurring and correcting, blurring and correcting, *ad nauseam*. Timing, i.e., day-night transition, is also badly mismanaged. For instance, it is already light when the prostitute is murdered under the boardwalk, but then pitch black again immediately after, when Tom and Gimpy return to Tom's apartment for a *tête-à-tête*. The pace is rather tedious too, with endless scenes of the fortune-teller haggling with customers. Repetition may equal comedy, but in horror it only equals boredom.

Perhaps *Carnival of Blood* is best remembered not for its technical gaffes, but for introducing the world to the acting stylings of Burt Young (*Rocky* [1976]). Here, Young essays the role of Gimpy, boardwalk hunchback. As this Carnie simpleton, Young often addresses the camera directly as he speaks. "You're drunk!" he accuses an off-screen customer at one point. Otherwise, Young functions adequately as a red herring, diverting audience attention away from the real killer of the piece, Mr. Garrison ... er ... Tom.

Overall, *Carnival of Blood* is a distasteful little picture about a traumatized child who grows up to be a sick, violent woman-hater. A good, suspenseful movie might have been made from such a template (witness *Psycho*!), but this film lingers on badly-realized gore at the expense of believable psychology or even horror thrills. Appropriately, the last shot of the film (after the closing credits) is of reddish paint (doubling as blood...), splattering and expanding on the ground as it turns the frame a sickly orange...

Cauldron of Blood

Cast and Crew

CAST: Boris Karloff (Badulescu); Viveca Lindfors (Tania); Jean-Piere Aumont (Marchand); Rosenda Monteros (Valerie); Milo Qeseda (Shanghai).

CREW: *Directed by:* Edward Mann. *Written by:* Edward Mann and John Nelson. *Produced by:* Robert Weinbach. *M.P.A.A. Rating:* PG. *Running Time:* 101 minutes.

DETAILS: Made in Spain, this film's primary claim to fame is that it also purports to be the last film of its star, Boris Karloff. Sadly, Karloff looks noticeably under the weather throughout the film, and the story is little more than an excuse for a series of bloody homicides, orchestrated by Viveca Lindfors (as Karloff's wife).

A Clockwork Orange (1971) ✶ ✶ ✶ ✶

Critical Reception

"...an evil motion picture ... the way Kubrick shot and edited all this makes it obvious he is trucking to today's alienated young, and promoting the kind of nihilism that has political purposes not all of which the young perceive ... the script is adolescent maundering, and sinks to the depths of buck-chasing."— Henry Hart, *Films in Review*, Volume XXIII, Number 1, January 1972, page 51.

"...situations are eloquent and highly stylized, with great impact. Technically, the film is flawless. The lighting, editing, photography, and art direction are expert. The battle sequences ... are among the most bizarre ballets ever filmed. The film is faithful in both theme and plot to the Anthony Burgess novel of the same name ... an arresting, rattling view of the near future."— Jeff Rovin, *A Pictorial History of Science Fiction Films*, Citadel Press, 1975, page 190.

"Certainly, there are some striking images; certainly there is some impudent wit; some adroitness. But the worst flaw in the film is its air of cool intelligence and very ruthless moral inquiry because those elements are least fulfilled. Very early on, there are hints of triteness and insecurity, and before the picture is a half-hour old it begins to slip into tedium. Sharp and glittery though it continues to be, it never quite shakes that tedium."— Stanley Kauffmann, *New Republic*, January 1, 1972, page 22.

"In the end, Kubrick is having a good laugh; at the world, at liberal pretensions, at law and order, at movie audiences. All satirists laugh with anger and sadness. But most satirists try to present a norm against which the horror they see can be judged.... In *A Clockwork Orange* perhaps no norm at all (hopefully not the priest, whose speech on free will is one of the weakest parts of the film). Maybe it's all singing in the rain. Or howling in the storm."— Robert Philip Kolker, *Journal of Popular Film*, Volume 1, #3, Summer, 1972, page 172.

"*Clockwork* is a violent film about a violent young man. The film might well be offensive and morally repugnant if Kubrick's skill and intelligence did not serve him so well. *Clockwork* is a moral and honest picture."— Kenneth Von Gunden, Stuart H. Stock, *Twenty All-Time Great Science Fiction* Films, 1982, page 231.

Cast & Crew

CAST: Malcolm McDowell (Alex); Patrick Magee (Mr. Alexander); Michael Bates (Chief Guard); Warren Clarke (Dim); John Clive (Stage Actor); Adrienne Corri (Mrs. Alexander); Carl Duering (Dr. Brodsky); Paul Farrell (Tramp); Michael Gover (Prison Governor); Miriam Karlin (Catlady); James Marcus (Georgie); Aubrey Morris (Deltoid); Godfrey Quigley (Prison Chaplain); Sheila Raynor (Mum); Madge Ryan (Dr. Branom); John Savident (Conspirator Dolin); Anthony Sharp (Minister of the Interior); Philip Stone (Dad); Pauline Taylor (Conspirator Rubinstein); Steven Beroff (Constable); Lindsay Campbell (Inspector); Michael Tarn (Pete); David Prowse (Julian); Jan Adair, Vivienne Chandler, Prudence Drage (Handmaidens); John J. Carney (C.I.D. Man); Richard Connaught (Billyboy); Carol Drinkwater (Nurse Feeley); George O'Gorman (Bottick Clerk); Cheryl Grunwald (Rape Girl); Gillian Hills (Sonietta); Craig Hunter (Dr. Friendly); Barbara Scott (Marty); Virginia Wetherell (Stage Actress); Katya Wyeth (Girl in Ascot); And: Barrie Cookson, Gaye Brown, Peter Burton, Lee Fox, Shirley Jaffe, Neil Wilson.

CREW: Warner Brothers Presents a Stanley Kubrick Production, *A Clockwork Orange*. *Produced and directed by:* Stanley Kubrick. *Screenplay by:* Stanley Kubrick. *Based on the novel by:* Anthony Burgess. *Executive Producers:* Max L. Rabb and Si Litvinoff. *Associate Producer:* Bernard Williams. *Assistant to the Producer:* Jan Harlan. *Production Designer:* John Barry. *Electronic Music composed and realized by:* Walter Carlos. *Film Editor:* Bill Butler. *Sound Editor:* Brian Blamey. *Sound Recordist:* John Jordan. *Dubbing Mixers:* Bill Rowe, Eddie Haben. *Art Directors:* Russell Hagg, Peter Shields. *Special Paintings and Sculpture:* Herman Makkink, Cornelius Makkink, Liz Moore, Christiane Kubrick. *Wardrobe Supervisor:* Ron Beck. *Costume Designer:* Milena Canonero. *Stunt Arranger:* Roy Scammell. *Casting:* Jimmy Liggat. *Location Manager:* Terry Clegg. *Assistant Directors:* Derek Cracknell, Dusty Symonds. *Construction Manager:* Bill Welch. *Property Master:* Frank Bruton. *Assistant Editors:* Gary Shepherd, Peter Burgess, David Beesley. *Make-up:* Fred Williamson, George Partleton, Barbara Daly. *M.P.A.A. Rating:* X. *Running time:* 137 minutes.

P.O.V.

"I could see very serious social unrest in the U.S. that would probably be resolved by a very authoritative government.... And then you could only hope you would have a benevolent despot rather than an evil one. A Tito rather than Stalin — though of the Right" (5).— Director Stanley Kubrick, on the political environment that led to his cautionary tale of freedom-lost, *A Clockwork Orange* (1971).

SYNOPSIS: In the not-so-distant future, society at large has become a more violent, brutal place. In this cold, lawless world, youngster Alex and his three "droogs" (Pete, Georgie and Dim) spend their evenings at the Korova Milk Bar drinking milk laced with drugs, a beverage that helps them work up an appetite for a little of the "ultra-violence" they enjoy so much. After a night of drinks, they beat up an old homeless man, then catch up with a rival gang of droogs, led by Billy Bob, and fight it out. As the police arrive, Alex and his cohorts flee to the country. They stop at a random residence, the home of writer Mr. Alexander. They worm their way into the home by claiming there has been an accident on the road. Once inside, however, Alex and his friends beat Mr. Alexander and rape his wife. To close out the fun-filled night, Alex and his droogs return to the milk bar and listen to a "sophisto" sing from Alex's favorite musical artist, Beethoven. The other droogs are bored by the performance, but Alex silences them with brute force.

As the morning comes, Alex returns to his home in Municipal Flatblock A, where he lives with his mother and father. He sleeps off the night after checking in with his pet snake, and masturbating to more Beethoven. The next day, he misses school and his guidance counselor comes to his house to warn he is just a step away from incarceration. The counselor leaves the premises after a half-hearted attempt to molest Alex. Later, Alex goes to a nearby mall, picks up two lovely

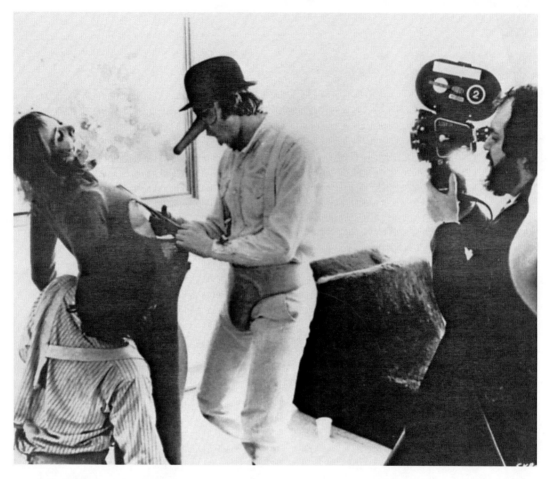

Just singing in the rain! Kubrick (right) directs Malcolm McDowell (center) and Adrienne Corri (left) during a "little ultra-violence" from *A Clockwork Orange* (1971).

girls, and brings them back to his room for a threesome.

By night, Alex's droogs gather and question his authority. Alex doesn't appreciate this, and puts down the challenge to his authority by throwing Georgie into a river and slicing open Dim's hand with a knife. Again, brute force wins the day, and Alex's leadership is re-established. He suggests they head next to Woodmere Health Farm for a little fun, and he proceeds to break in and brutally attack a woman (with a giant sculpture of a penis!). Unfortunately, this woman (an owner of many cats), has called the police, and Alex is incapacitated by his vengeful droogs and then apprehended by the authorities. After a brief trial, Alex is sen-

tenced to fourteen years in prison for the murder of the cat lady.

In prison, Alex is assigned to help a priest conduct Sunday services. He is a model prisoner until her hears of a new treatment that could get him released from prison quickly. Alex is promptly selected for the Ludovico treatment and transferred to a clinic. Under the supervision of a new "hard on crime" minister of interior, Alex's treatment begins. He is taken to a screening room and placed in eyelid-locks that force his eyes open as he watches violent film after violent film. In conjunction with these images of brutality, Alex has been given a nausea-provoking drug. Together, the drug and the images form a connection in his mind, and he grows sick, unable to stomach violence … or even sex. Unfortunately, Alex is also (inadvertently) conditioned to get sick whenever he hears Beethoven … his favorite composer!

After the treatment is complete, Alex is shown off to the government. He cannot fight, have sex, or even tolerate violent thoughts without growing physically ill, thus he is of no harm to society. A priest warns that Alex's humanity, his choice to do good or evil, has been taken away, but the government's response is that Alex is a "true Christian," finally capable of turning the other cheek.

Alex is released from prison and sent home. In his absence, his parents have rented out his room to a lodger and killed his pet snake. Ashen, Alex leaves home and is promptly beaten by the homeless men he once terrorized. Then he runs into George and Dim, now police officers! They beat him up and attempt to drown him. Bloodied and weak, Alex finds himself back at the home of Mr. Alexander, whose wife he raped. Mr. Alexander recognizes Alex and subjects him to Beethoven's *9th Symphony*. Driven mad by the nausea-provoking music, Alex attempts to kill himself. He jumps out a window … but survives.

Some time later, Alex awakens from a coma and learns he is a media celebrity, and that his so-called cure is the cause of controversy. He is nursed back to health, and even visited by the minister of the interior, who wants to be his friend. Alex is offered a job and a good salary in compensation for all he has suffered, and, best of all, he is cured of the Ludovico treatment…

COMMENTARY: In 1971, Stanley Kubrick's visual imagining of a future world dominated by sex, violence and corrupt bureaucracies was considered a far-fetched, even offensive, glimpse of a not-necessarily probable future world. However, by the year 2002, much of Kubrick's bleak vision had come to pass. We live in a media-saturated world where children are learning earlier than ever before about sex; there are violent outbreaks in schools; and political elections are bought and sold by corrupt special interests. Accordingly, the film's message is clearer than ever. Even in an age of excess, the citizen's right to choose right or wrong must never be corrupted … even if the choice is a morally degenerate one. In a free society, *A Clockwork Orange* seems to tell us, we must tolerate monsters like Alex (Malcolm McDowell) to ensure that the rest of us all retain our freedom.

It's both frightening and amazing to study the myriad places where Burgess's and Kubrick's film accurately predict (with some exaggeration), how a future world might look and feel. In today's reality, the world "sexualizes" young girls such as Britney Spears and Christina Aguilera (even as American girls reach puberty at a younger age than ever in history), and the media worships the hard-bodies of the international super models. In *A Clockwork Orange*, sex is likewise merchandised and sold. It has become as prevalent and generic as a Ronald McDonald sculpture at a fast food restaurant. To wit, at various bars, milk is dispensed through statuettes of naked women. Pull the lever, and out of the mechanical breasts pour a beverage. Nudity serves every consumer, and is no longer reserved for privacy, art or the like.

Men too are sexual objects in *A Clockwork Orange*, wearing enlarged codpieces as a sexual affectation. This latter image is not all that different from body piercings, tattoos or any other fad that now distinguishes those who wish to be seen as trendy and sexually desirable. Cleverly, *A Clockwork Orange* notes that the rampant sexuality is not so much a result of changing (or degenerating) morals as it is a reflection of an irresponsible media, where everyone and everything is viewed primarily as a commodity. One important scene in the film takes Alex to a futuristic mall filled wall to wall with magazines, music recordings (where we see the soundtrack to *2001: A Space Odyssey*), and a bevy of teenagers. This world of commerce is also the place where teens gather and meet, usually to have sex afterwards. It is all part and parcel of the consumer culture. Sex is on display right there with the CDs.

Yet *A Clockwork Orange* is most often noted for its themes about violence, not sex. That is appropriate too, since the film is rather brutal (meriting an X-rating when it was released in 1971). However, violence has progressed in film so far since *A Clockwork Orange* that Kubrick's movie seems almost quaint today. The oddball costume affectations immediately take the film out of the realm of pure realism into a land that, if no doubt plausible, also has a bit of make believe to it. Similarly, the rapes and beatings are orchestrated to classical or pop music (like "Singin' in the Rain"), which tends, again, to lift the film out of gritty reality into near-satire. A scene in which four droogs rape a helpless naked woman, and then are beaten down by Alex and his gang, becomes a ballet of violence, as beautiful and funny as it is disturbing. The blunt-faced rape scene involving Adrienne Corri and "Singin' in the Rain" is more harrowing, but Kubrick again distances the audience from the real horror by utilizing a familiar melody for purposes of irony. The audience is thus invited to retreat from the violence (to laugh with recognition as it were), instead of face the brutal rape with no escape. "Singin' in the Rain," a song of unadulterated joy, is forever linked to Gene Kelly's sure-footed dance of delight. Here, it is re-framed in a new context. To Alex, his joy involves beating others, and his foot delivers kicks, crushes and stomps rather than dance moves. The ironic use of music is entertaining, but it is also a ploy to appeal to the intellectual curiosity of the viewer. An audience member is not so tormented or disturbed by the break-in and ensuing violence when his brain is caught up acknowledging the irony of Kubrick's musical choice, cataloguing a reference to a musical classic.

The most disturbing facet of *A Clockwork Orange* is not actually the bald-faced violence, but the endemic cruelty of spirit that passes for the norm in Alex's world. His parents are cold, pitiable things with no real warmth or decency. They are objects to laugh at it in their mod clothes, eliciting no respect whatsoever. The priest, who insists that Alex must have the right to make his own moral choices, is a naïve dupe. He believes (wrongly) that Alex has a "genuine desire to reform," blissfully unaware that the boy is actually a monster. Politicians use any advantage, even rampant crime, to advance their position. Policemen — former droogs! — are corrupt, and even doctors and nurses are depicted in negative terms, more interested in sexual dalliances than in helping their wards, the sick and dying. No authority comes out of this film unscathed. Even those people audiences would be inclined to sympathize with, particularly the victims of violent crime, are shown to be obsessed with revenge. *A Clockwork Orange* is perceived as such a cold film not because of its violence, but because it clinically views man as an essentially cruel creature. There are few redeeming features to any character in the film.

And that brings us to Alex. Many critics were outraged with Kubrick because they feel his film actually engenders sympathy for Alex, a boy of violent impulses and immorality. There is a point there. In comparison with the brutal policemen, the self-obsessed bureaucrats, the other droog thugs (who don't even appreciate good music), and the empty-headed parents, Alex is the most identifiably human character in the film. He's a horrible person, no doubt, but at least we are privy to his thoughts. Even if those thoughts are brutal (and they are!), that identification humanizes the boy. He may be violent, but he loves Beethoven. He may treat his parents badly, but we see upon his release how deeply they wound him by disowning him. Though Alex is a victimizer, the film takes special pains to prove that he is likewise a victim. The overall picture of Alex is one of a boy who, in the absence of his parents, was raised by the violence and sex obsessed media. Is it any wonder then, that he is the way he is? A person must take some responsibility for his own actions, but just look at Alex's world. Even his guidance counselor is despicable; a pedophile! In such a world, Alex seems less culpable, less vile. He is a product of his environment, no more, no less.

So what is Kubrick's point? Why create a world of such horrors? The ultimate question of *A Clockwork Orange* involves choice. For whatever reason, this world of violence and immorality has been created by human choices. The politicians perpetuate it; parents permit it; Alex thrives in it. The film, however, never focuses on the dismantling of such a dystopia. Instead, it says that the world may degenerate, but humans must forever retain the right to make their own world — even if it's awful — or they won't be human anymore. For all his flaws, Alex has free will, an essential of the human condition, and as soon as that inalienable human right is taken away from him, he is nothing but an animal.

It seems then that, in one sense or another, Kubrick was predicting the rise of the PC and religious police, those self-appointed guardians of morality (such as the highly partisan William Bennett) who seek to steal choices away from others for the perceived greater good. It is bad and unhealthy to smoke, so now there are laws against smoking in public forums. There is moral decay in America, so students should be forced to pray in public classrooms, and courtrooms should display the Ten Commandments on the wall. Students should know how to read, so they will be given uniform standards and tested by our schools, *ad nauseam*, until the only thing anyone is learning is how to pass the test. All these acts attempt to take the freedom of choice away from the individual and put it in the hands of the bureaucrats, the priests, the police, the judges, and other authorities that Kubrick so evidently despised. As soon as these forces decide what is good for us, and force their choices on us, we lose our prerogatives as free, thinking human beings. We're just cattle.

And that is why Alex is nothing less than the protagonist of *A Clockwork Orange*. He is a violent, immoral monster, but he survives society's attempt to take away his individuality. He is not violent or immoral for the greater good, only for his own pleasures and selfish ends, but ... *and here's the rub* ... that's his choice. The question is, do we honor that choice, or seek to repress it? And if we forbid some acts, who is to say what will be forbidden next?

Crucible of Horror (1971) ✴ ✴ ✴

Cast & Crew

CAST: Yvonne Mitchell (Edith Eastwood); Michael Gough (Walter Eastwood); Olaf Pooley (Reid); Simon Gough (Rupert Eastwood); Sharon Gurney (Jane Eastwood); David Butler (Gregson); Nicholas Jones (Benji); Mary Hignett (Servant); Howard Goorney (Petrol Pump Attendant); Sam the Dog (Sam).
CREW: A Cannon Group, Inc, London-Cannon Film. *Executive Producers:* Dennis Friedland, Christopher Dewey. *Music composed and conducted by:* John Hotchkis. *Photography:* John Mackey. *Original screenplay by:* Olaf Poo-ley. *Directed by:* Viktor Ritelis. *Produced by:* Gabrielle Beaumont. *Editor:* Nicholas Pollock. *Dubbing Editor:* Max Bell. *Production Manager:* Michael Brown. *Art Director:* Peter Hampton. *Camera Operator:* Alan Tavener. *Second Cameraman:* Clive Tiekner. *First Assistant:* Colin Lloyd. *Sound Mixer:* Aubrey Lewis. *Gaffer:* Taffy Elkins. *Hairdresser:* Betty Glasgow. *Make-up:* Fred Willimson. *Wardrobe:* Mary Gibson. *Production Assistant:* Janet Elliott. *Titles and Opticals:* Abacus. Made on location and at Merton Park Studios with the cooperation of Abacus Productions Ltd. *M.P.A.A. Rating:* PG. *Running time:* 91 minutes.

SYNOPSIS: It is an existence of domestic torture for Jane and her mother, Edith Eastwood. Along with Jane's simpering sibling, Rupert, the Eastwood family lives under the thumb of the tyrannical, obsessive-compulsive Walter. Edith has resorted to the world of art, painting terrifying pictures of her boorish husband. Jane has rebelled in another way, stealing money and trying to hook up with boys behind her father's back.

One night during an interminable dinner, Mr. Gregson from the golf club arrives and informs Walter that Jane has stolen a considerable amount of cash from the club safe. Walter pays Gregson back and later beats Jane with a riding whip. As Jane is brutally abused, her brother and mother do nothing to stop the violence.

Seeing Jane's blood and bruises, Edith suggests the next day that she and Jane kill Walter once and for all. When Walter goes down to the cottage for the weekend, Jane and Edith decide to follow him, and do the deed. They steal one of his many hunting rifles, and confront him. Then, they force him to drink poison and liquor so it looks like he committed suicide. When the terrible Walter is finally unconscious, Edith and Jane carry him to the upstairs bedroom and undress him. There, they think they leave behind a corpse. Unseen by the culprits, Walter opens his eyes...

Jane and Edith return home and await the call announcing that Walter has been found dead at the cottage. The call doesn't come. Not that night, nor the next day. Finally, a worried Rupert telephones to say he has not heard from Walter. He tells Jane to drive to the cottage and check up on things. Jane and Edith go, reluctantly, and find the entire house spotlessly cleaned. But there is no sign of Walter's body! Outside the cabin, they find his corpse in a large crate. Before they can get rid of the evidence, a neighbor, Reid, shows up and starts to ask questions about Walter's whereabouts. His dog sniffs around at the crate, but doesn't find the corpse. After Reid has left, Jane and Edith heave the crate into the trunk of their car, drive to a dump, and throw the incriminating evidence over a hill.

Shaken, Jane and Edith return home. They hear a noise: someone has broken a window in their living room! Fearful, Jane and Edith wonder who might be playing tricks on them. Rupert telephones them, but the line goes dead. That night, Edith has a dream that something evil awaits in the attic. She awakens and checks the attic out, only to discover Walter, hanging upside down in the doorway. Edith flees in terror, and a very much alive Walter pursues her.

Later, Jane and Edith are forced to endure the same Hell as before. Walter is back, alive and well, treating them like nonpersons. In fact, Edith feels so invisible, she just fades away at the dinner table...

COMMENTARY: Sometimes, one character and one performance can make a movie memorable. Consider Hannibal Lecter (and Anthony Hopkins), in *Silence of the Lambs* (1991). *Crucible of Horror* doesn't quite offer anything so iconic in terms of the horror genre, but it comes close. In particular, Michael Gough (*The Boys from Brazil* [1978], *Serpent and the Rainbow* [1987], *Batman and Robin* [1997]) masterfully creates an absolutely intolerable fellow named Walter Eastwood. This character is obsessive-compulsive (we see him ritualistically cleaning his hands...), physically abusive (he beats his daughter...), a control freak (he also reads her mail...), haughty, and awfully fun to hate. In fact, much of *Crucible of Horror*'s considerable suspense comes from the fact that the audience hates Walter so much, and invests so much interest in seeing his demise orchestrated. Really, the picture serves little other purpose than that; it's a peek at a dysfunctional family that has become so broken that murder remains the only option for improving home life.

Ritelis is a capable director, and he has found good material and good performers to match his talents here. The film opens with some elaborate crosscutting between Jane's latest rebellion, and Walter's icy, silent stewing. The audience doesn't know what is going to happen with either character at this juncture, but a sense of discomfort and anticipation is forged as each character toils to opposite ends. Later in the film, the crosscutting technique recurs when Walter strikes Jane with a riding whip. This bit of brutality is intercut with shots of Jane's brother, Rupert, as he dons his headphones and conducts an invisible orchestra, alone in his own make-believe world. The crosscutting indicates Rupert's silent culpability in the domestic abuse. For letting it happen to Jane without struggle, he is just as guilty of the crime as his brutal father. The similarity in hand gestures (Walter striking Jane with the riding crop; Rupert waving in time to the music) forges a visual link, a bridge, between the acts. What it suggests is that Rupert's act is no less troublesome than Walter's, for he shuts himself off and enables the abuse to occur.

Crucible of Horror speaks the same language as *Straw Dogs* (1971), obsessing on matters of abuse, rape and violence — all of which are shown in disturbing flashes. But, Ritelis's primary focus is not on man's nature (as is Peckinpah's), but of a family's. Jane and Edith are desperate to find a way out of their domestic hell, and are surrounded by traitors (Rupert), and monsters (Walter). Does that give them the right to commit murder? Can it ever truly be declared that somebody deserves to die, let alone somebody who is part of our trusted inner circle? The reason Edith and Jane don't simply leave the abusive Eastwood household is that they want Walter's money ... they can't survive without it. So they are less than noble people, themselves. Why do some spouses stay? Why do some kill? *Crucible of Horror* offers some interesting thoughts on such dysfunction, and it meditates on them within a suspenseful framework.

Though there is nary a vampire or were-wolf in sight, *Crucible of Horror* is nonetheless a horror film because it invites the audience to watch a family's disintegration close up. Mother becomes unhinged, conversing with her bizarre art, and might as well be insane. Walter stalks his house and dominates everybody, a real-life monster in his modern-day castle. Rupert is locked away in his own world of imagination, and Jane's criminal acts are cries for attention. It's dysfunction junction, and part of the film's fun is in seeing how we (as viewers of dozens of similar movies) are smarter than these schemers when it comes to plotting the perfect crime.

Crucible of Horror earns its three stars mostly in its climactic moment, which finds a perfect visual metaphor for the quiet suffering that so many spouses endure in bad domestic situations. There is a family meal in the dining room, another interminable affair over which Walter arrogantly presides, and, without warning, Edith just fades away. Nothing has changed, nothing will change, and Ritelis visually suggests that Edith might as well be a ghost for all her importance to Walter and his domain. She literally disappears to nothing, no longer of value or concern. It's a daring final shot that uses a special effect (a fade-out style disappearance) not for supernatural ends, but for poetic, metaphorical ones. Inside, no doubt Edith faded away long ago. The last sequence of the film carries that process through to its logical, physical conclusion. She has shrunken to nothing before the domineering husband who fails to value her. Sadly, many spouses could probably relate to her plight.

As the vicious, officious Walter Eastwood, Gough has found a great role. Gough is a cold actor, and his face, so harsh and lined, is perfect for the part. Walter is every bit the monster that Dracula or the Wolfman is, but ever so much more frightening because he exists in our everyday reality. We don't need to make him up...

Crucible of Terror (1971) * *

Cast & Crew

CAST: Mike Raven (Victor); Mary Maude (Millie); James Bolam (John); Ronald Lacey (Michael); Melissa Stribling (Joanna); John Arnatt (Bill); Betty Alberge (Dorothy); Judy Matheson (Marcia); Beth Morris (Jane); Kenneth Keeling (George); Me Me Lay (Chi San).

CREW: A Peter Newbrook Production. *Director of Photography:* Peter Newbrook. *Production Executive:* John Brittany. *Art Director:* Arnold Chapkis. *Assistant Director:* Roger Simons. *Production Manager:* Ted Sturgis. *Camera Operator:* Kelvin Pike. *Make-up:* Jimmy Evan. *Hairstylist:* Jan Dorman. *Wardrobe:* May Gibson. *Continuity:* Ann Edwards. *Editor:* Maxine Julius. *Sound Editor:* Colin Hobson. *Assistant Editor:* Tariq Anwar. *Recorder:* Ken Ritchie. *Re-recording:* Nolan Roberts. *Dubbing Mixer:* Bob Jones. *Music:* Paris Rutherford. *Original Screenplay:* Ted Hooker, Tom Parkinson. *Executive Producer:* Peter Newbrook. *Producer:* Tom Parkinson. *Directed by:* Ted Hooker. Made at Shepperton Studios, London, England. *M.P.A.A. Rating:* R. *Running Time:* 95 minutes.

SYNOPSIS: A reclusive artist named Victor Clare premieres his latest body sculptures in a posh London art gallery. His most popular piece is a lead cast of a beautiful nude woman. But unknown to the patrons of the gallery, a real-life woman is dead inside the work of art.

The gallery wants more pieces from Victor Clare, but his son, the drunk Michael, is unwilling to smuggle out any more works because his father is a violent man. By night, a patron, George Brent, attempts to steal the already purchased sculpture, and is strangled in plastic by an unseen assailant.

The next day, John (the gallery curator) joins friends Michael, Jane and Millie for a trip to remote Jericho to meet Victor. There they are introduced to Michael's timid, not-quite-sane mother, and Victor's former-military buddy, Bill. They also meet Victor's new model, Marcia, with whom he is shacking up. Before long, Victor has asked Millie, John's wife, to model for him. She is creeped-out by Victor and unwilling to do so. Worse, when she dons an Asian kimono she purchased at a London bazaar, she has bizarre memories of a blood ritual involving a masked man, a sword, and a bucket of spilled blood. Despite Millie's reluctance to pose for him, Victor insists that Millie captures a unique beauty ... a beauty he has only seen once before.

While John returns to London to get the cash necessary to buy more pieces from Victor, the murderer strikes again, killing Michael on the beach. Millie's visions grow worse, especially when she meets with Bill, the military man and collector of Oriental artifacts. The sword she saw in her dream is hanging on his wall. While taking a walk on the beach, Millie is pursued by Victor to an old cave leading to a mine. Inside the mine, Millie runs into Victor's wife, who escorts her through a secret tunnel back to the safety of the lead furnace.

Growing impatient, Victor fires up the furnace, desiring to capture Millie's beauty in bronze forever. Meanwhile, John raises the money in London to buy more of Victor's "art," but his car breaks down on the return trip. When Marcia is murdered and Bill goes to fetch John, Millie is left to deal with Victor and his amorous needs. Millie ends up at the furnace, Victor's would-be victim, but strangely, a spirit enters her body and she kills Victor with Bill's Oriental sword before he can commit another murder. It seems that every time Millie wore her "cursed" kimono—belonging to one of Victor's previous victims—she channeled the spirit of a vengeful Asian girl who died for Victor's art.

COMMENTARY: What a wacky movie! *Crucible of Terror* is a modern day variant on *House of Wax*, with corpses providing the foundation for so-called works of art. Call it *Portrait of the Artist as a Psycho*. Though the film has a textbook horror movie set-up, and some not totally ineffective sequences, it is a badly jumbled mélange of elements that ultimately fail to cohere.

Crucible of Terror (not to be confused with the far superior *Crucible of Horror*) is one of those films that offer a good story, but a terrible script. Specifically, the setting and situations are filled with potential. There's a psychopath (identity indeterminate but suspected), a remote setting (complete with local superstitions and disturbing history), and a fresh supply of victims (including a beautiful blond). There's even a little hint of lesbianism thrown in for fun. Great horror movies have been made with lesser set-ups, no doubt.

But, sadly, the screenplay of *Crucible of Terror* is oddly vague. It sets up so many red herrings that it grows obvious by mid-movie that any one of them could legitimately be the killer. The military man, Bill, loves Victor's wife, and would do anything to protect her. He could be the killer. Victor's wife is a total psycho (she brings a toy stuffed dog to the dinner table and then spoon feeds it!). She too, could very well be a murderer. Victor, of course, is the obvious choice, since he is the philandering, obsessed artist. But then there is also Michael, his money-hungry son, and Victor's former mistress, now disenfranchised. With the stroke of a pen, any of these characters could have been the film's angel of death. Not unexpectedly, the movie is filled with ridiculous red-herring lines of dialogue like "Up to your old tricks again?" all of which indicate dark secrets and histories. Yet, when the conclusion finally comes,

none of these characters is the antagonist! Instead, the murders were carried out by the protagonist, who because of a haunted kimono (!?), was possessed by the spirit of a wronged model.

Not only is this resolution bizarre, it is out of left field. The film never suggests or even intimates that this is a world where the supernatural has presence, and then the film closes with … *surprise!* … the supernatural. It's a cop-out ending, and it leads one to realize that all the characters have been designed to be suspicious when in fact none of them are guilty.

"Great art demands great sacrifice," Victor notes in *Crucible of Terror*, and that would also suffice as a word of advice to director Ted Hooker. His film features lovely girls, pretty locations, an interesting enough story to keep it afloat, but a lazy, *deus ex machina* climax and a script that can only euphemistically be called banal. By the end of it all, even Hooker seems to know he's lost. Vanquished by his netherworldy opponent, Victor falls to his death, and Hooker's camera doesn't quite catch the pertinent action. Then, an awkward exposition scene follows suddenly, explaining what happened in basic, didactic terms … since the film's resolution is by no means clear to confused viewers who have been trying to keep track of the victims, the suspects, and their whereabouts at the time of various crimes.

If the rest of *Crucible of Terror* is just mediocre, then the end is downright messy. It's one of those rare, promising films that throw everything away at the climax, prompting audience hoots and hollers of derision. *Boo!*

Daughters of Darkness (1971) ★ ★ ★ ½

Critical Reception

"Kumel gets a lot of mileage out of only four significant characters…. The movie's effect is hypnotic and dreamlike…."—Michael Gingold, *Fangoria #172*, May 1998, page 77.

"While there is blood and gore, Kumel explores the dark side of human sexuality in fascinating fashion, using erotica and symbolism. Achieves an aura of decadence strangely compelling."—John Stanley, *Creature Features Strikes Again*, page 95, 1994.

Cast & Crew

CAST: John Karlen (Stefan); Delphine Syrig (Countess Elizabeth Battori); Danielle Ouimet (Valerie); With: Andrea Rau, Paul Esser, Georges Jamin, Jaris Collet, Fons Rademakers.

CREW: Showking Films and Maya Films present a Belgian-French-German co-production. Showking films (Brussels); Maya Films (Paris); Roxy Film (Munich); and Vog Films (Brussels). *Director of Photography:* Eduard van der Enden. *Music composed and conducted by:* François de Roubaix. *Screenplay:* Pierie Drouot, Jean Ferry, Harry Kumel. *In association with:* Joe Amiel. *Produced by:* Henry Lange, Paul Collet. *Associate Producer:* Alain C. Guilleaume, Pierre Drouot. *Directed by:* Harry Kumel. *Executive Producer:* Alain-Claude Guilleaume. *Production Managers:* Erwin Gitt, Jean-Marie Bertrand. *Location Manager:* Paul Collet. *Property Master:* Willy Dellaert. *Miss. Seyrig's Gown:* Bernard Perris. *Miss Ouimet's Wardrobe:* Cinelle, Malborough van Gelder. *Miss Seyrig's Hairstyle:* Alexandre. *Furs by:* Denoit. *Shoes by:* Lautrec. *Make-up:* Ulli Ullrich. *Make-up Assistant:* Pascale Kellen. *Wardrobe supervisor:* Marie-Paule Petignot. *Sound Mixer:* Jacques Eippers. *Boom swinger:* Henri Morelle. *Sound effects:* Hans W. Kramski. *Art Director:* François Hardy. *Set Dresser:* Henri Roesems. *First Camera Assistant:* Peter Anger. *Second Camera Assistant:* Jacques Fondaire. *First Assistant Director:* Paul Arias. *Second Assistant Director:* Jean-Marc Turine. *Continuity:* Magda Reypens. *Editing:* Gustav Schueren, Denis Bonan. *Assistant Editor:* Daniel Devalle, Edith Shumann. *Special Effects:* Eugene Hendrickx, Thierry Hallard. *Lighting Equipment:* localaflash. *Laboratories:* Meuter-Titra Brussels L.T.C. Shot on location in Ostend, Brussels. *M.P.A.A. Rating:* NR *Running time:* 100 minutes.

SYNOPSIS: A newlywed couple, Stefan and Valerie, make passionate love on a train returning from Sweden. Afterwards, Valerie is afraid Stefan's mother will not approve of her, and Stefan suggests a hotel stay for a time, so he can call his mother and tell her news of the marriage. They arrive at a grand old hotel and learn that they are the only guests there but for two glamorous women: Countess Elizabeth Battori and her traveling companion, a dark beauty. The hotel clerk is baffled by Battori's appearance because she closely resembles a woman who visited the hotel when he was but a busboy some thirty years earlier … and she hasn't aged a day.

Stefan and Valerie stay in an adjoining suite to the new arrivals, and are fascinated to learn of several local crimes. Four girls have been found dead in town. Valerie is concerned because Stefan seems fascinated by the deaths, and his sexual appetites are become increasingly violent. After a day on the town, Stefan and Valerie are followed by a suspicious policeman, who wonders if they know something of the deaths.

Elizabeth and her companion make

their move that evening, sharing drinks with Stefan and Valerie in the hotel lounge. Elizabeth tells the story of the "Scarlett Countess," a sadistic woman who drank the blood of hundreds of virgins to stay young. She chained them for their blood, bathed in it, clipped off their fingers, cut off their nipples with silver pincers, slit their throats, cut their veins with rusted nails, and performed other assorted atrocities. As Elizabeth speaks of these things, Stefan finds himself turned on by the images. Valerie is horrified by the morbid discussion, and excuses herself for the evening. In the hotel room, she is terrified that a shadowy figure is watching her from the ledge.

When Stefan beats Valerie with a belt preceding lovemaking, Valerie decides it is time to leave her husband. She packs her bags and leaves for the train, but is intercepted by Elizabeth at the station. Meanwhile, Stefan and Elizabeth's traveling companion make passionate love. Stefan and Valerie are unaware, at this point, that both strange women are actually vampires. Battori is the Scarlet Countess herself, and the other woman is one of her lovers.

Stefan inadvertently kills Elizabeth's companion when he forces her into the running water of the shower (a death sentence for vampires...). Just as Stefan kills the woman, Elizabeth and Valerie return to the hotel. Though angered by Stefan's betrayal, Valerie helps Elizabeth and Stefan get rid of the body. Not far away, the police officer watches in secret.

As the night passes, Elizabeth seduces Valerie, transforming her into a new love slave/vampire companion. Stefan is now convinced that Elizabeth is evil, and begs Valerie to leave the hotel with him. Valerie is under Elizabeth's spell, and can do nothing but obey her master. Stefan and Elizabeth fight for possession of Valerie, and Stefan loses. He ends up as dinner for the two vampires, who drink hungrily from his bloody wrists.

Together, Elizabeth and Valerie hide Stefan's body, steal a car, and strike the sus-picious police officer as he rides his bicycle on the road ahead of them. Unfortunately, daylight is coming, and Elizabeth will die if exposed. Valerie starts to speed, but as sunlight looms, loses control of the vehicle. The car spins and turns over, and Elizabeth is thrown from the burning vehicle and impaled on a tree.

A few months later, Valerie has adopted Elizabeth's decadent lifestyle (and voice), and leads another married couple down the path of temptation and ruin...

COMMENTARY: Harry Kumel's *Daughters of Darkness* is a kinky, erotic horror film, the genre equivalent of *9½ Weeks,* only smarter, more honest, and more provocative. The film artfully employs color and light to contrast the vampires (red) with the humans, Stefan and Valerie (blue). More importantly, the film makes some insightful connections between vampirism and the dark sexual appetites of its protagonists. Indeed, in *Daughters of Darkness*, vampirism seems just another avenue to sexual arousal, to sexual awakening. Countess Battori is merely a catalyst who opens up Stefan and Valerie to a dark sexual "experiment."

Daughters of Darkness commences with an explicit sexual coupling between Stefan and Valerie, bathed in a cool, azure light. There are close-ups and full shots of the nude couple, but the light suggests coolness, not passion. Blue is the color of ice, the color of cold, on film, and Kumel's choice reveals to the audience something about these characters. Though they are married, though they may be in love, their passion is such that it can only be described as restrained, courtesy of the sapphire lighting. When Countess Elizabeth Battori and her lover are seen, they recline in a hot red light, a remarkable contrast to the blue. Red represents fire, heat, and passion on film, so Kumel's choice of lighting is again revelatory: since Battori and her mistress openly express their desires (vampirism, homosexuality), they are seen in shades of scarlet. Not incidentally, crimson is also the color of blood, and the intimation seems to be that Stefan and Valerie's blood may run cold (blue), but Battori's is hot, burning, red.

This lighting concept, though simple, is consistent throughout the picture. Later in the film, Stefan and Valerie again make love, and again, they are seen in pale shades of blue. As the vampires watch the encounter from the ledge outside their room, the light shifts to red. Even by satisfying their desire to be voyeurs, to watch, then, the vampires are expressing their passion, and thus depicted in tones of red. Kumel adapts this tack later, too. After Stefan first expresses his repressed desire, to whip Valerie with a belt, the lighting turns to a golden yellow; not quite as hot as red, or as cold as blue, but somewhere between. The inference is that Stefan is changing, influenced perhaps by the red hue, the overt passion, of the vampires he has gotten to know.

Of course, lighting cues that indicate character temperament or desire would mean little in any film if the images did not reinforce the story and themes of the picture. Fortunately, *Daughters of Darkness* has a well-developed screenplay. It depicts a marriage that goes sour faster than Darva Conger's, as Stefan and Valerie are psychologically separated by both their secret (and kinky) desires, and by the manipulative Battori. When Battori tells the story of the Scarlet Countess, who drank the blood of hundreds of virgins to stay young, it is clearly a kind of "dirty" talk that arouses and excites Stefan. Valerie is not yet willing to be seduced by this stranger and her ways, but it is obvious that Sefan harbors a dark side which finds voice as he experiments with sado-masochism and other sexual "kinks." Indeed, in the first weekend of marriage, Stefan beats his wife, is unfaithful to her, and commits murder. Once released, Stefan's passions simply cannot be controlled.

That's appropriate, because *Daughters of Darkness* is a movie about appetites, sexual and violent, and how sometimes when we give voice to those darkest desires, we lose control. "What happened to us, Stefan? Why did she cross our path?" Valerie wonders to her husband, referring to the force of nature, Battori. What she seems to be expressing in that quote is the Pandora's box principle: that you can't open the box of "pleasure" without releasing a monster too. Had Stefan and Valerie not been open, at least in some sense, to the sexual freedom embodied by Battori, they would not be involved in murder, death, infidelity and the like. In this sense, the movie seems to be about the dangers of a threesome, about the alienation of affection in an unhappy marriage when an interesting, attractive third party inserts himself or herself into the intimacy of a couple.

Kumel has a gift for expressing this provocative material in an artistic way. A bathroom sequence late in the film is an unsettling mix of sex, nudity and violence that seems to suggest, in Battori's world anyway, that all three are the same. There's also some nice visual crosscutting between Stefan's neck and Ilona's hungry lips as they make love, a visual indicator of her everpresent need for blood. It's also rather clever the way Elizabeth's hands cast a reflection, but her face does not. It's a bizarre, but oddly effective updating of the "no reflection" aspect of vampirism.

Daughters of Darkness works best, however, when vampirism is used as a metaphor for passions unleashed. When the film actually depicts literal vampirism (Valerie and Elizabeth drinking hungrily from Stefan's wrists; Battori casting no reflection), it is less interesting, more obvious. For most of its running time *Daughters of Darkness* seems to understand that vampirism can be interchangeable with voyeurism, sadism, masochism, or any other outlet of repressed desire. Battori represents Stefan and Valerie's dark, experimental side, the side that is open to any and all of these things. When she acts independently as a long-lived vampire, drinking blood and actively trying to seduce Valerie, the picture loses some of its artistic luster. Thus *Daughters of Darkness* is quite exceptional because it works best as artistic metaphor, less so as vampire movie. It's a highbrow treat in a genre that has often been considered lowbrow. "I am just an outdated character," Battori bemoans at one point, and she is right — we've seen her ilk before in *Count Yorga*, *The Scars of Dracula* and the like — but Kumel puts the old clichés to new purpose in *Daughters of Darkness*, making the outdated seem daring, dangerous, and very, very erotic.

The Devils

Cast and Crew

CAST: Vanessa Redgrave (Sister Jeanne); Oliver Reed (Father Grandier); Dudley Sutton (Baron de Lombardemont); Murray Melvin (Father Mignon); Michael Gothard (Father Barre); Georgina Hale (Phillips); With: Max Adrian, John Woodvine, Judith Paris, Catherine Willmer, Iza Teller, Andrew Faulds.

CREW: *Directed by:* Ken Russell. *Based on the Play* The Devils *by:* John Whitney. *And Based on the Book* The Devils of Loudon *by:* Aldous Huxley. *Screenplay by:* Ken Russell. *Produced by:* Robert H. Solo and Ken Russell. *Music:* Peter Maxwell Davies. *Film Editing:* Michael Bradsell. *Special Effects:* John Richards. Made at Pinewood Studios, London, England. A Russell Production, Ltd., distributed by Warner Brothers. *M.P.A.A. Rating:* R. *Running Time:* 103 minutes.

DETAILS: This is Ken (*Altered States* [1980], *Lair of the White Worm* [1989]) Russell's stylish (and searing indictment) of religion, and the atrocities done in the name of religion. It might only marginally be called horror, but it does trade on some grotesque imagery (including a hunch-backed nun...). All the terror starts when the priest of Loudon refuses to cooperate with the French government. The King's men want to demolish the town's fortifications, but the priest (Oliver Reed) sees it as a defense should the government turn against its people. The government and the Church then go to some lengths to destroy the priest's reputation, marking him as a witch. The movie is about politically motivated witch-hunts, and is particularly relevant following the Clinton impeachment of 1999. In both film and reality, a man's sexual failings are the rope with which the rabid opposition hopes to hang him. As horror, the film lingers on a graphic depiction of Christ's crucifixion, and climaxes in a nasty burning at the stake. This is a controversial, spiky, even inflammatory film that fits in with the witch-hunt tradition of such gory 1970s films as *Mark of the Devil* (1972). Functions simultaneously as satire, indictment, horror picture, and political thriller.

Dr. Jekyll & Sister Hyde

Cast and Crew

CAST: Ralph Bates (Dr. Jekyll); Martine Beswick (Sister Hyde); Gerald Sim (Professor Robertson); Lewis Fiander (Howard); Philip Madoc (Ryker); Paul Whitsun-Jones (Sgt. Danvers); Virginia Wetherell (Betsy).

CREW: *Directed by:* Roy Ward Baker. *Written by:* Brian Clemens. *Produced by:* Brian Clemens and Albert Fennell. *Director of Photography:* Norman Warwick. *Editor:* James Needs. Hammer Studios. *M.P.A.A. Rating:* PG. *Running Time:* 95 minutes.

DETAILS: Hammer's unusual take on the Dr. Jekyll/Mr. Hyde mythos is energetic if nothing else. Here, Dr. Jekyll transforms into an evil woman (Martine Beswick), and all kinds of issues about sexuality and gender are raised ... and then abandoned in favor of horror tropes.

Duel (1971) ✶ ✶ ✶ ✶

Critical Reception

"...displays well Spielberg's ability to create an atmosphere laden with nerve-jangling tension." — John Brosnan, *Future Tense*, St. Martin's Press, 1978, page 217.

"Spielberg's direction is worthy of comparison with Hitchcock ... the nightmare in broad daylight recalls ... *North by Northwest*. The tense car drive and the use of recriminatory self-tormenting monologue reminds one of *Psycho*; the suggestion of malign intelligence in the strategy of the truck's attacks is similar to the way Hitchcock generates suspense in *The Birds*...." — Neil Sinyard, *The Films of Steven Spielberg*, Bison Books Ltd., 1986, page 14.

Cast & Crew

CAST: Dennis Weaver (David Mann); Jacqueline Scott (Mrs. Mann); Eddie Firestone (Cafe Owner); Lou Frizzell (Bus Driver); Gene Dynarski (Man in Cafe); Lucille Benson (Lady at Snakerama); Tim Herbert (Gas Station Attendant); Charles Seel (Old Man); Shirley O'Hara (Waitress); Alexander Lockwood (Old Man in Car); Amy Douglass (Old Woman in Car); Dick Whittington (Radio Interview); Gary Loftin (the Truck Driver); Dale Van Sickle (Car Driver).

CREW: Universal Studio Presents *Duel*. *Director of Photography:* Jack A Marta. *Art Director:* Robert S. Smith. *Set Decorator:* S. Blydenburgh. *Sound:* Edwin S. Hall. *Unit Production Manager:* Wallace Worsley. *Assistant Director:* Jim Fargo. *Film Editor:* Frank Morriss. *Stunt Coordinator:* Gary Loftin. *Titles and Opticals:* Universal Title. *Color:* Technicolor. *Music:* Billy Goldenberg. *Screenplay:* Richard Matheson. *Based on a short story by:* Richard Matheson. *Produced by:* George Eckstein. *Directed by:* Steven Spielberg.

SYNOPSIS: A lone driver on a business trip innocently passes a filthy old truck on a long stretch of desert highway. In response to this perceived insult, the truck takes the initiative and passes the confused driver. Irritated, salesman Mr. Mann passes the truck again, and speeds far away from the slow-moving diesel vehicle. When David Mann stops at a gas station, the truck stops too, though Mann is able only to make out the driver's hands and cowboy boots. A little spooked, David calls his wife, and then gets back on the road. Oddly, the truck follows him again. Not wishing to get involved in anything dangerous, Mann gestures the truck by, but it deliberately goes slow. Patiently, Mann waits for a passing lane, but the truck refuses to let him by on the treacherous mountain roads. Then, the truck driver gestures David by ... right into oncoming traffic, and Mann is nearly killed. Late for an appointment and tired of playing games, David races off-road and leaves the truck far behind in the dust.

Later, the truck returns, riding up on David's tailgate. The truck runs David off the road at nearly 100 miles an hour. Shaken but whole, David stops at a local diner to recover. When he returns to his table from the rest room, however, he sees the offending truck parked just outside ... waiting for him. David confronts a patron he believes to be the driver, but he angers the wrong man. Afraid, David bides his time and waits for the truck to leave. When it does, David gets back on the road and offers assistance to an overheated school bus. Just when David's vehicle is the most vulnerable, the truck returns for another pass. David escapes this unusual trap and races away. Unfortunately, his progress is slowed by a train crossing. The truck re-appears and attempts to push Mann's car into the oncoming train. Mann escapes again, but the truck will not give up the chase.

Mann stops at a gas station to phone the police, but the truck runs down the phone booth and then circles Mann, stalking him like a crazed predator. Mann makes it back to his car and returns to the road. He pulls into a ditch and decides to hide for an hour. When he resumes his trip, the malevolent truck is still waiting for him, just ahead. Mann asks the drivers of passing vehicles for help, but no one will assist him. When the truck gestures Mann ahead again, the final race is on. Soon, Mann's little Valiant is overheating after an extended chase, and dropping speed rapidly. Mann races down a mountainside, the truck in close pursuit. At the last minute, David jumps from his vehicle and the monster truck careens off the mountaintop in a fireball.

COMMENTARY: Including *Duel* in this book is no doubt a cheat. It is a film made for American television, not theatrical release, and this author has made the conscious decision to exclude TV product, because otherwise this book would be gigantic. TV movies would make for an excellent reference book, no doubt, all on their own. But, *Duel* is such a good and important film (and it did play theatrically in Europe...) that it seems a crime not to include it here. It is a bravura early film by Steven Spielberg (who helmed *Jaws*— one of the greatest horror films of the 1970s), and is important his-

torically in light of its director's subsequent career.

It's fascinating to see how *Duel* has been assembled into a taut engine of horror. An everyday situation (road rage) escalates quickly into horror, but Spielberg doesn't assemble his picture in the conventional manner that other directors might. Instead, *Duel* is constructed almost piecemeal from a collection of brief, informative detail shots: of spinning wheels, of headlights, of gauges, of mirrors, of train lights, and the like. The cumulative effect is riveting. It's as though the audience is being stalked, for it is we who monitor the speedometer along with Weaver, hear the hum of the motor, gaze out across the windshield, see the road rolling by, and even look down to view a foot pump the gas pedal. In essence, Spielberg puts his viewers in the driver's seat, and it is impossible not to identify with Weaver's character. We get sensory information about the chase as the protagonist does, as though we are driving the car (or at least co-piloting). Until virtual reality movies, *Duel* is about as close as you can get to interactive film. It's a brilliant way to direct a horror movie, and a clever way of fostering audience identification. Each shot is carefully constructed to convey important information about the race, the film's primary scenario.

Spielberg's technique is effective in other ways too. As he would do in *Jaws*, Spielberg hides the villain for as long as he can. In *Jaws*, the shark was rarely seen because of mechanical difficulties with the killer fish mock-up, but in *Duel*, Spielberg hides the driver of the truck so as to maintain the mystery of the villain. Who is this driver: Devil, demon or man? Why has he attacked so violently? Why is he so relentless? All these questions are raised, but Spielberg never answers them, and so *Duel* feels like a descent into a nightmare, into utter irrationality. What kind of world is it where passing someone on the road is a crime punishable by pursuit and murder? Is it just egregious road rage or the hand of a demon out to destroy Weaver's character? *Duel* is frightening because all those questions are raised.

Richard Matheson's *Duel* screenplay is a perfect launching pad for Spielberg, and is adept in the way it develops Weaver's driver. The audience is privy to his thoughts, and they feel pretty real. He escalates into full-scale panic, mulls over apologies, and acts out possibilities in his mind. This approach reveals to viewers how our minds keep replaying and reinterpreting traumatic events, trying to make them right in our heads so we can move on. Yet Mann, the driver, is denied any peace, because there is no rational explanation for the ambush against him. The audience identifies with him because his inner monologues keep trying to reason through the situation ... and keep failing. It is frightening to be confronted with the inexplicable, and Weaver's portrait of Mann, buttressed by internal soliloquies, presents a believable picture of an everyman confronted by the unusual, the terrifying, the unreal.

Until *The Road Warrior* (1982) and *The Hitcher* (1985), *Duel* is probably the best "road" chase movie ever made. The climax is a surprising reversal of expectations: after an extended fast chase (over 100 miles an hour), both vehicles overheat and fight to chug uphill, going ever more slowly as they arduously ascend a mountain, until the chase is actually a crawl. There are clever touches too (Mann drives a Valiant — a heroic car for a hero), and the truck blurts out a death rattle, like a dying monster, as it rolls off the mountain to its demise). But most of all, the movie is a supenseful, exciting chase.

"One stupid thing happens ... and there you are, right back in the jungle," Mann bemoans, under assault from the demonic driver and his mechanical steed. That's the key to *Duel*'s success: it shows how one incident at the wrong time and the wrong place can descend quickly and irrevocably into terror. Kudos to Steven Spielberg and his audacious, brilliant, ever-fluid camera work. *Duel* was his calling card to Hollywood, and it is bravura work — even if made for TV.

Equinox (1971) ★ ★ ½

Cast & Crew

CAST: Edward Connell (Dave Fielding); Barbara Hewitt (Susan); Frank Boers, Jr. (Jim); Robin Christopher (Vicki); Jack Woods (Asmodeus); Jim Phillips, Fritz Leiber, Patrick Burke, Jim Duron, Sharon Gray, Louis Clayton, Norvelle Brooks, Irving L. Lichtenstein.

CREW: Jack H. Harris Presents a Tonlyn Production, *Equinox. Special Photographic Effects:* Dennis Muren. *Associate Producers:* David Allen, Jim Danforth. *Based on a story by:* Mark Thomas McGee. *Music Supervisor:* John Capers. *Production Manager:* Sam Altonian. *Script Supervisor:* Jill Murphy. *Assistant Cameraman:* Ed Begley, Jr. *Production Assistant:* Bob Woods. *Gaffer:* Joel Chernoff. *Grip:* Ben Harwood, Jr. *Make-up:* Robynne Hoover. *Editor:*

John Joyce. *Sound Effects:* Edit International. *Opticals:* Howard A. Anderson, Co. *Mixer:* Bradley Lane. *Director of Photography:* Mike Hoover. *Color:* DeLuxe. *Producer:* Jack H. Harris. *Written and directed by:* Jack Woods. *M.P.A.A. Rating:* R. *Running time:* 82 minutes.

P.O.V.

"If you know which scenes were shot by Dennis and which scenes were done later by Jack Harris, shot by Mike Hoover, you can see the difference, because the stuff Hoover shot did not blow-up very well [to 35 mm]. The stuff Dennis shot is nice.... I still think the basic idea of the story for *Equinox* is kind of a viable thing. I was really impressed.... I was not pleased by the way Harris gave everybody the shaft" (6).— Special effects Artist Jim Danforth recalls his feelings about *Equinox* (1971).

SYNOPSIS: A young man named David Fielding is stalked in the woods by something evil after his three friends are killed. He makes it to a highway, and is struck by a driver-less car, but survives the collision.

A year and one day later, a reporter visits David, now a depressed "melancholic," in an asylum. David is non-communicative, but his attending physician shares information with the reporter about the disturbed patient. He plays a tape recording of an interview with David from the time of his admittance...

A year earlier, David, his blind date, Susan, friend Jim, and Jim's girlfriend Vicki went on a picnic to a remote cabin in the woods to meet with Dr. Johanson, a geology professor. They drove to the mountains, hit a dead end, and walked up a long cabin trail in search of Johanson's place, only to find it destroyed. They ran into a mysterious forest ranger named Asmodeus, who warned them to leave the woods.

The foursome walked a little further and spied a giant castle on a glen. En route to it, they heard a cackling emanating from a cave. Inside, a strange old man gave the four young adults a book. David attempted to translate the book, written in Latin, at least until Dr. Johanson showed up, transformed into a raving lunatic, and stole it. David chased the professor to a creek, where the old man died relinquishing the book. While the group investigated the text, some kind of medieval witch's book, Asmodeus attacked Susan, only to be repelled by her crucifix.

The special book, 1000 years old, soon revealed to the group that forces of evil co-existed with good on Earth, and the object of evil was to counteract its opposite. Johanson's scribbled notes in the text then revealed how he followed instructions and summoned evil manifestations. He saw physical instability in these manifestations, however, and was unable to control what he had released from Pandora's box. Frightened, David, Susan, Vicki and Jim returned to the castle, to discover it had disappeared, apparently into the instability of another dimension.

Meanwhile, Asmodeus summoned a giant simian monster to kill the group and steal the book. The attempt failed, primarily because David and the others had fashioned primitive protective icons out of available materials in the forest. When Susan lost her crucifix, she became evil, infected by Asmodeus, and David had to save her. She recovered sufficiently, but was frightened. Then Jim was confronted by Asmodeus, who still wanted the all-powerful book. When Jim was pulled across the barrier of dimensional instability in the grip of a giant, David followed him to the netherworld. There, Asmodeus tricked David and returned to reality, where he killed Vicki.

David and Susan combated Asmodeus, now transformed into a winged devil, with a crucifix, but Susan was injured in the ensuing explosion. David escaped into the woods, but not before hearing a warning that Asmodeus would kill him in one year and one day.

One year and one day later, a possessed Susan finds her way to the mental institution just as the reporter, having found nothing worth reporting, leaves.

COMMENTARY: There is one inexplicable fact of Hollywood: everyone has to start somewhere. And, some of today's greatest special effects legends, including Dennis Muren (*Star Wars: The Phantom Menace* [1999]), Jim Danforth (*They Live* [1988]) and Dave Allen (*Laserblast* [1978]) began their careers with a low-budget student film called *Equinox*. The picture was made for $8,000 dollars, took four years to make, and producer Jack Harris (*Dark Star* [1975]) bought the picture, re-shot some scenes and added others. The final result is a promising film,

Not the Jolly Green Giant, but an incredible simulation. One of the "demons" conjured by the Necrinomicon in *Equinox* (1971).

one rife with talent, but in the final analysis, somewhat lacking. Yet, despite its flaws, *Equinox* is an important film because many of its themes (and even some shots) have reoccurred in popular later productions such as *The Evil Dead* (1983) and *The Blair Witch Project* (1999).

Equinox is directed with plenty of energy and low-budget zeal, but the game effort is severely undercut by bland performances, and an obsession with special effects sequences that don't stand up to lingering attention. The performers and their characters are problematic. The heroes are pretty ineffectual, and the actresses sometimes appear only half-interested in what is occurring. On the level of a *Scooby Doo* episode, the characters come off as hopelessly square, and also somewhat confused. This may indeed be because several scenes were reshot and the talent may not have understood

how sequences would fit together. On that matter, the re-shoots are obvious. Vicki's haircut and weight vacillate from shot-to-shot, sometimes within the same scene. Pounds are lost, then gained, then lost again. The result is a film that seems jumbled.

Dialogue is a stumbling block. "Do you have a flashlight in the car?" One character asks. "No, I haven't," replies the other, in stilted, perfect English. A simple shake of the head would have done, and that's the problem. These student filmmakers (and it is important to remember they were students when the film was made) do not yet understand that film is a visual medium, and that it is not actually necessary to use dialogue to explain everything. The dubbing/looping of the dialogue is also less than quality work, but, again, this was a student film.

The effects in *Equinox*, though remarkable for their time and budget, don't stand up today, either. There are plenty of stop-motion junkies out there, and there is no doubt that stop-motion animation was still a viable special effects option in the '70s, but today the procedure seems dated, especially under the gaze of color photography. Also, there is an unfortunate tendency with stop-motion animation to show off. Monsters don't just fall over and die. They stagger, whinny, lunge, feint and then fall, giving audiences plenty of time to realize that we are looking at lifeless miniatures lovingly manipulated by invisible hands. This is true in *Equinox*, as it is in other films using the process, but it harder to stomach in color, and the stop-motion is, politely, not on the level of a Willis O'Brien or a Ray Harry-hausen. Make-up isn't very good either. When Jim is possessed by Asmodeus, black eyeshadow underlines his face, and what should have been a subtle effect is instead a kind of humorous forecasting of the 1980s punk look.

Despite all these flaws, *Equinox* has merit. It casts a creepy, unnerving atmosphere, features a good natural setting, and is ambitious in story and scope. In fact, it was a rather daring and bold an initiative for its time. Look at it this way: *Equinox* features an "adept demonologist" (Johanson) who discovers a demonic book, takes it to his remote cabin in the woods, and inadvertently conjures demonic forces. Those forces then kill him and run amok in the forest. As any horror fan will recall, that is the precise plot of Sam Raimi's brilliant (and far superior) *Evil Dead* films. *Evil Dead II: Dead By Dawn* (1987) even quotes directly from *Equinox* in its opening shot. A rotating book (the Necrinomicon) flies through a void (in stop motion). That is a shot lifted right from *Equinox*. Another moment, that of tape recorder wheels spinning, is also lifted from *Equinox* and inserted in the original *Evil Dead*. No doubt these moments are intended as homage, but they are nonetheless derivative.

The idea of a dark, supernatural evil in the woods, killing teens, is also at the core of *The Blair Witch Project*. The protective (and evil) icons fashioned in *Equinox* are even seen again in the Haxan symbol that came to be *Blair Witch*'s trademark. Considering its descendants, *Equinox* had quite an impact on horror filmmakers, even if those filmmakers created superior, more confident visions.

Equinox was clearly intended to be an ambitious horror picture on a grand scale. It featured spectacles (giant stop motion monsters, castles, and clashes with flying demons), and even a downbeat, nihilistic ending. Its makers should be commended for influencing the course of horror history with their powerful imagery and forward-thinking notions, even if, in the final analysis, their film isn't very good.

Hands of the Ripper (1971) ★ ★ ★ ½

Critical Reception

"...*Hands of the Ripper* has a good deal of ghoulish truck with the idea that the most storied Victorian killer, Jack the Ripper has passed his gory predilections on to his pretty blonde daughter...."—A.H. Weiler, *New York Times*, July 14, 1972, page 19.

"Offbeat ... ripping good."—John Stanley, *Creature Features Strikes Again*, 1994, page 173.

Cast & Crew

CAST: Eric Porter (Pritchard); Jane Merrow (Laura); Derek Godfrey (Dysart); Angharad Rees (Anna); Marjorie Rhodes (Mrs. Bryant); Keith Bill (Michael); Margaret Rawlings (Madame Bullard); Lynda Baren (Long Liz); Marjie Lawrence (Dolly); Norman Bird (Police Inspector); Elizabeth MacLennan (Mrs. Wilson); A.J. Brown (Reverend Anderson); Barry Lowe (Mr. Wilson); April Wilding (Catherine); Anne Clune (1st Cell Whore); Vicki Woolf (2nd Cell Whore); Katya Wyeth (1st Public Whore); Beulah Hughes (2nd Public Whore); Peter Munt (Pleasants); Philip Ryan (Police Constable); Molly Weir (Maid); Charles Lamb (Guard).

CREW: The Rank Organization Presents a Hammer Production. *Director of Photography:* Kenneth Talbot. *Production Manager:* Christopher Sutton. *Art Director:* Roy Stannard. *Editor:* Chris Barnes. *Music Composed by:* Christopher Gunning. *Musical Supervisor:* Philip Martell. *Assistant Director:* Arici Levy. *Sound Recordist:* Kevin Sutton. *Sound Editor:* Frank Goulding. *Continuity:* Gladys Goldsmith. *Make-up Supervisor:* Bunty Phillips. *Hairdressing Supervisor:* Pat McDermott. *Wardrobe Supervisor:* Rosemary Burrows. *Wardrobe Mistress:* Eileen Sullivan. *Special Effects:* Cliff Culley *Construction Manager:* Arthur Banks. *Dubbing Mixer:* Ken Barker. *Screenplay by:* L.W. Davidson. *From an original story by:* Edward Spencer Shew. *Produced by:* Aida Young. *Directed by:* Peter Sasdy. Made at Pinewood Studios. A Hammer Production, distributed by Rank Film Distributors Ltd. *M.P.A.A. Rating:* R. *Running time:* 82 minutes.

SYNOPSIS: In Victorian England, Jack the Ripper returns from a night of murder and mayhem to brutally kill the mother of his young daughter, Anna. Anna witnesses the crime, and comes to associate the glowing light of the fire, reflected on her brass bed, with terrible violence. After years spent in an orphanage, Anna is given a home by the fraudulent spiritual medium Mrs. Golding. In need of cash, Golding also prostitutes the 17-year-old girl to a wealthy customer, Mr. Dysart. When Dysart gives Anna a piece of jewelry that glimmers strangely in the light, Anna goes crazy and attempts to kill him. She impales Golding with a fireplace poker.

The police conduct an investigation, but a witness to the crime, one Dr. Pritchard, fails to place Dysart at the scene ... deliberately. Instead, he adopts Anna and, as a student of Freud and psychology, attempts to reform the murderous girl ... who has no memory of her violent activity. Dysart thinks Anna is possessed, but Pritchard believes psychoanalysis can help her. At the same time Anna becomes a houseguest, Pritchard's son, Michael, invites his blind fiancée, Laura, to stay there as well.

Before Pritchard can help Anna, she kills one of his servants, brutally slashing her throat. As before, the trigger for the violence is a piece of jewelry that shines a certain way. Pritchard sedates Anna, and then hides the evidence of her crime. When Dysart comes up empty-handed on trying to learn Anna's background, he makes an appointment for Anna and Pritchard with a psychic named Mrs. Bullard. A skeptical man of science, Pritchard instead hypnotizes Anna to learn the truth of her childhood. He is interrupted during the session, and Anna takes to the streets in a fragile state. There, she kills a prostitute. Too late to avert the violence, Pritchard finds her, and brings her home.

Desperate to help Anna shed the violent side of her personality, Pritchard relents and takes her to see Mrs. Bullard. The psychic reveals that Anna's father was Jack the Ripper. Furthermore, she sees the identity of the notorious criminal, and warns that Anna is possessed by the violence of her father. Anna kills Bullard, and Pritchard flees the premises. After witnessing the crime, Pritchard learns that flickering lights are key to Anna's violent episodes. He tests his theory, and Anna subsequently spears him in the gut with a sword.

Still in a hypnotic trance, Anna joins Michael and Laura for an afternoon carriage ride. Bleeding to death, Pritchard manages to warn his son of Anna's true nature. They race to St. Paul's cathedral, and the Whispering

Gallery, to save Laura before she is the next victim. Rather than let the Ripper's spirit lead her to commit a final act of violence, Anna jumps to her death ... and lands beside the corpse of Pritchard ... who has finally succumbed to his wound.

COMMENTARY: *Hands of the Ripper* is a rarity: A Hammer horror movie that is serious, gritty, and thoughtful. Its tale of a man of science's fall from grace also happens to be laced with enough explicit gore to satisfy the most hard-core horror fans. In all, it's an appealing mix of the grotesque, and a rather thoughtful film.

This is not the average Hammer horror picture, a decorative period piece with extravagant and opulent sets, and women prowling about in diaphanous gowns. Instead, the film presents a dark, disturbing and gritty image of Victorian London. In one of the early scenes, a woman pimps her 17-year-old girl without a second thought. "There, there girl, it happens to all of us." She calmly tells her ward. In another scene, a man is incarcerated in a jail cell with a group of ugly, hooting and hollering hookers. In other words, this film has no illusions about the Victorian world. It depicts a grungy, muddy London where old whores in garish make-up walk the streets trying to make a living. It's a new look for Hammer, and a very good one.

Perhaps more interestingly, *Hands of the Ripper* develops a rather mature screenplay that focuses on a tragic figure's fall from grace. Mr. Pritchard is a man of intellect, a man of science, and a man of the upper class. He is society's best, he is well read, and he is confident in his own knowledge. It is that confidence which ultimately proves to be his downfall. In attempting to study the criminal mind, Pritchard in fact develops his own criminal instincts: covering for Anna, hiding bodies, obstructing justice and the like. In the final analysis, Pritchard is killed trying to prove that his theory about Anna is correct,

and his son and daughter-in-law nearly pay the price for his hubris. In all, the downfall of Pritchard, a man who thinks he can solve the problem and learn all the answers, is a reminder of the old proverb that the road to Hell is paved with good intentions. If only he had left well-enough alone, Pritchard wouldn't have put himself or his family in danger.

This story of psychology, possession and tragedy is punctuated by moments of extreme gore. Mr. Golding is impaled through a door on a fireplace poker in one early set piece. In another, Anna sticks a hatpin in a prostitute's eye. At another moment, Anna slits the throat of Pritchard's servant, Dolly, and blood splatters everywhere. Yet, no doubt, the *pièce de résistance*, is Pritchard's own mortal wound, and his valiant attempt to recover from it. Anna sticks a sword in his side and escapes. Pritchard, still alive, hinges the handle of the sword (still lodged in his body) on a door knob, and then pushes himself off the lengthy, bloody blade. This is all far more bloody than most Hammer films, but it all works remarkably well in this gritty setting. The point of the film is that Anna's violence is total (and bloody), and that science can't explain it. Thus the violence is rather necessary. It also serves as a nice counterpoint to Anna's innocent demeanor. She is indeed quite murderous, but she is not a villain in the traditional sense, which as Al Gore might say, is a "distinction without a difference." In other words, she commits horrible acts but is ultimately not hated by audiences because she is in the grip of forces she cannot control.

Hands of the Ripper is a good film. Though its flirtation with the supernatural (the possession of the living by the dead) is only half-explored, the movie's notions of science's inadequacies, and Mr. Pritchard's arrogance, have resonance This is a world without happy endings, of grit and dirt, where even an innocent girl is plagued by the "sins of the fathers." Yet it's a world worth visiting.

Hatchet for a Honeymoon (1971) * * *

Cast & Crew

CAST: Stephen Forsyth (John Harrington); Dagmar Lassander, Laura Betti, Jesus Puente, Femi Benussi, Antonia Mas, Alan Collin, Gerard Tichy, Veronica Llimera, Fortunato Pascuale, Jose Ignacio Abadaz, Silvia Llenas, Monserrat Riba.

CREW: A Spanish-Italian co-production, Pan Latina Films and Mercury Films of Peliculas Ibarra & CIA, S.A, present *Hatchet for a Honeymoon*. *Screemplay* [*sic*]: Santiago Moncada. *Assistant Directors:* Ricardo Walker, Lamberto Bava. *Continuity Girl:* Patricia Zulini. *Assistant Producer:* Enzo Feria. *Cameramen:* Jaime Deu Casas, Emilio Barriano. *Assistant Cameramen:* Arcline Carla, Marcelo Anconetani. *Hairstylist:* Hipolita Lopez, Emilia Achini. *Stillmen:* Jose Adrian, Giuseppe Parrabano. *Film Editor:* Soledad Lopez. *Make-up:* Elisa Aspach, Piero McCacci. *Set Design:* Jesus Mc-Herrero. *Costumes:* Jose McTresserra. *Laboratory:* Fotofilm Madrid S.A, Technostampa, Roma. *Color:* Eastmancolor. *Studio:* Balcazar, Barcelona. *Sound:* Arcofon, Fono Roma. *Music:* Sante Romitelli. *Director of Photography:* Mario Bava. *Production Manager:* Jaine Fernandez Cid. *Assistant Manager:* Pedro Villanueva, Graciano Fabiani. *Producer:* Manuel Cano. *Directed by:* Mario Bava. *M.P.A.A. Rating:* PG. *Running time:* 84 minutes.

SYNOPSIS: John Harrington is a deranged psychopath who feels compelled to murder newlywed brides. A 30-year-old "paranoiac," this wealthy, handsome, playboy also happens to be married to a cold woman named Mildred, who does not suspect he has already killed five women. Harrington wants a divorce from Mildred, but she won't permit it. Meanwhile, John's business specializes in the fashion needs of newlyweds, his strange obsession.

When John goes to a séance with Mildred, his dead mother speaks through her and tells John to behave. Not long after, police investigate John in connection with the murders, and search the green house, where John has buried three bodies. Fortunately for John, the corpses are not discovered.

Meanwhile, a beautiful model informs John she will have to quit modeling for him because she is getting married. An aroused (and murderous) John asks to see her that evening, and offers her a wedding dress. When he sees her in the gown, he kills her, and feels he has started to come closer to understanding his compulsion. He believes it stems from a traumatic incident in childhood.

John's new model is actually the suspicious sister of the deceased girl. She courts John, even while suspecting he murdered her sister. Mildred, also suspicious, attempts to snare John in an infidelity, but he dresses up in a wedding veil and hacks her to death with a cleaver.

As John continues to kill and the police circle ever closer, he remembers his boyhood trauma. As a boy, he murdered his mother because he did not want her to re-marry. Even as this realization dawns, the ghost of Mildred starts to haunt John, saying she will never leave his side, even in death. John is finally captured by the police before he can kill again. He is arrested, and through it all, the shrewish Mildred remains at his side.

COMMENTARY: Despite its lurid title, *Hatchet for a Honeymoon* is a solid psychodrama. It's a little rough in spots, but on the whole is rather impressive. Director Mario Bava's gift is with imagery, not plotting or clarity, and this movie reflects that virtue and those faults. It is a child, or grandchild of Hitchcock's *Psycho* (1960), and an antecedent to *American Psycho* (2000), but possessed of a quirky Hitchcockian-style. The big surprise here is not a first act murder of a prominent character, but the third act shift to a more overt supernatural theme.

Unlike Norman Bates, John Harrington in *Hatchet for a Honeymoon* is known to be a psycho from the very beginning of the film. "The fact is, I'm completely mad," he acknowledges, after introducing himself to the audience. In these little internal monologues, John explains his hang-ups and his behavior the best he can. He sees his madness and his life as a "ridiculous" and "brief" drama. More to the point, he believes that "a woman should live till her wedding night, love once, and then die." As one might imagine, that anti-social philosophy causes him some problems in the end. But the decision to let Harrington narrate much of his own mis-adventure looks forward not only to *American Psycho*, with its delicious voice-over monologues, it grounds the audience in the character's plight before leaping into points unknown. Harrington is a psycho, but he's our psycho, and to some extent, we sympathize with him, despite his madness. Evil is attractive, and we simultaneously loathe him and hope he will elude capture.

As is typical for the work of Mario Bava, *A Hatchet for the Honeymoon* is filled with moments of cinematic inspiration. He brilliantly directs one suspense scene, wherein blood drips from a staircase onto a carpet, just beside a nosy police officer. Below the officer, a bloody hand is visible, reflected in a glass-top table. Throughout the scene, the audience is aware, and on edge, that Harrington's crime will be discovered, and Bava plays that anxiety for as long as possible. In another memorable moment, the ghostly Mildred ascends a grand staircase towards Harrington's room. Bava places his camera at floor level (at the top of the staircase), and Mildred's blurry head darts up suddenly in a jolting moment. Though psychologically speaking, the film is bunk (these movies, including *Psycho,* almost always are), Bava also has a good understanding of the material. It's nice the way he plays the supernatural. Is it "real" or is the ghostly Mildred just alive in the mind of a lunatic? The terrain is fertile for an artist of Bava's instincts.

"A madman can also have good reasons," John declares of his killing spree, and a mad movie can also be done with a level of ingenuity. Whether playing on the innate creepiness of mannequins, or gleefully dashing the expectations of blushing brides by marring their immaculate gowns with crimson blood, *A Hatchet for a Honeymoon* has delightful method behind its madness.

The House That Dripped Blood

Cast and Crew

CAST: Peter Cushing (Philip); Christopher Lee (Reid); Jon Pertwee (Paul); Ingrid Pitt, Denholm Elliott, Joanna Dunham, Geoffrey Bayldon

CREW: *Directed by*: Peter Duffell. *Produced by*: Max J. Rosenberg, Milton Subotsky. *Written by*: Robert Bloch. *Music*: Michael Dress. *Editor*: Peter Tanner. Cinerama Releasing. *M.P.A.A. Rating*: PG. *Running Time*: 101 minutes.

DETAILS: Another Subotsky/Rosenberg anthology, with material written by Robert Bloch (a la *Asylum* [1972]). A quartet of stories revolving around an evil "house," *The House That Dripped Blood* opens with "Method for Murder," about a writer whose monstrous, psychotic creation comes to life to attack his wife. "Waxworks" is just what it sounds like, the story of a twisted wax museum and its murderous owner. "Sweets to the Sweet" concerns a young girl who creates a voodoo doll. Finally, "The Cloak" (starring Pertwee and Pitt) involves a hammy horror movie actor who purchases an authentic vampire cape.

Jon Pertwee and Ingrid Pitt get close in *The House That Dripped Blood* (1971).

I, Monster

Cast and Crew

CAST: Christopher Lee (Dr. Marlowe/Edward Blake); Peter Cushing (Frederick Utterson); Mike Raven (Enfield); Susan Jameson (Diane).

CREW: *Directed by:* Stephen Weeks. *Written by:* Milton Subotsky. *Based on the Novel by:* Robert Louis Stevenson. *Produced by:* Max J. Rosenberg and Milton Subotsky. *Director of Photography:* Moray Grant. *Film Editor:* Peter Tanner. *Music:* Carl Davis. From Amicus. *M.P.A.A. Rating:* PG. *Running time:* 75 minutes.

DETAILS: Another Amicus production, this one a deadly serious version of *Dr. Jekyll and Mr. Hyde*. As its short running time indicates, there was precious little variation or inspiration here, though Christopher Lee is, as usual, remarkable. Reportedly shot to be a 3-D picture, but never released in that format.

Jack's Wife (1971) (a.k.a. *Hungry Wives* and *Season of the Witch*) ✶ ✶ ✶ ½

Critical Reception

"Today its sexual politics are obvious and off-putting.... Like most of Romero's work, it's made mostly of suburban locations and subtly acted by a de-glamorized unknown cast. The too-talky story can be seen as strict realism without any supernatural elements. In that respect, it's a companion piece to Romero's *Martin*, though not nearly as suspenseful or engrossing."—Mike Mayo, *VideoHound's Horror Show*, Visible Ink Press, 1998, page 316.

Cast & Crew

CAST: Jan White (Joan Mitchell); Virginia Greenwald (Marion); Ray Lane (Greg); Anne Muffly (Shirley); Joedda McClain, Bill Thunhurst, Nell Fisher, Esther Lapidus, Dan Mallinger, Dary Montgomery, Ken Peters, Shirlee Strasser, Bob Trow, Jean Wechsler, Charlotte Carter, Linda Creagan, Bill Hinzman, Marvin Lieber, Paul McCollough, Sue Michaels, Hal Priore, Luis Vochim.

CREW: This is a film from the Latent Image, Inc. *Cinematography:* George A. Romero. *Light and Additional Photography:* Bill Hinzman. *Sound Recordist:* Gerald Schutz. *Post-Production:* Bob Rutkowski. *Editorial:* Paul McCollough. *Properties:* H. Cramer Riblett. *Sound Assistant:* Rex Gleason. *Special Effects:* Rege Survinski. *Make-up:* Bonnie Priore. *Make-up Assistant:* Irene Croft. *Hair Styles:* Jim George. *Costumes/Furnishings:* Gimbels. *Production Supervisor:* Vince Survinski. *Associate Producer:* Gary Streiner. *Title Sequence:* The Animators. *Lab:* Du Art. *Color:* WRS Motion Picture Laboratories. Produced through the facilities of The Latent Image, Inc., Pittsburgh. *Song "Season of the Witch" sung by:* Donovan. *Original Electronic Music:* Steve Gorn. *Executive Producer:* Alvin Croft. *Written by:* George A. Romero. *Produced by:* Nancy M. Romero. *Directed by:* George A. Romero. *M.P.A.A. Rating:* R. *Running Time:* 105 minutes.

P.O.V.

"*Jack's Wife* was really sort of a feminist picture. The beginning days of women's liberation, and so forth. Even though I wrote it, I wrote it based on the feelings and observations of some female friends of mine. This was a script I liked very much, but due to the financial muddle, I had to work with half the anticipated budget and without the technical and creative support I needed" (7).— George Romero, on his horror follow-up to *Night of the Living Dead*.

SYNOPSIS: Forty-year-old Joan Mitchell sees herself as "Jack's wife," and little else. In her dreams, she walks subserviently six paces behind her husband as he carelessly snaps tree branches in her face and reads the morning paper. In the same dream, Jack puts Joan on a leash and collar, and leaves her at a kennel while he goes away to continue his life. The kennel soon transforms into the Mitchell home, and Joan sees herself as a lifelong inmate there. Worse, when she confronts herself in the mirror, she sees her reflection as a withered, decrepit hag. Joan awakens from this dream, and tells her therapist about it. He informs her that the only person isolating and imprisoning Joan is Joan herself.

One night, Jack and Joan go to a party at their friend Larry's house, and Joan finds herself secretly tantalized when she learns of a new neighbor who claims to be a witch. A few days later, Joan and her friend Shirley go to visit the witch, Marion. Shirley sits for a tarot card reading, and Marion's fortune-telling abilities prove uncannily accurate about the failure of Shirley's romance with her husband, Larry. The cards also reveal that Shirley has been having a secret affair with a man named David. All the while, Joan finds herself attracted to the world of the occult, though she is appalled it has become a trendy hobby for local WASPs and disillusioned wives.

On returning home, Joan meets her daughter Nikki's boyfriend, a sociology teaching assistant named Greg. Almost immediately, Joan is attracted to Greg, but is furious when he gets Shirley drunk on martinis and tricks her into believing that she has been smoking marijuana. Afterwards, Greg apologizes to Joan for the game but reminds her that she was complicit in the con. Later, Joan overhears Nikki and Greg making love and is driven to physical distraction by it. Nikki is upset that her mother has listened in on this intimate moment and leaves the house with all of her belongings. Making matters worse, Jack blames Joan for the situation, and slaps her across the face for failing to stop Nikki's deflowering in their very own house.

Though questioned by the police about Nikki's abrupt departure, Joan protects Greg. Then she dismisses her maid so she can be alone in the house while Jack goes away on a business trip. Excited, Joan visits Greg at the college and he tells her he is available. Joan feigns disinterest, unable to commit adultery, and returns home—frustrated. That night, Joan detects an intruder outside the house. A masked madman with a knife breaks into the Mitchell home and sexually assaults Joan ... but it is only a nightmare. This strange vision is the impetus Joan needs to explore her dark side. Alone in her house, she purchases the necessary books and materials to become a witch. Joan throws herself into her witchcraft, and conducts a spell to bring Greg to her. He accommodates, and they make passionate love. Later, Joan sees

Marion and asks to become a member of her coven.

All the while, Joan continues to have disturbing dreams in which a masked man breaks into the house and attacks her. She also continues to have sexual escapades with Greg. She even informs him that she's a witch, and that her powers brought him to her bed. He refuses to believe in superstitious nonsense and they have a falling out. Later, Joan conjures another spell, invoking a dark "lord."

As she sleeps that night, Joan hears an intruder for real and, armed with a shotgun, shoots him dead. In reality, there was no intruder, only Jack returning home early from his business trip. Joan is found innocent of murder, and now continues her life as a single woman. At the local parties, a black clad Joan now introduces herself to others as a witch.

COMMENTARY: George Romero is one of the genre's greats, no doubt. *Night of the Living Dead* (1968) was arguably the most influential and oft-imitated horror film of the 1960s (with the possible exceptions of *Psycho* [1960] and *Rosemary's Baby* [1968]). His work in the early '70s (*Jack's Wife, The Crazies*) is not usually as highly regarded as his "zombie" pictures, like *Dawn of the Dead* [1979] or his camp treat, *Creepshow* (1981), yet in many ways these efforts remain more interesting. Take *Jack's Wife*, for instance. It is written, directed, and perhaps most importantly, filmed and edited by Romero. He wears many hats here, and thus the film can be seen as a more accurate and concentrated (rather than diffuse) reflection of his own personal ethos. The film is very good, though overlong, and benefits enormously from Romero's visual sense and keen understanding of film editing.

Jack's Wife opens with an informative, thematically rich dream sequence. Joan is seen on a wooded trail, walking well behind her husband as he reads a newspaper, oblivious. He is unaware that he is snapping branches in her face. The inference is obviously that he is hurting his wife by not paying attention to her. This is important because the film does not see Jack as a brutal or ritual abuser of woman (though he does strike Joan at one point in the film). Instead, he is seen as being a rather average middle class husband, and his crime is in neglecting Joan, and not seeing her as a person.

The wooded trail itself seems to represent the path of Joan's life, with things lost on the trail: a baby that died, *et al.* This sequence supplies much detail, and reveals much about Joan's vision of her life, but it is a bit long, and in parts obvious. Indeed, this is the primary fault of most early Romero films: he carries on with good scenes too long, thereby lessening their impact. After the wooded trail, the same dream sequence continues, with Joan leashed and caged like a dog. Then it continues even further, depicting Joan's home as a kind of nursing home/prison. The trail sequence is strong enough on its own without two further variations defining Joan's sense of irrelevance. Nonetheless, the scene is splendidly edited and well conceived.

Romero's central arguments in the film are twofold. The first is that the supernatural is only the latest fad for a bored suburban community. It actually has no power unless given power. "Voodoo only works because you believe it works. Your mind does the work," one character acknowledges in the film. This is a common Romero conceit, repeated in *Martin*, the story of a boy who fancies himself a supernatural vampire but is in fact just a lonely, sick kid. Thus, everything that occurs in *Jack's Wife* can be interpreted two ways. Either Joan is a witch summoning the supernatural, or she believes she is a witch summoning the supernatural. The illusion of the supernatural gives Joan the personal confidence to call Greg, but is there really a dark power at work outside Joan? Probably not, but the film walks a fine line. Religion (including the wiccan way) is a convenient scapegoat when you want to

blame the Devil for your own misdeeds, but is also, inevitably, empowering to those who truly believe. The ambiguity surrounding Joan's witchcraft is fascinating, but is probably less than thrilling to the average horror fan, who wants "evil" to be tangible, and real. As usual, Romero confounds those expectations, making a balanced, interesting, and intelligent film instead of a simple genre one.

The second argument in the film is actually about suburbia more than it is about female power (or imprisonment). Romero sees it as a realm of boredom, no matter what. Boredom can result in infidelity, drug-use, or even … witchcraft. Joan is something of a hypocrite. Like Greg, she claims to want people to be honest, to confront the substance of their life. Yet Joan is obsessed with appearances. Several times in the film she confronts her own reflection in the mirror, and it shows her prematurely aged. It is that fear that she is unfulfilled and getting older that informs her choice to become a witch. She is horrified that many see witchcraft as a fad, but she jumps on board the trend anyway. *Jack's Wife* is about the image of things, of witchcraft, of sex, and of marriage, and how people manipulate those images to create an outward image of oneself for the community. Yes, Joan is bored and unhappy, but aren't we all responsible for our own boredom to some degree? Witchcraft is merely the filter through which Joan finds her suburban existence tolerable.

In fact, some of the final images of the film imply that Joan has merely traded one trap for another. In her coven ritual, a red rope is put around her neck, and she is dragged by it, as if on a leash. This sequence echoes the opening dream sequence, in which Jack leads Joan around on a leash. Yet in this case, despite the continued enslavement, Joan finds the bondage acceptable.

Also, the film closes with an echo of another early scene. Near the start of the picture, Joan is identified as "Jack's wife." At the end of the picture, she identifies herself as a "witch." The label has changed, but has anything else? She still seeks attention in either regard and is still living in a society that does not value her. As long as Joan lacks the self-confidence to break free of the establishment mind-set for women that they should marry, have babies, stay at home, and be happy, she will be enslaved.

Jack's Wife is really only a feminist picture in the sense that it acknowledges that women are treated as subservient in affluent, middle-class America. Joan's therapist tells Joan that only she can imprison herself, but the audience senses immediately that his comments are off the mark. As Romero's camera follows her from one emotionally empty task to another (a grocery trip, a stop at the dry cleaners), viewers realize the deck has been stacked against her. It is harder for her to find emotional fulfillment because her chores are repetitive and meaningless and her mate values her only for her ability to take care of them — not for any intrinsic value she brings to their pairing.

As one might guess from this review, *Jack's Wife* is a rich, meaningful, and even important film. George Romero handles it well, and the movie is a strong glimpse of one woman's quest for self-relevance in a society that makes her second to men. Yet, the film is overlong, and Romero overfilms scenes. The same points can be made with a degree of brevity. Though Romero is nothing less than a genius at forging meaning through editing, he lacks the discipline to "cut" his work down to an efficient length.

Thus *Jack's Wife* feels bloated. There are lots of good things in it, but they sometimes come too far apart. The art in editing films is push the good stuff as close together as possible, while removing the bad stuff in between. It is clear that Romero is still struggling with that process here. Also, some technical credits are barely adequate. The film's sound is not mixed right, and background noises are too loud. This may sound like nit-picking, but it is a real flaw when so much of the film depends on smart dialogue. The audience strains to hear Romero's witty words, instead of synthesizing their meaning and importance.

The stereotypical "horror" aspects of *Jack's Wife* really play second fiddle to the character study, but that's fine. When Romero does need to mine the imagery of nightmares, he is as adept as ever. When an intruder breaks into Joan's house and tries to rape her, Romero's frenetic cutting makes it memorable, and quite frightening. Even the look of the attacker, a masked, willowy creature in black, is unnerving.

Made on an exceedingly low budget, *Jack's Wife* is really worth seeking out. It is not Romero's best work, but it is a critical juncture between *Night of the Living Dead* and *Martin*. It shows consistency with his *oeuvre*, and has a lot on its mind. If one is into cerebral horror, there are few more interesting genre pictures.

Let's Scare Jessica to Death (1971) ★ ★ ★ ½

Critical Reception

"With the exception of Zohra Lampert's subtle and knowledgeable performance, no one in the cast has enough substance even to be considered humanoid. And after the first reel, the vampires seem to have lost their bite."— Stanley Kanfer, *Time:* "Batgirl," September 20, 1971, page 74.

"Director John Hancock is to be congratulated for a multi-layered horror film with frightening visuals. There isn't much logic to the story, yet the overall effect is unsettling ... the film has a dream-like quality...."— John Stanley, *Creature Features Strikes Again*, 1994, page 226.

"...it tends to lose much sense of what kind of movie it is.... Among the actors only Miss Lampert develops a characterization. And although she is beautiful and as always, breathlessly appealing, she projects a personality too forcefully complex for a role that requires only sympathetic passivity...."—Roger Greenspun, *New York Times*: "Hippie Vampire," August 28, 1971, page 15.

Cast & Crew

CAST: Zohra Lampert (Jessica); Barton Heyman (Duncan); Kevin O'Connor (Woody); Gretchen Corbett (Girl); Alan Manson (Dorker); Mariclare Costello (Emily).

CREW: Paramount Pictures Presents *Let's Scare Jessica to Death. Directed by:* John Hancock. *Produced by:* Charles B. Moss, Jr. *Film Editor:* Murray Solomon. *Director of Photography:* Bob Baldwin. *Music:* Orville Stoeber. *Co-Producer:* William Badalato. *Written by:* Ralph Rose, Norman Jonas. *Assistant Editor:* Ginny Katz. *Assistant Camera:* Sal Guida. *Set Decorator:* Norman Kenneson. *Costume Designer:* Mariette Pinchart. *Gaffer:* Myron Odeguard. *Continuity:* Randa Haines. *Make-up:* Irvin Carlton. *Grip:* Melvin Noped. *Production Assistant:* Judith Spangler, Joanne Michels, Barbara Reynolds. *Sound:* Joe Ryan. *Electronic Music:* Walter Sean. *Color:* Deluxe. *M.P.A.A. Rating:* R. *Running Time:* 89 minutes.

SYNOPSIS: After recovering from a nervous breakdown, Jessica decides to start over. With her husband Duncan and their friend, Woody, in tow, Jessica embarks on a trip to rural Connecticut. En route to their new home, Jessica stops at a cemetery to take rubbings of two gravestones. There, she sees a woman in a pale dress beckoning her, and wonders if she has regained her sanity at all. After a ferry ride to a secluded island, Jess and her fellow travelers arrive at their new home—the old Bishop place. Again, Jessica questions her sanity when she imagines that someone is sitting in a rocking chair on the front porch.

Once inside the house, Duncan and Woody share Jessica's concern. They all spot a woman upstairs. There, they meet the beautiful Emily, a young "traveler" who has

been squatting at the remote Connecticut home. Jessica takes a liking to Emily and asks her to spend the night, even though it is clear that Duncan is attracted to her. After dinner, the "groovy" Emily suggests a séance, and the others agree. Emily calls upon all those who have died in the house to give a sign of their presence. Terrified, Jessica soon hears whispers in the house. Later, while she combs the old attic for antiques, Jessica senses a dark shadow nearby. Even more disturbing, while out in the cove for a swim, Jessica feels a hand try to pull her down to the bottom, calling her name.

The next day, Jessica and Duncan head to the nearby town to sell off the antiques they have gathered. They find the odd local people—all strange old men—distinctly unfriendly. A bit further down the road Jessica and Duncan meet Dorker, the proprietor of an antique shop. He is hesitant to buy their goods because he knows they came from the old Bishop homestead. Apparently, there is a great deal of local superstition about the home now owned by Jessica and Duncan. In 1880, Abigail Bishop drowned in the cove on the eve of her wedding. Now myth suggests that Abigail still lives, and that she roams the idyllic countryside as some kind of vampire. Jessica is terrified by this story, especially because she found a wedding dress and a very sharp knife stowed away safely in a trunk in her attic...

On another day, Jessica takes a walk in the country, and is shocked to discover Dorker's dead body near a creek. Unfortunately, she is the only person who sees the corpse, and Emily, Duncan and Woody again suspect that she has not recovered from her nervous breakdown. Even weirder, Jessica again runs into the mute girl in the white dress, the one she saw at the graveyard. This girl tries to warn Jessica about something before she runs away.

Fearing the worst about his wife, Duncan suggests it may be time to return home to New York City. Jessica and Duncan then quarrel, and spend the night sleeping apart. In the middle of the night, Emily seduces Duncan and makes love to him. The following morning, Jessica finds that her pet mole has been murdered.

Upset, Jessica goes off by herself. In the attic, she sees a framed picture of the Bishop family, and notices that Abigail is a dead ringer for Emily. Emily brushes aside the resemblance, and suggests that Jessica go swimming in the cove with her. There, Emily tries to kill Jessica. Terrified, Jessica realizes that Emily is Abigail. Abigail chases Jessica to the house, where Jessica hides for many hours, awaiting Duncan's return from town. Meanwhile, Abigail seduces Woody too.

After some time, Jessica works up the courage to flee the house. She runs to town, but the men there all have strange wounds on their necks, and are resolutely unhelpful. When Jessica returns home, Duncan reappears. He takes her to bed, comforting her. As they prepare to make love, Jessica realizes that her husband bears the same strange slash-mark on his neck. When Jessica looks up from her bed, she sees all the old men of the town — a mob — staring at her. And, Abigail is there too. Abigail slices Jessica's neck, and starts to drink her blood. Fleeing the community of vampires, Jessica seeks Woody only to find him dead, drained of blood. Desperate, Jessica hops into a rowboat and escapes from the island of vampires. On the shore, Abigail and her army of servants watch her coldly.

Crying in a rowboat, Jessica wonders if she is really, truly insane, of if the strange events she has witnessed could possibly be true...

COMMENTARY: The bottom line is that horror movies are supposed to be scary. But how movies reach that common denomina-

tor is a matter of debate. In Hollywood today, many executives think CGI effects can scare the audience (witness the tepid remakes of *The Haunting* [1999] or *House on Haunted Hill* [1999]). Contrarily, Alfred Hitchcock believed that he could terrify audiences with misdirection, surprise, and shock (*à la Psycho*). *The Exorcist* (1973) worked so splendidly because William Friedkin adopted an almost documentary-style approach to the horrific material, making it feel "real" to involved audiences. Already in this text, it has been noted how lighting (*Daughters of Darkness*), or clever editing (*Jack's Wife*) can contribute to a successful, frightening film too.

But there is another way to scare. It is more difficult, and ultimately more subjective, as it involves the auspices of texture, feeling and mood. *Let's Scare Jessica to Death* may be one of the best examples of this very complex approach. The film's story makes little sense if taken as a whole; there are few dramatic "action" scenes (save for one exquisite "jolt" early on), and even fewer special effects. Yet the film is, in the best sense of the word, creepy. It is a scary little film that gets under your nerves and puts you ill at ease almost instantly.

How is this mood achieved? It's not easy to dissect it, frankly. One might make mention of the brilliant cinematography, for one thing. The film is hazy at times, like a dream, and it is filled with gothic images. The beautiful opening shot reveals a fog settling over the still waters of a cove. The sun is orange and low in the apricot sky, forecasting night, and a sad woman (Jessica) sits alone in a canoe, a post-modern Lady of Shallotte. The villain is a porcelain woman in flowing white dress, a contemporary Rappaccini's daughter, who brings terror and death to anyone who gets too close.

On a simple level, Jessica's abandoned old house is an imposing bit of architecture, well filmed from multiple low angles to indicate menace. These visuals play on old dreads, but effective ones, and *Let's Scare Jessica to Death* is a lovely and even poetic horror film in a visual sense.

John Hancock has also taken special care to "hint" at rather than definitively show his most horrific moments. That's another trick for moody horror movies. Consider for a moment the impact of *The Blair Witch Project*. Almost nothing horrific is shown, but the cumulative effect of seeing the witch's icons and figures (which she leaves behind), the uncertainty of being lost, and the paranoia of the kids lost in the woods, combine to create a mood of abject terror. *Let's Scare Jessica to Death* selects a similar method. There's an unsettling moment in an attic when a shadowy figure shifts (in the foreground) while Jessica is seen in the background. This dark blur is never seen clearly. It is visible merely as black movement. What is it? Who is it? We don't know, but we're unnerved by its presence.

Similarly, the old men of the town are often referred to as vampires, as is Abigail, but these aren't the garden-variety cape-and-fangs sort. They're more like a mob of undead zombies, moving slowly, strangely gnarled in their old age, and enigmatic in their purpose. Had Hancock desired to do so, he could have provided clarity about these specters, their nature, and their history. Instead, like the blur in the attic, he merely hints at what they are. A tried and true method of scaring audiences is to remove clarity from reality's equation. The audience starts to wonder, along with Jessica, if it has really seen or understood what is occurring.

Let's Scare Jessica to Death's macabre touches flow throughout the film. In particular, the film is obsessed with images of death. Jessica and her friends drive to her new life in Connecticut in a hearse, a vehicle of the dead. Jessica's hobby, gravestone rubbings, also brings to light a connection to death as she reads grave inscriptions that speak of life and joy, and decay. Hancock so carefully forges his atmosphere of fear that even the grave rubbings, blowing on a wall by night, seem terrifying. With silences and intervals of noise (like squawking chickens in a coop!), Hancock keeps the viewer unbalanced. It's a spooky, spooky film.

Then there's another trick: *whispering.* Everybody whispers in this film. Jessica calls upon the spirits of the dead to talk to her, and odd, evil whispering surrounds her. Many of Jessica's own interior monologues (*"look at the blood, Jessica, look at the blood!"*) are whispered. If anyone seriously doubts that whispering is an effective way to raise goosebumps, this author suggests they check out *The Sixth Sense* (1999) as evidence. There is something immediate, impassioned and troubling about the mode of the whisper. It seems to be directed at the audience, as if it is a secret the viewer shouldn't know. Whatever the reason of its effectiveness, it adds to the general feeling of unease generated by this film.

Those seeking a linear, sensible horror show will no doubt find *Let's Scare Jessica to Death* a bit disappointing. It does not subscribe to any sense of reality most viewers are familiar with. Yet, and this is important, its decision to be inscrutable, enigmatic, and ambivalent echoes the film's central theme: Jessica's uncertain mental state. It's almost as if this film is seen through Jessica's eyes (an effect heightened by her frequent voice-overs). We might very well be in the mind of a crazy woman … or a woman terrorized by something truly and deeply evil. It isn't clear, but it doesn't need to be. Hancock's camera sees as if through Jessica's (possibly) mad eyes and the result is a very disturbing film.

New England Gothic — that's the mood of *Let's Scare Jessica to Death*. There's an ancient evil, a town with a dark secret, a struggle with sanity, and a coven of blood-thirsty men. What else could one want out of a horror movie? Director Hancock sets the mood, and viewers get to revel in it for 89 hypnotic minutes. This reviewer, for one, will take mood over CGI any day.

The Man Who Haunted Himself

Cast and Crew

CAST: Roger Moore (Pelham); Hildegard Neil (Eve); Alastair Mackenzie (Michael); Hugh Mackenzie (James); Thorley Walters (Bellamy); Anton Rodgers (Alexander); Olga Georges-Picot (Julie); Freddie Jones (Psychiatrist).

CREW: *Directed by:* Basil Dearden. *Written by:* Basil Dearden and Michael Ralph. *Music:* Michael Lewis. *Produced by:* Michael Ralph. *M.P.A.A. Rating:* PG. *Running Time:* 94 minutes.

DETAILS: A pre–Bond Roger Moore headlines in this British-made thriller about a man who learns he as an exact duplicate, a Doppelgänger. Moore is supported ably by the fetching Hildegard Neil, but this is one bizarre movie.

The Mephisto Waltz (1971) ⋆ ⋆ ½

Critical Reception

"*Waltz* stands on its own as a sleek and scary piece of movie necromancy... Director Paul Wendkos has ... taken ... his title ... too literally. He seizes every available opportunity to dance his camera around, photographing from acrobatic angles and utilizing a full spectrum of weird color filters ... he succeeds in achieving a good sense of clammy terror ... spooky enough to make you wonder just a little the next time you attend a piano recital."— Jay Cocks, *Time:* "Spook The Piano Player," May 3, 1971 page 89.

"...the year's most expensively mounted 'horror film' and it will probably be the year's most corrupt one. For its story ... not only centers upon satanism but also involves incest. Fortunately, it doesn't make any sense."— Eunice Sinkler, *Films in Review*, Volume XXII, May 1971, page 313.

"...a miserably infantile botch of occult suspense.... The picture ... is terrible. Style and subtlety might have done the trick.... But this shrill, heavy-handed exercise only makes us appreciate *Rosemary's Baby* all over again."— Howard Thompson, *New York Times*, April 10, 1971.

"...generates an effective atmosphere of evil and makes a satisfying, eerie thriller.... Wendkos mistakes a frenetic camera for genuine style."— Alan Frank, *The Horror Film Handbook*, 1982, page 96.

Cast & Credits

CAST: Alan Alda (Myles Clarkson); Jacqueline Bisset (Paula Clarkson); Barbara Perkins (Roxanne DeLancey); Brad Dillman (Bill Delancey); William Windom (Dr. West); Kathleen Widdoes (Maggie West); Pamelyn Ferdin (Abby Clarkson); Curt Jurgens (Duncan Ely); Curt Lowens, Gregory Morton, Janee Michelle, Illyan Chauvin, Khigh Dhilegh, Alberto Morin, Barry Kroeger, Terence Scammell.

CREW: 20th Century–Fox Presents a Quinn Martin Production, *The Mephisto Waltz. Music:* Jerry Goldsmith. *The Mephisto Waltz by Liszt performed by:* Jakob Gimpel. *Costumes:* Moss Mabry. *Director of Photography:* William W. Spencer. *Art Direction:* Richard Y. Haman. *Film Editor:* Richard Brockway. *Set Decorator:* Walter M. Scott, Raphael Bretton. *Property Master:*

Sidney Greenwood. *Special Photographic Effects:* Howard A. Anderson Co. *Main Title:* Phill Norman. *Unit Production Manager:* William Eckhardt. *Assistant Director:* David Hall. *Orchestration:* Arthur Morton. *Camera Operator:* Gene Evans. *Sound Supervisor:* John A. Bonner. *Sound Mixer:* Don J. Bassman. *Makeup Supervisor:* Joe DiBella. *Hairstylist:* Pat Abbott. *Color:* DeLuxe. *Associate Producer:* Arthur Fellows. *Screenplay:* Ben Maddow. *Based on the Novel by:* Fred Mustard Stewart. *Produced by:* Quinn Martin. *Directed by:* Paul Wendkos. Produced by QM Productions. Released by 20th Century–Fox. *M.P.A.A. Rating:* R. *Running Time:* 109 minutes.

SYNOPSIS: The famous (and arrogant) pianist Duncan Ely summons writer and amateur musician Myles Clarkson to his palatial home to grant him an interview. The aged Ely lives with his beautiful daughter, Roxanne, and immediately finds himself fascinated with Myles … particularly his "pianist's" hands. After Roxanne affirms that she also approves of Myles, Duncan's haughty tone softens and he takes the impressed Clarkson under his wing. Duncan encourages him to give up writing and return to his first love, the piano, despite the fact Myles was not well received by the critics after his debut concert.

Clarkson's beautiful wife, Paula, instantly dislikes the eccentric old Ely, as well as the seductive Roxanne. She also finds herself less than thrilled when compelled by Myles to attend Duncan's raucous New Year's Eve party. The party turns out to be a wild bacchanalia, and Paula seeks solace from the noise and debauched activity in Duncan's private study. There, she finds evidence (a spell book and a strange vial of blue liquid) that Duncan is actually a devil worshiper.

Over Paula's objections, Myles spends increasingly more time with Ely and Roxanne. Myles confides to Paula that Duncan is dying of leukemia, and Paula softens her stance against the older man for a time. One night, Myles agrees to sit for Roxanne, an aspiring artist, and she makes a plaster life-mask of the young musician to hang on the wall in Duncan's study. Though Myles is unaware of it, this mask is a crucial piece of a diabolical satanic ritual. As Duncan lies dying in his bed of disease, Roxanne conducts a ritual which implants the old man's immortal soul into Myles' young, healthy body … presumably sending Clarkson's soul to some kind of oblivion or Hell. After Duncan's physical body has expired, the "transplanted" Ely starts to live a new life inside Myles.

Ely's will bequeaths the Clarksons one hundred thousand dollars as well as a Steinway piano. And, Ely leaves his murderous dog, Robin, to Paula's daughter, Abby. Swayed by the money, and Myles' new amorous qualities, Paula fails to notice at first that her husband has changed. However, she grows increasingly unhappy and jealous when Myles continues to spend time with Roxanne. One day, Paula hears Myles playing the piano and is amazed that he is suddenly a brilliant musician … every bit the equal of Duncan Ely. Also impressed, Roxanne arranges for Myles to take over Duncan's concert schedule.

Paula finds herself increasingly drawn to Myles, astounded by his newfound sexual prowess and appetites. She confides in a friend, Maggie, that he has the appetite of three men, and that she feels unfaithful making love to him because he is so different … and so good. Even as Paula enjoys this "perk" of marriage, she experiences a terrible nightmare in which Ely kills her daughter Abby, telling Paula that it is all part of the bargain. When Paula awakens from the terrible dream, she finds that Abby really is sick. Myles and Paula rush Abby to the hospital, but the young girl dies soon after their arrival there. Paula now believes that Roxanne and Duncan somehow made a bargain with the Devil to steal Myles' body. In return, she thinks, they had to give the Devil a prize: Abby's life. Terrified, Paula seeks a rendezvous with Roxanne's ex-husband, an attorney named Delancey. He affirms that Duncan and Roxanne are devil worshipers, but does not believe they have any real powers beyond those of suggestion. Before long, Delancey dies too (with a blotch of mysterious blue fluid on his head) and Paula becomes convinced that she will be the next victim.

When Paula narrowly survives a car accident, she is spurred to action. While Myles is in San Francisco at a concert with Roxanne, Paula visits the Ely estate and steals the devil's prayer book and special blue oil used for a satanic ritual. Becoming a Satanist herself, Paula arranges for a switcheroo that will bring her new, and wonderful, lover, Duncan, back to her forever. Embracing evil, Paula initiates the ritual, and switches bodies with Roxanne. Roxanne's soul is cast to oblivion in Paula's vacated corpse, and now Paula, alive in Roxanne's body, is free to enjoy the wonderful sexual pleasures dispensed by Duncan.

COMMENTARY: Here's a movie that starts ambitiously as a meditation on old age and creative failure, but then ends off-message, focusing on one woman's quest for good sex at the expense of her daughter's life and her husband's soul. The final act seems not only exploitative, but out of character, for star Jacqueline Bisset had hitherto given a solid, believable performance as a woman in the center of a satanic conspiracy. Thus *The Mephisto Waltz* is an engaging, well-directed, competently acted horror film that, simply put, springs a leak in the final act.

The opening sections of the film are powerful, interesting, and a metaphor for a situation many young artists, whether musicians, writers or painters, have faced. Specifically, the movie focuses on a creative genius (Duncan Ely) who covets his success as an artist (a pianist). Yet, he is dying, so he steals the thunder of the next generation—literally. He possesses the body of Clarkson, basically stealing Clarkson's talents. This is not an uncommon situation in Hollywood (or anywhere where creativity is at a premium, truthfully). The old power, fortified by a powerful reputation, absconds with the talents of the younger generation, which is trying to establish itself and is eager to please. *The Mephisto Waltz* takes that concept literally, with the old talent literally stealing the life of the young talent, yet the metaphor is plain. The old don't want to give up their grip on fame or fortune, and so resort to theft to remain in the public eye. As for the young, they are so desperate to do important work, to be known, that they settle for apprenticeships that don't always favor their best long-term interests. It's a great relationship to explore in a horror movie.

Wendkos' film explores this conceit with some really nice visual touches. Hands seem to be a leitmotif, as images of hands are repeated throughout the film. During the opening credits, disembodied hands pop off a candle flame, and the camera examines them. Later, Ely notes of Clarkson that "hands like" his are "one in a hundred thousand." For a pianist, hands are the focal point of talent, and *The Mephisto Waltz* obsesses on them. Hands, also, play a part in sexual satisfaction no doubt, and the film makes quite clear that Ely has the hands of an artist in more ways than one. The repetition of "hand" imagery ties much of the film together, as does the piano music, which underscores various important moments.

The "horror" of the film is also handled well. During the satanic ritual which robs Clarkson of life, Wendkos' camera adopts a high angle, and the edges of the frame are soft, blurred, as if a third party (possibly devilish) is watching it all dispassionately from a distance ... not quite inside our reality. Though all films come to audiences from a third-person perspective, this sequence, this series of shots, feels as if events are being watched from the edge of existence, through eyes not quite our own. It is a solid choice, and well executed.

Even scene transitions in *The Mephisto Waltz* are powerfully handled. The film is erotically charged, and scene transitions forge a link between sex and darkness. Miles and Paula make love ... and then the film cuts to that creepy party at the Ely estate. Paula and Miles make love, and then the film cuts to a funeral, and so on. *The Mephisto Waltz* seems to be linking sex and death in a visual fashion.

The problem is that Alda and Bisset are not just two randy lovers screwing around. The film takes special pains to establish them as a couple in love. In their first scene together they are in bed and the dialogue establishes their intimacy through romantic banter. Alda is especially effective in these early scenes, which establish a quirky, attractive personality with very little screentime. Bisset too creates an endearing individual who is concerned for her husband. They are obviously in love, and they adore their child, Abby. Yet, for the final act of the film to work, one must believe that Paula would willingly accept the death of her daughter and husband just so she can continue to experience good sex with Ely. That's just too hard to swallow. Had the film established Bisset's character as a libidinous, unfaithful wife given to sexual infidelity, one might understand her willingness to accept evil into her life for such passion.

The Mephisto Waltz takes a decidedly wrong turn when it loses track of its core relationship: that between Paula and her husband. "I want Miles ... whoever he ... just once more." Bisset's character enthuses, blown over by Ely's sexual prowess. In fact, he is so good in bed that Paula becomes a Satanist, and switches bodies with Roxanne just to get him. That decision is way out of character with the Paula of the rest of the film, and leaves one shocked. It's an ending out of leftfield. In a sense, Wendkos is sabotaged by his performers: they do such a good job of creating intimacy on screen that one never believes that Paula would give up her child and her husband (and her religious convictions, and her very soul) for terrific sex. Asking the audience to accept that unbelievable development is worse than asking it to believe in body switches, devilish dogs, and any other horror aspect of the script. This is so stylish, so interesting a film that one can merely gasp at the wrong turn it takes at its denouement. *The Mephisto Waltz* could hit some great notes, but the script has a tin ear.

Night of Dark Shadows (1971) *

Critical Reception

"...the script ... depends a good deal on visual effects that aren't particularly effective.... Dan Curtis ... hasn't given his cast much to work with.... The attraction of this dour adventure is Lyndhurst, the ... mansion ... where the film was shot.... The somber story, ... however, is strictly for the low rent district."— A. H. Weiler, *New York Times*, October 14, 1971.

Cast & Crew

CAST: David Selby (Quentin Collins/Charles Collins); Grayson Hall (Carlotta Drake/Sarah Castle); Lara Parker (Angelique Collins); John Karlen (Alex Jenkins); Nancy Barrett (Clair Jenkins); James Storm (Gerard Styles); Thayer David (Reverend Strack); Christopher Pennock (Gabriel Collins); Diana Millay (Laura Collins); Kate Jackson (Tracy Collins); Monica Rich (Young Sarah Castle); Clarice Blackburn (Mrs. Castle).

CREW: Metro-Goldwyn Mayer Presents a Dan Curtis Production, *Night of Dark Shadows*. *Assistant Director:* Stanley Panesoff. *Assistant Producer:* Robert Singer. *Director of Photography:* Richard Shore. *Production Supervisor and Associate Producer:* George Goodman. *Music*

Composed and Conducted by: Robert Cobert. *Screenplay:* Sam Hall. *Story:* Sam Hall and Dan Curtis. *Produced and Directed by:* Dan Curtis. *Film Editor:* Charles Goldsmith. *Assistant Editor:* Aviva Slesin. *Camera Operator:* Ronald Lautore. *Casting:* Linda Otto. *Production Assistant:* William Schwartz. *Sound:* John Bolz, Al Gramaglia. *Wardrobe Designer:* Domingo Rodriguez. *Make-up:* Reginald Tackley. *Hair dresser:* Edith Tilles. *Stunt Coordinator:* Alex Stevens. *Titles:* The Optical House. *Technical Adviser:* Hans Holzer. *M.P.A.A. Rating:* PG. *Running Time:* 95 minutes.

———————————

SYNOPSIS: Quentin Collins and his wife Tracy move into the abandoned Collinswood Estate in Collins Port, Maine. There, they meet the odd housekeeper, Carlotta Drake, who seems to know more about the home's history than she lets on. Once moved in, Quentin, a painter, almost immediately starts to dream about a beautiful blonde woman named Angelique Collins, who was hanged as a witch 150 years ago and was a former tenant of the estate. While riding his horse on the land, Quentin experiences a vision of Angelique's funeral and sees a little girl, Sarah Castle, peering out of the Collinswood house windows.

Friends of Tracy and Quentin, Clair and Alex Jenkins, come to visit Collinsport and Quentin reveals that he has been imagining things since his arrival. Later, he experiences a strong sense of *déjà vu* when he visits the Tower Room, a painting studio at the top of the house. In his new studio, Quentin unearths a painting of Angelique and imagines that he is Charles Collins, a painter who had a lustful affair with the witch in centuries past. Consumed with this vision, Quentin beats up the groundskeeper, Gerard, whom he somehow mistakes for the brother of Charles and the very man responsible for Angelique's death so many years ago.

The next day, Alex Jenkins spots a mysterious woman when patrolling the grounds, and is nearly killed by falling glass panes in an old greenhouse. At the same time, Quentin decides not to paint in the Tower Room, feeling that it may be responsible for his odd behavior. This decision irritates Carlotta Drake, who claims that she is the reincarnation of Sarah Castle, the little girl from a century and a half ago who has an eternal love and regard for Angelique. Worse, Carlotta expresses the belief that Quentin is the reincarnation of Charles and that Angelique has been waiting for him. A witch during her life, Angelique is powerful even in death, and Carlotta warns Quentin that Tracy should leave the house lest she face Angelique's wrath. Quentin ignores the advice and remains in the home with Tracy. He resumes work in the Tower Room and is soon overcome by the personality of Charles Collins.

Tracy visits Quentin's painting studio while he is away in town and discovers his newest painting—a portrait of Quentin bringing a sacrifice in the form of a dead Tracy to a lounging Angelique. Meanwhile, Alex and Clair have uncovered another painting that reveals Quentin as a dead-ringer for Charles Collins. They race to save Tracy and Quentin, but find that Quentin has tried to drown Tracy in the abandoned pool house. Tracy survives the encounter, and Quentin returns to normality. Then, all hell breaks loose as the groundskeeper, Gerard, tries to kill Tracy and Quentin for some wrong committed in a past life. Gerard is killed in hand-to-hand battle, and Quentin realizes that Angelique will always be a part of his spirit unless he kills Carlotta, who keeps the evil ghost alive with her undying "love." Carlotta jumps from the roof of the Collinswood estate rather than face capture, and dies.

Alex, Clair, Tracy and Quentin decide to flee Collinswood, but Angelique's spirit is still a presence to be reckoned with. When Quentin goes inside the haunted home to gather his painting supplies, a dark figure strikes again.

———————————

COMMENTARY: One might think it would be difficult to create a less interesting film than 1970's *House of Dark Shadows*, which recycled the "Barnabas" plot of the famous TV soap opera. One would be wrong. The sequel to that film, *Night of Dark Shadows*, is a slow-paced, badly written regurgitation of the program's lesser material, the "B" storyline. Yet, oddly, this sub-par material, once an integral part of Barnabas's story, makes nary a mention of that vampire. It is a stand-alone adventure that makes only a modicum of sense, and seems to have no real connection to the TV series.

The plot of *Night of Dark Shadows* consists of Quentin Collins' discovery of a previous life via dreams and visions. These phantasms are told without thrills or jolts, and are pretty repetitive. Damningly, the dreams always convey relevant information at exactly the right time. In fact, all these characters, from Quentin to Carlotta Drake, remember an awful lot as reincarnated souls, so much so that it is hard to understand why their souls returned with "new" names in the next life at all. As for Carlotta, she's that hoary cliché, the strange housekeeper, but even worse she exists in this film solely as a convenient mouthpiece for exposition. Through a reincarnated Sarah Castle, she remembers things precisely enough to explain the plot to a befuddled Quentin.

Actually, all the characters are pretty weak, at the whim of a confusing story. Quentin seems to be bipolar, insisting one moment that he loves Tracy, while at the next moment trying to kill her. There is no link or transition between these two approaches, and the result is distancing. The audience never feels it knows Quentin, and thus does not really care about his plight. The supernatural mechanisms that apparently seize control of him remain vague, and it is impossible to tell when he is himself, or when he is possessed. Kate Jackson's Tracy isn't delineated in terms much better. She is a submissive character that lets Quentin's strange behavior go unquestioned for far too long. The fallacy of haunted house movies is that the characters must remain in the house, the place of danger, beyond all reason and logic. That is nowhere more obvious than in *Night of Dark Shadows*. It is blatantly obvious to everybody that Tracy and Quentin just need to get in their car and drive away … but they never do.

And Gerard the groundskeeper? He's another character in service of a bad plot. He goes crazy at the right time to facilitate two necessary action scenes (a car chase and a fist fight). Who is he? Why is he nuts? Who knows! He's there only to present a physical conflict, because the film could not, apparently, afford a climax featuring a ghost.

Which brings us to Angelique. In the TV series, she was the witch who damned Barnabas to his life of vampirism. He had scorned her, and that was her revenge. None of that information appears in *Night of Dark Shadows,* and Angelique is just a ghost haunting a house with little rhyme or reason. She is not made terrifying by the low-tech, primitive opticals the film employs, and is hardly interesting at all. Fans of the TV series should have been outraged.

Night of Dark Shadows is a boring movie, with a few effective moments. The scene in the dilapidated greenhouse, buffeted by wind, works rather well. The use of Lyndhurst as a Gothic mansion is inspired. And, the climactic car chase is shot ably and is professionally edited, though this is a horror movie, not *The French Connection*. In the end, this film is a staggering disappointment because it is uninteresting, nonsensical, confusing, and a rip-off of the TV series. Why call this film *Dark Shadows*, when it is so unlike the TV show, and Barnabas is nowhere to be found? No wonder this sequel killed the franchise. That said, look for the climax of *Night of Dark Shadows* to recur in Dan Curtis's far superior 1976 outing, *Burnt Offerings*.

LEGACY: In January of 2001, *Wicked* magazine reported that director Dan Curtis' cut of *Night of Dark Shadows*, which apparently runs over two hours, would be released on a special edition DVD. According to Curtis, the film was cut to 90 minutes against his will for theatrical release.

The Night Visitor (1971) ✶ ✶ ✶

Critical Reception

"As a tense how-was-it-done, *The Night Visitor* is an uncommonly fascinating film ... the motivations for all the machinations and Gothic horrors are merely touched on and hinted at ... in the convoluted goings-on. But the methods of madness are the thing here ... a captivating, moody and scenic thriller."— A.H. Weiler, *New York Times*, February 11, 1971.

"It's incredible that any film with a cast which includes Max Von Sydow, Liv Ullmann, Per Oscarrson and Trevor Howard could be as bad as *The Night Visitor*. If there were ever proof that talented actors cannot save a bad script — it is here. Nor save a mediocre director (Laslo Benedek). Nor an addled producer (Mel Ferrer)."— Gloria Ives, *Films in Review*, Volume XII, Number 3, March 1971, page 175.

Cast & Crew

CAST: Trevor Howard (Inspector); Liv Ullmann (Ester Jenks); Per Oscarsson (Dr. Anton Jenks); Max Von Sydow (Salem); Andrew Keir (Dr. Kemp); Jim Kennedy (Carl); Arthur Hewlett (Pop); Hanne Bork (Emmie); Gretchen Franklin (Mrs. Hansen); Rupert Davies (Mr. Clemens); Bjorn Watt-Booksen (Mr. Torens); Lotte Freddie (Britt Torens); Erik Kuhnau (Police Doctor).

CREW: Sidney Glazier Presents a Hemisphere Production, *The Night Visitor*. *Production Manager:* Katinka Farago. *Assistant to Director:* Pamela Davies. *Camera Operator:* Peter Klitgard. *Second Mixer:* Robert Allen. *Dubbing Mixer:* Hugh Strain. *Sound Editor:* Ian Fuller. *Production Designer:* P.A. Lundgren. *Art Director:* Viggo Bentzon. *Props:* Karen Bentzon. *Make-up:* Bengt Ottekil, Ruth Mahler. *Production Secretary:* Romy Watt Torrance. *Film Editor:* Bill Blunden. *Director of Photography:* Henning Kirstiansen. *Music:* Henry Mancini. *Screenplay:* Guy Elmes. *Based on an Original Story by:* Sam Roecca. *Produced by:* Mel Ferrer. *Directed by:* Laslo Benedek. Filmed Entirely on Location in Denmark and Sweden and at Asa and Laterna Studios, Copenhagen. *M.P.A.A. Rating:* PG. *Running Time:* 102 minutes.

SYNOPSIS: In frozen Sweden, a farmer named Salem has been termed "criminally insane" and incarcerated at an impregnable, inescapable mental asylum. Salem's crime was the axe-murder of a farmhand, but in truth Salem was framed in a devious, wide-ranging conspiracy. His sister, Ester Jenks, and her husband, Dr. Anton Jenks, actually murdered the farmhand themselves, and framed Salem for the crime so that they, not Salem, could control the financial future of the farm. Salem's alibi in the case was Britt Torens, a young lover he was with when the farmhand was killed. Unfortunately, Britt did not speak up in court to clear Salem, instead protecting her own virginal reputation at the cost of his freedom. Damningly, even Salem's lawyer, Mr. Clemens, was involved in the cover-up. Without Salem's permission, Clemens changed his client's plea, and thereby assured that Salem would not go to prison but rather to an insane asylum where there was no possibility of parole.

For two long years, Salem has stewed in his tiny cell and plotted how to wreak revenge against those who conspired against him. Using a mixture of psychological warfare and death-defying athletics, Salem manages to escape from the fortress-like asylum each night and turn the tables on his many accusers and betrayers. He kills Britt Torens, and implicates Jenks in her death. When the police become involved, they immediately question both Jenks and Salem, but the inspector quickly comes to realize that Salem could not possibly escape from the well-fortified asylum to commit murder. And, even if he did so, why would he then return to his cell each night?

Salem's plan, which requires split-second timing, then frames Anton Jenks in a new series of murders, including the chopping death of his very own wife, Ester ... who implicated him to the police shortly before her death.

All of Salem's well-laid plans seem to be working quite well, conquering harsh weather, personal loyalties, and even timing. However, there is one loose cannon in Salem's revenge scenario. Dr. Jenks and his late wife Ester own a parrot ... a parrot with knowledge of their crimes, as well as an extensive vocabulary. During Salem's many night visits to the family farm to enact his plan, the bird is inadvertently freed from its cage. Now that Jenks has been framed for all the murders and Salem is to be freed, found innocent of the crime he was charged with, this final wild card is played in a surprising way.

COMMENTARY: With a cold, psychologically frigid setting and the presence of Max Von Sydow in the lead role, *The Night Visitor* looks a lot like an Ingmar Bergman picture. Yet, it is more immediately accessible a film than, say, *Persona*, and it focuses not so much on inner conflict as it does on action. This is Bergman re-imagined as action director, and it works rather well.

The film is built like a puzzle box. How does the protagonist, Salem, escape from the asylum each night? How does he pass through the bars in the hallway outside his room? How does he survive the fall to the courtyard 60 feet below his cell? How does he commit his perfect, but bloody crimes? Those are the questions that *The Night Visitor* concerns itself with, and that narrow focus makes for a compelling film that is equal parts crime caper and suspense film.

There's a Hitchcockian precision to the set-up here, and one has to admire director Laslo Benedeck for his detail-minded helming. Benedek builds his movie brilliantly.

The picture opens with Salem free and on the loose in the icy terrain (garbed only in his underwear, no less), so the audience is immediately aware that he is escaping each night. Then, Benedek follows a police inspector who demonstrates, rather compellingly, that such an escape is absolutely impossible. Each impediment, from the asylum's stone gray walls of great height, and the impassible prison bars, to the locked cell, is highlighted, tested and reinforced. Finally, after establishing both Salem's freedom and the utter impossibility of that freedom, Benedek depicts precisely how the escape is managed. Amazingly, there are no tricks in this final portion of the movie. The audience is not asked to suspend disbelief, or accept a physical impossibility (like the mine car jump in *Indiana Jones and the Temple of Doom* [1985] or the bus freeway jump in *Speed* [1994]). Instead, the film thoughtfully reasons out every impediment in reasonable and logical fashion, and Salem's escape is revealed to be part psychology (the tricking of inmates and guards), part crafty theft (there are hidden tools to use, such as keys), and, finally, and most harrowingly, physical prowess. In this last regard, the film is truly impressive as Max Von Sydow is seen scaling trees and walls, and racing from one part of his plan to another. As methodical, well-conceived action flick, *The Night Visitor* is no less than brilliant.

An impossible escape in a bleak, forbidding terrain is the centerpiece of *The Night Visitor*, but the film is also interesting in the way that it asks the audience to first perceive Salem as a resourceful hero, a framed man, and then, finally as something of a monster. He is, after all, a murderer. Despite this fact, the audience is with him all the way, since his enemies, the conspirators, all richly deserve their fate. The final third of the film is an exercise in suspense as Salem crosses one hurdle after another in an attempt to get back to his asylum cell before the inspector discovers he has escaped. Of course, as one might expect, there is a final twist that exposes Salem, but how and why that twist occurs makes for a fun, heart-pounding conclusion.

Probably the only flaw in this amazing caper is that (at least in the U.S.) a competent police inspector would have men sta-tioned all over the asylum grounds, just in case Salem was somehow escaping. That doesn't happen here, but that's a very minor quibble with a well-thought-out film. For its splendid action scenes (such as Sydow swing-ing down a high exterior wall), and its thoughtful construction of the perfect crime, *The Night Visitor* is a welcome guest in the VCR anytime.

The Omega Man (1971) ✳ ✳ ✳

Critical Reception

"...The film is best in its middle-third … peppered with some sharp, even amusing dialogue, the story temporarily shelves the heavy allegory and slips into good, slam-bang suspense. But it doesn't last. And the climax is as florid and phony as it can be…."— Howard Thompson, *New York Times*, August 14, 1971, page 13.

"This version has a large budget; unfortunately it also has uninspired direc-tion, a script that strays too far from its source material, and a dull and stodgy performance from Heston. A totally wasted opportunity."— Alan Frank, *The Horror Film Handbook*, 1982, page 108.

Cast & Crew

CAST: Charlton Heston (Colonel Robert Neville); Anthony Zerbe (Matthias); Rosalind Cash (Lisa); Paul Koslo (Dutch); Lincoln Kil-patrick (Brother Zachary); Eric Laneuville (Richie); Jill Giraldi (Little Girl); Anna Aries (Woman in Cemetery Crypt); Brian Tochi (Tommy); DeVeren Bookwalter, John Dierkes, Monika Henreid, Linda Redfearn, Forrest Wood (Family Members).

CREW: Warner Brothers Presents a Walter Seltzer Production, *The Omega Man. Director of Photography:* Russell Metty. *Art Director:* Arthur Loel, Walter M. Simonds. *Set Decora-tion:* Donald Roberts. *Film Editor:* William Ziegler. *Unit Production Manager:* Frank Baur. *Music:* Ron Grainer. *Action Coordinator:* Joe Cannutt. *Sound:* Bob Martin. *Costumer:* Margo Baxley. *Make-up:* Gordon Bau. *Screenplay:* John William and Joyce H. Corrington. *Based on the Novel by:* Richard Matheson. *Producer:* Walter Seltzer. *Director:* Boris Sagal. *Filmed in* Panav-ision and in Technicolor. *M.P.A.A. Rating:* PG. *Running Time:* 98 minutes.

P.O.V.

"Our basic decision to demythologize the story was, I think, a good one. Maybe it wasn't — maybe we should have left the vam-pires in. But somehow, when you're doing a last man on Earth story that involves all kinds of scientific plausibility, it seemed that vampires would not fit very well…. Instead we tried to render the spooks in scientific terms, with a blood disease and albinoism and photophobia and all" (8).— Charlton Heston, star of *The Omega Man* (1971), on the differences between Matheson's source material and the finished film.

***

SYNOPSIS: In March of 1975, a biological plague wipes out the vast majority of mankind, leaving only one man alive, Colonel Robert Neville. By 1977, the lonely Neville is locked in a life-and-death struggle with a "new world order": a race of neo-luddite, albino mutants, sick with the plague themselves, who are bent on destroying Neville and all evidence of mankind's technological civilization. Calling itself the "Family," these mutants are led by a former TV news anchorman, Matthias. Matthias has a special hatred for Neville, as Neville was part of the military establishment that contributed to the downfall of humanity.

Living a life of isolation, Neville spends his nights holed up in his museum-like penthouse apartment, and his days attempting to exterminate the light-sensitive, homicidal mutants in their nests. One night, Neville returns home late and narrowly avoids a trap set by the Family. Neville survives the attack, and recalls how he came to be in this situation. When the plague came, Neville injected himself with an experimental vaccine. This vaccine now keeps him immune from the disease and courses through his blood, but it also isolates him from the undead creatures of Los Angeles.

While out on the city one day attempting to find the hideout of Matthias, Neville spots a fellow survivor, the beautiful African-American woman named Lisa. When Neville is captured by Matthias and brought to a sports arena to be burned at the stake, Lisa rescues him with the help of a young former med student named Dutch. Once free of the Family, Lisa, Dutch and Neville flee the city, and Neville is introduced to an encampment of seemingly normal children. In truth, the children, Lisa, and Dutch are all living on borrowed time. Because they are not immune, the plague will soon transform them into albino mutants. In fact, Lisa's own younger brother, Richie, is going through that very process. Realizing his blood may carry the means to save his fellow humans, Neville tends to Richie. With Lisa and Dutch, Neville takes the boy back to his apartment laboratory in the city. There, he develops a serum from his blood and injects

Richie with it. Meanwhile, Neville and Lisa become romantically attached. Before they can consummate their relationship, Neville's apartment generator fails, plunging the apartment into darkness. Thinking the humans to be easy-pickings, Matthias orders an attack. Brother Zachary, a Family member who wants Neville dead at any cost, ascends the exterior wall of Neville's building. Neville manages to re-start his generator, and kill Zachary, just in time.

With Richie on the mend, Lisa, Dutch and Neville plot to leave the city permanently. Lisa heads out to gather supplies by day, while Neville makes more serum from his blood. A healthy Richie is troubled by Neville's attitude about the "Family." He wants to save Matthias and his people using the serum, much the way he was saved. Neville refuses to help, calling the mutants "vermin." Without Neville's knowledge or consent, Richie visits Matthias and the Family at their headquarters in a courthouse. There, he is captured and murdered. At the same time, the deadly plague takes hold of Lisa, turning her into an albino, homicidal mutant. When Neville fails to save Richie, he returns to his apartment and is led into a trap by Lisa. Matthias and his people smash and destroy all of Neville's art and artifacts, and plot to kill him. Neville manages to escape with the last vial of his precious blood serum, and Lisa. However, he does not get far. In the courtyard below his apartment, Neville is killed when Matthias hurls a spear through his chest.

Daylight comes, and Dutch and the children find Neville dead in the courtyard, crucified in the position of Christ, on a strange work of modern art. With Neville's precious blood serum, Dutch resolves to restore Lisa to health, and to get the children to safety. One of the children, a little girl, wonders if Neville was "God."

COMMENTARY: Charlton Heston *is* legend. To children who grew up in the 1970s, he is neither the "religious" figure of *The Ten*

"From my cold, dead hands…" A heavily armed Neville (Charlton Heston) searches for the "Family" in ***The Omega Man*** (1971).

Commandments, nor the 1990s NRA hawk ("From my cold, dead hands…"). Instead, he is the ultimate science-fiction anti-hero, the best "bad-ass" in the business. In *Planet of the Apes* (1968), *Beneath the Planet of the Apes* (1970), *The Omega Man* (1971), and *Soylent Green* (1973) — all rerun continually on WABC New York's *4:30 Movie*—Heston played humanity's reluctant defender, an outsider standing against a new social order whether it be simian, mutant, albino, or even cannibal. Heston seems perfect for this role, and all these films benefited enormously from his presence. As Pauline Kael once observed of the Academy Award-winning actor (in relation to *Planet of the Apes*):

> Physically, Heston, with his perfect, lean hipped, powerful body, is a god-like hero, built for strength, he's an archetype of what makes Americans win. He

doesn't play nice guy; he's harsh and hostile, self-centered and hot-tempered. Yet we don't hate him, because he's so magnetically strong; he represents American power — the physical attraction and admiration one feels toward the beauty of strength as well as the moral revulsion one feels toward the ugliness of violence…. He is the perfect American Adam to work off some American guilt feelings or self hatred on…. [9].

The same could very well be said of Heston's role in *The Omega Man,* a film that once again portrays the actor as a flawed messiah, a symbol of both American virtue and American arrogance. For even though his blood will save humanity, Heston is seen in the film as a right-wing ideologue, a closet racist who refers to his enemy as "vermin," non-humans to be exterminated with extreme prejudice. It's true he has a relationship with an African-American woman in the film, but his character, Neville is resolutely incapable of seeing the whiter-than-white family members as anything other than monsters. The intense dislike is mirrored by the Family, a "race" that views Heston's Neville in similarly hateful terms. But the casting of Heston is a masterstroke because he represents so many things. He's comfortable as a religious messiah (à la *The Ten Commandments*), a man alone in a topsy-turvy world (*Planet of the Apes*), and a flawed outsider trying to right a system he is not a part of (*Touch of Evil* [1958]). In a movie where the plot pits one man against a society (and usually a corrupt one), it is important that "the man" be strong, powerful, and charismatic. Heston fits the bill. There's no doubt that the presence of this 1970s science fiction icon enhances *The Omega Man*.

The film also benefits from the fact that the set-up of the picture is a primal male fantasy. Every guy wants to be the last man on Earth so he can drive the fast cars, carry the baddest guns, wear the coolest clothes, live in the best house, and romance a hot woman — who, because of her limited options, sees him as powerful and worthwhile. Though the film attempts to play against this fantasy with its themes of isolation and racial division, who can truthfully deny that such an existence fulfills every male's innate desire to be a hero? You get to save the world, your blood is considered precious, and when you die, you become a messiah figure, remembered for generations. It may not make a lot of sense, and it certainly isn't admirable, but *The Omega Man* plays into the hero complex that drives so many men.

But beyond the iconic presence of Charlton Heston and the hero complex set-up of the film, *The Omega Man* succeeds in other ways. The earliest sequence of the film, as Neville's car speeds through an empty city, a metal valley of sorts, is very effectively shot. These scenes were lensed in a sleeping L.A. during the early morning hours before and around dawn, and the feeling of emptiness is authentic, and a little scary. It *feels* like a

dead world. And the music, courtesy of Ron Grainer (*The Prisoner*) also lends the picture a melancholy but groovy 1970s mood. There's a jaunty, militant feel to the music of *The Prisoner*, a show about a man's psychological and physical imprisonment, and that same tone is generated here. Neville is every bit as much a prisoner as Patrick McGoohan was: alone and unable to escape a village that is, perhaps, of his own making. Good production values, coupled with some nice stylistic camerawork (such as the hand-held shaky material when the plague attacks passersby on the street), make this film nothing less than a guilty pleasure.

Why a *guilty* pleasure? Well, scribe Richard Matheson might well tell you that this film significantly changes the details of his book, *I Am Legend*. Secondly, *The Omega Man* much less meaningfully deals with the idea of a new social order than did George Romero's *Night of the Living Dead* (also inspired by Matheson's book, no doubt). In that picture, the tenets of western, Christian society had to be cast off to survive in a world of the ghouls. There was no time for funerals, family relationships disintegrated once a brother or daughter became undead, and man found himself sheltered in a 20th century cave, helpless before a mob usurper who controlled the outdoors and the night. Rather empty in comparison, *The Omega Man* settles for action and romance, and some shallow commentary about race warfare. It should be an infinitely more meaningful film. If this truly is a passing of the guard, then shouldn't the film also reveal Neville from the perspective of the new order? Like the last dinosaur in an age dominated by rodents, he is a curiosity, but also an outlier, a symbol of the past. All those things could have been explored outside the confines of "us vs. them" physical conflict or action set pieces.

The film's heavy-handed dialogue sometimes feels forced, such as Richie's comment of idealistic pacifism that "at times," Neville scares him more than "Matthias does." The film never legitimately tackles that fact, that Neville isn't a particularly nice guy, and that, as part of the military establishment, he does bear a measure of guilt for the biological war that destroyed most of humanity. Instead, the film only brings up those points, and then hides them, while contrarily canonizing Neville as a Christ figure (as seen in that famous crucifixion pose). Also, there is an uncomfortable undertone of fascism to the picture. Think of it this way: a lone man protects his blood against the colored (ivory white) hordes that hope to destroy him and his hold on the traditional ways (which destroyed the world, by the way!). In the end, this "pure" blood is valued above understanding or tolerance or even communication with the new social order. There's something distinctly wrong about the whole set-up. If this movie were really about racial divisions, a détente would be declared, and humanity and the Family would find some way to co-exist. Instead, the colored are seen as vermin, an ugly reminder of American racial violence in the 1960s and 1970s, and the blood of the white man is seen as the legacy that will heal the future. One has to wonder how minorities might view that message.

Still, there's the presence of Heston, the ultimate right-winger, battling for humanity, and living the ultimate male fantasy (though admittedly megalomaniacal…). Those factors mitigate a lot of the confusing rhetoric. It's almost like there are two Omega Men. The intellectual side of the picture knows it's full of untruth, and even fascist. But on the surface the picture is an entertaining, rollicking adventure that appeals to the heroic needs of every red-blooded American male. In some cases, it is best not to think too much about a movie's implications, especially if that movie is as exciting, and downright enjoyable as *The Omega Man*.

Play Misty for Me (1971) ★ ★ ★ ½

Critical Reception

"…the terror sequences, though seemingly swiped from *Psycho*, are good and scary. Eastwood should also be credited with drawing a flamboyantly neurotic, wild performance from Jessica Walter…. But the film flags principally because Eastwood can't discriminate between the really good stuff he's got and the draggy scenes that kill suspense. Any shrewd director would have excised a long, essentially useless romp along the Carmel coast with Eastwood and Donna Mills making love beneath a waterfall." — Paul D. Zimmerman, *Newsweek*: "Special Request," November 22, 1971, page 120.

"…Clint Eastwood, the director … has made too many easy decisions about events, … atmosphere, … performances — including the rather inexpressive one of Clint Eastwood the actor, who is asked to bear more witness to a quality of inwardness than his better directors have yet had the temerity to ask of him." — Roger Greenspun, *New York Times*, November 4, 1971, page 52.

"…the scariest portrait of a female psycho the screen has yet given us is Jessica Walter's neurotically obsessive and insanely possessive groupie in *Play Misty for Me*…. As the psycho fan whose spurned ardor leads to wrathful vengeance, she is astonishing. Her quick changes of mood are terrifyingly unpredictable; she literally makes the hairs bristle on the back of one's neck." — John McCarty, *Psychos: Eight Years of Mad Movies, Maniacs and Murderous Deeds*, St. Martin's Press, 1986, page 126.

Cast & Crew

CAST: Clint Eastwood (Dave Garvey); Jessica Walter (Evelyn Draper); Donna Mills (Tobie Williams); John Larch (Sgt. McCallum); Jack Ging (Frank); Irene Harvey (Madge); James McEachin (Al Monte); Clarice Taylor (Birdie); Donald Siegel (Bartender Murray); Duke Everts (Jay Jay); George Fargo (Man); Mervin W. Frates (Locksmith); Tim Frawley (Deputy Sheriff); Otis Kadan (Policeman); Brit Lind (Anjelica); Paul E. Lippman (2nd Man); Jack Kosslyn (Car Driver); Gina Patterson (Madalyn); Malcolm Moran (Man in Window).

CREW: A Universal Release of a Jennings Lang Presentation, a Malpaso Company Production, *Play Misty for Me. Director of Photography:* Bruce Sertees. *Art Director:* Alexander Colitzer. *Set Decorator:* Ralph Hurst. *Assistant Director:* Bob Larson. *Script Supervisor:* Betty Abbott. *Dialogue Coach:* Jack Kosslyn. *Sound:* Waldon O. Watson, Robert Martin, Robert L. Hoyt. *Painting:* Don Heitkolter. *"Misty" by arrangement with* Octave Music Publishing Corp. *Costumes:* Helen Colvic. *Cosmetics:* Cinematique. *Titles and Opticals:* Universal Title. *Mr. Eastwood's Wardrobe:* Brad Whitner of Carmel. *Color:* Technicolor. *Film Editor:* Carl Pingitore. *Associate Producer:* Bob Larson. *"Misty" Composed and Performed by:* Erroll Garner. *Original Music by:* Dee Barton. *"The First Time Ever I Saw Your Face" Sung by:* Roberta Flack. *Produced by:* Joel Dorn for Atlantic Records. *Screenplay:* Jo Helms, Dean Riesner. *Story:* Jo Helms. *Produced by:* Robert Daley. *Directed by:* Clint Eastwood. A Universal-Malpaso Company Picture. *M.P.A.A. Rating:* R. *Running Time:* 102 minutes.

SYNOPSIS: In the quaint little town of Carmel in scenic, coastal California, jazz DJ Dave Garvey runs a late-night radio show. During every show, a sultry-voiced woman calls in to request the song "Misty," and Dave obliges. On one late night, Dave meets Evelyn Draper at a bar and takes her home. She tells him she is his "Misty" girl and that she wants to make love to him. Dave tells Evelyn he is involved, but Evelyn replies that they could spend just one night together, no strings attached. Dave agrees, and leaves the next morning after a night of passion.

Later, Evelyn arrives unannounced at Dave's place, with bags of groceries. He is disturbed by her arrival but lets her stay, and they make love again. Afterwards, Evelyn proves a bit temperamental when a neighbor asks her to pipe down. She responds by laying on a car-horn and cussing.

Soon Dave meets up with his ex-girlfriend, Tobie, whom he still has strong feelings for. She left him because of his womanizing, but he convinces her that she is really the one he desires to be with. While Dave courts Tobie, Evelyn remains in the picture and tracks Dave down at a bar. There, she gets pushy with him, stealing his car keys and making demands on his time and freedom. She shows up at Dave's house that night, naked but for a jacket. Dave sleeps with her again and afterwards promises to call. He does not call her, and later forgets to confirm plans she is making for a late night date during the week. After Evelyn calls Dave at KRML to talk about the aforementioned date, Dave goes over to her place to straighten things out. They fight, break off the affair, and Evelyn flies into an angry frenzy. Later, she calls Dave at home to apologize, but he rebuffs her.

Dave resumes his romantic relationship with Tobie while Evelyn spies from the shadows. She appears at Dave's house one night, protesting, then goes to the bathroom and slits her wrists with a razor blade. Feeling guilty, Dave spends the day caring for Evelyn, even though he has a date with Tobie. He misses the date and awakens the next morning to find that Evelyn has borrowed his car. While she is out, she makes a duplicate set of keys to his house. Her behavior growing ever more questionable, Evelyn insults a businesswoman, Madge, who was planning to hire Dave to host the Monterey Jazz Festival. Evelyn's actions cost Dave the job and he finally realizes how disturbing an influence Evelyn has become. He meets with Tobie and tells her the truth about Evelyn. Evelyn flies off the handle, trashes Dave's house, and stabs David's maid, Birdie, with a butcher knife.

The police take Evelyn away, and Dave thinks the nightmare is over. He and Tobie make love in a beautiful forest, then enjoy the jazz festival, unaware that Evelyn is planning her final revenge. On the job a few days later, Dave gets a call from Evelyn asking him to play "Misty." She claims that she is better and headed to Hawaii for a new job. She quotes a poem by Edgar Allen Poe and says goodbye to her obsessive love. By midnight, however, Evelyn has had a dangerous turnaround. She appears in Dave's bedroom and tries to murder him. Dave escapes this attempt, and informs the police of the situation. Sgt. McCallum warns him to change the locks in his house, and then McCallum plans to use the radio show to track Evelyn down. If she calls to request "Misty," the cops will trace the call.

However, Evelyn is one step ahead of her opponents. She has moved in with Tobie under the name Annabel, the latest in a long line of revolving roommates, and now she plans to kill Tobie and Dave. A suspicious Dave remembers that "Annabel Lee" is the name of the Edgar Allan Poe poem Evelyn quoted him one night and races from the radio station to help the endangered Tobie. When he arrives, Dave finds that Evelyn has already murdered Sgt. McCallum with a very large pair of scissors. With Tobie in mortal danger, Evelyn and Dave fight to the death. The fight carries them to the ledge overlooking the shoreline far below, and only one of the lovers will survive.

COMMENTARY: Before celebrity stalking was a national concern in America, Clint Eastwood nailed the concept with *Play Misty for Me*, an effectively directed (and shot) suspense picture with a strong villain in Jessica Walter.

From the opening montage, Clint Eastwood declares his intention to throw every trick in the book at his directorial debut. The film opens with Clint driving through scenic colorful California. The scenery is beautiful, and jazz blares on the soundtrack as various helicopter shots capture the beauty of the location. As Eastwood fans would later learn, jazz music, and Carmel, California, are two of Eastwood's favorite things in the universe, and so those predilections form the bedrock of *Play Misty for Me*. Surprisingly, the jazz music and the natural beauty work together thematically too. The gorgeous ocean, the lush trees, and the beautiful scenery all indicate Dave's 1970s paradise, a "groovy" existence unencumbered by many concerns, either moral or financial The playful and relaxing jazz reinforces the idea of a casual existence (in which casual sex is the order of the day). That Dave's existence is so beautiful and blissful is important, because it shows the audience immediately what he has to lose. Evelyn threatens his perfect life, and we see evidence of that perfect life in his job, in his choice of car, in his home, and even in his music.

Play Misty for Me is really a good old fashioned morality play, a story about the downside of the sexual revolution. It reveals how encounters with strangers can cause unwanted entanglements. People who you don't really want in your life are suddenly granted access to the most intimate details of your life, by virtue of a casual sexual experience. In the scene involving Dave and Evelyn's first meeting, the camera seems to be positioned so that it is almost peering up Walter's skirt. This is a nicely composed shot, and a significant one, because it tells us exactly what function Evelyn is to serve for Dave. She is a sex object, nothing more, and a receptacle for his desires. So, as per the order of the early 1970s, he takes her home, sleeps with her, and has little use for her beyond that biological function. Slam bam.

In depicting this casual sex affair gone awry, Eastwood points the way to 1987's *Fatal Attraction*. Though that film's essence was all 1980s and yuppiesm (rather than being representative of the 1970s ideal of "whatever feels right"), there is nonetheless much similarity. In *Play Misty for Me*, a sexually hungry male brings a woman to his bed, claiming there will be "no strings attached." But she can't let go of the attractive, charismatic and powerful male figure, and even attempts to commit suicide to keep him. All that, including the suicide attempt, happens in *Fatal Attraction* too, of course, but the stakes are different. In the 1970s, what was at stake was Eastwood the bachelor's freedom. Evelyn was cramping Dave's life-style, affecting his job, and messing up his good thing with that hot little number Donna Mills. Reflective of its age, *Fatal Attraction* jeopardized not freedom, but the family and hearth of Michael Douglas's unfaithful rogue. Glenn Close's sexual predator threatened to destroy his security in that motion picture by queering things with his wife and child, and destroying his image as a respectable businessman.

Still, the films are alike in their view of casual sexual relationships: a man's desire for sex with strangers inevitably leads to the endangerment of that which he values most, whether it is freedom or security (and family). Of the two films, it is hard to say which is better, since they are both highly effective thrillers. All that can be said definitively is that *Play Misty for Me* came first, and that both films have more in common than initially meets the eye.

Eastwood is lucky, however, that his casting was so good in this film. Jessica Walter is effective in transmitting her character's neuroses and psychoses a piece at a time, thus escalating the audience's unease with her. Clearly, Evelyn gives audiences the creeps. She has a broad smile, an annoying demeanor, a foul mouth (an early signal of her instability), and keeps crossing the line of appropriate behavior with defiance. It is a powerful and menacing performance that could have come across as clichéd. Instead, Walter is unpredictable and eruptive as Evelyn. She's not easily forgotten. One has to remember too that she is threatening a basic American symbol of power (no, not Charlton Heston!), and if she weren't truly a powerful and scary figure, people would laugh

instead of cringe at her confrontations with the stolid Eastwood.

Alas, Donna Mills does not fair so well in the film, perhaps because her part is less flashy and is weighted down by the ballast of clichés. Every romantic conversation she shares with Eastwood is made up of ridiculous, hopeless lines that have been uttered in romantic subplots since the beginning of film history. "I gotta figure where I'm at," says one character. "I don't want to get on that revolving door again," says another. It's all terribly interchangeable, and one feels that any problems in the Eastwood-Mills relationship is more an example of plot necessity than genuine differences or problems among the characters. The romantic scenes are pretty underwhelming and bland, even though Eastwood stages them in the most beautiful locales imaginable, and accompanies them with soft, romantic music, such as Roberta Flack's "The First Time Ever I Saw Your Face."

Eastwood himself is the center of this love triangle, and he is an appropriate choice for the role of Dave. He does not have the warmest screen presence, but his harshness works for the picture since Dave is supposed to be a love 'em and leave 'em kind of guy. And, what is known of Eastwood's personal life seems to verify that this character is closer to the real Eastwood than, say, *Dirty Harry*, or the gunslinger of *Unforgiven*. The bottom line is that Dave is a pretty shallow guy who thinks that his great house, his great car, and his love of great music make him "deep." But he treats people as objects, and he pays the price for it. He is not particularly heroic, he's just an average joe who likes a piece of ass now and then, and Eastwood captures the character's selfish and shallow nature very well.

The horror sequences in *Play Misty for Me* are powerfully staged, and even jolting. When Evelyn strikes, she inevitably does so directly at the camera (a cliché of the 1970s). Eastwood deploys a hand-held camera during the many surprise attacks, and that shaky, unhinged look provides for some startling, effective, and very real-looking bloodletting. The scene wherein Dave's maid, Birdie, is assaulted is a vicious little bloodbath, made more so by the fact that the ambush is completely undeserved. Only the climactic attack, which sees Dave tossing the insane Evelyn over a ledge, seems ineffectually staged: it is over too fast, and poorly lit.

Through his confident handling of the love triangle, Dave's inner world of jazz, nature and sex, and even Evelyn's violence, Eastwood makes a very compelling thriller. The only place his skills come up lacking is in the arena of pacing. The film is too long for a thriller, and Eastwood fritters away too much time at a jazz festival. There is an extended sequence filled with colorful shots of musicians and crowds playing and listening to good music, but the sequence is irrelevant to the picture as a whole. We know it's there because Eastwood is a jazz fan, but a clever director would have realized it was extraneous material and dropped it. A solid thriller depends on timing, pace and the snowballing of disturbing events to create a mood. A languorous, slow-moving montage of a jazz festival works against the overall tapestry of the film.

But *Play Misty for Me* lives on in horror film history because it is a cautionary tale every person can relate to, an explicit warning to playboys (or girls) to be careful who they bring home to their pads. One night, you might just get a wacko. On that level, even thirty years later, *Play Misty for Me* has lost none of its visceral punch.

LEGACY: *Play Misty for Me* was the first picture directed by Clint Eastwood, and twenty some years later, he accepted the best director Academy Award for *Unforgiven* (1993). His most recent directorial effort was *Space Cowboys* (2000). The themes, events, and characters of *Play Misty for Me* were later regurgitated in the hit 1987 film *Fatal Attraction*.

See No Evil (1971) ★ ★ ★

Critical Reception

"The whole story is possessed of a staggering imbecility, and proceeds at a trudging gait that seems to be Richard Fleischer's natural pace…. The fondness for half-calf shots is a new trait: Bunuel's fetishism without the humor, the sensuality, or the intelligence…."— Penelope Gilliatt, *New Yorker*: "Soaked Uncle," September 15, 1971, page 69.

"Sarah [Mia Farrow] manages to wander through … hazards obliviously…. Prolonged this way, the tension and suspense keep turning into a delightfully shaggy dog story, the sort that Hitchcock used to tell so expertly. Throughout these scenes, Fleischer's camera slithers and crawls in front of Sarah's movements, incidentally revealing the bodies and other evidence as it stays focused on her. This snake's eye view is contrived enough to get laughs and yet appropriately menacing as well."— Colin L. Westerbeck, Jr., *Commonwealth,* October 22, 1971, pages 88–89.

"Scenarist Brian Clemens offers no motivations and precious few plot twists. Nor is his head-on, harum-scarum approach improved by Richard Fleischer's blunt direction, which favors sudden cuts to broken corpses and sadistic close-ups of a girl precipitously tumbling into catatonia. Manifestly, Fleischer is out for only one thing: to inspire sudden fear. That he does, but at the expense of taste."— Stanley Kanfer, *Time*: "Blind Fear," September 20, 1971, page 74.

Cast & Crew

CAST: Mia Farrow (Sarah); Dorothy Alison (Betty Rexton); Robin Bailey (George Rexton); Brian Rawlinson (Barker); Diane Grayson (Sandy Rexton); Paul Nicholas (Jacko); Norman Eshley (Steve Reding); Barrie Houghton (Gypsy Jack); Michael Elphick (Gypsy Thom); Lila Kaye (Gypsy Mother); Christopher Matthews (Frost); Max Faulkner, Scott Fredericks, Reg Harding (Steve's Men); Donald Bisset (Doctor).

CREW: Columbia Pictures and Filmways Present a Martin Ransohoff/Leslie Linder Production, *See No Evil. Production Manager:* Jilda Smith. *Art Director:* John Hoesli. *Director of Photography:* Gerry Fisher. *Film Editor:* Thelma Connell. *Music Composed and Conducted by:* Elmer Bernstein. *Camera Operator:* Bernard Ford. *Set Decorator:* Hugh Scaife. *Assistant Director:* Terry Marcel. *Sound Mixer:* Robert Allen. *Sound Recording:* Ken Scrivener. *Continuity:* Pamela Carlton. *Wardrobe:* Stuart Freeborn. *Hairdresser:* Betty Glasgow. *Lighting Equipment:* Kee Electric (Lighting) Ltd. *Associate Producer:* Basil Appleby. *Written by:* Brian Clemens. *Produced by:* Martin Ransohoff, Leslie Linder. *Director:* Richard Fleischer. Filmed in Eastmancolor. The Film was photographed on location in Berkshire, England, by Genesis Productions Ltd. M.P.A.A. *Rating:* PG. *Running Time:* 90 minutes.

SYNOPSIS: A recently blinded young woman, Sarah, leaves the hospital to recuperate with her aunt and uncle at their horse farm. Soon after moving in, Sarah is driven to a meeting with her boyfriend, Steven. Though she lost her sight in a riding accident, Steven gives Sarah a new horse, and helps her overcome her fears of the animal.

While Sarah is away, a stranger wearing cowboy boots shows up at the house of Sarah's Uncle George and murders the entire family (including George, Aunt Betty and young Sandy). Then Sarah returns home — to what she believes should be an empty house, completely unaware of the massacre and its aftermath, which is all around her. Night falls and Sarah's handicap prevents her from seeing all the signs of danger in the house, such as broken glass and gun shells. As she goes to sleep, Sarah is not even aware that Sandy's bloody corpse is just feet away. The next morning, Sarah starts to run a bath … without realizing that Uncle George's corpse has been strewn into the tub. Before she discovers the corpse, Steven calls and brings Sarah her new horse. They go riding together in a rainstorm, and afterwards Steve reluctantly leaves the independent Sarah home alone again. This time, she discovers George's body, and falls down the cellar stairs in shock.

Meanwhile, the murderer realizes he has left an identifying bracelet behind at the crime scene, and returns to the house to find it. Sarah escapes from the killer, and runs into the yard-hand, Barker. He's been shot and is dying, but warns that the killer left a silver bracelet and has returned for it. Unaware there is writing on the bracelet, Sarah retrieves it and flees the house on horseback. The killer has heard her, and gives chase. Sarah is thrown from the horse, and wanders lost in the woods, until she runs into a family of gypsies. Unfortunately, the gypsies think the killer is one of their own, a man named Jack, and lie to Sarah about the name engraved on the jewelry.

While Sarah is in jeopardy, her horse arrives at Steven's farm, signaling trouble. He rushes to her house, finds her family dead, and starts to search for her. At the same time, Sarah has been locked in a cabin in a muddy dump. Steve finds her there and goes after the gypsies. But there has been a mix-up. The gypsy Jack is not the killer … the bracelet actually reads "Jacko"—the name of one of Steve's farm-hands!

While Steven rushes home, Sarah is alone at his house with the killer. Jacko watches Sarah bathe, and then tries to drown her. Steve arrives just in time to save Sarah and dispatch the psychotic Jacko.

COMMENTARY: *See No Evil* is an extremely deft, psycho-film that hinges on the following conceit: You're blind; you don't know where you are, and you don't know who to trust. It is the story of what happens when a critical sense (sight) is lost, and how that loss affects all the other senses, and the capacity to trust. Is it a sadistic film, as many critics have suggested, since it takes a helpless blind girl and puts her through the wringer? Perhaps so, but audiences go to horror movies to be terrorized, and this film uses every tool at its disposal, innocent blind girls included, to do just that. One can hardly fault a suspense film for being suspenseful, after all.

Since "blindness" is a core tenet of *See No Evil* (even in the title!), it is appropriate that director Fleischer obsesses on the way the camera sees things. For instance, the killer is never seen (until the climax) except as a pair of cowboy boots and jeans. Yet, the camera nicely reveals that he is evil in the opening sequence, as this figure walks a busy city strip that offers pertinent clues to his nature. The theater behind him is showing a double feature: *The Convent Murders* and *The Rapist Cult*. Other images of violence abound. We see toy guns, violent headlines on newspapers, and images of violence on TV. There are those viewers who complained that *See No Evil* never explained why Jacko was a killer, but the answers are all around him. Everything, from movies to TV, to newspapers, is filled with violence. By association, he is just one more violent component of a violent world. It is no coincidence that every image that accompanies this booted killer on his walk through the metropolis is related to death. This guy is death, himself! Or, at the very least, this is how the killer sees his world, made up of death, and again we should remember that sight is important to the film.

Fleischer plays his "game of vision" throughout the picture. His camera tracks Sarah's path into her house as if to count the footfalls, to chart the distance from the front door to the stairs. Why is this important? Again, this is how the character in the drama "sees" the world: a space to be navigated. To her, the walk from house to stairs is not a visual trip, but a set number of footsteps, a path, in darkness, from one place to another. The camera, by tracking this distance, expresses Sarah's perception of the walk.

Fleischer's camera spends much of the film's running time perched at ground level, making viewers acutely aware of space and distance, a very effective stance to adopt in a film in which every step to freedom is a challenge. Furthermore, by not revealing Jacko's face, Fleischer again creates an empathy with Sarah. Like this blind woman, we do not know who the killer is; we are literally left in the dark. Just as Sarah would not know the killer if she ran into him again, nor would we. Unless, of course, we recognized the boots...

See No Evil is one of those movies that is so successful at creating empathy for its star (and in expressing her limited point of view), that it becomes anxiety provoking. Accordingly, Fleischer has some wicked fun at the audience's expense as Sarah makes her way through a house that she does not realize is littered with corpses. Fleischer revels in revealing this massacre, again and again, until a real dread about it has been formed. When Sarah drops a pen, the camera tracks down to the floor, and we see the feet of a corpse in the background. Again, Sarah has no access to this information. To the blind, the dead are literally invisible. This tense setup, in which the audience is aware of something the protagonist is not, is very effective in generating suspense.

In another startling moment, Sandy's dead hand pops into the foreground of a frame, animated by rigor mortis. It's an unexpected jolt, as is the sight of poor Uncle George, bloodied and dead in the bathtub.

Watching Mia Farrow tumble down stairs, slip in the mud, fight her way out of captivity, and get lost in the woods, one senses how exhausting a film this must have been to make. The actress gives it her all and is ably supported by the director, who makes the agony of her situation almost tangible. We identify with her misery, and consequently begin to pull for her to survive.

Though there are clearly echoes of *Wait Until Dark* (1967) in the film, *See No Evil* is determined to cross all lines of good taste and appropriateness in its effort to scare. Really, it is a harrowing film.

Of course, there are some problems. Sarah seems way too agile for someone who has only recently been blinded. Also, the sequence with the gypsy — a red herring — seems an unnecessary twist in an already twisted story. Furthermore, wind seems to function selectively (and with purpose) in the film, blowing open doors just at the precise moment Sarah might be affected by them, and so forth. That's a cheat, but for the most part Fleischer plays fair with the audience, showing them only what they need to see, not what they want to see. As a critic,

this reviewer likes the way his camera reveals just a bit at a time, providing necessary, sometimes contradictory tidbits of information. The camera keeps the audience blinded with tunnelvision, and it is a nice metaphor for Sarah's condition. Those who objected to this film did so primarily on the basis that it feels manipulative. Yet, remembering the words of Alfred Hitchcock, a good suspense film should "play an audience like a piano." *See No Evil* accomplishes that directive, and reaches a crescendo of horror ... even if it doesn't play nice.

LEGACY: *See No Evil* is on the re-make trail for 2003.

Straw Dogs (1971) ✶ ✶ ✶ ✶

Critical Reception

"The subject of *Straw Dogs* is machismo. It has been the obsession behind most of Peckinpah's other films; now that it's out in the open, his strength and follies are clearly visible.... The setting, music, and the people are deliberately disquieting. It *is* a thriller — a machine headed for destruction ... the goal of the movie is to demonstrate that David *enjoys* the killing, and achieves his manhood in that self-recognition ... it confirms the old militarists' view that pacifism is unmanly, is pussyfooting, is false to nature.... [This is] a fascist work of art."— Pauline Kael, *New Yorker*, January 29, 1972, pages 80 — 85.

"...literally sophomoric. It resembles the horrified reaction of an adolescent to the discovery that evil really exists in the world, and his brief, if passionate, contemplation of the possibility that it might be universal. This, of course, is a no more realistic appraisal of the world than the unblemished cheerfulness of a TV sitcom's microcosms. It is the obligation of the mature artist to reconcile and integrate these half-truths, and that is precisely where Peckinpah's vision fails him. *Straw Dogs* is a meaningless attack on a straw man — unredeemed, unrelenting evil."— Richard Schickel, *Life*: "Don't Play It Again Sam," February 11, 1972, page 14.

"What makes the violence of *Straw Dogs* particularly disturbing is that Peckinpah steers clear of the stock responses to it. On the one hand, he does not equate violence with heroism.... On the other hand, Peckinpah does not equate violence with villainy by implying that it could and should have been avoided... Peckinpah is not concerned with putting labels of right or wrong on the violent actions and reactions in the film. Here, as in his earlier films, he is focusing on the tension between the individual and the disintegrating forces of society."— William Johnson, *Film Quarterly*, 1972, pages 61–64.

"...most critics seem to have missed the point, and believe it [*Straw Dogs*] advocates violence as some kind of rite of passage, glorifies it as heroic act.... In *Straw Dogs*, Peckinpah's point is the horrible inevitability of human brutality, especially when an individual attempts to evade it." — Robert Philip Kolker, *Journal of Popular Film*: "Oranges, Dogs, and Ultra-Violence," Summer 1972, pages 159–172.

Cast & Crew

CAST: Dustin Hoffman (David Sumner); Susan George (Amy Sumner); David Warner (Henry Niles); Ken Hutchison (Norman); Peter Vaughn, T.P. McKenna, Del Henney, Jim Norton, Donald Webster, Len Jones, Sally Thomsett, Robert Keegan, Peter Arne, Cherina Scher, Colin Welland.

CREW: From Cinerama Releasing Corp, ABC Pictures Corp. Presents Dustin Hoffman in Sam Peckinpah's film of a Daniel Melnick Production, *Straw Dogs*. *Director of Photography:* John Coquillon. *Production Design Consultant:* Julia Trevelyan Oman. *Music:* Jerry Fielding. *Screenplay:* David Zelag Goodman, Sam Peckinpah. *Producer:* David Melnick. *Director:* Sam Peckinpah. *Production Design:* Ray Simm. *Art Director:* Ken Bridgeman. *Set Dresser:* Peter James. *Titles Designed by:* Anthony Goldschmidt. *Assistant Director:* Peter James. *Assistant Director:* Terry Marcel. *Continuity:* Pamela Davies. *Camera Operator:* Herbert Smith. *Sound Recordist:* John Bramail. *Make-up:* Harry Frampton. *Wardrobe:* Tiny Nicholls. *Hairdresser:* Bobbie Smith. *Dialogue Director:* Katie Haber. *Special Effects:* John Richardson. *Stunt Coordinator:* Bill Cornelius. *Film Editors:* Roger Spottiswoode, Paul Davies, Tony Lawson. *Editorial Consultant:* Robert Wolfe. *Sound Editor:* Garth Craven. *Associate Producer:* James Swann. *Production Supervisor:* Derek Kavanagh. *Casting:* Miriam Brickman. *Based on the novel* The Siege of Trencher's Farm *by:* Gordon Williams. *Filmed on location in* the west of England and at Twickenham Film Studios, Twickenham, Middlesex, England, for Talent Associate Films Ltd. and Amerbroco Films Ltd. *M.P.A.A. Rating:* R. *Running time:* 117 minutes.

SYNOPSIS: A nerdy American mathematician, David Sumner, and his gorgeous wife, Amy, rent a cottage in the remote English village where she grew up. There, David hopes to write a book in peace, but soon finds that the locals are not very accepting of him or his foreign ways. Amy's old boyfriend, Charlie, is a macho guy who leads a crew of thugs and lowlifes. David hires the bunch to repair the roof over his cottage garage, but when he and Amy are gone shopping, the men go into the house and steal a pair of Amy's underwear. Charlie is convinced that Amy still wants him, not David.

Charlie and the others delay work on the roof, irritating David. Meanwhile, they leer at Amy, who strips for a bath in plain view of the rowdies because she's angry with David. Another signal of trouble occurs on a tight country road when Charlie and his buddies try to run David into the path of oncoming traffic. When the family cat goes missing, Amy is sure Charlie has killed it. The cat shows up hanged in the bathroom closet, and Amy believes it was displayed there to prove to David that the fellas could get into his bedroom. But David is slow to point fingers and act decisively. Instead, he invites the thugs into his house and asks their help in carrying in a bear trap. He even shares a beer with them. Amy thinks David is a coward pure and simple, and is dead set against it when Charlie and his crew invite David to go out hunting with them.

While on the hunting trip, the crew ditches David at the first opportunity (saying he must wait for the ducks to show up...). They circle back to his cottage, and Charlie rapes Amy. She protests at first, but eventually gives over. Then, the others show up for a piece of the action too, and Amy is raped repeatedly. David arrives home and argues with Amy, who doesn't tell him what has happened. Finally shoring up his courage, David fires the men from the roof job, still unaware of their worst infraction.

The deadly events come to a head when the village idiot, Henry Niles, son of the town drunk and head troublemaker, accidentally kills the beautiful young Janice. When David accidentally hits Niles with his car, he gives him sanctuary in his cottage. But Charlie and his boys show up, spitting-mad, and demanding David turn over Henry. David refuses to turn the boy over to a mob, and Charlie's gang lays siege to the house. The town magistrate arrives to straighten things out, but is soon murdered by the thugs. Something snaps inside David, and he decides he will fight all five men, till death if necessary. He methodically defends his home with boiling water, bear traps, and anything else he can find. In the end, David is victorious, and for the first time in his life feels he is a man worthy of Amy's respect. Newly confident, David drives Henry Niles to the authorities...

COMMENTARY: Say what you will about the violent films of the 1970s, but at least they were generally about something. *A Clockwork Orange, Deliverance, Straw Dogs, The Last House on the Left*, and *The Wicker Man* were all appallingly brutal, it's true, but unlike *Rambo*, any *Friday the 13th* or the first-person video game shoot 'em ups of the 1990s, at least they had reasons and rationale for their intense violence. The violence in those pictures revealed something important, such as middle-class hypocrisy in *Last House*, or the freedom to choose in *A Clockwork Orange*. Nowhere is violence more clearly examined than in Sam Peckinpah's *Straw Dogs*, a film that attempts to discern the real meaning of courage, and looks at what it means to be a "man."

There are legions of viewers who hate this movie, and what they perceive it stands for. They look at David's choice to resolve conflict with violence, his bold post-ambush affirmation that he "did it," and that he "got 'em all" as some kind of vindication of brutality and killing. Contrarily, the film seems to go to great pains to state the argument that David becomes a killer only when it is a last resort. It is Amy, his wife, and the local thugs, who meet with the film's venom because they are the ones with the retrograde assumptions about what it means to be a man, a hero.

The conflict in *Straw Dogs* arises out of two factors. The first is that David is an outsider, and his ways are different. He is an intellectual man, a thinker, in a town where men make their livings as farm workers, repairmen, carpenters and the like. In other words, he is mind-oriented; they are body-oriented. Thus David and Charlie are opposites. This plays out even in the physical casting. Charlie (Hutchison) is large, physical and imposing. David (Hoffman) is short, wormy, and wears glasses. He is the evolved modern man versus Charlie's caveman. The town is fascinated with David because he is so totally different from what villagers are used to seeing. Some people (like Janice) are attracted to him, and others, like Charlie, feel threatened by him. If Europeans had rednecks, these townspeople would certainly qualify (they even sing songs about sexual intercourse with livestock...). This culture clash makes David feel the inferiority that all nerds feel when faced with physically capable, athletic men. It also causes Charlie and his gang to snicker at David behind his back. He is not accepted by the gang because he is not big and strong, and physically powerful.

The second conflict involves Amy. One must remember that she too has grown up in this town. In fact, she dated Charlie — she grew up with Charlie — and hence has more in common with his mindset than with David's. To Amy, David is different from any man she has ever known, and she has contempt for him because he is not strong in the way that Charlie is, the way she is familiar with. She doesn't understand David's true strength is as a civilized human being. For instance, Amy expects to be carried away in love, but David is a methodical and unromantic person. Before sex, he takes off his watch, his glasses, and then pauses to set his alarm. Though he is interested and playful, he is not overwhelmingly erotic or "forceful," and Amy sees this, in comparison with the macho Charlie, as less than manly.

Amy criticizes David, arguing that she should leave him "alone" with his blackboard. Her ego can't take David's attitude towards romance. She is used to a man who will command and dominate her, and just does not know what to make of David.

And that's just in the bedroom. Clearly, Amy also does not understand David in other avenues of interpersonal communication. When the cat is killed, David feels it is not right to blatantly accuse Charlie of murder until he knows the situation. He shows too much rationality in this stance, and not enough emotion. Amy takes his stance as one of cowardice: he doesn't have enough backbone for her taste. Were the situation reversed, Charlie would come out and brutalize David over a suspected wrong. Again, it is the battle of evolved man versus unevolved man, but in this case, David is sabotaged by his choice of women. Amy cannot understand why David treats his enemies with respect and courtesy, and even sees such behavior as weakness. And, no doubt, there is some truth to that. By growing up in an environment where he never had to fight, David is slow to act, and reluctant to fight. His delays give rise to Amy's rape in one sense or another (though she leads Charlie on, and parades around in front of him half-naked...).

But, the interesting thing about these characters is that David, for all his flaws, is seen as superior to the natives because he shows one quality that everybody else lacks: empathy. When David takes care of Niles, the village idiot, he notes that the villagers must be worried about Janice. "I know how I'd feel if I had a daughter missing," he says with a sense of mercy. So he sympathizes with his enemies, and with someone of a lesser intelligence (Henry Niles). In fact, it

is so important to him that the matter be handled justly that he risks his life to save Niles from the mob. That, finally, is what prompts David to violence: the protection of the innocent.

It is in this crucible of pressure that Amy shows her true colors (and her inclination towards the townspeople who have refused to accept her choice of husband). "I don't care!" She says of Niles, showing no empathy for him whatsoever. All she cares about is her own protection. But David does fight, and win, not for himself, but for the "intellectual" principle of justice. What Peckinpah seems to be saying is that civilized man has the capacity to use violence (and to use it intelligently) when the situation warrants it. He may be slow to act because he reasons that violence usually solves nothing, but eventually he will act, and act definitively. It's a little sad, however, that Amy only comes around when David, acting as she would expect of a man, starts to slap her around and talk to her in the language she is accustomed to. Some people, the film says, don't change. They're stuck in their parochial perceptions.

Does *Straw Dogs* advocate violence? No, not really. What it actually advocates is justice. There is that moment when David declares "I did it, I beat 'em all," but one should note that the victory is immediately followed by another attack — the final assault from one of the surviving gang. The moment of David's victory is immediately undercut by another battle, one in which Amy comes to his defense. The fact of the matter is that he didn't beat the gang alone, he needed Amy to help. So it is hard to see how the film advocates violence or a sense of machismo. Indeed, David's declaration of victory is less a statement of the film's philosophy than a reiteration of a popular horror movie cliché. David declares victory, fostering a false peace, and then *BOOM!* Up pops another villain! It's the old lull before the peak, the calm before the storm, and it is a technical necessity in horror film finales.

It seems clear that in *Straw Dogs*, David

is violent when it is a matter of protecting that which he loves and cherishes (both people and principles). When Charlie is violent, it is to take what he wants, whether that "want" be Amy, Niles, or the cat. He is at the whim of his violence, and unable to express his desires in any but brutal fashions. David is more evolved, but he can fight on Charlie's level when push comes to shove. It's not so much "the savage within us all," as it is meeting brute force with brute force when the situation warrants it.

All this meditation on violence, and what it means to be a man, is handled expertly by Peckinpah, a director who films violence as though a dance. Slow-motion photography, tight framing, quick cuts, cockeyed angles and other formalist techniques combine beautifully to form the film's final siege. This battle is long in coming (and some people find the film boring up to this point), but it caps off the thematic point of the film: that David is finally roused to violence when he has exhausted all civilized means of dealing with Charlie.

Straw Dogs is built on a strong horror foundation. The siege is a popular conceit for genre films (witness *Night of the Living Dead* and *Assault on Precinct 13*). The idea of an outsider in a strange land is another oft-seen set up (witness *And Soon the Darkness* and *The Wicker Man*), and even the family versus family nature of the film's conflict is one that has been seen many times (*Last House on the Left*, *The Hills Have Eyes* and other work of Wes Craven come to mind immediately). Even the idea of civilized man versus uncivilized man is horror fodder (seen in *Deliverance* and *The Texas Chainsaw Massacre*, among others). Yet *Straw Dogs* is valuable and distinct for the manner in which it goes beyond these cornerstones to sketch interesting and provocative characters.

There is ample reason, for instance, to believe that Amy was at least half courting Charlie's sexual advances. The character is sexualized from the start, and we see her with erect nipples in no less than the second or third shot of the film. Later, she refuses to wear a bra, and gallivants about naked. The feminists out there will no doubt say that she was not courting rape — but in this town, in this environment, with these guys around? Isn't her action inflammatory at the least, considering the tenor of the locals? That's just one topic that *Straw Dogs* leaves open for debate, but there are more.

For instance, is David so far out a leftie (i.e. liberal) that he puts the defense of a known murderer (Niles) above the defense of his wife? There's evidence of that too. Basically, all the characters are shaded by their foibles and biases, and events can be interpreted in different ways.

There are no easy answers about man's violent nature, and so *Straw Dogs* cannot hope to easily answer the questions it so artfully raises. As is so often the case in film, it is the discussion that's important, not the solution. And the words, the punctuation to that discussion are the formalist techniques of Sam Peckinpah, a director who knew a thing or two about violence. A challenging picture, *Straw Dogs* is one of the 1970s' most endlessly fascinating, and endlessly debated, horror films.

Vampire Circus

Cast & Crew

CAST: Adrienne Corri (Gypsy); Thorley Walters (Bürgermesiter); Lynne Frederick (Dora Mueller); Richard Owens (Kersh); Robin Hunter (Hauser); Robin Sachs (Henreich); David Prowse (Strongman); Laurence Payne (Mueller).

CREW: *Directed by:* Robert Young. *Written by:* Judson Kingberg. *Director of Photography:* Moray Grant. *Produced by:* Wilbur Stark. *Film Editor:* Peter Musgrave. A Hammer Production. *M.P.A.A. Rating:* R. *Running Time:* 88 minutes.

DETAILS: In early 19th century Eastern Europe, a circus run by vampires and other ghouls makes its home in a village infected with the plague. Before long, the town is in double trouble. One of Hammer's few non–Dracula, non–Carmilla vampire tales, with some interesting moments.

Werewolves on Wheels

Cast & Crew

CAST: Severn Darden (One); Stephen Oliver (Adam); Duece Berry (Tarot); D. J. Anderson (Helena).

CREW: *Directed by:* Michel Levesque. *Written by:* David M. Kauffman, Michel Levesque. *Produced by:* Paul Lewis. *Director of Photography:* Isadore Mankofsky. *Film Editor:* Peter Parsheles. *M.P.A.A. Rating:* R. *Running Time:* 85 minutes.

DETAILS: A bold (yet bizarre) attempt to meld "biker" movies like *Easy Rider* (1969) with the horror genre. It starts rolling when a gang of roaming cyclists is transformed into werewolves after confronting a demonic cult.

Who Slew Auntie Roo? (1971) * * *

Cast & Crew

CAST: Shelley Winters (Mrs. Forrest); Mark Lester (Christopher); Ralph Richardson (Mr. Benton); Judy Cornell (Clarine); Michael Gothard (Albie); Hugh Griffith (the Pigman); Lionel Jeffries (Willoughby); Chloe Franks (Katy); Rosalie Crutchley (Miss Henley); Pat Heywood (Dr. Mason); Richard Beaumont (Peter); Jacquelin Cowper (Angela); Marianne Stone (Miss Wilcox); Charlotte Sayce (Katharine).

CREW: American International Pictures, James H. Nicholson and Samuel Z. Arkoff present an American International/Hemdale Production. *Casting:* Sally Nicholl. *Production Manager:* Donald Toms. *Assistant Director:* Colin Brewer. *Wardrobe Supervisor:* Bridget Sellers. *Color:* Movielab. *Film Editor:* Tristam Cones. *Art Director:* George Provis. *Director of Photography:* Desmond Dickinson. *Camera Operator:* Norman Jones. *Sound Recorder:* Ken Ritchie, Richard Langford. *Sound Editor:* Peter Leonard. *Make-up:* Eddie Knight, Sylvia Craft. *Hairdressing:* Pat McDermott, Joyce Jones. *Continuity:* June Randall. *Music:* Kenneth V. Jones. *Executive Producer:* John Pellatt. *Original Screenplay:* David Osborn. *Screenplay:* Robert Blees, James Sangster. *Additional Dialogue:* Gavin Lambert. *Executive Producers:* Samuel Z. Arkoff, James H. Nicholson. *Directed by:* Curtis Harrington. Filmed at Shepperton Studios, Middlesex, England. *M.P.A.A. Rating:* PG. *Running Time:* 90 minutes.

SYNOPSIS: In the midst of a terrible storm in the 1930s, a medium named Benton arrives at the Forrest mansion to conduct a séance. Old Mrs. Forrest, Auntie Roo, is a show-business has-been who is desperate to contact her dead daughter, Catherine. She is unaware that her servants and Mr. Benton are scamming her. Others in the community are likewise unaware that every night, Auntie Roo cradles and sings to the rotting corpse of her dead child in a secret nursery...

At the annual Christmas party at Auntie Roo's house, two orphans (Katie and Christopher) stow away in the trunk of Inspector Willoughby's car, and attend the party. Auntie Roo welcomes them along with the other children, stuffs them all with fine food, and showers them with presents. On Christmas morning, it snows and Roo invites Katie, who resembles her beloved Catherine, to come live with her permanently. She doesn't extend the same offer to Christopher. A suspicious Christopher uses the house dumbwaiter to spy on Auntie Roo, and learns how she caters to the corpse in Catherine's room. Chris escapes Roo's detection, but is now convinced that she is evil, like the witch in *Hansel and Gretel*.

When it is time for the children to leave for the orphanage, Katie is nowhere to be found, and Chris is convinced Roo is hiding her, fattening her up to eat her. In fact, Roo now believes Katie is Catherine's reincarnation, and has trapped her in the house! No one at the orphanage believes Christopher's story because he has a reputation as a liar, and Roo is known as a kind benefactor of children. Christopher sneaks back to Roo's house to rescue his sister, and steal Roo's valuable jewels. He finds Katie in the secret nursery, and convinces her to leave Roo the witch before they are both eaten for supper. Unfortunately, Roo re-captures the children before they can escape. She then fires all the house help when she learns of their plan to scam her. Now it is just her and the two children in the giant mansion.

Inspector Willoughby drops by the next morning to search the house for the two missing children. He does not find the secret room where they are trapped, and goes on about his business. Christopher matches wits with Roo, with his sister's freedom the prize.

Roo locks the children in a closet as she prepares a meal, but they outsmart her, escape and lock her inside. Then they start a fire in the house, killing Roo. They escape "the evil witch's" dungeon with Roo's jewels.

COMMENTARY: If you think about it, most good horror movies come from stories we first encountered in childhood. For instance, *The Blair Witch Project*, with kids lost in the woods, evokes portions of *Hansel and Gretel*. So it's only natural that along comes *Who Slew Auntie Roo*, a mild horror film that mines territory all too familiar to the young. It is one part *Hansel and Gretel*, and one part *The Boy Who Cried Wolf*. The result is an entertaining, resonant picture that explores horror in a decidedly minor key.

"Crazy" Auntie Roo, played by Shelley Winters as a smothering psychopath, doubles for Hansel and Gretel's witch, of course, and Christopher and Katie represent the title characters themselves. They lose their way, are entrapped by a witch, and fear a terrible end. What's interesting, however, is that this comparison is mostly in the mind of the children. They know the story of *Hansel and Gretel*, and so put Roo into that context. Naturally, she never intends to eat them, only to take care of them. This may represent two different things. Firstly, the childish misperception that Roo is a witch could be an indication that children see the world in a different light and that their defense mechanisms come up when they are threatened. Hence, when they meet a psychopath, their minds categorize her as a witch, like the one from a familiar story. Oppositely, the children may simply be wrong about Roo. She seems more pitiful a character than an evil one, and there is some sympathy generated for her at the end of the story when the children lock her up and burn her alive (as if in an oven...). That fate hardly seems deserved.

Who Slew Auntie Roo also plays on elements from the tale of the boy who cried wolf. Specifically, Christopher has lied so frequently and so effectively that no one believes him when he tells them his crazy story about Roo and Katie, which happens to be true. In this case, it is fair to say that the characters are archetypal. They are also Dickensian: orphans, out of *Oliver Twist*, perhaps. Whatever the intended source material, *Who Slew Auntie Roo* seems to be a chillingly good fairy tale put to celluloid. It is never really scary, and Roo is a villain only by virtue of her insanity, but it is important to remember that the images of horror movies are also the images of fairy tales.

For how different from the giant in *Jack and the Beanstalk* is Leatherface, when push comes to shove? Both the fairy tale and the horror film play on basic fears (of being eaten; of being captured; of being taken away from family) with basic villains (giants; witches; ghouls; flesh-eating cannibals...). *Who Slew Auntie Roo* simply takes the logical step of making the connection a tad more obvious. One cannot watch this film without thinking of *Hansel and Gretel,* and the like. Thus there's a pleasantly nostalgic feeling to the film.

The same feeling is generated by *Who Slew Auntie Roo*'s setting: Christmas time. The Christmas holiday has, for whatever reason, frequently been the locale of horror stories. *How the Grinch Stole Christmas* is, after all, a story about a green monster who subverts the holiday for his own purposes. Perhaps it is an effective setting because people generally associate pleasant things with snow, Christmas trees, presents, and turkey dinners, and when something terrible happens, it is all the more jarring. *Gremlins* (1984) traded on this fact with a ghoulish story about Santa Claus and a chimney. *Silent Night, Deadly Night* (1984) and all its dreadful sequels likewise mined the holidays for gruesomeness and gore instead of nogg and cheer. But, besides again feeling Dickensian (à la *A Christmas Carol*), *Auntie Roo* somehow feels classic with this combination of fairy tale and holiday settings

Fans of the hard stuff are not going to be really fond of this film. Despite the corpse in the nursery (which dissolves in Roo's grip...), and tense moments in dumbwaiters, this is might accurately be described as a horror film for children.

The Wicker Man (1971) ✶ ✶ ✶ ✶

Critical Reception

"Robin Hardy directed the well-researched film so skillfully that second and third viewings are enjoyable. Richly photographed, beautifully paced and intelligently directed."— Frank Manchel, *An Album of Modern Horror Films*, Franklin Watts, Publisher, 1983, page 45.

"Literate and intelligently conceived horror story with strong sexual and religious overtones, building to a shocking and disturbing climax."— Howard Maxford, *The A to Z of Horror Films*, Indiana University Press, 1997, page 290.

Cast & Crew

CAST: Edward Woodward (Sgt. Howie); Britt Ekland (Willow); Diane Cilento (Miss Rose); Ingrid Pitt (Librarian); Christopher Lee (Lord Summerisle); Roy Boyd (Broome); Walter Carr (School Master); Lindsay Kemp (Aldo MacGregor); Kevin Collins (Old Fisherman); Russell Waters (Harbor Master); Leslie MacKie (Daisy); Irene Sunters (Mrs. Morrison); Ian Campbell (Oak); Aubrey Morris (Old Graveyard Groundskeeper); Donald Eccles (T.H. Lennox); Geraldine Cowper (Rowan Morrison); Barbara Ann Brown (Woman with Baby);

Juliette Cadzow (Villager on Summerisle); Ross Campbell (Communicant); Penny Cluer (Callie); Michael Cole (Musician); Myra Forsyth (Mrs. Grimmond); John Hallam (P. C. McTaggert); Alison Hughes (Fiancée to Howie); Charles Kearney (Butcher); Fiona Kennedy (Holly); John MacGregor (Baker); Jimmy Mackenzie (Briar); Jennifer Martin (Myrtle Morrison); Bernard Murray (Musician); Helen Norman (Villager on Summerisle); Lorraine Peters (Girl on Grave); Tony Roper (Postman); John Sharp (Doctor Ewan); Elizabeth Sinclair (Villager on Summerisle); Andrew Tompkins (Musician); Ian Wilson (Communicant); Richard Wren (Ash Buchanan); John Young (Fishmonger).

CREW: British Lion Presents a Peter Snell Production, *Anthony Shaffer's The Wicker Man. Sound Editor:* Vernon Messenger. *Assistant Editor:* Denis Whitehouse. *Casting Director:* Maggie Cartier. *Publicity:* Frank Law. *Stills:* John Brown. *Wardrobe Supervisor:* Masada Wilmot. *Make-up:* Billy Partleton. *Hairdresser:* Ian Dorman. *Assistant Director:* Jake Wright. *Location Manager:* Jilda Smith. *Unit Manager:* Mike Cowans. *Continuity:* Sue Merry. *Production Secretary:* Beryl Harvey. *Camera Operator:* Jimmy Devis. *Focus:* Mike Drew. *Sound:* Robin Gregory, Bob Jones. *Production Manager:* Ted Morley. *Choreographer:* Stewart Hopps. *Costume Designer:* Sue Yelland. *Second Unit Photography:* Peter Allwork. *Associate Musical Director:* Gary Carpenter. *Music Performed by:* Magnet. *"Corn Rigs" Sung by:* Paul Giovanni. *Art Director:* Seamus Flannery. *Music Composed by:* Paul Giovanni. *Director of Photography:* Harry Waxman. *Film Editor:* Eric Boyd-Perkins. *Screenplay:* Anthony Shaffer. *Produced by:* Peter Snell. *Directed by:* Robin Hardy. *M.P.A.A. Rating:* R. *Running time:* 84 minutes.

SYNOPSIS: Sgt. Howe, a by-the-book, prim-and-proper English police officer, flies to the island of Summerisle off the west coast of Scotland to investigate reports of a missing girl named Rowan Morrison. On arrival, he visits Rowan's family, and finds that they are unconcerned about her disappearance. That night, he stays at the Green Man Inn, and Willow, the innkeeper's beautiful daughter, attempts to tempt him with an alluring

nude dance. Howe summons all of his Christianity to avoid temptation, remembering his fiancée at home, and forces himself to sleep in peace.

The next morning, Sgt. Howe witnesses the games and rituals of the people of Summerisle, most of which concern fertility and phallic symbols. Howe abhors the rampant sexuality, but continues his search nonetheless. He discovers Rowan's name in the teacher's roll book, though neither the teacher nor the students claim to know her. The teacher informs the sergeant of Summerisle's pagan beliefs, and that Rowan is, in Christian terms, considered dead.

Howe proceeds to the graveyard to find Rowan's corpse, and leaves a crucifix at her grave, horrified by the paganism of the people. He then visits the island's leader, Lord Summerisle, and they debate their respective religions. Summerisle grants Howe permission to exhume Rowan's body, and determine the cause of death, but Howe finds only a dead rabbit in the coffin. It slowly dawns on Howe that Rowan was murdered in some barbaric ritual, and he informs Summerisle that he intends to launch a full-scale inquiry into the matter. His specific fear is that Rowan was sacrificed as part of last year's May Day festival. Howe resolves to remain on the island for the upcoming May Day celebration, just to be sure the atrocity is not repeated.

At the town library, Howe reads about May Day and learns that the ritual involves human sacrifices and a huge bonfire around wicker effigies ... all conducted with the intent of improving crop fertility, which has been bad in recent years. When Howe finds his plane sabotaged and the rituals beginning, he steals a costume and joins the processional as it marches through the town, down the mountainside and finally to the beach. There, on a cliff, the ritual sacrifice to the Sun God will occur. There, he also finds his quarry: Rowan Morrison alive and well.

Strangely, Rowan is in no need of rescuing. Her disappearance was merely a ruse to bring Howe to the island. Howe realizes he has been led about step by step by Summerisle and his heathen people. It is Howe, a Christian crusader, a virgin, and now a participant in the parade, who is to be the human sacrifice for the year! At Summerisle's instruction, Howe meets his appointment with the giant wicker man, a cage in which he is burned alive in honor of pagan gods.

COMMENTARY: One of the most cleverly crafted films to come out of the 1970s, *The Wicker Man* is a stinging indictment of religion in general, and Christianity in particular. It is structured as a mystery, but as usual, the best mysteries are those which end with a total, yet logical, surprise. *The Wicker Man* satisfies that requirement and so much more as it reaches its terrifying apex.

It is not too difficult to view *The Wicker Man* as a culture clash. An outsider, a prim and proper Christian policeman (Howe), arrives in Summerisle, an island with its own customs. Yet, oddly, the values of the outsider are not, in this situation, lauded above those of the natives. Instead, Howe is shown to be a hypocrite as director Robin Hardy spells out a well-defined Christianity vs. Paganism debate. His point seems to be, correctly, that there are absurdities and contradictions in all religions, so it is useless and wasteful to bother debating which one is better or superior. Yet, Sgt. Howe is unable to see past his faith to determine the fallacies of his own chosen belief system. He is an arrogant Christian who arrives in a culture he knows nothing about, and then rapidly determines that it is inferior because Christianity has not taken hold there. When Howe brazenly deposits a makeshift crucifix upon Rowan's tomb, he is imposing his own belief system on someone (and the family of someone) that has already thoughtfully developed a different set of beliefs. What right does he have to supersede that decision, simply because *he* values Christianity? What arrogance!

The battle of the religions rages in other ways throughout the film as well. Howe is upset that the Summerisle people are pagans. He thus sees them as primitives who are "raving mad." This is because they embrace sexuality (rather than repressing it, as is typical of Christianity), and believe that when human life ends, the soul returns to trees, fires, air, the water and other elements. For Howe, that is a leap of belief he will not take. Yet what does he believe? That Jesus walked on water? That Jesus returned from the dead in the resurrection? That Jesus was born without an earthly father? That the wine and wafer of communion are the Lord's body and blood? Isn't that last bit representative of ... *gasp* ... cannibalism? This is the connection Howe is unable to make. He can't see that his religion is no more or less believable than anybody else's.

The Wicker Man artfully brings home this point, and raises the possibility that Christianity's ascent in the world is little more than a fluke. The people of Summerisle, after all, live in an alternative society in which they are quite happy, and quite religious. No, they don't have churches, or ministers, and yes, their rites feature nudity and fertility, but that just makes so-called "paganism" different from Christianity, not necessarily wrong.

But, going even deeper, *The Wicker Man* is impressive because by pitting two disparate religions against one another, it makes an interesting point. At the finale of the film, the Summerisle residents pray to their God, killing Howe, as he prays to his own savior while awaiting his death. There is a feeling of futility here, that both parties are, in fact, deluded. Man shouldn't be killing his brother over religious differences, and the film becomes an indictment of the idea of religion as a whole. It is seen as a false comfort. It won't grow the crops, and it won't give you peace everlasting. It is just an excuse by which people kill each other. That's a well-thought-out point, and whenever this author is confronted with people who seem to believe that horror movies are a bad influence on society, he politely reminds

Christopher Lee and Britt Ekland prepare for location shooting on *The Wicker Man* (1971).

them that, in point of fact, religion is a worse influence on society. Whether Muslim or Christian, more people have killed each other over religion than have ever killed each other over a venue of ideas (such as a genre of film, like horror). *The Wicker Man* likewise understands how religion can be poisonous.

What is rather remarkable about this film is not that it has so unique a theme, but that it explores it with such depth and success. The film leads us, like Howe, to a wholly unexpected destination. At first, the people of Summerisle merely seem different, then seductive, then mysterious. It is not until it is too late that the audience realizes just how dangerous the island is, and that Howe has walked into a well-designed trap. Indeed, the Summerisle folk have been waiting for just such a powerful sacrifice for a long time. Howe is a man who came of his own free will. He is a man who came as a virgin (no

pre-marital sex, thank you, Ms. Ekland!). He is a man who came as a voice of the law, and, finally, as a fool. All these things make him the perfect target. It is only in understanding all this that one sees why the film has gone to such a great effort to delineate Howe as a rigid prude, as a religious zealot. Those are the very things that cost him his life!

The Wicker Man is a highly sexual film, another reason that the right wing probably wouldn't appreciate it. However, it uses sex to delineate another difference between Howe and the natives of the island. Ekland comes to Woodward, naked and irresistible, beckoning him to sex. Had he wanted to survive his trip (and had he understood the plan), he would have made love to her … and that would have mitigated his strength as a sacrifice. Instead, Woodward's Howe stuck to his "holy" guns, and evaded her seduction … thereby becoming a fool instead. He doesn't get that pre-marital sex, taboo in Catholicism, is encouraged on Summerisle.

The Maypole song (and ritual) is also highly sexual, and it is clear that the film benefits from the new freedom of the 1970s. Thus *The Wicker Man* can show a flashback of Christian communion at one moment, yet in another moment depict an orgy in the grass, with naked men and women making love over a grave. It's an odd, but potent combination that reminds us how very different belief systems can believe very different things.

The full breadth of *The Wicker Man*'s horror does not come until its climax. Howe has been led to a giant wicker man, where he pleads for his life. Seen from a low angle, this pagan statue is a gigantic and imposing symbol of inevitable doom. Outnumbered, Howe goes to his death, put inside the wicker man. He is then forced to watch as the natives light the wicker effigy from below, and fire starts to lick and lap closer and closer. It is a terrifying moment, as the audience realizes there will be no escape for Howe. This is the end of the line. It is a kind of sick joke, however, that the Summerisle people don't see it as murder. After all, they're giving him a martyr's death … what more could a good Christian want? If Howe truly believes that Heaven awaits him, he should have nothing to fear, right? Somehow, as the fire surrounds him, one gets the idea that the closed-minded Howe is *finally* questioning his beliefs.

The Wicker Man is not only a great and meaningful film, it is one of the ten best horror movies of the 1970s. It makes us look at our own religion and ask why it looks the way it does. It makes us question the things that organized religions want us to take for granted. It's a film about a man who is so cowed by his religion's dogma that he walks unwitting into a flame. That's a testament either to his faith, or his stupidity. You choose.

Willard (1971) ★ ★ ★ ½

Critical Reception

"…in its simple-minded way, *Willard* taps into a couple of good, common fantasies, … and its cleverness and appeal lies [*sic*] in the way … it imperceptibly modulates from the former to the latter…. *Willard* transcends its genre; becomes a metaphorical representation of what we have come to understand as … the tragedy of them — the tragedy of multiplication. The analogy might be between Willard and Mayor Lindsay, Willard and Robert McNamara, Willard and the chief executive of any sprawling social organism … where the population under his nominal control has outrun the known techniques of rational governance."— Richard Schickel, *Life*, August 27, 1971, page 11.

Cast & Crew

CAST: Bruce Davison (Willard Stiles); Sondra Locke (Joan); Elsa Lanchester (Henrietta Stiles); Michael Dante (Brandt); Jody Gilbert (Charlotte Stassen); William Hansen (Brasin); John Myhers (Carlson); J. Pat O'Malley (Jonathan Farley); Joan Shawlee (Alice); Ernest Borgnine (Al Martin); Almira Sessions (Carrie Smith); Pauline Drake (Ida Stassen); Helen Spring (Mrs. Becker); Alan Baxter (Spencer); Sherri Presnell (Mrs. Spencer).

CREW: From BCP, A Service of Cox Broacasting Corporation. *Music Composed and Conducted by:* Alex North. *Executive Producer:* Charles A. Pratt. *Screenplay:* Gilbert A. Ralston. *Based on the novel* Ratman's Notebooks *by:* Stephen Gilbert. *Produced by:* Mort Briskin.

Directed by: Daniel Mann. *Director of Photography:* Robert B. Hauser. *Art Director:* Howard Hollander. *Editorial Supervision:* Warren Low. *Assistant Director/Unit Production Manager:* Robert Goodstein. *Casting:* Irving Lande. *Set Decorator:* Ralph S. Hurst. *Chief Electrician:* Don Johnson. *Head Grip:* Robert Moore. *Sound Mixer:* Harold Lewis. *Construction Coordinator:* Harold Nyby. *Special Effects:* Bud David. *Properties:* Alan Gordon. *Script Supervisor:* Hazel Hall. *Make-up:* Gus Norin. *Hairstylist:* Hazel Washington. *Costumes:* Eric Seelig, Dorothy Barkley. *Socrates and Ben trained by:* Moe DiSesso. *Post-Production Supervisor:* Houseley Stevenson. *Assistant Film Editor:* Howard Deane. *Music Supervisor:* Milton Lustig. *Sound Effects:* James J. Klinger. *Recorded by:* Glenn Glenn Sound. *Photographic Effects:* Howard A. Anderson Company. *Color:* Deluxe. A Cinerama Release. *M.P.A.A. Rating:* PG. *Running Time:* 95 minutes.

P.O.V.

"Since it takes only 21 days for a rat to have a litter of ten to twelve, we bought a dozen and left it up to them" (10).—Moe Di Sesso, *Willard*'s rat trainer and wrangler, on the economics of rat breeding.

SYNOPSIS: Meek and mild clerk Willard Stiles lives a miserable existence. At home, he lives with an overbearing and sick mother who demands attention. At work, he must kowtow to the boss, the tyrannical Al Martin. Martin is the very man who stole the family business out from under Willard's family, and he takes a particular delight in humiliating young Stiles. Making matters worse, the Stiles mansion is falling apart from disrepair, and the once-wealthy family has fallen on hard times financially. Willard works 80 hours a week, but can only just manage to pay the bills. Although Al Martin has assigned Willard a beautiful temp, Joan, to help him sort out his job responsibilities, Willard is sure it is only a matter of time before he is fired.

On Willard's birthday, Willard's mother invites all of her old friends (all of whom want something from the family) for a party, and Willard gets angry. Blowing off steam, he goes to the backyard, and unexpectedly befriends several rats he finds living in the empty rock pool. Unlike the human beings all around him, Willard finds the rats responsive to his kindness, and sets about to train them. He has soon made friends of the little creatures. His favorite is the white mouse, Socrates, but the smartest of the bunch is a black rat that Willard names Ben.

When Al Martin refuses to give Willard a raise, he suggests that Willard sell the house to him. Willard refuses, and Martin berates him for being just like his old man. To get back at Martin, Willard releases his army of trained rats at Martin's anniversary party. A swarm of rats overrun the shindig, sending Martin's clients and high-society friends screaming away in terror.

The next day, Willard is forced to leave work when he learns that his mother has passed away. At her funeral, Willard gets news that the house is heavily mortgaged, and that there is no money left in his mother's estate. Before long, Martin and other vultures descend on the house, offering to help Willard in exchange for favors and ownership of the Stiles mansion. Willard holds the buzzards at bay, but overhears Martin's plan. The nasty old bastard wants to fire Willard, buy the house, and then level it so he can put up cheap apartments.

Soon, Willard's rat army has moved out of the backyard and into the cellar. Willard treats Socrates with real kindness, allowing him to sleep in his bedroom, but is inexplicably cruel to Ben. One day, Willard purchases a car with his mother's last sum of money, and drives Socrates and Ben to work with him. He stashes them in an out-of-the-way records room that only he visits. On the job, Willard starts to develop feelings for Joan, and she reciprocates, even buying a pet cat for him. Knowing a cat would never live with rats, Willard ditches the cat at his first opportunity. Even as all seems to be going well with the rats and Joan, another financial snafu strikes. As it turns out, Willard owes back taxes on his house. Unfortunately, not one of his mother's good-for-nothing friends will even consider lending him money. In desperate need of cash, Willard resolves to steal it from a rich client of Martin's. He uses his army of rats to spook Mr. and Mrs. Spencer, and then steals 8,000 dollars from their bedroom.

At home, the mistreated Ben starts to show signs of rebellion. At work, Martin hatches his plan to get the Stiles house, firing Willard and Joan. Then, to make matters worse, Martin discovers Socrates in the records room and bludgeons him to death. Avenging the death of his best friend, Willard and his army of rats pay Martin a visit at the office one night. Willard orders the rats to tear the bastard up, and they do. Horrified by his own actions, Willard decides it is time to cut bait. He abandons Ben and the rats at the office and drives home. Then, he drowns all of the rats at the house, destroying any evidence of his army of rodents. Ben is not about to be ignored, however. With his own army of rats, Ben finds his way home. Rather than make peace with Ben and the rats, Willard attempts to poison them with arsenic. For the intelligent Ben, this is the last straw, and the rats turn on their former master.

COMMENTARY: Though preceded by Alfred Hitchcock's *The Birds*, *Willard* is the film that began the "when animals attack" craze of the early '70s. It was a whopping (and unexpected) success at the box office, and it is not hard to see why. The film has quite a bit of depth and solid characterization. On the surface it's a tale of revenge, of a boy who trains rats to right the wrongs that the world has inflicted on him. But more than that, *Willard* is about the cycle of abuse. The film ultimately realizes that its protagonist, Willard Stiles, is no better than its villain, Martin.

The first half of the film spends a great deal of time depicting Willard Stiles' bleak, hopeless existence. He lives with his crazy mother, who he takes care of night and day. She is a nag who is constantly prodding him about something ("you're letting everything go," she complains from the comfort of her bed). Martin fills in, unfortunately, as Willard's father: the male authority figure in his life. Martin takes special pleasure in humiliating and embarrassing the boy, and it is no wonder that Willard feels empty and of no use. He takes a bus to work, and everybody tells him what to do and when to do it. He is psychologically abused by everyone from his mother and Martin (whose desk is decorated with a sign which reads "Do Unto Others Before They Do Unto You"...) to his mother's nosey friends. And the responsibilities! He has to keep the house up; he has to pay taxes; he has to go to work; he has to bring work home after hours. It's a miserable, unhappy life and Willard feels he has no control over it.

At this critical juncture, Willard starts to befriend the rats. Interestingly, this is the one point in the story where he could have opted to be kind and decent. But instead, Willard realizes he can be cruel to the rats, since he trains them and has control over them. Sadly, the cycle of abuse continues, and Willard opts to control the rats much the way Martin and his mother try to control him. The rat who takes the brunt of this abuse is the black one, Ben. While love and rewards are lavished on the white Socrates, Ben is treated like a poor cousin. "I'm the boss here!" Willard warns the rat, sounding like a carbon copy of Martin, the man he hates. Ben, though smart, is not allowed to sleep in the bed with Willard, like Socrates. And, he is unduly punished when he disappoints his master. Thus Willard does to Ben as Martin did unto him, and the miserable cycle continues.

For a time, Ben obeys his master, but then Willard grows even crueler (as Martin became increasingly cruel). Willard even abandons Ben at the scene of the crime, and then murders all of his rat brothers. Ironically, the cycle of abuse and hate goes one more round: Ben, fed up, turns on Willard.

As he dies, Willard tells Ben that he was "good to him," a comment that the arrogant Martin might have made while begging for his own life.

Beyond being a personal story of abuse perpetuated from one generation to another, there are racial undertones in the film. Is it of any significance that the favored rat, Socrates, is white, and the abused, less favored rat (Ben), is black? While the white Socrates is given a life of comfort in the bedroom, black Ben must toil in the basement as a slave, used by his master for terrible purposes. Thus *Willard* might also be seen to be a bizarre comment on Civil Rights. When Ben fights against his benevolent master (who claims he was "good to him" in the manner of so many plantation-owning Southerners), he is rising up against a system that has judged him not as good as his white brother. That may be stretching the matter a bit, but it seems to fit.

Indeed, in the sequel, *Ben,* all the rats rebel against the human society (representing their masters), causing violent riots in the streets. Not surprisingly, they are repelled by fire hoses ... an ever present symbol of white repressive authority in the Civil Rights movement.

If that's stretching the issue, no matter. The point of *Willard* is that it can be read as more than a simple horror movie wherein rats attack people. It is a story of the disenfranchised rising up against those who have mistreated them. Though it may sound insulting to compare rodents to humans (specifically humans of color), one must again remember the era. Fantasy films about race relations were coming out by the droves in the 1970s, and there have been significant books about the racial implications of the *Planet of the Apes* series. If simians can represent or signify minorities, so then too can rats. And, it is a fact that *Willard* and *Ben* were disproportionately popular in inner city movie theaters. The disenfranchised of those neighborhoods were able to empathize with the disenfranchised animals of the film, even though they were "rats."

But the joy of this movie, and indeed, of most really good movies reviewed in this book, is that they can also be seen simply as what they are: ripping good horror pictures. The scenes of rats swarming in *Willard* are highly effective, and realistic. And Davison is in close proximity to the animals in much of the film. Really, it's all rather astounding. The Stiles house, teeming with hundreds of rats, is an image one is not likely to soon forget.

Of all the rat attack scenes, only Martin's death seems weak. In this case it looks uncomfortably like stagehands are simply throwing rats on him. But otherwise, the rats are great actors, and an effective threat. Some mention should also go to Bruce Davison, who acts his heart out to make a memorable and interesting character. Most horror movies don't feature such a well-defined, deeply delineated character. In *Willard*, we feel his pain, and we hate the fact that, in the end, he becomes what he despised. *Willard* is the best of the best 1970s "animal" pack because it is about people, not critters, and how they fail to escape the prison of their lives.

LEGACY: *Willard* was the surprise hit of 1971, grossing more than $8.2 million, and setting off an "animals attack" sub-genre that would come to include its own sequel, *Ben* (1972), *Frogs* (1972), *Stanley* (1972), *Sssssss* (1973), *Night of the Lepus* (1972), *Squirm* (1976), *Day of the Animals* (1977), *Kingdom of the Spiders* (1977) and others. For actor Bruce Davison, *Willard* offered a high-profile leading role that propelled his career to critical accolades (*Longtime Companion* [1990]), and cult popularity (*The X-Men* [2000]). *Willard* is being re-made for a 2003–2004 release.

1972

Asylum (1972) * * *

Cast & Crew

CAST: Peter Cushing (Smith); Britt Ekland (Lucy); Herbert Lom (Byron); Patrick Magee (Dr. Rutherford); Barry Morse (Bruno the Tailor); Barbara Parkins (Bonnie); Robert Powell (Dr. Martin); Charlotte Rampling (Barbara); Sylvia Syms (Ruth); James Villiers (George); Geoffey Bayldon (Max); Ann Firbank (Anna); Meg Jenkins (Miss Higgins); John Franklyn-Robbins (Stubbins); Sylvia Marriott, Daniel Jones, Frank Forsyth, Richard Todd, Tony Wall.

CREW: Harbor Productions Inc. Presents an Amicus Production, *Asylum*. *Director of Photography:* Denys Coop. *Art Director:* Tony Curtis. *Editor:* Peter Tanner. *Production Manager:* Teresa Bolland. *Assistant Director:* Anthony Waye. *Camera Operator:* Neil Binney. *Continuity:* Pamela Davis. *Casting Director:* Ronnie Curtis. *Chief Make-up:* Roy Ashton. *Chief Hairdresser:* Joan Carpenter. *Wardrobe Mistress:* Bridget Sellers. *Sound Mixer:* Norman Bolland. *Sound Editor:* Clive Smith. *Dubbing Mixer:* Robert Jones. *Set Dresser:* Fred Carter. *Titles:* G.S.E. Ltd. *Color:* Technicolor. *Music composed, arranged and conducted by:* Douglas Gamley. *Executive Producer:* Gustave Berne. *Produced by:* Max J. Rosenberg, Milton Subotsky. *Written by:* Robert Bloch. *Directed by:* Roy Ward Baker. Produced at Shepperton Studios, Shepperton, Middlesex, England. *M.P.A.A. Rating:* PG. *Running time:* 95 minutes

NOTE: *Asylum* features four stories by Robert Bloch in the following order: "Frozen Fear," The Weird Tailor," "Lucy Comes to Stay" and "Mannikins of Horror."

SYNOPSIS: Dr. Martin visits Dunsmoor Asylum for the incurably insane, and learns that the head psychiatrist, Dr. Starr, has gone crazy. Martin is offered a job at the asylum, but only if he can determine which of four disturbed patients is actually Dr. Starr. He accepts the conditions, and is led upstairs to the patient rooms by an orderly named Max.

The first patient Martin sees is named Bonnie. He listens as she tells of her adulterous relationship with a man married to a woman versed in African voodoo and superstition. Bonnie recalls how her lover, Walter, chopped up his wife with a hatchet and stuffed her body parts in a basement freezer. Walter was then killed when the body parts, working independently, attacked and murdered him. Bonnie arrived at the scene of the crime some time later, and was also confronted by the murderous limbs of Walter's wife. Dr. Martin concludes that the scarred Bonnie is actually a paranoid psychotic.

Moving on, Dr. Martin meets Bruno, a tailor. Bruno soon reveals his story. He recounts how a strange man named Smith visited his shop and asked him to sew a suit out of an odd reflective material. Bruno did not know it at the time, but the suit was designed to re-animate the corpse of Smith's son! In a scuffle over payment, Mr. Smith was killed, and Bruno stole his book of the occult only to find that the strange suit could ... and did ... bring life to a store mannequin.

In his third case, Dr. Martin consults with Barbara, who claims she is not ill at all. She tells of a friend named Lucy who murdered her brother and a nurse with scissors. Martin quickly learns that the murderous Lucy is actually Barbara's alter ego.

Finally, Dr. Martin meets Dr. Byron, a

strange fellow who creates perfect little figurines that he claims are alive. His final creation is a miniature version of himself, right down to the correct placement of internal organs. Byron believes he can will his mind into the toy body, and sets out to do just that.

Dr. Martin is tired of playing games, and tells Mr. Rutherford, the man that offered him the job in the first place, that he will have none of it. At the same time, Byron is successful at transferring his soul into the little toy figure. The doll escapes its cell unnoticed, even as Martin refuses to name the disturbed patient he believes is Starr. The doll then stabs Rutherford in the neck, killing him in Martin's sight. Martin destroys the doll ... and it bleeds! Before Martin can make his escape from this most strange asylum, he discovers the identity of Dr. Starr. This discovery costs Dr. Martin his life...

COMMENTARY: *Asylum* is a good horror anthology that plays out a bit like a shaggy dog joke. The premise sounds like something one might overhear at a bar: a doctor goes to an asylum and visits four patients, trying to figure out which one of them is the former head psychologist... It's a workable scenario, and an opportunity to unify the four stories by Robert Bloch, author of *Psycho* (the novel). Of the four stories, the first and second are probably strongest.

"Frozen Fear" may be the best of the four tales. A chopped-up body tries to wriggle its way out of a basement freezer, much to the dismay of the murderer. The terror begins when a decapitated head appears on the floor just beyond the basement door, a spectral warning that reality is not as it seems. From there, it becomes a multi-pronged (or limbed) attack, as various body parts attack the murderer, Walter. A hand reaches out of the freezer and strangles Walter in a jolting moment, and the horror is simultaneously funny and scary.

The second story, "The Weird Tailor" is more an acting set piece, a two-man con-

frontation between Peter Cushing, and *Space: 1999*'s Barry Morse. Rather than being an out-and-out horror escapade (as was "Frozen Fear"), the second story is more deliberate, more suspenseful, more involved, and it builds a sense of anticipation. Only the ending is a letdown.

Story #3, "Lucy Comes to Stay," though glittering with the beauty of both Britt Ekland and Charlotte Rampling, is the weakest story of the bunch. It is a garden-variety psycho story about a schizophrenic murderess. The audience is way ahead of the filmmakers on this one, realizing early on that Ekland's oft-referred-to imaginary friend is but the inner voice of a tormented woman.

Finally, "Mannikins of Horror" (which was later remade on the first season of the Laurel TV anthology *Monsters*), puts *Asylum* back on track, with surprise and horror as a crazy doctor constructs a murderous little homunculus. Herbert Lom is effective as the psycho, and though the murderous doll is but a wind-up robot, the horror scenes are strangely frightening. It's more than a bit disturbing to see a malevolent wind-up toy work its way through the asylum and commit murder.

The wraparound pieces, involving Dr. Martin, tend to be pretty effective. Director Roy Ward Baker's camera is careful to capture the disturbing artwork on the walls of the asylum: portraits of bizarre, insane-seeming caricatures. These works seems to indicate that the building itself is filled with evil, a nice touch that paves the way for the supernatural stories. When Ward is ready to transition from wraparound to flashback, his camera focuses on a black-and-white sketch, and then spins about. It's as if the glimpse of artistic insanity has spurred the camera to go crazy itself. That's a good transition tool, because the film is taking the audience from the normal world (ostensibly), to the world of the deranged.

Though *Asylum* is a well-crafted horror anthology, it is unlikely that it will appeal to today's younger genre fans. The stories are rather short and undeveloped, especially considering the recent history of such anthologies as *Tales from the Crypt*, *Monsters*, and *Tales from the Darkside*, and none of the stories stands out as being an overwhelming highpoint. Droll but so-so.

The Asphyx (1972) ✶ ✶ ✶

Cast & Crew

CAST: Robert Stephens (Hugo); Robert Powell (Giles); Jane Lapotaire (Christina); Fiona Walker (Anna); Alex Scott (President); Terry Scully (Pauper); Ralph Arliss (Clive); John Lawrence (Mason); David Grey (Vicar); Tony Caunter (Warden); Paul Bacon (First Member).

CREW: A Peter Newbrook film. *Production Designer:* John Stoll. *Production Manager:* Ted Sturgis. *Assistant Director:* Roger Simons. *Continuity:* Phyllis Crocker. *Camera Operator:* Chris Holden. *Make-up:* Jimmy Evans. *Hairstylist:* Stephanie Kay. *Costumes:* Evelyn Gibbs. *Set Decorator:* Arthur Taksen. *Special Effects:* Ted Samuels. *Editor:* Maxine Julius. *Sound Effects:* Peter Bond. *Sound Supervisor:* John Cox. *Recordist:* Ken Ritchie. *Re-recording:* Bob Jones. *Music Composed and conducted by:* Bill McGuffie. *Filmed in:* TODD AO-35. *Director of photography:* Freddie Young. *Associate Producer:* Maxine Julius. *Screenplay:* Brian Comport. *Based on an original idea "The Asphyx" by:* Christina and Lawrence Beers. *Produced by:* John Brittany. *Directed by:* Peter Newbrook. *M.P.A.A. Rating:* PG. *Running Time:* 96 minutes.

SYNOPSIS: Sir Hugo, a photographer interested in psychical research, photographs the dead and dying as a hobby. Strangely, a variety of his pictures taken at the precise moment of expiration reveal an odd smudge. A society of researchers believe it is a representation of the soul leaving the body. Hugo is not so sure.

One day, while vacationing on the lake with his family, Hugo's son Clive and Hugo's wife are killed during a boating accident while Hugo is filming them with a new "moving picture" (film) contraption. After a period of mourning, Hugo develops the film, and detects a moving shadow near Clive at the moment of his death. Furthermore, it seems to be moving towards, not away, from him as the soul ostensibly would. Hugo becomes obsessed with understanding the phenomenon. He comes to believe that the smudge is actually a spirit of death that the Greeks called an "asphyx." Did it possess his son at the moment he died? Did it somehow rob him of life?

Since the asphyx seems to manifest itself only when mortals are in real danger of death, Hugo tests his theory during a public hanging. He films the execution, and utilizes a machine he has developed, which renders the asphyx visible to all the bystanders in the audience. Furthermore, he records it on film. Despite his success, Hugo is unnerved because he feels the asphyx saw him … and that it actually has a malevolent intelligence.

With the assistance of his daughter's beau, Giles, Sir Hugo sets about to capture the asphyx, using a guinea pig as the endangered life form. The attempt is successful, and with its asphyx captured, the guinea pig will never die. It has attained immortality because the spirit of death is trapped in a bottle!

The next "guinea pig" is a human being, a poor wretch from Bede House who is dying of tuberculosis. Sir Hugo believes that by capturing the man's asphyx, he can restore him to health, and even grant him eternal life. During the experiment, the ungrateful wretch splashes acid on Hugo's face, and the operation fails.

The accident in the lab gets Hugo thinking. He desires to be immortal, so he asks

Giles to trap his asphyx for him. Giles is a reluctant partner in this experiment, but his father-in-law-to-be is most persuasive. After devising a method of slow electrocution to "kill" himself (and force the asphyx to appear), Giles and Hugo capture the entity. Giles locks it away in a safe that only he knows the combination to. Buoyed by his success, Hugo decides that his daughter Christina must also live forever. He wants to trap her asphyx. Christina and Giles are dead set against the plan, which will put Christina in danger of death, but Hugo promises he will give them his blessing to marry if they agree to his plan. The experiment proceeds, and Christina is unexpectedly decapitated when it fails. A furious Hugo, damned to eternal guilt and eternal regret at the death of his daughter, plans to release his own asphyx, and die himself. Embittered, Giles refuses to help. He kills himself in the next experiment, leaving Hugo without the means (and the lock combination!) to free his asphyx.

One hundred years later, Hugo is still alive ... ancient, twisted ... but living ... and still atoning for his crimes.

———————————

COMMENTARY: This is one case where premise trumps execution. The norm in the horror genre is to obsess on style, mood, art direction and even special effects to the exclusion of logic, common sense, and sometimes, humanity. Believability is often sacrificed at the altars of shock, suspense, or gore. The Asphyx is an interesting anomaly because it has the opposite problem. It is directed with ham-handed earnestness, and a general lack of style, yet its premise is so powerful, so appealing, that the film actually surmounts its stylistic miscues.

So many horror movies obsess on the fear of dying, of attempting to escape death before it strikes. Final Destination (2000) is one notable example. Yet few films genuinely explore what happens to the human essence at the time of death — when the grim reaper actually strikes. The Asphyx focuses solely on

that moment, and posits that there is an entity, a bizarre creature, which brings death to all humans at times of extreme danger. The film then makes the logical leap that if this personal demon can be captured, a person will be immortal, freed to live forever. It is a fascinating concept, and The Asphyx mines it for its story about mortality and morality.

Perhaps the above paragraph makes The Asphyx sound purely philosophical, and less than involving. That's an incorrect assumption. The concept of the film is couched in an intriguing way, in a great personal story of human invention, and frailty. Think about the concept this way: What if Kodak developed a new brand of film for cameras that, as an unexpected side effect of its chemical properties, captured the presence of ghosts? Once this "side effect" has been established, The Asphyx then examines, in moral terms, what such a discovery would mean.

Not surprisingly, The Asphyx, for much of its length, echoes the storyline of Mary Shelley's Frankenstein. Because he has lost a son and a wife, Hugo, a man of science and social standing, becomes obsessed with death. Like Victor Frankenstein, Hugo believes that if he can accomplish just one thing (in this case catching the asphyx of each of his loved ones), they never need die. The film then provides the requisite argument that life and death should remain in the hands of the deity, not man. "It's wrong," Christina declares of immortality. "We're merely creatures of God, not God!" Yet the obsessed Hugo cannot stop, and his gradual loss of balance and perspective echoes Frankenstein's development into a psychotic. Finally, in the end, Hugo, like Frankenstein, creates a process whereby he kills those he loves, the very people who should benefit from his discovery. So, even while exploring a fascinating premise, The Asphyx pays homage to a classic horror story, again warning about the dangers of science's overreaching.

Like Frankenstein, Hugo pays quite a price for his actions. Since his asphyx is trapped away, never to be released, Hugo goes on eternally. His punishment (which is much less merciful than the death penalty he objects to so vehemently in the film) is eternal torment. He will live forever with a mistake, knowing that he killed his own daughter. Here the film reaches a new moral plateau beyond the obvious confines and "don't tamper in God's domain" didacticism of the Frankenstein story.

Finally, in the end, with no asphyx to permit death, there's no individual choice. Even when life is miserable, there is no opportunity to die. Fate is taken out of human hands, and the picture ultimately states that it is important for humans to have the ability to self-terminate. It is an unpleasant truth, but one that is important. Is eternal life, spent in misery, preferable to death? And, is eternal life responsible? Is not a primary human responsibility in life the decision to relinquish control of the world to the next generation, to our children, and our children's children? *The Asphyx* raises all of these moral issues in clever ways.

The Asphyx effectively deals with all of its concepts, even the frightening, genre ones. A large component of its outline involves a Lovecraftian tenet. It speculates, in essence, that a horrid, screeching monster with malevolent intelligence exists side by side with man, just outside his field of vision. This thing is visible by a fluke and is discovered by accident. Like the old ones waiting outside our dimension, these creatures have the ability to affect our world, and that's a really scary thought, as is the "newly discovered" cause of death. Man expires, *The Asphyx* tells us, because an invisible creature preys on us. There is no such thing as "natural causes"; all deaths are generated by a malevolent, *thinking* thing.

Buoyed by so many great ideas, *The Asphyx* is thought provoking almost in spite of itself. It has a compelling moral conflict, and a great premise, even though it is undercut at times by some clumsy visualization. The special-effects depiction of the asphyx, for instance, reduces the awe and power one feels at the nature of such a creature. The spirit of death is represented by a primitive optical effect that at time looks like a floating mutant shrimp! But, perhaps it is too much to ask that a film be literate, challenging and possessed of top-notch special effects. Like the best of its genre, *The Asphyx* articulates questions about the nature of life and death, and the morality surrounding our understanding of those concepts. The special effects, weak as they are, aren't terribly important.

The Baby

Cast & Crew

CAST: Ruth Roman (Mrs. Wadsworth); Anjanette Comer (Ann Gentry); Marianna Hill (Germaine); Michael Pataki (Dennis); David Manzy (The Baby).

CREW: *Directed by:* Ted Post. *Written by:* Abe Polsky. *Produced by:* Elliott Feinman, Ralph Hirsch, Abe Polsky, Milton Polsky. *Director of Photography:* Michael Margulies. *Editor:* Bob Crawford Senior. *Music:* Gerald Fried. *M.P.A.A Rating:* PG. *Running Time:* 84 minutes.

DETAILS: A surprised social worker finds a family taking care of a very strange "child" in this disturbing, off-kilter film. The social worker attempts to liberate the "infant" (a 21-year-old mental simpleton) from its mother (Roman), but there is a surprise twist in the tale. Recently released on DVD.

Baron Blood (1972) ＊ ＊

Critical Reception

"Under Mario Bava's pedestrian direction the concocted creaking, scream-ing, gory murders and Miss Sommer's frightened racing through dark passage-ways largely add up to a spectral schlock."— A.H. Weiler, *New York Times,* February 8, 1973, page 36.

"Strengths include some great location shooting, fine cinematography and a cameo appearance by Joseph Cotten."—Anthony Tomlinson, *Shivers* # 30, June 1996, page 27.

Cast & Crew

CAST: Joseph Cotten (Alfred Becker); Elke Sommer (Eva Arnold); Massimo Girotti (Karl Hummel); Rada Rassimov (Christine Hoff-man); Antonio Cantafora (Peter Kleist); Humi Raho (Police Inspector); Alan Collins (Fritz); Dieter Tressler (Herr Dortmunat).

CREW: Alfred Leone Presents *Baron Blood. Executive Producers:* Sam Lang, J. Arthur Elliot. *Original Story and Screenplay:* Vincent Fotre. *Adapted for the Screen by:* William A. Bairn. *Music:* Stelvio Cipriani. *Produced by:* Alfred Leone. *Directed by:* Mario Bava. *Lighting:* Anto-nio Rinaldi. *Art Director:* Enzo Bulgarelli. *Edi-tor:* Carlo Reali. *Cameraman:* Emilio Varriano. *Make-up:* Silyana Petri. *Assistant Director:* Lamberto Bava. *Special Effects:* Franco Tocci. *Hairdresser:* Rossana Gigante. *Production Man-ager:* Bruno Fasca. A Leone International Pro-duction in Association with Cinevision, Ltd. Filmed in Technicolor. *M.P.A.A. Rating:* R. *Running Time:* 90 minutes.

SYNOPSIS: American Peter Kline arrives in Austria and meets his Uncle Karl. He has traveled across the world to learn the truth about an ancestor on his father's side known as "Baron Blood," a sadist who reveled in the torture of others. He goes to visit the baron's castle (known as the Castle of Devils…) and learns it is being restored for sale. Oversee-ing the operation is a beautiful blond wo-man, Ava, whom Peter befriends. Living in the castle is Fritz, a slightly bonkers grounds-keeper. Soon, Paul reveals why he has really come. In his possession is a document cre-ated by a witch named Elizabeth Holly, a document which is purported to have the power to resurrect Baron Blood!

By night, Peter and Ava steal into the castle and recite the resurrection incantation. They read aloud from the parchment, and almost immediately, a bell tolls indicating the baron has awakened. When a rattling is heard somewhere upstairs, Peter and Ava panic and revoke the incantation. The house is silent again, but Ava remains shaken.

The next day, work progresses on the castle, and Peter and Ava return in search of a secret passage. They find it, and the baron's secret room beyond. They resolve to try the incantation again that night. They do so, and deep within the castle, the baron awakens. Ava begs Peter to send the baron back to oblivion again, but the parchment has fallen into the fireplace and can no longer be refer-enced.

Awake for the first time in centuries, the disfigured baron leaves the castle for a nearby clinic. He kills the doctor there, and then murders one of Ava's close friends. Police suspect a run-of-the-mill murder, but Ava and Peter fear the baron is responsible.

The baron's castle is sold at auction, and the winning man is a crippled fellow named Becker. He asks Ava's assistance in further restoring the castle. Ava and Peter tell Becker the curse of the baron, but he brushes it off.

By night, Ava is pursued through the house by a dark figure she believes to be Baron Blood. Peter rescues Ava, but the Baron persists in coming after her.

Realizing the depth of their danger, Peter and Ava seek the assistance of a clairvoyant named Christina Hoffman. She is a medium, and is fearful of the baron. She informs them that the baron wants them dead because only they have the power to send him back to oblivion. Then, Hoffman presents Peter and Ava with a medallion owned by Elizabeth Holly, the witch who destroyed the baron the first time.

Before long, Peter and Ava have returned to the castle. Becker shows them the newly restored dungeon, and then reveals his true identity as the baron! Peter and Ava try to use the medallion, but he refers to it as a trinket. He tortures them, starting with Peter, but Ava remembers part of the incantation, and that the medallion can resurrect Baron Blood's victims. One at a time, those victimized by the baron return from the dead, and the baron is forced to suffer for his crimes all over again.

COMMENTARY: "I would not play with the occult, if I were you," one of the characters in Mario Bava's *Baron Blood* warns. That's good advice, for this is a film in which the evil dead, awakened by a resurrection incantation, threaten the living. Unfortunately, the film is rather dull, and not particularly scary, revealing little of the psychological depth or cinematic style of Bava's *A Hatchet for the Honeymoon.*

Part of the problem is that warning. All the characters ignore it, and so this becomes one of those predictable horror tales in which hip, attractive youngsters fool with a power beyond their comprehension and are made to pay the price for such irreverence. The error is compounded in *Baron Blood* when the hip idiots in question (Ava and Peter) resurrect the sadistic baron not once, but twice. They just don't learn from their mistakes, do they?

Baron Blood loses points in other regards, besides character motivation. The translated dialogue is atrocious, obvious and inartistic. "There is something terrible and horrifying out there and we have released it!" one character breathlessly declares, helping sleeping viewers catch up on the plot. "You really had a terrifying experience," another character tells Elke Sommer, after she has been attacked ... as though she were not smart enough to figure that out for herself. Still, at least Sommers seems invested in the ludicrous action. Contrarily, Joseph Cotten gives a rote, unmenacing performance that might as well have been phoned in.

But the main disappointment of the film is that it could have been so much better if just a little more thought had gone into it. The core of the picture should have been Peter's interest in the baron. Why is he so fascinated by the evil of this particular ancestor? The film could have explored the reasons that good, normal people are sometimes drawn to evil and destruction. Another scene suggests another tack Bava could have taken if inclined to really contemplate his material. There is an effective scene wherein a man is killed at a soda machine that has been brought into the ancient mansion/ hotel. That is an interesting juxtaposition of the past and present, and the ramifications of the baron's home becoming a vacation resort could have been mined for a little irony. Sadistic past versus commercial present, and all that. But no, not here. That would have been too clever.

The real problem with *Baron Blood* is that it feels diluted, like a sequel to a better film — a latter entry in the *Hellraiser* or *Nightmare on Elm Street* series, perhaps. The Baron is not terribly frightening, though one feels he could have been with a little bit of tweaking, and his antics seem vaguely familiar, and vaguely rote ... like it's all been done before. There are some nice images, like the foggy blue exteriors where lots of light shines through tree branches, but most of the film feels off-key. Even the color of the blood drops is wrong — too pink. A little more care could have resulted in smarter characters, better dialogue, a scarier villain, a more interesting theme, and the right color blood. This movie is a primary example of why so many horror films are not taken seriously by critics. Rather than actively face its real subject matter (the allure of evil), *Baron Blood* settles for lazy situational logic and plotting. It is all bells and whistles, when it could have been meaningful and scary.

Ben (1972) ★ ★ ½

Critical Reception

"The way in which you respond to *Ben* will depend on a number of variables, including how you feel about the possibility of Los Angeles shutting down, trick photography, dreadful acting, the decline and fall of Phil Karlson as a director and a screenplay that never has the courage to acknowledge its comic impulses."—*New York Times*, June 24, 1972.

"...starts off briskly ... but then tends to sink into a fairly maudlin relationship between the sick boy and the lead rat."— Alan Frank, *The Horror Film Handbook*, 1982, page 18.

Cast & Crew

CAST: Joseph Campanella (Cliff Kirtland); Arthur O'Connell (Billy Hatfield); Rosemary Murphy (Beth Garrison); Meredith Baxter (Eve Garrison); Kaz Garas (Joe Green); Lee Harcourt Montgomery (Danny Garrison); Norman Alden (Policeman); Paul Carr (Kelly); James Luisi (Ed); Kenneth Tobey (Engineer); Richard Van Vleet (Reade); Lee Paul (Carey); Scott Garrett (Henry Gray); Arlen Stuart (Mrs. Gray); Richard Drasin (George).

CREW: From Cinerama Releasing and BCP — A Service of the Cos Broadcasting Company. *Director of Photography:* Russell Metty. *Art Director:* Rolland M. Brooks. *Unit Production Manager/Assistant Director:* Floyd Joyer. *Animals Trained by:* Moe Di Sesso. *Marionettes by:* Rene. *Casting:* Irving Lande. *Set Decorator:* Antony Mondello. *Chief Electrician:* Earl Williaman, Jr. *Head Grip:* Dick Borland. *Construction Coordinator:* Ed Shanley. *Special Effects:* Bud David. *Properties:* William Waness. *Script Supervisor:* Joan Evemin Buck. *Make-up:* Jack H. Young. *Hairstylist:* Hazel Washington. *Costumes:* Ray Harp, Mina Mittelman. *Post-Production Supervisor:* Houseley Stevenson. *Sound Editor:* James J. Klinger. *Music Editor:* Jack Tillar. *Sound Recording:* Leon M. Leon, David Dockendorf. *Recorded by:* Glenn-Glenn Sound. *Color:* DeLuxe. *Second Unit Photography and Photography Effects:* Howard A. Anderson Co. *Film Editor:* Harry Gerstad. *Associate Producer:* Joel Briskin. *Music:* Walter Scharf. *"Ben's Song" and "Start the Day" lyrics by:* Don Black, *Music by:* Walter Scharf. *"Ben's Song" sung by:* Michael Jackson. *In charge of production operations:* John E. Pommer. *Executive Producer:* Charles A. Pratt. *Based on characters created by:* Stephen Gilbert. *Written by:* Gilbert A. Ralston. *Produced by:* Mort Briskin. *Directed by:* Phil Karlson. A Cinerama Release. *M.P.A.A. Rating:* PG. *Running Time:* 97 minutes.

SYNOPSIS: Police in L.A. investigate the death of Willard Stiles, the strange young man who was murdered by his army of rats and its leader, Ben. The police discover a diary detailing Ben's training at Willard's hands, and attempt to prevent a public panic about rats. Two officers remain at the crime scene until late in the night, and are murdered when they discover Ben and his hidden army of vermin.

The rats spread out across the neighborhood, using the sewers as a subway system of sorts, and Ben meets a little boy with a heart condition named Danny. Danny performs puppet shows about Ben, and the two become fast friends even as Ben's rats attack a truck delivering fish and poultry. Danny's mother and older sister (Eve) think Danny has a new imaginary friend when he sings "Ben's Song," a melody about his new friend. Meanwhile, the rats attack a grocery store and lay waste to it. Danny learns of Ben's nocturnal activities, and scolds the rat for organizing so much destruction, but Ben is still stinging from his cruel treatment at Willard's hands.

The police comb the neighborhood and Danny's house for rats. Danny hides Ben in a shoebox to conceal him, and then teaches him how to avoid poison rat-traps. When a neighborhood bully attacks Danny, Ben and the rats respond in kind — biting and attacking the bully. Before long, the rats also overrun a nearby candy factory and a gymnasium.

Growing more trustful, Ben takes Danny to the sewer where the rats hide. Danny sneaks into the tunnels and sees thousand of rats hidden there. He returns home and spends the night sleeping peacefully in his room until Eve sees rats on his bed and panics. The police question Danny and he is uncooperative with them, but they search the storm drains to find the rats.

The police cordon off the sewers, and Danny races inside the tunnels to warn his friends of imminent danger, with Eve in hot pursuit. Danny finds Ben and begs him to leave before it is too late. The police use flamethrowers to burn out the rats and an all-out battle occurs in the sewers. Eve and Danny escape the tunnels as hoses are used to flush the animals out. The police catch the rats in the ensuing crossfire, and the battle is lost for Ben.

Sometime later, Ben shows up at Danny's house, beaten but not dead. Danny tends to his friend, and Ben lives to fight another day.

COMMENTARY: Before *Stuart Little* (1999) charmed the hearts of little tykes across America, there was *Ben*. This film is a sequel to 1971's unexpected hit *Willard*, but very few characters from the first film return for this one ... since Ben (inconveniently) killed most of the humans at the end of the original picture. Instead, Ben, that scamp of a rat, returns to befriend a little sick boy with a bad heart.

As a film, *Ben* is simultaneously pulled in contrary directions. On one hand, the film goes to great lengths to depict rat attacks (or rather, rat riots, since the attacks are not directed at people usually). Indeed, there are many more rat confrontations in this sequel than were in *Willard*. Yet, on the other hand, the film also takes special pains to stress the cloying, sappy and irritating emotional bond between Danny and Ben. It makes for an odd combination as the film crosscuts from scenes of extreme property destruction and violence to tender dialogue sequences with children and puppet shows. It's *The Yearling* meets *King Kong*, or some other unholy blend of crap. Not surprisingly, the mix doesn't work.

Also, it is clear that the tendency of this sequel, like so many sequels, is to edge further towards camp, towards humor, when there is no real human or legitimate way to further the story of the progenitor. *Willard* was a serious, straight-faced, and effective horror film about a disenfranchised young man and his "revolt" against society (using rats). When his army of rats was dispatched to attack people, it was serious business. In *Ben,* not so. The rats attack a grocery store, and the audience sees the little buggers chowing down on Kellogg's Frosted Flakes ("*They're Greeeeeat!*"). The rats attack a health center and are seen running on an exercise conveyer belt while a surprised client (in leotard) doubletakes at the rascally antics.

Yet, the rat stunts are amazing. As if in military formation, rats dash through a maze of pipes in a sewer, obey commands, run and jump, brave fire and water, and perform other tasks that would seem beyond the limits of rodent behavior. It is all rather well done (especially considering there was no such thing as CGI in 1972). The effects are impressive, but the rat attacks themselves have lost their bite.

And, frankly, the reason is because every franchise needs a hero. A decision was made, prior to production apparently, that Ben and his army of rats were to be the heroes of this particular film. So Ben is now a fella just like Rocky, a little guy bucking the system, aiming for greatness, and just wanting to live his life. It is inherently silly, but the picture is framed that way. If one thinks about it, Ben's heroic journey in this film is almost Biblical in its proportions. After freeing his people (who were enslaved by Stiles), Ben leads them across a body of water (in the sewers) to the promised land (Danny's house; the grocery store). In the end, Ben is betrayed, and the evil police attempt to destroy his army, but he survives to fight another day. Is he a Moses figure? A Christ figure? Or just a furry little four-legger?

Even Campanella's character, the police detective, is completely unsympathetic. He's the villain of the piece, destroying the rats and getting his just deserts. Never mind that he's trying to protect thousands of Los Angelenos from a thousand or so rampaging rats...

So, audience sympathy is overtly with the rats in *Ben*. They may be a health hazard; they may carry diseases; but gosh darn it, they're the best friends a kid could have. That sounds sarcastic, yet there is no doubt that *Ben* is in a different league than *Willard*. This movie represents the "franchise-ization" of a horror concept. *Willard* was about people, about characters and their choices, about their traps, and the cycle of abuse. *Ben* is just playtime with vermin, with a top-40 tune by Michael Jackson thrown in to help sell it. Oddly enough ... and rather embarrassingly, it almost works. This viewer was nonplussed by most of the film as a whole, but became increasingly supportive of the rats as those nasty policemen attempted to eradicate them with superior firepower. And, this reviewer actually felt relief when cuddly little Ben showed up alive and well at the end.

As the end credits rolled, this author felt another bit of relief too, specifically that *Ben* did not generate another sequel. At this rate of concept erosion and canonization, the third film would have seen the United States government hiring Ben and his stalwart rodent army to rescue POWs in Vietnam...

Beware! The Blob!

Cast & Crew

CAST: Robert Walker, Jr. (Bobby); Gwynne Gilford (Lisa); Richard Stahl (Ed); Richard Webb (Sheriff); Godfrey Cambridge (Chester); Carol Lynley (Leslie); With: Larry Hagman, Burgess Meredith, Dick Van Patten, Cindy Williams.

CREW: *Directed by:* Larry Hagman. *Written by:* Richard Clair, Anthony Harris and Jack Harris. *Produced by:* Jack Harris. *Director of Photography:* Al Hamm. *Editor:* Tony De Zarraga. *Music:* Mort Garson. *M.P.A.A. Rating:* PG. *Running Time:* 87 minutes.

DETAILS: Larry Hagman, J.R. Ewing himself, directed this follow-up to the 1958 cult classic *The Blob*. This time around, the orange jello-mold is played mostly for laughs by a cast of TV stars. The blob surfaces in a barber shop, in an easy chair, and other unlikely locations before finally being put on ice. Brought to the world by Jack Harris, of *Equinox* (1971) and *Dark Star* (1975) fame.

Blacula (1972) ✻ ✻ ✻

Critical Reception

"...an above-average morality play, due mostly to the talent of the distinguished Shakespearean actor William Marshall.... Black humor and music effectively mask the weak acting of the supporting cast. Suspense, rather than violence, was the keynote." — Frank Manchel, *An Album of Modern Horror Films*, Franklin Watts, Publisher, 1983 page 19.

"...an awkward mixture of romance, vampire-pic clichés, and shocks (a few effective)." — Donald C. Willis, *Horror and Science Fiction Films II*, Scarecrow Press, 1982, page 36.

"Anybody who goes to a vampire movie expecting sense is in serious trouble and *Blacula* offers less sense than most." — Roger Greenspun, *New York Times*, August 26, 1972.

Cast & Crew

CAST: William Marshall (Blacula); Vonetta McGee (Tina/Louva); Denise Nicholas (Michelle); Thalmus Rasulala (Dr. Gordon Thomas); Gordon Pinsent (Lt. Peters); Emily Yancy (Nancy); Lance Taylor, Sr. (Swenson); Logan Field (Barnes); Ted Harris (Bobby); Rick Metzler (Billy); Kitty Lester (Juanita); Charles Macauley (Count Dracula); Jit Cumbuka (Skillet); Elisha Cook (Sam); Eric Brotherson (Real Estate Agent).

CREW: An American International Release. Samuel Z. Arkoff Presents *Blacula*. *Director of Photography:* John M. Stevens. *Art Director:* Walter Herndon. *Executive Producer:* Samuel Z. Arkoff. *Executive Production Supervisor:* Norman T. Herman. *Screenplay by:* Joan Torres and Raymond Koenig. *Producer:* Joseph T. Naar. *Directed by:* William Crain. *Production Manager:* Jack Bohler. *Post-Production Manager:* Salvatore Billitterri. *Locations:* Cinemobile Systems. *Music Composed and Conducted by:* Gene Page. "*Main Chance*" *sung by:* Billy Page and Gene Page. *Music Coordinator:* Al Simms. *Editor:* Allan Jacobs. *Assistant Editor:* Tom Neff. *Special Effects Editor:* Sam Horta. *Titles Designed by:* Imagic. *Special Effects:* Roger George. *Assistant Director:* Phil Cook. *Wardrobe:* Ermon Sessions and Sandy Stewart. *Camera Operator:* John Kiser. *Hairdresser:* Lola Kemp. *Script Coordinator:* George Fisher. *Sound:* Ryder Sound Services. *Color:* Movie Lab. *Cars furnished by:* Chrysler Corporation of America. *M.P.A.A. Rating:* PG. *Running Time:* 93 minutes.

SYNOPSIS: In Transylvania in the year 1780, the regal African prince Mamawaldi and his beautiful wife, Louva, visit with Count Dracula on a diplomatic mission to end the slave trade. When Dracula makes unwanted advances upon Louva, Mamawaldi responds with anger. The count, a vampire, shows his true colors, and an army of the dead attack Mamawaldi. Dracula bites the African prince, dubs him "Blacula," and dooms him to an eternal life of bloodlust as a vampire. Poor Louva is sealed in the tomb where Blacula's locked coffin sits, and there she rots and dies.

Some two hundred years later, Dracula is long dead, and his castle is up for sale. Two gay American antique dealers look the place over and determine that they could make a killing by selling off the count's antiques. Among the items purchased is the coffin of Blacula (still locked), and it is transported back to America.

Once in the United States, Blacula awakens and feeds on the two antique dealers, making them vampire servants. Then, at a funeral for one of the men, Blacula spots a beautiful woman, Tina, who is a dead ringer for his beloved, Louva. Unfortunately, Tina is also a friend of Michelle, who happens to be seeing Dr. Gordon Thomas, a prominent agent for the Scientific Investigation Division of the government. Thomas spies the puncture marks on the neck of the corpse, and refuses to believe the official explanation: that it was a fatal rat bite. He suspects a vampire.

That night, Blacula follows Tina home, and inadvertently scares her. Once she escapes safely, Blacula bites the neck of an obnoxious city cabbie that nearly ran him over in the street. This murder becomes part of Dr. Thomas's investigation, and he seeks the help of white police detective Lt. Peters in exploring his theory that a vampire is responsible.

Mamawaldi courts Tina and tells her that she is the reincarnation of his beloved wife. As strange as this story is, it makes sense to Tina, and she finds herself drawn to this tall, dark stranger. Mamawaldi also reveals that he is a vampire, and that Tina can be with him for all eternity if only she gives herself willingly to him. While Tina considers her future, and Blacula continues to rack up victims (including a beautiful photographer at a local club who has seen that he casts no reflection), Dr. Thomas and Lt. Peters close in on the vampire. Understanding that the coffin is the key to killing the vampire, the police hunt Blacula down to the antiques warehouse. There they are confronted by an army of the undead, and they use oil burning lamps to start a fire and kill the ghouls.

Though Blacula's minions are dead, the prince himself still prowls the night. He communicates telepathically with Tina, and she obeys his directive to come to him. The police trail Tina to a factory, where she meets Blacula. In the shoot-out that follows, Tina is killed, and Blacula has no choice but to turn her into a vampire so she can live some form of life. Even this reunion of lovers is short-lived, however. Lt. Peters drives a stake through Tina's heart during a battle. Shat-

tered by the loss of his love, Blacula staggers into the daylight and faces his own destruction.

COMMENTARY: To survive from generation to generation legends often change tenor, style and feel. In the 1970s, moviemakers were starting to realize that there were African-American audiences hungering to see many such film legends and styles modulated to reflect their lives in a post–Civil Rights movement 1970s America. Thus was born blaxploitation. Some people see that as a negative term, but the impulse behind the black cinema of the 1970s was actually a positive and even empowering one. Though blacks were appearing in exploitation films of often dubious quality, at least the African-American constituency was being addressed rather than ignored. Hollywood was acknowledging the need to speak meaningfully to the black experience in America, and it paid heed to their wants with a series of Afrocentric films.

Thus black private eyes (*Shaft* [1972]) graced the silver screen, as did African-American re-inventions of the popular monsters. *Blacula* was a dark *Dracula*, *Blackenstein* was an ebony *Frankenstein*, and *Abby* was an African-American reflection of Linda Blair and *The Exorcist* (1973). The most interesting aspect of this re-imagination of the classic monsters is that the classic characters were not only updated for the 1970s, but also altered to specifically mirror the experience of African-Americans in a country where discrimination and racism were still important issues. *Blacula* is probably the best example of this trend, and is fascinating because of the changes it makes to the *Dracula* story.

The film opens with a European white man (Dracula) enslaving a powerful African diplomat, Mamawaldi. That Blacula becomes a monster at all is not his fault. He is captured by Dracula, locked away, and made a vampire against his will. This very experience of becoming a vampire is thus related to the abomination of slavery and the early black experience in the United States. The African slaves who came to America to serve the agricultural South always did so against their will, separated from their families, and forced to serve under harsh white masters who treated them as chattels. Likewise, it is clear that when Dracula re-names Mamawaldi in his own image, as Blacula, the film is equating the white plantation masters with the white vampire master. It is an apt comparison, and one that immediately generates sympathy for Blacula. "Blacula" is Mamawaldi's slave name.

And sympathy is the one facet of his character that separates Blacula from Dracula, Yorga or most other vampires (besides Angel, Spike or Nick Knight). Most vampires in film are depicted as evil, monstrous, and without souls. But Blacula is not that way, at all. He is regal born, decent, honorable and proud ... but betrayed into vampire enslavement. His vampiric entanglements in this film involve not the ruling of the world or a sating of his sexual appetites, but an earnest attempt to win back the wife who was stolen from him by a white master. Again, the specter of slavery is there: Mamawaldi was ruthlessly separated from his beloved wife, and from his family in the northeast of the Nigerian delta. It is no stretch to view him, in fact, as a disenfranchised black man, awakened in a white-dominated world and seeking to re-connect with the heritage that he was robbed of.

Though Dracula's primary opponent is also African-American (Thomas), much of the film nonetheless involves Blacula's clashes with the Caucasian police force. And indeed, Blacula only turns Tina into a vampire when a white policeman shoots her in the back, leaving him no choice but to "turn" her to keep her alive. An act of aggression and conquest in the context of a "white" Dracula has been, in the black cinema, transmuted into an act of mercy, of kindness. That even the ritual taking of the beautiful female, a rite of all screen vampires, is re-packaged in contemporary, ethnic terms, is significant. Blac-

ula does not enjoy making vampires, he does so only because of police brutality ... and that transforms him into a protagonist, a hero, rather than a villain.

Thomas, the Van Helsing of *Blacula*, is also depicted as combating the white establishment. He suspects a ghoul is at large, and even has evidence of such, but is clearly fighting the bankrupt white police establishment. He can't get permission to exhume a body, and the reports he requests on the matter keep getting lost at the hands of a white man. Because he can't stop Blacula sooner (due to these impediments), it is again white America that is to blame for bloody murder. As a black man in a white hierarchy, Thomas's is a voice that, if heard at all, is rarely listened to.

Again, it should be noted that these touches are all handled extremely well. This is not a political film, but merely one which reflects its times and the core concerns of its audience. *Blacula* looks at Thomas and Mamawaldi as two extraordinary men of color who live in a world that does not value them. Remember, a powerful impulse in many horror movies is to create a situation that is believable and identifiable to your audience. *Blacula* does that. It reflects the fear of the African-American audience that they are not heard, not appreciated, and indeed, not even protected, by a police force they do not necessarily trust.

Lest someone believe that *Blacula* is merely a polemic about race, the film is also highly entertaining. William Marshall is one of the all-time great screen vampires, regardless of skin color, and his booming, Shakespearean delivery magnificently captures the regal demeanor, and tragic happenstance, of this once-proud man. Though *Blacula* is hardly what would be considered a scary film today, it is still strong, like so many Hammer films, because it is stylish. When Blacula attacks the photographer for instance, he glides suddenly across the room, his arms upraised like batwings. It is a bizarre, surreal moment, but an interesting one nonetheless. The film is energetically performed by all of its principals, who seem fully invested in re-fashioning the Dracula myth for a new time and a contemporary audience. There are bloodcurdling moments aplenty (such as the slow-motion attack by a vampirized cabbie, her fanged mouth gaping), some fine music, and even a touching ending. Blacula is a creature of such dignity, a "black prince" as Dracula calls him, that when he has lost all chance of reclaiming his love, he takes his own life. Rather than giving his enemies the satisfaction of a victory, he courageously faces sunlight, and ends his life. It is a pow-erful sacrifice, and another moment that speaks to the fact that, though cursed by Dracula, Mamawaldi is a man of noble char-acter.

If *Blacula* fails anywhere, it is in its crude, stereotypical depiction of two gay antique dealers. It seems disingenuous for a film so beautifully reflective of one minor-ity's American experience to then turn around and reinforce the most ridiculous and bigoted views of another disenfran-chised group: gay men. These guys are por-trayed as mincing, swishy queens, which is funny, but which somehow manages to undercut the grace and style of Blacula's world.

Other flaws are ones typical of low-bud-get films. We see the same close-up of a police pistol firing at least three times dur-ing the climax of the picture. That's a small price to pay, however, for such an enthusi-astic re-imagining of a story that had grown stale through infinite repetition and so little variation.

———————

LEGACY: With *Blacula,* the '70s blaxploita-tion hit horror with a bang. After *Blacula,* one sequel, *Scream Blacula Scream* (1973), followed. The blaxploitation cycle ran its course with AIP's *Blackenstein: The Black Frankenstein* (1973), *Blood Couple* (1973), and 1974's *Abby* (also starring William Mar-shall), an African-American variation on *The Exorcist,* directed by William Girdler, and *J.D.'s Revenge* (1976). The success of *Blacula* paved the way for other vampires of color, including Eddie Murphy in Wes Craven's *A Vampire in Brooklyn* (1995), and Wesley Snipes' heroic *Blade* (1998).

Children Shouldn't Play with Dead Things (1972) ★ ★ ½

Critical Reception

"Genuinely weird … an uneasy combination of comedy and … *Night of the Living Dead.*"— Alan Frank, *The Horror Film Handbook,* 1982, page 31.

"Lamely acted … and rather weirdly didactic."— Donald C. Willis, *Horror and Science Fiction Films II,* Scarecrow Press, 1982, page 57.

"Indescribable, improbable tale of a repertory theater group, two gay grave robbers, and several bargain basement zombies on an island cemetery. Starring the unforgettable husband-and-wife team of Alan and Anya Ormsby."— Harry and Michael Medved, *The Golden Turkey Awards,* A Perigee Book, 1980, page 211.

Cast & Crew

CAST: Alan Ormsby (Alan); Valerie Mamche (Kat); Anya Ormsby (Anya); Jeffrey Gillen (Jeff); Jane Daly (Terry); Paul Cronin (Paul); Roy Engleman (Roy); Robert Philip (Emerson); Seth Sklarey (Orville); Bruce Solomon (Vims); Alecs Blair (Caretaker); Robert Sherman, Debbie Cummins, Hester Phebus, Dick Sohmer, Brendan Kenny, Curtis Bryant, Gordon Gillert, Stuart Mitchell, Sandra Laurie, Stephanie Laurie, Jean Clark, Paula Hoffer, Harry Boehme, Robert Smedley, Peter Burke, Lee O'Donnell, Gamille MacDonald, Al McAdams, Carl Richardson, Andy Herbst.

CREW: Geneni Film Distributing Company Presents A Brandywinde Motionarts Film, *Children Shouldn't Play with Dead Things*. *Art Director:* Forest Carpenter. *Set Designer:* David Trimble. *Director of Photography:* Jack McGowan. *Musical Score:* Carl Zittrer. *Special Make-up Created by and Screenplay Collaboration:* Alan Ormsby. *Film Editor:* Gary Goch. *Second Unit Director of Photography:* Michael McGowan. *Production Manager:* Chris Martell. *Costumer:* Bruce Solomon. *Make-up:* Lee James O'Donnell, Benita Friedman, Judy Whalen. *Camera Operator:* Randy Franken. *Assistant Cameraman:* John McGowan. *Script Supervisor:* Sandy Ulosevich. *Acknowledgments to:* Dade County Department of Parks, City of Miami. *Sound Recording:* Location Recording Company. *Production Assistant:* Mike Harris, Joe Bonvosu, Oliver Rish. *Titles and Opticals:* The Optical House. *Color:* Capital. *Produced by:* Gary Goch and Benjamin Clark. *Directed and Written by:* Benjamin Clark. *M.P.A.A. Rating:* R. *Running time:* 87 minutes.

SYNOPSIS: A group of actors set out for a "burial island" by boat on a dark night. There is an old graveyard on the island, and the leader of the repertory company, Alan, is planning to dig up a dead body as part of a bizarre prank-cum-initiation ritual. The rest of the theatrical group includes Jeff, Kat, Anya, and newcomers Paul and Terry. Paul considers himself the "new Brando" and Terry is intimidated by Alan, who openly expresses his desire to have sex with her.

When the actors reach the island, Alan provides a tour of the cemetery and tells a brief history of the place, reporting that it is "Satan's sanctum," and that malevolent forces gather in the dark there. Alan leads his cohorts to the caretaker's vacant cabin, and inside they find a bathroom teeming with rats. As midnight nears, Alan opens his "sorcerer's sourcebox" and prepares to summon the dead. Using a grimoire, a spell book, he plans to call forth the dead from their graves. First, however, he forces his companions to exhume the body of a corpse named Orville. Then, suddenly, two zombies attack and the group panics. It is all a prank, however, and the two zombies are really just Emerson and Roy, two flamboyant members of Alan's troupe who were waiting on the island to pull off the practical joke.

After the others have recovered from his joke, Alan prepares the corpse, Orville, for the summation. He draws the pentagram, the symbol of Satan, atop a coffin and lights the black candles for the dark mass. He summons the dead, but nothing happens. Disappointed, Alan loudly insults Satan and renounces the power of the grimoire. Flustered by Alan's lousy performance, Kat conducts the same spell in much more dramatic fashion. She calls on the power of Satan and gives the performance of a lifetime. Upstaged by Kat, Alan resolves to re-capture his thunder. He decides to bring Orville back to the caretaker's cottage for a party. There, he arranges a sick wedding and is married to Orville in a mock ceremony conducted by Jeff. Terry objects to the proceedings and Anya warns that Orville should be respected, lest he become angry, but Alan is determined to go so far over the top that no one will ever question his commitment to the theater. He even takes Orville to his bedroom and resolves to sleep with the corpse.

Down in the graveyard, the corpses buried there begin to rise. The hungry ghouls feed on Roy and Emerson, and devour the real caretaker of the island, who has been held captive by Alan and the others. Unaware of the events transpiring outside the cabin, the troupe decides to leave Alan and get back to the boat. They are confronted by an army of the dead and are forced to retreat into the cottage as zombies surround the dwelling. The surviving performers barricade the house, but the undead keep walking. Kat, Alan, Jeff and Anya distract the zombies while Paul runs out in the night to retrieve a gun from the boat. Unfortunately, Paul does not make it very far, and is devoured by hungry ghouls. Trying to rescue him, Terry is also dragged away by the ravenous corpses.

Terrified, Alan and the others resolve to perform a counter-ritual that will send the dead back to their graves. Unfortunately, they cannot complete one part of the ritual: they cannot return Orville, the ceremonial corpse, to his grave, because the zombies are all around. Alan conducts the spell anyway, and it seems to drive the zombies back. Relieved, Alan, Anya, Kat and Jeff flee the house. Halfway to the boat, the zombies spring their trap. They have been waiting, and surround the actors. Jeffrey and Kat are devoured by the monsters but Alan and Anya make it back to the cottage. As zombies swarm in after them, a selfish Alan throws them Anya and runs upstairs to a room he hopes is safe.

Alan locks himself in his bedroom only to discover that Orville is there, waiting for him. Alan screams in terror as Orville lunges for him, and the zombies break in.

———————————

COMMENTARY: Evil can hide in plain sight, and so can terror. That's one lesson of the ultra-bizarre but not ineffective movie entitled *Children Shouldn't Play with Dead Things*. Much of the suspense generated by the film comes from the ever-present — but unmoving — threat embodied by a character called Orville. Orville is a corpse, you see, and a bunch of inconsiderate actors have stolen him from his grave, and peaceful slumber, as part of a prank to raise the dead on a so-called "burial" island. The prank fails, apparently, and Orville then functions in the film as a kind of human prop ("He's my straight-man!" the cruel Alan declares),

to be used, abused and debased by the *dramatis personae*. It's like *Weekend at Bernie's* (1987) for the cemetery set. All through this portion of the film, the audience waits with a sense of growing dread for Orville's response to the mockery. It waits for him to come to malevolent, vengeful life. To this movie's credit, it holds back that eventuality until the last possible moment, and consequently every scene featuring Orville exhibits an underlying, commendable tension. Of course, this is but a variation on Alfred Hitchcock's old trick (put a bomb under a table ... but don't let it explode), yet it works well, granting this low budget horror picture a boost in its fear quotient. There Orville sits: exploited, teased, manipulated ... and ostensibly angry. But any minute that situation could change. And finally, horrifically, it does.

The skillful placement of Orville within the film's action (so that he almost becomes background) is indicative of writer/director Benjamin Clark's facility at tapping effectively into the horror mythos. Don't we all fear waking a sleeping juggernaut? Aren't we all afraid that what should be dead is actually still alive, and watching us? The film plumbs those terrors nimbly, even if overall the movie is darn silly.

What really sinks the movie fastest is a conjunction of two weaknesses: amateurish acting and florid, overly theatrical dialogue. The acting is bad, all right, but even the best and most studied performer would have a hard time mouthing phrases like "the magnitude of your simplitude overwhelms me," and such. Yet, thematically, this florid dialogue is acceptable because the characters involved are all pompous, self-important acting wannabes, part of a repertory company. As anyone who has ever spent time with fledgling actors is aware, GAS (great actors syndrome) is a real threat, and this film works that syndrome into its narrative. Still, whether the dialogue is valid or not, it is tough on the ears and stagey to the point of absurdity (which just may be the point...). Still, there are not many forms of torture worse than listening to two amateur performers (playing swishy gay to boot) announce that they've "peed" their pants (four times!!!).

Despite the poor acting, the atrocious dialogue, and only barely coherent editing at times, *Children Shouldn't Play with Dead Things* manages to be a rather endearing picture in spite of itself. It operates on a simple (yet distinctly primal) level of nightmare. A group of nasty "children," as the script repeatedly terms the actors, disrespect the dead and are forced to pay a price for their sacrilege. Not unlike an E.C. comic of the 1950s, *Children Shouldn't Play with Dead Things* is oddly moral in that it metes out punishment for the wicked, and establishes that there is a higher order of morality, an order of justice (of the eye-for-an-eye variety, no doubt).

Alan, the perpetrator of most of the wrong-headed pranks in the film, is a particularly arrogant sort who demonstrates no respect for the dead, the occult, his fellow man, or even the sanctity of wedding vows. At one especially disgusting juncture, Alan even intimates that he will have sex with Orville's corpse — a perverse desecration that spurs the anger of the "powers that be." Appropriately, Alan is eventually done in by the revivified Orville, who waits silently in a bedroom, ready to defile his would-be defiler. It is a moment of just deserts, and a chilling one; it is also satisfying, as the audience has been anticipating (and even desiring) the moment when Orville would spring to life and avenge the wrongs heaped upon him.

Of all of *Night of the Living Dead*'s children (zombie movies of the 1970s), *Children Shouldn't Play with Dead Things* seems to have the most distinct and separate ethos. Though the living dead, graveyards, and even

a climactic siege on an isolated house are all ingredients transferred from George Romero's seminal cult flick, they are arranged to have different meanings here. *Night of the Living Dead* shows humanity as essentially heroic, even if disorganized and bickering. Ben protected Barbara, engineered an escape (though a failed one), and battled the living dead with an almost innate sense of decency. It wasn't his fault the deck was stacked against him. Such decency is clearly missing from *Children Shouldn't Play with Dead Things*, a film which reduces adults to "children," sees man as monstrous and disrespectful, and metes out supernatural justice. In *Night of the Living Dead*, there is no justice at all; Ben survives the night of the ghouls, but is picked off by trigger-happy rednecks who mistake him for the enemy. Contrast that climax with *Children*'s, in which the unpleasant self-important characters get the bruisin' they have been cruisin' for all along.

In the final analysis, *Children Shouldn't Play with Dead Things* passes the most important of tests for horror movies: it is scary. The isolated burial island, the "sleeping" Orville quiescent amidst the action, and the manner in which the cutting gets faster as Alan summons the dead — thereby working the movie into a visual frenzy — all lend the production a sturdy platform on which to build scares. That the characters are all dinner theater rejects prone to pomposity and lacking redeeming value only adds to the film's moral underpinning and tension. We know these bastards are going to get it for their blatant disrespect of a "higher power," but the fun of *Children Shouldn't Play with Dead Things* is not knowing exactly when justice — and Orville — will awaken from a long slumber.

Countess Dracula

Cast & Crew

CAST: Ingrid Pitt (Countess Elizabeth); Nigel Green (Cap'n); Sandor Eles (Toth); Lesley-Anne Down (Ilona); Maurice Denham (Fabio); Patience Collier (Julia).

CREW: *Directed by:* Peter Sasdy. *Written by:* Jeremy Paul. *Produced by:* Alexander Paal. *Director of Photography:* Ken Talbot. *Film Editor:* Henry Richardson. *Music:* Harry Robinson. *M.P.A.A. Rating:* PG. *Running Time:* 93 minutes.

DETAILS: The legend of Countess Bathory (the subject also of *Daughters of Darkness* [1971]) is the prime focus of *Countess Dracula*. Ingrid Pitt plays the aristocratic vampire that maintains her youth by soaking in the blood of virgins. Try that out, Madge!

Daughters of Satan (1972) ✳ ½

Critical Reception

"A coven of local, modern witches … entice Miss Grant into satanic shivarees … so we can have some metaphysical mumbo jumbo, a few obligatory seminude scenes, and explicitly sexy talk…. Miss Grant and Miss Guthrie are photogenic, if little else, and Mr. Selleck … is natural in his confusion."—A.H. Weiler, *New York Times*, November 2, 1972, page 80.

Cast & Crew

CAST: Tom Selleck (James Robertson); Barra Grant (Chris Robertson); Tani Phelps Guthrie (Kitty Duarte); Paraluman (Juana Rios); Vic Silayan (Dr. Dangal); Vic Diaz (Carlos Ching); Gina Laforteza (Andrea); Ben Rubio (Tommy Tantuico); Paquito Salcedo (Mortician); Chito Reves (Guerilla); Bobby Greenwood (Mrs. Postlewaite).

CREW: United Artists presents *Daughters of Satan. Camera Operator:* Jun Rasca. *Boom Operator:* Tindy Corpuz. *Chief Electrician:* Julian Baldonado. *Wardrobe:* Vicente Cabrera. *Set Design:* Hernando Palon. *Set Dresser:* Mario Carmona. *Make-up Artist:* Fred C. Blau, Sr. *Assistant Make-up Artist:* Ricardo Villomin. *Hairdresser:* Carmelita Sidson. *Assistant to Producer:* Ann Tait. *Unit Manager:* A. Corpuz. *Assistant Director:* Jose Velasco. *Sound Recordist:* Levy Principe. *Sound:* Glen Glenn Sound. *Sound Effects Editor:* Gene Eliot. *Director of Photography:* Monong Pasca. *Film Editor:* Tony DiMarco. *Color:* DeLuxe. *Music composed and conducted by:* Richard La Salle. *Associate Producer:* Vicente Nayve. *Screenplay:* John C. Higgins. *From a story by:* John Bushelman. *Produced by:* Aubrey Schenck. *Directed by:* Hollingsworth Morse. *M.P.A.A. Rating:* R. *Running Time:* 90 minutes.

SYNOPSIS: In Manila, American art collector James Robertson visits a curio shop called "Treasures of the Orient," and ends up purchasing a painting of a witchburning (set in the 16th century). He is so interested in the painting because his wife, Christine, resembles the leader of the three witches on the canvas.

The painting disturbs Chris, who is instantly fearful of it. Worse, she seems to recognize the burning depicted on the painting, as one from 1592. Chris even has nightmares about the work of art, and hears someone calling her name.

Before long, figures from the painting are materializing in reality, specifically a devil dog named Nicodemus, and a satanic housekeeper, Juana Rios. James watches Christine change, and with suspicion, attempts to track down the dog's owner to house #666 on a busy street. He fails to find anything, but is nearly killed by a gang of knife-wielding lunatics, all Satanists out to get him. Jim confides in his psychiatrist, Dr. Dangal, about the situation, and meets one of his other patients, Kitty. Like Juana and Chris, Kitty resembles one of the three witches burned in the painting.

After Dr. Dangal is killed in a suspicious car accident, Jim drives Kitty home from the funeral. She shows him that she owns the third in a series of "The Burning of the Witches" paintings. In this particular piece of art, Robertson sees himself as the head inquisitor. Kitty then tells him of a witches' vengeance pact: all descendants of the inquisitors have died young. Jim realizes he is related to the inquisitors, and that the people in his life are being possessed by the spirits of the witches. A possessed Chris fails to kill James, and is tortured by a coven of Satanists, the Manila Assembly of Lucifer. She is ordered to spit on a crucifix, is reconfirmed in the faith, and ordered to kill Jim again.

Understandably, Jim wants to move from Manila immediately, but Juana and Chris poison his drink, and knock him unconscious. They deposit him in his car, and position it to go over a ravine. The car flies off the cliff, erupting into flame. At midnight, Juana, Kitty and Chris snap out of their possession, with no knowledge of the crime they have committed. Chris returns home and wonders where Jim is, feeling guilty for some reason. Miraculously, Jim shows up, alive but confused, having escaped the burning car. Suddenly re-possessed, Chris stabs her husband in the back, and completes the centuries-old pact.

COMMENTARY: Besides introducing the world to Tom Selleck, *Daughters of Satan* points the way to a new generation of reality/game show TV programming, if only the intrepid producer would look at it. As a woman is tortured by a satanic cult early in the film, her feet impaled on rows of spikes, her torturess suddenly demands of her: "Repeat the nine names of the principal powers of darkness!" It is kind of like *Jeopardy* meets *Survivor*, meets *The Weakest Link*, with a cult twist thrown in. A contestant could answer questions not for the opportunity to win prize money, but to avoid bloody punishment, thus granting a whole new meaning to the idea of a "lifeline." Some people already say Anne Robinson is evil, so this show would be a shoo in...

But all kidding aside, this tale of karmic revenge and past lives is no boost to anyone's resume, certainly not Selleck's. The poor guy spends much of the picture unaware of the danger his (possessed) wife represents to him. "Does the fly rest easily caught in the web?" Selleck's psychologist asks of him ... and the answer seems to be "yes," since Selleck's character never catches on to the ramifications of the situation.

A film of rudimentary style and acting, the low budget *Daughters of Satan* at least looks interesting, having been lensed in the Philippines. That bit of local color aside, the film relentlessly relies on horror clichés such as evil dogs, evil domestics (both better handled in *The Omen* [1976]) and paranormal phenomena such as possession and reincarnation. One might think when surrounded by so many evil characters and unusual circumstances, the average person would be pretty concerned, or at least a tad suspicious. Consider these facts: a 25-year-old wife suddenly (and spontaneously) reveals intimate knowledge of an obscure historical event (a witch burning). A dog miraculously disappears out of a painting and then shows up in the flesh at your house (wearing a collar that identifies his place of residence as being apartment # 666). A poison gas suddenly suffuses your bedroom. Thugs miraculously appear in your backyard and beat you up. After your wife fixes you a cocktail, you fall unconscious … only to awaken in your car as it is speeding off a cliff. *Hmmm.* Could something strange be happening?

One would think that one or two of these events might really send up some warning signals to the average husband. Naturally, Selleck, like a chicken with his head cut off, dodges back and forth gathering information, never quite understanding the full picture or the real breadth of his danger. Naturally, Selleck's last scene in the film depicts him returning to his wife's loving embrace … as she prepares to plunge a knife into his back. Frankly, at that point it is difficult to empathize with a character so dumb.

The actors aren't aided much by *Daughters of Satan*'s hilarious dialogue either. When Christina is asked where she has been, by husband Jim (Selleck), she casually replies: "I was at a meeting." Strictly speaking, that report is true. What she fails to report is that the meeting was a gathering of the Manila Assembly of Lucifer, and that she was tortured there for hours on end. Still, at least she didn't lie!

In another funny moment, a hot-to-trot Satanist makes a pass at Selleck, noting that in "eleven years" her husband "never once touched" her breasts. Now *there's* a come-on! Perhaps the most ludicrous (under)statement comes from the future *Magnum P.I.* star himself as he notes of the devil canine (affectionately named Nicodemus), "that dog has been bugging the hell out of me!"

In a movie populated by idiots, the horror sequences of *Daughters of Satan* take on

an unusual air, and a high degree of unintentional humor. In a picnic sequence, Christine sits behind Jim, comforting him and telling him he's not crazy, while at the same time she cravenly fingers a ceremonial dagger and plots to murder him. Amusingly, every time Jim turns to face his wife, she hides the knife behind her back. Oddly, this shtick seems to be timed for comedy rather than suspense. It is well rehearsed, and even well acted, but is utterly ridiculous. After all, if you were planning to murder your husband, does it matter in the slightest if he turns around to face you while you deliver the death blow? Instead of killing Jim, the diffident Christine can't seem to make up her mind, hiding the knife, then brandishing it in a comic ballet that just keeps going and going.

If all of this isn't bad enough, *Daughters of Satan* even fails to keep track of its own plot. Late in the film, Kitty recommends to Chris that she see psychiatrist Dr. Dangal. Oddly, Christine does not recognize the doctor's name … even though the film establishes that Dangal has already been her therapist for some time! Apparently, a side effect of possession is stupidity … or maybe that's just an affliction that everyone in *Daughters of Satan* suffers from…

LEGACY: Though *Daughters of Satan* might best be left forgotten, it did launch the career of Tom Selleck. Still, Selleck must have been chargrined in the summer 2000 to see the film resurrected on TNT, just as his TV movie *Running Mates* was receiving critical accolades.

Dear Dead Delilah (1972) ★ ★ ½

Cast & Crew

CAST: Agnes Moorehead (Delilah); Will Geer (Ray Jurroe); Michael Ansara (Morgan); Dennis Patrick (Alonzo); Anne Meacham (Grace); Robert Gentry (Richard); Elizabeth Eis (Ellen); Ruth Baker (Buffy); Anne Gibbs (Young Luddy); John Marriott (Marshall); Patricia Carmichael (Luddy).

CREW: Southern Star Productions and Jack Clement Present *Dear Dead Delilah*. *Art Director:* James Tilton. *Costume Designer:* Nancy Potts. *Music:* Bill Justis. *Director of Photography:* William R. Johnson. *Assistant Cameramen:* Wilson Hong, John Packwood. *Sound:* Robert Janus. *Gaffer:* Murray Cohan. *Unit Manager:* Michael Kenner. *Music Coordinator:* David Davis. *Music Editor:* Ken Johnson. *Sound Mixer:* Al Gramaglia. *Production Manager:* Fred Carmichael. *Assistant to Producer:* Tilla Marshall. *Script Continuity:* Phyllis Pestaino. *Makeup:* Vincent Loscalzo. *Hairdresser:* William Chiarelli. *Wardrobe:* Clifford Capone. *Stunt Coordinator:* Alex Stevens. *Casting Assistant:* John Murrey. *Technical Advisor:* K. Baker. *Editor:* Ron Dorfman. *Associate Producer:* Susan Richardson. *Produced by:* Jack Clement. *Written and directed by:* John Farris. *M.P.A.A. Rating:* R. *Running Time:* 97 minutes.

SYNOPSIS: In Tennessee in 1943, young Luddy brutally murders her mother with an axe after fighting about the G.I. boyfriend who impregnated her...

Twenty-five years later, an older, fatter and sadder Luddy is released from prison. She saw her baby only once, and has spent her adult life wondering what became of the child. Luddy soon finds employment at South Hall Plantation, the exclusive home of the rich Charles family. There, she cares for the wealthy but wheelchair-bound Delilah Charles, family matriarch and cold-hearted shrew. Delilah has been scheming, along with her lawyer, Ray, to find a way to cut her greedy siblings, Grace, Morgan and Alonzo, out of the family estate.

Luddy befriends Ellen, Delilah's pretty young niece, and her husband Richard, but finds a special kinship with Alonzo, a sad drug addict and family physician. Like Luddy, Alonzo loves children, and longs for the child he lost many years earlier during a botched abortion.

At a family dinner one night, Delilah reveals that she only has 30 days to live. She then announces to her siblings that she is leaving the South Hall estate to the state of Tennessee — not her family. However, Delilah also reveals that she has found her dead father's secret stash of cash worth $600,000. She reports that the sibling who finds this "horse money" (cash earned from the sale of the family horses during the Great Depression) can keep it. Soon, the avaricious siblings are at each other's throats looking for the hidden cash.

One night, Luddy discovers a bloody axe on her pillow, and finds the family lawyer, Ray Jurroes, butchered nearby. She believes she committed the murder, and sets out to hide the attorney's death with the help of a sympathetic Alonzo.

Meanwhile, Morgan reveals to Delilah that he is in deep financial trouble — $40,000 worth — and that he needs the horse money to set things right. Delilah refuses to help, and so Morgan and his girlfriend begin searching for the horse money. They dig near a recently installed plumbing line after finding $50 in cash nearby. That night, an unseen assailant murders Buffy, Morgan's girlfriend, and then Morgan, with a very sharp axe.

The next night, Delilah's sister, Grace, is decapitated by an assailant dressed up to resemble her dead father. The killer reveals himself to be Richard, Ellen's husband. He has found the horse money in the tomb of Mr. Charles, and, having learned about Luddy's past, is murdering his relatives with an axe in order to frame Luddy and take the money for himself! After finishing off Grace,

Richard even murders his wife, Ellen! Then, he sees to it that Alonzo is given an apparently fatal drug overdose.

Finally it comes down to Luddy and Richard, but Richard has forgotten about the stubborn Delilah ... who disappeared into the tomb of her father and was believed to have expired there. She crawls out of the tomb, summoning all her failing strength, blasts Richard's head to smithereens with a shotgun, and finally passes away. This leaves Luddy and a recovered Alonzo to keep the horse money and start a home for orphaned children.

COMMENTARY: *Dear Dead Delilah* is a mildly intriguing story of family politics, dysfunction, and murder. Madness, greed, duplicity and even excessive gore are the primary players in the drama. A sturdy B-movie cast, including Michael Ansara and Agnes Moorehad, tether the film to reality and make some of the suspects seem more than just ciphers.

The film opens with some interesting drawings over the opening credits. These sketches of murder and violence (by Luddy), not only remind audiences of her murderous past with her mother, but forecast her future at South Hall Plantation. What's rewarding about the film is that it is a successful game of audience misdirection, beginning with these disturbing works of art. The film opens with Norman Bates-like story of Luddy's youth (and murderous infraction). She defies her mother, kills her, and goes to jail for it. The rest of the film is built on the assumption that she is going to go nuts again and resume her homicidal ways. However, that never happens, and what results is a moderately effective "time bomb" effect.

Alfred Hitchcock always said it was interesting to put a time bomb under a table, and then *not* have it go off. That's Luddy's

function in the plot. She is a logical suspect, and a convicted murderer ... but not the real villain in this case. Rather surprisingly, Luddy runs into a group of people who are far more nasty and brutal than she ever was. She's small time compared to the decadent, rich and powerful Charles family.

Dear Dead Delilah is brutal not only in its violence, but in its depiction of the Southern social upper crust. This is clearly a family that has been pampered for far too long. Delilah is purposefully cruel, and her siblings are spoiled wretches for the most part. The primary concern of all these folks is money, whether it be who gives it or who receives it. Morgan blows his money on bad business schemes, and never learns from his excessive mistakes. Richard is a hungry young buck, willing to marry, beg, plead or kill to be wealthy. The family dynamic is so bad that sensitive Alonzo has become an addict, unable to cope with a Machiavellian home life. Luddy, a poor girl out of rural Tennessee, is the only character who does not care about money, and in a nice twist, she is the character who walks away with it at the end of the picture.

Where *Dear Dead Delilah* focuses much of its creative energy is in its depiction of gory violence. In the prologue, a severed arm is seen on the floor, and Luddy's mom is garbed in a blood-spattered dress. Later, Ray staggers out of a stable, clutching a bloody hand. Richard receives a bullet to the face in a really bloody climax, and so on. It probably isn't necessary to go to these violent lengths to make the film's twin points (that insanity is not reserved for the poor, and that the rich exploit the poor). Still, the violence enlivens what might have been a rather pedestrian affair.

Dear Dead Delilah is not particularly good, or particularly bad. Some of the twists work just right, some don't. The title, and the blood and guts, are the best part.

Deliverance (1972) ✶ ✶ ✶ ✶

Critical Reception

"…it works like a very smooth and exciting piece of toy machinery for men at Christmas…. It is the long-windedness and banality of some of the dialogue and action that startle you in the midst of the bashing plot and subtle look of the picture…. Strongly made, and a fine yarn as long as the story of the delivered ones isn't taken as metaphysically as the title suggests it should be."—Penelope Gilliatt, *New Yorker*, August 5, 1972, pages 52–53.

"Between director Boorman and cameraman Vilmos Zsigmond exists an understanding that film is a visual experience. The imagery in this film is spectacular and the worthy result of delicate interplay of natural setting, sensitive composition, sophisticated work with the telephoto lenses, an eerie filter or solarization effects … an engaging experience with considerable impact on a multiplicity of levels."—Hal Aigner, *Film Quarterly*, Volume XXVI, Number 2, Winter 1972–73, page 41.

"The film starts out with heavy emphasis on nature, on its hidden savagery, and the despoilment of nature by technology. The first thing we see is a lumpy editorial, intercuts of bulldozers and sylvan beauty. But the only real drama comes from the encounter with two bestial mountaineers, who would have been what they are if bulldozers had never been invented…. Beyond the unfulfilled theme, the moral parallelisms of the script are intolerable…. The glory-of-nature shots are trite, the drama is clumsy, and the editing clanks."—Stanley Kauffmann, *The New Republic*, August 5, 1972, pages 24, 35.

Cast & Crew

CAST: Jon Voight (Ed); Burt Reynolds (Lewis); Ned Beatty (Bobby); Ronny Cox (Drew); Bil McKinney (Mountain Man); Herbert "Cowboy" Coward (Toothless Man); James Dickey (Sheriff Bullard); Lewis Crone (First Deputy); Ken Keener (Second Deputy); Ed Ramey (Old Man); Johnny Popwell (Ambulance Driver); John Fowler (Doctor); Jathry Rickman (Nurse); With: Bill Redden, Seamon Glass, Randall Deal, Louis Coldren, Pete Ware, Macon McCalman, Hoyt Pollard, Belinda Beatty, Charlie Boorman.

CREW: Warner Brothers Presents a John Boorman film, *Deliverance. Director of Photography:* Vilmos Zsigmond. *Editor:* Tom Priestley. *Art Director:* Fred Harpman. *Property Master:* Syd Greenwood. *Script Supervisor:* Ray Quiroz. *Technical Advisors:* Charles Wiggin, E. Lewis King. *Production Supervisor:* Wallace Worsley. *Assistant Directors:* Al Jennings, Miles Middough. *Production Secretary:* Sue Dwiggins. *Special Effects:* Marcel Vecoutere. *Wardrobe Master:* Bucky Rous. *Make-up:* Michael Hancock. *Hairstylist:* Donoene McKay. *Sound Mixer:* Walter Goss. *Sound Editor:* Jim Atkinson. *Dubbing Mixer:* Doug Turner. *Assistant Editor:* Ian Rakoff. *Second Unit Photography:* Bill Butler. *Camera Operator:* Sven Wainum. *Assistant Camera:* Earl Clark. *Electrical Supervisor:* Jim Blair. *Casting:* Lynn Stalmaster. *"Dueling Banjos" arranged and played by:* Eric Weissberg with Steve Mandel. *Screenplay by:* James Dickey. *Based on the novel by:* James Dickey. *Produced and Directed by:* John Boorman. *M.P.A.A Rating:* R. *Running time:* 110 minutes.

SYNOPSIS: A foursome of suburban weekend warriors (Ed, Lewis, Drew and Bobby) head to the country to navigate a river that will soon be destroyed by the creation of a dam and an artificial lake. While filling up their cars with gas at a remote country station, Drew, the liberal of the bunch, attempts to befriend a little boy with music, and the two musicians duel playfully with banjo and guitar. Afterwards, Drew's attempts at friendship with the boy are rejected outright because he is a stranger in those parts. The macho survivalist, Lewis, then hires two locals to drive the cars to the bottom of the river, at the town of Aintry, while they canoe there. After a few near misses, Lewis finds the river and the foursome land their canoes into the water at last. Ed, an average family man, and Drew take one boat; Bobby, the sarcastic city slicker, and Lewis man the other. As they head down the river, the banjo-playing mountain boy looks after them with an expression of suspicion.

On the river, rapids come fast, and the weekenders navigate them with flying colors, exuberant in their defiance of nature. On the first night, they camp on the riverside, eating fish Lewis has caught. The next morning, Ed hunts a deer, but finds himself unable to kill it with his bow and arrow, his hands quaking at the moment of truth.

The four return to the river, this time with Bobby and Ed sharing a boat. For a time, Ed and Bobby are separated from the other team. They go ashore and are confronted by two armed locals. These burly mountain men demand that the trespassers go up into the woods with them. Ed and Bobby try to defuse the situation, but are left with no choice but to obey the armed men. Ed is consequently tied to a tree while one of the mountain men sexually assaults Bobby, forcing him to squeal like a pig during an act of anal penetration. Ed is in line for an even more horrible treatment, but Lewis arrives in time and kills the offending mountain man with an arrow. The other man, a toothless simpleton, escapes.

The four vacationers debate how to handle the corpse, and whether or not to notify authorities. Drew thinks the law should be involved in any decision they make, but Ed casts the deciding vote against such action, and the men bury the body. They continue downriver.

On the journey through deep rapids, a despondent Drew fails to wear his life jacket, and is consequently ejected from the boat — lost. The others, fearing he has been shot, search for him, and their boats collide and are overturned. Lewis, Bobby and Ed are cast overboard, one canoe destroyed, and thrown into the harsh water. Though the three survive the accident, Lewis's leg is badly broken. He also reports that Drew was definitely shot ... which means that the surviving mountain man has returned for vengeance. Worse, he is waiting on top of the nearest mountain, the area directly above the three men's position!

By dark of night, Ed scales the peaks of the mountain to confront the killer who waits above. He makes it to the top, exhausted, and waits for the redneck assassin to make a move. His hands shaking at the moment of kill, Ed manages to control his fear, and kill his enemy.

Ed, now the acknowledged leader of the group, the wounded Lewis, and Bobby continue downriver. Along the way, they discover Drew's body, and realize that it too must be done away with so as to hide the evidence of armed conflict with locals. They sink the body after an abrupt, halting eulogy, and take one last turn at the rapids. They survive, and make it to the town of Aintry, where they are greeted with suspicion by the authorities.

As the three men heal from their wounds, police probe more deeply into their story ... and recover a shattered canoe at a different point on the river than where Ed and the others claimed it was lost. In the final analysis, the police have nothing to hold the men on, and they are allowed to leave town.

Returning home to his wife and children, Ed is haunted by nightmares, and of a dead hand rising from a still lake...

COMMENTARY: *Deliverance* is one of the most powerful, profound, and harrowing horror films of the 1970s. It scared a whole generation away from camping in the woods, and remains one of the most stirring and exciting film testaments of man's violent nature. The secret to its success is found somewhere in its unique combination of thematic depth and exhilarating action. It is a film that doesn't pause long on big issues, but which nonetheless raises all kinds of questions about mankind.

Based on James Dickey's novel, *Deliverance* is a film that seems deceptively simple at first blush. Four weekend warriors meet with local hostility on a wild river, and must confront not only nature and their fellow man, but their own instincts and morals. From that elegant template is forged a brilliant action story that can be interpreted on a number of thematic levels.

First and foremost, the film tracks clearly as a metaphor for American involvement in the Vietnam War. Like that conflict (which was raging when the film was produced), *Deliverance* reveals an American intrusion into a more "primitive" world where the local culture is misunderstood, and treated with disrespect. What is plain almost from the beginning of the film is Lewis's and Bobby's disdain for the locals, and their existence on the fringes of the wild. "We've got a live one here," Bobby sarcastically states within earshot of one local. "I love the way you wear that hat," he mocks another.

It's almost as if the locals are not fully human beings, and therefore somehow incapable of understanding sarcasm. These folks don't talk a different language, as it were, though Bobby and Lewis treat them that way … like foreigners. In point of fact, that is much the same way that many American soldiers treated the people who spoke their own native tongue in Vietnam. They were treated as primitives in their own homes, not as simply different but equal.

Furthermore, Lewis (Burt Reynolds) is a symbol of American arrogance and potency, especially in relation to the Vietnam conflict. Though he is a stranger to the river, he believes he knows the land better than those who inhabit it. He is certain he knows

exactly where the river is, and takes special pains to lead the way to it, ignoring and bullying the locals who are more familiar with the terrain. Reynolds is perfect for this role because, like Charlton Heston, he typifies American strength — he is both macho and physically beautiful. Like America in Vietnam, Reynolds' character believes he is tough stuff, invincible even, yet he is completely out of his element when faced with the truth of just how tough the terrain truly is. It is no accident that Reynolds is rendered impotent half way through the film, disabled by a crippling wound. His strength is useless in this land, much as America's strength, technological and military, proved useless in Vietnam.

On a more personal level, *Deliverance* also concerns man, and what kind of creature he is. "The savage within" rears its head, and the film suggests that brutality and violence are forces that can be summoned within every human, that violence may be repressed in a civilized society, but if forced into service, it will arise. "Sometimes you have to lose yourself before you can find anything," Lewis states meaningfully, early in the film, and that might well be *Deliverance*'s mantra. There is a distinct macho side to the film that suggests you never really know yourself until you confront the worst.

In that regard, *Deliverance* is about four people who have lost touch not only with nature, but the human imperative to survive. On a day-to-day basis in the city nothing challenges these weekend warriors. So what do they do? They choose a form of recreation that requires them to put themselves in danger. It's as if to feel like men in today's unchallenging world, they must face mortal threats. It says something pertinent about our society that we must artificially generate such challenges for ourselves. We have advanced to the point where the circle of life, the battle for life and death, is distant, yet somehow we crave it.

Tellingly, it is not distant on the river. The instincts to fight, to struggle, to kill, are re-awakened in the visitors. Ed is unable to kill a deer because, intellectually, he knows it is not necessary. Yet, when his life is in danger, he is capable of killing a man. The battle for survival makes monsters of us all, doesn't it? Clearly, the transition from "civilized man" to survival-oriented organism is not an easy one. Even after Bobby's brutal rape, the group of four wastes valuable time debating the morality of their situation. They are blissfully unaware that they are still on enemy soil, in mortal jeopardy. They are literally babes in the woods, unable to grasp where they really are, and the gravity of their situation.

Each character in *Deliverance* represents some facet of the modern man. Drew is the liberal, the intellectual. He acts as the group's conscience. He still sees the world in moral absolutes. "It's a matter for the law," he declares of the mountain man's murder. Yet there is no law out there ... or perhaps only the law of the jungle. It is no wonder that Drew is killed first. The voice of society, the voice of morality, has little effect in the Darwinian world of the forest, in the kill-or-be-killed world of the rapids. He is unable to adapt to a world without the artificial structures he has imposed, and so dies first.

Lewis represents American arrogance and authority. Yet the jungle doesn't allow for vanity, or arrogance either. You can't beat nature, and the over-confident Lewis is taken out of the action early too, wounded so badly he can't even sit up. He thought he was more powerful than his surroundings, but he wasn't.

Bobby is a symbol of American flab and laziness. He depends on everybody else to help him survive the weekend. He is "rescued" first by Lewis, then by Ed. He is a flabby, weak representative of a modern urban man. He survives by luck, but not before being humiliated.

Ed, the film's protagonist, symbolizes the everyman. When he scales the mountain and kills the second redneck, it is a rite of passage, and Ed replaces Lewis as the expedition leader. This could be interpreted as recognition of the fact that nature does not appreciate extremes. Drew, the liberal, is too weak to survive. Lewis fails because there is no room for arrogance in the wild. Ed survives because he is temperate, and because, of all the characters, he seems genuinely to be fighting for something beyond survival. Of all the characters, he is the only one who is constantly defined in terms of family life. At the end of the picture, the audience sees his wife, briefly. He kills to protect himself, but also to return to the nurturing environment of hearth. Like the American soldier in Vietnam who keeps a photograph of his wife in his uniform, Ed keeps his eye on the prize, and balances his behavior to assure he can attain it.

This sounds like a lot to digest in a two-hour motion picture, but *Deliverance* moves like a rollercoaster, confidently sailing from scene to scene. The principal actors look to have performed all their stunts on the river, and the authenticity of those action sequences is amazing. The river scenes appear legitimately dangerous, and that's another area where Boorman's approach excels: he captures nature as inherently dangerous, and doesn't shy away from showing it as both beautiful and menacing.

Besides pace and distinctive action, *Deliverance* remains memorable. The legendary dueling banjos sequence nicely reveals how disparate cultures can come together for music. Music is the universal language, and for a moment, when the banjo and guitar join, the film is euphoric. Peace can be made, and it doesn't have to be forged through violence.

And, no review of *Deliverance* would be complete without mentioning the scene that has had men squirming for almost thirty years. That central rape scene is incredibly powerful, and disturbing. The rape represents man's worst fear, a harrowing, terrible sequence that exposes, once and for all, that rape is about power, not sex. The rape scene actually mirrors much of the action on the rapids: both scenes focus on power, and who will command power, whether it be locals, or nature itself. The scene is also about humiliation, and bringing the city-folk down to size. Bobby, who was so sarcastic and arrogant to the local men, learns the hard way that he's not in charge in that part of the woods.

There is another rape in the movie too— the rape of the river by man for his own purposes. Bulldozers encroach on trees. Dams force back the river's edge, and nature's path is circumvented for development. By springing to life one last time to attack the city four, the river is issuing its death rat-

tle. Before it falls to man once and for all, it strikes a blow at its enemy. "Don't take me for granted. You'll regret it."

In whatever way one chooses to view *Deliverance*, it is a powerful adventure yarn, filled with danger, suspense, and action. And for those who say it isn't a horror movie, take one more look at a certain scene in the woods, and how it is constructed to convey not only inevitability, but impotency, and terror.

Demons of the Mind (1972) ✶ ✶ ✶

Cast & Crew

CAST: Paul Jones (Carl); Patrick Magee (Dr. Falkenberg); Gillian Hills (Elizabeth Zorn); Robert Hardy (Baron Zorn); Michael Hordern (Priest); Yvonne Mitchell (Hilda); Kenneth J. Warren (Klaus); Virginia Wetherell (Inga); Barry Santon (Ernst); Robert Brown (Felschinger); Deidre Costello (Magda); Shane Briant (Emil Zorn); Sidonie Bond (Zorn's Wife); Thomas Heathcote (Coachman); John Atkinson (First Villager); George Cormack (Second Villager); Mary Hignett (Matronly Woman); Jan Adair (First Girl); Jane Garew (Second Girl).

CREW: A Hammer Production, in association with Frank Godwin Productions, Ltd. *Director of Photography:* Arthur Grant. *Designer:* Michael Stringer. *Production Supervisor:* Roy Skeggs. *Editor:* Chris Barnes. *Music Composed by:* Harry Robinson. *Musical Supervisor:* Philip Martell. *Production Manager:* Christopher Neame. *Assistant Supervisor:* Ted Morley. *Continuity:* Gladys Goldsmith. *Casting Director:* James Liggat. *Camera Operator:* Neil Binney. *Sound Recordist:* John Purchas. *Dubbing Mixer:* Len Abbott. *Sound Editor:* Terry Poulton. *Wardrobe Supevisor:* Rosemary Burrows. *Wardrobe Mistress:* Eileen Sullivan. *Make-up:* Trevor Grole-Rees. *Hair Dresser:* Maud Onslow. *Screenplay:* Christopher Wicking. *From an original story by:* Christopher Wick-

ing and Frank Godwin. *Produced by:* Frank Godwin. *Directed by:* Peter Sykes.

SYNOPSIS: In rural England of the late 1800s, a disturbed but beautiful girl, Elizabeth Zorn, is lost in the woods near Zorn Manor and befriended by a handsome stranger, Klaus. Later, she is returned to the estate of her wealthy family. Her brother Emil is imprisoned there by the tyrannical patriarch of the clan, Baron Zorn.

Meanwhile, a woman in the nearby village is attacked and murdered in the woods by a dangerous, hidden assailant. Subsequently, a Christian priest arrives in the village, claiming that God has much work for him to do there.

Inside Zorn Manor, Elizabeth is subjected to a cruel bloodletting procedure at the hands of her father and aunt. Emil objects to the barbaric procedure, but his father forcibly keeps Emil and Elizabeth apart in accord with some bizarre secret plan.

Amidst all this strangeness, a psychologist banished from polite society, Dr. Falkenberg, is retained by the Zorn family to see to the strange siblings. When he arrives at Zorn's house, there has been another murder in the local village, and Dr. Falkenberg immediately detects that Baron Zorn is psychologically responsible for all the insanity and violence. When hypnotized by Falkenberg, Zorn reveals that he feels a terrible bloodlust. He is impotent, and fears that his insanity has passed into the blood of his children. His obsession with such depraved thoughts led his late wife to madness and suicide.

A weakened Elizabeth and an anemic Emil attempt to escape the clutches of the their father, but are intercepted before they can leave the house. Falkenberg attempts to cure them, and proposes a strange treatment for their ailment, which, it turns out, is an incestuous sexual desire for each other. To cure them, Emil enlists the services of a town wench to "play" as Elizabeth. But instead of making love to her, Emil kills the wench.

Falkenberg then realizes that the baron has been orchestrating and encouraging this homicidal behavior in his son. He has been using Emil as the living embodiment, the instrument, of his own lust. He's been letting Emil out of the house to rape and kill local women.

The villagers soon witness the baron dumping the wench's body into the river, and are enraged. Emil kills his aunt, and attempts to escape with Elizabeth, but Elizabeth's young lover, Klaus, tries to intervene. Emil knocks him out, and flees into the woods with his sister. The baron kills Dr. Falkenberg, and realizes he must wipe out his entire bloodline so the madness will stop. He takes off after his children, but the villagers form a mob and chase the baron. Though Zorn shoots and kills Emil, the mob, led by the priest, in turn, kills the baron. They chop off one of his hands, and impale him on a giant cross. Elizabeth and her lover are reunited, but she is still beset by madness.

COMMENTARY: Hammer delves deep into psychological horror in the gritty, disturbing *Demons of the Mind*. This film concerns itself with incest, madness, and hysteria with an admirable seriousness, and even a flair for the artistic. It is an unhappy, unpleasant film, but one that has the courage to see its convictions through to the bitter end.

Demons of the Mind opens with several sepia-tone photographs displaying homes and people from the late 1800s. It's a decidedly romantic view of the past, and it is instantly cast aside as the film then goes to some lengths to suggest a life of unfettered "chaos." In particular, the focus is on the dysfunctional Zorn family. Brother and sister Zorn share incestuous feelings for one another, Daddy Zorn is an impotent rageaholic, and Mommy Zorn committed suicide rather than deal with a family life of major dysfunction. Into this mix of mental illness comes a controversial early psychologist (based on Mesmer), who wants to find order in the chaos, and thereby cure the Zorn family. But, as he discovers too late, some diseases just cannot be cured.

Director Peter Sykes does not flinch from making the material gritty and unpleasant. So many Hammer films (specifically of the *Dracula* and *Frankenstein* variety) are romantic views of the past — essentially lush period pieces. The model here (as in *Hands of the Ripper* [1971]) is one of unromantic, ugly reality. In one thoroughly nauseating (though riveting) scene, Sykes takes viewers step by step through the arcane process of bloodletting. The torturous procedure is shown in nauseating, graphic detail. A small device embedded with razors is inserted in the supple flesh of Elizabeth's hip (where there are already scars from previous applications...). Then a heated cup is attached to the razor wounds, creating a kind of suction. Before long, thick red blood is draining by torrents into the cup ... and it looks very, very real. If there is a more disturbing image in the films of Hammer Studios, this author hasn't seen it.

The remainder of the film is an intimate, head-on look at madness. "The place reeks of madness and decay," one character aptly states of the Zorn homestead, and Sykes' camera accommodates that perspective by filming many of the scenes from an askew, cockeyed angle. Not so much as to be exaggerated or cartoony though, just enough to make the point that things are off-kilter.

Sykes also cleverly equates sex with death in at least one important sequence. When Emil kills his aunt, he jams a set of keys into her throat in a thrusting, violent motion that reeks of phallic symbolism. Another phallic image occurs when Elizabeth makes contact with Emil through a keyhole. She pushes a rose and its long stem through the hole, and on the other side of the door, Emil rapturously smells the intruding shaft. It's decidedly kinky, but done in an artistic manner that gets the point across. Sex is the issue between these two disturbed characters, so the imagery is contextually appropriate.

Demons of the Mind isn't really a scary movie. It's just a blunt, disturbing one. It reveals a Hammer that has grown up a bit,

and is willing to look at stories of an unromantic, gritty nature. Maybe *Straw Dogs* or its ilk had made an impression with the studio. Whatever the cause of this experiment, that "new freedom" in cinema is evidenced here. And, in a particularly gory sequence, the baron has his hand severed in full view of the camera. Bloody good.

While several moments in *Demons of the Mind* are quite strong and well played-out, it seems necessary to note that there are also some rather jarring jumps from scene to scene, as if the idea of transition was too much for the editor to grasp. Still, if one is interested in the old taboo of incest and the archetypal idea of a father killing his own children (a theme that has all kinds of psychological possibilities...) then *Demons of the Mind* is a pretty involving picture. And a gross one, too.

Dr. Phibes Rises Again (1972) ✱ ✱ ✱

Critical Reception

"Crowded with mad villainy, stuffed with hair-raising perils and escape, it's a serial fan's dream of the ultimate cliffhanger. In the best serial traditions, its action is maxi and its plausibility mini.... *Phibes* also makes gentle fun of movie styles of the 1930s, and with its Art Deco sets and costumes is a treat for your ... eyes." — Margaret Ronan, *Senior Scholastic*, March 5, 1977, page 18.

"The second *Phibes* epic shows few signs of the ingenious touches and little of the wit of the first." — Alvin H. Marill, *Films in Review*, Volume XXIV, Number 3, March 1973, page 182.

Cast & Crew

CAST: Vincent Price (Dr. Anton Phibes); Robert Quarry (Darius Biederbeck); Peter Jeffrey (Trout); Fiona Lewis (Diana); Hugh Griffith (Ambrose); John Cater (Waverly); Gerald Sim (Hackett); Lewis Flander (Baker); John Thaw (Shavers); Peter Cushing (Captain); Beryl Reid (Miss Ambrose); Terry-Thomas (Lombardo); Valli Kemp (Vulnavia); Keith Bickley (Stewart); Milton Reid (Manservant). CREW: James H. Nicholson and Samuel Z.

Arkoff Present *Dr. Phibes Rises Again*. *Production Manager:* Richard Dalton. *Assistant Director:* Jack Wright. *Continuity:* Jane Buck. *Casting Director:* Sally Nicholl. *Director of Photography:* Alex Thomson. *Camera Operator:* Colin Corby. *Camera Assistant:* John Golding. *Make-up:* Carol Trevor-Rees. *Hairdresser:* Bernadette Ibbetson. *Supervising Electrician:* Roy Bond. *Sets Designed by:* Brian Eatwell. *Assistant Art Director:* Peter Withers. *Costume Supervisor:* Ivy Baker Jones. *Construction Manager:* Harry Phipps. *Properties:* Rex Hobbs. *Editor:* Tristam

Cones. *Sound Recordists:* Les Hammond, Dennis Whitlock. *Sound Assistant:* Fred Tomlin. *Dubbing Editor:* Peter Lennard. *Original Music:* John Gale. *Written by:* Robert Fuest, Robert Blees. *Based on Characters Created by:* James Whiton, William Goldstein. *Executive Producers:* Samuel Z. Arkoff, James H. Nicholson. *Produced by:* Louis M. Heyward. *Directed by:* Robert Fuest. *M.P.A.A. Rating:* PG. *Running time:* 89 minutes.

SYNOPSIS: Three years after he disappeared in his tomb, the evil Dr. Phibes awakens and walks upon the Earth once more. The moon is in the astral position it held 2000 years earlier, when a portal in Egypt was last open, and Phibes believes the doorway leads to the river of life ... a place that can bring his beloved wife, Victoria, back to life. Phibes teams up once more with his beautiful assistant Vulnavia, to look for the River of Life in the land of the pharaohs. The plan hits a snag, however, when Phibes realizes his mansion has been destroyed, and his safe (with the secret map to the River of Life!) stolen.

The map is now in the hands of Phibes' archrival, the pompous Professor Biederbeck. Biederback also desires to learn the secrets of the River of Life, and his quest is personal: he is extremely long-lived thanks to a special elixir, but now he has run out of the life-giving fluid, and needs another tonic to maintain his unnatural life.

With his usual murderous zeal, Phibes sends an army of snakes into Biederbeck's house to murder his bodyguard and steal back the papyrus map. Once the map is safe, Phibes sets sail for Egypt while befuddled police investigate the theft.

Not surprisingly, Biederbeck is also aboard the ship bound for Egypt. One of his colleagues finds Victoria's corpse in the ship's hold, and Phibes traps him in a giant gin bottle (part of a publicity display) and throws the meddler overboard.

Phibes arrives in Egypt, and proceeds to the tomb he prepared years ago just for this occasion. Meanwhile, in Scotland Yard,

the police realize they are once more dealing with Phibes and also head to Egypt ... well out of their jurisdiction. As the authorities look for Phibes, he murders an interloper in the tomb, using a hawk to peck the man to death. Undeterred, Phibes finds a secret room deep in the caverns, and inside is a sarcophagus and key — the route and means to gain access to the River of Life and restore Victoria. Meanwhile, Vulnavia seduces one of Biederbeck's men to his death with the help of scorpions, no less.

Biederbeck soon finds the tomb, and steals the key, the sarcophagus, and Victoria's body, causing Phibes to swear vengeance. The police warn Biederbeck about the mad doctor, but he is determined to be the first to gain access to the River of Life. By night, Phibes employs a giant fan to attack the Biederback camp, and then he crunches a guard in a giant vise. He steals back Victoria and the sarcophagus, but learns that Biederbeck has the key on his person. Phibes thus captures Diana, Biederbeck's lover, and agrees to an exchange: Diana's life for the key.

Biederbeck is unable to rescue Diana, who has been trapped in a rapidly flooding pyramid! As Diana faces submersion, Biederbeck gives up the key rather than see her die. Phibes spares Diana, and with key in hand, vaults down the River of Life with his beloved Victoria. Without the magic elixir, Biederbeck ages rapidly and dies...

COMMENTARY: No better or worse than its predecessor, *Dr. Phibes Rises Again* is every bit as fun. Nothing more than a collection of bloody set pieces strung together between witty asides, the film is macabre, ghoulish, silly, and at times downright disgusting. It is performed with real relish, and is a tasty dessert for the fun-minded horror fan.

The tone of this sequel is set at the very outset when a narrator, like one out of an old-time chapter play, enables viewers to catch up on events so far. It's a perfect opening touch, because this film is very much in the tradition of those old 1930s cliffhangers, with hissable villains, bizarre action scenes, and art deco sets galore. The fun in the picture results from seeing two horror icons of the era (Vincent Price and Robert Quarry) squaring off, trying to outdo the other in the quest to find the River of Life. As for Price, he's again in fine form. Together, Phibes and Vulnavia form the Pat Sajak and Vanna White of the horror set, forever dwelling in a perpetual game show of terror. Quarry is an especially good villain, pompous and arrogant, though less feral than Count Yorga. He has the stature and charisma to equal Price's, and he's a better foil for Phibes than Cotten was in the first film.

The best reason to see this film is to watch these two fine actors crack wise over half a dozen gory set pieces. A hawk pecks an intruder to death; a man is crushed in a vise; scorpions are released from a ceramic statue to teem all over an innocent man, biting him to death, and so forth. It's all pretty gross, but pretty fun. After one really disgusting murder, one character states of the victim, "I don't know about his body, but we should give his head a decent burial…" For tongue-in-cheek absurdity, one can do no better than this silly film, again an obvious forerunner to the tongue-in-cheek *Nightmare on Elm Street* sequels of the 1980s.

Dracula AD 1972 (1972) ★ ★ ★

Critical Reception

> "…abysmal fang-and-cross flick without even the saving grace of humour. The worst of the Hammer Draculas, its would-be hip dialogue has to be heard to be believed."— Howard Maxford, *The A to Z of Horror Films*, Indiana University Press, 1997, page 87.

Cast & Crew

CAST: Christopher Lee (Count Dracula); Peter Cushing (Professor Van Helsing); Stephanie Beacham (Jessica Van Helsing); Christopher Neame (Johnny Alucard); Michael Coles (Inspector); William Ellis (Joe Mitcham); Janet Key (Anna); Michael Kitchen (Greg); Caroline Munro (Laura); Marsha Hunt (Gaynor); Phillip Miller (Bob); David Andrews (Detective Sergeant); Lolly Bowers (Matron); Constance Luttrell (Mrs. Donnelly); Michael Daly (Charles); Artro Morris (Police Sgt); Jo Richardson (Crying Matron); Penny Brohms (Hippy Girl); Brian John Smith (Hippy Boy); Rock Group (Stoneground).

CREW: Warner Brothers Communication Company Presents a Hammer Production, *Dracula AD 1972. Director of Photography:* Dick Bush. *Processed by:* Humphries Laboratory. *Production Supervisor:* Roy Skeggs. *Designer:* Don Mingaye. *Editor:* James Needs. *Production Manager:* Ron Jackson. *Assistant Director:* Robert Lynn. *Continuity:* Dorean Dearnsley. *Casting Director:* James Ligget. *Camera Operator:* Bernie Ford. *Special Effects:* Les Bowie. *Make-up:* Jill Carpenter. *Hairdresser:* Barbara Ritchie. *Assistant Art Director:* Ron Benton. *Sound Editor:* Roy Baker. *Recordist:* Claude Hitchcock. *Dubbing Mixer:* Bill Rowe. *Music Composed by:* Michael Vickers. *Musical Supervision:* Philip Martell. *And Introducing:* Stoneground. *Songs:* "Alligator Man," and "You Better Come Through." *Screenplay:* Don Houghton. *Produced by:* Josephine Douglas. *Directed by:* Alan Gibson. A Hammer Production Made at Elstree Studios, Hertfordshire, England. *M.P.A.A. Rating:* PG. *Running time:* 96 minutes.

SYNOPSIS: In 1872, Lawrence Van Helsing defeats the Prince of Darkness known as Dracula. After the vampire is staked in daylight, he dissolves ... but a stranger steals his ring and collects his ashes. Van Helsing dies from wounds suffered during the battle.

In 1972, a gang of groovy youngsters crash a stodgy estate party and dance to the tunes of Stoneground, a new rock sensation. One of the rebellious youngsters, Johnny Alucard, suggests a different kind of high after the police end the party: a date with the devil. Led by Johnny, the group decides to a conduct a black mass in a de-sanctified church due for demolition.

Among the teens is Jessica Van Helsing, whose grandfather is an expert in all matters of demonology and the occult. He is concerned that Jess is hanging with the wrong crowd, but she assures him of her virtue. That night, Jess, her boyfriend Bob and the others convene over the grave of Lawrence Van Helsing in the cemetery. They perform the black magic ritual and Johnny even uses the blood of one of the group, Laura, to resurrect Dracula. The Prince of Darkness is reborn to claim his first victim, Laura, and the rest of the gang runs in terror.

The next day, Alucard tries to convince his freaked-out friends that the group witnessed a hoax, but Jessica is not convinced. And then Laura's body turns up at a construction site! The police seek the help of Van Helsing, remembering his assistance on a case of witchcraft not long before. Van Helsing suspects the presence of a vampire, and soon Jessica reveals everything, including the specifics of the black mass. Van Helsing then realizes that Alucard is an anagram for Dracula, and that he must face not just any vampire but the king.

At the same time, Dracula claims another victim, though he desires to take Jessica Van Helsing and destroy the Van Helsing family line. Alucard wants immortality from Dracula and promises him Jessica's life in return for it. The deal is sealed and Jessica is delivered to the vampire, even as Alucard becomes a murderous vampire.

Van Helsing attempts to rescue his daughter. He fights Alucard at his apartment and uses the running water of a shower stall, in conjunction with daylight, to kill the vampire. He discovers Dracula's plan to marry Jessica — the ultimate ruin of the Van Helsings, and makes for the church. He makes preparations to destroy Dracula as night falls. At last, Dracula and his nemesis meet for a final struggle. The battle is won by Van Helsing when he douses Dracula with holy water and sees the vampire impaled on a bed of spikes in sanctified ground.

COMMENTARY: Though not well-liked by Hammer aficionados (primarily because it takes the good Count Dracula out of his time period and into ours), *Dracula AD 1972* is nonetheless a solid and substantial addition to Hammer Studios' seemingly immortal Dracula franchise. For a change, new ideas are in evidence, and the film actually has a thesis concerning contrasting time periods: holy past versus unholy present. The film handles this comparison of disparate eras in a unique visual way, and actually generates some interesting debate about sex, religion, and even the generation gap.

Dracula AD 1972 opens in the past, 1872 to be precise, before it voyages forward a century to 1972 and director Alan Gibson immediately states his argument about contrasts. In 1872, leaves blow freely on an earthen firmament, and the camera is positioned behind several trees. There is an idyllic country road in evidence too.

In 1972, the landscape has morphed dramatically, and Gibson's camera captures the hustle and bustle of a construction site and a busy freeway. Racing automobiles have replaced the horse-drawn carriage, and the audience has traveled from a time of natural beauty to one of man's technological ascent. The viewer has gone from a time of superstition and belief (as demonstrated by the presence of Dracula) to one of reason, rationality and science.

The images of these disparate eras are joined together by a brilliant transitional conceit. The camera tilts up from Van Helsing's gravestone (circa 1872), and *boom!*—a

Count Dracula (Christopher Lee) gets the point in the finale of *Dracula AD 1972* (1972).

jumbo jet flies overhead, and the soundtrack turns to rock-'n'-roll as the picture greets the latter half of the 20th century. Like Kubrick's famous bone-into-spaceship transition (encompassing centuries of evolution) in *2001: A Space Odyssey* (1968), this little tilt from grounded past to technological future overhead is an economical, artful juxtaposition that visually captures how much has changed in the intervening century.

Perhaps more significant than the physical/technological changes from 1872 to 1972, Gibson (and Houghton's screenplay) chart the moral changes. Dracula came out of the Victorian era, an epoch of moral rectitude and a concentrated repression of desire. Dracula emerges in an age of moral, political and sexual revolution and relativism. The freedom of this new age extends beyond sexual freedom into deviant religious freedom, to Satan worshipping even. No doubt this is a comment on how easy it is to be decadent in a society of perceived social freedom.

The physical changes in the film's central church reflect the moral decline of the intervening century. The church is beautiful, vibrant, alive in 1872, but out of use, dilapidated, and abandoned in freewheeling, freethinking 1972. Apparently, the creators of *Dracula AD 1972* see the new world as a venue in which evil can more easily flourish because the boundaries between good and evil have been blurred by a "do whatever feels right for you" mentality. This argument, cogently expressed in dialogue, production design, and even editing, grants this Dracula update a kind of relevance and importance missing from *Scars of Dracula*.

In some ways, the plot of *Dracula AD 1972* is one of teenage rebellion against authority figures too—another relevant topic since the phrase "the generation gap" was being bandied about so much, and youngsters were actively encouraging one another not to trust "anyone over thirty." Specifically, Van Helsing's lovely granddaughter, Jessica, informs her stodgy grandpa that she hasn't "dropped acid," "doesn't shoot up," and is not "sleeping with anyone ... yet." What she

fails to mention, however, is that she has experimented with the black arts. She has dabbled in the occult, importantly the one and only real taboo area in her particular family. In other words Van Helsing might not really care if Jessica went to bed with a boyfriend, but he would *certainly* object to her practicing Satanism, considering his field of study and family lineage. Is it not always that way with adolescent rebellion? Does not the teenager always know precisely how to strike at the core of the parent's bedrock values?

Likewise, Dracula in this picture is a rather obvious surrogate for Charles Manson, an "evil" cult figure from that period. In the new age of freedom, youngsters could be drawn to evil via charismatic leaders ... and there is no more charismatic an evil than that represented by vampires in general, and Count Dracula specifically. The generation gap, Dracula as cult guru, today's society as decadent anti–Victorian—these modern touches permit *Dracula AD 1972* the luxury of a new interpretation of an old myth. The details of vampirism, Dracula, and even Van Helsing are all highly familiar elements by now, but a "mod" setting of 1972 makes this film feel fresher, looser, and more fun than recent entries in the franchise. The underlying message, that sometimes old values still need to be adhered to in an era of too much moral relativism, feels fresh too. Even Dracula gets a new bag here: revenge!

The only disappointment in *Dracula AD 1972* stems from the handling of the Dracula character in the present. Though top billed, Christopher Lee appears infrequently on camera (in only about four or five scenes), and is not even permitted to leave the church where this Prince of Darkness is re-born. Producers may have rightly feared that a man in a black cape would seem less than imposing in hip '70s London, but an opportunity was missed. Imagine, for a moment, a resurgent Dracula suddenly awakened in a world where all appetites are valid, and where all appetites can be sated without moral judgment or condemnation. With that picture in mind, one can detect immediately how this film might have been genuinely great rather than merely good.

––––––––––––––

LEGACY: Liked or disliked, *Dracula AD 1972* proved to have an enduring central concept.

The idea that Dracula might awaken in the present was resurrected in *Wes Craven Presents Dracula 2000* (2000), another re-invention of Bram Stoker's classic character.

Frenzy (1972) ✶ ✶ ✶ ✶

Critical Reception

"…Hitchcock's return to the realm he commanded so long: the fears and excitement felt when viewing and hearing the stories of a diabolical narrator…. Shaffer should work with Hitchcock again."— Albert Johns, *Film Quarterly*, Volume XXVI, Number 1, Fall 1972, pages 58–60.

"…a return to old forms by the master of suspense, whose newer forms have pleased movie critics but not his public. This is the kind of thriller Hitchcock was making in the 1940s filled with macabre details, incongruous humor, and the desperation of a man convicted of a crime he didn't commit."— Roger Ebert, *Roger Ebert's Movie Home Companion* (1993 Edition), Andrews and McMeel, 1993, page 236.

"A fundamentally simple story spiced with dramatic invention, crackling suspense, and liberal doses of sardonic humor serving as counterpoint to horror are all present in *Frenzy*. And Hitchcock has stirred the brew with his old skill, imagination and contrivance."— Hubbell Robinson, *Films in Review*, Volume XXIII, Number 7, August-September 1972, pages 429–430.

"…a psychological thriller that ranks among his [Hitchcock's] very best and shows the 72-year-old director in triumphant command of his unmatched artistic powers…. Hitchcock uses the vehicle of the thriller as a conveyance for more serious social and psychological material. And, once again, he manipulates us like marionettes."— Paul D. Zimmerman, *Newsweek:* "Return of the Master," June 26, 1972, pages 83–84.

Cast and Crew

CAST: John Finch (Richard Blaney); Alec McCowen (Inspector Oxford); Barry Foster (Robert Rusk); Billie Whitelaw (Mrs. Porter); Barbara Leigh-Hunt (Brenda Blaney); Vivien Merchant (Mrs. Oxford); Anna Massey (Babs Milligan); Bernard Cribbins (Felix Forsythe); Michael Bates (Sergeant Spearman); Jean Marsh (Monica); Clive Swift (Johnny Porter); Madge Ryan, Elsie Randolph, Gerald Sim, John Bower, George Tovey, Jimmy Gardner, Noel Johnson.

CREW: Universal Presents Alfred Hitchcock's *Frenzy. Camera Operator:* Paul Wilson. *Coordinator:* Angela Martelli. *Sound Mixer:* Peter Handford. *Wardrobe Supervisor:* Dulcie Midwinter. *Casting:* Sally Nicholl. *Special Photographic Effects:* Albert Whitlock. *Make-up:* Harry Frampton. *Hairdresser:* Fay McDerrmott. *Set Dresser:* Simon Wakefield. *Production Designer:* Syd Cain. *Art Director:* Bob Laing. *Production Manager:* Brian Burgess. *Assistant Director:* Colin M. Brewer. *Film Editor:* John Jympson. *Director of Photography:* Gil Taylor. *Associate Producer:* William Hill. *Music*

Composed and Conducted by: Ron Goodwin. *Screenplay:* Anthony Shaffer. *Directed by:* Alfred Hitchcock. Made at Pinewood Studios, London, England, and on location in England. A Universal Release. *M.P.A.A. Rating:* R. *Running Time:* 116 minutes.

P.O.V.

"Where cinema is concerned, I am a puritan. I believe in telling a story visually. I believe in using the medium for what it is, the medium of montage, of cutting. A lot of films are only photographs of people talking, merely extensions of the theater. To me, the visual is first and the oral is supplementary... It's tremendously satisfying to be able to use cinema to achieve a mass emotion...."(11).— Director Alfred Hitchcock as he prepared *Frenzy* (1972), an adaptation of *Goodbye Picadilly, Farewell Leicester Square* by Arthur Labern.

———————————

SYNOPSIS: As a politician stands on the bank of the Thames to proclaim to a gathering crowd that the river has finally been cleaned of refuse and debris, the corpse of a strangled woman washes up nearby to interrupt the event. This unfortunate lady is the most recent victim of a serial killer terrorizing London: the Neck Tie Murderer!

Elsewhere in London, Dick Blaney, bartender at a pub called the Globe, is fired after his boss accuses him of stealing liquor from the stock. Dick leaves in a huff, says goodbye to his girlfriend Babs, and heads over to the fruit market to meet with his friend Bob Rusk. Bob recommends that Dick bet on a horse to make some extra cash, but Dick does not have the money for such a bet. Consequently, he is quite angry when Bob's horse pays off big. In a rotten mood all around, Dick drops by at a "lonely hearts" dating service run by his ex-wife, Brenda. She is sympathetic to his woes and invites him out for dinner. Angry at life for ruining his career, his marriage and his prospects, Dick makes quite a scene at the restaurant. Brenda pities him and drops some money in his coat

pocket. Dick does not discover the gift until a bum tries to lift the money from him during his stay at the Salvation Army that night.

The next day, Bob Rusk visits with Brenda at the lonely-hearts office while the prissy receptionist, Monica, is away at lunch. Bob demands that Brenda find him a girl who will bend to his perverse sexual demands. He becomes threatening and eventually forces himself on Brenda. Poor Brenda prays for deliverance as Bob rapes her and then strangles her with his necktie. Bob, the Neck Tie Murderer, flees the scene, but Dick goes to the office shortly afterwards. He is locked out, though Monica has seen him leave the building. She discovers Brenda's corpse inside, and informs the police. She reports to Inspector Oxford of Scotland Yard that Dick, a violent and angry man, was the last person she saw at the office before finding her boss dead. A citywide manhunt for Dick Blaney begins.

Meanwhile, Dick is blissfully unaware that he has become the object of such a hunt, and spends the night at a fancy hotel with girlfriend Babs. The porter reads the newspapers, which publishes an identification of Dick Blaney as the Neck Tie Murder, and calls the police. Dick and Babs also read the paper and flee the hotel before they can be caught. After Dick convinces Babs of his innocence, they decide to hide out at the home of Johnny Porter, a friend. Unfortunately, Johnny's wife is convinced that Dick is a violent murderer and has serious reservations about harboring such a criminal. Dick and Babs decide to go to Paris, and Babs returns to the Globe to pick up some clothes for the trip. Unfortunately, she runs into Bob Rusk there. He takes her up to his apartment on a pretense and then strangles her. Bob attempts to dispose of Babs' body by putting it in a potato sack and throwing it on the rear of a potato truck. Only later does Bob realize that he has lost his "R" tie-pin, and that Babs may still be clutching it in her dead hand! Bob returns to the potato truck and has several close calls before retrieving his pin. Moments after his narrow escape, two policeman watch flabbergasted as Babs' body rolls off the back of the potato truck on a highway.

The next morning, Dick is on the run and he seeks Bob's help, unaware that he is seeking sanctuary from the Neck Tie Murderer himself. Bob obligingly hides Dick in his apartment, then turns over Dick to the police immediately. Dick is sentenced to life in prison after being found guilty of murder. But, Inspector Oxford has some doubts about the case. He discusses these doubts with his busybody wife, a woman obsessed with cooking bizarre meals, and comes to the conclusion that Bob Rusk is actually the man who should be in jail. Dick has come to the same conclusion. He arranges a jailbreak and heads immediately to Bob's apartment. Oxford does likewise, and there, Dick Blaney, Inspector Oxford and the Neck Tie Murderer all meet in one room to end the killing spree once and for all.

COMMENTARY: Alfred Hitchcock was over 70 years old when he directed *Frenzy*, his 52nd motion picture, but the film proves that the master of suspense had not lost his ability (or propensity) to play his audience like a piano. In keeping with Hitch's other thrillers (particularly *Vertigo*, *Psycho* and *The Birds*), *Frenzy* is psychologically facile, an examination of a man who commits murder because of a problem with dear old mum in particular, and women in general. Despite this simple explanation, *Frenzy* is wickedly stylish and funny. For students of Hitchcock, there is that old dichotomy too: *Frenzy* is a brilliant balancing act, confident in its deployment of film technique, while at the same time the content (and thematic thrust) of the picture seems distinctly misogynistic. At least one murder (of a woman) is lingered on so lovingly and beautifully by the master's camera that one nearly forgets the brutality of what is being depicted. And oddly, Hitchcock strives for identification with, not distance from, the man committing these horrible acts.

Frenzy opens with a gliding, aerial shot over London to the tune of a very royal-sounding overture. The camera soon finds a dead woman washed up on the beach of the Thames, a new victim of the Neck-Tie Murderer, just as a politico is informing a crowd that the river is being "cleaned up." That's the kind of irony Hitchcock excels in framing, contrasting images with words to foster a kind of icy good humor in his audiences. Viewers do not identify with the murder victim, but are instead encouraged to laugh (or at least feel amused) because the corpse is a punchline in a visual joke. That is clearly Hitchcock's m.o. for much of *Frenzy*: the distancing of the audience from Robert Rusk's murderous acts, while actually bolstering sympathy for him as a person.

Much later in the film, Rusk murders the protagonist's girlfriend, Babs. But again there is a distancing aspect to his crime. As Rusk leads unknowing Babs to her second floor apartment and eventual death, Hitchcock's camera retreats, literally backing down the staircase, out the front door of the building, and back across the street. To some, this "withdraw" from the murder has been read as a disapproval of Rusk's behavior. The camera is backing away in disgust from it.

Indeed, in John Carpenter's *Halloween* (1978), the prologue climaxes when murderer Michael Myers is revealed to be a child and Carpenter's camera backs up and away in horror from the revelation. But *Frenzy* is a different matter simply because it has not revealed Rusk's horrid crime against Babs on-camera. Therefore, it simply cannot be registering disgust at his action, not having witnessed it first-hand. Right?

Instead, the pull-back and withdraw, like the humor, distances the audience from the act of murder, an act which, if seen close up, might have fostered sympathy for Babs and killed audience identification with Rusk that, for whatever reason, Hitchcock planned to engender.

In another sequence in *Frenzy*, perhaps the most suspenseful, Rusk hides Babs' corpse in a potato sack at the rear of the truck, and then realizes that he has left incriminating evidence behind. Desperate, he returns to the truck and is nearly caught. All along, the scene heightens identification with Rusk. Will he be caught? Will he escape? Will he leave behind evidence that dooms him? These questions are raised (as Vincent Canby and Roger Ebert have both noted in their reviews of the film), and consequently the audience wishes for him to succeed ... to pull this one off. But remember, Rusk is a terrible person, a serial killer of women, and yet viewers are on pins and needles, encouraged to wonder if he'll escape the grasp of the law!

Further identification with Rusk is generated by Hitchcock's food motif, which underlies the film. Throughout *Frenzy*, characters are constantly associated with food, and hence with appetites. The inspector is constantly being served odd meals, courtesy of his strange wife. Fish soup, quail with grapes, pig's feet in tripe, and so on. He endures all of these things, but is left unsatisfied, longing for a good old-fashioned plate of fish and chips.

In comparison, Rusk is a man of appetite who is also unable to sate his hunger with even the ordinary "meals" of his domestic setting. Instead, he must commit murder to feel satisfied. There is a line in the film, "don't squeeze the goods until they're yours," which indicates that Rusk, a grocer, sees women as his "meals" as much as human beings. The on-screen, brutal death of Brenda is a notable example of appetite sated.

Just as Hitchock's camera lingers on shots of food (bread sticks snapping as the breaking of human fingers is discussed; potatoes rolling about in the truck bed as Rusk seeks desperately to hide Babs' feet and toes in a potato sack), so does he face Brenda's murder with the attitude and energy of a starving man contemplating his feast. Rusk strangles Brenda after raping her, and there is a shot of her eyes going dead, her tongue bulging from her mouth. Here, as in the sequences featuring food, the camera does not shy away from appetites and desires sated. The inference is clear: Brenda sates Rusk's murderous appetites. He kills to feel satisfied the way most of us eat. That connection makes him seem more human, more understandable in his crimes ... hence easier to empathize with. Not surprisingly, the scene concludes with Rusk eating an apple, a kind of after-dinner snack. He's already had his main course: Brenda.

Hitchcock utilizes humor in at least two critical sequences involving corpses. First, there's the opening scene at the Thames, and secondly the moment when Babs' dead foot kicks Rusk in the face. This sort of humor makes Rusk a figure of amusement, of fun, rather than menace. And then, by backing away from the details of a homicidal spree (the purposeful withdrawal from Babs' apartment) and by linking Rusk's appetites for sex and death with food (thereby forging common ground with the audience since we all have appetites), Hitchcock truly makes his murderer the hero of *Frenzy*.

The "real" star, John Finch, plays Blaney, a character who is violent (he breaks a whiskey glass), self-destructive (prone to drinking), and not particularly likeable. So audience sympathy goes to Rusk almost by default. What does this mean? Is *Frenzy* a debauched entertainment because it deposits viewers into the camp of a serial killer? At least some critics seemed to think so.

Victoria Sullivan, an assistant professor in the English department at New York's City College, wrote an essay about the film for the *New York Times* in July of 1972. She found the film to be primarily about the degradation of women, and furthermore accused critics (such as Vincent Canby) of giving Hitchcock a "pass" anyway because of the technical prowess with which he directed the picture. She wrote:

> I suspect that films like *Frenzy* may be sicker and more pernicious than your cheapie humdrum porno flick, because they are slicker, more artistically compelling versions of sado-masochistic

fantasies, and because they leave me feeling more angry and more impotent simultaneously [12].

Sullivan undoubtedly has a point about content, but it is important to note that film criticism is not always the same thing as social criticism. As Roger Ebert is fondly (and rightly) prone to remind his readership, it is not *what* a film is about that's important, but *how* that film is about the subject. *Frenzy* tells its story of a psycho killer with visual aplomb, a sense of humor, and a master's skill for pacing. In other words, how it is about Rusk (through visual associations, through visual contrasts, through film language, and through connections with food, of all things) is more important than the fact that contextually it is about Rusk, clearly a monstrous man and all-round rotten human being.

Sullivan takes the opposite approach, that technique means nothing if the subject matter is degrading or inappropriate. For her, the issue is not how Hitchcock tells the story of Rusk, but that Rusk's spree is glorified at all on film.

What is presented for us then is a debate between two camps of criticism. This reviewer tends to side with Canby only because the other road can lead, ultimately, to censorship. *Frenzy* is violent. It is about a nasty, horrible man who brutalizes women. But it is also the film Hitchcock — an artist — wanted to make ... and he made it well. It would be a mistake to take away his right to make the film simply because the subject matter was not deemed worthy by some aspect of society.

Yet, Sullivan is not at all wrong in her assertion that Hitchcock champions Rusk in *Frenzy*, and one has to wonder what he was up to there. Though critics who look for a deeper psychological meaning in Hitchcock's films might quibble, especially considering the violence directed against women in *Psycho* and *The Birds*, this reviewer senses that in *Frenzy* Hitchcock was simply doing something he couldn't do before.

The 1970s brought what was known as "the new freedom" to films, a liberty to show more violence and more nudity. In *Frenzy*, Hitchcock was simply taking advantage of that, pushing the boundaries as it were. And, when one considers his fly-in-the-ointment, sardonic nature, one might put forward an even better answer. He makes his audience identifiy with Rusk in *Frenzy* simply because he *can*. Hitchcock enjoys playing his audience like a piano, and here he pulls off the ultimate high-wire act: depicting graphic violence against women, at the same time making the perpetrator of such actions a figure of heroism, or at least empathy. It is a daring move, but Hitchcock had an unmatched expertise with the building blocks of film (*mise en scène* and editing, particularly), and *Frenzy* seems to be a bid to reestablish his eminence in this domain.

On some thematic level, *Frenzy* may be reprehensible, dangerous even, but on the technical level it is close to perfect. And besides, an opposite argument about *Frenzy* could easily be made. By asking his audience to identify with Rusk, Hitchcock is acknowledging that that there is the seed, the capacity for evil, in all men, and that we should have sympathy nonetheless. That's not an unworthy message in an age (and a genre) where horror is often seen as coming from outside of humanity (*The Exorcist*, *Blood on Satan's Claw*) rather than being engendered by it. And, the idea of the anti-hero was quite popular in the 1970s, so Hitchcock, in his inimitable way, gives cinema the ultimate anti-(social) hero: Robert Rusk, the smiling grocer and devourer of women.

Frogs (1972) ✭ ✭

Critical Reception

"…doesn't quite pack the punch that *Squirm* does, but it still comes across as an enjoyably hokey thriller … enough uneasy moments to pass the time."— Dr. Cyclops, *Fangoria # 30*, October 1983, page 44.

"Most of the cast, beginning with Ray Milland, deserve annihilation. Selfish and boring, they weigh the picture down so that what happens to them is unimportant."— Deirdre Mack, *Films in Review*, Volume XXIII, Number 5, May 1972, page 311.

Cast & Crew

CAST: Ray Milland (Jason Crockett); Sam Elliott (Pickett Smith); Joan Van Ark (Karen Crockett); Adam Roarke (Clint Crockett); Judy Pace (Bella); Lynn Borden (Jenny); Mae Mercer (Maybelle); David Gilliam (Michael); Nicholas Cortland (Kenneth); George Skaff (Stuart); Lance Taylor, Sr. (Charles); Holly Irving (Iris); Dale Willingham (Tina); Hal Hodges (Jay); Carolyn Fitzimmons (Lady in Car); Robert Sanders (Boy in Car).

CREW: American International Pictures, and Samuel Z. Arkoff and James H. Nicholson present an American International Production in Association with Peter Thomas Productions and George Edward, *Frogs*. *Director of Photography:* Mario Tosi. *Production Manager:* Elliot Schick. *Production Executive:* William J. Immerman. *Post-Production Supervisor:* Salvatore Bilitteri. *Music composed and played by:* Les Baxter. *Music Supervisor:* Al Simms. *Electronic Effects:* Joe Sidore. *Film Editor:* Fred R. Feitshans. *Assistant Editor:* James L. Honore. *Effects Editor:* Gene Corso. *Title:* Rabin. *Sound:* Ryder Sound Services. *Color:* Movielab. *Cars Furnished by:* Chrysler Corp. *Boats by:* Glastron Boat Company. *Assistant Director:* Rusty Meek. *Wardrobe:* Phyllis Garr. *Camera Operator:* Jose L. Mignone. *Gaffer:* Michael Jones. *Key Grip:* Myron Schindler. *Property Master:* Mike Ross. *Sound Mixer:* John Speak. *Script Supervisor:* Tom Moore. *Make-up:* Tom Burman. *Hairdresser:* Jean Austin. *Publicity:* Julian E. Myers. *Transportation Captain:* Skip Hitchcock. *Production Associate:* Chuck Minsky, Carolyn Fitzsimmons. *Production Secretary:* Christine Minsky. *Assistant to Producer:* Sal Grasso.

Executive Producer: Norman T. Herman. *Produced by:* George Edwards, Peter Thomas. *Screenplay by:* Robert Hutchison, Robert Blees. *Story by:* Robert Hutchison. *Directed by:* George McCowan. Shot entirely on location in Eden Park Historical Museum, Florida, U.S.A. Locations by Cinemobile Systems. An American International Picture. *M.P.A.A. Rating:* PG. *Running time:* 91 minutes.

P.O.V

"I'm not touching one damned frog" (13).— Ray Milland, on his amphibian co-stars.

"I hate them. They're cold, slimy and they pee all over you" (14).— Producer George Edwards echoes Milland's sentiments.

SYNOPSIS: Photographer and environmental enthusiast Pickett Smith photographs the wildlife in and around Crockett island until he is thrown from his canoe by a motorboat drive-by. The motorboat is manned by Clint Crockett and his beautiful sister, Karen, and the duo quickly returns to fish Pickett out of the drink. Clint apologizes, and offers to take Pickett back to the luxurious Crockett estate to dry off and share a meal. While befriending Karen, Pickett accepts the offer.

Once on the island, Pickett meets the patriarch of the family, Karen's grandfather, Jason. He is a nasty, selfish tyrant who rules his family with iron fist. Among his guests for this Fourth of July weekend are Clint's wife and children, Jason's other son, Michael, dotty old Aunt Iris, fey cousin Kenny, and his African-American girlfriend, Bella. All of them fear Jason Crockett, but obey his wishes because they stand to inherit the family fortune when he dies. Today, Crockett has a bee in his bonnet about Grover, a family employee who has disappeared in the woods. Worse, there is an overabundance of frogs on the island this season and they are becoming an irritant. Pickett offers to search the island for Grover and examine the frog problem. Once in the swampland, he finds Grover's jeep ... and his half-eaten corpse.

Pickett reports to Jason Crockett that the island wildlife, including frogs, snakes and lizards, seem to be rallying for a battle against the Crockett family ... which has poisoned and polluted much of the island environment. Crockett believes this a preposterous idea, and does not even inform the family of the death, not wishing to spoil the Independence Day celebration (or his own birthday party).

The holiday, however, does not go well. Crockett's son Michael is killed in the woods by spiders. Kenneth is murdered in the greenhouse by lizards that asphyxiate him (by knocking over poison bottles in the secluded area). Then Iris is killed in pursuit of a butterfly as leeches and snakes take their turns at the old woman.

The survivors plan to flee Crockett's island, but Jason refuses to let his special day be spoiled. Bella will take no more of Crockett's nonsense and plans to leave the island with Jason's black servants. They all meet an untimely end thanks to attacking birds. At the same time, Clint is killed near his motorboat by poisonous water snakes. Clint's wife is drowned ... by a large turtle.

Pickett plans to torch the frogs, now surrounding the Crockett estate, with gasoline, but the frogs scatter, sensing the danger. Pickett realizes that the best plan is one of escape, and with Karen and Clint's children in tow, plots to leave the island. But stubborn old Crockett won't leave his land on his special birthday. Pickett gathers every-

one else, and they canoe off the island, battling frogs, snake and lizards all the way. They even fight crocodiles, but finally manage to get to the mainland and catch a lift from a passing motorist.

Alone on his island, Crockett watches in horror as swarms of frogs invade his house, smashing through windows. The frogs surround Crockett and hop all over his body as he dies of a heart attack.

COMMENTARY: Nature strikes back in *Frogs*, one of the first "revenge of nature" films of the 1970s. The culprit in this case is decadent, overstuffed man, who pollutes his environment, and causes wildlife (snakes, frogs, birds, crocodiles, spiders, and the like) to challenge him for planetary supremacy.

The film starts rather promisingly, as actor Sam Elliott canoes through a swamp, snapping photographs of the wildlife. As the beautifully lensed scene continues, litter is seen on the landscape and then polluted water and refuse comes into view. The film thus states its point with visuals, revealing how nature and garbage must exist side by side, thanks to human civilization.

Sadly, from that evocative start, the film degenerates rapidly into a series of highly improbable animal attacks. At one point, the preposterous screenplay even has the audacity to suggest that frogs have cut the phone lines at Ray Milland's mansion! The attacks are also poorly integrated into the action, possible only because each of the characters (or victims) persists in stupidly venturing off alone. Spiders attack Michael while he wanders alone into the swamp. A crocodile (with mouth visibly taped shut), kills another solitary fellow. Yet another character dies when lizards dump over jars of poison in a greenhouse, and he is asphyxiated (!?). You know a movie is struggling for believability when a lizard outsmarts a human being.

This author's wife is an excellent barometer for bullshit in horror movies. After the third or fourth character in *Frogs* had spontaneously wandered off alone to be killed by little buggers, she tuned out of the film with this *bon mot*, "I can't watch people do stupid things over and over again."

The actors struggle vainly to make some of this hokum meaningful but are sabotaged by a dreadful script that requires them to be idiots. Ray Milland's character, typified by his line "we are the filthy rich," stubbornly plans his birthday party after many of his family and friends have bit the dust. When asked what should be done, he states that he'd like his original dinner menu, as planned. Would anyone, even a jerk, be so stupid and callous? Joan Van Ark is wasted as Milland's spunky daughter, but does provide a great deal of leggy appeal. Elliott has the meatiest role, but still has to contend with corny lines like "What if nature is trying to get back at us?"

With films like this, it is sometimes illuminating to compare it to others of its kind. *Willard,* a movie about rat attacks, was infinitely deeper. The main character seemed to be a real individual, and his "rat revolu-

tion" arose logically out of his situation. 1977's *Kingdom of the Spiders* also casts man (and his pesticides) as a villain, but the heroes in that picture (William Shatner, Tiffany Bolling) follow the mystery logically from one step to another, and avoid putting themselves in stupid situations. The spider attacks in that film are relentless, and well orchestrated rather than humorous and improbable.

Another disappointment is the finale. Ray Milland is purportedly surrounded (and then set upon...) by the army of angry frogs. Yet, Milland is never seen in the same shot with even a single frog. Again, *Kingdom of the Spiders* is a helpful contrast. In the climax of that film, spiders literally *rain* upon the besieged Shatner, and the authenticity brings gasps of shock. In *Willard,* Bruce Davison interacted with the rats in several key shots. Here, either the frogs or Milland seems to be phoning in his performance. Or maybe they both are...

Horror Express (1972) * * *

Critical Reception

> "...absurdities make it entertaining — it puts Christopher Lee and Peter Cushing on the Trans-Siberian express together with Telly Savalas as a murderous Cossack and a prehistoric apeman that comes to life and turns out to be possessed by an alien." — John Brosnan, *Future Tense,* St. Martin's Press, 1978, page 217.

Cast & Crew

CAST: Christopher Lee (Dr. Alexander Saxton); Peter Cushing (Dr. Welles); Angel del Pozo (Yevtushenko); Telly Savalas (Captain); Alberto deMendoza (Miroff); Silvia Tortosa, Julio Pena.

CREW: *Camera Operator:* Teodor Escavisa. *Focus:* Luis Pena. *Assistant:* Simon Lopez. *Sound supervisor:* Antonio Ilan. *Mixing Recordist:* Enrique Molinaro. *Location Recordist:* Luis Lopez Diaz. *Wardrobe Supervisor:* Charles Simminger. *Wardrobe:* Andres Fernandez, Carmen Manzano. *Make-up Supervisor:* Julian Ruiz. *Make-up Assistant:* Fernando Florido, Rafael Berraquero. *Hairdressing assistant:* Maria Nieves Ruiz, Romania Gonzalez. *First Assistant Director:* Gil Curretero. *Second Assistant Director:* Vicente Escrimi. *Script Clerk:* Maribel Ruiz-Cipilas. *Production Assistant:* Jose Luis Rubio. *Property Master:* Juan Gracia. *Set Assistant:* Rafael Perez Marcia. *Special Effects:* Pablo

Perez. *Optical Effects:* Brian Stevens. *Production Supervisor:* Jose Maria Ramos. *Art Director:* Ramiro Gomez. *Editor:* Robert Dearben. *Editorial Assistants:* Carmen Alonso, Fernando Megino. *Music:* John Carav. *Screenplay:* Arnaud D'Usseau and Julian Halevy. *From an original story by:* Gene Martin. *Produced by:* Bernard Gordon. *Directed by:* Gene Martin. *M.P.A.A. Rating:* PG. *Running Time:* 86 minutes.

SYNOPSIS: In 1906, Alexander Saxton reports to the Royal Geological Society about the strange disaster that befell his expedition to Manchuria and the mountains of the Province of Szechuan in China...

There, in the remote mountains, Saxton and his assistants discovered a strange humanoid frozen in the ice. They packed it up in a crate and brought it back to civilization. They booked passage on the Trans-Siberian express with the corpse in storage, only to learn that it was demonstrating amazing powers. It blinded and killed two people early on. Dr. Saxton's competitor, Dr. Wells, was also on the train, and he hired someone to break open the crate ... for the sake of curiosity. What resulted was yet another murder (of a baggage man), and a monster on the loose. Saxton feared that his missing link was alive after 2 million years and sure enough, the mysterious creature began to kill again, murdering soldiers that scoured the train to learn its hiding place.

Later, Wells and Saxton made a terrifying discovery. The victims of the monster had completely smooth brains with no wrinkles, which suggested that their minds had somehow been drained of memory and knowledge. Wells hypothesized that it was in this way that the monster was able to absorb knowledge from other life forms. After several more encounters, the creature was killed and the threat believed over, but in fact, the monster merely jumped into or "possessed" another living human being. Events became even more complicated when it was learned that the final image in the monster's eye could be displayed—as if in a photograph. What Saxton and Wells saw in

that image was staggering: dinosaurs and the Earth, as they would look from outer space. Saxton now believed that the creature was an alien life form that had crashed on Earth and existed in several bodies, including that of the missing link, for aeons. And now it was awake, and malevolent. Wells agreed with that notion, and suggested that the monster was like a disease, infecting new bodies. Wells and Saxton then scanned the eyes of all train passengers to determine if they too were monsters.

In fact, the monster had jumped into the body of an inspector and was hoping to find a way to escape into space and return home. To this end, he absorbed the train engineer, who had a rudimentary knowledge of rocketry.

Just when it seemed things couldn't get worse, a team of heavily armed Russian soldiers boarded the train and put everyone under arrest as the situation was studied. The monster made short work of the soldiers, and then did the unthinkable, reviving them as an army of evil.

Saxton, Wells and the surviving passengers fled the army of the walking dead, and sought safety in one compartment. They wired Moscow with orders to destroy the train, and then unhooked their car from the rest. Saxton and Wells watched with satisfaction as the remainder of the train—and the monster from space—went over the edge of a cliff and burned on the side of a mountain far below.

COMMENTARY: *Horror Express* is like *The Thing* (1951) meets *Murder on the Orient Express* meets *The Hidden* (1987). And, surprisingly, it's a pretty good yarn too. Its tale of an identity-absorbing alien trying to get home (and escape from Earth) benefits from its isolated setting (the Trans-Siberian Express ... in motion), and the solid, restrained performance of its leads, old hands at this material both, Christopher Lee and Peter Cushing.

The first shot of the film, a long pan

across a wide mountain range, establishes a sense of place. There is a pale sky overhead, the sound of wind roaring ferociously on the soundtrack, and the audience's instinctive reaction is to hunker down and shiver from the almost tangible sense of cold. The fog-covered mountains of Szechuan then reveal something much more frightening than the cold, a cave containing a frozen humanoid (no, not Trog...).

The thrill of such a discovery quickly gives way to horror as people start to die, and it's a good set-up. With its frozen setting one thinks immediately of both versions of *The Thing*, and even its source story, "Who Goes There?" The reality of the picture is also heightened by Christopher Lee's opening voice-over narration, told in the form of a report to the Royal Geological Society. This narration, which reads and sounds like a correspondence, lends the early sequences of *Horror Express* an almost documentary-style feel. Considering the amazing developments that soon follow this opening, it's a good idea to ground the film in what, on first blush, could be mistaken for scientific minutiae.

In a film like this, the monster is very important. How many horror movies have failed because their monsters simply could not live up to expectations once revealed? *Night of the Blood Beast* (1958), *It, the Terror from Beyond Space* (1958) and even Hawks' *The Thing* pop to mind immediately. So, for a "monster" picture to work, the creature has to be scary. In crafting their "beast," the makers of *Horror Express* have created a memorable monster, because, for the most part, very little is revealed (beyond the ape-man at the start of the picture, which is actually just a "shell" hiding the *real* monster). What can be deciphered for sure is that the alien boasts glowing red eyes, and the mental ability to mesmerize its victims. Then, as it sucks dry their minds, the victims bleed profusely out of their eyes and nose, a horrible side-effect of the absorption. Finally, before dying, the victims go blind, their eyes shifting to a stark white. That series of images, first of blood streaming like tears

from eye sockets, then of corpses defiled by those blank, white, eyes, are extremely effective ones. So, the alien is defined not so much by how it looks, by what it does. An elegant solution to the fact that there was not yet technology (or the money) to create an *Alien* (1979)-caliber monster.

Impressively, *Horror Express* is rather ambitious in its thinking, even beyond the details of the creature. The movie keeps throwing in inspired twists, most of them unexpected. For instance, Lee and Cushing, in typical dispassionate fashion, determine that the eye fluid of the monster retains the last image the creature saw before dying. They find a way to magnify that image, and see the Earth as viewed from outer space—proving the existence of alien life. That discovery sheds some light on the monster's motives, as it absorbs human after human in hopes of discovering the knowledge that will help it return to its home in the stars. This is an unexpected turn of events, but one that gracefully leads to the final act.

The "jumping from body to body" alien is a genre cliché today, but one must remember it had not been done so frequently in the early '70s, when *Horror Express* was made. *The Hidden* plumbed the same material in the mid–'80s, offering the world a rock-'n'-roll alien who loved fast cars. *Horror Express* never gets that jiggy with the material, content instead to fill a moving train with death and horror.

Contrarily, one must also note that instead of looking forward, *Horror Express*'s climax references Romero's *Night of the Living Dead*. The dead return to life as white-eyed ghouls to attack the living. Yet even if the finale is derivative, the remainder of the film is notably ambitious in keeping audience expectations rattled. The monster is first a missing link, a beast, then a shape-shifter, then an alien, and finally a puppet master pulling the strings of the dead. These shifts in technique (and shape) keep the film's horror rolling, and generate a fair amount of paranoia.

What differentiates *Horror Express* from

a truly brilliant picture of this category, like *John Carpenter's The Thing* (1981), is that there seems to be no real sub-text in *Express*. Carpenter's picture explored the frailty of the flesh, how humanity could be warped and perverted by the unseen intruder (disease). It also explored human relations to a high degree, calling into question our ability to trust our neighbors, our friends, when frightened. *Horror Express* lacks the visual artistry, as well as the thematic depth, to be anything beyond what it appears to be: a fast-paced horror movie that pauses to validate the concept of evolution ("It's a fact, and there's no morality in fact," says Christopher Lee's character, of evolution). It's a clever hybrid of *Murder on the Orient Express*, with every character on the train hiding a secret identity or agenda, and the horror films of the 1950s. And it moves.

All aboard...

I Dismember Mama (aka *Poor Albert and Little Annie*) (1972) *

Critical Reception

> "...the title here is not only tasteless, it is misleading. Though psychotic killer Albert demonstrates his carving technique on assorted nurses, housekeepers, department-store mannequins and ladies of the night, he never does get to work on his mother. The title tells us more about the psychological hang-ups of the filmmakers than it does about the action on-screen." — Harry and Michael Medved, *The Golden Turkey Awards*, A Perigee Book, 1980, page 27.

Cast & Crew

CAST: Zooey Hall (Albert Robertson); Joanne Moore Jordan (Mrs. Robertson); Greg Mullavey (Detective); Marlene Tracy (Alice); Frank Whiteman (Dr. Burton); Elaine Partnow (Nurse); Rosella Olson (Girl in Poolroom); James Tartain (Attendant); Roger Christopher (Man in Poolroom); Geri Reischl (Annie).

CREW: From Simitar Entertainment Inc., and Screen Gems. *Director of Photography:* William Swenning. *Camera Operator:* Mark Rasmussen. *Sound:* Kirk Francis. *Lighting:* Parker Bartlett. *Script Supervisor:* Joseph Bean. *Assistant Editor:* Justin DuPont. *Boom Operator:* John Westmoreland. *Grips:* Terry Meacham, Reuben Leder. *Music Composed and Conducted by:* Herschel Burke Gilbert. *Song "Poor Albert" Lyrics by:* Rocket Roden. *Music by:* Herschel Burke Gilbert. *Sung by:* Rocket Roden. *Screenplay:* William Norton. *Associate Producer:* Jack Marshall. *Producer:* Leon Roth. *Director:* Paul Leder. *Color by:* Pacific Film Industries.

M.P.A.A. Rating: R. *Running Time:* 85 minutes.

SYNOPSIS: Albert Robertson is incarcerated in a low-security mental hospital, where he watches movie after movie on his projector. Then, one day, Albert attacks his nurse, disrobing her and attempting to strangle her. Although this attempt is thwarted by two security guards, it signals a bad downturn in Albert's behavior.

Albert informs his psychiatrist, Dr. Burton, that his mother is to blame for all his problems. He accuses his mother of being "a whore," and Dr. Burton replies that Albert's problems stem from his belief that all women are whores. Though Albert wants to be released from the hospital, his violent behavior assures that it will not happen, and in fact, a transfer to the maximum-security state hospital is highly likely. As Dr. Burton calls Mrs. Robertson to inform her of the bad news, Albert kills a guard and escapes from the hospital. The police are informed of the situation, and the hunt for Albert Robertson is on.

Soon, Albert calls to tell his mother that he cannot wait to see her. He steals a white convertible, and heads to the fancy Robertson estate. Once at home, Albert terrorizes the new housekeeper, Alice, asking if she is a virgin. He attacks her with a knife and then orders her to take off her clothes and sing and dance for him. At the end of this little show, a sexually confused and impotent Albert kills Alice. Then, little Annie, Alice's pre-pubescent daughter, arrives at the Robertson home. She meets Albert, and he lies to her, telling her that her mom is away at a doctor's appointment. Believing young Annie to be the only pure woman he has ever known, Albert takes a shine to the girl and performs a bullfighting dance for her. He gives her candy and then takes her to an amusement park called Magic Mountain.

When Magic Mountain turns out to be closed, Albert escorts Annie on a romantic trolley ride, and later a boat ride on a lake. Meanwhile, the police discover Alice's corpse, and realize that Albert has come home. At the same time, Albert caters to young Annie's every wish because she is "undefiled." He takes her to a hotel, built in the Victorian age, and they share the bridal suite, going so far as to have a mock wedding ceremony. Happy with his new "friend," Albert telephones home again and tells his mother that he needs money so he can go away with Annie.

That night, Albert's psychosis surges and he fights the urge to attack little Annie as she sleeps. Instead, he leaves the suite, seeking sex at a local pool hall. He meets a sexy blonde there, and brings her to the room. He asks her to dance for money, and she disrobes and tries to seduce him. Albert responds with anger and strangles the woman. Annie witnesses the crime and flees the hotel room, seeking sanctuary in a dark

mannequin storeroom. There, Albert has a change of heart and decides that Annie is just as much a whore as the rest of womanhood. Armed with a meat cleaver, Albert pursues Annie, but at the last moment of a chase he missteps and falls from a high window to the alley far below. The police arrive to save Annie, and Albert's days of freedom are over.

COMMENTARY: Disclaimer: No mothers are dismembered in this movie. Instead, the title is probably the cleverest aspect of this rather underwhelming, illegitimate grandchild of *Psycho*. For those who don't remember, the film's name is a bizarre reference to the classic TV series *I Remember Mama* (1949–1956), and the feature film of the same name. As a title for an exploitation flick, *I Dismember Mama* is actually rather good. It suggests a droll, fun quality of horror. It hints of a satire or spoof of the "white bread" sitcom life depicted in the old *Father Knows Best*-era TV series. Sadly, none of those elements come to play in the actual production. Instead, the title is mere exploitation, the film is not smart, not even in the neighborhood of funny, and its bad taste, not the sort you'd see in *Scary Movie*, is of a genuinely disturbing, and depraved variety. Succinctly put, the film's horror comes from a sensitive topic: an adult's sexual obsession with an eleven-year-old girl. It isn't exactly a savory or sensitive bit of work.

To get the good out of the way first, the performances and technical credits for this low-budget cheapie are solid. Though the film is shot to resemble a colorful TV series more than a film, it is a competent job. However, what is thoroughly objectionable about the film is its script, a screenplay that repeatedly puts a little girl in real physical danger from a murderous sexual predator.

There is a longstanding debate in horror circles about the role of children in the genre. Some critics immediately "sign off" a movie when a child's life is put in jeopardy on-screen. The late Gene Siskel, for instance, gave *Aliens* (1986) a "thumbs down" vote because little Newt was constantly endangered. This viewer does not subscribe to that kind of thinking. Newt was an important character in that film, and it would not have made sense for a race of gruesome, slimy aliens to treat a child as though she were special. Imagine how the critics would have complained if drooling, acid-spitting gutbursters showed favoritism to a small child?

Similarly, the remake of *The Blob* (1988) also endangered children (and in fact, killed one), but again, it did not seem inappropriate considering the context.

Yet *I Dismember Mama* makes one feel dirty about watching because its main concern is not just violence, but sex. The film makes it plain that Albert sees little Annie as a possible sexual conquest, and that is a really disturbing thing to see in a film with no aspirations to be anything but entertainment. Here is a character that treats all women as whores, unless they are children. That could make for an interesting film, no doubt, since terrible things do happen to people; and there are many strange points of view in the human world. The problem here is that it is done with little skill or artistry. Is it possible to make a good movie about child molestation, or sexual predators? Probably, but is a grade Z horror movie with a lurid title really the right place to attempt the tackling of so serious-minded a topic?

Perhaps it comes down to where one draws the line. For instance, this film features some effective, suspenseful scenes, all based on the main notion (again) that Albert is finally going to lose his mind, and rape little Annie (an eleven year old). The suspense is genuine because the threat is genuine. The audience is afraid for the little girl, having seen Albert's violence. But the question remains: Is it necessary to go to such lengths to make a suspenseful movie? Annie could have been 14, 16, or 18, and the same suspense would have been generated, but the film would not have openly endangered a girl who is clearly a child.

As an objective reviewer, this author can note with a sense of appreciation how thoroughly effective it is to crosscut between the antics of Annie and Albert, and the dead body of her mother in an upstairs bedroom. However, is it really something one wants to see in a horror film? The point is clear: Albert has already terrorized this child (by killing her mother), and she is not even aware of the danger she is in, or the damage that has been done. Yuck.

Part of the problem is that *I Dismember Mama* goes to special lengths to sympathize with Albert's twisted point of view. "Poor Albert, can you tell me where you are? Poor Albert, can you take your lover very far?" the sympathetic theme song croaks melodically. Poor Albert? Poor *Albert*? What about poor Annie, who has lost the love of her mother forever, and is caught in the hands of a psychotic killer? Why is there no song to help the viewer identify with *her* plight? And the song's lyrics even identify Annie as Albert's lover ... another really icky moment. She certainly does not see herself in those terms, and that the music would do so is really troubling.

It is hard to say when a horror movie is out of bounds, and indeed, many critics differ on that point. For this author, *The Last House on the Left* is a brilliantly constructed film that rejects violence outright, but which is nonetheless violent. Wes Craven's picture is artistic, even though its subject is brutal, messy, and ugly. Others see the same work as an incitement to violence, and a really sick movie. For this reviewer, *I Dismember Mama* is in bad taste because it exploits a serious, ugly topic (child molestation) but makes no final, deep, or interesting point about the so-called "beautiful" game that Albert plays.

In what may be one of the sickest scenes in horror cinema, Albert dresses Annie in a nightgown, and they celebrate a wedding ceremony. At Annie's age, she has no idea what this "dress up" is a precursor to. Adult viewers are all too aware of what it portends for Annie. Unfortunately, there are sick people in this world who hurt children. Unfortunately, there is pain in the world. But is it really necessary to feature this particular ugliness in (bad) entertainment?

This author does not believe in censorship. He is not part of the moral majority. He believes horror should be free to express whatever demons drive its creators. Yet, by the same token, he makes choices as a viewer, and perhaps there is no way to objectively validate those choices. Some movies go too far (and are perceived to go too far), and for this reviewer, *I Dismember Mama* is one of those. Other viewers may draw the line somewhere else, and that's fine too.

The Last House on the Left (1972) ✶ ✶ ✶ ✶

Critical Reception

"…contains moments of squirm-in-your seat horror which genre movies of ten times its budget and sophistication cannot or dare not approach. The movie amply displays Craven's unique talent for tapping into the middle American nightmare … even as a beginner, Craven had a knack for setting up a tense, frightening situation and keeping his audience off balance with a mix of visceral shocks and black humor."— David A. Szulkin, *Wes Craven's Last House on the Left, the Making of a Cult Classic*, A Fab Press Publication, October 1997, page 8.

"*Last House* begins by depicting opposites, gradually blurring barriers, until the audience's emotional involvement with violent actions leads not to catharsis but self-disgust and self-awareness…. It is an extremely complex film that unveils an ugly sadistic lust most horror films pander to."— Tony Williams, *Hearths of Darkness: The Family in the American Horror Film*, Associated University Presses, 1996, page 130.

"The filmmakers seem to get great pleasure from the torture, sexual humiliation and killing of two truly sweet teenage girls. *The Last House on the Left* is a sick sexual fantasy for predators that is indeed an 'incitement to violence.'"— Danny Peary, *Cult Movies*, Delacorte Press, 1981, page 348.

"The film has little style and little humor but it is marked by documentary-like intensity."— Darrell Moore, *The Best, Worst and Most Unusual: Horror Films*, Publications International, Ltd., 1983, page 147.

Cast & Crew

CAST: Sandra Cassell (Mari Collingwood); Lucy Grantham (Phyllis Stone); David A. Hess (Krug Stillo); Fred Lincoln (Fred "Weasel" Podowski); Marc Sheffler (Junior Stillo); Jeramie Rain (Sadie); Gaylord St. James (John Collingwood); Cynthia Carr (Estelle Collingwood); Ada Washington (Ada); Marshall Anker (Sheriff); Martin Kove (Deputy Harry); Ray Edwards (Postman).
CREW: Sean S. Cunningham Films Ltd., The Night Company. *Director of Photography:* Victor Hurwitz. *Original Music:* David Alexander Hess. *Producer:* Sean S. Cunningham. *Writer/ Director:* Wes Craven. *Film Editor:* Wes Craven. *Assistant Editor:* Stephen Miner. *Costume Design:* Susan S. Cunningham. *Assistant Director:* Yvonne Hannemann. *Associate Producer:* Katherine D'Amato. *Sound:* Jim Hubbard. *Gaffer:* Dick Donovan. *Production Assistant:* Steve Miner. *Wardrobe and Make-up:* Anne Paul. *Special Effects:* Troy Roberts. *Mix:* R.S.I. *Sound Mixer:* Gary Leibman. *Opticals and Blow-Up:* The Optical House. *Title Design:* David Miner. *Unit Production Manager: Larry*

Beinhart. From Lobster Enterprises. MPAA Rating: R. *Running Time:* 82 minutes.

————————————

SYNOPSIS: Beautiful Mari Collingwood turns 17 and prepares to go to a "Bloodlust" concert in New York City. Her parents argue about her revealing attire and the violent nature of Bloodlust, a band that once dismembered a chicken on stage. After the quarrel, Mari and her friend Phyllis drink champagne in the beautiful woods behind the Collingwood house, and imagine what it would be like to make love to the members of the band.

Phyllis and Mari arrive in New York City and find reality far different from their imagination. While trying to score some weed, the two girls are abducted by notorious prison escapee (and psychopath) Krug Stillo, a child molester called Fred "the Weasel" Podowsky, Stillo's junkie son Junior, and a "feral" lesbian named Sadie. While the Collingwoods unknowingly bake a birthday cake for Mari in clean fun, Mari undergoes a catalogue of horrors, and is forced to watch Stillo rape Phyllis. The next morning, the thugs shove the two girls into their car trunk, and drive them out to the country to have some vicious fun with them.

Mari learns that she has been taken to the woods behind her parents' very house, but is unable to call for help. Krug and his buddies murder Phyllis when she tries to escape, and Krug rapes Mari while the others watch. After he has carved his name into Mari's chest with a knife, Krug shoots her in the head, and puts her out of her misery. The thugs clean up, but find their car has broken down. While local police race to the scene to stop the convicts, the thugs stay for dinner at the Collingwood house.

That night, Mrs. Collingwood learns that the four guests in her home are actually the murderers of her daughter. With Mr. Collingwood, she conspires to give the criminals a taste of their own medicine. The cops are still en route, but their car runs out of gas, leaving the Collingwoods to take justice

into their own hands. Mrs. Collingwood lures Fred outside, and under pretense of fellatio, bites off his penis. She then wrestles Sadie in the family pool and slashes her throat with a switchblade. Junior, the sensitive guy of the gang, commits suicide by blowing his brains out with Krug's pistol. The police arrive just as Mr. Collingwood carves up the villainous Krug Stillo with a chainsaw...

————————————

COMMENTARY: When Wes Craven wrote the screenplay for *The Last House on the Left* (reportedly over a period of four days), he designed the film as a re-interpretation of the 1958 Ingmar Bergman film called *The Virgin Spring*. Accordingly, there are many similarities between Craven's loose adaptation of the material and Bergman's acclaimed motion picture. What makes each film particularly interesting is context. Bergman tells his story in a world of religion whereas Craven depicts his in a world completely lacking it. *The Virgin Spring* template — now re-imagined for the Vietnam/hippie generation — results in a highly thoughtful, provocative, and disturbing film. Though *The Last House on the Left* has been reviled as a violent, ugly picture, it is also an honest one. It does not glorify violence, and, indeed, depicts how violent impulses dwell within us all.

Briefly summarized, *The Virgin Spring* is a re-telling of the medieval German ballad known as *Tore's Daughter*. It's the story of a physician (played by Max Von Sydow in the film) and the events leading up to the murder of his beloved, and much-indulged daughter, Karin. Her murderers are three unwashed herdsmen, who intercept her while she is on the way to church to light candles for the Virgin Mary.

In *Last House on the Left*, it is spoiled middle-class American Mari Collingwood (daughter of Dr. Collingwood) who is murdered by thugs. She is also on the way to a so-called pilgrimage, this time a rock concert — a fact revealing how civilization has changed.

In *The Virgin Spring*, Dr. Tore and his wife (Mareta) commit revenge against the herdsmen, who by a strange twist of fate stay at their home for the evening. This unexpected plot twist is also established in Craven's film, but with John Collingwood brandishing a chainsaw against his enemies rather than a butcher's knife.

The innocent youth tortured by the images of the dead girl is also translated to Craven's universe. In *The Virgin Spring* he is a ten-year-old child (who Tore kills mercilessly anyway...), but in *The Last House on the Left* he is Junior, a young adult, who commits suicide because of his anguish.

Even Mareta's (Tore's wife's) overriding hatred for the servant girl Ingeri is carried over in *The Last House on the Left* when Estelle Collingwood expresses severe disapproval of Phyllis, a girl from a different social class than Mari.

Where these two stories differ is not in detail or character type, but in religious conviction. In *The Virgin Spring*, Dr. Tore's wife blames herself for Karin's death because she loved her daughter more than she loved God. For Dr. Tore, the matter is one of faith. He wonders how God can allow such monstrosities to occur in his world. "You see it and you allow it! The innocent child's death and my revenge, you allowed it!" He cries in despair. In his confusion, Tore swears to erect a church in the wild where Karin's corpse now lies cold. In response to this act of faith, God causes a spring to bubble there. In a high angle shot focusing on the dead Karin, Bergman's camera captures the mystery of faith, and the birth of this beautiful spring. With the questioning of God and the miracle of the virgin spring, Bergman's film confirms the existence of a Christian God who watches over man, even if he does not intervene when horrible events occur.

Clearly then, *The Virgin Spring* views the world in a religious context, and the characters are overtly demonstrative in their faith. They pray before every meal, and Mareta burns her wrists with the fire of a candle every Friday, in memory of Christ's day of agony. Perhaps more significantly, the protagonists in the Bergman picture question God and their own faith and in the climax are rewarded when God grants them a miracle to buttress their faith.

In pointed contrast, there is no suggestion of an afterlife or God in *The Last House on the Left*. The theme song of the picture, oft repeated during the film, is titled "The Road Leads to Nowhere" and it implies that life is a voyage with but one destination: death. Since God is non-existent and the road leads nowhere, *The Last House on the Left* reveals itself to be existentialist, even nihilistic, in its approach to horror.

To wit: terrible things happen to innocent people in the Craven film, and "good people" like the Collingwoods resort to brutal violence and bloodlust with little regret. Though Mari prays before she is killed, in a scene staged in nearly identical fashion to Karin's rape in *The Virgin Spring*, there is no salvation for her, or redemption for her fallen parents. Unlike the Tores in *The Virgin Spring*, the Collingwoods are not enlightened by the existence of God, or an awareness of some divine method. Instead, they are left in a shattered living room filled only with the blood of villains. Craven's camera does not swoop heavenward to give the impression of God's presence, because in *The Last House on the Left*, God is dead.

A flaw of most remakes is the slavish nature by which they attempt to recreate the original. *The Last House on the Left* is a great film because Craven has excised the theological context of *The Virgin Spring* and substituted an equally provocative secular philosophy. His film reflects a godless world. Unlike Bergman, Craven does not treat Karin, Dr. Tore, Maretta and the servant girl Ingeri (Phyllis in *Last House*) as game pieces to be manipulated by God's master plan, but as realistic people caught in a universe of purposeless, random violence. After Mari's rape, any sensible viewer of *The Last House on the Left* will thirst for Krug's death. Yet when Craven finally depicts this murder (and the murder of Krug's cohorts), there is no sense of joy or accomplishment, only a deep-seated sense of shame and anger.

The Last House on the Left's final moment is not a reaffirmation of faith or a celebration of violence, but a moment of grim contemplation. The Collingwoods have been as ruthlessly violent and merciless as Mari's attackers, and nothing has been gained by their savage revenge. Mari is dead, and the road still leads nowhere. The climactic shot of The Last House on the Left indicates that John and Mrs. Collingwood have lost more than their child. They have lost themselves and the life of "innocent" morality they imagined they shared. They have committed murder, and for what? Their house is still empty; as the film's soundtrack asserts, "The castle stays the same."

By freeze-framing on the faces of the shattered middle-class family, the closing shot of The Last House on the Left reveals the futility of bloodshed and retribution in a manner the uplifting finale of The Virgin Spring does not. The final image of human agony lingers, and is therefore forced down the throats of theatergoers. It is the image they leave the theater with; that they carry home. There is no triumphant music on the soundtrack, no heroic overture indicating the issuance of "justice," only a still-life photograph of faces in pain. By concluding with such a downcast note, the film actually serves as an argument against violence and revenge. It is clear that it is not so much the death of Mari that has taken its toll on the Collingwoods, but rather the unexpected realization that they are no better than the people who so casually murdered her.

In at least one way, The Last House on the Left is a more responsible and moral film than The Virgin Spring because of this thorough condemnation of violence. The final image of Craven's film is not a beautiful, bubbling spring that puts aside the violence of the past and suggests the existence of God, but rather the frozen portrait of two shattered human beings. The Last House on the Left finds no validation for revenge, whereas The Virgin Spring suggests that horrible acts of violence will be forgiven by God and that there is redemption, if one looks for it in religion. Erecting a church in God's name, for instance, washes one's hands forever of bloodshed. In an age and society where people bomb abortion clinics or murder doctors who perform abortions, this is a dangerous argument.

Where The Virgin Spring takes Dr. Tore and his wife off the hook for their violence by allowing God to forgive their trespasses, The Last House on the Left leaves the Collingwoods responsible for their own actions. And, because it so daringly re-interprets the context of Bergman's story, as a tale of man's violent nature (instead of one wherein God moves in mysterious ways), it is far more meaningful to a society where retribution, via capital punishment, is legally mandated.

If the final frame of the movie, that of the shattered Collingwoods presiding over an empty castle, is Craven's destination, it is fascinating to examine how he arrives there. The two families (Krugs and Collingwoods) are paralleled throughout the film to suggest that they have more in common than first meets the eye. First, both families are seen in the same circumstances. As the film begins, John Collingwood sits in the living room of his home and reads the newspaper while ignoring his wife. The camera later finds Krug in his home where the mother figure, Sadie, is similarly ignored.

After the first few scenes indicating parallel family circumstances, and an interesting segment wherein Sadie yearns to be a lady with the noble-sounding name Agatha Greenwood (not unlike Estelle Collingwood), Craven's film crosscuts between the activities of the two families with regularity. In the Collingwood home, husband and wife frolic in their kitchen as Estelle spreads creamy icing over Mari's birthday cake. After crosscutting to the Krug household, the thug declares to Sadie that he is the "cream" of American manhood and makes similar, if more blunt, advances on the matriarch of his family.

After Mari and Phyllis are detained,

Craven again cuts back to the Collingwoods as John declares to his wife, "I want to attack you." From there, the scene switches back yet again as Mari and Phyllis are physically assaulted by Krug and Weasel.

The cross-cutting establishes a spiritual connection between the two families even before they have met. John expresses his will to attack, and Krug does just that. This bond will blossom throughout the movie, and the final similarity between families is that they both stoop to heinous acts of violence before the movie's end. The final freeze-frame on the Collingwoods is not dissimilar to an earlier shot of Sadie, Weasel and Krug at the lake following Mari's rape. The killers realize what they have done — raped two girls and murdered them — and they stand in the composition looking ashamed, much as John and Estelle feel after dispatching their opponents in the film's denouement.

The Last House on the Left is a powerful debut for director Craven, and is not an easy film to watch. But sometimes the best films aren't easy to watch, are they? *Platoon* (1986), *Natural Born Killers* (1994), *A Clockwork Orange* (1971), *Schindler's List* (1994) and *The Virgin Spring* (1958) are critically praised films that also face human ugliness, and *The Last House on the Left* has a great deal in common with them. However, it is a far less palatable vision to many viewers and scholars because there is no barrier separating the filmmaker from his audience. *Platoon* is set in Vietnam. *Natural Born Killers* is pointedly satirical, existing outside the confines of our real world. *A Clockwork Orange* occurs in a future society. *Schindler's List* remembers a specific time and place: Germany in the era of the holocaust. *The Virgin Spring* is a medieval story told in a religious context. All of these films thus have an element of safety to them because they do not confront the audience with horrors in a place and time where those horrors dwell on a day-to-day basis. After *Platoon*'s climax, a viewer can click off the TV and satisfy himself that Vietnam, and its remembered atrocities, are halfway around the world, and the result of a different decade.

As its title reminds us, *The Last House on the Left* happens next door. There is no artifice in the movie's structure to protect the audience, no setting as remote as Vietnam, World War II or Sweden to make the movie's message more palatable. Instead, Craven's first film makes its well-considered points about violence and retribution in our living rooms and our backyard. Now. For that reason, it is a powerful film, and far harder to accept than the others mentioned here. Since *The Last House on the Left* does not unfold within the safe confines of any given genre, its raw power incites all kinds of uncomfortable feelings, from voyeurism and curiosity, to disgust and shame ... but certainly not violence, as many have claimed.

On the contrary, *The Last House on the Left* is a movie that despises violence in every frame. It is less offensive than "popular" vigilante movies such as *Death Wish* (1975), because it doesn't laud "eye-for-an-eye" justice. Instead, it offers a succinct (if bloody...) statement about the role of violence in our society and our families.

The Mark of the Devil (1972) *

Cast & Crew

CAST: Herbert Lom (the Witch Finder); Olivera Vuco (Vanessa Benedict); Udo Kier (Baron Christian); Reggie Nalder (Albino); Herbert Fux, Michael Maien, Ingeborg Schoener, Johannes Buzalski, Gaby Fuchs, Gunter Clemens, Doris Von Danwitz, Dorothea Carrera, Marlies Peterson, Bob Gerry.

CREW: World Distribution and Atlas International Present *The Mark of the Devil. Original Story and Screenplay:* Sergio Casstner and Perry Parker. *Director of Photography:* Ernst M. Kalinke. *Assistant Camera Operator:* Fuarhim Gitt, Michael Georg. *Art Director:* Max Mellin. *Decorator:* Walter Karsch. *Costumes:* Barbara Grupp. *Make-up:* Gunther Kulier, Alena Heidankoba. *Film Editor:* Siegrun Jager. *Sound:* Hans-Dieter Schwarz. *Production Manager:* Gerhard Motil. *Production Assistant:* Gerhard Cepe. *Unit Manager:* Heinz Scheloks. *Music:* Michael Holm. *Produced by:* Adrian Hoben. *Directed by:* Michael Armstrong.

SYNOPSIS: In the 15th century, witch-hunters and a mob of angry citizens capture two nuns on the run. The nuns are accused of witchcraft, and then raped. The priest accompanying them is tarred and feathered, and the two nuns are burned alive upon a scaffold.

Later, Lord Witch Finder Cumberland plans to visit town to hunt down more witches. There are so many, apparently, that the local witch-hunters can no longer handle the job adequately. This jurisdictional dispute angers the local witch-finder, the scarred Albino, not only because he does not appreciate having his authority questioned, but because he has conducted no legitimate trials, coerced no valid confessions, and left no documentation of his cruel activities. Accordingly, Albino orders his underlings to forge the appropriate documentation before Cumberland's impending examination.

In the local tavern, Albino makes amorous advances toward Vanessa, a beautiful barmaid. When she refuses his lustful passes, Albino denounces her as a witch. His attempt to try her for witchcraft is prevented by the handsome Baron Christian, an assistant to Cumberland. Albino is whipped for his inappropriate behavior, and Vanessa and Christian become romantically involved. Albino, however, is not satisfied, and drafts an indictment against Vanessa formally accusing her of witchcraft. Vanessa is arrested and whipped as Lord Cumberland arrives in town, and starts conducting trials.

One local woman, accused of witchcraft, claims that the local bishop raped her. Cumberland does not believe the story, and orders the woman's tongue ripped out. A young noble who owns land the Church wishes to possess is also incarcerated and tortured. Cumberland also finds the indictment against Vanessa to be sufficient. This disturbs Christian, who admits to Cumberland that he feels weakness and uncertainty in this particular case. After affirming his belief in Vanessa's guilt, the witchfinder releases Albino from custody. Almost immediately, Albino accuses Cumberland of impotence, and Cumberland strangles him for his words. Christian witnesses the crime but says nothing at first. However, when Cumberland's judgments become even harsher, Christian starts to doubt that Cumberland still serves God. This suspicion grows when Cumberland detains an innocent family of puppeteers, and tortures them as witches.

Disturbed, Christian challenges Lord Cumberland over his murder of Albino, and the teacher and student hurl angry accusations. Convinced that Lord Cumberland has crossed the line, Christian frees Vanessa. He also intends to free the young baron with the hotly desired land, but Cumberland prevents his escape and captures Christian.

Vanessa foments an insurrection in town. Cumberland orders all those who stand against him killed, and sides clash. In the melee, the young baron is beheaded. The peasants free Christian, and he pursues Cumberland. Chased and beaten, Cumberland flees the town. Then the villagers turn on Christian, an emissary of the evil Cumberland, and execute him, even as Vanessa runs to his side in tears.

COMMENTARY: Since its release in 1972 (with the rating "V" for "violent"—a brilliant publicity gimmick), *The Mark of the Devil* has developed a cult reputation in some horror movie circles. Yet the film is memorable not so much because of its quality (in fact, it is terrible…), but because it is an unrepentant, almost gleeful gore-fest. The film opens with the brutal rape of two nuns. It then proceeds to depict dismemberment (a priest's hand is chopped off...), the violent excision of an innocent woman's tongue, torture on the rack, torture on a row of spikes, more rape, more torture, and so forth. Finally, it is plain that the film exists solely to catalogue man's brutality against man.

After the initial rape, hand severing, and torching at the stake, *The Mark of the Devil* pauses momentarily for an on-screen crawl reporting the crushingly obvious information that this period of history was brutal, awful and unjust. Really! Following this brief interruption in the bloody narrative, the film then continues to wallow in the details of those facts. The ugly truth this movie bears witness to is that people enjoy hurting people. That is not a bad point to make (and it has been made well in good films such as *The Crucible* [1996] and *The Devils* [1971]), but by wallowing in the violence (often in close-up), *The Mark of the Devil* inadvertently makes another, far more disturbing (and telling) point.

Specifically, the violence of this movie implies that humans find enjoyment in watching others suffer ... for entertainment, no less. That the film should attempt to appeal to some ethical or moral standard in its opening crawl is rather hypocritical. On one hand, the film wants viewers to be disgusted that human beings can do such things to one another, but on the other hand, it stoops to the level of Cumberland's corrupt witch-finders by depicting the violence with loving detail and attention.

Audiences are invited to feel good about their impulse to view this violence negatively by the moral stirrings of the scripts. "Gee, aren't we above all of this ... aren't we lucky we got out of this terrible time?" the film asks at the same time that it zooms in to capture another atrocity.

No doubt fans of *The Mark of the Devil* would argue that the film is actually anti-violence since it views the witch-finders as amoral, monstrous and impotent men. In response, such apologists are best advised to remember Roger Ebert's oft-quoted thesis on the movies: it is not what a movie's about, it's how it is about it. In other words, *The Mark of the Devil* may indeed have a good point about man's inhumanity to man, but the way it covers such subject matter is both appalling and exploitative. The film never makes the case for its own morality because the camera spends more time lingering on blood and gore than it does reviling those who conduct the violence.

Contrast this approach with *The Last House on the Left*, Wes Craven's film about violence and retribution. In that picture, intense violence (including rape and disembowelment) was also depicted, but with purpose. The early part of that film spent much time visually comparing and contrasting a so-called civilized family (the Collingwoods) with a not-so-refined one (the vicious Krugs), and it used the technique of cross-cutting to do it. By film's end, the distinctions between families had disappeared, and the Collingwoods resorted to the same level of violence as their enemies. In the famous final shot of the film, accompanied by music which indicated no good had been done ("the castle stays the same..."), Craven established that violence solved nothing.

And *The Mark of the Devil*? It understands that violence is wrong, and that witch-hunters used immoral and unethical means to further their own agendas, but it has no stylistic or artistic comment about its world. The plot is so lazily constructed that the town denizens flit from side to side with no rhyme or reason. When it is necessary to the story, they support Cumberland. When it is necessary to the story, they turn against Cumberland. When it is necessary to feature a tragic ending, the townspeople — having just participated in his rescue — kill Kier's character in cold blood.

It's unclear why the citizens take up arms and fight Cumberland, since the opening scene with the nun defines them as bloodthirsty, and Vanessa incites them to violence with ridiculous ease. It is possible that a statement was trying to be made about the "mob," how it is fickle, how it turns on all sides, eventually. Yet there is no consistency within the picture. In *The Mark of the Devil* people kill others indiscriminately, with no justification or reason, and again the picture seems to say only that people enjoy hurting each other. Worse, that we, as viewers, find enjoyment from watching such violence.

Visually, *The Mark of the Devil* is a mess, depending, like other films of the time, on the dated and overused technique of the zoom. The camera zooms in so close sometimes that the object it hopes to highlight blurs out of focus. The dubbing of the dialogue is inadvertently ridiculous, and much of the acting is cornball. Keir is a striking, effective performer, but cast in the role of a complete innocent, his character seems merely daft. "Vanessa, do you know that you're dangerous?" he asks earnestly. "This is my truth — what I can touch and feel," replies a dreamy Vanessa. Any actor would have difficulty with such naïve-sounding banter, and perhaps that is why it is the das-

tardly, pompous Lom who remains most memorable. He is a steely-eyed devil in this film, an impotent woman hater. His performance as a powerful hypocrite who says one thing and preaches is another is central to the film, but since he is unlikable, the focus on this character only serves to make the film even less likable, less accessible.

There's a kernel of an idea in *The Mark of the Devil* that, if developed, could have raised the film's discourse beyond torture, pain and dismemberment. In Baron Christian's development to maturity, he comes to reject the faults and learning of his teacher. That rejection of a once-trusted authority, that stirring of independence, is a human emotion that all young people go through. As children become adults, they question what was once accepted quietly, and the results are not always pretty ... yet it is a natural part of maturity. Had *The Mark of the Devil* more narrowly focused on the Christian-Cumberland relationship, son to father, apprentice to mentor, it might have felt more meaningful, and all that violence and brutality would have had a more valuable context.

Night of the Lepus (1972) ⋆ ⋆

Critical Reception

"...the producers have come up with the most ludicrous concept in cinema history ... and they are 100 percent serious about it ... rabbits, even when photographed in slow motion close-ups to make them look huge and menacing, will inspire fear in absolutely no one."— Harry and Michael Medved, *The Golden Turkey Awards*, Perigee Books, 1980, pages 66–67.

"Take away the seventies color and gore and this could be an archetypal fifties monster movie. Quite fun, although the enlarged rabbits, shown in slow motion with thunderous hooves on the soundtrack, don't really carry a genuinely monstrous charge."— Alan Frank, *The Horror Film Handbook*, 1982, page 103.

"*Night of the Lepus* ... doesn't even reasonably try to make a rabbit seem scary ... the film relies almost entirely on slow-motion shots of ordinary rabbits running through miniaturized settings... It is this technical laziness as much as the stupid story or the dumb direction that leaves the film in limbo...."— Roger Greenspun, *New York Times:* "*Night of the Lepus* Shows Peter Rabbit's Other Side," October 5, 1972, page 56.

Cast & Crew

CAST: Stuart Whitman (Roy Bennett); Janet Leigh (Gerry Bennett); Rory Calhoun (Cole Hillman); DeForest Kelley (Elgin Clark); Paul Fix (Sheriff Cody); Melanie Fullerton (Amanda Bennett); Chris Morrell (Jackie Hillman); Chuck Hayward (Jud); Henry Wills (Frank); Francesca Jarvis (Mildred); William Elliott (Dr. Leopold); Robert Hardy (Professor Dirkson); Richard Jacome (Deputy Jason); Inez Perez (Housekeeper); G. Leroy Gainther (Walker); Evans Thornton (Major White); I. Stanford Jolley (Dispatcher); Robert Gooden (Leslie); Walter Kelley (Taxi Driver); Frank Kennedy (Doctor); Don Starr (Cutler); Peter O'Crotty (Arlen); Phillip Avenetti (Officer Lopez); Russell Morrell (Priest); Donna Gelgur (Wife in Car); Stephen DeFrance (Husband in Car); Sherry Hummer, Rick Hummer (Children in Car); Jerry Dunphy (Television Newscaster).

CREW: Metro-Goldwyn-Mayer Presents *Night of the Lepus. Music:* Jimmie Haskell. *Director of Photography:* Ted Voigtlander. *Production Designer:* Stan Jolley. *Film Editor:* John McSweeney. *Set Decorator:* William Calvert. *Sound:* Jerry Jost, Hal Watkins. *Special Effects:* Howard A. Anderson Company. *Unit Production Manager:* John Wilson. *Assistant Director:* Ted Schiltz *Second Unit Director:* Stan Jolley. *Animal Trainer:* Lou Schumacher, Henry Cowl. *Make-up:* Wes Dawn. *Hairdresser:* Alma Johnson. *Wardrobe:* Norman Burza. *Screenplay:* Don Holliday and Gene R. Kearney. *Based upon the novel* Year of the Angry Rabbit *by:* Russell Braddon. *Produced by:* A. C. Lyles. *Directed by:* William F. Claxton. *M.P.A.A. Rating:* PG. *Running Time:* 99 minutes.

P.O.V.

"*Night of the Lepus* was made at the time of pictures like *Willard, Ben* and *Frogs* ... it read very well. No one put a gun to my head and said I had to do it. What no one realized was that, no matter what you do, a bunny rabbit is a bunny rabbit. A rat, that can be menacing.... But a bunny rabbit?!" (15).— Janet Leigh, star of *Night of the Lepus* (1972).

SYNOPSIS: Near Ajo, Arizona, rancher Cole Hillman fights a war with a rabbit population explosion. A friend from a nearby university, Elgin Clark, recommends that two scientists, Roy and Gerry Bennett, help Hillman find a solution to the environmental crisis, lest Hillman use deadly poison to stop the infestation. Roy and Gerry agree to help, and soon strike on the notion of manipulating the rabbits with special hormones. Upset about the cruelty of the experiments, Roy and Gerry's young daughter, Amanda, releases her favorite rabbit after it has been injected with the hormone concoction. The rabbit escapes into the wild, and returns to the general population.

Meanwhile, angry ranchers plan to burn the rabbits out of their holes. Some days later, Gerry and Roy find an abnormally large rabbit footprint on Cole's land. At the same time, Amanda and Cole's son, Jackie, go to play in an old gold mine but find a local, Captain Billy, missing. In the mine, they locate his corpse just as it is devoured by giant rabbits! Terrified, Amanda goes into shock and is taken to the hospital. That night, a herd of killer rabbits murder a trucker who has stopped on the side of the road. The police, led by Sheriff Cody, discover the body and a coroner declares it has been gnawed by something huge ... like a saber-toothed tiger!

Convinced the rabbits are to blame, Elgin, Terry, Roy and Cole search for the mutant strain at the gold mine. They determine that the monsters are hiding inside and plant dynamite charges at all the mine exits. Before killing the rabbits, Roy and Cole venture into the mine to photograph the beasts. A herd of the giant animals attack, and Roy and Cole barely escape as the dynamite is detonated.

Unfortunately, this measure proves ineffective. The oversized rabbits dig themselves free, and attack Cole's ranch. They massacre his horses, and rampage across his land. Out of control, the rabbits break into Cole's house as he and his family hide in the basement. Then, the animals attack Main Street of a nearby town. The next morning, Roy sends Gerry and Amanda to safety in nearby Woodale, while he and Elgin meet with Sheriff Cody and call in the National Guard. When Cole Hillman reports that the rabbits are nearing Ajo, Sheriff Cody evacuates town.

Roy comes up with a plan to trap and stop the rabbits with an electrical fence erected at a nearby railroad junction. Meanwhile, Gerry and Amanda have driven into a sandpit, and are trapped on the side of the road as the rabbits mass for an attack. As authorities plan to destroy the herd, Roy goes to his family's rescue in a helicopter. Gerry uses a flare to hold the rampaging rabbits at bay as they surround her RV. Roy flies in and evacuates his family just in time.

In Ajo, the authorities are warned that thousands of giant rabbits are on the warpath. With Roy's assistance, the electrified fence is charged. The gambit is successful, and the mutant rabbits are destroyed in a spectacular firestorm.

COMMENTARY: *Night of the Lepus*, a film about giant killer rabbits, may be the most ridiculous horror film ever conceived. It wants to be a tale about environmental balance and the necessity of respecting nature, but instead it emerges as a comedy of hilarious proportions as giant rabbits attack a town and a cast of stalwart B players. The poor stars of the film do the best they can mouthing the inane dialogue, but how do you compete with killer rabbits?

"Do not tamper in God's domain." That was the message of umpteen giant bug movies in the 1950s, and it is repeated, with minor variation, in the "revenge of nature" films of '70s. In the fifties, atomic radiation was the bugaboo that had everybody frightened. Twenty years later, it was the notion that man was destroying his environment through pesticides (*Frogs, Kingdom of the Spiders*), genetic manipulation (*Night of the Lepus*), pollution (*Empire of the Ants*), and other human errors. Yet the story remains the same: mankind's irresponsibility and hubris leads him to face undreamed of threats, whether they be giant insects or giant ... rabbits.

Of course, purely as a matter of practicality, insects are a lot more fearsome than are sweet, fuzzy bunnies...

And that, no doubt, is the central flaw of *Night of the Lepus*. Had the rabbits mutated into fanged, disease-ridden, mutated creatures, they might have been scary (*maybe...*). But the giant, oh so cute bunnies of this film only make one long for Easter.

In all seriousness, the film is hampered by primitive special effects that never convince the audience that the bunnies have grown to enormous (and threatening) dimensions. Basically, life-size rabbits mill about randomly on miniature sets in slow motion and hardly seem threatening. Extreme close-ups are frequently used to indicate that these rabbits are gigantic, but that does not work either. These close-shots are inevitably framed against a black, blank background rather than "on set." So the effect is that the rabbits never seem to be where they are supposed to be.

It is also a stumbling block that there is very rarely any connective material between man and lepus. Only rarely are the actors and the rabbits "composited" in shots together. Instead, it's a visual mish-mash, a back and forth between principals and rabbits, and hence there's no sense of menace. Though a paw occasionally "swats" into the frame, it does not seem scary either. In those rare hand-to-hand scuffles between man and beast, the rabbit is clearly a man in a fluffy suit and a rabbit helmet. As one expects, it looks ridiculous...

Furthermore, there appears to have been a shortage of usable rabbit footage. These dazed, sleepy-looking animals are seen in the same sequences of shots, over and over again. The shots of rabbits running under a bridge and leaping across a chasm are seen at least twice. The editing is sloppy too, with bad mismatches between effects and live-action. For instance, one attack features rabbits (in blackest night) supposedly approaching grazing cows (in blue, early evening).

The special effects depiction of "monster" rabbits may have been an impossible hurdle to climb, but *Night of the Lepus* is further plagued by some of the funniest dialogue you'll ever hear in a horror film. The movie opens with a very serious radio broadcast about the rabbit population explosion. "Rabbits ... which seem so cuddly ... can become a menace," the grave-sounding announcer declares. It might have been a good idea *not* to start the film with the idea that its main antagonist was considered "cuddly."

Later, the film awkwardly tries to explain the concepts surrounding "hormones." Little Amanda consequently asks her mother (Leigh), "Mommy, what's a control group?"

Yet the funniest dialogue is reserved for the action sequences. "Attention!" shouts a harried police officer to a crowd at a drive-in movie, "there's a herd of killer rabbits headed this way!"

Another funny moment, during a surprise attack, has one character warn another "Behind you!!!" as a giant rabbit stealthily approaches.

This author's favorite moment occurs when a sincere Leigh, trying to calm a survivor of a vicious bunny attack, soothingly declares that it is all right, that "the rabbit's gone..."

It's all such a mismatch. The funny monsters and the lousy special effects play off the earnest actors to generate a really amusing picture.

DeForest Kelley, Stuart Whitman, Janet Leigh, Paul Fix and Rory Calhoun deserve better material than they find in *Night of the Lepus*, and one has to admire them all for so ably keeping straight faces as they heroically stand against the onslaught of the bunnies.

LEGACY: In 1999, footage from *Night of the Lepus* showed up in the mega-hit *The Matrix*, starring Keanu Reeves. Watch the TV screen as Keanu (as Neo) arrives at the home of the Oracle. Behind him on the tube is footage of rampaging rabbits in slow-motion.

Nothing but the Night

Cast & Crew

CAST: Christopher Lee (Inspector Bingham); Peter Cushing (Sir Ashley); Diana Dors (Anna Harb); Georgia Brown (Joan Foster); Keith Barron (Dr. Haynes).

CREW: *Directed by:* Peter Sasdy. *Produced by:* Anthony Nelson Keys. *Screenplay by:* John Blackburn. *Director of Photography:* Kenneth Talbot. *Music:* Malcolm Williamson. *Film Editor:* Keith Palmer. *M.P.A.A. Rating:* PG. *Running Time:* 95 minutes.

DETAILS: A terrible bus accident may be linked to a series of murders once thought suicides, and detective Bingham (Lee) is on the case. The investigation takes him to a strange Scottish orphange in this unusual supernatural thriller.

The Other (1972) ✻ ✻ ✻

Critical Reception

"...it confronts us with the same problems of identity, of something lurking beneath the surface, of the supernatural and evil that Edmund Wilson explored so brilliantly in Henry James' *The Turn of the Screw*.... As a psychological thriller, *The Other* is a good film that might have been great."—Hugh James, *Films in Review*, Volume XXIII, Number 7, August-September 1972, page 432.

"Like erotica, horror thrives on suggestion, an approach hopelessly at odds with a period in films in which audiences are calling for increasingly explicit celebrations of violence. It is to Mulligan's credit, then, that he treats his spooky story in the ambiguous style of Henry James's *The Turn of the Screw*, constantly keeping us wondering whether Holland, the bad brother is or isn't a projection of his twin's fevered brain ... but his Cain and Abel story with its constantly changing sets of clues, conveys neither surprise nor horror, only the heavy machinery of essentially 19th century Gothic fiction."—Paul D. Zimmerman, *Newsweek:* "Which Twin?" June 5, 1972, page 98.

"I was never quite sure which twin was the bad one and therefore whether the evil was psychological or supernatural. I did not much care either. Though director Robert Mulligan has handled the children well and achieved a fine feel for the "not so long ago" period setting and atmosphere, the story ... does not generate enough sense or substance to balance its shock value gimmicks."—Moira Walsh, *America*, June 17, 1972, page 635.

"Visually effective, the chilling *The Other* gave fans some memorable goosebumps."—Frank Manchel, *An Album of Modern Horror Films*, Franklin Watts, Publisher, 1983, page 42.

"...the more the audience was prepared to work with it, the more frightening it became in its implications...."—William K. Everson, *Classics of the Horror Film*, A Citadel Press Book, 1974, page 242.

Cast & Crew

CAST: Uta Hagen (Ada); Diana Muldaur (Alexandra); Chris Udvarnoky (Niles Perry); Martin Udvarnoky (Holland Perry); Norma Connolly (Aunt Vee); Lou Frizzell (Uncle George); Loretta Leversee (Winnie); Jenny Sullivan (Torrie); Victor French (Mr. Angelini); Portia Nelson (Mrs. Rowe); Jack Collins (Mr. P.C. Pretty); Ed Bakey (Chan-Yu); John Ritter (Rider); Clarence Crow (Russell).

CREW: 20th Century–Fox Presents a Robert Mulligan Production, *The Other*. *Assistant Directors:* Dan Kranze, Mark Sandrich, Bert Gold. *Sound:* Jack Solomon, Don Bassman. *Set Decorator:* Ruby Levitt. *Costumes:* Tommy Welsh, Joanne Haas. *Make-up:* Joe DiBella. *Hairstylist:* Dorothy White. *Orchestration:* Arthur Morton. *Color:* DeLuxe. *Production Designed by:* Albert Brenner. *Film Editor:* Folmar Blangsted, O. Nicholas Brown. *Director of Photography:* Robert L. Surtees. *Associate Producer:* Don Kranze. *Music:* Jerry Goldsmith. *Executive Producer:* Thomas Tryon. *Screenplay:* Thomas Tryon. *Based on the novel by:* Thomas Tryon. *Produced and Directed by:* Robert Mulligan. Produced by REM-Benchmark Productions. Released by 20th Century–Fox Film Corp. *M.P.A.A. Rating:* PG. *Running Time:* 100 minutes.

SYNOPSIS: In rural Midwest America in the 1930s, little Niles Perry raises hell with his twin brother, Holland. Their mother seems oddly disconnected from reality, apparently in mourning over a death in the family. On one afternoon, the boys' Russian grandmother, Ada, teaches Niles how to use his special gift of insight to get in psychic touch with other organisms, like a crow. In his mind, Niles imagines himself flying like the crow. In that state, he sees a child friend impaled on a pitchfork in a haystack and his twin, Holland, running guiltily from the scene of the crime. At other points, Niles plays the psychic "game" to determine how a magician at a local fair accomplishes a disappearing act.

Meanwhile, Niles keeps his dead father's severed finger, complete with ring, in a tin of special items. One day, Holland dresses as a magician, and scares an elderly neighbor to death by pulling a rat out of his hat in her living room. When Ada visits old Mrs. Rowe with Niles, they find her dead.

Niles' mother soon finds the severed finger and demands to know where Niles got it. Holland intervenes and Mrs. Perry falls down a flight of stairs. She is now paralyzed, and Niles is horrified. He flees to the church, where he admits to Ada that Holland terrifies him. Niles tells Ada that Holland killed Mrs. Rowe by accident. Angry, she leads Niles out to the graveyard, where she forces him to see Holland's tombstone. It seems that the twin, Holland, died on his birthday when he fell into a well. Niles is flabbergasted by the revelation, but appears to accept the death of his brother.

That night, Niles is visited by the dead Holland, who leads him to a coffin and tells him to "remember." There, Niles views Holland's corpse. That very night, Ada overhears Niles talking to Holland again, even though she warned him not to continue playing this particular game.

While Niles cares for his older sister's newborn one night, the baby disappears from its cradle ... replaced by a ceramic doll, just as in Niles' favorite story, *The Changeling*. Authorities arrive to search for the baby, but Niles is convinced Holland has stolen it. He tells Ada his story, blaming everything, including the death of his father, on Holland.

The baby is soon found drowned and discolored in a barrel of wine.

Realizing that it is Niles, not Holland, who is a murderer, Ada locks herself and Niles in a barn, and starts a fire that will kill them both. Niles manages to escape his grandmother's trap, and lives on, his evil unsuspected.

COMMENTARY: *The Other* is a slow-moving, but often atmospheric horror film. It is gloomy, dread-filled, and, frankly, rather confusing. The movie never clarifies whether Niles is merely schizophrenic or actually being haunted by his malevolent, dead brother. The film lacks outright scares (as well as a linear story line), yet is remarkably effective in creating a sense of mood and place. It is also buttressed by the film's allusions to *The Changeling*, a fairy tale that has thematic meaning and that places this story of insanity and childhood into perspective.

Robert Mulligan has a flair for landing viewers in another world, a different time and place. Accordingly, the film is exquisitely photographed, a lush evocation of the 1930s. The details feel just right, and there is a lyrical nostalgia in the set design, the art direction, and the costuming. Period horror films are notoriously hard to pull off, yet Mulligan has taken pains to re-create a world of bygone days. Skies are blue, the landscape is gorgeous, and a simpler era is recreated in terms that stand in stark contrast to the horror to come.

Rewardingly, Mulligan also has a keen eye for creepy images and touches, if not outright jolts or scares. These disturbing images are many, and they linger in the mind long after the film is done. Niles imagines a baby in a jar; his mother is permanently disassociated from reality, in a glaze. A boy unwraps a package and inside is a severed finger; a rat's neck is snapped before our eyes. A gloved white hand unexpectedly enters the frame; the freak show features a hairy boy, a deformed man, and an obese woman, and one feels Niles would be right at home with them. And so on. This is not so much an out-and-out scary picture as it is a disturbing one. The sight of a baby drowned in a barrel of wine is the final, unsettling horror, and it too is a kicker. The corpse has become a sick violet, as the skin has soaked up the wine. A grim, sick, image.

The children, Chris and Martin Udvarnoky, are very good in the film, and one is reminded again just how disturbing "scary" children can be. The notion that a little bottle of innocence could actually be evil, a harbinger of death, is a potent one in the genre, exploited in everything from *Village of the Damned* (1960) to *The Exorcist* (1973). This film adds to the "evil child" equation by making prominent mention of the story of the changeling, a terrible creature that replaces the soul of a baby. This story is one of Niles' favorites, and is obviously a metaphor for his character. Is he simply a child, or is he a creature of evil?

Likewise, Niles' final act in the film is to "steal" a baby, replacing it with a doll, acting again like in *The Changeling*. The changeling allusion works rather nicely, giving the film a literary feel, yet one still feels there could be additional clarity. The film goes out of its way *not* to make a decision about Niles. He could be crazy, and a monster, or just a little boy besieged by tragedy. Still, the film works despite the cloudy narrative. What Niles actually "is" may be less important than where he is (the depiction of his world), and what he represents (a changeling).

The Possession of Joel Delaney (1972) * ½

Critical Reception

"Whatever sinister quality the picture has stems from the ambience of Puerto Rican Harlem and not from the direction of Waris Hussein or the acting of Miss MacLaine.... Although Hussein has learned some of the tricks of suspense from Hitchcock, most of the time we're treated to nonsense...."—*Films in Review*, Volume XXIII, Number 3, June-July 1972, pages 375–376.

"I presume that Miss MacLaine was attracted to the story because its sardonic examination of contrasting life styles seemed to her a forceful indictment of white racism. But she missed the point that its unflattering depiction of Puerto Ricans could have the opposite effect. Director Waris Hussein has a blind spot too. He can't tell the difference between frightening an audience and disgusting them."—Moira Walsh, *America*, June 17, 1972, page 635.

"...works its way towards its sickening climax with such predictability that only a newborn baby would have trouble guessing whose head will be severed next."—Paul D. Zimmerman, *Newsweek:* "Terror Tonic," June 12, 1972, page 98.

"...so nauseating and downbeat, its climax so pointlessly revolting, that it was not worth the effort of working with it."—William K. Everson, *Classics of the Horror Film*, a Citadel Press book, 1974, page 242.

Cast & Crew

CAST: Shirley MacLaine (Norah Benson); Perry King (Joel Delaney); David Elliott (Peter Benson); Lisa Kohane (Carrie Benson); Lovelady Powell (Erika); Barbara Trentham (Sherry); Miriam Colon (Veronica); Edmundo Rivera Alvarez (Don Pedro); Teodorina Bellow

(Mrs. Perez); Robert Burr (Ted Benson); Ernesto Gonzalez (Young Man at Séance); Peter Turgeon (Detective Brady); Earl Hyman (Charles); Marita Lindholm (Marta Benson); Paulita Iglesias (Brujo at Service); Stan Watt (James); Michael Hordern (Justin); William Hawley, Aukie Herger.

CREW: Paramount Pictures and ITC Present *The Possession of Joel Delaney*. *Director of Photography:* Arthur J. Ornitz. *Production Designer:* Peter Murton. *Film Editor:* John Victor Smith. *In Charge of Post-Production:* George Justin. *Art Director:* Philip Rosenberg. *Costumes:* Frank Thompson. *Casting:* Jennifer Levy. *Extras Casting:* Vic Ramos. *Set Decorator:* Edward Stewart. *Wardrobe:* Marilyn Putnam. *Make-up:* Saul Meth. *Hair-stylist:* Lee Trent. *Assistant Director:* Alan Hopkins, Alex Hapsas, Mike Haley. *Camera Operator:* Lou Barlia. *Script Supervisor:* Robert Hodes. *Sound:* Dick Gramalia. *Dubbing Editor:* Dino DiCampo. *Sound Mixer:* Gerry Humphreys. *Music Composed and Directed by:* Joe Raposo. *Screenplay:* Matt Robinson, Grimes Grice. *Based on a novel by:* Ramona Stewart. *Directed by:* Waris Hussein. Filmed entirely on location in New York. Post-Production at Twickenham Studios, England. *M.P.A.A. Rating:* R. *Running Time:* 102 minutes.

SYNOPSIS: Norah Benson, a rich New York City socialite, is disturbed when her younger brother, Joel Delaney, begins to act strangely. She checks up on him, visiting his apartment, and finds that the police have beaten her to the building. The police drag Joel away, and put him in Bellevue hospital. Norah searches Joe's apartment for some clue to his odd behavior. She finds a switchblade, and then goes to see Joel at Bellevue. There, she learns Joel is incarcerated for an attack on his landlord, Mr. Perez. So that he will be released from Bellevue, Joel admits to taking drugs, but he must see a psychologist, family friend Dr. Larens.

Joel's odd behavior grows worse, and he becomes cruel. He questions Norah about her sex life, frequents bar, and makes love to his girlfriend in violent fashion. When Norah sees Joe next, at his birthday party,

Joel is even weirder. Suddenly, he speaks Spanish fluently, and nearly burns his girlfriend's hair in his birthday cake. When Norah checks up on her the next morning, she finds her in bed, decapitated. The police arrest Joel.

The police promptly question Norah about her brother. His girlfriend's death is identical to three murders in Spanish Harlem that took place a summer ago. Confused, Norah visits Spanish Harlem after researching the late Tonio Perez, the suspected murderer. Norah's domestic, Veronica, suggests Norah check out a shop in Spanish Harlem where there may be help for Joel. There, Norah meets Don Pedro. He reveals that Joel has been possessed by Tonio's spirit! Norah is reluctant to believe this, but Pedro arranges a séance to draw out Perez's restless soul. The ritual appears successful, and Norah is relieved.

But Joel is not better. Instead, he goes into a psychotic frenzy! Norah seeks help from the therapist, who instructs Nora to take her children and get out of town. Norah follows the advice, and stays at a remote beach house.

After a quiet night, terror strikes. Dr. Laren's severed head is found in the beach house refrigerator, and Joel arrives. He threatens the children, demands they take their clothes off, and then dances with them. The police arrive outside the beach house, but inside things get worse. Joel makes Norah eat dog food out of a bowl on the floor. When Norah fights back, Joel attempts to rape her. Norah's children escape, and the cops shoot Joel. He dies on the shore, but, once and for all, is himself again

Suddenly, Norah is possessed...

COMMENTARY: In *The Possession of Joel Delaney*, a rich white boy is struck by the horror movie equivalent of white liberal guilt, and possessed by the spirit of a murderous Hispanic. Though the plot has possibilities, the filmmakers exploit audience prejudices to heighten suspense. Worse, the film features a really cheap ending that soaks up the last ounce of the viewer's good will.

In the early part of the film it is clear that Joel is grappling with his identity. He feels guilty that his family is so rich, and thus moves to a poor district in the city to be with what he calls "the real people." That impulse to try to understand those less fortunate than himself turns out to be Joel's undoing, since it is his proximity to a local, an ethnic American, that ends up causing his possession. There's an unpleasant message here, to be sure. When you leave your own "kind," you face the possibility of losing your true nature, of being overcome by the spirit of the poor. It's not only anti-tolerant, it is anti–American, to suggest that Joel's better impulses, to question his wealth and superiority in a class society, is the cause of his ultimate downfall. Implicitly, the movie warns that people should stay within their own social circles, with those of the same skin color and religion. If not, those "voodoo" ways might get ya!

The film goes further downhill by taking Norah (MacLaine) to the poorest streets in Spanish Harlem, where she looks and feels threatened among Puerto Ricans. The location shooting, the scads of authentic "Hispanic" extras, and MacLaine's fear all add up to an exploitation scene of the ugliest order. It reveals the white man's fear of ethnic minorities in America, in a manner that is neither pleasant nor nice. The audience is supposed to identify with MacLaine because she is so "obviously" in danger, surrounded by other than her own people. That MacLaine's very presence with non-whites

should seem scary presumes that audiences share the character's (and filmmaker's) biases. In essence, the movie resorts to racist fear to generate scares and suspense, and that is simply not playing fair. It is an unsavory way to try to inject life into a very lifeless film.

But the worst is yet to come. Just when you think the movie cannot sink any lower, or be any more offensive, it ends with a nasty "hostage" situation in which a little boy is forced to undress and then dance naked before Hussein's camera. It is a mean-spirited, sick move (replete with frontal nudity…), and it is wholly unnecessary. It gives the movie no additional power, making it only more repellant. Why abuse a child actor in this fashion? Why humiliate him? Is there any dramatic reason for it?

Finally, the last moment of the film reveals that Norah — ostensibly our heroine — has been possessed by the "evil" Puerto Rican. This is the kind of lame-brained ending that causes audiences to hurl objects at the screen. A tragic ending, built up to, can be a very powerful thing. *The Wicker Man* and *The Blair Witch Project* are just two horror films which earn their downbeat endings, being terrifying and clever throughout. The ending of *The Possession of Joel Delaney* is just another trick, another gimmick thrown out for lack of genuine invention. The climax doesn't inform; it doesn't chill. It merely infuriates. One suspects that a lot of money went into the production of *The Possession of Joel Delaney*. That money might have been spent on a better script.

Return of Count Yorga (1972) ✳ ✳ ✳

Cast & Crew

CAST: Robert Quarry (Count Yorga); Mariette Hartley (Cynthia Nelson); Roger Perry (David Baldwin), Philip Frame (Tommy); Craig Nelson (Sgt. O'Connor); Yvonne Wilder,

Tom Toner, Rudy De Luca, George MacReady, Walter Brooke, Edward Walsh, David Lampson, Karen Houston, Helen Baron, Jesse Wells, Mike Pataki, Corrine Conley, Alden Joseph, Peg Shirley, Liz Rogers, Paul Hansen.

CREW: A Michael MacReady & Bob Kelljan

Production. *Production Manager:* Carl Olsen. *Chief Electrician:* Dennis Bishop. *Script Supervisor:* Joyce King. *Wardrobe:* Jeannie Anderson. *Make-up:* Mark Busson. *Sound Mixer:* Rod Sutton. *Property Master:* Eric Nelson. *Set Designer:* Vince Cresseman. *Special Effects:* Roger George. *Assistant Director:* Jack Oliver. *Animal Trainer:* Vee Kasegan. *Sound:* Ryder Sound Services. *Sound Effects:* Edit International Ltd. *Optical Effects:* Modern Film Effects. *Film Editors:* Fabien Tordjmann, Laurette Odney. *Director of Photography:* Bill Butler. *Songs: "Think It Over,"* written and performed by: Marilynn Lovell; *"This Song,"* written by: Marilynn Lovell, Yvonne Wilder, Bob Kelljan, Bill Marx. *Music composed and conducted by:* Bill Marx. *Screenplay by:* Bob Kelljan, Yvonne Wilder. *Produced by:* Michael MacReady. *Directed by:* Bob Kelljan. *M.P.A.A. Rating:* R. *Running time:* 97 minutes.

––––––––––––––––

SYNOPSIS: As night falls in rural California, a young orphan, Tommy, inadvertently rouses the dead in a nearby graveyard … and is turned into a vampire by the master of the night, Count Yorga. Then, at the Westwood Orphanage, beautiful instructor Cynthia Nelson meets Yorga on Halloween night as she attends a masquerade ball. Before long, one of the partygoers, Mitzi, turns up with strange bite marks on her neck. Claiming to be European royalty, Yorga suggests it is time to believe in vampires.

That night, Cynthia has trouble sleeping, and awakens feeling disturbed. Ironically, her entire family feels the same way, citing a sense of uneasiness. Suddenly, Yorga's undead brides attack the house. An unconscious Cynthia is taken to Yorga's castle after her family is killed in the attack. There, Yorga hypnotizes her into forgetting the incident, and believing that he is her friend. He informs her that she must rest at his home for a few days.

Meanwhile, a deaf orphan finds Tommy in the aftermath of the massacre and authorities are notified. When they arrive, however, all signs of the attack have been cleaned up. Tommy, a servant of Yorga, lies about the incident. Brudeh, Yorga's manservant, dumps the bodies in quicksand on the count's property.

In San Francisco, Cynthia's boyfriend, David Baldwin, suspects vampire activity on Yorga's part, and seeks the help of an expert in the occult. Meanwhile, back at Gateway Mansion, Yorga believes he can experience love with Cynthia, although a soothsayer warns him not to even try. By night, Yorga hunts the ill Mitzi and her boyfriend. Craving blood, he follows them to their houseboat, and drains Mitzi dry.

That very night, Tommy lures another victim to the mansion, even as Yorga informs Cynthia of his love for her. As she rejects him, David, the Reverend Thomas and two police detectives head to Yorga's castle to investigate him. While David and the cops (Madden and O'Connor) search the house, the reverend attempts to distract Yorga. The count sees through the ruse, and lures the reverend to a pit of quicksand … where the man of the cloth drowns.

Inside the castle, Yorga's vampires attack David and the cops. The forces of good are separated, and O'Connor and Madden are done in by Yorga's vampire minions. David and Cynthia attempt to escape the house, but Yorga captures Cynthia, and attempts to run off, with David in close pursuit. Cynthia finally remembers that Yorga is responsible for the death of her family, and plants an axe in the vampire's chest. David pushes the vampire over the ledge of a bell tower … presumably to his death. Cynthia is relieved, until she realizes that David has been bitten, and is now a vampire himself.

––––––––––––––––

COMMENTARY: The second time is the charm for *The Return of Count Yorga,* a fun sequel to the 1970 cult-horror hit. Not only is this sequel scarier than its predecessor, but it possesses an admirable (but not distracting) sense of humor. Buoyed also by Robert Quarry's central performance, this is a vampire film that delivers the goods.

Return of Count Yorga opens with a sense of anticipation and danger. A young boy, Tommy, plays ball all alone on the grounds of Yorga's expansive estate as night falls, and a high angle shot reveals that he is in real danger from an unseen terror. From there, referencing *Night of the Living Dead,* the dead walk, and an ill wind (the "winds of Santa Ana") blow across a seemingly sedate orphanage. These moments of fear — the resurrected corpses, the attack on the boy and the promise of more horrors to come (carried on the wind) — all lend the film a quality that *Count Yorga, Vampire,* truly lacked: a sense of atmosphere. The first film, burdened by a clunky opening narration seemed almost amateurish at times, but this sequel rectifies any mistakes from the franchise's past, reveling in a gothic atmosphere. Even the characters take note of this new focus on texture. "Night winds do stir the imagination," Yorga acknowledges. Perhaps that's an admission on the part of the producers that they have learned some new tricks since creating the initial film.

The zombie attack on Cynthia's house is also well staged, and frightening. There is a shocking "jolt" moment after a long interval of silence, and much use of lenses that distort the frame. And, the director also understands well how slow-motion photography can effectively sell the terror. Even the common touches of "taunting laughter" and "mysterious whispers" from dark corners feel fresh in this film, which reveals energy not hinted at in the original film.

Yet despite all these improvements, *Return of Count Yorga* remembers it has a history — in a way. During a beautifully composed sequence overlooking the Golden Gate Bridge in San Francisco, director Kelljan stages a scenic "walk/talk" scene, much like one in *Count Yorga, Vampire.* In both films, the director adopts a distant stance (in long shot), and actors "loop" their dialogue over authentic local footage. This is a stylistic bridge between films. Even though the location has changed, the subject (vampires in a modern world) remains the same.

In another nice touch, Roger Perry has been invited back to duel with Yorga in this sequel, though he plays a different (and less interesting) character this time around.

Humor also flourishes in this vampire sequel. When David seeks help from a professor in the occult, he is disturbed to find the old man is hard-of-hearing, and unable to assist. He mistakes the name "Yorga" for "Yoga." This scene is not only amusing, but it helps to set up the climax, revealing that, essentially, David will have no help in defeating the vampire master. In another wicked moment, Yorga sits down in front of a TV screen and watches an Ingrid Pitt vampire movie on TV, straight from the vaults of Hammer Studios! Also, any true horror aficionado will love one of the film's absurd, but fun moments. Near the climax, an off-screen Yorga makes a threatening — yet funny — overhead announcement to his nemesis. "David Baldwin ... this is Count Yorga ... you're going to die...," the vampire informs Baldwin, in a ridiculous moment. First of all, the threat comes off like an important announcement on a high school PA system. And secondly, why does Yorga bother to introduce himself before issuing his threat? Does he thinks his nemesis has forgotten his name? It is an absurd, silly moment ... and totally wonderful in a million ways.

Quarry seems quite energized in this film, adding a tragic quality to Yorga's character. He says he believes in a "cold, emotional truth," yet is blind-sided by Cynthia, and disarmed by feelings of love. This is an interesting twist on so cool a character, and one quite unexpected. The image heretofore of Yorga was one of hedonistic delight. He was a slick, seedy vampire with a taste for the ladies ... literally. This film gives Quarry some more substantial emotions to sink his teeth into. And, in the kill scenes, Quarry is still commendably icy. Near the end of the picture, his cool dismissal of the reverend — leading him to quicksand and watching him sink to his demise — establishes the real danger of this creature of the night.

If *Return of Count Yorga* fails in any category, it is that the climax of the film degenerates into a repeat of the first film's denouement: a search through the castle by those who suspect Yorga's identity as a vampire. And, sadly, the characters populating this world are still not very smart. Early in the film, Yorga (dressed in stylish vampire cape) enters a masquerade party, and informs his fellow partygoers that he believes in vampires. Moments later, a girl is found unconscious with two bites on her neck, and nobody suspects there might be a connection between Yorga and a vampire attack! If that moment had been played with the tongue-in-cheek delight of Yorga's threatening, yet strangely matter-of-fact announcement to David, the picture might have worked even better.

Stanley (1972) * ½

Cast & Crew

CAST: Chris Robinson (Tim); Alex Rocco (Thomkins); Steve Alaimo (Crail); Susan Carroll (Susie); Mark Harris (Bob); Rey Baumel (Sidney); Paul Avery (Psycho); Marcie Knight (Gloria); Gary Crutcher (Dr. Everett); Mei Pape (Guard); Butterball Smith (Stage Manager); Pamela Talus (Girlfriend); Bill Marquez (Wachula).

CREW: *Film Editor:* Julio Chavez. *Director of Photography:* Cliff Poland. *Assistant Director:* Gayle DeCamp. *Director of Sound:* Howard Warren. *Camera Technician:* Mike Davis. *Property Master:* Jack Johnson. *Make-up:* Marie Del Russo. *Animal Sequences Filmed at:* Homasassa Spring, Florida. *Color:* Capital Labs and Deluxe. *Titles:* Visual Productions. *Sound:* Warren Sound Systems & McLeod Films); Filmed in Everglades and Ivan Tors Studio, Miami Florida. *Written by:* Gary Crutcher. *Executive Producer:* John H. Burrow. *From an original story by:* William Grefe. *Songs "Sparrow" and "Star a New World" written and sung by:* Jack Vino. *Produced by:* Steve Alaimo, Bobby Radeloff. *Musical Score:* Post Production Associates. *Produced and Directed by:* William Grefe. *M.P.A.A. Rating:* R. *Running time:* 92 minutes.

SYNOPSIS: Tim is a Native-American, Vietnam veteran whose father was shot while trespassing on the land of a local robber baron, Thomkins. Understandably, Tim is not happy with his lot in the world, and has forsaken his village to care for snakes. He now lives isolated from mankind in the Florida everglades, but takes special care of a family of snakes. In fact, snake parents Stanley and Hazel have just mated, and little baby snakes are on the way.

One day, Thomkins travels out to Tim's place to make him an offer. He will buy Tim's snakes, kill them, and then sell their skins on the lucrative fashion market. Tim is none too happy with the idea of this exploitation, and has been using the snakes for a positive goal instead: providing venom samples for the local hospital. Thomkins and his half-wit enforcer, Crail, warn Tim that he will do as they say or else. In revenge, Tim attacks Thomkins' snake-collecting operation, freeing the exploited snakes before they can be killed. At the same time that Tim proves to be a thorn in his side, Thomkins is bedeviled by his 17-year-old daughter, Susie. She has become sexually active with many of the locals, and downright rebellious. Susie tells Thomkins that she hates him, and Thomkins warns her to watch her step. He then hires Marty "Psycho" Simpson to keep Tim at bay and if need be, kill him.

Before long, Tim has struck again. He leads Crail and another henchman, Bob, to a quicksand pit ... where Stanley the snake promptly bites them. The poisoned men sink into the quicksand and die. An irate Psycho seeks vengeance, and kills Hazel and Stanley's snake brood. This murder drives Tim over the edge of sanity, and he and Stanley kill Psycho.

Tim is further enraged when a local stripper, Gloria, and her husband abuse snakes on-stage as part of her cabaret act. In one vicious moment, Gloria (dressed as Cleopatra) bites the head off a live snake. By night, Tim rights this wrong, and Stanley and his fellow snakes kill the offenders.

The next day, Tim takes the fight directly to Thomkins. He dumps snakes in the pool, and Thomkins dives in for his morning swim, unaware of the danger. He dies quickly, leaving Tim to kidnap the beautiful Susie. He takes her back to the Everglades, and asks her to be Eve to his Adam. Once at Tim's place, Susie and Tim make love, but the party does not last. Susie accuses Tim of playing god with his snakes. She decides to leave, and Tim orders Stanley to kill her. When Stanley will no longer be used, Tim is infuriated, and grows violent. Defending himself, Stanley bites his master … multiple times. A lamp falls off a table inside the cabin and starts a fire. Susie and the snakes escape, but the hate-filled Tim dies. He asks Stanley, his old friend, if in Hell he will finally learn to accept who he is…

COMMENTARY: "The lowest thing on this Earth are snakes," says a character in *Stanley*, a low-budget variation of *Willard* (1971) and *Ben* (1972). Oddly, the movie itself seems to suggest otherwise, depicting a world of unsavory men and women, where people hurt people. Stanley the snake is actually one of the nicer characters in a movie that makes viewers realize just how good a film *Willard* really is.

Calling *Stanley* a *Willard* with snakes is pretty accurate. There's the one word title (which happens to be the name of an animal, as in *Ben*), and a story of a disenfranchised man training animals to kill his enemies. In this situation, Thomkins the snake killer is like the Ernest Borgnine character in *Willard*, and Chris Robinson's Tim is the equivalent of the much-abused Willard Stiles (Bruce

Davison). Stanley, like Ben before him, comes to realize that his master is no better than his enemies and ultimately turns on the man he once protected. It couldn't be much more on the nose.

What truly differentiates *Stanley* from *Willard* is that the snake variation is done without a modicum of wit, style, or even meaningful subtext. Where *Willard* had a compelling character in Stiles (and even in Sondra Locke as his love interest), *Stanley* goes out of its way to present really unattractive people. Thomkins makes incestuous advances toward his 17-year-old daughter, Susie. Susie is depicted as a cruel nymphomaniac (the best kind!). The strip club is a hellhole filled with fatty, unattractive strippers and hiccupping drunks. One over-the-hill stripper, who Tim visits backstage, has baggy-looking underwear hanging from her clothesline … a not very appealing image. Taken as a whole, it's like a lingering ride down a sewer, with even Tim emerging as an unlikable psycho, damaged perhaps by his experiences in Vietnam. And the only subtext comes in when Tim demands that Susie "touch" his snake, an obvious penis metaphor. "Touch him!" he orders, and one cannot help but think of Mike Myers' character Dieter, who demanded that guests on his TV show (Sprockets) touch his monkey. Susie's response to this invitation is equally charged with sexuality. "It's my first time," she purrs. Yeah, right.

Like *Night of the Lepus, Ben, Frogs, Kingdom of the Spiders*, or any other "revenge of the animals"-themed pictures of the 1970s, *Stanley* wears its environmental heart on its sleeve. Thomkins is bad because he exploits snakes for profit. Tim, like the snakes, feels exploited by white American society, and so he becomes riddled with a "cancer of hate." It's all meant to be meaningful, but the film is not sincere in its assertions. For instance, Tim does not want any animals hurt, yet he feeds live mice to the snakes. Isn't there a contradiction worthy of note there? How does he rationalize the death of some animals, but not others?

The hazy metaphor that Indians, like snakes, are exploited does not really work either. When Tim says that maybe in Hell he will find out who he is, it's as if the film is blaming his American Indian heritage and genetic make-up for his character failings. Or maybe Vietnam is an excuse. The film doesn't really decide, except that Tim becomes "evil." He sees himself as Adam, Susie as Eve … and Stanley, the serpent, represents the Devil? That metaphor does not really fit, since it is Adam (Tim) who destroys the paradise of Eden, by turning on his friend, Stanley, and on his "would-be bride," Susie. There's all this classical allusion but it means nothing in relation to what actually occurs in the picture.

Snakes and people do interact in the same shots in this film, a fact that at least lends *Stanley* a believability missing from *Frogs* (wherein Ray Milland and the frogs were never seen in the same shot…). At one point Tim drops a bag of snakes on the camera, and snakes fall towards the lens. That's pretty cool. Then, in a series of dissolves, the snakes land on a stripper and her husband as they writhe in bed. It's a bizarre moment in a bizarre movie, and probably one that doesn't bear too much scrutiny.

"Your idea of a dream is my idea of a nightmare," Susie says of her incestuous father in *Stanley*. She might have added that this movie is the viewer's idea of a nightmare too.

LEGACY: Chris Robinson went onto play a popular character on the ABC daytime soap opera *General Hospital* for many years, but never again acted with snakes.

Superbeast

Cast & Crew

CAST: Antoinette Bower (Dr. Pardee); Craig Littler (Dr. Fleming); Harry Lauter (Stewart Victor); Vic Diaz (Diaz); Jose Romulo (Vigo).

CREW: *Written, Produced, and Directed by:* George Schenck. *Director of Photography:* Nonong Rasca. *Film Editor:* Tony DiMarch. *Music:* Richard LaSalle. United Artists. *M.P.A.A. Rating:* R. *Running Time:* 93 minutes.

DETAILS: Shot in the Philippines (by *Daughter of Satan*'s cinematographer, Nanong Rosca), *Superbeast* is an odd hybrid of *The Island of Dr. Moreau* and *The Most Dangerous Game*. Here, a big game hunter (Lauter) tracks down and kills criminals who have been transformed into monsters courtesy of a scientist's (Littler's) "rehabilitation" formula. Bower plays the pathologist who runs afoul of the goings-on deep in a lush forest.

Tales from the Crypt (1972) ★ ★ ½

Cast & Crew

CAST: Joan Collins (Joanne); Peter Cushing (Grimsdyke); Roy Dotrice (Gregory); Richard Greene (Jason); Ian Hendry (Maitland); Patrick Magee (Carter); Barbara Murray (Wife); Nigel Patrick (Rogers); Robin Phillips (Elliot); Ralph Richardson (Crypt Keeper); Geoffrey Bayldon (Guide); David Markham (Father); Robert Hatton (Neighbor); Angie Grant (Susan); Susan Denny (Wife); Chloe Franks (Daughter); Martin Boddey (Husband); Oliver MacGreevy (Maniac); With: Manning Wilson, Kay Adrian, Carlos Baker, Dan Gaalfield, Melinda Clancy, Paul Glere, Sharon Glere, Clifford Earl, Edward Evans, Frank Forsyth, Peter Frazer, Irene Gawre, George Herbert, Harry Locke, Stafford Niedhurst, Jayne Soffano, Peter Thomas, Tony Wall, Hodger Wallace.

CREW: Metromedia Producers Corporation Presents an Amicus Production, *Tales from the Crypt. Screenplay by:* Milton Subotsky. *Based on stories by:* Al Feldstein, Johnny Craig and Bill Gaines originally published in the Comic Magazines *Tales from the Crypt* and *The Vault of Horror* by Bill Gaines. *Music composed and conducted by:* Douglas Gamley. *Director of Photography:* Norman Warwick. *Art Director:* Tony Curtis. *Editor:* Teddy Darras. *Production Manager:* Teresa Bolland. *Production Supervisor:* Arthur Stolnitz. *Assistant Director:* Peter Saunders. *Camera Operator:* John Harris. *Continuity:* Penny Daniels. *Casting Director:* Ronnie Curtis. *Make-up:* Roy Ashton. *Chief Hairdresser:* Joan Carpenter. *Wardrobe Mistress:* Bridget Sellers. *Sound Mixer:* Norman Bolland. *Sound Editor:* Pat Foster. *Dubbing Mixer:* Nolan Roberts. *Set Dresser:* Helen Thomas. *Production Executive:* Paul Thompson. *Produced by:* Max J. Rosenberg and Milton Subotsky. *Executive Producers:* Charles Fries. *Directed by:* Freddie Francis. Produced at Shepperton Studios, Middlesex, England. *M.P.A.A. Rating:* R. *Running Time:* 92 minutes.

P.O.V.

"We had Ralph Richardson for two days and things were going slightly awry because the script was much too short. We made it up as we went along, and dear old Ralph didn't mind … he was quite happy in his dressing room, reading his books" (16).—Director Freddie Francis discusses the making of *Tales from the Crypt* (1972).

SYNOPSIS: Five tourists become lost in a crypt. They find themselves locked in an underground chamber with a strange, elderly crypt keeper. One at a time, the crypt keeper analyzes his new guests, and shows them each a disturbing vision.

In the first vision ("And All Through the House"), a beautiful woman named Joanne murders her husband on Christmas Eve. As she disposes of his body, she hears a report on the radio that a psychotic maniac dressed as Santa Claus has escaped from a mental institution. Before long, this madman is knocking at Joanne's door. Joanne fights to keep the killer out, but her young daughter, believing the man to be Saint Nick, lets him in. Santa Claus kills Joanne, who has been very naughty this year…

Next up, the crypt keeper reveals a fantasy ("Reflection of Death") to a man named Maitland. Maitland has left his wife for his mistress. While out driving with his new lover, there is a terrible accident on the highway. For two long years, Maitland staggers about as a ghoul until he visits the apartment of his mistress. She's been blinded, and believes him dead. When he looks at the mirror, he sees that he is a monster. Suddenly, Maitland awakens from this nightmare to find himself back in the car with his mistress, just before the accident. Then the accident happens again.

Back at the crypt, the crypt keeper shows a wealthy young aristocrat, Jason, a vision of his life ("Poetic Justice"). This nasty man hates his neighbor, a lonely and meek widower named Grimsdyke. Jason causes Grimsdyke to lose his job, and then drives him to commit suicide on Valentine's Day by sending him a bundle of nasty Valentine cards. A year later, Grimsdyke rises from the grave on Valentine's Day, and sends Jason his own bloody valentine.

The crypt keeper next reveals a series of images to a man called Carter ("Wish You Were Here"). In this vision, Carter and his wife have gone bankrupt and are forced to sell their belongings. Together, the couple takes notice of an Oriental statue that bears a legend about three wishes. Carter's wife wishes for money, and Carter is promptly killed, allowing her to inherit his life-insurance money. Carter's wife wishes him back, but that wish goes wrong too, because Carter has already been embalmed...

Finally, the crypt keeper reveals a phantasm to Major Rogers, an uptight military man ("Blind Alleys"). Rogers becomes superintendent at the Elmridge Home of the Blind and sets out to cut costs by skimping on heat, blankets, and even food. When one of the sightless wards dies because of malnutrition and the cold, the blind men take action. They abduct Rogers and his brutal dog, and lock them in separate cages. Then, the blind men starve the dog for days, until it is literally starving to death. Finally, they release Rogers to walk a narrow passageway lined with razor blades. At the end of the gauntlet, Rogers' hungry dog waits to maul him. Desperate, Rogers is forced to run the wall of razor blades ... with bloody results.

Inside the crypt, the keeper informs his five guests that they may now leave. When they open the door, however, they discover that their destination is Hell. The crypt keeper reveals that his five visions are not their futures ... but their pasts. They are now leaving the crypt where those who have died without repentance must relive their sins...

COMMENTARY: Like *Asylum*, Amicus' *Tales from the Crypt* is an omnibus of horror stories, lumped together under an umbrella of unity. Here, the connection between the five tales is a crypt where tourists have (they believe) become lost. Based on the source material by Bill Gaines, three of the five stories are of the "comeuppance" variety where the scales of justice are righted. The stories are short and bloodily sweet, but only the final one, "Blind Alleys," remains memorable.

"And All Through the House" (later remade for the HBO series, with Larry Drake as the crazed Santa) is a fun story with some macabre touches. Director Francis contrasts the homicidal actions of Joan Collins with the holy, peaceful music associated with Christmas, and the irony is good for a few giggles. In her desire to clean up her crime, Collins also evokes a little bit of Lady Macbeth, attempting to cleanse her hands of spilled blood. Otherwise, its just routine "stalk'n'slash" as Collins is menaced by a murderous Santa Claus, and undone by her child ... who mistakes the killer for the real thing.

"Reflection of Fear" is the weakest story of the bunch. Ian Hendry stars as a man who has taken up with a mistress, and is consequently punished in two ways. First, he comes back to life as a monstrous ghoul after a car accident. Secondly, the accident, and his fate, seem to repeat. It's all handled in such a speedy, careless fashion that one can't tell if the accident is a flashback, a premonition, or part of an ongoing time loop. And, of all the characters in the film, Hendry seems to least deserve his fate. Sure, infidelity is bad, but does this guy really deserve to be tortured for eternity because of a decision to leave his wife? Murder of a spouse ("And All Through The House"), and exploitation of the poor ("Blind Alleys") are much worse abrogations of the human moral code.

Tales from the Crypt gets itself back on track in "Poetic Justice" as a nasty rich man victimizes kindly old Peter Cushing so as to sell his property and make money. This is the only story to really reach the viewer on an emotional level, as it is downright difficult to watch people being nasty to this kindly old man — a widower no less. When Grimsdyke (Cushing) finally commits suicide, the comeuppance begins, and his tormenter becomes the tormented. A bloody Valentine is delivered, and the perverse chill of the magazine is re-captured. It is fun seeing bad people punished in "poetic" ways, and by forging sympathy with Cushing's character, Francis tells this story effectively.

The fourth story, "Wish You Were Here," is a detour into ghoulish humor as a series of wishes go badly wrong. It is the kind of uninspired story one might see on *Tales from the Darkside*, *The Hitchhiker*, *Monsters* or any other low-grade TV anthology. Like "Reflection of Fear" it brings the film to a grinding halt.

Fortunately, momentum is revived with "Blind Alleys," another comeuppance story, but one that is, like "Poetic Justice," rather effective. Here, a nasty superintendent running a home for the blind skims money for himself by cutting back on heat, food, and other necessities. When a blind ward dies, the superintendent shows no remorse and the blind work together to teach him a lesson. In the end, he is forced to run an alleyway of razor blades to avoid the jaws of his own starving pet … a frightening climax. The most developed of the five stories, "Blind Alleys," culminates in a truly harrowing scene that has become legendary, as a wall of razor blades is confronted. This set piece gives the film a necessary lift to its climax.

Today, all of the *Tales from the Crypt* stories seem rather rudimentary, though "Poetic Justice," "Blind Alleys," and to a lesser degree "All Through the House," provoke a feeling of the creeps. The moral aspects of the film are a little dreary, and as an anthology this film is probably less cohesive than either *Asylum* or 1973's *From Beyond the Grave*. The crypt keeper sequences are flat, and don't contribute much of value to the film. In *Asylum*, there was a solid, dramatic reason to pay attention. Each new "patient" in the asylum was introduced so as to present information and clues about the identity of the mysterious Dr. Starr. Audiences wanted to know who he/she was, and so remained engaged in each succeeding tale.

In *From Beyond the Grave*, it is understood that each character is getting a comeuppance for some wrong done at a "haunted" antique store, as effect follows cause. However, the crypt keeper sequences in *Tales from the Crypt* are pretty purposeless … until the surprise ending. By the end, the reason these five people have been drawn together in Hell's alcove is quite clear, but you have to get to the climax (and five stories) to find out the answer. Also, *Tales from the Crypt* does not seem to build from story to story. There is a feeling of momentum in both *Asylum* and *From Beyond the Grave*, but "Reflection of Fear" and "Wish You Were Here" kill forward momentum, taking the anthology back to ground zero, and leaving the remaining stories to pick up the slack.

LEGACY: A sequel to *Tales from the Crypt* followed in 1973 entitled *Vault of Horror*. Though these films were mostly forgotten after the 1970s, the *Tales from the Crypt* property (including a far more decomposed, yet animated, crypt keeper) was re-imagined in the late '80s for the HBO TV series (1989–96) of the same name. The pilot episode of the new *Tales from the Crypt* was "And All Through the House," the initial story of the 1972 feature film.

Terror at Red Wolf Inn (1972) ✶ ✶ ✶ ½

Cast & Crew

CAST: Linda Gillin (Regina McKee); John Nielson (Baby John Smith); Arthur Space (Henry Smith); Mary Jackson (Evelyn "Evie" Smith); Janet Wood (Pamela); Margaret Avery (Edwina); Michael Macready (Jonathan the Deputy); Earl Parker (Paul the Pilot).

CREW: Manson International and International Releasing Corporation Presents *Terror at Red Wolf Inn*. *Production Manager:* Erik Nelson. *Art Director:* Mike Townsend. *Set Decoration and Props:* Elizabeth Nelson. *Chief Electrician:* Al York. *Key Grip:* Leo Behar. *Script Supervisor:* Patty Sue Townsend. *Sound Mixer:* Bruce Bisense. *Casting:* Sheila Manning. *Sound:* Ryder Sound Service. *Sound Effects:* Rich Harrison. *Titles and Opticals:* Modern Film Effects, Steve Orfanos. *Post-Production:* The Film Place. *Assistant to Producer:* Ted Petit. *Girl on the Set:* Nola. *Original Music:* Bill Marx. *Associate Producers:* Herb Ellis, Allen J. Actor. *Director of Photography:* John McNichol. *Film Editor:* Al Maguire. *Screenplay:* Allen J. Actor. *Produced by:* Michael Macready. *Directed by:* Bud Townsend. "*My Dream*" *lyrics Written and Sung by:* Marilynn Lovell. *M.P.A.A. Rating:* PG. *Running time:* 80 minutes.

SYNOPSIS: Regina, a young and naive college girl, returns to her dorm one afternoon to discover she has won a contest: a vacation to the remote resort called Red Wolf Inn. Without contacting anyone, even her mother, Regina takes a charter flight to her isolated destination. Upon landing near the resort, Regina is driven to the old Victorian bed and breakfast by "Baby" John Smith, grandson to Red Wolf Inn owners Henry, a former butcher, and Evelyn. There, Regina meets the other guests, the beautiful model Pamela, and friendly Edwina. When Regina tries to telephone her mother, she learns the phone is out of order. All thoughts of trouble are erased, however, when Henry and Evelyn serve a magnificent meal of ribs.

After the feast, Regina gets sleepy and goes to bed. Meanwhile, something strange seems to be happening with Baby John in the walk-in freezer…

The next morning, Pamela has disappeared without a trace, and Regina hears flies buzzing about an out-building. She discovers one of Pamela's dresses hanging there, but no sign of Pamela, who has apparently left. Regina eats lunch with Baby John and becomes attracted to him, if frightened by his violent side. When he catches a baby shark at the beach, he bludgeons it to death.

That night, Henry and Evelyn throw a party for Edwina on her last night at the resort. They all drink champagne and celebrate over another grand meal. After dinner, Edwina packs up to leave, and then sleeps. But, by dark of night, she is chloroformed by Evelyn and Henry, and carried down to the walk-in freezer … where she is chopped up.

Regina grows suspicious about Edwina's disappearance, and does not believe Evelyn's story that the young woman simply "left" without saying farewell. Suspecting something is amiss, Evelyn attempts to call home, but is prevented from using the repaired telephone by Evelyn. When the police arrive at Red Wolf Inn, Regina thinks she is safe, but the deputy is Baby John's brother, and in on the secret. Regina seeks help from John, but he is afraid to question his grandma's authority. Then, Regina makes a discovery: the decapitated heads of Edwina and Pamela in the freezer. Their bodies have been cut up, and served as meals! Terrified, Regina escapes the house, but is re-captured.

Evelyn and Henry prepare a party for Regina's "last night" at the resort, but Baby John has fallen in love with the visitor, and does not want to eat her. Baby John frees Regina, and they attempt escape, Henry and Evelyn in hot pursuit. There is a final confrontation in the Red Wolf greenhouse, and Baby John kills his grandparents with a meat cleaver.

Sometime later, Regina and Baby John, happily married, have resumed Evelyn and Henry's bizarre culinary habits...

COMMENTARY: The Australian-made *Terror at Red-Wolf Inn* is a scrumptious dessert, a tasty slice of cannibal horror. In the 1970s, the culinary appetites of cannibals were the subject of a variety of notable horror films, including *The Texas Chainsaw Massacre* (1974), *Shriek of the Mutilated* (1974), and Wes Craven's *The Hills Have Eyes. Terror at Red Wolf Inn* is a variation on the themes explored in those films, but the cannibal set is depicted here with a heightened sense of irony, and even fun. In *Red Wolf Inn*, a college girl is tormented by two smiling, senior citizen cannibals who not only run a bed and breakfast, but who want to eat her for dinner. Unlike The *Texas Chainsaw Massacre* or *The Hills Have Eyes, Terror at Red Wolf Inn* offers a light, almost tongue-in-cheek approach to the gruesome material. Though there are chases and moments of high suspense, the feeling of relentless madness so successfully generated in those other memorable pictures is forsaken in favor of a deep, rewarding sense of irony, and a commendable thematic focus on the underlying subject. *In Terror at Red Wolf Inn,* the impulse beneath cannibalism is considered. Specifically, the film deals with appetites and addictions, and how they become unhealthy if carried to extremes.

In fashioning this cinematic banquet, director Bud Townsend focuses repetitively on the meals served at the Red Wolf Inn. Henry and Evelyn constantly talk about eating, and the camera emphasizes close-ups of food in all its succulent forms, whether they be meat, vegetables or starches. It is impossible not to note how central a concern "eating" is in this group, thanks to Townsend's insistence on showing actors shoveling food into their mouths and smacking their lips. It is an opera of chewing and crunching rapture, almost a sexual orgasm, as the cast of characters fill their cheeks, masticate, sigh, and pause to fill up on drink.

The point is made explicitly through these "dining" montages that humans get hungry, and sate that appetite by eating ... sometimes too much. This is important because one gets the sense that Henry and Evelyn, despite their peculiar pastime, are not bad people. They have just let their appetites get the better of them. The scene is further heightened by the director's choice of music. "Pomp and Circumstance" plays on the soundtrack during one gluttonous meal, and the ironic implication is that the characters have "graduated" beyond normal tastes and desires, into the realm of the truly dangerous.

The link between food and other human appetites is a running motif in *Terror at Red Wolf Inn.* For instance, when Regina dreams of being "with" Baby John in a sexual sense, food is again called up as the explicit signifier of appetite. In her phantasm, Regina envisions herself making love to John, and then, importantly, stuffing her face with a delicious cake. The desire to fulfill an appetite, to be gluttonous, is the same, *Terror at Red Wolf Inn* tells us, whether in the arena of sex or eating.

The film is about the feelings and desires we crave as humans, whether they be acceptable (as sex often is not), or unacceptable. Some people eat till it is unhealthy, and are actually addicted to food. Some people enjoy sex too much, and become promiscuous sex-aholics who put themselves in danger with their needs. This film equates those impulses to Evelyn and Henry's appetite to eat human flesh. Regina's dream forecasts her own lack of control, and at the end of the film she gives into her appetites, not only taking John sexually, but becoming a cannibal just like the rest of his family.

It is not an exaggeration to state that everything in *Terror at Red Wolf Inn* is geared towards food. As soon as one understands that fact, and makes the connection between the desire to eat, and what is actually being eaten, it is possible to really enjoy this bizarre, off-beat look at an addiction that is ... outside the mainstream. Every line is fraught with double meanings, considering that the Red Wolf Inn menu consists of human flesh. "Wait till you see what we have for breakfast," Evelyn enthuses. "Eat some lunch, it's your last day," she insists cheerfully, and the audience realize it really will be Regina's last day … of life. "This is choice, Grade A," Henry states of the lovely and succulent Edwina. And so on. It's all rather funny, and the end credits finally tread outright into humor, presenting the names of the cast and crew as though they were items on the Red Wolf Inn Menu. The film even closes with a line on that menu: "We Reserve the Right to Serve *Anyone*," and it might as well be the picture's ad line.

Like the crazed family in Tobe Hooper's *The Texas Chainsaw Massacre*, the cannibals in this film see their "victims" as delicious meals, not people. Trying to reason with them is like talking to a wall. They aren't going to change, and they just want to eat you. You are no more than a cow, a chicken, or any other livestock.

And that is why *Terror at Red Wolf Inn*

is scary as well as funny. It is a basic human fear to be eaten. In *Hansel and Gretel*, children fear being "fattened up" and deposited in the witch's oven to be devoured. In *Jaws*, the fear of the shark is coupled with the fear of being eaten alive by another living creature. *Terror of Red Wolf Inn* understands just how frightening it is to be viewed as "meat" by another being. Since Regina is isolated, all alone in remote Australia, there is no help for her, and the film becomes a deadly game she must escape lest she end up on a platter. *Terror at Red Wolf Inn* is not deeply scary, as are *The Texas Chainsaw Massacre* and *The Hills Have Eyes*, but it is notably suspenseful and fun, a more palatable look at cannibalism, one might even say. Savor it!

LEGACY: The initial set-up of *Terror at Red Wolf Inn*, a college girl lured to a remote vacation spot with a ruse that she has "won a contest," was repeated in 1998's *I Still Know What You Did Last Summer*.

The Thing with Two Heads (1972) ★ ★ ½

Cast & Crew

CAST: Ray Milland (Dr. Max Kirshner); Rosey Grier (Jack Moss); Don Marshall (Dr. Fred Williams); Roger Perry (Dr. Phillip Desmond); Kathy Baumann (Patricia); John Dullaghan (Thomas); John Bliss (Donald); Chelsea Brown (Lila); Bruce Kimball (Police Lieutenant); Jane Kellem (Miss Mullen); Lee Frost (Sgt. Hacker); Wes Bishop (dr. Smith); Roger Gentry (Police Sergeant); Britt Nilsson (Nurse); Rick Baker (Gorilla); Phil Hoover (Policeman); Rod Stecle (Medical Salesman); Michael Viner (Prison Guard);.

CREW: American International Pictures and Samuel Z. Arkoff Present a Saber Production of Rosey Grier and Ray Milland as *The Thing with Two Heads*. *Production Supervisor:* Ed Forsyth. *Post-Production Sound Supervisor:* Edward Schryver. *Production Manager:* Roger Gentry.

Key Grip: Jerry Deats. *Cinematographer:* Jack Steely, Chuck Minsky, Edward Schryver. *Assistant to Producer:* Fred Nyquist. *Production Sound:* Clark Will. *Medical Advisors:* Dr. Cadvan Griffiths, Rod Steele. *Optical Effects and Titles:* Modern Film Effects. *Re-recording Mixer:* George Porter. *Sound:* Ryder. *Prints:* DeLuxe. Vehicles Courtesy of Chrysler Corporation. *Music Produced and Supervised by:* Michael Viner. *Music score by:* Robert D. Ragland. *"The Thing Theme/Police chase"* Composed and Performed by: Porter Jordan. *Additional Music Composed and Performed by:* David Angel and Peter Jordan. *Screenplay:* Lee Frost, Wes Bishop, James Gordon White. *Story by:* Lee Frost, Wes Bishop. *Executive Producer:* John Lawrence. *Produced by:* Wes Bishop. *Directed by:* Lee Frost. *With Thanks to friends:* William Smith, Jerry Butler, George E. Carey, Tommy Cook, Albert Zugsmith, Dick Whittington. *Mr.*

Milland's and Mr. Grier's heads re-created by: Dan Striepeke, Gail Brown, Tom Burman, Charles Schram, James White, Pete Peterson. *M.P.A.A. Rating:* PG. *Running time:* 90 minutes.

SYNOPSIS: Dr. Max Kirshner, an expert in transplants, is dying. But instead of going calmly into that good night, Max develops a revolutionary method to transplant a head onto another creature's body. His guinea pig is a gorilla that now has two heads. Eventually, the original head will be removed, leaving a new head to control the original organism's "appropriated" body. Unfortunately, the gorilla breaks free during an operation, flees Kirshner's laboratory, and attacks patrons in a grocery store. It is re-captured and the experiment is successfully completed.

At the Kirshner institute, Dr. Kirshner — a racist and a bigot — is dismayed to learn that a new doctor on his staff, Williams, is African-American. He attempts to fire Williams because of his skin color, but Williams holds him to their legally binding contract and stays on staff. Meanwhile, Kirshner's condition worsens and he grows desperate to survive. Unwilling to let his "genius" die, Max requires a human donor, someone with a healthy body, so his head can be transplanted to it.

Dr. Desmond, Kirshner's friend and associate, arranges with a prison warden to allow a death row convict to donate his body to science for this very cause. Jack Moss, a man sentenced to die for a crime he did not commit, volunteers for the procedure in hopes of gaining extra time to prove his innocence. Moss is transported from prison to Kirshner's private lab. The only hitch is that Jack Moss is black … and Kirshner hates all blacks. Still, there is no time for such matters because Max is dying.

The operation is conducted, and when Kirshner awakes, he is horrified to learn that his white head has been transplanted onto a black man's body. Jack awakens and is equally displeased to be joined with the big-

oted Kirshner. Jack (with Max's head attached to his shoulders…) escapes from the laboratory and demands that Dr. Williams drive him to safety so he can prove his innocence to the world. Williams complies and the police chase the "thing with two heads." The authorities set up a roadblock, but Jack evades it. Moss and Williams run across a dirt bike race, steal a bike, and continue to evade police in an incredible demolition derby of police cars.

Jack and Williams then hide out at Jack's girlfriend's apartment, even as Max complains. Lila has trouble coping with Jack's extra head, and Max slowly starts to gain control of Moss's body. When Williams takes Jack to a hospital where he can amputate Max's head, Max finally asserts control over Jack's body and plans to do the surgery to rid the world of Moss. Lila and Williams save Jack at the last moment, and amputate Max's head. While Williams, Lila and Jack flee for freedom, Max demands that Desmond find him another body…

COMMENTARY: *The Thing with Two Heads* is a cult classic simply because of its ridiculous premise, which one-ups the formula of *The Defiant Ones* by attaching a white man's head to a black man's body. Yet much of the enjoyment of the film is the contemplation of that premise itself, and not the execution of the concept. This is a film that should be outrageously funny, and pointed in its societal satire, but which settles instead for car chases and dopey cop humor. The film's trailer is actually more entertaining than the movie, as Grier and Milland trade racist barbs and put-downs in rapid-fire succession. That same material is spread pretty thin through the actual movie, and the film consequently emerges as a squandered opportunity.

In fairness, *The Thing with Two Heads* actually has some real promise. This is the "Frankenstein" story that 1973's *Blackenstein* wishes it could have been. The white man (with his science gone awry) experiments on the black man, thus making for a pretty clear allegory of white exploitation of black culture. After all, *The Thing with Two Heads* is a literalization of the notion that the white man has been on the black man's back for a long time. No longer content merely to wipe out African-American identity, culture and economic fortune, white America now hopes to sap the very physical strength of the black man! White society has punished a black man (Jake) for a crime he didn't commit, and so now plans to "enslave" his very body under the direction of a white master, Kirshner. That plot line, picking up on the racial divides of the 1970s, opens up all kinds of humorous and satirical possibilities on any number of fronts. The only way it would work better is if Archie Bunker's head had been put on George Jefferson's body (now there's an idea for a sitcom...).

Yet the film doesn't live up to this promise. After a tense and ugly early scene in which Kirshner attempts to fire Williams because of his skin color, the race card is played merely as a tongue-in-cheek joke with toothless references to eating "watermelons" and singing "spirituals." Ultimately, Kirshner learns nothing from his experience perched atop Jack's body, and in the end, Jack doesn't even win back his good name in the eyes of the American people or the law. The film simply ends when white and black are again segregated back to their individual bodies. The law has not been corrected, and racism has not been addressed in any significant way. And, though the film has a few funny lines, it doesn't have nearly enough humor to make the trip worthwhile. Still, one has to giggle at Lila's opening line to Jack (with friend Max attached): "I know you don't like to answer a lot of questions ... but how did this happen?"

The Thing with Two Heads has some convincing special effects and make-up for the 1970s, an impressive, if deeply silly, car chase, and some likable performers, but it never takes the final step and actually explores its premise. It would rather distract the audience with humorous doubletakes than address what it means for white and black to be together in one body. This is one of those movies that would be more fun to read about than to actually watch. On the page, it sounds incredibly funny, but on the screen it's ho-hum, despite the occasional outrageous bits of dialogue (such as Milland's notation to his friend that a particular skull is "not the gorilla's original head...."). Imagine for a moment that this film was remade today with Jim Carrey's head on Martin Lawrence's body, with Spike Lee directing the affair. Now *that* would be a thing (with two heads...) to see!

Three on a Meathook

CAST: Charles Kissinger, James Pickett, Sherry Steiner.

CREW: *Written and Directed by:* William Girdler. *Produced by:* John Asman, Joseph Shulten. *Director of Photography:* William L. Asman. *Film Editor:* Henry Asman. *Music:* William Girdler. *M.P.A.A. Rating:* R. *Running Time:* 80 minutes.

DETAILS: William Girdler meets *The Texas Chainsaw Massacre* in this underlit, gory variation of the Ed Gein crimes. Girdler star Kissinger (*Asylum of Satan* [1971]) is the leader of a barbaric clan that kidnaps and tortures women. Not as charming as its title indicates.

Tombs of the Blind Dead (1972) * * *
(La Noche del Terror Ciego)

Cast & Crew

CAST: Lone Fleming, Cesar Burner, Helen Harp, Joseph Thelman, Rufino Ingles, Veronic Llimera, Simon Arriaga, Francisco Sanz, Juan Cortes, Andres Speizer, Antonio Orengo, Jose Camoiras, Maria Silva.

CREW: Una coproduccion Hispano-Portuguesa. Plata Films S.A.—Madrid and Interfilme—Lisboa. *Art Direction:* Paulino Gonzalez, Rafael Ablanque. *Camera:* Luis Alcolea, Felix Miron. *Special Effects:* Jose Gomes Soria. *Sound Effects:* Luis Castro. *Set Decorator:* Juan Garcia. *Director of Photography:* Pablo Ripoli. *Music:* Anton Garcia Abril. *Executive Producer:* Salvador Romero. *Producer:* Jose A. Perez. *Director:* Amando De Ossorio.

SYNOPSIS: In Lisbon, two old friends, Betty and Virginia, are unexpectedly reacquainted at a pool near the beach. Virginia's friend Roger suggests they all go camping together, and the next day, they board a train. Virginia is troubled, however, because of an adolescent sexual flirtation she once had with Betty. Disturbed by the memories, as well as Roger's attraction to Betty, Virginia jumps off the train at a remote spot, the deserted village of Berzano.

Alone in the isolated, rural area, Virginia happens upon the ruins of a monastery and graveyard. She spends the night there, unaware it is a hotbed of local legend. Berzano is believed to be haunted by excommunicated Knights Templar who worshipped the devil. Their eyes plucked out by crows, these immortal, bloodsucking zombies roam the countryside by horseback, seeking new victims. Unfortunately for Virginia, the legend is true, and she is chased and attacked by ambulatory, bony corpses on horseback. She flees for the train tracks, but dies just short of them, even as daylight comes.

Meanwhile, Roger and Betty feel guilty about leaving Virginia behind. They hear the story of Berzano, and ride there to find Virginia. When they arrive at the ruins, a policeman tells them that Virginia has been found dead. They go to the morgue to identify her body and the coroner reports that Virginia was tortured and set upon by at least a dozen animals … or something *animal-like*. Later, Virginia's corpse stirs in the morgue, attacks an attendant, and drinks his blood.

Roger and Betty visit Professor Cantal at a library, and he tells them more about the Templars and their black magic. In the 13th century, Berzano was the seat of a Templar hierarchy. Now, their evil lives by night. Contrarily, the police suggest the Templar myth is really just a cover for Cantal's son, a small-time thief named Pedro, to cloak his illegal activities. Betty and Roger resolve to meet with Pedro, and learn if he is responsible for Virginia's death. At the same time, the re-animated Virginia heads to the mannequin shop where Betty works. She attacks Betty's co-worker, but is set ablaze and killed.

After meeting Pedro and his girlfriend, a hot-to-trot sort, Betty and Roger ask them to join them in Berzano to assess the truth of the legend. They spend the night in the ruins, and Pedro's moll makes a play for Roger, even as Pedro rapes Betty, an avowed lesbian. Midnight then arrives, and so do the Templars. They kill Pedro first, drinking his blood hungrily. Then they attack Robert, chopping off his arm and killing him. Next they descend upon Pedro's girlfriend, leaving Betty the sole survivor. She runs for her life, and makes for a passing train. The train stops to rescue her, and the Templars follow her on board, killing all the engineers and passengers.

A shell-shocked Betty survives the terror as a train crowded with the cannibal zombies pulls into a populated station. She screams in terror as the Templars attack, her hair now a stark shade of gray....

COMMENTARY: George Romero's *Night of the Living Dead* (1968) was so inspired an initiative that its undead ethos informed a whole generation of zombie imitators, some of them quite good. In one way or another, *The Omega Man* (1971), *Children Shouldn't Play with Dead Things* (1972), *The Return of Count Yorga* (1972), *Zombie* (1979), and even Romero's own *The Crazies* (1973) owe something to the power of his seminal zombie film. Likewise for *Tombs of the Blind Dead*, a stylish and successful horror picture that takes Romero's prototype as its template and then moves confidently into new, creepy terrain. Though spartan in dialogue and even logic, the film remains a masterpiece of visual horror, and its climax is a riveting, frightening one.

In *Night of the Living Dead*, nobody understands exactly why the dead return to life (though there is the media's explanation of the Venus probe explosion and ensuing radiation). In *Tombs of the Blind Dead*, there is the faintest suggestion of a strange reason behind the Templar terror: *passion*. All of the characters in the film boast barely contained passions that threaten to get out of control. Everybody wants to have sex with everybody else. Betty is interested in Virginia. Virginia is interested in Roger. Pedro rapes Betty, and so forth. Even the Templars are sexual creatures in their own way: sucking, lapping and biting their victims. Each character is defined in terms of sexuality, and one has to wonder if it is this barely contained passion that causes the world to spiral out of control ... as if in response to the hidden desires of the population. If one looks at the construct of the film, the Templars seem to attack when provoked by passion. Virginia, alone in the ruins, is one object of passion, and is killed. Later, Pedro rapes Betty, and the Templars strike again, murdering Pedro. It seems that

in this world, sexual desire and aggression lead to attack, and destruction. That's not an uncommon conceit for horror movies, considering the "sex = death" equation of most 1980s slasher films, but it is interesting here as something of an undercurrent.

The idea of co-mingling sexuality, sadism, cannibalism, and vampirism is nowhere more obvious in *Tombs of the Blind Dead* than in the flashback to the Templar immortality ritual. Their swords cut up a female sacrifice in a truly bloody scene, and Templars then drink her blood. They suck and nurse on her body, a hungry mob, and this is clearly a gross metaphor for some demented sexuality.

The characters are also defined almost entirely in terms of sex. Virginia once had a sexual flirtation with Betty during adolescence. Roger is "with" Virginia but is interested in Betty. Betty identifies herself as a lesbian who has "never been interested in men" because of a "bad experience" in childhood. Pedro, of course, is a rapist, and his girlfriend affirms that she likes "rough men" just as the blind dead arrive to devour her.

In conjunction with all the sexual tension, this material is also highly effective as horror. The Templars, arriving in the dead city on horseback, are photographed in slow motion. The slow motion extends the terror, and heightens the suspense of the chase, yet the climax is probably the most frightening (and best orchestrated moment). Since the Templars are blind, they can only detect victims by sound. As Betty tries to hide from them, she is betrayed by the beating of her own heart, and the monsters detect her. From there, it is an anxiety-provoking race to a passing train, and an unexpected twist as the Templars leave their necropolis, board the vehicle, and massacre all of the passengers! This unexpected blood bath is followed by a series of "still photos" (freeze-frames), a touch right out of *Night of the Living Dead*.

Tombs of the Blind Dead plays on a lot of effective horror tropes, including the trip gone awry, a "scare" scene involving mannequins, and, of course, hungry zombies. Yet what separates this film from the rest of the ghoul pack is its visual aplomb. After a great first act, the film loses some momentum, but the Templars are genuinely scary. They are slow moving all right, but those bony, decayed hands are going to reach out and grab you, and even your heartbeat could give you away. That's quite an effective image, and this film makes the most of it, while also making some odd commentary about human passions.

Twins of Evil

Cast & Crew

CAST: Peter Cushing (Gustav Weil); Harvey Hall (Franz); Alex Scott (Herman); Frieda Gellhorn (Madelaine Collinson); Maria Gellhorn (Mary Collinson); Katya Wyeth (Kathleen Byron/Mircalla); Roy Stewart (Joachim); Luan Peters (Gerta); Damien Thomas (Count Karnstein); Dennis Price (Dietrich).

CREW: *Produced by:* Harry Fine, Michael Style. *Written by:* Tudor Gates. *Based on Characters Created by:* J. Sheridan Le Fanu. *Director of Photography:* Dick Bush. *Directed by:* John Hough. *Music Conducted and Composed by:* Harry Robinson. *Editor:* Spencer Reeve. *M.P.A.A Rating:* R. *Running Time:* 85 minutes.

DETAILS: This is the final movement in the Carmilla/Mircalla cycle initiated by *The Vampire Lovers* (1970) and *Lust for a Vampire* (1970). Set in the 19th century, it's the story of a witchhunter (Cushing) who must save the souls of two lovely damsels (The Gellhorn twins, models in real life). As might be expected, there is plenty of nudity and lesbian overtones to go around, but disappointingly, no Ingrid Pitt!

Westworld (1972) * * *

Critical Reception

"The movie's Orwellian idea has real possibilities, but writer Michael Crichton ... who also does the directing, falls back on the primitive humor of Benjamin as sissy-coward and the tired old cliché of the Revolt of the Machines. The scenario begs for daring, but even in Roman World the orgiasts keep their togas on. What's the point of fantasy if it's rated PG?"— Paul D. Zimmerman, *Newsweek*: "Draw, Robot!" December 10, 1973, page 135.

"...moderately entertaining ... its major disadvantage is that Crichton's idea is—potentially—too ingenious for what he was able to do with it ... you can see that everything has been skimped and that the idea isn't fully developed."— Pauline Kael, *New Yorker*, November 26, 1973, page 183.

Cast & Crew

CAST: Yul Brynner (Gunslinger); Richard Benjamin (Peter Morton); James Brolin (John Blane); Norman Bartold (Medieval Knight); Victoria Shaw (Medieval Queen); Dick Van Patten (Banker); Linda Scott (Arielle); Steve Franken (Technician); Michael Mikler (Black

Knight); Terry Wilson (Sheriff); Majel Barrett (Miss Carrie); Anne Randall (Servant Girl); Julie Marcus (Girl in Dungeon); Anne Bellamy (Middle Aged Woman); Chris Holter (Stewardess); Charles Seel (Bellhop); Wade Crosby (Bartender); Nora Marlowe (Hostess); Lin Henson (Ticket Girl); Orville Shennan, Lindsey Workman, Lauren Gilbert, David Roberts, Howard Platt (Supervisors); Richard Roat, Jared Martin, David Frank, David Man, Kenneth Washington, Robert Patten, Kip King, Larry Delaney (Technicians); Will J. White, Ben Young, Tom Falk (Workmen).

CREW: Metro-Goldwyn-Mayer Presents *Westworld. Produced by:* Paul N. Lazarus III. *Written and directed by:* Michael Crichton. *Music:* Fred Karlin. *Director of Photography:* Gene Polito. *Art Director:* Herman Blumenthal. *Camera Operator:* Joseph August. *Set Decorator:* John Austin. *Property Master:* Arthur Friedrich. *Special Effects:* Charles Schulthies. *Filmed in:* Panavision and Metrocolor. *Film Editor:* David Bretherton. *Associate Producer:* Michael I. Rachmil. *Unit Production Manager and Assistant Director:* Claude Binyon Jr. *Second Assistant Director:* James Boyle. *Sound:* Richard Church, Harry W. Tetrick. *Make-up:* Frank Griffin, Irving Pringle. *Wardrobe:* Richard Bruono, Betsy Cox. *Hairdresser:* Dione Taylor. *Visual Effects Coordinator:* Brent Sellstrom. *Casting:* Leonard Murphy. *Roman World Sequences Filmed at:* Harold Lloyd Estate, Beverly Hills, California. *Action Sequences Coordinated by:* Dick Ziker. *Automated Image Processing:* Information International Inc., John Whitney, Jr. *Presented by:* MGM. *M.P.A.A. Rating:* PG. *Running time:* 90 minutes.

SYNOPSIS: Delos is the amusement park of the future, a realm where rich vacationers can play, love and even "kill" in three robot-populated arenas based on historical epochs: Medieval World, Roman World and Westworld.

A futuristic hovercraft transports a boatload of vacationers to Delos, including Peter and John, two fellas bound for Westworld. Upon arrival at the park depot, Delos employees provide them with cowboy hats, boots, holsters, guns, and all the accouterments of the lawless American frontier of the 1880s. Once inside Westworld, Peter finds the robot humanoids remarkable, and the setting incredibly accurate ... even a little uncomfortable. At the bar, Peter is challenged by a black-garbed gunslinger. In a shoot-out, Peter is victorious, and the vanquished android gunslinger gets dragged away, presumably for repair by Delos personnel.

Later, Peter and John enjoy themselves with robot prostitutes. While the resort sleeps, the town scenario is "re-set" by technicians and workers, and even cleaned by park janitors. Unbeknownst to the guests, Delos scientists, operating under the park in a vast computerized vault, are growing concerned because of an increase in robot breakdowns.

The next morning, the black-garbed gunslinger android returns to kill John, but Peter shoots him dead again ... and is promptly incarcerated in the Westworld jail for murder. John breaks Peter out of prison, and shoots the sheriff during the escape attempt. Consequently, the two men play at being desperados, and ride off into a nearby canyon. There, John is bitten by an android rattlesnake, an indication that something is wrong since none of the robot automatons are supposed to be able to hurt "real" people in Delos.

Scientists manning the park are warned that they are seeing central mechanism "psychosis," a very disturbing sign, but they agree not to close the park until the current guests have completed their vacations and gotten their money's worth.

A more devastating breakdown occurs in Medieval World when the Black Knight, another robot, skewers a human guest. Back in Westworld, the black-garbed gunslinger confronts Peter and John on the streets, resurrected once more, and shoots Peter dead with live bullets. The gunslinger, now augmented with infra-red vision and ultrapowerful hearing mechanisms, chases Peter out of town.

Peter flees Westworld for the canyons beyond, and finally makes it to Roman

World. He finds a culvert there that leads down into the scientific underbelly of the amusement park. Inside, Peter finds the scientist operators dead: asphyxiated in their hermetically sealed, temperature-controlled computer vault! With the robot gunslinger still in hot pursuit, Peter tries throwing acid in the thing's face. This has virtually no effect, and Peter is forced to run for his life to Medieval World. There, he is able to use the royal banquet hall's fiery torches to fool the gunslinger's infrared sensors. Using a torch, Peter sets the gunslinger aflame. Charred and blackened, the vengeful machine keeps coming for Peter, seemingly unstoppable…

COMMENTARY: Though *Westworld* is set in a futuristic amusement park, the picture is all horror, rather than science fiction. At its core, it is the story of a chase, of a man being pursued by an unstoppable, inhuman opponent. That's the stuff of nightmares (and the horror genre), but there is much more to appreciate in the film than its "invincible" enemy antagonist. The film is also a prototype of two future mega hits in the genre, *The Terminator* (1984) and *Jurassic Park* (1993). Yet the historical view of *Westworld*, in the end, may not be as important as what the film reveals about mankind as a species.

Taking the notion of Disneyland's animatronic robots one step beyond contemporary reality (as *The Stepford Wives* [1975] later would, also for purposes of satire and social commentary), *Westworld*'s central action piece is a sustained, relentless pursuit. Yul Brynner's silver-eyed, menacing gunslinger pursues Richard Benjamin's Peter from venue to venue, unstoppable, and bent on murder … even revenge. Cleverly, this chase occurs only after the strength and adaptability of the technological villain has been thoroughly established. Brynner, so effective here, creates an iconic villain, an unstoppable machine with no mercy. Mankind has built him, but he sees better than

humans, reacts faster, and has the mind of computer. He is the walking, talking embodiment of man's technology out of control. Yes, my friends, science has gone awry.

The film also makes an interesting point by featuring not only a black gunslinger in Westworld, but a black knight in Medieval World. The message is implicit: in every historical time period there is an "evil" for man to beat. Even in his own entertainment constructs there must always be a "bad" guy for man to vanquish.

In positing the notion of a merciless, unstoppable robot, *Westworld* forecasts *The Terminator*, a 1984 film by James Cameron. Like Arnold Schwarzenneger's Terminator, *Westworld*'s android is equipped with a false "human" face that starts to peel off after sustained battle. Like the Terminator, this android is ultimately consumed with flames, burning away the illusion that he is "like" the men that surround him. And, like his cinematic cousin, the gunslinger ultimately emerges from the flames with no face — only machinery — for one last scare. At that point, the illusion is gone, and the villain boldly represents technology, not man. Of course the idea of unstoppable terror is universal (witness the success of Michael Myers in the *Halloween* franchise!), but it is important to note that both the terminator and the gunslinger represent man's machines gone awry and turned back against him. Even the casting of a "star" in the role of emotionless, pitiless robot villain is carried over in *The Terminator*. The charisma of a Brynner or a Schwarzenneger is sublimated in the protocol of machines.

Yet, truly, *Westworld* has as much in common with Crichton's own *Jurassic Park* as it does *The Terminator*. It is clear that Crichton finds fascination with the ideas of amusement parks (whether it be Jurasssic Park or Westworld) breaking down, and threatening the very vacationers it is supposed to welcome. But, the similarities go beyond identical premises. A voiceover on the hovercraft, describing the creation of Westworld, states that "no expense was spared." This *exact phrase* is repeated in *Jurassic Park*, as park creator Hammond (Richard Attenborough) describes the work that went into that amusement center. What's that about?

Even beyond that specific dialogue, the stories are structured in similar fashion. In both films, the park control center is ruined and the scientists who might stop the horror are killed before they can be of help. The progenitors of the terror are thus the first to die. In both stories, the park is a vast area, featuring diverse, geographically separated attractions. In *Westworld*, these various places (which provide for action set pieces) are Roman World, Medieval World, and Westworld. In *Jurassic Park*, these attractions are T-Rex paddocks, velociraptor paddocks, and the like.

Also, there are "instructional" videos in each film, describing the layout of the park, and the methods by which the attractions have been created. Clearly, *Jurassic Park* is different only in that it substitutes on-the-loose dinosaurs for on-the-loose robots.

Yet, of the two films, *Westworld* is ultimately the richer, because there is a succinct point to all the violent mayhem. Though *Jurassic Park* warns that man should not be arrogant and use his technology to recklessly bring dinosaurs into the 20th century, *Westworld* has a more radical message about humanity. What does it say about mankind that his idea of recreation includes murder? "Killing" robots (not unlike shooting down human-like images in first-person-shooter-style video games...) has become a form of entertainment. It is a sport, a recreation, and relaxation. The androids in the film exist solely to be killed, to be exploited by mankind. Is it any wonder that these "new"-style slaves ultimately revolt against their masters? Consider also that in addition to murdering androids, the vacationers at Delos also engage in sexual relations with the androids. They are mechanical prostitutes,

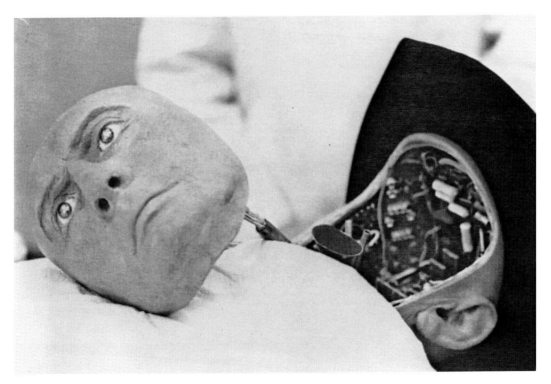

Technology is the new face of terror: The gunslinger's mechanical innards are revealed in *Westworld* (1972).

given no opportunity to choose or reject which "john" they sleep with. Is it any wonder that the park's central mechanism undergoes "psychosis" after this kind of ritual exploitation and abuse?

And what is man's response to an environment where he can kill, and have sex indiscriminately, and not worry about the rights or feelings of slaves? Peter states that he feels like a "real man" for the first time. That's a very disturbing thought, and the 1970s were the era in which the "macho man" was vying for superiority with the intellectual, sensitive man of the hippie era. Peter clearly feels inferior to John (Brolin) in the film, because he is not that macho stereotype. When he kills, he feels vindicated, alive. So *Westworld* indicates that what makes us feel good as people (and as males) is hurting and controlling others.

There are other nice touches in *Westworld* that give the film the aura of reality. Dick Van Patten plays an incompetent vacationer. He is slow at the "quick draw," but nonetheless finds success in this user-friendly tourist trap. His presence captures the notion of "regular folks" out of their element, on vacation. He's responsible to no one for his own inadequacies and coddled by a corporation that has been well paid to provide him a fantasy and illusion.

Also, Crichton pauses the main action to reveal the inner workings of the park in a terrific (and surreal) sequence set at night, in which Delos employees (dressed in blue jumpsuits) thoughtlessly carry out robot corpses (to be repaired and returned to the arena). Mass killing has become just a hassle then, a thing to be cleaned up.

Westworld is a fast-paced, action-packed look at an environment that is designed to appeal to the worst in human nature. On the surface is the false reality of Westworld, and underneath is the inner working of that world — the technology and effort necessary to maintain the park and allow the humans to keep whoring, killing, and sating other base appetites. That's a highly workable premise, and when Yul Brynner, a slave to human vanity, finally stands up and refuses to take it anymore, the film kicks into horror gear, and the message is plain. What man has forged to serve him will dominate him unless stopped, or, conversely, treated with common decency.

LEGACY: A sequel, *Futureworld*, premiered in 1976, with Peter Fonda assuming Richard Benjamin's role. In 1980, a TV series starring Connie Selleca, *Beyond Westworld*, saw the murderous androids return for three episodes ... before a hasty cancellation. *Westworld* is being re-made for a 2003 release with Arnold Schwarzenneger in the Yul Brynner role.

1973

And Now the Screaming Starts

Cast & Crew

CAST: Peter Cushing (Dr. Pope); Herbert Lom (Henry Fengriffen); Ian Ogilvy (Charles Fengriffen); Stephanie Beacham (Catherine Fengriffen); Patrick Magee (Dr. Whittle); Guy Rolfe (Maitland).

CREW: *Directed by:* Roy Ward Baker. *Produced by:* Max. J. Rosenberg, Milton Subotsky. *Executive Producer:* Gustav Berne. *Written by:*

Roger Marshall. *Director of Photography:* Denys Coop. *Film Editor:* Peter Tanner. From Amicus. *M.P.A.A. Rating:* PG. *Running Time:* 91 minutes.

DETAILS: This Amicus film revives the old "evil severed hand" horror cliché, satirized in modern fare such as *Evil Dead II: Dead by Dawn* (1987) and *Idle Hands* (1999). Peter Cushing leads an all-star British cast in this gothic story of a severed limb killing "cursed" denizens of the House of Fengriffen.

Blackenstein: The Black Frankenstein (1973) ⋆ ½

Cast & Crew

CAST: John Hart (Dr. Stein); Ivory Stone (Dr. Winifred Walker); Liz Renay (Woman in Bed); Roosevelt Jackson (Malcolm); Andrea King (Eleanor); Nick Bolin (Bruno Strager); Joe De Sue (Eddie Turner/ The Monster); Jim Cousar (Police Sgt. Jackson); Bob Brophy (Hospital Attendant); Beverly Hagerty (Girl in Car); Dale E. Bach (Girl in Dune buggy); Cardella De Milo (Night Club Singer); Andy E (Night Club Comedian); Daniel Faure (Boy in Car); Don Bodie (Police Lt. Turner); Jerry Soucie (Man in Bed); Karen Lind (Hospital Supervisor); Yvonne Robinson (Hospital Receptionist); Robert L. Hurd, Maria Farmer (Couple in Car).

CREW: Frank R. Saletri Presents *Blackenstein*. *Executive Producer:* Ted Tetrick. *Director of Photography:* Robert Caramico. *Music:* Cardella De Milo, Lou Frohman. *Written and Produced by:* Frank R. Saletri. *Directed by:* William A. Levey. *Production Manager:* F.A. Miller. *Assistant Director:* Paul Heslin. *Second Assistant Director:* Don Goldman. *Assistant to Producer:* Don Brodie. *Film Editor:* Bill Levey. *Assistant Editor:* M. Indergand. *Assistant Cameraman:* Bob Isenberg. *Production Sound:* Dick Damon. *Script Supervisor:* Judy Redland. *Boom Man:* Ray Hill. *Property Master:* Bud Costello. *Gaffer:* Larry Lapoint. *Key Grip:* Earl Tunberg. *Best Boy:* Frank Smith. *Electrician:* Stu Spohn. *Make-up:* Gordon Freed. *Prosthetic Construction:* Bill Munns. *Make-up Staff:* Jerry Soucie. *Wardrobe Mistress:* Sharon Lally. *Special Effects:* Frank R. Saletri, Ken Strickfaden. *Production Assistant:* Edward A. Interrera. *Production Secretary:* Christine Trill. *Stunt Advisor:* Joe Pronto. *Stunt Man:* Robert Hurd, Jay Goldher. *Post-Production:* The Jamez. *Music and Sound Effects:* Walco Productions. *Titles and Opticals:* Cinefx. *Color:* Deluxe. *M.P.A.A. Rating:* NR. *Running time:* 93 minutes.

SYNOPSIS: The beautiful African-American Dr. Winifred Walker arrives at the palatial home of Nobel Prize–winning Dr. Stein. His black assistant, Malcolm, escorts her to the doctor's laboratory. Walker tells Stein of her fiancé Eddie Turner, who lost his arms and legs in the Vietnam War, and is living without hope. Stein, who won his honors for solving the "DNA code," agrees to take a look at his case. They visit Eddie at the veterans' hospital, unaware that a sadistic orderly has been mistreating him, and arrange for him to be transferred to Stein's home laboratory at once.

Winifred studies Stein's work, becoming familiar with patients Eleanor and Bruno. Eleanor is ninety years old, but Stein has made her look considerably younger by tampering with her genetic code, and he has modified Bruno's DNA so he could grow a replacement leg. Together, Stein and Winifred conduct a three-part experiment on Eddie, using genetic material to spur the growth of new limbs.

Meanwhile, Malcolm reveals to Winifred that he has fallen in love with her. She politely rejects him, saying she hopes to marry Eddie when he is made whole again. Malcolm becomes jealous of Eddie, and decides to sabotage his treatment.

On the verge of recovery, Eddie suddenly fills ill, and evidence is shown that his medication has been tampered with. Instead of the stable DNA serum, he has been given an unstable RNA serum, which spurs the growth of animal-like appendages as well as encouraging "throwback" physical development. Eddie develops a neanderthal brow (and a giant afro…) and awakens as a lumbering monster. By night, he returns to the veterans' hospital and murders the cruel orderly who tormented him. Then he kills a white couple at their house. Though he returns to Stein's home by day, Eddie goes rampaging again the following night, murdering a teenager.

The police soon arrive to question Dr. Stein about the murders, but he reveals nothing of his work. By night, Eddie escapes once more, and kills a black couple making out behind a local nightclub. Back at the lab, Malcolm attempts to rape Winifred. Eddie saves her, and kills Malcolm. Then he kills Stein and all his patients. Eddie leaves the lab, abducts another woman, and kills her too. The police send in vicious attack dogs to bring the monster down, and they succeed.

COMMENTARY: *Blackenstein: The Black Frankenstein* is a very bad film. The 1970s blaxploitation trend resulted in some solid, well-acted horror movies (including *Blacula* [1972] and *J.D.'s Revenge* [1976]), but this is not one of them. The film is hampered by a very low budget, and by a weak script that seems to have only been half completed when shooting was finished.

It is important to note that the idea to re-arrange horror legends for contemporary black audiences is a good one. As clumsy as this film is, legends like *Frankenstein* need new faces, new focus, new energy, new per-

spectives and new creators to stay relevant in today's fast-moving pop culture. The African-American, post–Vietnam experience could have been a very powerful context for this timeless story, and resulted in a daring re-interpretation of the *Frankenstein* ethos. That said, none of that happens in this movie.

Blackenstein's low budget is clearly a stumbling block. Dr. Stein's lab is a bare room decorated with equipment that looks to be on loan from the 1940s Universal Studios. The lighting in the lab is garish, half-red/half-dark, in an attempt to hide the skimpy props. But more importantly, the film could not apparently afford a master actor, like the great William Marshall. Consequently, the performances here are not up to the level established by *Shaft*, *Blacula* and other films of the time. William Marshall, a man of great intelligence and dramatic strength, surely would have helped matters, for he understands the literary tradition and weight of roles such as Dr. Frankenstein.

The script is weak too, more explicit than witty. Indeed, it appears the script was abandoned (or left unfinished). About half way through the film, all dramatic action stops, and the movie is a shambles. Eddie (the monster) kills, kills, kills, and we lose track of Winifred, the doctor, and the story set-up.

Part of the problem involves Eddie's attacks. After dispatching the cruel orderly, he randomly kills unsuspecting, unfamiliar people, whether they deserve it or not. The last battle of the film involves Eddie's pursuit of a white woman, who has never been seen before. Since she is a random victim, randomly selected by the monster, the audience has no identification with her and no suspense is generated. The audience does not even know her name! It is also a huge disappointment that Eddie becomes a murderous monster with little or no memory of who/what he was in a human sense. The pathos of the *Frankenstein* legend is that the monster has some traits of humanity remaining within him. Those traits are absent in *Blackenstein*, and so is the pathos. There is no sense of loss, because Eddie never seems to realize how his humanity has slipped away. He never has a moment of hesitation or reflection.

Put bluntly, race *should* have been an issue in *Blackenstein*. More succinctly, it should have been the primary issue of the film. Why else revise *Frankenstein* with an African-American cast? The black experience in America in the early '70s should have been the context of this story, yet it is ultimately just a backdrop that is quickly tossed aside in favor of violent murders. For instance, Dr. Stein is a white Jew. Shouldn't some significance be attached to that fact? That he is a white man, literally exploiting the bodies of blacks for his experiments, seems important. It is never even mentioned, and worse, Stein and "his" monster seem to have no relationship to one another at all. That relationship, of creator and monster (or master and slave?), could have made this film really interesting, and it is usually the core of any *Frankenstein* story. Considering the patronizing "father" relationship that many whites impose on blacks, a great story could have been forged here about arrogant creator and rebellious son.

What about the fact that Eddie lost his limbs fighting a war for the white establishment? That is another story point that might have added purpose to Eddie's killings. Had he been avenging himself against the white America that sent him to Vietnam and than renounced its responsibility to take care of him, the film would have had a powerful narrative thrust. As it is, that idea is only minimally enunciated. That Eddie attacks a white girl, and drags her away off-screen (implying he will do more than just kill her…), is a racially charged image that also could

have been used to the film's advantage. What if the police had hunted Eddie down because they perceived him as a different kind of monster, a "big black man" raping a white woman? Again, the racial overtones could have added significance to a story just crying out for some kind of theme or meaning.

Perhaps the point is that *Frankenstein* need not be re-imagined in an African-American coloring unless it addresses the concerns and experience of that community. Instead, this film wants to be color blind, content to update the story but not consider how that updating should actually affect the story. It is a terrible fact that all plotting in *Blackenstein* ceases completely the moment Eddie is transformed into a "monster." That is a mistake, because the film does not address why he is a monster. Malcolm (a black man) sabotages his serum. Shouldn't that fact mean something in the context of African-American culture and relationships? There are so many possibilities for a "black" Frankenstein, but this movie seizes on none of them. It is content to stick an afro hairdo on the Frankenstein monster's square head, and then set the monster loose on random people.

This film is a terrible disappointment, considering the potential, and one cannot help but be reminded of *Blacula* again. That film depicted a proud African prince sold into "vampire" slavery and re-named by a white Dracula. That film depicted a Van Helsing who had to cope not only with a vampire, but a white police force that was disposed to distrust him. Black culture was celebrated at the same time that a black man's role in white society was exposed. And it was scary, involving and well acted. *Blackenstein* is a very empty film in comparison, blind to the implications of its own colorful story.

Blood Couple (1973)
(aka *Ganja & Hess*) ✶ ✶ ✶

Critical Reception

"As a black-oriented contemporary horror study, *Ganja & Hess* ... is dedicated to what is obviously meant to be a serious theme. The artistry for which it strives, however, is largely vitiated by a confusingly vague mélange of symbolism, violence, and sex."—A. H. Weiler, *New York Times*: "Gunn's Ganja & Hess Opens," Saturday, April 21, 1973.

"At the heart of the film lies vampirism as a metaphor for capitalism and cultural imperialism, dramatizing in horror movie iconography how some human beings live off the blood, sweat, and toil of others.... Thus *Ganja and Hess* symbolize the "real life" issues that plague the African-American community, such as drug abuse or selling out to materialism ... *Ganja & Hess* attempted to use the horror film as a means of interrogating race, ... gender, sexuality, religion, and class. Pigeonholed into the existing categories of blaxploitation genre film or independent art film, *Ganja & Hess* satisfied neither audience...."—Harry M. Benshoff, *Cinema Journal*: "Blaxploitation Horror Films: Generic Reappropriation or Reinscription?" Volume 39, No. 2, Winter 2000, pages 43–45.

"This deals with black traditions in a well-intended but mind-dulling fashion, its pacing is slow and its moments of action infrequent.... Good black music accompanies the tale, but nothing saves this from its own stuffiness."—John Stanley, *Creature Features Strikes Again*, 1994, page 48.

Cast & Crew

CAST: Duane Jones (Dr. Hess Green); Marlene Clark (Ganja Meda); Bill Gunn (George Meda); Sam Waymon (Reverend Luther Williams); Leonard Jackson (Archie); Candece Tarpley (Girl in Bar); Richard Harrow (Dinner Guest); John Hoffmeister (Jack Sergeant); Betty Barney (Singer in Church); Mabel King (Queen of Myrthia); Tommy Lane (Pimp); Tara Fields (Woman with a baby); With: The Congregation of Evangel Revivaltime Church.

CREW: Kelly-Jordan Enterprises, Inc., in association with Heritage Enterprises, Inc., Presents *Blood Couple*. *Written and Directed by:* Bill Gunn. *Director of Photography:* James E. Hinton. *Editor:* Victor Kanefsky. *Production Designer:* Tom John. *Executive Producers:* Quentin Kelly, Jack Jordan. *Produced by:* Quentin Kelly, Chiz Schultz. *Associate Producer:* Joan Shigekawa. *Production Supervisor:* Ed DeSisso. *Production Manager:* Lou Pastore. *Assistant Director:* Anthony Major. *Script Supervisor:* Renoir Darrett. *Musical Director:* Ed Bland. *African Instruments Played by:* Nadi Qamar. *March Blues Sung by:* Mabel King. *Special Audio Effects:* Mike Lobel. *Costumes Designed by:* Scott Barrie. *Sound:* Ron Love. *Second Cameraman:* Charles Blackwell. *Lighting Director:* Bill Lister. *Final Mix:* Gary Leibman. *Property Master:* James Walker. *Key Grip:* Rex North. *Best Boy:* Dennis Murphy. *Rerecording:* Emil Nerod. *Assistant Sound:* Bill Meredith. *Make-up:* Scott Cunningham. *Hair Stylist:* Annie De Mille. *M.P.A.A. Rating:* R. *Running time:* 110 minutes.

P.O.V.

"There are times when the white critic must sit down and listen. If he cannot listen and learn, than he must not concern himself with black creativity.... I want to say that it is a terrible thing to be a black artist in this country ... for reasons too private to expose to the arrogance of white criticism...." (17).—director Bill

Gun, in a letter to the *New York Times*, regarding reviews of *Ganja & Hess* (1973).

SYNOPSIS: Dr. Hess Green, a wealthy scholar in the long-dead Nigerian civilization of Myrthia, befriends a colleague, George Meda, and invites him to stay at his opulent home. Green is gratified to learn from Meda that a Myrthian ceremonial dagger has been discovered, and wonders how this artifact fit into the culture, which died of vampirism and pernicious anemia so long ago.

As Green studies the dagger, he also learns that Meda is unstable, even suicidal. He prevents George from hanging himself that night, but later George goes on a bloody rampage. He stabs Hess repeatedly with the ceremonial dagger and then commits suicide. To Green's shock, he does not die from his stab wounds. Instead, the dagger has infected him with the same form of vampirism that destroyed Myrthia. He drinks George's spilled blood, and hides the corpse.

Vowing never to kill another human being, Green gets his "fix" from local blood banks. His rule soon falls by the wayside, however, when his habit grows too strong, and he murders a hooker and her pimp to drink their precious blood.

Before long, George's beautiful wife, Ganja, returns to the United States from Amsterdam, looking for her husband. She moves in with Hess, unaware that George is dead. Though she is suspicious of Hess at first, Ganja and Hess soon develop a romance. Later, Ganja discovers George's corpse in the freezer behind Hess's wine cellar, and confronts her lover. Hess reveals that George took his own life, and further confesses that he drank George's blood. Ganja accepts his explanation and his peculiar perversion, and asks Hess to marry her.

Ganja and Hess wed, but Hess is so smitten with Ganja that he wants her to live forever. One night he murders his beautiful wife, and revives her as a vampire. To satiate their appetites, Ganja and Hess then invite an attractive black man for dinner one night. Ganja makes love to him, and then murders him, drinking his blood. Despite her indoctrination into the way of the vampire, Ganja is troubled by her new existence. Hoping to end their torturous, eternal lives, Hess and Ganja learn that only the shadow of the crucifix can bring them the peace of death. Hess goes to a chapel, seeking redemption in Jesus Christ, and then enlists Ganja's help in dying before the shadow of the cross.

After Hess dies, Ganja continues to live…

COMMENTARY: Perhaps Bill Gunn hasn't created a masterpiece in *Blood Couple*, but he has directed a challenging, and interesting … if muddled … film. Though the version reviewed here was cropped awkwardly for home video release, and it appears that a low-budget hampered the look of the film, overall *Blood Couple* is an inventive, ambitious work that seeks to re-interpret vampirism in the context of the African-American community and experience. It's a film that will not satisfy most plot-minded or detail-oriented horror fans, but it is valuable nonetheless for the debate it fosters about addiction, the role of Christianity in the black community, and the essence of vampirism (defined here as, essentially, the feeding on others).

Gunn has written that white critics are not equipped (or willing) to appreciate his 1973 contribution to horror cinema. That may be true, for *Blood Couple* clearly flouts accepted critical expectations and traditions. The film develops in an unconventional manner, at its own languorous pace, and the narrative is, at times, secondary to symbolism.

And, Gunn has chosen as his mode of expression the horror genre, a format critics are predisposed to denigrate anyway, so his film already has two strikes against it. In this case, the low budget, coupled with the horror concept, was probably enough to turn away most reviewers willy-nilly. This is not institutional racism, however, so much as genre discrimination, pure and simple. Many horror films, have, over the years, failed to get a fair shake from critics because of subject matter. One can glance over reviews for *The Exorcist* and reel at the vicious critical attacks heaped upon it. No quarter was given the film upon its initial release, no notice of its inherent artistry. *Blood Couple* is not in the same class as *The Exorcist*, but it met the same kind of unfriendly reception.

Bill Gunn is a director with a lot on his mind in *Blood Couple*, and the "surface" story of two African-Americans who become vampires, is co-joined with a number of interesting sociological points. On its most transparent level, the film notes uneasily that Hess, despite his wealth, is still part of the American underclass. "I'm the only colored man on the block," he anxiously reveals to George Meda at one point, fearful of a confrontation with the (white) police establishment. This notation also reminds the audience, paradoxically, that Hess is apart and separate from other members of the African-American community. Because of his wealth and status, he has chosen to live away from his "own kind." Thus he is at home in neither world.

That's an important distinction, because, ultimately, Ganja and Hess only "feed" on their own kind. When they become vampires, they kill pimps, hookers, and the poor … notably all inner city black people, not suburban whites. Without reaching too deep into the well of film analysis, it is easy to see that Gunn is making a statement about blacks who "leave behind" their brothers and sisters. They become vampires (like the white man), literally feeding on and exploiting those who are less affluent.

Accordingly, when Hess dreams, he is torn. On one hand, the priestess from Myrthia beckons him to Africa, his ancestral home. In the same dream, however, he sees a masked white man laughing at him. Each one of these figures represents a "side" of

Hess. On one hand is the African origin, the family and the history of his people. On the other is a cackling white man whose true motives are obscured by that mask. The white man of Hess's dreams may represent a society Hess can never be a part of, though he attempts to inhabit it. He senses that the white man is laughing at him for attempting to integrate himself into a world where he will always be marked as different, or outside.

Blood Couple is also pretty clearly an indictment of drug use. Hess abhors the fact that vampirism is an addiction, and that he now has a "habit to support." Worse, his values and morals do not survive the overriding addiction to blood. When he first becomes a vampire, Hess establishes that he will not kill to eat. That edict goes out the window in no time flat, when he hungrily feeds from a pimp and a hooker in the African-American community. The point is plain: morality does not survive in the face of an overwhelming addiction. Hunger becomes everything, and the beast must be fed.

What's a little odd about *Blood Couple* is that it so clearly supports the Christian religion. The soundtrack establishes that Africans (like the Myrthians) were "cursed to walk the Earth till the Christians came." Likewise, Hess ultimately finds salvation in a community church. He is freed of his curse (vamprisim) by his belief in and acceptance of Jesus, and his final surrendering to that icon of Christianity, the crucifix.

Yet, and here's the contradiction, Christianity is, no doubt, a construct of "white society." Christianity was "given" to Africans and other blacks (ex-slaves) by Christian missionaries. Yet the black culture has embraced Christ and his teachings in a very deep way. So, in *Blood Couple* there is a lauding of white religion, and even a sense that the Myrthians died because, in essence, they were pagans who fed on themselves. That's where the muddle part comes in. Is one to believe that the film is actually an indictment of black culture and origins, because they didn't imagine Christ the Messiah? Or, is the film noting that, in the final analysis, a "white" religion can save the black man? It takes a more insightful reviewer than this one to be certain, but director Gunn will be gratified, at least, to know that I have my ears up.

What is highly rewarding about *Blood Couple* as a film is that Gunn has apparently felt no pressure to express his messages within the confines of "acceptable" film technique. He has not created an easy film that draws on a century of "white" filmmaking dogma. Instead, he uses film in a wholly individual way. There is a formality and theatricality in the way the characters of *Blood Couple* talk, and it is as much stage play as film. Also, scenes are included in the film not for their contribution to the narrative, but rather for their enhancement of the overall mood.

One of the climactic scenes in the film is set in the African-American chapel to a choir's singing. It goes on and on and on ... almost endlessly. It has not been cut with an eye for pacing, speed, or narrative clarity. On the contrary, the scene continues for sometime and thereby builds an interesting feel and texture the longer it lasts. This scene evokes a curious feeling in the viewer. It starts slow, builds a tempo, and leads ultimately to a sort of rapturous release. It is not done through writing, directing, or any editorial technique. It is done primarily through song ... and sweat. Gunn's camera holds back, lets the audience soak in the music, and watches Jones swaying to the music that can deliver him from vampirism. It's interesting.

But if Gunn is inventive with his approach to this material, he is also insightful about how to manipulate more common film techniques. There are many high-angle shots throughout the film, in which the participants are, literally, looked down upon. This shot, accepted film language for entrapment or doom, helps to create the sense that these characters are all marching to an unpleasant fate. The crosscutting between the marriage celebration of Ganja and Hess and the removal of George's corpse from the Hess residence is also ironic, and clever. One life begins, another ends, and the crosscutting (serving as counterpoint) reminds the audience of that fact.

This is clearly a director who understands film technique, but who is also willing to be innovate as well as to kowtow to tradition. One of the best scenes in the film is an erotic sex scene that entangles physical lust with blood lust. Like the scene in the congregation, this sequence is nearly mesmerizing.

Blood Couple is a film to grapple with. It is filled with poetic voice-overs, fascinating imagery, and mood-altering moments. It is saddled with some awkward scene bridges and a sense that more could have been achieved with greater resources. The message may be a muddle, but the pictures are highly memorable. As an art film, it's pretty provocative. But for a viewer conditioned to the pacing, style and feel of more traditional horror movies, it's only moderately successful.

The Crazies (1973) ★ ★ ★ ½

Critical Reception

"...evenly split in its virtues and flaws. The plot is close to George C. Scott's *Rage*, about the effects of germ warfare.... The approach is different, with scenes utilizing various styles: mock documentary, drama, melodrama, and some inspired sequences of horror and comedy which often touch on the cinema of the absurd … good, cinematic fun."—Roy Frumkes, *Films in Review*, Volume XXIV, Number 4, May 1973, page 306.

"…much less pretentious than *The Omega Man*, much nastier, and also more fun."—John Brosnan, *Future Tense*, St. Martin's Press, 1978, page 200.

Cast & Crew

CAST: Lane Carroll (Judy); W.G. McMillan (David); Harold Wayne Jones (Clank); Lloyd Hollar (Colonel Peckman); Lynn Lowry (Kathy); Richard Liberty (Artie); Richard France (Dr. Watts); Harry Spillman (Major Ryder); Will Disney (Dr. Brookmyre); Edith Bell (Lab Technician); Will Thunhurst, Jr. (Brubaker); Leland Starnes (Shelby); A.C. MacDonald (General Bowen); Robert J. McCully (Hawks); Robert Karlowsky (Sheriff Cooper); Ned Schmidtke (Sgt. Tragesser); Tony Scott (Deputy Shade); Roy Cheverie (Army Doctor); Jack Zaharia (Priest). With: Stephen Liska, David Meek, Roger Brown, Kim Smith, Billy Hinzman Richard Lewick, William C. Kennedy, Malynda Parker, Walter Cook, Pig Tilbrook, Vince Survinski, Norman Chese, Ross Harris.
CREW: Lee Hessel presents *The Crazies. Produced by:* A.C. Croft. *Directed by:* George A. Romero. *Director of Photography:* William Hinzman. *Edited by:* George A. Romero. *Based on an Original Script by:* Paul McCollough. *Screenplay by:* George A. Romero. *Production Managers:* Rob Rutkowski, H. Cramer Riblett, Vince Survinski. *Post-Production Coordinators:* Bob Rutkowski. *Sound Recordists:* Rex Gleeson, John Stoll. *Sound Technicians:* Eric Bacca, Michael Gornick. *Production Coordinator:* Edith Bell. *Script-Girl:* Bonnie Hinzman. *Miss Carroll's Make-up:* Doris Dodds. *Make-up Consultant:* Gloria Natalie/Justine Ltd. *Make-up:* Bonnie Priore. *Special Effects:* Regis Survinski, Tony Pantanello. *Assistant Cameraman:* John Fitzpatrick. *Assistant to Editor:* Joe Colazzi. *Medical Advisor:* Barry J. Rosenbaum, MD. *Grips:* David Meek, Robert Karlowskiy, John Atkinson. *Military Advisor:* Colonel Bernard Garred, Ret. *Song: "Heaven Help Us" Composed by:* Carole Bayer-Sager and Melissa Manchester. *Sung by:* Beverly Bremers, Courtesy of Scepter Records, Inc. *Musical Director:* Stephen Metz. *Musical Score:* Bruce Roberts. *Associate Producer:* Margaret Walsh. *Color:* Movielab. *Produced by:* Pittsburgh Films through the facilities of the Latent Image Inc., Pittsburgh. A Cambist Film. *M.P.A.A. Rating:* R. *Running time:* 105 minutes.

SYNOPSIS: In Evans City, a man goes crazy in his house, kills his wife, attacks both his children and then sets his home on fire. The local fire department responds, along with a nurse named Judy. More surprisingly, the U.S. army intervenes, garbed in gas masks and white environmental suits! Judy learns that her quiet little town is now under quarantine. This frightens her because she is pregnant, and her physician friend suggests she hide with lover David until things quiet down. He then gives her a single hypodermic of vaccine. Judy flees the doctor's office at his urging, and meets up with David.

The U.S. government believes that a plane crash in the area caused the release of Trixie, a deadly chemical agent, in Evans City. The military brass decides to launch a plane carrying a nuclear bomb, just in case the situation gets out of hand. Martial law is declared, and the army rounds up a defiant populace, breaking into private residences and herding citizens into a makeshift infirmary in the high school gym. The truth is that Trixie is no virus, but a bacteriological weapon accidentally released by the government into the water supply.

Meanwhile, soldiers capture Judy and David before she can share the vaccine with him. They are thrown in the back of a truck with other townspeople, but soon escape. With friend Clank and with Mr. Arties and his grown daughter, Kathy, Judy and David seek refuge in a country club away from town. They have good reason to be scared because the army has confiscated all weapons in the area, and is shooting down anyone who stands up to it.

While David and the others squabble over what course to take, army scientists fight too. They burn the bodies of the dead, seek a cure, and argue over who is to blame. Trixie is particularly insidious because it causes insanity, and it is difficult to judge when someone is merely panicked or actually raving mad...

Before long, David and Judy get a look at the madness close up. Mr. Arties tries to rape his daughter ... revealing they are both infected. Even Clank falls ill, becoming a homicidal maniac who shoots soldiers down in cold blood without a second thought. David comes to believe that he's immune to Trixie, and thus of vital importance to the scientists, but soon he, Judy and Clank are on the run from soldiers again.

Dr. Elston, a scientist from the Trixie project, works long hours and eventually finds an antidote to the disease. But, through military blundering, he is put in with the Evans City crazies, and shot dead before he is able to share his data or stop the epidemic.

Judy falls ill while on the run, and the army kills her. David is captured as Trixie spreads to Louisville. David is brought to the makeshift lab but conditions are so bad that no one remembers to test him for immunity. A hostile David, mourning the murder of his wife and unborn child, doesn't say a word. Desperate, the military pulls out of Evans City ... a town that now belongs permanently to the crazies. At least until the nukes...

COMMENTARY: In a bizarre coincidence, this reviewer screened George Romero's *The Crazies* on Easter Sunday of the year 2000, exactly one day after a government raid was staged in Miami, Florida, to recover Elian Gonzalez. There is, of course, an infamous photograph of that raid featuring a helmeted federal soldier breaking into a civilian household and taking the 6 year old by force, and at gunpoint. No doubt, George Romero never intended such a connection, but *The Crazies*, a tale of military power run amuck,

looks markedly less paranoid in light of this contemporary situation.

Unlike *Night of the Living Dead*, which was a personal apocalypse set around a societal one, *The Crazies* casts a wider net, detailing the societal apocalypse, but with a sampling of personal stories to flavor the tale. Romero's primary target of ridicule this time is the government controlled military, an "invasion army" set loose in suburban modern America, and his images are provocative, and even inflammatory.

In its highlighting of martial law in middle-class America, *The Crazies* pulls no punches. There are multiple shots of armed soldiers breaking into homes, into bedrooms, into private residences, with no restrictions and no explanations. We see the federal army occupy a town's main street, stationed in front of a post office, and shooting down U.S. citizens (in the back, no less...) as the people run. The soldiers steal wallets, loot jewelry and similarly misbehave in the homes they occupy, revealing themselves to be little more than thugs and thieves. Romero's point is, perhaps, that freedom in America is just one executive order away from destruction. An army with free reign, capable of killing those who resist the occupation, can destroy every principle America is founded upon.

The Crazies is a stunning view of the manner in which a government equipped with a strong military can turn on its own people who are powerless to stop it. Why tell such a story? Well, remember that *The Crazies* was made in 1972-1973, a time when much of the country was decrying President Richard Nixon as "King Richard," a monarch who seemed especially fond of his own executive authority. The Vietnam War—an unpopular conflict with many American people—continued to rage with no end in sight, and the voices of the community—who wanted it stopped—were not being heard.

Indeed, much of *The Crazies* plays out as a Vietnam War allegory. Without warning, the full power of the American military arrives in a smaller community, a simple, rural town. The people are rounded up and killed because their perceived condition (insanity) is believed to be a threat to United States national security. It is not hard to read "insanity" as "Communism" in this setting. Indeed, the Vietnamese people become, in a way, the people of Evans City. A priest, driven to madness by the situation, pours gasoline over his body and then immolates himself, a direct parallel to that famous image of a Buddhist monk during the Vietnam conflict. And, importantly, who is the one person who has a natural immunity to Trixie? It is David, a Vietnam War veteran. Why is he immune? Because he has seen insanity before ... in Vietnam, in fact.

The Crazies is an existentialist movie, a picture that reveals how life and death hinge on ridiculous circumstances. A scientist discovers a cure for Trixie, but is shot by the military before he can save the world. David is immune to Trixie, but the confused military never tests him for immunity, and so on. It is an absolutely absurdist and paranoid depiction of what life in America would look like under martial law, and it is a frightening, cold image.

Romero's filmic style (which inevitably includes frenetic, rapid-fire editing) contributes to the film's sense of insanity. A city "up to its ass" in soldiers (dehumanized by the white environmental suits and gas masks they wear...) is assaulted, all because of a government "accident." There are resonances of *Night of the Living Dead* too because family relationships are perverted by the plague. Here a father has sex with his daughter instead of a brother devouring his sister, but the point is the same. A country club replaces a farmhouse as the remote setting of choice, and authorities continue to make fatal mistakes. In *The Crazies*, the military murders a healthy Judy (just as the healthy Ben was shot dead in *Night*). Yet *The Crazies* is an even darker film because there is no dependable way to differentiate hero from villain. The military, though ostensibly trying to help, is

the film's biggest danger. The good people of Evans City slip into insanity without any warning or signals, unlike the dead that walk the night in *Living Dead*. Because the line between heroes and villains is blurred, *The Crazies* is also much, much more paranoid than its predecessor. It is a well-made, beautifully shot film, but watching it is not a pleasant experience.

It would be easy (and convenient) to dismiss *The Crazies* as a paranoid "what if" scenario, a playing off of the fear that an overreaching federal government will send soldiers against its own populace, trampling the United States Constitution in the process. But the events of Easter Sunday, 2000, make a viewing of this film a far more sober, far less "fantastic" experience. George Romero's warning about freedom lost in America, if anything, is more timely today than it was in 1973.

Though Vietnam and Richard Nixon are far behind us, here in Miami, today, the government broke into a private residence — armed — with the intent of righting a wrong. The object of that quest may have been a little boy instead of the "containment" of a plague, but the point of *The Crazies* is that motives do not matter. Once the army is let loose on its own people, a Pandora's box is opened.

George Romero never makes "easy" or "simple" horror films. His movies are always about something important, whether it be equality among sexes (*Jack's Wife*), religious persecution (*Martin*), or martial law (*The Crazies*). This film offers some of Romero's most stylish and meaningful work, and in some ways is a better film than *Dawn of the Dead* (1979) because it gives free reign to its feelings of anarchy. Humor, violence, absurdity and terror co-mingle in a frenetic, but somehow cohesive whole. That balance was overstepped in *Dawn of the Dead* (remember the pie-throwing incident with the zombies and bikers!?) but is revelatory here. *The Crazies* reminds us of an old lesson. It can happen here.

The Creeping Flesh

Cast & Crew

CAST: Christopher Lee (James Hildern); Peter Cushing (Emmanuel Hildern); Lorna Heilbron (Penelope Hildren); Duncan Lamont (Inspector); Kenneth Warren (Lenny); Maurice Bush (Karl).

CREW: *Directed by:* Freddie Francis. *Written by:* Peter Spenceley and Jonathan Rumbold. *Produced by:* Norman Priggen, Tony Tenser, Michael Redbourn. *Director of Photography:* Norman Warwick. *Editor:* Oswald Hafenrichter. *Music:* Paul Ferris. *M.P.A.A. Rating:* PG. *Running Time:* 94 minutes.

DETAILS: A spectacularly creepy film set in the Victorian era. A prehistoric skeleton found in New Guinea is brought back to malevolent life by that perennial dabbler in mad science, Peter Cushing. A disturbing and moody horror film, buttressed by the presence of Christopher Lee and the experienced directing chops of Freddie Francis. Chilling.

Don't Look in the Basement (1973) *

Cast & Crew

CAST: William Bill McGhee (Sam); Jessie Lee Fulton (Jane St. Claire); Robert Dracup (Ray Daniels); Harryette Warren (Jennifer); Michael Harvey (Dr. Stephens); Jessie Kirby (Donny); Hugh Feggin (Sgt. Jaffee); Betty Chandler (Allyson); Camilla Carr (Harriett); Gene Ross (Oliver W. Cameron); Anne MacAdams (Dr. Masters); Rosie Holotik (Charlotte Beale); Rhea MacAdams (Mrs. Callingham).

CREW: Camera 2000 Productions in Association with Century Studios Presents *Don't Look in the Basement.* *Cinematographer:* Robert Alcott. *Camera Operator:* Dale Johnson. *Assistant Camera:* David Ceika. *Art Director:* Lynda Pendleton. *Continuity:* L. J. Feagin. *Wardrobe:* Florence Baker. *Make-up:* Jill Esmond. *Production Coordinator:* Annabelle Weenick. *Editor:* Jerry Caraway. *Assistant Editor:* Lynn Lenau. *Unit Manager:* John Jacobie. *Sound:* Edward Motteram. *Special Effects:* Jack Bennett. *Sound Effects:* Brian Hooper. *Location Coordinator:* Joe Eakin, Joe Copeland, Calvin Praytor. *Original Screenplay:* Tim Pope. *Music:* Robert Farrar. *Executive Producer:* Walter L. Krusz. *Color:* Movielab. *Produced and Directed by:* S. F. Brownrigg. *M.P.A.A. Rating:* R. *Running Time:* 89 minutes.

SYNOPSIS: At the isolated Stephens Sanitarium, a long-time nurse informs a simple-minded inmate, Sam, that she is planning to quit her job. Sam, a once-violent man who now has the mind of a child because of a lobotomy, is upset by the sad news. Meanwhile, another inmate, the Judge, uses an axe to kill Dr. Stephens. Desperate to maintain order, a psychotic patient who believes she is a doctor (and who calls herself Dr. Geraldine Masters) takes charge of the asylum. Before the departing nurse can leave the asylum, she is murdered.

Later that very night, Charlotte Beale, the sanitarium's new nurse, arrives at the hospital unaware there has been a "change" in administration. She reports to Geraldine Masters, who is still playing at being a psychiatrist. Masters informs Charlotte that Dr. Stephens is dead and that she is changing his administrative objectives. Still, she offers Charlotte a post. That night, Charlotte learns her room is on the same hall with the inmates, and is more than a little disturbed.

The next morning, Dr. Masters and Charlotte review the inmates together. There is Sam, who has the mentality of an 8 year old. Sarge is a military officer who went crazy after losing his platoon in combat. The Judge, formerly of the court of appeals, is a homicidal maniac. Harriet, who believes a doll is a living baby, is facing her own internal trauma. Mrs. Callingham, an old lady, Danny, a mischievous brat, and a nymphomaniac named Allyson make up the remainder of the contingent. Each one of these unfortunate souls was part of Dr. Stephens' experiment to prove that insanity was not a break with reality, but actually a pattern of obsession.

Even as Charlotte becomes familiar with her new wards, Dr. Masters cuts the phone lines so the new arrival cannot communicate with anyone outside the sanitarium. When a phone repairman arrives to fix the line, Allyson accosts him. Later, Dr. Masters murders him.

After an inmate tries to murder her, Charlotte starts to have serious doubts about her career move. Complicating matters, Sam continues to insist that Dr. Stephens is alive and trying to help Charlotte. Charlotte thinks Sam is delusional, but later finds the doctor, half-dead in the basement. Terrified, Charlotte tries to flee the asylum as another coup erupts. The psychotic Masters, a cruel taskmaster, is murdered by the other inmates, many of whom she has wronged.

As Charlotte flees the rural home for the criminally insane, Sam has another break with reality. He goes crazy, and murders all the surviving patients. After the bloody deed is done, he absently gets an ice pop from the refrigerator and starts to cry like a baby.

COMMENTARY: "Willing suspension of disbelief." We've all heard that term, and we all know what it means. To buy into a movie (and subsequently enjoy it), a viewer must set aside some reservations and just let events happen. However, suspension of disbelief becomes harder the less probable and less realistic a movie seems. Suspension of disbelief becomes downright impossible when a movie blatantly breaks the rules of reality,

yet purports to be realistic. *Don't Look in the Basement* is just such a movie. It is 89 minutes of overacting, implausible plotting, and crazy, irrational tics.

Let us begin with the setting. The Stephens Sanitarium is a rural insane asylum, a two-story house. The film is so badly directed that no sense of location is established. Whose room is where? How many rooms are there? What is the relationship of one room to another? When are we on the first floor? When are we on the second? The asylum exterior is filmed many times, so it is clear that it cannot be a large enough structure to accommodate Charlotte's absence from the plot for such long stretches of time.

Leaving that issue aside, there are others about the location. Charlotte has just moved in to the house/asylum. Would she not want to know where the nearest grocery store is? Is there a car nearby in case of emergencies? Does nobody, not even a medical supply team, bring equipment, supplies or even groceries to this location? It is simply not easy to believe that this asylum, populated by insane people, is so completely isolated from the rest of the world. Do any of the inmates have relatives that might visit? Psychiatrists? Case workers? It is the kind of asylum that can only exist in a horror film because it is patently unbelievable.

Still, horror movies have survived such ill-conceived settings. One is reminded immediately of *Halloween II* (1981), a movie in which a city hospital was virtually abandoned, and always dark, despite the fact that it was one of the busiest nights of the year. Still, the movie had some tension, and enough reality to just pass muster. *Don't Look in the Basement* fails its second test of believability by presenting a lead character, Charlotte, who is a total idiot. This woman is supposed to be a trained psychiatric nurse, yet she is not observant, bright or even very curious.

No alarms ring in her vacant little brain when she learns that there is no lock on her bedroom door, and that the staff of the hospital sleep on the same floor with the murderous patients? In fact, new arrival, Nurse Beale, does not even think to ask which of her new wards was the person who killed Dr. Stephens! One might think that would be an important bit of information, at least for self-protection, if not clinical clarity.

Later, Charlotte is awakened in the middle of the night when a patient, armed with an axe, walks freely in her room and attempts to molest her right there in bed. Though frightened, she doesn't suspect that things are amiss.

Then, finally, when Charlotte realizes something is wrong at the asylum, she bemoans the fact that she cannot escape from the establishment. Why? There are glass windows all around her, on both floors of the building. "BREAK A WINDOW!" one wants to shout at her. Indeed, there is one scene in the film that speaks beautifully to Charlotte's lack of intelligence. She runs breathily to a telephone, picks it up, and realizes it is dead. She looks straight at the telephone handle and says, accusingly, "Why don't you work?" Brilliant.

As for the other characters in *Don't Look in the Basement*, they make Nurse Beale look like a rocket scientist. Dr. Stephens hands a murderous patient an axe, an act that doesn't seem very smart, and thus his subsequent death scene is anticipated rather than unexpected. The actors playing the lunatics all ham it up beyond belief, filling their performances with irrational facial expressions and outbursts of laughter. They are the insane as imagined by a writer who knows nothing about psychology, nothing about human behavior, and nothing about filmmaking.

So, a director has made a terrible movie filled with dumb characters, and a hard-to-swallow "isolated" setting. How does he top it off? Well, at the end of the picture, he can rely on that charming old movie tradition of showing a montage of your cast, along with their names. But, instead of picking out their best moments (as in the closing credits of *Scream*, or *Last House on the Left*), the director opts to show the cast members bloodied and in pain, reliving their hammy, and bloody death scenes! This must be a first in motion picture history, a totally tasteless way to cap off a totally ridiculous motion picture.

"Get out! Get out and never come back!" warns a little old nutcase in extreme close-up (facing the camera) in one of *Don't Look in the Basement*'s bizarre, unintentionally humorous moments. That was also this reviewer's reaction to the videotape as he popped it out of the VCR.

Don't Look Now (1973) ✶ ✶ ✶ ✶

Critical Reception

"*Don't Look Now* does not aim to convert anyone to a belief in the occult; but by the end of the film, even the most skeptical may feel chilled, uneasy, unable to still the doubts and fear stirred in the dark, secret places of the imagination."— Stephen Farber, *New York Times*: "*Don't Look Now* Will Scare You — Subtly," December 23, 1973, pages 147–148.

"...a highly professional piece, more serious than satisfying.... Wintry Venice is the locale ... it has exactly the crypt-like patina called for by such a tale of cloistered terrors. The picture misses in the compounding of its effects; it fails Roeg's intentions to achieve a delicate balance between montage and muddle."— Roy Frumkes, *Films in Review*, Volume XXV, Number 1, January 1974, page 49.

"Puzzling, brilliantly detailed and thoroughly absorbing thriller which makes excellent use of its locations and has many thought-provoking passages. A modern-day classic."— Howard Maxford, *The A to Z of Horror Films*, Indiana University Press, 1997, page 82.

"...the picture is the fanciest, most carefully assembled Gothic enigma yet put on the screen; it's emblazoned in chic and compared to such Gothics as *Seance on a Wet Afternoon*, it's a masterwork. It's also trash."— Pauline Kael, *New Yorker*, December 24, 1973, pages 68–69.

"...Roeg successfully plunges us into a formerly peaceful, ordered world now smashed into jagged arcs and shards by sudden pointless death.... It is a tribute to Roeg's artistry that this originally tricky conclusion, like the rest of *Don't Look Now*, can transcend itself, even imperfectly."— Michael Dempsey, *Film Quarterly*, Volume XXVII, Number 3, Spring 1974, pages 39, 42, 43.

"...a ghost story for adults. It is a film packed with compelling ideas about time and space, life and death, certainty and doubt. The film offers clues, ideas, associations, and images, but it never provides answers. *Don't Look Now* rewards intellectual curiosity and confounds literary interpretation."— Darrell Moore, *The Best, Worst, and Most Unusual: Horror Films*, Crowne Publishers, 1983, page 93.

Cast & Crew

CAST: Julie Christie (Laura Baxter); Donald Sutherland (John Baxter); Hilary Mason (Heather); Massimo Serato (Wendy); Clelia Matania (Bishop Barbarrigo); Renato Scarpa (Inspector Longhi); Giorgio Trestini (Workman); Leopoldo Trieste (Hotel Manager); David Tree (Anthony Babbage); Am Rye (Mandy Babbage); Nicholas Salter (Johnny Baxter); Sharon Willkins (Christine Baxter); Bruno Cattaneo (Detective Sabbione); Adelina Poerio (Dwarf).

CREW: A Peter Katz and Anthony B. Unger Production. Julie Christie and Donald Sutherland in *Don't Look Now* from a story by Daphne Du Maurier. *Executive Producer:* Anthony B. Unger. *Screenplay:* Alan Scott and Chris Bryant. *Produced by:* Peter Katz. *Directed by:* Nicholas Roeg. *Associate Producer:* Federico Mueller. *Director of Photography:* Anthony Richmond. *Art Director:* Giovanni Soccol. *Set Dresser:* Francesco Chinanese. *Film Editor:* Graeme Clifford. *Sound Editor:* Rodney Holland. *Assistant Editors:* Tony Lawson, Peter Holt. *Music:* Pino Donnagio. *Arranged and Conducted by:* Giampiero Boneschi. *Unit Manager:* Franco Coduti. *Assistant Director:* Francesco Cinieri. *Camera Operator:* Luciano Tonti. *Assistant Cameraman:* Simon Ransley. *Sound Recordist:* Peter Davies. *Dub Mixer:* Bob Jones. *Production Accountant:* Terence O'Connor. *Miss Christie's Wardrobe:* Marit Lieberson, Andrea Galer. *Wardrobe Mistress:* Annamalla Fea. *Make-up:* Giancarlo Del Brocco. *Hair-Stylist:* Barry Richardson. *Hairdresser:* Maria Luisa Garbini. *Casting:* Miriam Brickman, Ugo Mariatt. *Continuity:* Rita Agostini. *Gaffer:* Luciano Marrocchi. *Key Grip:* Spartaco Pizzi. *Stunt Coordinator:* Richard Grayden. *Publicity:* Hubert Doyle. *Production Executive:* Steve Previn. *M.P.A.A. Rating:* R. *Running time:* 110 minutes.

SYNOPSIS: On a sunny day at their home in England, John and Laura Baxter are shattered when their daughter, Christine, drowns unexpectedly in a backyard pond. Oddly, John seems to have foreknowledge of the tragedy, and races to save his red-slicker–garbed daughter from this terrible accident. Unfortunately, he arrives too late, and Christine dies.

Sometime later, John and Laura go to Venice, where John has been hired to restore a magnificent cathedral. One day, John and Laura run into a blind woman named Heather, and her sister, Wendy. The blind Heather claims to possess psychic powers, or "second sight." She tells the mourning Laura that Christine is still with John and Laura, and that she is happy. Laura faints at this news, and is rushed to a hospital. She tells

John about Heather's revelation, and John is immediately wary of the sisters, fearing some con or "mumbo jumbo." Still, Laura is happy for the first time since the accident, and she and John make love before an evening out in Venice.

After dinner, they get lost in one of the city's twisting back alleys and hear a man scream in terror. John glimpses a strange, diminutive figure wearing a red slicker running from the scene, and his suspicion is aroused.

Heather and Wendy meet with Laura on another day, as John continues his assignment at the cathedral. Heather tells Laura that John possesses the gift of second sight too, and that Christine is trying to communicate with him. The sisters ask John to meet with them, but he refuses. Instead, Laura visits their hotel room and watches with horror as Heather experiences a psychic seizure. She warns that John's life is in danger as long as he remains in Venice. Terrified, Laura wants to leave for England. That night, John and Laura receive a call from their son Johnny's boarding school that he has been injured in an accident. Laura decides to take the first flight back to England, leaving John in Venice.

After John has sent Laura on her way, he mysteriously spies Laura back in Venice, on a funeral boat — and apparently in mourning — with Heather and Wendy at her side.

While John tries to determine if the sisters have abducted his wife, he sees a corpse pulled out of the Venice canals. This is just another brutal death in a series of murders plaguing the city. Afraid that Laura is somehow in danger, John goes to the police and tells his story to a skeptical Inspector Longhi. The police set out to find Heather and her sister, while simultaneously keeping a tail on John … who they fear may be their serial killer.

Searching desperately for Laura, John prowls the streets of Venice and again catches a glimpse of a figure in a red slicker. Eventually, John ends up at the sisters' hotel and learns they have moved. When a desperate John calls home to England he is surprised to discover that Laura is still there, with Johnny, and apparently unharmed. Confused, John tells the police that he made a mistake.

As Laura flies back to Venice, John visits with Heather and takes her to her new hotel, where she meets up with Wendy. When John attempts to leave the hotel, Heather has another seizure and begs John to stay. Frightened, John leaves the hotel and sees the specter in the red slicker again. As he pursues the ghoul, Laura arrives at the hotel, just missing him. In the midst of a dark, fog-ridden night, John pursues the stranger in the red slicker, thinking it to be his dead daughter, Christine. He corners the specter in a dark church chamber but is confronted not with his daughter, but a deformed, monstrous dwarf … the serial killer of Venice. The diminutive monster slices John's neck with a razor blade, and kills him.

Later, a mourning Laura stands with Heather and Wendy on a funeral boat. When John saw Laura in Venice earlier, he was actually glimpsing the future … and his own death.

COMMENTARY: The year 1973 brought two landmark films to grateful horror aficionados: William Friedkin's *The Exorcist,* and Nicholas Roeg's intense, and disturbing *Don't Look Now.* Both films belong on any critic's ten best horror list for the decade, and both sustain a terrifying world-view. Where *The Exorcist* re-imagines the ancient "evil" of Satan and debunks modern science and medicine in the process, *Don't Look Now* instead posits a frightening world in which the unfathomable hand of fate leads mortals step by step to disaster. The film is especially powerful because director Nicholas Roeg goes to great (and dramatic) lengths to present the lead characters, John Baxter (Donald Sutherland) and Laura Baxter (Julie Christie), as likable, tender and identifiable human beings.

Horror movies are always more powerful when populated by characters the audience cares about, and *Don't Look Now* focuses strongly on the relationship and intimacy of its two primaries. This focus is well-placed because the last ten minutes of the film, in which the lines of fate finally converge, are all the more shattering since the audience has come to love the film's leads.

How does a director forge so powerful a link between character and viewer? In *Don't Look Now*, Nicholas Roeg aggressively marshals formalist film technique, particularly crosscutting, to build to that very effect. Early in the film, Laura and John Baxter make love in their hotel room. Instead of merely "recording" that sensuous experience, Roeg cross-cuts the intense love-making with a lyrical period of post-coital "dressing up," in which a satisfied John and Laura prepare for their night out in Venice.

By seeing the couple acting intimately, not just sexually, but in their own "space" together, the audience catches the characters in the act of being human. Roeg's camera watches them undressing, bathing, experiencing their own nakedness (sometimes with modesty, as when John runs across the maid and is embarrassed by his lack of dress), and even sharing laughs. Their sex scene, though erotic, is also remarkably tender. It begins with a simple, gentle touch, and then escalates, slowly, into outright passion. There's something very right and very natural about the pacing and shooting of this sequence, and the sex scene never feels forced, arty, or artificially "erotic" (like the overblown sexcapades of a film such as *Basic Instinct* [1991]). It all takes place on a far more human playing field and the act of getting dressed together after sex importantly follows one act of intimacy with another.

And, by crosscutting future time (dressing and getting ready for dinner) with present time (sexual intercourse), the lovemaking scene defies movie sex-scene convention. It does not build up to sexual gratification and orgasm as most filmed sexual encounters would. Instead, the crosscutting of the sexual present with the post-sex future takes the crescendo and the "build up" out of the sexual equation. This is appropriate because it is the intimacy of sex, not the final ejaculation and orgasm, that is important to director Roeg in this case.

He wants us to experience the lovemaking with the couple as a moment shared, not an appetite sated. It's as if we're suddenly privy to flashes of a real person's life, and the sex scene creates empathy in the audience for these characters. We have experienced a sensitive moment with this couple, as well as a tragedy (the death of their child, Christine), and that is a one-two punch of "likeability" that propels the audience, unwittingly into the horror that comes next. The sex scene played against those romantic preparations for a night out is touching rather than vulgar, emotional rather than merely lustful.

The juxtaposition of intimacies in the sex scene is part of the overall film's *modus operandi* as well. Roeg is constantly juxtaposing like and unlike moments in *Don't Look Now* to suggest a connection, or disconnect, in the hands of fate. The first scene of the film is positively pastoral, for instance. A child (Christine) plays carelessly near a pond on a dewy green morning. An orange sun hangs lazily in the background, and the girl is seen wearing a red slicker. Just yards away, inside the house, Christine's father gazes at a slide of a church interior. He spies someone sitting in a pew, wearing a similar red slicker. What's the connection? Why has one image bled into the other?

This "overlap" or coincidence happens, quite literally. When Christine falls into the water, John simultaneously spills his drink on the slide, and in both situations the person in the slicker (either in reality or image) is "drowned" in wetness. Is this part of John's second sight, or merely a connection that the "world" is aware of, but which the human characters are not? How can John know that his daughter is dying, and that she will die in a way that eventually leads him to his own death? It seems random, but the crosscutting suggests it is not at all random, but by some

strange design. The hands of fate are operating to a purpose, but as human beings, we
do not understand the mechanism or the
purpose.

Similarly, fate conspires to keep Laura
and John apart as the end of his life draws
near. Why? Why should he end up on the
exact street with the ghoulish serial killer at
that one moment of time? Why should Laura
always be one step behind him, unable to
reach him or save him? Why should John die
at the hands of a malevolent troll who, in
passing, seems to resemble the daughter he
misses so very much? There are no answers
to these questions in *Don't Look Now*, and
the audience is left to feel that though there
is an order to the universe, it is one that John
has only barely glimpsed.

When John dies, images flash in front
of the camera: images of life and death, of
love and fear, of pain and joy. His death is
pointless, but for John his death represents
a moment, a summit, of understanding. The
tangle of images in this montage suggest that
this is how it was *meant* to be. By design.
Every blind corner, every misstep, led John
directly to this moment, and to the razor
blade of that dwarf. It was preordained,
decided long ago, and John fulfilled his role
in it all, unconsciously.

Don't Look Now is a terrifying film
because it is all about the connections in our
lives, connections that we either see or fail to
see. Why should the dwarf look mysteriously
like a gargoyle on the cathedral John is ren-
ovating? Why should the dead girl and the
serial killer both wear a red slicker? Why are
the sisters, Heather and Wendy, seen to be
laughing maniacally in a moment alone?
Why should John experience a vision of the
future, a warning, that instead leads him
straight to his own demise? These questions
are not answered, but as John's life flashes
before his eyes, there is a feeling of synthesis
and calm following the shock and surprise of
his murder.

Unlike the rest of us, John has found his
answers at last. He knows why bad things
happen to good people ... but, like all those
who leave this mortal coil, he cannot share
the secret with the rest of us. Again, we are
cut off from the answers we desire.

Set in Venice, a frightening city of "too
many shadows," that's like a "dinner party
where the guests are all dead," *Don't Look
Now* not only makes the most of the city's
twisted alleyways, it actually mirrors them.
Like Venice, *Don't Look Now* is a labyrinth
with dead ends, false starts, and circles. Like
Venice, life seems in this film to be a cruel
trick in which there is no direct route to
answers, or any sense of clarity. The final revelatory shot of the film — a dwarf hidden in
the corner, monstrous and horrifying — is as
much a question as an answer. What is this
thing? Where did it come from? Why does it
kill? Who is it? What is it? There are no
answers, only the end of a human life. But
there is also terror in this not knowing.

It is a profound terror more akin to that
in *Picnic at Hanging Rock* (1975) than to that
in *The Exorcist*. The final moment, when the
stranger in the slicker is revealed, remains
one of horror's most terrifying and powerful images, even today. It is terrifying because, all at once, it makes sense *and* fails to
make sense. On a purely subconscious level,
we understand what it is. On a rational, daylight level, the existence of this ... thing, is
too much to contemplate. We want it to be
a child, somehow brought back from the
dead, but instead it is a twisted reflection of
us, a monster delivered to us by the hand of
fate.

Don't Look Now is a perfect title for this
film. In that final revelatory moment, the
film's title warns the audience to hide. If you
look, if you watch, all your fears about life
and death, and the connections in your life,
will be validated. Even the nicest people will
meet the grim reaper one day, and the form
of that reaper, as in our worst nightmares,
will make sense and fail to make sense at the
same time. Chilling.

The Exorcist (1973) * * * *

Critical Reception

"This is the most scary picture I've seen in years.... The acting, the lighting, the soundtrack, and above all, the special effects have been ordered up carefully by the director and used precisely. Even the music is faultless.... During most horror pictures that I see, I keep watching how it's done.... Here the director-ial hand is quicker than the eyes; the ears. Here I got frights and the pleasure of unmediated visceral response. Disbelief was canted, if not suspended. And virtually all of this was Friedkin's doing.... *The Exorcist* will scare the hell out of you."— Stanley Kauffmann, *New Republic,* February 9, 1974, page 23.

"If movies are, among other things, the opportunities for escapism, then *The Exorcist* is one of the most powerful ever made.... During the movie there are no reservations, but only experiences. We feel shock, horror, nausea, fear, and some small measure of dogged hope.... *The Exorcist* is one of the best movies of its type ever made; it not only transcends the genre of terror, horror, and the supernatural, but it transcends such serious, ambitious efforts in the same direction as Roman Polanski's *Rosemary's Baby*."— Roger Ebert, *Roger Ebert's Movie Home Companion* (1993 Edition), Andrews and McMeel, 1993, page 204.

"...a terrifying motion picture.... Friedkin's direction is expert: he has left much of the filmic excitement to supervising editor Jordan Leondopoulos, who emphasizes the struggle between good and evil ... the horror film will never be the same."— C.P.R., *Films in Review,* Volume XXV, Number 2, February 1974.

"...an exceedingly well-made bad picture. It invokes snobbish admiration of people rich enough to own a Mercedes and a butler, it denigrates medicine and psychiatry, it involves the Catholic Church in mumbo jumbo and, by grotesque make-up and camera trickery ... it turns a 12-year-old girl into a spectacle of loathsome ugliness for the sole purpose of mindless entertainment. It should be scorned, and when it opened every critic I read did indeed scorn it."— Robert Hatch, *Nation*, February 2, 1974, page 157.

"...the movie is vile and brutalizing.... Von Sydow has a presence of unshad-owed strength. Jason Miller ... makes a very impressive first film appearance with a performance full of swift undercurrents of psychic pain. Linda Blair per-forms bravely as the tormented girl; the rasping voice of her demon is haunt-ingly dubbed.... Ellen Burstyn, a good actress who is especially adept at portraying beleaguered strength is stuck here with an assignment that might have once suited Fay Wray: look hysterical and scream. The role, alas, is the very essence of *The Exorcist*."— Jay Cocks, *Time Magazine,* January 14, 1974, page 38.

"...the trash bombshell of 1973, the aesthetic equivalent of being run over by a truck ... a gloating, ugly exploitation picture, a costlier cousin of those ghoulish cheapies released in drive-ins and fleapits almost weekly in major American cities."— Michael Dempsey, *Film Quarterly*, Volume XXVII, Number 4, Summer 1974, pages 39, 42, 43.

"Instead of characters we are not exactly given caricatures; the figures on screen strike me more as witnesses whose main task is simply to stand atten-tively at bay, observing the weird and unnatural events in the Georgetown house.... In lieu of developed plot we get what Aristotle called 'spectacle,' unadulterated and unrelenting depiction of the horrible ... despite the movie's obvious flaws, it possesses undeniable power to shock."— Robert F. Willson, Jr.

Journal of Popular Film: "*The Exorcist* and Multicinema Aesthetics," Volume 3, Number 2, 1974, page 183.

"*The Exorcist* is the kind of movie you get when you leave religion to screenwriters and businessmen." — Eugene Kennedy, priest and professor of psychology at Loyloa, *New York Times*, August 4, 1974, page 4.

"Blatty's 'problem of good' treatise gave the big-budget treatment to horror, and as a canvas for provocative scares, has never really been equalled. Today, it's kind of slow moving and a little overblown, but it certainly shows how we longed for some spiritual healing after the chaotic 1960s. Best moments: the nearly subliminal flashing 'Death mask' appearing for a split second during Karras's dream and once during a possession scene." — Bill Latham, *Mary's Monster*, Powys Books.

"Director Friedkin treats his subject very seriously, wrapping us up in the lore of demonology and scrupulously taking us through the process of the exorcism. Unexpected shocks — such as the sudden close-up of the spinal tap — wear us down and weaken our resistance towards the confrontations that we do expect. The story is compelling, the acting first-rate, the pacing taut, and the shocks original. The acting and the script lift *The Exorcist* to a level beyond standard horror." — Darrell Moore, *The Best, the Worst, the Most Unusual: Horror Films*, Crowne Publishers, 1983, page 82.

Cast & Crew

CAST: Ellen Burstyn (Chris MacNeil); Max Von Sydow (Father Merrin); Lee J. Cobb (Lt. Kinderman); Kitty Winn (Sharon); Jack Mac-Gowran (Burke Dennings); Jason Miller (Father Karras); Linda Blair (Regan); Mercedes McCambridge (the Voice of Evil). Reverend William O'Malley, S.J., Barton Heyman, Peter Masterson, Rudolf Schundler, Gina Petrushka, Robert Symonds, Arthur Storch, Reverend Thomas Bermingham, S.J., Vasiliki Maliaros, Titos Vandis, Wallace Rooney, Ron Faber, Donna Mitchell, Roy Cooper, Robert Gerringer.

CREW: A William Friedkin Film of William Peter Blatty's *The Exorcist. Directed by:* William Friedkin. *Written by:* William Peter Blatty (based on his novel). *Executive Producer:* Noel Marshall. *Associate Producer:* David Salven. *Director of Photography:* Owen Roizman. *Make-up artist:* Dick Smith. *Special Effects:* Marcel Vercoutere. *Production Designer:* Billy Malley. *First Assistant Director:* Terence A. Donnelly. *Set Decorator:* Jerry Wunderlich. *Music:* Mike Oldfield (Tubular Bells), Hans Werner Henze (Fantasia for Strings). *Additional Music:* Jack Nitzsche. *Director of Photography (Iraq Sequence):* Billy Williams. *Production Manager:* William Kaplan. *Sound:* Jean-Louis Ducarme.

Film Editor: Bud Smith. *Assistant Film Editor:* Ross Levy. *Supervising Film Editor:* Jordan Leondopoulos. *Film Editors:* Evan Lottman, Norman Gay. *Assistant Film Editors:* Michael Goldman, Craig McKay, Jonathan Pontell. *Sound:* Chris Newman. *Dubbing Mixer:* Buzz Knudson. *Sound Special Effects:* Fred Brown, Ross Taylor. *Special Sound Effects:* Ron Nagle, Doc Siegel, Gonzalo Gavira, Bob Fine. *Sound Consultant:* Hal Landaker. *Music Editor:* Gene Marks. *Property Master:* Joe Laracciolo. *Script Supervisor:* Nick Sgarro. *Costume:* Joe Fretwell. *Hairstylist:* Bill Farley. *Casting:* Nessa Hyams, Juliet Taylor, Louise D. Giamo. *Assistant Art Director:* Charles Bailey. *Technical Advisors:* Reverend John Nicola, Reverend Thomas Bermingham, Reverend William O'Malley, Norman E. Chase, MD., Herbert F. Walker, MD., Arthur I. Snyder, MD. *M.P.A.A. Rating:* R. *Running Time:* 122 minutes.

P.O.V.

"*The Exorcist* goes back to a case of alleged demon possession that I heard about in 1949 when I was a junior at George Washington University — not an overly credulous and pious account from medieval times. This was in a sophisticated capital city, with psychiatric experts in attendance" (18).—Author/producer William Peter Blatty recounts his inspiration for *The Exorcist* (1973).

"A psychiatrist friend of mine has told me that he is seeing new patients all the time whose troubles can be directly traced to their having seen this film. They report recurring nightmares and problems they never had before. My friend is concerned, as I am, that there will be even more of it, if people continue to flock to the box office" (19).—The Reverend Billy Graham denounces *The Exorcist*.

———————

SYNOPSIS: In Northern Iraq, a Catholic priest, Father Merrin, participates in a massive archeological dig. As he works at the site, he unearths a tiny statue buried in the dirt, one with the face of a mythical demon. This discovery, coupled with some bizarre incidents, affects Merrin deeply and he plans to return stateside, though he is hampered in part by his weak heart.

Meanwhile, movie star Chris MacNeil shoots a movie for director Burke Dennings in Georgetown, Washington, D.C. She is renting a house with her 12-year-old daughter, Regan, and lives in the chi-chi world of movie star celebrity; she is troubled when strange noises are heard in her attic. Before long, cute little Regan also has an unusual experience. She has been playing with a Ouija board, and contacts a spirit called "Captain Howdy." To Regan and Chris, this event is only part of a silly child's game, but it is to be the catalyst for terror.

One night at a party, Regan walks downstairs long after her bedtime and warns a visiting astronaut that he will die "up there" on his next visit to space. Then, as if for punctuation, she urinates on the carpet. Chris is concerned, though Regan's odd behavior is first dismissed as a case of "nerves." Before long, the strange behavior intensifies, and Regan is taken to see a doctor for her shocking descents into obscenity and violence.

At first the doctor suspects a chemical disturbance, a lesion, in Regan's temporal lobe, but X-rays reveal no signs of a seizure disorder. Regan suffers through a battery of painful medical tests, but medicine completely fails to diagnose her condition.

The last straw occurs when Chris finds a bloody Regan masturbating with a crucifix. Regan's physical appearance and voice have changed too: she seems to be inhabited by another, monstrous creature. Worse, she commands inexplicable powers, including the ability to hurl furniture around the room by power of thought.

Before long, there is also a suspicion that Regan somehow managed to kill Burke Dennings. A local police detective, Lt. Kinderman, visits Chris, and questions how a girl Regan's size could hurtle an adult man out her bedroom window and down the long flight of stairs outside.

At a loss to explain Regan's condition, the medical community recommends psychiatry. A prominent psychiatrist informs Chris that Regan may have a split personality, but even that answer does not explain Regan's strange and horrifying transformation into a monster. The psychiatrist attempts to hypnotize Regan, but the child grabs him by the testicles, and attacks him. Later, a panel of psychologists recommends to Chris that her daughter be committed. When Chris refuses, the same panel offers another suggestion: *religion*.

Specifically, Regan needs to be "exorcised" of the demon that has possessed her. Though Chris is shocked that learned men of science and medicine have recommended the approach of a "witch doctor," she realizes an exorcism may be her last opportunity to save Regan.

Chris seeks out Father Karras, a psychologist and Jesuit priest. Karras is struggling with his own demons, of a different variety. His old mother recently died, and Karras feels partially responsible. He did not look in on her during her last hours, and it was days before her corpse was discovered. Struggling with issues of faith, Karras agrees to see Regan, but as a psychologist, not a priest. He meets with her, and a close analysis of Regan's speech reveals that she is speaking English in reverse. Regan even volunteers that she is actually "the Devil." Karras comes to believe this terrible fact when Regan miraculously reveals knowledge of his dead mother, and the words "help me" appear carved on the girl's belly!

Karras goes to the Catholic Church to request an exorcism, and after some initial resistance, is able to secure the talents of Father Merrin, the wizened priest who recently returned from Iraq. One dark night, Merrin arrives at the MacNeil house to do the job. With Karras assisting him, Merrin prepares to battle the Devil. However, even the experienced Merrin is unprepared for the array of evil tricks he soon witnesses. The demon inhabiting Regan proceeds to levitate off the bed, projectile vomit a foul green substance, and spin Regan's head 360 degrees.

Arguing that "the Power of Christ" compels the demon to vacate Regan's innocent vessel, Merrin continues the exorcism. Unfortunately, his weak heart gives out, and Merrin dies before the battle is won.

Alone now, Karras confronts Regan and the demon within her one more time. As she taunts him with the knowledge that his "mother sucks cocks in Hell" and other atrocities, Karras abandons the Bible and grows dangerously physical, even throttling the girl madly. Karras finally tells the demon to "take him," and the monster obliges. The demon flees Regan and possesses Karras, but in a last moment of humanity the priest summons the will to throw himself out the nearest window. He plunges down the long flight of stairs outside, and dies, taking the evil with him.

In time, Regan recovers from her ordeal, and the MacNeils leave Georgetown for good. A thoughtful Father Dyer, friend to Father Karras and priest to the MacNeils, gazes at the staircase where good and evil collided, and ponders the nature of man, and existence itself.

COMMENTARY: Although such pronouncements are notoriously difficult to prove, not to mention highly contentious, it hardly seems an exaggeration to state that *The Exorcist* is the greatest horror film of the 1970s, and indeed, perhaps the greatest genre picture ever produced. The key to the film's artistic success rests in the unique collaboration of two artists, writer William Peter Blatty, and director William Friedkin. Blatty's story is a literate template, even-handedly contemplating the hierarchy of the universe (and the existence of God). And Friedkin's studied approach to this material is nearly revolutionary. Instead of straining to shock and jolt audiences throughout the picture with exploitative effects and "bumps," Friedkin assumes the perspective of observer, almost a documentarian. Thus, when he is finally ready to release the shock effects (in the final act of the picture), they are not only disconcerting, but terrifying.

The Exorcist opens in Iraq, and were the picture made today, this entire scene would no doubt be excised as being irrelevant and too slow. Yet, as Friedkin understands, the preamble to the action in Georgetown sets up the film's debate about the nature of human existence and the universe. The picture opens with a black-and-white view of the sun that quickly fades into a deep orange. This shot might be seen as a metaphor for the picture's view of the world. This isn't a typical "black-and-white" horror film with easy answers, but rather a full-blooded, colorful examination of questions that humans have yet to fully answer. In the opening shot, *The Exorcist* leaves behind the tradition of *Dracula* (1931), *Frankenstein* (1931), *The Wolfman* (1941) and their ilk by going further, and deeper, into what it means to be human, and what it means to be scared. The shedding of black and white is a visual cue that genre traditions have been cast off.

From that provocative opening, the picture instantly achieves vast scope as Friedkin's camera prowls a colossal archeological dig, and focuses on Father Merrin's discovery of a small statue. The slow-moving camera, the tracking shots, the inscrutable faces of Iraqi extras, and the heavy focus on

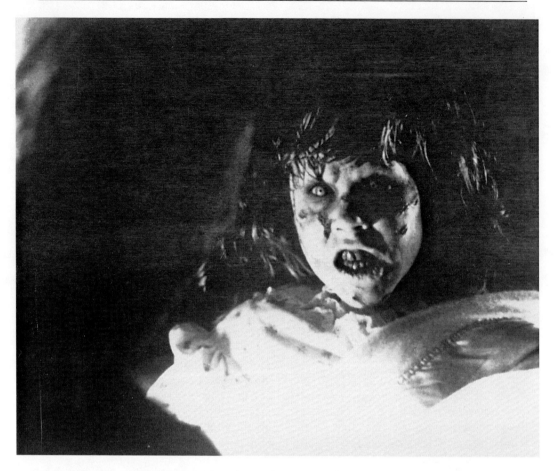

Regan MacNeil (Linda Blair) prepares to vomit pea soup during a confrontation in *The Exorcist* (1973).

authentic locations establish immediately the reality of this world. It might as well be a travelogue, for the narrative is clearly secondary to the exploration of place. Viewers are discomforted not because of special effects or depictions of monsters, but because this world seems unsettling and alien. Father Merrin is outside the safety of America, and outside the shelter of his religious beliefs. The statue he discovers, that of some ancient Middle Eastern icon, either a demon or a god, raises further doubt in the audience. What is it? What does it represent? Was it buried for a reason, and has some ancient evil been unearthed by its discovery?

Interestingly, there is no linear narrative here informing us that Merrin is a priest on sabbatical, searching a dig, recovering from his previous brush with evil. That information is all projected backwards, from an understanding fostered later in the film, and for the time being, the audience is left with a simple, but disturbing picture: an old priest finding a mystery in the dirt. The conjunction of foreign detail, and audience uncertainty about the narrative's direction, creates a strange tension, an uneasiness that escalates throughout the film.

To Friedkin's credit, the sounds and sights of Iraq are recorded by his camera without the bias of overt formalism. In film, there are two schools concerning approach: the formalistic and the realistic. In the realistic vein, the camera merely records action, letting audiences draw conclusions. In the formalist school, the camera expresses something, whether it is emotion, perception, or implication. *The Exorcist* is so effective because Friedkin artfully blends these approaches. The film reads as mostly realistic (with documentary-style excursions to Iraq and a modern American hospital), with bursts of the formalistic (the Georgetown bedroom climax) injected to chill the blood. The opening prologue is realistic, and it leaves enough psychic "space" for viewers to form their opinions about what is being depicted and suggested on-screen. This is critical, for the audience will receive no solid answers about the events that follow, only competing theories. Nobody ever knows or understands why Regan is chosen to be the vessel of evil, but questions raised throughout *The Exorcist* lead viewers to glean and synthesize their own understanding based on the totality of Friedkin's images. It is as close to artistic as a horror film ever gets (except, perhaps, *Don't Look Now*), and the critical backlash against *The Exorcist* may have resulted simply because critics were unwilling to accept Friedkin's artistic approach in that most reviled of dark horses: a genre film.

Here, for once, was a horror film to be taken seriously, to be examined rigorously, and most critics at the time simply weren't up to the task. They didn't go into a horror movie expecting so high a level of discourse (and so effectively scary a film), and most critics, disturbed by what they felt and experienced, termed the film debauched. Art in the service of the vulgar, or so they argued. As time has proven, they missed the boat.

The second interlude of realism in *The Exorcist* is perhaps more effective even than the prologue in Iraq. It finds the audience accompanying Regan and her mother to a metropolitan, state-of-the-art hospital in America. There, in excruciating detail, the film details Regan's battery of "medical tests." We watch in shock and disgust as she receives a hypodermic in her neck, then dye in her veins. We see her blood spurt out as a tube is capped in her throat, and we watch with horror as arcane, vibrating machinery has its way with the girl.

Again, it is important to note that this scene is not constructed in the manner most horror directors would, no doubt, assume. There are few close-ups of grimacing faces, or bloody tools. This isn't the autopsy scene of *Alien³* (1992), where bloody bone saws and scalpels are observed in extreme, discordant close-up. Instead, these procedures and their participants are all viewed by the auspices of restrained long shot. The camera pointedly does not *express* the horror of Regan's experience with modern medicine, it only *records* it, allowing the audience to take away from it what it will. Indeed, the medical procedures are horrifying enough that they do not require any tarting up or shading of any type whatsoever.

In some ways, the hospital interlude is the most horrifying scene in the film because it looks, sounds and feels totally real. The audience is at the hospital with Regan and her mother, looking through the observation glass as a spinal tap and other procedures are performed with clinical detachment. For a time, it is medicine that possesses Regan, not the Devil, it seems.

In discussing a film like this, it is often rewarding to look at the choices the director didn't make. For instance, is it truly necessary to *The Exorcist's* narrative to depict these scenes of medical torture? *Not really*. It might all have been accomplished with a short scene in which a doctor announces that the tests on Regan are complete. But Friedkin again plays the role of documentarian, escorting the audience inside a modern hospital, and exposing its procedures, step by methodical step. He need not comment on the horror; this plain recording of it is enough to be unsettling. Sympathy for Regan and her mother is evinced, and that's an important point. Another is clearly that modern medicine is cold, de-humanizing, out of touch, and inefficient. These monstrous tests result, after all, in no insight into the problem. Even the "best" of 20th century technology and know-how cannot save this girl from evil.

Much has been made of the sequence in

which the physicians refer Chris to the psychiatrists, and then finally recommend she seek out religion. In other words, science fails utterly to help Regan. This doubt and concern about man's knowledge is the factor that most distinctly marks *The Exorcist* as a film of the 1970s. At the time of *The Exorcist,* America was still at war (in Vietnam), Richard Nixon was fighting scandal (Watergate), crime was skyrocketing, an energy crisis was looming, and there seemed to be no answers for any of these considerable problems. In a nutshell, the world seemed to be going to Hell in a hand-basket, and Americans were openly wondering, perhaps for the first time in the country's history, if their know-how and ingenuity was capable of leading them out of the darkness. The old answers, those of philosophy and religion, seemed to carry a new meaning, a new validity even, because pillars like science, government, and technology were exposed as failures. It is no wonder that Ronald Reagan won the presidency in 1980. A simple, optimistic man, he appealed to America's deep need to believe in itself again. Here was a man who championed simple, "traditional" values, like good and evil, good guys and bad guys, and that basic characteristic encouraged Americans, who had seen a decade of doubt and self-recriminations. The conservative 1980s were a backlash against the more open, more provocative 1970s.

The Exorcist is, perhaps, the ultimate film of the 1970s because it so accurately reflects the temperature of the times. It acknowledges the uncertainty of its era, and anticipating the 1980s, it leads the nation back to a consideration of the basics. Forget science, technology, psychiatry and the other "*bullshit*"— what finally saves Regan in the end of Friedkin's film is a rite of exorcism ... a *religious* ritual.

For that reason, the religious backlash against *The Exorcist* is especially hard to comprehend. There has rarely been a more moral, more overtly religious film. Reading it in its most simple forms, the film reaffirms the Christian belief that the universe is separated into forces of good and evil. The Church is even seen in a mostly positive light (the dedicated Father Merrin, the hip Father Dyer, the brilliant Father Karras).

On another, equally simple level, *The Exorcist* is about a priest who loses faith, discovers evil is real, and recovers that faith. What's for the Church not to like there? Or, is the notion that there might not be a God simply something that religious zealots find unacceptable, and therefore worthy of censorship and dismissal?

Leaving religion behind, the fear that is ultimately being expressed so effectively in *The Exorcist* is one about the future. If technology, science, medicine, government and other so-called human authorities are ineffective, what possible future can exist? It is no accident then that *The Exorcist* is about a child in distress, for children, more than anything else in the human spectrum, clearly represent the future. Without children, our traditions don't continue. Without children, the human race dies. Some conservatives, including ultra-right wing author David Frum (*How We Got Here: The 70's: The Decade That Brought You Modern Life— For Better or Worse*) have read *The Exorcist* as a diatribe against children, stating that it represents a rampant fear of the time: a fear of having children and maintaining family. He even rattles off statistics about how birth rates were down in the 1970s (a factor on which he blames women, liberals and abortions...). Yet, as is so typical for these cultural warriors, he has misread the facts regarding an entertainment. *The Exorcist* is not afraid *of* children, it is afraid *for* children. Reading the film purely on a social level (again, not representing the totality of the film's artistry), this is a movie in which a mother loses her child to evil influences, and the pillars of community (including science, medicine and psychology) are useless. What helps? *Religion.* Pure and simple.

The Exorcist sees an order in the universe beyond the vicissitudes of '70s life and technology. Furthermore, it believes that order may be all that can save children.

Taken on the most extreme terms, one could even argue that Regan is metaphorically possessed by the disco decade. She suddenly has knowledge of and interest in sex (a result of the decade's sexual liberation?), her language grows coarse, and she abandons "right" principles. She is only cured when she is again re-acquainted with religion ... by force.

In the preceding paragraphs, one can read and analyze how technique (realism injected into a traditionally formalist genre) and theme (the nature of evil, fear of the future, *et cetera*), combine to create a memorable horror film. What few words can adequately express is the sense of growing terror so palpably generated in *The Exorcist*. The unsettling (Iraq, the death of Karras' mother) builds to the disturbing (Regan's urinating, her experience at the hospital), to terrifying (the bedroom set piece) with such confidence that there are few opportunities for reservations. By building slowly to the head spins and the pea soup regurgitation, *The Exorcist* achieves its effects with absolute legitimacy. All the right questions are asked (is this a mental illness?), and all the right notes are hit, particularly in Karras' subplot, which sees him struggling with issues of faith.

Ultimately, history writes its own reviews. Today, any discussion of *The Exorcist* immediately conjures images of Linda Blair masturbating with a crucifix, spitting up pea soup, or spinning her head 360 degrees. Those were all shocking and stunning moments in 1973, and they remain so today, but in a sense these special effects triumphs mean less to the film than the opening in Iraq, or that visit to the hospital. The bedroom mechanics and pyrotechnics, though terrifying and well orchestrated, are only the icing on a very satisfying cake. They punctuate the horror, but would serve no purpose had not Friedkin opted to take every moment in the film seriously, and bring his considerable knowledge of film technique and mood to bear on the project. Most films are lucky to have one intellect calling the shots, but *The Exorcist* has two, Friedkin and Blatty,

and they have combined to create one of the great cinema experiences of the 20th century.

One of the most memorable images in horror cinema comes early in *The Exorcist*. Father Merrin, in Iraq, gazes at a giant statue of a gargoyle or demon. In one frame, there is both good (Merrin), and evil (the statue), and a gulf between them. It is in that gulf that most of us probably dwell, between the worst and best impulses of our human nature. *The Exorcist* is a great, and important, film because it makes viewers imagine that there may be something greater outside us: an order beyond that which we perceive in our daily lives. Any horror film that can make an atheist stop and really wonder about God is a wonder itself, and *The Exorcist* does just that. It accomplishes this task not with bells and whistles (as most critics argue) but with its persistent intelligence, and its conjunction of the realistic with the formalistic. Ultimately all horror films are about the human condition, and man's place in the universe. *The Exorcist* is the best of this genre because it does not tiptoe around that fact, but confronts it head on. The uncertainty it leaves in viewers is the uncertainty of our very lives.

———————————

LEGACY: Despite a series of critical assaults from all sides, *The Exorcist* went on to become the highest grossing moneymaker of all time (a title taken away two years later, when *Jaws* premiered). The film was so successful that it not only spawned two sequels, the mediocre *Exorcist II: The Heretic* (1977) and the decent, Blatty-directed *Exorcist III: Legion* (1990), but a host of horrific and horrible progeny. *Abby* (1974) was a blaxploitation spin on the material, *Beyond the Door* (1975), an Italian spin-off, *House of Exorcism* (1976), another Italian botch-job, and so on. *The Exorcist* spawned a new wave not only of "possession" films, but Devil-oriented supernatural horror pictures such as *To the Devil a Daughter* (1976), *The Omen* (1976), and *The Manitou* (1978).

As a result of her head-spinning performance in Friedkin's film, young Linda Blair immediately became a superstar before fading to obscurity. Her other horror credits include *A Stranger in Our House*, a 1978 TV movie directed by Wes Craven, *Hell Night* (1982) and *Re-Possessed* (1989), in which she spoofed the film that made her a success. Blair also had a cameo in *Scream* (1996).

Today, *The Exorcist* is recognized as a classic of the horror genre, and few viewers remember how caustic the reviews were more than twenty-five years ago. The film was re-released with new footage in 2000 as *The Exorcist: The Version You've Never Seen*, and it was the top-horror grosser of the year.

Fear in the Night (1973) ★ ★ ½

Critical Reception

"One of those neatly constructed but slightly mechanical psycho-thrillers which makes you feel as if someone is pushing buttons connected to electrodes in your brain… There is a sporadically effective use of prowling camera movements and atmospheric sounds, but Hammer fans will soon recognize the plot as a thinly disguised reworking of *A Taste of Fear*…." — Geoff Andrew, *Time Out Film Guide*, Seventh Edition, Penguin Books, 1999, page 291.

Cast & Crew

CAST: Judy Geeson (Peggy); Joan Collins (Molly Carmichael); Ralph Bates (Robert); Peter Cushing (the Headmaster/Michael Carmichael); James Cossins, Brian Grellins, Gillian Lind (Mrs. Beamish), John Bown.
CREW: A Hammer Production. *Production Supervisor:* Roy Skaggs. *Production Manager:* Christopher Neame. *Assistant Director:* Ted Morley. *Continuity:* Gladys Goldsmith. *Casting:* James Liggat. *Director of Photography:* Arthur Grant. *Camera Operator:* Neil Binney. *Make-up:* Bill Partleton. *Hairdresser:* Helen Lennox. *Wardrobe Supervisor:* Rosemary Burrow. *Art Director:* Don Picton. *Set Dresser:* Penny Struthers. *Construction Manager:* Bill Greene. *Editor:* Peter Weatherley. *Sound Recordist:* Claude Hitchcock. *Sound Editor:* Ron Hyde. *Dubbing Recordist:* Denis Whitlock. *Recording Director:* Tony Lumkin. *Music:* John McCabe. *Musical Supervision:* Philip Martell. *Screenplay:* Jimmy Sangster, Michael Syson. *Produced and Directed by:* Jimmy Sangster. A Hammer Production Made at Elstree Studios, Hertfordshire, England. *M.P.A.A. Rating:* PG. *Running time:* 90 minutes.

SYNOPSIS: On the eve of her departure to live at an exclusive boys school of 150 with her husband, a young newlywed, Peggy, is attacked in her apartment by a shadowy figure with a prosthetic arm. Her bizarre story is dismissed by the kindly landlady, Mrs. Beamish, because Peggy recently recovered from a nervous breakdown, and still doubts her full recovery. Peggy's husband, Bob, dismisses the attack too, and takes Peggy away from London, to their new haunts.

Peggy and Bob's cottage stands on the grounds of an exquisite, though strangely isolated and quiet school. Not long after their arrival on campus, Peggy thinks she sees someone standing outside her window. The next day, she explores the vast school on her own, and meets Michael Carmichael, the creepy headmaster. Even more strangely, the school appears abandoned, though Peggy distinctly hears the voices of young men emanating from various chambers. On her return home, Peggy is attacked by the same assailant, and Bob still refuses to believe her.

The next morning, Peggy meets Molly Carmichael, the headmaster's bitchy wife (and splendid sharpshooter...). Immediate dislike arises between the two women, but Peggy is more disturbed by the fact that Bob must return to London for an overnight conference ... leaving her alone at the cottage. Peggy's fears are justified, and that very night, she confronts an intruder downstairs, shooting him. Surprised, Peggy discovers her assailant is Michael, the headmaster! Carmichael is miraculously uninjured by the bullet, and pursues Peggy out of the cabin into the quiet, dark school. There, Peggy corners herself in a dormitory room and fires her weapon again, but strangely, Carmichael keeps coming...

When Bob returns from London, he finds Peggy in a near catatonic state, and then sets about to find evidence that she has killed Carmichael. When he cannot find such proof, Bob tells Peggy an odd story. Bob claims that the school has not been occupied since 1963, when a fire killed several students and cost Mr. Carmichael his arm. Bob, it turns out, was Carmichael's medical caregiver after the incident, and he came to like the bizarre headmaster. Now, Michael prowls the school alone (with his mechanical arm...), teaching and lecturing to a group of boys who only exist as voices on audio tape recordings.

What Bob fails to tell Peggy is that he and Molly Carmichael are lovers, and that he has arranged everything, including his marriage to the unstable Peggy, to get rid of Michael and inherit the headmaster's wife and money. The only problem is that Michael's body cannot be found, so Bob and Molly set out to torture Peggy into "confessing" her crime, and revealing where she hid the headmaster's body. The tables turn unexpectedly when the headmaster turns out to be very much alive, and in league with

Peggy to stop the conspirators from completing their nasty little plan.

COMMENTARY: The clichés fly fast and thick in *Fear in the Night,* a "psychological" Hammer Studios film that relies on some of the hoariest horror ideas imaginable. Despite the reliance on age-old material, the film is enjoyable, and supported by a dream B-movie cast including (you already know, don't you?) Peter Cushing, the beautiful Judy Geeson, and "super bitch" Joan Collins.

Fear in the Night is immediately reminiscent of *Diabolique,* and its title might more accurately have been *Let's Scare Peggy to Death.* The film trots out the old clichés of the genre including (in no particular order): the secret lovers, the disbelieving husband, the woman with a history of mental problems, and the "crime from the past" (in this case, 1963). Despite such threadbare material, there is an interesting sexual undercurrent to the film, and director Sangster keeps surprise in the air as long as humanly possible considering the derivative nature of the material.

Fear in the Night starts with a pan across a field, as leaves blow across it. We then see the abandoned school that is the film's central setting, and experience a feeling of isolation and foreboding. Then the soundtrack broadcasts eerie sing-songy young voices lifted in song, as the camera probes the gym, the dining room, the bunk room, et cetera ... all mysteriously devoid of life. It's a strange tour of a seemingly haunted or perhaps cursed place, and the (effective) punctuation to the montage is a view of a hanging corpse (with the house in the background, the corpse's feet dangling in the foreground...).

It's an artistic, interesting way to set the scene for the story proper, but the film never again recovers the icy, morbid precision of its opening. Instead, it labors for effect, lingering on clues such as Mr. Carmichael's prosthetic arm, or his wife's fascination with hunting. Peggy's psychological problems are revealed in flashbacks of her therapy sessions, but one is never convinced she is out of her mind. Her husband, the school and its bizarre occupants are all highly suspicious, so *Fear in the Night* never plays as ambiguous. It's clear there is a conspiracy from the beginning. This fact doesn't necessarily ruin the film, it just makes it all the more predictable.

Peter Cushing has a small but crucial role in the film, and one senses he is in the film simply to grant it a little marquee value. Ditto Joan Collins, who is missing in action for the early part of the film, until arriving to portray an all too familiar character in her repertoire (a bitch…). Still, it is undeniably fun to see Cushing as a psycho, prowling the halls of the school, and Collins can do no wrong while playing a sexually promiscuous manipulator. As for Judy Geeson, she has always been an underrated actress, and has given good performances on TV (*Space: 1999*: "Another Time, Another Place") and film.

She's an effective lead, and it is easy to sympathize with her plight. Indeed, the best sections of the film are those that find her in imminent physical danger, stalked and pursued by a dark figure with a mechanical arm. All the mental games (is she or isn't she nuts?) are a wash, but Geeson's screen presence makes the threats to her feel immediate.

Fear in the Night is a Hammer film through and through, meaning it is neither overtly scary, ambitiously artistic, nor particularly bad. Production values are good, the cast has fun with the material, and the story is interesting in an unchallenging way. But, like its later *Frankenstein* and *Dracula* films, this Hammer entry is sort of thriller-"lite." It doesn't have the intelligence or weight to merit comparison to a truly interesting (or dark) psychological thriller like *Frenzy*, *Psycho*, or even *And Soon the Darkness*.

From Beyond the Grave (1973) ★ ★ ★ ½

Cast & Crew

CAST: Peter Cushing (Shopkeeper); Ian Bannen, Ian Carmichael, Diana Dors, Margaret Leighton, Donald Pleasence, Nyree Dawn Porter, David Warner, Ian Ogilvy, Lesley Anne Down, Jack Watson, Angela Pleasence, Wendy Allnutt, Rosalind Ayres, Tommy Godfrey, Ben Howard, John O'Farrell, Marcel Steiner.

CREW: An Amicus Production. *Director of Photography:* Alan Hume. *Camera Operator:* Derek Browne. *Camera Focus:* Michael Frift. *Prints:* Technicolor. *Production Design:* Maurice Carter. *Art Director:* Bert Davey. *Set Dresser:* Simon Wakefield. *Construction Manager:* Vic Simpson. *Editor:* John Ireland. *Sound Mixer:* Peter Handford. *Sound Editor:* Peter Keen. *Dubbing Mixer:* Nolan Roberts. *Unit Production Manager:* Teresa Bolland. *First Assistant Director:* John Peverall. *Continuity:* Penny Daniels. *Second Assistant Director:* Graham Easton. *Chief Make-up:* Neville Smallwood. *Chief Hairdresser:* Milos Parker. *Wardrobe Supervisor:* John Hilling. *Wardrobe Mistress:* Ruth Knight. *Music Composed and Conducted by:* Douglas Gamley. *Associate Producer:* John Dark. *Screenplay by:* Robin Clarke, Raymond Christodoulou. *Based on Stories by:* R. Chetwynd-Hayes. *Produced by:* Max J. Rosenberg, Milton Subotsky. *Directed by:* Kevin Connor. *M.P.A.A. Rating:* PG. *Running Time:* 98 minutes.

SYNOPSIS: A malevolent shopkeeper dispatches cursed goods to a quartet of patrons.

Edward, the first customer at the store, thinks he is conning the dealer out of a valuable mirror by claiming it is a reproduction, but the con is on him. During a séance, an evil spirit inhabiting the mirror possesses him. This ghoul demands that Edward commit murder so he may be released from his reflection prison. Edward reluctantly complies, and is trapped inside the mirror until he too is freed in similar fashion.

Meanwhile, a henpecked husband steals a war medal from the antique shop. He befriends a beggar and his beautiful daughter, and claims that he was awarded the medal in war. Before long, the thief is at the center of a family dispute, murder and an illicit relationship. In the end, he finds that it has all been part of his son's conspiracy to get rid of him.

Another customer at Temptation Ltd., Reggie, switches prices on two snuff-boxes, so as to purchase the one he wants more cheaply. Thinking he has gotten away scot-free, Reggie takes his box and boards a train. There, an occultist promptly informs him that an invisible, bodyless creature called an elemental is feeding off him. Soon afterwards, people begin to complain that Reggie is hurting them, though he has not made any physical contact. That night, his wife feels him holding her hand in bed ... when Reggie is doing no such thing. Realizing that he is haunted by this elemental, Reggie hires Madame Orloff, the occultist, and she exorcises the spirit. Unfortunately, the elemental leaves Reggie, and possesses Susan ... with fatal results for Reggie.

The fourth customer, Seaton, buys an antique door and installs it inside his house. The door leads not to a closet, but a dank, blue room. Seaton and his wife explore it, and realize it is the sanctuary of a sadist and witch named Sinclair. The dungeon-like room borders our reality and Seaton soon realizes it must be destroyed. He rescues his wife from Sinclair's grasp, smashes the door to bits, and breaks free of the evil dimension, family intact.

Back at the store, the shopkeeper continues his evil ways.

COMMENTARY: Amicus has a way with anthologies, and *From Beyond the Grave* is one of its best in this format. Director Kevin (*Motel Hell* [1980]) Connor, who began his film career as an editor, has a special understanding of pace and technique, one that he successfully applies to the low-budget film.

The film thus builds momentum from story to story, ultimately seeming far more cohesive than the scattershot *Tales from the Crypt* or its even less satisfying sequel, *Vault of Horror.*

The first story in *From Beyond the Grave* is one that could have inspired *Hellraiser* (1987). A man lures unsuspecting low-lifes (i.e. prostitutes) to his dreary apartment so he may murder them and bring back to life an evil spirit who holds sway over him. It's good, gory fun, with Warner in the lead role. This descent into madness, with the arrogant Warner ultimately becoming the servant of evil, trapped himself in the "other world" of the mirror, is pretty messy stuff. Connor, who has a flair for this sort of material, stages it all with relish. A spinning camera enlivens a séance, and blood splatters like water on numerous occasions. It's frightfully gruesome.

The second story is a bit kinder and gentler. It's all a matter of misdirection as a cheating husband thinks he is in charge, when in fact, there is another game being played all along. It's less overtly horrific than the opening story, but the characters are more interesting, and the film's rhythm is established. That's why *From Beyond the Grave* is actually pretty good. The film is structured not as the typical anthology might be, with each story an entity in and of itself with distinct highs and lows and other characteristics, but as one overall film with different movements. It works.

The third story at first blush might look to be a spoof of *The Exorcist,* with a funny medium hoping to cast out an elemental that is bothering a poor chap. There are *Exorcist*-style manifestations as a murderous, invisible spirit goes nuts. Plates crash, ceramics explode, lamp shades fly about, and so on. Yet when this author talked to director Kevin Connor at the Main Mission 2000 convention in September of 2000, he learned that *From Beyond the Grave* was made before *The Exorcist* was released. That the story plays as a spoof of that popular film is merely a happy happenstance. Of all of *From Beyond the*

Grave's stories, the third tale is the most overtly tongue-in-cheek, but it still has enough bite to keep the swell of momentum going into the fourth, and most horrific story.

In the last tale, a doorway opens into the realm of an undead sadist, and the story really chills. When the murderous Sinclair comes out of the shadows to pursue Seaton, that precious adrenaline rush that horror movie fans treasure so much is delivered. The set-up is basic, but that's the case in most horror films. Connor's camera clearly establishes the rules. Behind the door, Sinclair reigns. Beyond the door lies the normal. The fun of the story comes in when Connor violates these rules, blurs the territories, and leaves the audience unnerved and uncertain. It is the climax of the film not just because it is the fourth and final story in the mix, but because it is the most intense of the bunch.

From Beyond the Grave is a fun, energetically directed horror movie. Its director loves the genre, and it shows.

LEGACY: In 1987, Paramount Studios syndicated *Friday the 13th: The Series* (1987–1991). The premise? An evil shopkeeper dispenses cursed antiques to his unsuspecting customers, until the shopkeeper's cousins take over the business, and attempt to retrieve the evil goods. It owed more than a bit to *From Beyond the Grave*.

It's Alive (1973) ★ ★ ★ ★

Critical Reception

"Schlock shock is a proliferating subspecies: the horror flick that will do anything, show anything, to churn a stomach.... *It's Alive* is the latest example of schlock shock.... What's most troublesome about *It's Alive* even beyond its shoddiness, is the cynicism with which it was concocted."—Jay Cocks, *Time*: "Scarred at Birth," March 3, 1975, page 6.

"A slick throwback to the old monster days, though using the topical gimmick of pollution, was *It's Alive*.... Cohen has a nice line in black humour, best demonstrated in a scene where we see a milkman fall victim to the hungry little monster.... Definitely not a film for expectant mothers."—John Brosnan, *Future Tense*, St. Martin's Press, 1978, pages 221–222.

"...never less than ridiculous and absurd, but it has a strong kinetic force that carries you through to the end. The film isn't exactly clever, but it certainly seems to have some new ideas about horror. The ending is predictable, yet compelling."—Darrell Moore, *The Best, Worst and Most Unusual: Horror Films*, Crowne Publishers, 1983, page 150.

"Over padded horror comic whose effective moments are rather too few and far between."—Howard Maxford, *The A to Z of Horror Films*, Indiana University Press, 1997, page 151.

Cast & Crew

CAST: John P. Ryan (Frank Davis); Sharon Farrell (Lenore Davis); Andrew Duggan (the Professor); Guy Stockwell (Bob Clayton); James Dixon (Lt. Perkins); Michael Ansara (the Captain); Robert Emhardt (the Executive); William Wellman, Jr. (Charley); Shamus Locke (the Doctor); Daniel Holzman (Chris) and Mary Nancy Burnett, Patrick McAllister, Diana

Hale, Gerald York, Jerry Taft, Gwil Richards, W. Allen York.

CREW: Warner Brothers Communications Company Presents a Larco Production, *It's Alive. Photographed by:* Fenton Hamilton. *Edited by:* Peter Honess. *Filmed with*: Panavision Equipment. *Make-up:* Rick Baker. *Production Assistants:* Rob Cohen, Reid Freehman. *Sound Effects:* Robert Biggart, Patrick Somerset. *Titles and Opticals:* Imagic, Inc. *Production Consultant:* Steve Salkin. *Executive Producers:* Peter Sabiston. *Co-Producer:* Janelle Cohen. *Music:* Bernard Herrmann. *Written, Produced and Directed by:* Larry Cohen. A Larry Cohen Film, Distributed by Warner Brothers. *M.P.A.A. Rating:* PG. *Running Time:* 91 minutes.

SYNOPSIS: Frank Davis's expectant wife, Lenore, awakens in the middle of the night as she goes into labor. Frank wakes their son, Chris, who is worried that his mother might die while delivering the child. Frank quiets Chris's fears, and takes one last look around the new nursery: a beacon of hope in their house. Then he drives his family to the hospital for what should be a routine delivery.

While Frank waits to hear about his new baby, something goes terribly wrong in the delivery room. The Davis baby is not normal, and it kills an entire surgical team. After committing these bloody deeds, the baby then disappears into the night, leaving a traumatized Davis family behind. While the police begin a search for the homicidal infant, the doctors ask Lenore and Frank about radiation exposure. They want to test the entire Davis family, but Frank refuses.

On the long ride back home, Frank hears a radio newscaster announce his name as being the father of a mutant baby. He is horrified at his new infamy, and at work, he is sent on a three-week vacation because of the incident. Then, Davis is unexpectedly fired. At home, a reporter masquerading as a nurse tries to get a story out of Lenore, but is dismissed by Frank. Meanwhile, the Davis

Baby's first steps: The mutant of *It's Alive* (1973) looks for Mommy...

baby blazes a killing streak across Los Angeles, making its way into a milk truck and murdering the driver.

A local university wants to examine the mutant infant, and a representative approaches Frank about getting the rights to the baby's corpse after the police kill it. Eager to have the whole affair behind him, Frank signs off on the document. The police corner the infant at a school on Hawthorne Street, and Frank heads to the scene. The baby escapes after killing another cop. The baby finds its way to the Davis home and Lenore, who still considers the monster her child, begins to care for the baby in secret.

When Frank learns of the baby's proximity, he takes down his pistol to kill it. It escapes, killing another neighbor, and Frank takes part in the manhunt with the police. The wounded infant makes its way into the sewers, and eventually it is Davis himself who finds his son. He corners it and talks to it, and suddenly sympathizes with the solitary, lonely creature in the dark. Davis has a change of heart and realizes the monster — for all its horrible qualities — is a living thing worthy of love. He flees with the baby as the police bear down on him. The cops corner Frank, and he begs for them to let his child live. They ignore his pleas and kill the mutant child, leaving Frank and Lenore to mourn another terrible loss.

As Frank and Lenore head for home after the ordeal, they learn a shocking bit of news. Another mutant baby has been born in Seattle.

COMMENTARY: Low-budget as it may be, Larry Cohen's *It's Alive* is a brilliant horror film. It speaks meaningfully about the fears of its time, and despite some descents into gore, actually focuses on character and relationships rather than vicious murders.

Cohen develops audience sympathy for the Davis family from the first frame of the film. They are depicted as a normal, middle-class American family living blissfully in the suburbs. They have a cat, a car, and even a nursery, and they await their blessed event with a combination of eagerness and anxiety. Before Lenore goes to the hospital, Frank pauses to silently consider the home nursery, and the audience can't help but think of all the hopes and fears associated with pregnancy. Then, at the hospital, there are shots of normal babies, seen across a glass barrier. Expectations are raised again, and acknowledged. "I hope we have one like that," Frank says, full of hope.

Like the best horror scenarios, *It's Alive* begins with the routine, the normal, and then takes a turn into the unexpected. Here, Cohen documents that normality — the dreams and aspirations of a "typical" family — and twists them.

After the depiction of the normal, Cohen introduces the threat, the cause of all the horror. Interestingly, there is no specific threat or cause for the horrible events that follow in *It's Alive*. Instead, Cohen's film provides a laundry list of possible explanations for the baby's mutant nature. A group of tense fathers-to-be sit together in a waiting room, and their discussion lingers on some interesting dreads. "There's an overabundance of lead in everything we eat," one father declares, afraid. "There's smog outside," another notes warily. When the baby is born "wrong," this kind of speculation continues undeterred, this time coming from medical professionals. "You've never been exposed to radiation or extensive x-rays, have you?" The Davises are asked. At another juncture, Lenore's previous use of the birth control pill (for 31 months) is raised as the culprit for the odd mutation. Science has no answers, but the human mind fills in the gaps. There are a million reasons why something could have gone wrong with this baby...

The possible reasons for the mutation just keep coming in *It's Alive*, and wisely, Cohen never settles on one as the answer. Instead, the cumulative effect of all the hysterical, desperate guesswork is that the audience gleans a different, but critical, message about causation: *it's just the time we're living in.* That's what was so great (and so troubling) about the 1970s. People were questioning everything. What would be the end result of pollution? Ozone depletion? Dependence on nuclear power? Radiation? The birth control pill? Proximity to microwave ovens? Acid rain? Bad meat?

You name it, and people were concerned about it. Why were the '70s such an era of worry? Consider again that people were very aware in the early '70s that the government was not being straight with them. Whether it was about the Vietnam War or the Watergate break-in, there seemed to be secrets and lies everywhere. Unsettled, America's people began to wonder what else might be hidden. *It's Alive* is the ultimate expression of such fear: that things we don't know are actually killing us, and threatening our future (i.e. our children).

But *It's Alive* is a damned good film because it makes these fears personal ones, rather than merely societal. Frank Davis returns to his nursery after his wife has given birth to the homicidal mutant. He walks into the chamber, hopeless, shattered. He gazes at himself in the mirror, and his unspoken question is obvious. *Is it me?* What's wrong with me? Did I create this monster? Davis is unable to accept the child as his own because he fears that somehow, in some way, he is responsible for its anti-social behavior. Is that not the fear of all parents, when it comes down to it? Are not all parents afraid that they made a mistake in child rearing? How often have we seen the parents of serial killers struggling with the notion of responsibility? What could they have done differently to prevent the atrocities committed by their children? *It's Alive* walks meaningfully in that territory too, as Ryan is first repulsed by his monster child, and later realizes that, for all its evil, it is still a living creature that he helped bring into the world. *It's Alive* is about people, not ghoulies, because it concerns Davis's struggle, and the stages of his acceptance. It asks the question: can we still love something that has done wrong? Can we love a creature that is unlike us, and yet accept it as our own?

It's interesting that the Davises own a cat. There, already, they have accepted something different, and "feral" in their household. The monster child, so anti-social, is acting according to its nature too, but is not treated with the same love as even the cat ... because expectations for it were different.

The reason for such rejection may simply be a result of society's pressure. The Davises are immediately ostracized for having conceived something "different." Davis loses his job, the press tells all kinds of stories, and the police are suspicious. In its own way, *It's Alive* is about the ways that society forms its own answers about things. Really, what happens to the Davises in *It's Alive* is not that different from what has happened to the parents of JonBenet Ramsey. Nobody knows who killed their daughter, but the Ramseys are considered guilty *a priori*. Whether they killed their own child or not, the Ramseys have been judged as "bad" by the public. That little girl should not have been wearing so much make-up. Mrs. Ramsey should not have been so hard on Jon-Benet about bedwetting. And so on. Suddenly, every decision made by those parents is second-guessed and judged in context of a perceived crime. Similarly, in *It's Alive*, people start to ask questions about the Davises. Aren't they a little old to be having children? Did they ever consider abortion? Was Mrs. Davis on the birth control pill for too long? What did they do wrong that *this* should have happened to them? The implication is obvious: society blames the parents.

So *It's Alive* is really the story of Frank Davis and his wife as they face two apocalypses. One involves their own fear that they have created something monstrous. The other is society's condemnation of them for creating that monstrous thing. Though people may call it schlock, the film is rather meaningful when viewed in this context.

And, Cohen does not go over the top to achieve his effects, even sparing the audience the expected birthing sequence. Instead, Mr. Davis happens upon the operating theater, post-massacre. Blood is everywhere, the team of doctors is dead, and there is gore galore. But, imagine how much worse it could have been, had Cohen's camera witnessed the "actual" delivery. It's true that the budget could not have afforded that, but had Cohen wanted to be graphic, he could have been. Instead, he opts only to show the aftermath, letting the audience wonder about the actual birth. Smart move. Our idea of the birth is probably far more disgusting than anything that might have been achieved.

Another horror sequence is shot to maximum thematic effect too. The mutant baby kills a milkman, and his crimson blood mixes with the white, creamy, spilled milk. That's a perfect image for this film. The Davises were expecting a baby who would be nourished on milk. Instead, they got one who lusted for blood. Yet, interestingly, the monster still needs the love any baby would. The milk and the blood mix, just as the monster is both innocent and culprit. Like the bloody milk, it is neither fish nor fowl.

Many critics have indicated that *It's Alive* is actually about abortion. Some see it as pro-choice (had the baby been aborted, none of this would have happened!), but others argue it is blatantly pro-life. Davis tries to save his baby, and see its value, even though it is deformed and murderous. The movie does seem to state that the creature deserves to live, despite its crimes. But abortion is a contentious issue, and one senses *It's Alive* is about humanity more than some political football. It's about people who, through no fault of their own, give birth to something horrible. Society condemns them, and tries to destroy both their creation and their reputation. Amidst that pressure, the family clings together, and even tries to love what has caused them so much strife. In this regard, the movie is actually about the human heart, and the capacity to love unconditionally. It is a remarkable film.

LEGACY: On the strength of *It's Alive*, independent filmmaker Larry Cohen became a popular horror/cult director with his own cadre of admirers. In addition to two "monster baby" sequels (*It Lives Again* [1978] and *It's Alive III: Island of the Alive* [1986]), Cohen has contributed several memorable (and low-budget) pictures to the genre, including *God Told Me To* (1976), *Q— The Winged Serpent* (1982), *A Return to Salem's Lot* (1987) and *The Ambulance* (1990). *It's Alive* shows up regularly around 3:00 A.M. on national cable channels, a mainstay of '70s schlock.

The Legend of Boggy Creek (1973) * *

Cast & Crew

CAST: Chuck Pierce (Jim as Boy); William Stump (Jim as Adult); Willie E. Smith (Himself); Lloyd Bowen (Himself); B.R. Barrington (Himself); Smokey Crabtree (Himself); Travis Crabtree (Himself); John M. Oates (Himself); Buddy Crabtree (Himself); Jeff Crabtree (Fred Crabtree); Judy Dalton (Mary Beth Searcy); Mary B. Johnston (Sister); Louise Searcy (Herself); Dina Louise Sorell (Baby); Philip Bradley (Teenage Hunter); Herb Jones (Himself); Steve Lyons, Patty Dougan (Teenage Couple); Dennis Lamb (Mr. Kennedy).

CREW: From Cinema Shares International Distribution Corporation. Pierce-Ledwell Productions Presents *The Legend of Boggy Creek*. *Screenplay:* Earl E. Smith. *Music:* James Mendoza-Nava. *Narrated by:* Vern Stierman. *Executive Producers:* L.B. Ledwell, Jr., and Charles B. Pierce. *Produced and Directed by:* Charles B. Pierce. *Editor:* Tom Boutrose. *Associate Producer:* Earl E. Smith. *Photographed by:* Charles B. Pierce. "*The Legend of Boggy Creek*" *written by* Earl E. Smith, *sung by* Chuck Bryant.

"Nobody Sees the Flowers but Me" written by Earl E. Smith, *sung by* Jimmy Collins. *Filmed in* Techniscope. *M.P.A.A. Rating: G. Running Time:* 87 minutes.

SYNOPSIS: There's a quiet little town in Southwest Arkansas called Fouke, a town that borders on Texas and has a population of approximately 350. It's a simple town of farmers and hunters that's "a right pleasant" place to live ... until the sun goes down, that is. By black night, a hairy man-beast living near Boggy Creek ventures into civilization. Years ago, a seven year old boy named Jim saw the "Fouke Monster" in a sprawling field, and now he has returned to Fouke to narrate the story of the Boggy Creek monster.

Long after Jim's childhood encounter with the creature of Boggy Creek, reports of the monster's activity have spread. The creature came up from the bog and carried off both of John Oates' 200 lb. hogs on one occasion, and another resident, Willie E. Smith, shot at the shaggy creature with a shotgun. On a different evening, the Fouke monster followed the shore of Boggy Creek to the isolated Searcy home, where two sisters were alone for the evening with no phone, and the nearest neighbors were a mile or so away. Mary Beth Search fainted after seeing the hairy beast outside her window, and the family kitten died from fright at the sight of the monster. In the following weeks, a teenage hunter wounded the beast with his rifle while tracking a deer.

No longer able to ignore their problem, the good citizens of Fouke organize a big hunt on foot and horseback, and the creature retreats — not to be seen again for some eight years. Consequently, backwoods hermit Herb Johnson refutes the creature's existence to his friend Travis Crabtree. If such a creature existed, Herb is certain he would have seen it by now.

Years later, farmer O.H. Kennedy, who lives on the outskirts of Fouke, reports finding monstrous footprints (with 3 toes) in his bean field. The national press catches wind of the local story, and investigates the area around the creek to determine if there is a "sasquatch" on the loose. Growing bold, the Boggy Creek monster ventures upstream and attacks a house where three teens are having a pajama party. Later, he kills a dog in front of a mobile home.

Then, on one especially frightening occasion, the creature almost gains entrance to a house where two young married couples are staying. The creature reaches in through an open window and is subsequently shot at. Angry, the creature attacks again, injuring a resident.

Jim, the narrator of this unusual local legend, returns to his old home — the field where he once encountered a monster — and reminisces about the beast and his fear of it. He also shares a warning with his audience: if you're ever in Arkansas after nightfall, beware of the hairy man-beast that roams the land around Boggy Creek. Satisfied that "there's still a bit of wilderness" and still "some mysteries" left in the world, Jim signs off.

COMMENTARY: Before *The Blair Witch Project* (1999), before *The Amityville Horror* (1979), there was this low-budget curiosity, a home-spun Arkansas film based on a "true story" about a local monster who dwelled in the wilds of Arkansas. Ironically, the best and worst elements of *The Legend of Boggy Creek* derive from the same source: the film's ability and willingness to capture a sense of place.

Boggy Creek opens with mystery. A prowling camera (in a boat) searches the land and water around Boggy Creek in a slow, almost dreamy, state. Beavers, turtles, lizards and birds all go about their business, unimpeded, as the cameraman (director Pierce) captures the action in workman-like, but not inefficient fashion. There are some creaky zooms, a photographic technique indicative of the times, and a few clumsy rack focuses that nonetheless capture the natural beauty of the land. But mostly there is a real feeling for the sprawl of the wild. Sounds of the wilderness punctuate the soundtrack, and in its opening moments, *The Legend of Boggy Creek* lives up to its final meditation: that there are still some mysteries left in the world. In this half-explored universe of gnarled trees, criss-crossing branches, eerily calm waters and varied wildlife, a viewer is able to temporarily suspend disbelief. What mysteries lurk here? How did this world, often unseen by man, evolve? Is it possible that out here, in the dark woods of Arkansas, some kind of monster dwells? The opening montage of *The Legend of Boggy Creek* permits room for such ruminations, and wisely puts the viewer in the right frame of mind to consider what is supposedly a "true" story.

Yet even in his observance of this untapped setting, director Pierce, and editor Tom Boutrose, missteps. There are no less than 23 shots of Boggy Creek and its wildlife in the opening montage, some shots held for as long 30 seconds. Though the dedication to creating backdrop and mood is commendable, the same feeling, the same rhythm could probably have been generated with half as many shots. But that fact is part and parcel of this film's problem. It is competently made, and even modestly clever, but it never reveals itself to be artistic, at least not in the manner that the brilliant *Blair Witch Project* manages. The *Boggy Creek* approach does reveal to viewers a different and mysterious world, the backwoods of Arkansas, but it never generates the kind of fear and tension the filmmakers seemingly desire.

Part of that failure may have to do with something else that *The Legend of Boggy Creek* manages to establish expertly with its "authentic" feel and local color. Quite simply, the people "dramatized" in this film are not well served by the straight-faced, solemn approach to the material. These people, Arkansas natives all, either of their own free will or at the direction of Charles Pierce, say some very funny, very stupid things. The result of the unintentionally funny dialogue, coupled with the distinct Arkansas accent, is a feeling that everyone who lives in this particular region of the country is a bumpkin. Of course, such an assertion is not at all true. Arkansas has many smart people living there, but few (it seems from the movie) dwell anywhere in the vicinity of Boggy Creek.

The Blair Witch Project was a clever film because it depicted the locals of Burkittsville (formerly Blair) with a sense of irony and distance. They were local yokels, all right, but the three visiting film students were outsiders who judged everything with irony and contempt. Thus the film, which found the arrogant students facing their comeuppance in the woods, was a comment on slacker cynicism and the post-modern, media-driven Generation-Next.

By contrast, *The Legend of Boggy Creek* is respectful, even worshipful of those from whom it gleans its critical testimony. That these people may be a little weird, a little uneducated, or even just perhaps a bit different, is never suggested, never whispered, never hinted at. For instance, the narrator of the film, a wise-sounding authority, expresses delight that a big hunt is being organized to catch the Boggy Creek monster. Excited, he enthuses that even "famous dogs from Tennessee" have been recruited for the important mission.

All that can be said about that is that you know you live in a small southern state when the canines of another state are your local celebrities.

Even more comically, local fisherman Travis Crabtree visits a hermit named Herb Johnson at one point in the film. Herb, who lives in a tent on the banks of Boggy Creek and is proud of his "bottle tree" (literally a tree in which large moonshine bottles have been hung...), is treated like the town oracle, as a wise and knowledgeable elder. That in itself is not funny, but the narrator's opening revelation about him is. Herb, you see, shot off "half of his foot" during a "boating accident" some 14 years back.

Again, a town is in real trouble when its elder statesman is a guy who blew his toes off fishing.

That Travis is seen rowing a canoe to

the strains of his very own folk song ("Hey Travis Crabtree, Do You See What I See?") adds to the comedic aura of the sequence.

Okay, it is easy to make regional jokes, and one can make all kinds of cruel-hearted jokes about New Jersey, Virginia, South Carolina, Arkansas, California or just about any other region in the United States with equal sarcasm. The point of these criticisms is not that Arkansas is a state of bumpkins, but that the film, by recording these "real" people in this bizarre light, suggests that, indeed, the good people of Fouke are, well … idiots.

Take for example the nighttime siege that leads up to the climax of the picture. The Boggy Creek monster has just attacked a house during blackest night, and what does one concerned character do? Well, he takes the opportunity to go to the toilet, of course! Then, while he is *in medias res* there, the monster breaks into the bathroom, causing the terrified man to fly skittering off the toilet, his pants still half-down, screaming. The timing, setting and direction of this "jolt" incline one to laugh, not scream, and yet Charles B. Pierce probably intended the opposite. So, even as Pierce manages to create suspension of disbelief by capturing the wilds of Arkansas and allowing for the possibility of a Big Foot–like animal, he inadvertently creates humor and ridicule by revealing the "real" people of Fouke (playing themselves…) to be somewhat less than intelligent.

The final straw, perhaps, is that even the creature of *Boggy Creek* merits its own folk song, which is heard not just once, but twice in the picture. "Here the sulfur river flows … this is where the creature goes … safe within a world he knows," the singer warbles, creating another very funny effect in what is obviously intended as a serious picture.

While watching *The Legend of Boggy Creek,* this author's wife, his barometer of the bad, expressed the notion that so inept and toothless a horror picture could only be meant for the eyes of children. It is rated G, after all. However, one must again wonder if the film's lack of thrills is intentional.

When the monster attacks the Searcy house, the family's cat dies of sheer terror. Subsequently director Pierce treats his audience to an intense close-up of the dead-cat, its eyes wide, its mouth agape with terror. Though inherently silly, the image of a dead household pet is not exactly suitable for children.

Actually, this scene leads back to the earlier conclusion that, well, the people of this town are just not very smart. Mary Beth Searcy (who eerily resembles Paula Jones…) is home alone at night, and she hears something strange outside her living room window. Her little black kitten meows with fear and terror at the sound. Oddly, the very next shot is of Mary Beth putting the poor, terrified kitten out on the porch! The next morning, Searcy is shocked to find it expired, "scared to death," but what the hell did she expect by putting it out in the night when it was so obviously terrified of whatever was lurking in the bushes?

By utilizing a shaky camera and tight framing in the film's pajama party attack sequence, it is clear Pierce is hoping to generate suspense, thrills and chills in *Legend of Boggy Creek.* These effects are out of his reach because the titular creature never actually does anything scary, or even particularly significant. Pierce is unable to deliver on any of his action scenes, perhaps because of budgetary restraints, perhaps because the monster is fairly harmless. Regardless of the reason for the failure, each action set piece results in what can only kindly be termed anti-climax.

In one attack scene, the creature "attacks" a house and "smashes flowerpots" (out of what the film terms "lonely frustration"…) and then disappears. Two other times, he comes out of the woods, shambles around, and disappears. Since he never actually threatens anybody with physical danger, these scenes literally have nowhere to go. And, if one is being analytical about this, one cannot really blame old Boggy for the dead cat. He was just a bystander, and could not help if it his "sour, pig-pen" odor and hideous appearance are fatal to others. Thus the action scenes build and build, and then lead to nothing except smashed garden pottery and a fatal feline infarction.

Is *The Legend of Boggy Creek* presented believably? The opening card of the film establishes it "is a true story" and that "some of the people in this motion picture portray themselves—in many cases on actual location" (meaning, inevitably, mobile homes…), but the film techniques unfurled by Pierce undercut the notion that any of this really happened. For instance, there is no attempt to document the passage of time. Jim (the narrator) sees the monster when he is at the tender age of 7. The creature goes on the attack for several years, then disappears for eight years, and then returns. Yet hairstyles, clothes, even car models, never change to acknowledge the passage of time. Judging by the film, it seems to have been 1970 for ten years at least.

Also, the narrator never attempts to indicate that what the audience is seeing is actually a "dramatization" of the events, rather than documentary footage of the events. This is troubling for a number of reasons. Firstly, how is one to account for all the well-considered cuts and camera angles if this is "occurring as live?" When little Jimmy runs across a golden field at sunset (a beautiful image, by the way), the audience is treated to a long shot, a close shot, a tracking shot, and even what appears to be an aerial shot from tree level. The rest of the movie follows suit, even revealing the monster in a fairly detailed medium shot. The movie cannot be considered "documentary" because of the very film techniques it exploits. If it were a documentary, we would be lucky to catch a fleeting glimpse of the monster, let alone such lingering shots of the hairy beast.

As dramatization, the film fails to persuade as well. Fully three eyewitness participants in this legend are from the same family, the Crabtrees, and that seems more than a tad suspicious. No compelling evidence is presented (not a single audio recording, a photograph, or a super 8 film is anywhere.) What results is a film that tries to sneak by under the auspices of being true without really ever reaching legitimacy. Even bogus TV series such as *In Search of* or *Sightings* interview authorities on paranormal or supernormal events, and acknowledge their re-creations as such.

The best way to appreciate *The Legend of Boggy Creek* is to watch the opening montage, and imagine just how scary and interesting it would be if a monster did dwell out there, in that beautiful but dangerous realm of the unknown. Then, when the first character opens his mouth, turn off the VCR . That way, one can maintain respect for the great state of Arkansas, as well as preserve the commendable notion that there are still "some mysteries" out there in the dark, in the night.

LEGACY: A surprise box office winner, *The Legend of Boggy Creek* spawned two less-successful sequels, *Return to Boggy Creek* (1978), and *Boggy Creek II* (1985). Perhaps more importantly, its documentary approach to horrific material was revived, generally to kudos, in the 1999 sleeper *The Blair Witch Project*. Director Charles B. Pierce returned with another low-budget hit in 1976, *The Town That Dreaded Sundown*, this one about a masked serial killer in Texarkana.

The Legend of Hell House (1973) ✳ ✳ ✳ ✳

Critical Reception

"It's a supernatural thriller; it's a shocker, with things leaping out of corners … and its an almost-convincing pseudoscientific study of psychic events … a tightly wound and really scary story, which has been directed by John Hough with a great deal of sympathy for the novel's spirit."— Roger Ebert, *Roger Ebert's Movie Home Companion* (1993 Edition), Andrews and McMeel, 1993, page 367.

"Genuinely frightening haunted house chiller with just the right style and atmosphere. Not for the nervous."— Howard Maxford, *The A to Z of Horror Films*, Indiana University Press, 1997, page 171.

"…the grooviest, ghastliest ghost story to come along since *The Haunting.…* The movie is so harrowing that the let-down ending is a relief."— Margaret Ronan, *Senior Scholastic*, September 20, 1973

"While not perfect, this film pulled a series of time worn threads from the science fiction arena into a horror sub-genre that lives with us today in *The X-Files*— science versus things that go bump in the night (as opposed to giant grasshoppers). The cynic learning to believe in evil is as old as horror, but the cynic in scientist's garb, having taken an evolutionary step up from being the cause of the evil, is certainly an interesting approach, and one of a handful of times a Richard Matheson novel has survived a big-screen treatment."— Bill Latham, *Mary's Monster*, Powys Books.

Cast & Crew

CAST: Roddy McDowall (Ben Fischer); Pamela Franklin (Florence Tanner); Clive Revill (Dr. Lionel Barrett); Gayle Hunnicut (Ann Barrett); Roland Culver (Mr. Deutsch); Peter Bowles (Haney).

CREW: Academy Pictures Corporation Presents a James H. Nicholson Production, *The Legend of Hell House. Music and Electronic Score:* Brian Hodgson, Delia Derbyshire. *Executive Producer:* James H. Nicholson. *Screenplay:* Richard Matheson. *Based on His Novel* Hell House. *Produced by:* Albert Fennell, Nortman T. Herman. *Directed by:* John Hough. *Production Manager:* Ron Fry. *Assistant Director:* Bert Batt. *Continuity:* Gladys Goldsmith. *Casting Director:* Sally Nicholl. *Technical Advisor:* Tom Corbett. *Director of Photography:* Alan Hume. *Camera Operator:* Tony White. *Make-up:* Linda Devetta. *Hairdresser:* Pat McDermott. *Photographic Effects:* Tom Howard. *Sets Designed by:* Robert Jones. *Assistant Art Director:* Kenneth McCallum Tait. *Special Effects:* Roy Whybrow. *Wardrobe Mistress:* Eileen Sullivan. *Editor:* Geoffrey Root. *Sound Recordist:*

Les Hammond, Bill Rowe. *Dubbing Editor:* Peter Lennard. Made on location at EMI-MGM Elstree Studios, Boreham Wood, Hertfordshire, England. Produced by Academy Picture Corporation. Released by 20th Century–Fox. *M.P.A.A. Rating:* PG. *Running Time:* 94 minutes.

P.O.V.

"Just after they made *The Legend of Hell House*, people began making the really classy A-picture-type horror films, starting with *The Exorcist*, so had I held on to *Hell House* a few more years, it might have gotten that kind of treatment, too. It's a B-plus, but it didn't make A" (20).— Richard Matheson, author of *Legend of Hell House* (1973), discusses his perception of the film.

___

SYNOPSIS: Physicist Lionel Barrett is paid handsomely by an old millionaire, Mr.

Deutsch, to confirm or disprove that life exists after death. To this end, Barrett is to spend five days with a team inside the Belasco House, a dwelling known as "Hell House" and the "Mount Everest of Haunted Houses," to get his answer. The only sane survivor from the last expedition (in 1953), Fischer, joins the team. Florence Tanner, a mental medium also joins Barrett, Fischer and Barrett's beautiful wife, Ann.

The team arrives at the strange old house, and finds that the windows are all bricked up by Belasco, the eccentric owner who did not want guests looking out or outsiders looking in. Once inside, the team acquaints itself with the house, including the cellar, the chapel and a grand living room. On an old record player, Belasco's voice welcomes his new guests to Hell House.

Florence Tanner soon arrives at the theory that the house is being haunted by multiple surviving personalities, and Fischer tells Ann the history of the house. Built in 1919 by Belasco, a "Roaring giant" with some frightening hobbies including necrophilia, sadism, cannibalism, alcoholism, drug addiction and sexual fetishes. Then, in 1929, 27 guests were found dead inside Hell House, but Belasco was not among them. His body was never found. Later, Tanner conducts a sitting and senses the spirit of a disturbed young man, Daniel Belasco. In a changed voice, Daniel/Florence warns the others to get out of the house before he kills them. The sitting is repeated, this time under Barrett's scientific supervision. Electromagnetic energy is detected, as well as ectoplasm, but when Barrett insults Tanner's capabilities, the house responds in force. Barrett barely survives a poltergeist attack, and he blames Tanner for the occurrences.

By night, Ann is possessed by sexual visions and longings. She attempts to seduce Fischer, but he slaps her to break her out of the trance. Meanwhile, Florence searches for Daniel's corpse and finds it between the walls of the wine cellar. The boy is given a Christian burial, but the hauntings don't stop. Daniel's spirit returns to Florence and

informs her he can only be free if she willingly makes love to him. Florence does so, and is unhinged by the experience.

On the following day, a special machine called a "reverser" is delivered to Hell House. Barrett's invention, the device is capable of reversing the electromagnetic radiation of the house and rendering it dead. Fischer warns Barrett not to fight Hell House, but Barrett ignores his warning even as his wife's sexual behavior becomes more pronounced. Barrett activates the machine as Tanner works up the courage to visit the chapel, the one room in Hell House she is afraid to enter. There, she learns the truth about Belasco, and is killed for her knowledge.

To Fischer's surprise, the reverser cleanses Hell House … except for the chapel. The house strikes out, killing Lionel and leaving Fischer, who has been reluctant to open his mind up to the house, to fight Belasco once and for all. Putting together clues from Barrett and Tanner, Fischer learns the secret of Belasco. He was no roaring giant at all, but a vain, short man who was so embarrassed by his small stature that he cut off his own legs and replaced them with artificial ones. Fischer's discovery destroys the spirit of the humiliated Belasco, and Ann and Fischer discover a lead room behind the chapel. There, the corpse of Belasco sits. There was no Daniel, no other spirits, just one evil man who found a kind of horrible life after death.

COMMENTARY: The highest compliment one can pay to 1973's *The Legend of Hell House* is that it would have made an outstanding episode of *The X-Files* (1993–). For, like that now-classic series, the film gracefully mixes horror and science to illuminating effect. In fact, the film is probably the most logical and intelligent "haunted house" movie yet created. More than just a film with a supernatural foe, *Legend of Hell House* artfully balances two opposing "religions," science and mysticism.

The idea that a group of disparate, and

quarrelsome, people should be forced to spend time together in a haunted house is not a new one. It was the fodder of *The Haunting* (1963) and *The House on Haunted Hill* (1959), to name but two. Yet *Legend of Hell House* takes this common premise further than other similar productions because of the manner in which it defines the characters that walk, eyes open, into the danger.

One character, Barrett, is a staunch advocate of science and rationality. He is so grounded, in fact, that his defense of science in the face of the supernatural actually seems irrational. He just can't accept something that doesn't fit his perception of Euclidian reality.

Another character, Tanner, subscribes to the idea that the universe is mystical, and rife with the supernatural. Like Barrett, Tanner is blind to anything that opposes her point of view.

Between these two poles of thought stand a non-aligned person (Barrett's wife), and a clever medium named Fischer (McDowall), who tries to balance the competing approaches. What's good about the film is the manner in which each "advocate" (Barrett and Tanner respectively) is seduced by his or her own beliefs. Each is so obsessed with being right that the actual puzzle of the haunting is shunted aside. Over and over again, these competitors argue about who knows more in the situation. "She had to destroy my beliefs before they could destroy hers," a haughty Barrett declares at one important point. For him, anything anti-science is a personal assault. Tanner is the same way, a reflection of his closed-mindedness.

The importance of being right, ironically, is the very weakness, the character flaw, that the malevolent spirit of Belasco exploits against both Barrett and Tanner. These two opposites have more in common than they know, as they both suffer from their philosophical blindness. Barrett believes his scientific device can wipe out any "negative" energy in Hell House, and is proven wrong most drastically. Tanner believes that there are competing multiple spirits in the house,

and is raped and ultimately murdered for her beliefs. They are both tricked, duped, and rather ruthlessly so.

The reason *Legend of Hell House* holds together so well is that the ghostly attacks orchestrated by Belasco have logical purpose and motivation. The right people are attacked at the right time, so to speak. In most films of this type, it is all supernatural fire and fury. It is rarely clear why the hauntings unfold as they do. In the case of *Hell House*, one detects that Belasco has been acting according to a consistent personal strategy. Every attack is part of his deliberate mind game to undermine his "visitors." He wants to have sex with Tanner, so he tricks her, utilizing her own pride as a weapon of undoing. She believes an innocent spirit named Daniel can be freed if only she has sex with him, and is so desperate to prove to Barrett that she is right that she goes through with the insane act. Of course, there is no Daniel after all, only Belasco, and he gets exactly what he wants … roughly too.

It is no accident that science and mysticism both fail to stop Belasco's hauntings. The force that is finally proven effective against this "beast" is psychology. Fischer understands human nature, and he is able to defeat Belasco when he uncovers Belasco's personality flaw. He realizes that the "Roaring Giant" suffers from a Napoleon complex. He has a giant ego, but a little body. Thus Fischer uses neither mysticism nor hard science to destroy the villain, but a comprehension of humanity, of psychology. In a sense, it is a reversal of everything Belasco has done in the film. The psychological brinksmanship has been reversed, turned against the perpetrator, and Belasco is vanquished.

Ironically, Fischer reaches his conclusion by pulling together elements of Barrett's philosophy, and Tanner's too. He is able to blend approaches, and that's why he survives the horror of Hell House.

The Legend of Hell House tries to get its details right, and that is another reason why it is an admirable horror film. At the same time that it is a frightening film, it asks the right questions about the paranormal. In particular, it wonders: do living people cause disturbances, like those attributed to Belasco, or are such manifestations actually the work of spirits? Parapsychology has still not answered that very important question, and *The Legend of Hell House* plays with the idea. For a time, Barrett suspects Tanner is actually causing the manifestations. She then accuses Fischer of being the origin of the supernatural happenings. He counter-accuses Tanner, and so forth. Nobody knows where the evil of Hell House originates, and that's what makes it so hard to defeat ... and so compelling. It's a mystery.

And indeed, that may be why, in the final analysis, the film is a trifle anti-climactic. This movie has the courage to stick to its guns. It has a statement to make about psychology and human nature, and once that statement is made, there are no further fireworks to share. Fans of the horror genre long for the last "jolt," the sting in the tale, or the spectacular finale, and *Legend of Hell House* only marginally delivers that. It isn't interested in such razzmatazz, only logic. For this reviewer, that's quite satisfactory. This movie plays by the rules, and there is no non-sensical ending to take a viewer out of its well-crafted reality. Once Belasco is defeated the film is over.

One might contrast this subdued approach with the re-make of *The Haunting* (1999), in which special effects were all-important, and the story made little or no sense. To this viewer's eyes, *Legend of Hell House* remains far scarier because, for the bulk of its running time, it only hints at evil forces, rather than depicting them through overwrought CGI effects. That the end of *Legend of Hell House* fails to unleash a firestorm of effects on the audience is probably a testament to its integrity. It would rather scare audiences with ideas than with expensive pyrotechnics.

John Hough directs *The Legend of Hell House* with a welcome restraint and intelligence. In the moments where fear should be felt, he provides it. In the moments where awe should be generated, he crafts that too. The entire film is directed with an eye toward the artistic. Moving reflections in a coffee pot open one important scene. A cat crawls warily in the foreground of the foreboding house, obscured partially by mist, in the background of another scene. There is a long pan (in close up), establishing the scientific tools of Barrett, and so on. It's a restrained, but effective use of camera work throughout. The electronic music gets under one's skin, and the moments of pure horror — such as the poltergeist attack on Barrett — are staged with a terrifying zeal, equal to any mechanical effects one will find in *The Exorcist*.

The Legend of Hell House is often thought of as a good, not great film, and that may, ultimately, be because it has the courage of its convictions. It stands by its thesis, and doesn't succumb to the audience desire to be blown away. How rare, and how wonderful.

Phase IV

Cast & Crew

CAST: Nigel Davenport (Dr. Hobbs); Michael Murphy (James); Lynne Frederick (Kendra).

CREW: *Directed by:* Saul Bass. *Produced by:* Paul B. Radin. *Screenplay by:* Mayo Simon. *Director of Photography:* Dick Bush. *Music:* Brian Gascoigne. *Film Editor:* Willy Kempler. *M.P.A.A. Rating:* PG. *Running Time:* 93 minutes.

DETAILS: Out in the desert, a colony of ants begins to show signs of a "hive mind." Scientists (Davenport and Murphy) set up an outpost from which to observe the ants, but the critters strike back, in several strikingly photographed sequences. The ending, in which the ants seduce Murphy to their cause with a "possessed" Frederick, is strange and disturbing. The ant footage is amazing, and the direction of Bass is thought-provoking. A bizarre, but interesting "revenge of nature" film.

The Pyx (1973) ⋆ ⋆ ½

Critical Reception

"Director Harvey Hart has worked well with film editor Ron Wisman in using flashbacks and cutting, giving pace and excitement and a good deal of suspense to a plot which opens with the death of Karen Black…. Miss Black gives a fine performance, ably assisted by Christopher Plummer, a policeman investigating her death."— Beatrice McKenna, *Films in Review*, Volume XXIV, Number 10, December 1973, page 628.

"Neither devotees of murder mysteries nor devotees of the occult … are likely to come away satisfied. Point the finger of guilt to a screenplay that tells less than enough about Christopher Plummer … and so much about Karen Black."— Lawrence Van Gelder, *New York Times*, March 28, page 34.

Cast & Crew

CAST: Karen Black (Elizabeth Lucy); Christopher Plummer (Detective Sgt. Jim Henderson); Donald Pilon (Detective Sgt. Pierre Paquette); Jean-Louis Roux (Keerson); Yvette Brina'Amour (Meg); Jacques Godin (Superintendent); Terry Haig (Jimmy); Lee Broker (Herbie Lefram); Robin Gammel (Werther); Louis Rinfret (Sandra). With: Gerard Parkes, Francine Moran, Therese Merange, Henry Gamer, Jean Dubost, Julie Wildman, Wally Martin, Gerard Richard, Jean-Guy Dubuc, Pierre Jolicoeur, Gilles Desormeaux, Jacques Galipeal, Petronella Van Duk, John A. Sullivan, Laurence Luczko, Bob Wyngaert, Robert Viens, Robert Bealieu, Marcel Fournier, Pierre-Paul Belisle, Charles Beauchamp, Brian R. Erb.

CREW: From Cinerama Releasing, Maxine Samuels Presents a film by Harvey Hart, *The Pyx*. *Songs Composed and Sung by:* Karen Black. *Miss Black's Music Consultant:* Bob Johnston. *Director of Photograpy:* Rene Verzier. *Film Editor:* Ron Wisman. *Production Designer:* Earl Preston. *Costume Designer:* Estelle Leiter. *Supervisor of Make-up:* Julia Grundy. *Hairstyles:* Pierre Taylor. *Continuity:* Tatania Mihailoff.

Music: Harry Freatman. *Conductor:* Victor Feldbrill. *Choir Conducted by:* Giles Bryant. *Location Manager:* Minou Petrowski. *Location Sound Mixer:* Richard Lightstone. *Sound Editor:* John Kelly. *Technical Consultant:* Pierre Sangollo, Jean-Guy Dubuc. *Production Supervisor:* Tolly Reviv. *Production Consultant:* Willard Goodman. *Associate Producer:* Paulle Clark. *Screenplay:* Robert Schlitt. *Based on the novel* The Pyx *by:* John Buell. *Produced by:* Julian Roffman. *Executive Producer:* Maxine Samuels. *Directed by:* Harvey Hart. *Casting:* Ian DeVoy. *Boom:* Normand Mercier. *First Assistant Camera:* Denis Gingras. *Second Assistant Camera:* Jean-Jacques Gervais. *Camera Grip:* Gerge Grenier. *Gaffer:* Don Saari. *Electrician:* John Sawyer. *Grip:* Raymond Lamy. *Assistant Directors:* Mark Bourgault and Samuel Wendel. *Property Master:* Fernand Durand. *Set Decorator:* Peter Hopkins. *Assistant Props:* Jacques Godbout. *Set Carpenter:* George Savard. *Assistant Editor:* Sandy Altwerger and Pamela Lewis. *Production Assistant:* Diane Marcoux. *Stunt Advisor:* Guy Marcenais. *Laboratory:* Quebec Film Labs. *Post-Production:* Film House. *Titles:* Film Optics/Film Design. *Sound Mixer:* Paul Coombe. Filmed entirely on location in Montreal, Quebec. A Host-Rohar Production. *M.P.A.A. Rating:* R. *Running Time:* 111 minutes.

SYNOPSIS: Detective Sgt. Henderson of the Montreal Police arrives at a crime scene to discover the corpse of a beautiful woman who apparently fell to her death from a high apartment ledge. Another cop recognizes the dead woman as a hooker, Elizabeth Lucy. Henderson commences his investigation, learning that Elizabeth was a Catholic, and a heroin addict. He grills Elizabeth's madam, the duplicitous Meg, but learns little.

Henderson searches the apartment from which Elizabeth fell, and unexpectedly finds himself grappling with the cagey landlord. From the landlord, Henderson learns of the involvement of two mystery figures: Lefram and Keerson. When Henderson returns to Meg's place to question her about these two strangers, he finds the madam and her girls have been brutally murdered.

Taking another tack, Henderson studies the items found on Elizabeth at the time of her death, a black Satanic crucifix and a "pyx," a small container for "the host" during communion. Suspecting some kind of cult activity, Henderson runs down more information on Lefram, the stooge who hired Elizabeth for his boss, Keerson.

Next, Henderson question's Elizabeth's homosexual roommate, Jimmy, but the young man is shot by a sniper as he reveals details of Elizabeth's last night alive, and her fateful meeting with the rich customer, Keerson. Henderson pursues the sniper, Lefram, and there is a bloody shoot-out on a boat. Finally, Henderson gets to Keerson, and learns that the lonely but good-hearted Elizabeth was sacrificed during a black mass.

Henderson is unsettled, however, when Keersen seems to know secrets about him that none should know … none but the Devil. Henderson shoots Keerson dead, but Keerson insists with his dying breath that Henderson has only "freed" him.

COMMENTARY: From Canada comes *The Pyx*, a rather depressing descent into the last hours of a noble prostitute named Elizabeth (Karen Black) who is ultimately sacrificed in a satanic rite. Though the picture is dark, tedious, heavy, and mired in an uninteresting police procedural format (fronted by a bored-looking Christopher Plummer), *The Pyx* nonetheless has some substance to it, and even aims to parallel its fallen heroine with Jesus Christ.

There are miscues aplenty in *The Pyx*. It opens with a dreadful folk song written and performed (or warbled…) by Karen Black herself. The lyrics in this tune and others (such as: "It all turned out like I planned it, if I planned it, but I didn't plan it…") are circular to the point of insanity, and uniformly embarrassing. In addition, some of the supporting actors don't seem comfortable with English. True, the dialogue is mostly awkward but it could have passed muster if more smoothly delivered. And, on top of these flaws, *The Pyx* could have been improved by omitting Plummer's character (Henderson), and his lackluster investigation. The good detective never achieves three dimensions, often coming off as that old "hard boiled" cliché that Hollywood loves so much.

In point of fact, Henderson needed to go on an inner journey too. Merely solving Elizabeth's death is not enough, since Henderson is one of the two leads in the picture. How does he feel about Elizabeth? Her death? Her life? Her choice of careers? How is he changed by his involvement in her case? The audience is never let in on Henderson's thoughts in these matters, and so he remains remote. The climax of the film, which reveals that Henderson is actually confronting a "real" satanic evil as much as a human one, intimates that more could have been investigated in this man. A cult leader looks into him, and somehow sees that Henderson was glad when his wife died in a car accident. That's quite a surprise, and maybe *The Pyx* should have stressed Henderson's personality and emotional complexity more broadly.

Even if *The Pyx* could have done without her vocal stylings, it does benefit strongly from Black's acting presence in the other lead role. She has a sad countenance here, and the film makes the most of her soulful, sad look. And Black has been given an interesting character to play. Although the movie starts with Elizabeth's death, as her body falls from a high rise skyscraper, the flashbacks of the film take her from the role of fallen woman to Christ-like savior.

As *The Pyx* commences, Elizabeth is fallen, both literally and metaphorically. Not only has her body crashed from a great height, but Elizabeth is a lapsed Catholic, a prostitute who sells her body to men. In a scene set in a church, a guilty looking Black gazes longingly at Catholic religious icons, and desires to take communion, but is visually separated from this rite of redemption by a physical barrier, a gate. This obstacle visually symbolizes Black's status as seeking salvation, cut off from it, and in need of redemption.

That redemption comes for Elizabeth when she seeks to save the souls of others. In this pursuit, the film clearly wants to establish Elizabeth as a Christ figure. She is thus canonized in *The Pyx* in both dialogue and action. "I looked up … *she* was there" states an awe-filled homosexual who had contemplated suicide until receiving counseling from the sage Elizabeth.

More to the point, Elizabeth willfully takes the place of a "good" girl, the innocent Sandra, in the cult of death, thus ascending to a point of sainthood. When Black's character is dragged against her will into the satanic rite, the film is also establishing her as martyr. The Satanists substitute for the Romans, and the satanic rite substitutes for Crucifixion, but the result is the same. Elizabeth is "saved" by her good deed. She dies for the sins of a world that led her into prostitution and made a place for such evil.

In its depiction of a life of despair (drugs, joyless sex, serial dissatisfaction and unhappiness) wherein only a meaningful death can save and give life purpose, *The Pyx* is a deeply sad, and deeply Catholic picture. There was once a woman named Elizabeth; her life was valuable, even if she did not treat it that way, and now it is over. To her, saving a friend's life was more important than continuing her own flawed existence. In an age of graphic violence in video games and on TV, this sober point about sacrifice is still worth making.

But *The Pyx* is not nearly artful enough in its approach to this stance. The symbolism is nice, and the ritual montage edited to a speeded-up Gregorian chant is disturbing, but the general feeling of the film mimics Christopher Plummer's detachment. It is ho-hum, and Black's death, revealed in the opening frames, casts a pall over the remainder of the film.

The Satanic Rites of Dracula (1973) ✶ ✶

Cast & Crew

CAST: Christopher Lee (Count Dracula); Peter Cushing (Lorimar Van Helsing); Michael Coles (Inspector Murray); William Franklyn (Torrence); Freddie Jones (Professor Julian Keeley); Joanna Lumley (Jessica Van Helsing); Richard Vernon (Mathews); Patrick Barr (Lord Carradine); Barbara Yu Ling (Chin Yang); Lockwood West (Freeborne); Richard Mathews (John Porter); Maurice O'Connell (Hanson); Valerie Van Ost (Jane); Peter Adair (Doctor); Maggie Fitzgerald, Pauline Peart, Finnuala O'Shannon, Mia Martin (Girls); John Harvey (Commissionaire); Marc Zuber (Guard #1); Paul Weston (Guard #2); Ian Dewar (Guard #3); Graham Rees (Guard #4).

CREW: *Assistant Director:* Derek Whitehurst. *Camera Operator:* Eric Anstiss. *Wardrobe Supervisor:* Rebecca Breed. *Construction Manager:* Ken Softley. *Sound Recordist:* Claude Hitchcock. *Continuity:* Elizabeth Wilcox. *Hairdresser:* Maude Onslow. *Dubbing Mixer:* Dennis Whitlock. *Special Effects:* Les Bowie. *Sound Editor:* Terry Poulton. *Make-up:* George Blackler. *Assistant Art Director:* Don Picton. *Casting Director:* James Liggat. *Production Manager:* Ron Jackson. *Art Director:* Lionel Couch. *Editor:* Chris Barnes. *Associate Producer:* Don Houghton. *Director of Photography:* Brian Probyn. *Music:* John Cacauas. *Music Supervisor:* Philip Martell. *Screenplay:* Don Houghton. *Produced by:* Roy Skeggs. *Directed by:* Alan Gibson. A Hammer Production made at EMI/MGM Elstree Studios, Boreham Wood, Hertfordshire, England. *M.P.A.A. Rating:* R. *Running time:* 86 minutes.

P.O.V.

"It was poor…. The producers were desperately trying to update Dracula. He was made the head of a corporation… Dreadful. Oh, how I fought that. It was very sad for me to see the role deteriorate from film to film" (21).— Christopher Lee sounds off on the "revisionist" Count Dracula of *The Satanic Rites of Dracula* (1973).

SYNOPSIS: In 1973, a British agent escapes a satanic cult, and is rescued by fellow government agents. He dies shortly thereafter, but not before informing his superiors that several high-ranking members of the British government and business community are involved in a satanic cult.

Dr. Lorimar Van Helsing, professor of the occult, is brought in to consult on the case, along with his beautiful granddaughter, Jessica. Van Helsing is shocked to learn that an old college friend, Dr. Keeley, is involved in the cult. He speaks with his friend to ascertain his level of involvement in the dark matter. Keeley seems shaken, confused and downright out of his mind about the project he has been working on. Van Helsing learns, to his horror, that Keeley has developed a

new strain of bubonic plague, more virulent than any yet imagined by man. A cultist sniper shoots Van Helsing after learning the truth, but Van Helsing is only knocked unconscious. He awakens some time later to find Keeley hanged.

Inspector Murray and Jessica investigate the house where the cult is headquartered. Jessica finds the sleeping chambers of several vampire females, and is surrounded by them. Murray rescues her, and they flee the premises, pursued by Satanists on motorcycles.

Van Helsing soon realizes they are facing a master of the undead, Count Dracula himself, and his ultimate plot to destroy mankind. A satanic equinox is rapidly approaching, a time in which the Prince of Darkness commands the balance of power. At this time, Dracula plans to release a plague that will destroy humanity.

Jessica and Murray stake out the Palomar cultist house, while Van Helsing prepares silver bullets with which to ward off the vampire. Jessica and Murray are captured by cultists and held hostage, as Van Helsing visits a rich industrialist named Denham, the front man, and moneybags, for the cult. Denham, of course, is Dracula himself. Like his granddaughter, Van Helsing is captured.

Incarcerated at the Palomar house, Murray awakens in a dungeon just in time to stake one of Dracula's brides. He then kills the other brides by activating a sprinkler system, and dousing the undead with running water. Meanwhile, Dracula wants Van Helsing to watch as he makes Jessica his consort. Then, Dracula decides to expose Van Helsing to the plague. As a fire starts, Murray rescues Jessica, and Van Helsing and Dracula face off one last time. Van Helsing leads Count Dracula into a thicket, and ushers the vampire to his death, impaled on thorns. Then Van Helsing finishes Dracula off with a good, old-fashioned, stake to the heart.

COMMENTARY: Without getting on too much of a high horse about it, it's pretty

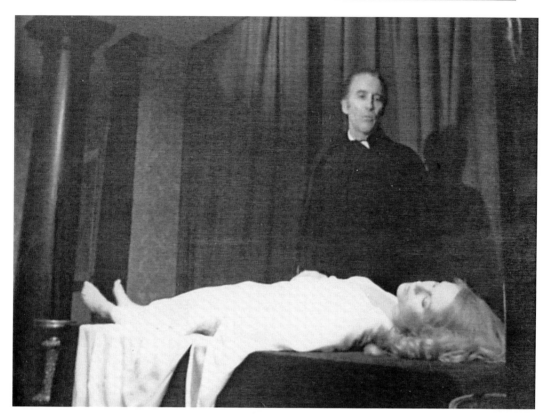

Down for the count: Jessica Van Helsing (Joanna Lumley) sleeps under the gaze of Dracula (Christopher Lee) in *The Satanic Rites of Dracula* (1973).

sickening what they've done to Count Dracula in *The Satanic Rites of Dracula*. In a move that inspires irritation, if not downright anger, the Transylvanian vampire has been transformed into a James Bond movie villain ... bent on world determination, and easily defeated. It's a crying shame.

It's also a surprise, since the resourceful Hammer Studios is behind this uninspiring update of the character. Dracula had served the studio well over the years, and had proven to be the headliner for a durable, long-lived franchise. After the lackluster *Scars of Dracula* (1970), the fun *Dracula AD 1972* updated the character by bringing him into contemporary London. Yet even that advance in setting was apparently not deemed enough to perpetuate a moribund franchise. Instead, this movie is all tacky trend and fad, as it cashes in on two kinds of popular contemporary film: the Satan movies (embodied

by films such as *Brotherhood of Satan, Asylum of Satan*, and *Daughters of Satan*), and the long-lived James Bond film series. Like the latter franchise, this film features secret agents, a mission briefing, the efficient government secretary, gadgets, and otherworldly, Ken Adams–like set designs. Dracula is not just an evil vampire who drinks blood, he is a madman running a corporation who wants to unleash a plague across the Earth. It's Nosferatu by way of Blofeld. And it's wholly uninspiring.

The thing about James Bond villains is they always lose, whether it's Goldfinger, Scaramanga, Blofeld, Renard or Drax. They're as disposable as paper towels, so why put the magnificent horror icon Dracula into the same category? Perhaps it was all just an elaborate audition. In 1974, Christopher Lee actually played a Bond villain in *The Man with the Golden Gun...*

Still, perhaps the overall idea of Dracula manipulating the business world to his own nefarious ends is not terrible in and of itself. In fact, it was the premise of *Dracula: The Series* in 1990. Yet even that relatively mundane TV series had the intelligence to equate Dracula's vampirism with corporate greed and yuppieism. There's no overriding context here, and *The Satanic Rites of Dracula* does not find much motivation for its action. Dracula apparently wants to release bubonic plague on the world to bring about "final peace." He wants to end his existence, and take the universe with him.

Well, if Dracula wants "final peace," can someone explain why he keeps coming back, again and again, after Van Helsing kills him? If all the Christopher Lee/Hammer Dracula movies take place in the same universe, this vampire has had more than his fair shot at "final peace," since he dies at the end of every movie, without fail. Couldn't he just stay dead, rather than continue his cycle of death and resurrection?

As if the character motivation isn't weak enough, director Gibson seems to have little clue about how to direct action. His camera is static most of the time, frozen and seemingly afraid to move. Besides which, why waste time with snipers and secret agents, when there's a master vampire to be offed? If the audience wanted a James Bond film, presumably it would go to see one. When horror fans see a Dracula movie, they want to be scared. This installment just doesn't deliver.

Also, it must be noted that the climax of this picture is as blatantly absurd as any scene Hammer ever committed to celluloid. Dracula is vanquished when he is chased into a thicket and beset by thorns. That's right, he's "stung" with thorny brush, and dies! Let's re-cap then: vampires can be killed by electricity (*Scars of Dracula*), running water (*Dracula AD 1972*), impalings (*Dracula AD 1972*), and now thorns too? Jeez, why be afraid of this guy? It is to Hammer's detriment that it has not only de-mythologized Dracula in this film, it has made him easily killable. This Dracula wouldn't last a round with Buffy the vampire slayer, that's for certain.

From desperation often comes inspiration. *Satanic Rites of Dracula* is clearly an attempt to do something different with Dracula, but it feels more like exploitation than a creative hail-mary pass. Next up for the franchise was 1974's *The Legend of Seven Golden Vampires*, which melded Hong Kong kung fu action with Hammer-style horror. It sounds absurd, but that movie is actually a lot better than the *Satanic Rites of Dracula*. This is the bottom of the Hammer barrel.

Scream, Blacula, Scream! (1973) ✶ ✶ ✶

Cast & Crew

CAST: William Marshall (Blacula); Don Mitchell (Justin); Pam Grier (Lisa Fortier); Michael Conrad (Sheriff Harley Dunlop); Janee Michelle (Gloria); Lynn Moody (Denny); Barbara Rhoades (Elaine); Bernie Hamilton (Ragman); Richard Lawson (Willis); Arnold Williams (Louis); Van Kirksey (Professor Walston); Bob Minor (Pimp # 1); Al Jones (Pimp # 2); Eric Mason (Milt); Sybil Scotford (Librarian); Beverly Gill (Maggie); Don Blackman (Doll Man); Judith Elliotte (Prostitute); Dan Roth (Cop); Nicholas Worth (Dennis); Kenneth O'Brien (Joe); Craig Nelson (Sarge); James Payne (Attendant); Richard Washington (Cop #1); James Kingsley (Sgt. Williams); Arnita Bell (Woman).

CREW: American International Pictures and Samuel Z. Arkoff Present *Scream Blacula Scream*. *Director of Photography:* Isidore Mankofsky. *Edited by:* Fabien Tordjmann. *Post-Production Supervisor:* Salvatore Billitteri. *Music Composed by:* Bill Marx. *Title Song "Torment" Lyrics by:* Marilynn Lovell, *Music by:* Bill Marx. *Main Title:* Sandy Dvore. *Executive Producer:*

Samuel Z. Arkoff. *Screenplay by:* Joan Torres and Raymond Koenig and Maurice Jules. *Story by:* Joan Torres and Raymond Koenig. *Produced by:* Joseph T. Naar. *Directed by:* Bob Kelljan. *Production Manager:* Frank Beetson. *Art Director:* Alfeo Bocchicchio. *Casting:* Joe Scully, Bernard Carneol. *Additional Editing:* Bruce Schoengarth and Kent Schafer. *Sound Effects Editor:* Edit International Ltd. *Sound:* Ryder Sound Services. *Color:* Movielab. *Locations:* Cinemobile Systems, Inc. *Opticals:* Imagic Inc. *Cars Furnished by:* Chrysler Corporation. *First Assistant Director:* Reuben Watt. *Second Assistant Director:* John Poer. *Camera Operator:* Ed Koons. *Sound Mixer:* Donald Johnson. *Set Decorator:* Chuck Pierce. *Script Supervisor:* Joyce King. *Wardrobe:* Ermon Sessions and Sandra Stewart. *Property Master:* Thomas Fairbanks. *Special Effects:* Jack DeBron, Jr. *Make-up:* Alan Snider. *Hairstylist:* Ruby Ford. *Music Editor:* Ving Hershon. An American International Picture. *M.P.A.A. Rating:* PG. *Running Time:* 98 minutes.

SYNOPSIS: In a secret voodoo cult, a power struggle erupts over the priesthood. Big Willis thinks that, by rights, he should be the new leader, but his powerful mother died without naming a successor, and now the decision favors beautiful Lisa Fortier, a priestess herself, in a democratic vote. A defeated Willis seeks vengeance by conducting a dangerous fire ritual that will bring life back to the vampire known as Blacula. Using Blacula's bones, Willis resurrects the dark undead lord, and Blacula immediately bites Willis, turning him into a vampire slave. Willis is a particularly vain man, and is upset that he no longer casts a reflection. Blacula puts the fool in his place, and warns him that he exists only to serve Blacula's agenda. When two friends, Elaine and Lewis, visit Willis's house to pick him up for a party, Blacula strikes again, this time in tandem with the vampirized Willis.

Later, Blacula goes to the party instead of Willis, and encounters Lisa Fortier there. Befriending an African historian named Justin, Blacula also recognizes some ancient African jewelry which once belonged to his

dynasty. After the party, Blacula expands his army, killing Gloria, Lisa's friend. The police arrive on the scene, and immediately suspect that Lisa's voodoo cult is involved in the unusual biting death. Meanwhile, Blacula kills two pimps who accost him on a street, and Willis vampirizes his own girlfriend.

The next evening, Lisa sits with Gloria's corpse, and the undead creature soon rises from her coffin to strike. Blacula intervenes, saving Lisa's life for a very special job. He needs her help because of her great voodoo powers, and warns his minions not to attack Lisa because she is under his protection. Still bearing a grudge, Willis attempts to defy Blacula, but the head vampire threatens to rip out Willis's "worthless heart" should he proceed with his plan of vengeance.

Meanwhile, Justin suspects that a vampire has killed Gloria and the others, and goes to the library to research the subject. After failing to convince the police of his theory, Justin narrows his search and comes to the conclusion that Blacula is his man. Justin confronts the undead lord with his suspicions at a tense meeting. Not wishing to kill Justin, Blacula warns him to abandon his theories lest he find himself in mortal danger. After the encounter, Blacula informs Lisa that he wants her to exorcise the demonic monster dwelling within him, and restore his humanity before he kills again. Lisa agrees to help Blacula find redemption, and starts to conduct the voodoo ritual. Unfortunately, the police and Justin bear down on Blacula and his army of vampires just as the spell seems to be working. The police are unprepared for the vampire counter-attack, but Justin is prepared with pickets from a fence, and methodically stakes the undead creatures in their hearts.

When Justin ruins his restoration ritual, Blacula goes on a killing spree. Left with no choice if Justin is to survive, Lisa kills Blacula by jabbing an arrow through his voodoo doll effigy. An agonized Blacula dies, looking heavenward for release.

COMMENTARY: This sequel to 1972's *Blacula* also expands that film's subtext. The black vampire, again personified by the dignified William Marshall, is no villain, but a cursed man seeking redemption, a victim of white "enslavement." But despite its extension of this familiar material, *Scream, Blacula, Scream!* is no mere rehash. The first film had to concern itself with the business of "origin." The audience had to see how Blacula was created, and the overarching idea was to spin Dracula into an African-American context, but with all the same horror touches that viewers are familiar with.

While remaining consistent with the ideas informing its predecessor, *Scream, Blacula, Scream!* heads for new narrative territory with commendable focus. This time, the story revolves around Blacula's attempt to be fully restored to humanity. He hates being a vampire (read: a slave), and he kills men and women only to further his attempts at restoration. What's so interesting is that the film depicts a black culture that does not support this particular brother. Willis, and even the heroic Justin, fail to understand Blacula's motives, and interfere with his attempt to be redeemed. He is a tragic hero, undone by the lack of understanding of his own people.

Scream, Dracula, Scream! is at its best when it follows Blacula's forays into the streets of the contemporary world. There is a really interesting scene wherein Blacula walks a city strip, stopping to gaze at the sights of modern life. This is a brand new world to him, and the movie pauses to acknowledge that. The movie's best moment comes, however, when Blacula confronts two pimps in the city. He chastises these black criminals for involving a black girl in prostitution. "You made a slave of your sister," he tells them. "You're slaves, imitating your slave masters." It's a chilling moment and Blacula, the regal outsider and former noble, is the only one who could say it and get away with it. This scene plays as an acknowledgment that some aspects of African-American society have imitated the worst parts of the corrupt white society. Blacula, a man enslaved by Dracula, recognizes what it means to enslave others, and is disappointed to see that "slavery," even sexual slavery, has survived in his own kind. This movie works because Blacula, the outsider, is allowed to comment on what he sees, and his perspective isn't as simple as "black and white."

In the first film, the white establishment (its law enforcement, in particular) was targeted for excluding and marginalizing black citizens. The sequel is even more bold, turning the mirror back on black society. It's an interesting and provocative tack to take. Racism and discrimination exist within the African-American community too, and *Scream, Blacula, Scream!* is an entertainment with enough smarts to realize that. It also makes a cogent point about exploitation. Blacula feeds on his brothers and sisters out of necessity. It's a curse he wishes to rid himself of. The pimps exploit their brothers and sisters out of greed, out of the desire to be rich. Willis is the same way: he's a power-hungry, wealth-craving tyrant.

It's clear that *Scream, Blacula, Scream!* desires to make Blacula the ultimate anti-hero, speaking out against injustices of any color, and William Marshall refines his performance here. He's more charming and more menacing, but also more the tragic figure. There's a great depth to his performance, a depth that is missing from films like *The Satanic Rites of Dracula*.

Also worthy of note is the fact that voodoo plays as large a role as vampirism in this film. It's another tacit acknowledgment that the history and culture of the black community is worth exploring. Vampirism may be a European horror, popularized by Hollywood, but the tenants of voodoo are just as fascinating, and if, anything, this film takes an equal opportunity to mythologize this misunderstood (and much feared) religion.

Scream, Blacula, Scream! is fast-paced, jam-packed with impressive stunt work, and every bit the success as *Blacula*. Pam Grier is a gorgeous, involving heroine (as always), and the movie has visceral chills to match its story about enslavement. One can only wish Marshall might have donned the cape for a third and final outing. If the quality were kept as high as in this screen double feature, a franchise would have been cemented, probably well beyond the 1970s.

Silent Night, Bloody Night (1973) * ½

Cast & Crew

CAST: Patrick O'Neal (John Carter); James Patterson (Jeffrey Butler); Mary Woronov (Diane Adams); Astrid Heeren (Ingrid); John Carradine (Towman); Walter Abel (Mayor Adams); Fran Stevens (Tess); Walter Klavun (Sheriff Mason); Phillip Bruns (Wilfred Butler—1929); Staats Cotsworth (Voice of Wilfred Butler); Ondine (Chief Inmate); Tally Brown, Lewis Love, Harvey Cohen, Hetty NacLise, George Trakas, Susan Rothenberg, Cleo Young, Kristin Steen, Jack Smith, Leroy Lessane, Bob Darchi (Inmates); Candy Darling, Barbara Sand (Guests); Jay Garner (Dr. Robinson); Donelda Dunne (Marianne Butler at age 15); Michael Pendrey (Doctor); Lisa Richards (Maggie Daly); George Strus (Doctor); Grant Code (Wilfred Butler at age 80); Debbie Parness (Marianne Butler at age 8).

CREW: Ami Artzi and Cannon Releasing Corporation in Conjunction with Armor Films Incorporated Present a Cannon Production in Association with Jeffrey Konvitz Productions, a film by Theodore Gershuny, *Silent Night, Bloody Night*. *Director of Photography:* Adam Giffard. *Color:* Deluxe. *Equipment:* Cameramart. *Sound:* Magnasound. *Screenplay by:* Theordore Gershuny, Jeffrey Konvitz, Ira Teller. *Editor:* Tom Kennedy. *Music:* Gershon Kingsley. *Produced by:* Jeffrey Konvitz, Ami Artzi. *Directed by:* Theodore Gershuny. *Art Director:* Henry Shrady. *Assistant Art Director:* Sam Bender. *Props:* Jim Walker. *Wardrobe:* Bill Christians. *Make-up:* Pat Pizza. *Hairstylist:* Neil Barbella. *Sound Recordist:* Bruce Perlman. *Sound Assistant:* Paul Bang. *Assistant Director:* Andrew Geygerson. *Assistant Cameraman:* Sal Guida. *Gaffer:* Aristides Pappidas. *Script Continuity:* Helga Petrashevics. *Grip:* Joe Bruck. *Production Assistants:* Jeff Kahan, Brad Pagota, Melanie Mintz, Thomas Sturges, Everett Sherman, Gary Rich. *Assistant to Producer:* Carole Sobel. *Sound Editor:* Nobuko Oganesoff. *Music Editor:* James Korris. *Assistant Editor:* Jonathan Kroll, Charles Baum. *Re-recording Engineer:* Raun Kirves. *Mixer:* Jack Cooley. *Special Effects:* Louis Antzes. *Title Design:* Sal Vitale, Hugh Valentine. *Associate Producers:* Frank Vitale, Lloyd Kaufman. A Cannon Release. *M.P.A.A. Rating:* R. *Running Time:* 83 minutes.

P.O.V.

"*Silent Night, Bloody Night* was terrible. We were given a weird script, and Ted [Gershuny] tried to spark it up. He tried to make it an artistic statement, but it didn't work. It didn't even make much sense. Most people couldn't understand what was going on—which is not good, particularly for a horror film" (22).—Mary Woronov, star of *Silent Night, Bloody Night*.

SYNOPSIS: On December 24, 1950, Wilfred Butler is set aflame in his own house, a former insane asylum. The coroner rules the death accidental, and the Butler house is willed to Butler's young grandson. The grand house stands untouched for twenty years until sold by Mr. Carter, a lawyer from the big city.

Carter meets with the town elders, who are quite suspicious about Carter's client, the Butler grandson. They also warn Carter not to stay in the house alone for the evening. He ignores their warnings and remains in the house with his mistress. While Carter and his mistress make love, a stranger breaks into their room and hacks them to pieces with an axe. The killer then phones the police to tell them Carter is "gone."

Young Jeffrey Butler arrives in town to check out the house he is selling after so many years. He meets the mayor's lovely daughter, Diane, and they plan to go to the house together to check it out. Meanwhile, the axe murderer kills Tess, the city telephone operator, who has also dropped by to check out the Butler place. Soon, other town elders (including the newspaper man and the sheriff) are being murdered with an axe for some dark reason.

Jeffrey finds his grandfather's diary and learns the truth. His mother, Maryann, was only a young girl when Wilfred, her own father, raped and impregnated her. Consequently, Maryann lost her grip on sanity. Hoping to rectify his terrible crime, Wilfred turned the Butler place into an asylum for the insane — believing Maryann could be cured there. But the doctors who came to the asylum were debauched and unwilling to help the sick. To redeem himself yet again, Wilfred released all the psychotic inmates, who promptly killed the doctors, and poor little Maryann too. Then, the inmates who killed both Maryann and the doctors became the town elders including Tess, the sheriff, and Diane's father, the mayor! Now, Wilfred is still alive and conducting his vengeance against the town elders for the murder of his daughter all those years ago!

When Jeffrey learns the truth, he confronts the mayor, and they end up killing each other in a shoot out, leaving Diane alone to confront Wilfred Butler ... who staged his own fiery demise in 1950.

COMMENTARY: Today, bad movies like *The Haunting* (1999) or *The House on Haunted Hill* (1999) cost tens of millions of dollars. *Silent Night, Bloody Night* manages to be just as terrible, but at a fraction of the cost. Therefore, some people might be tempted to see it as a bargain. After all, half way through a viewing of *The Haunting*, the audience is still discerning that, underneath the all-star cast and the great special effects, the movie actually stinks.

Silent Night, Bloody Night is more honest, more blatant in its badness than that. It bears all those reassuring tell-tale signs of a bad movie, signs that today's garbage might avoid through expense: amateur editing and filming, bad sound, bad film stock, atrocious dialogue, and the rest. Still, at least you know where you stand with a movie like *Silent Night, Bloody Night*. It doesn't take long to realize that you're trapped in bad movie hell.

First off, a bit of editorial business: This is not a review of *Silent Night, Deadly Night*, the infamous slasher flick that highlighted a homicidal maniac dressed as Santa Claus. Instead, this is *Silent Night, Bloody Night*, the ultra-low-budget horror movie that probably only six or seven people in the world actually remember. Didn't want there to be any confusion about that.

Also, it seems only fair to note that other than the inclusion of the song *Silent Night* over the opening credits, this film has absolutely nothing to do with the holiday season. There's nary a Christmas decoration, tree or accouterment anywhere to be found. There's no suggestion at all, actually, that any of the events of this film take place on a holiday. It's just an exploitation title, pure and simple.

What follows the opening credits is a badly lit mess that is damned near impossible to follow. The film looks grainy, and appears to have been cut together by someone with attention deficit disorder. John Carradine is wasted in a nothing part, and events don't seem to connect. When does Tess die? When does Jeffrey leave Towman? Who is going where, and why? It's a really messed-up jumble of ideas that never connect to one another. Eventually, even the film gives up trying to understand itself, and voice-over exposition is added in an attempt to explain the over-complicated story. As a rule, voice-over narration of this extent is usually a bad sign, an indication that a movie needed to be rescued in post-production. *Silent Night, Bloody Night* adheres to that rule.

The film starts with one well-executed idea, a rehash of the famous *Psycho*/Janet

Leigh trick, and then moves on to a strange tale that recalls *Don't Look in the Basement* by way of *An Enemy of the People*. In other words, *Silent Night, Deadly Night* begins as though Patrick O'Neal is the star of the film. But, *surprise!*—he's not. About a quarter of the way through, he gets murdered in bed during a pretty well staged and brutal axe attack. From there, it's the old chestnut about loonies controlling the nuthouse, only this time, they actually control a whole town.

From what this reviewer can gather, this is the story: a man raped his daughter, felt bad, turned his house into an insane asylum, boarded her there, and let her be. The doctors at the asylum were bad, though, and the inmates killed them, and took over the nearby town. Now, years later, the father is back, and he's really mad because the inmates killed his daughter, and are now ensconced as the town elders. It's really two (bad) stories for the price of one: trauma in the 1930s (told in gloomy sepia tone), and a massacre in the 1970s (told in shades of dark and black). Any further examination of the film's plot could cause harmful side effects including (but not limited to) nausea, headaches, and confusion.

But at least *Silent Night, Bloody Night* is perfectly up front about its quality (or lack thereof). Watching it, one is reminded how bad movies have really changed since the '70s. Even the worst movies of today are technically competent (even extraordinary, in some cases). Even the worst films made today can be seen and heard adequately. Technology is always solid. Back in the '70s, rotten films like *Silent Night, Bloody Night* were rough, difficult to hear, and painful to watch. They were technologically incompetent, bungled in the editing, and so forth. Somehow, this approach seems more honest. One can at least buckle down early on, grit one's teeth, and get on with the business at hand, fully cognizant that pain will soon follow.

Sisters (1973) ✶ ✶ ✶ ✶

Critical Reception

"…DePalma's most self-sufficient chiller to date in that his penchant for 'quoting' Hitchcock had not yet reached the level of parody that it would attain in his future films. Nor does he send up his story *à la* Godard. The result is a film that is less characteristic of the future DePalma, but a more effective psycho-film because of it."—John McCarty, *Psychos: Eighty Years of Mad Movies, Maniacs, and Murderous Deeds*, St. Martin's Press, 1986, page 124.

"…Brian DePalma's best film; it has humor and gore and is adept at balancing the two."—Darrell Moore, *The Best, Worst, Most Unusual: Horror Films*, Crowne Publishers, 1983, page 125.

"…comes close enough to his [DePalma's] underground films to remain one strange and scruffy piece of work; the final half hour set in a rural Bedlam is particularly bent."—Ty Burr, *Entertainment Weekly*: "Hitchcraft," January 15, 1993, page 56.

Cast & Crew

CAST: Margot Kidder (Danielle); Jennifer Salt (Grace Collier); Charles Durning (Larch); Bill Finley (Emile); Barnard Hughes (McClennon); Dolph Sweet (Lieutenant). With: Lisle Wilson, Mary Davenport.

CREW: American International Pictures and

Pressman-Williams Present a Brian DePalma Film, *Sisters. Directed by:* Brian DePalma. *Assistant Director:* Alan Hopkins. *Unit Production Manager:* Jeffery Hayes. *Gaffer:* William W. Lister. *Casting Director:* Sylvia Fay. *Recordist:* Russell Arthur. *Sound Editor:* John Fox. *Associate Producer:* Lynn Pressman, Robert Richie. *Production Supervisor:* Louis A. Stroker. *Production Designer:* Gary Weist. *Director of Photography:* Gregory Sandor. *Editor:* Paul Hirsch. *Music:* Bernard Herrmann. *Screenplay by:* Brian DePalma and Louisa Rose. *From an Original Story by:* Brian DePalma. *Produced by:* Edward R Pressman. *M.P.A.A. Rating:* R. *Running Time:* 90 minutes.

SYNOPSIS: A beautiful model named Danielle appears on the local New York TV game show called *Peeping Toms*, and then goes out to dinner with a contestant, Philip Wood. Her strange ex-husband follows her to the restaurant, and makes a scene. A worried Philip takes Danielle home to Staten Island. And though her crazy husband stands watch outside her apartment, Danielle and Philip spend the night together. Philip fails to notice the terrible scar on Danielle's hip ... the spot where a co-joined twin was removed.

The next morning, Philip overhears Danielle talking to her sister, Dominique, in another room of the apartment. She seems a bit unhinged. Upset by the encounter, Danielle sends her new beau to the local pharmacy to fill a prescription. When Philip returns, he has brought a birthday cake for Danielle, but Dominique stabs him to death before Danielle can enjoy it.

Grace Collier, a nosy reporter who lives in an apartment building across from Danielle's, witnesses the crime and calls the police. Meanwhile, Danielle's husband Emile arrives and helps Danielle clean up Domi-

A demented Dominique (Margot Kidder) disrobes in Brian DePalma's homage to Hitchcock, *Sisters* (1973).

nique's mess. They hide Philip's body in a sofa bed, and clean up as the police, skeptical of the reporter, delay Grace in the lobby. When they finally search Danielle's apartment, they find nothing suspicious.

Now Grace's reporter's instincts are aroused, and she follows a lead (Danielle's birthday cake) to the local bakery, and learns that Philip purchased it. With a hapless private detective named Larch at her side, she investigates further. Though disagreeing with Larch's methods, Grace works with him to illicitly get into Danielle's apartment. Danielle and Emile return to the dwelling while Larch is inside, but he evades detection even as they remove the sofa that hides the bloody evidence of murder.

Larch realizes the body is hidden in the sofa, and trails the truck transporting it. Grace looks at Dominique's stolen medical records and realizes she is a separated Siamese twin. Grace meets a writer who has written about these particular twins, and he shows her a video of the co-joined siblings. She sees their residence at the Loisel Institute, and learns that Dominique is psychologically damaged, dangerous. She watches as the separation is performed, and McClennon (the writer) reveals that the operation went badly, that Dominique didn't survive the surgery.

Grace pursues Emile and Danielle to a madhouse on Staten Island. Emile insists that Grace is a patient there, and has her held and drugged against her will. He attempts to hypnotize her into believing that there was no murder. As Grace soon learns, Danielle is schizophrenic. She becomes Dominique in her mind, and then becomes violent, just like her dead sister. Even as Grace is hypnotized, Danielle turns into Dominique and kills Emile. The police arrest Danielle, but Grace, a victim of Emile's mind programming, now insists there was no murder.

Meanwhile, Larch sits watching the sofa bed in rural Quebec, waiting for someone to pick it up.

COMMENTARY: For many years, Brian DePalma has been touted as the "next Hitchcock" and his first thriller, *Sisters*, explains why. It's an inspired, out-of-this world homage to the master's *Psycho*. The "Janet Leigh trick," that a lead character should die early in the film, is carried over here, as is a surprise twist in identity, and a focus on schizophrenia. But DePalma's brilliance is revealed not so much in his contextual references to Hitchcock, but in his thorough understanding of film technique. In particular, he deploys split-screen photography to ends both dramatic and clever.

In 1976, Brian DePalma staged the climactic scenes of *Carrie* using split screens. There, he created a visual cause-and-effect relationship with opposing film frames. In one frame, Carrie would gaze at something. In the other frame, her psi energy would cause explosions, or other pyrotechnics. In *Sisters*, DePalma has somewhat different purposes. He uses the split screen to ease the audience through the transition from one protagonist to another.

As Philip lies dying in Danielle's apartment, the image is split. On one side (filmed from inside the window) the audience sees Philip seeking help, dying. On the other side of the screen, from outside the window, viewers become aware that someone else is watching the bloody act, Grace Collier. As one protagonist dies then, another is simultaneously introduced. It is a visual passing of the torch.

DePalma also utilizes the split screen for purposes of contrast. In one sequence, Grace Collier and the detectives are seen arguing in the lobby in one half of the screen, while the bloody clean up of the murder in apartment 3R is depicted in the other screen. Here, "time" is the notion held in common between the two images. One image reveals time wasted, as the police delay Collier. The other image (Danielle and Emile's hiding of evidence) reveals time used fruitfully.

In its totality, *Sisters* concerns a split. Danielle's mind has split so as to accommodate two distinct, competing personalities. Her schizophrenic nature is reflected in DePalma's pervasive use of the split screen. The audience is privy to two lives, two images simultaneously, just as Danielle is. It's an oddly reflexive technique, but one that is used brilliantly. The film's double vision reflects Danielle's.

DePalma also understands irony and suspense, and how the two interrelate. In one tense moment, Grace sits down heavily on the sofa where Phillip's body is hidden. The camera pans down to a bloody spot on the back of the couch, and reveals information that the characters in the drama are not privy to. Will Grace see the spot? Will she discover the body? These are suspenseful questions that DePalma's camerawork raises. At the same time, the audience notes the irony: Grace's behind is very close to the quarry she seeks, if only she would notice.

Hitchcock blended suspense and irony like no director in film history, and DePalma orchestrates scenes towards similar ends. His film is designed for moments such as these, and it is clear he relishes them.

The direct references to other Hitchcock films are many. Danielle's struggle with "the Dominique within" echoes Norman's battle with his own internal "Mother" in *Psycho*. The very idea that people (like Grace) don't mind their own business, is a reflection of elements of both *Vertigo* and *Rear Window*. And, then, of course, there's the stunning violence, which Hitchcock included in all his best suspense films.

DePalma's unconventional sense of humor belies his admiration for Jean Luc Godard, and the final sequences of *Sisters* owe more to Godard's sensibilities than they do Hitchcock's. For instance, it is outrageously funny, and utterly purposeless, that Grace is ultimately undone by her curiosity. After harassing the police about a murder for the entirety of the film, the hypnotism causes Grace to suddenly do an about-face and declare that there has been no homicide. At the end of the film, she is not restored to her right mind ... she is completely muddled. That's how we leave her, and it's a development Hitchcock would never have permitted, and one reason why *Sisters* is more than a Hitchcock pastiche. DePalma's twin (one might say "split") sensibilities in *Sisters* (part Godard/part Hitchcock) make it simultaneously suspenseful and absurd, a potent, uncommon mix.

Sssssss (1973) ★ ★ ½

Cast & Crew

CAST: Strother Martin (Dr. Stoner); Dirk Benedict (David Blake); Heather Menzies (Kristine Stoner); Richard B. Shull (Dr. Daniels); Tim O'Connor (Kagen); Jack Ging (Sheriff); Kathleen King (Kitty); Reb Brown (Steve Randall); Ted Grossman (Deputy); Charles Seel (Old Man); Ray Ballard (Waggish Tourist); Brendan Burns (Jock # 1); Rick Brokner (Jock # 2); James Drum (Hawker # 1); Ed McCready (Hawker # 2); Frank Kowalksi (Hawker # 3); Ralph Montgomery (Hawker # 4); Michael Masters (Hawker # 5); Charlie Fox (Arvin Loy Deux); Felix Silla (Seal Boy); Nobel Craig (Tim/Snake Man); Bobbi Kige (Kootch Dancer); J.R. Clark (Station Attendant); Chip Potter (Postal Clerk).

CREW: A Zanuck/Brown Production. *Executive Producers:* Richard D. Zanuck, David Brown. *Screenplay by:* Hal Dresner. *Story by:* Dan Striepeke. *Produced by:* Dan Striepeke. *Directed by:* Bernard L. Kowalski. *Director of Photography:* Gerald Perry Finnerman. *Color:* Technicolor. *Art Director:* John T. McCormack. *Set Decorator:* Claire P. Brown. *Sound:* Waldon O. Watson, Melvin Metcalfe. *Technical Advisor:* Ray Folson. *Animals Furnished by:* Hamosa Reptile, and Wild Animal Farm, Inc. *Film Editor:* Robert Watts. *Unit Production Manager:*

Doc Herman. *Assistant Director:* Gordon Webb. *Second Assistant Director:* Charles Dismates. *Titles and Opticals:* Elkin/Universal. *Creative Make-up Design:* John Chambers, Nick Marcellino. *Graphic Montage:* John Newhart. *Music:* Pat Williams. *Associate Producer:* Robert Butner. *M.P.A.A. Rating:* PG. *Running time:* 90 minutes.

P.O.V.

"All the reptiles shown in this film are real. The King Cobras were imported from Bangkok, the Python from Singapore. We wish to thank the cast and crew for their courageous efforts while being exposed to extremely hazardous conditions."—the opening card of *Sssssss* (1973).

SYNOPSIS: Dr. Stoner, a professor obsessed with snakes, goes to see Dr. Daniels at the local university to request an extension of his grant, and the help of one of the students for the summer. Daniels recommends the contemplative David Blake, and Blake soon goes to work with Stoner, befriending his beautiful daughter, Kristine, as well as his huge boa constrictor, Harry.

Stoner familiarizes David with his lab and his menagerie of rare snakes. He then introduces a series of "immunization" shots to David, claiming it is a protective measure. In fact, Stoner's work involves evolution and the survival of man. He believes man would survive better as a cold-blooded, snake-like creature. He transformed his last assistant, Tim, into a snake-hybrid and then sold him to a local freak show. Soon, David feels the effects of the inoculations, and begins to feel sick.

Soon after David's arrival, Stoner stages a public demonstration of his skill with snakes, extracting the venom of a dangerous king cobra. Days later, David's skin begins to peel, and Stoner insists it is a normal reaction to the injections. The police visit Stoner and question him about his last assistant, Tim McGraw, who has officially disappeared.

Meanwhile, David and Kristine grow close and skinny dip together in the nearby lake. When they go out on a date to the carnival, David sees Tim — a half-man/half-snake — and is bothered by his appearance.

A local bully, Steve, then confronts David, trying to make time with Kristine. The police break up the fight, but Steve attacks again later, attempting to sexually assault Kristine in her bedroom. Harry the snake defends her, but Steve kills the snake. Angry, Dr. Stoner follows Steve home, and leaves a poisonous snake in the shower. Steve is killed quickly by the critter

David and Kristine become intimate, but Dr. Stoner catches them fooling around and grows angry. The next morning, David awakes to discover that his face has changed. Stoner claims it is an allergic reaction to the shots, but David's transformation to snake-man continues as Kristine leaves town to pick up a rare snake.

When the university cuts off support for Dr. Stoner's experiments, Stoner abducts Dr. Daniels and locks him in a basement with a boa constrictor.

Kristine happens by the carnival, suspicious about the snake-man, and recognizes Tim. Worried about David, she returns home. By now, David has turned into a full-fledged king cobra snake. Meanwhile, Stoner is bitten while attempting to catch another snake, and is killed by the venom. When Kristine is threatened by David, now completely hostile in his snakish demeanor, the police kill the strange creature.

COMMENTARY: *Sssssss* is an absurd but highly entertaining film that is saddled with a terrible title. The film features some fine B movie acting, some interesting ideas about snakes, and some really dangerous-looking stunts involving the main actors. On the negative side, *Sssssss* is stuck with a weak ending (highlighted by some dopey time-lapse special effects), and a few derivative moments.

Dirk Benedict (*Battlestar Galactica*

Heather Menzies and Dirk Benedict share a happy moment before the terror of *Sssssss* (1973) slithers into full swing.

[1978]), Heather Menzies (*Logan's Run* [1977], *Piranha* [1978]) and Strother Martin (*Brotherhood of Satan* [1971]) give this material their all, and attempt to create memorable, or at least interesting characters. Bene-dict and Menzies are particularly appealing as the young couple in love, and Benedict's only flaw is that he seems too smart to play so dumb a person. As *Battlestar Galactica* also proved, Benedict has an intelligent, witty screen persona, and that high level of charm and intellect carries over into this film … which nonetheless requires him to be stupid throughout.

But kudos to the cast for a willingness to interact (on camera) with a variety of wriggly, and apparently dangerous, snakes. Accordingly, some of the snake footage is rather startling. Strother Martin, in particular, really handles these snakes like a pro, even while mouthing tongue-tying scientific dialogue. Martin's is a bravura B-movie performance, and one that heightens the reality of the movie significantly.

And, to its benefit, *Ssssss* has some pretty heady stuff on its mind. The film unconventionally views snakes as a minority group, victims of dangerous generalizations and stereotypes, a viewpoint that the title character of *Stanley* would have no doubt appreciated. It then notes that snakes are also a cultural icon representing "evil." There was a serpent, after all, in the Biblical garden. And that fact raises the question, is Stoner doing God's work, or the Devil's? This metaphor is carried over when David Blake starts to feel the effect of snake "blood" in his own veins. He experiences a dream that features Biblical images of Heaven and Hell, as if the snake is really a religious symbol, rather than just an animal. This may sound preposterous, but the connection to myth grants the film a little bit of class.

But, negatively, the film also genuflects to the king of this genre, 1971's *Willard.* The "nice" snake in *Ssssss* is named Harry, but might as well be Socrates, the moniker of the "nice" rat in *Willard,* who also met with an unpleasant fate. Also, after some great makeup and special effects of a half-devolved snakeman, *Ssssss* loses credibility in literally its final moment, by showcasing (in timelapse photography, no less) Benedict's transformation into a creature that looks a lot like a glow-worm. As the movie has been building toward this metamorphosis, its inherent silliness kills much of the suspense and interest.

But, if you want to see a snake fight a mongoose, or coil around in angry parries, this is your movie. It's a lot better than that other snake movie of the '70s, *Stanley* (1972).

Tales That Witness Madness

Cast & Crew

CAST: Donald Pleasence (Dr. Tremayne); Jack Hawkins (Dr. Nicholas); Georgia Brown (Faye); Donald Houston (Sam); Joan Collins (Bella); Michael Jayston (Brian).

CREW: *Directed by:* Freddie Francis. *Written by:* Jay Fairbank. *Produced by:* Norman Priggen, Milton Subotsky. *Director of Photography:* Norman Warwick. *Film Editor:* Bernard Gribble. *Music:* Bernard Ebbinghouse. *M.P.A.A. Rating:* R. *Running Time:* 90 minutes.

DETAILS: It's *Asylum* (1972) redux, as another Amicus anthology is set inside a mental institution. There are four stories this time, only barely connected thematically. The stories, "Mr. Tiger," "Mel," "Penny Farthing" and "Luau," unfold as star Donald Pleasence encounters four deranged inmates.

Theatre of Blood (1973) ★ ★ ★ ½

Critical Reception

"Some of the do-ins are funnily horrible as director Douglas Hickox uses his DeLuxe color cinematography to emphasize Robert Morley's outrageously blond hairdo as well as all the blood flowing…. If you know the Shakespeare plots, you'll get some fun trying to guess how scripter Anthony Greville-Belle has adapted them for each murder."—Deirdre Mack, *Films in Review*, Volume XXIV, Number 6, June-July 1973, page 379.

"Comedy-horror that really does give Vincent Price a chance to show his stuff, with deliciously absurd results … but unfortunately the overlong script eventually runs out of steam, and the ending is feeble."—David Pirie, *Time Out Film Guide*, Seventh Edition, Penguin Books, 1999, page 903.

"The movie is bright and, a good deal of the time, quite funny. It is farce as broad as Shaftesbury Avenue, but its high spirits are not entirely consistent with the great gobs of gore that director Douglas Hickox leaves smeared about."— Jay Cocks, *Time*, May 21, 1973, page 70.

"Few horror films are written with English majors in mind, but … *Theatre of Blood* surely can make such a claim… Director Douglas Hickox skillfully handles the material, allowing his camera to bear witness as Price steals the show, gliding between delightfully over-the-top camp and sheer irony…. But what is most intriguing about *Theatre of Blood* is the extent to which it can be said to have influenced some of the best modern offerings."—Gina McIntyre, *Wicked*, Volume 3, Number 1, Spring 2001, pages 74–75.

Cast & Crew

CAST: Vincent Price (Edward Lionheart); Diana Rigg (Edwina Lionheart); Ian Hendry (Peregrine Devlin); Harry Andrews (Trevor Dickman); Coral Browne (Chloe Moon); Robert Coote (Oliver Larding); Jack Hawkins (Solomon Psaltery); Michael Hordern (George Maxwell); Arthur Lowe (Horace Sprout); Robert Morley (Meredith Merridew); Dennis Price (Hector Snipe); Diana Dors (Rosemary); Madeline Smith (Maisie Psaltery); Joan Hickson (Mrs. Sprout); Renee Asherson (Mrs. Maxwell); Milo O'Shea (Inspector Boot); Eric Sykes (Sgt. Dogge); Bunny Reed, Peter Thornton (Policemen); Charles Sinnickson (Vicar); Brigid Erin Bates (Maid); Meth Drinkers (Tutte Lemkow, Stanley Bates, Eric Francis, Sally Gilmore, John Gilpin, Joyce Graeme, Jack Maguire, Declan Mulholland (Meth Drinker).
CREW: *Director of Photography:* Wolfgang Suschitzky. *Camera Operator:* Ronnie Taylor.

Editor: Malcolm Cooke. *Color:* DeLuxe. *Music Composed and Conducted by:* Michael J. Lewis. *Screenplay:* Anthony Greville-Bell. *Based on an Idea by:* Stanley Mann and John Kohn. *Executive Producers:* Gustav Berne and Sam Jaffe. *Produced by:* John Kohn and Stanley Mann. *Directed by:* Douglas Hickox. *Production Manager:* David Anderson. *Continuity:* Angela Allen. *Set Decorator:* Ann Mollo. *Construction Manager:* Peter Verrand. *Wardrobe Assistant:* Terry Smith. *Assistant to Producers:* Sarah Romilly. *Sound Mixer:* Simon Kaye. *Sound Editor:* Lois Wiggins. *Dubbing Mixer:* Douglas Turner. *Make-up:* George Blackler. *Hairdresser:* Pearl Tipaldi. *Assistant Editor:* Chris Kelly. *Stunts:* Terry York. *Special Effects:* John Stears. *Choreographer:* Tutte Lemkow. Filmed on Location in London, England, by Cineman Films Limited. *M.P.A.A. Rating:* R. *Running Time:* 105 minutes.

SYNOPSIS: Edward Lionheart has spent twenty glorious years on the British stage proving himself to be the greatest Shakespearean actor of his generation. Unfortunately, the critics don't like Lionheart's work, and repeatedly snub him. Then comes the ultimate humiliation. After an incredible year of performing Shakespeare, Lionheart loses the Critics Circle Actor of the Year Award to a marbles-in-his-mouth method actor! Humiliated, Lionheart confronts the Critics Circle and, finally, throws himself over a ledge in defeat.

Then, on March 15, 1972, critic George Maxwell is killed in a brutal crime that resembles Caesar's stabbing death at the hands of the Senate in Shakespeare's *Julius Caesar*. Occurring on the ides of March, this terrible murder sends ripples of fear through the Critics Circle, including the youngest and most fit of the reviewers, Peregrine Devlin. The police are soon investigating the incident, but are too late to prevent the death of a second critic, Hector Snipes. Snipes is stabbed with a spear and then displayed at a funeral, his corpse dragged from a horse's tail and torn apart. Oddly, this death mimics exactly Hector's death in *Troilus and Cressida*!

Convinced that someone is killing the critics of London, Peregrine Devlin confronts Edwina Lionheart, thespian daughter of the deceased Edward Lionheart. Could she be the culprit? Edwina denies any knowledge of the murders and claims that her father died of a broken heart.

Before long, more critics are dying. One is decapitated as he sleeps, in an elaborate re-enactment of *Cymbeline,* and another has his heart, "a pound of flesh," removed in an odd re-working of *The Merchant of Venice*. Though the police are reluctant to believe it, Edward Lionheart is still alive and, with demented glee, re-staging his last season of Shakespeare dramas with a bloody twist. His murder of the critics is his final revenge for losing the Critics Actor of the Year Award.

Refusing to believe that Lionheart is still alive, the police arrest Edwina for the crimes. However, Devlin assures her release when he survives a face-to-face fencing duel with Lionheart in his gym (in a re-enactment of the duel from *Romeo and Juliet*). The police release Edwina and put security around all the survivors of the Critics Circle, but even that is not enough to stop the great actor, Lionheart! Using *Othello* as his template, Lionheart spurs a jealous reviewer to murder his wife in a fit of jealousy. Another critic, Chloe Moon, is electrocuted in an updated version of Joan of Arc's burning at the stake from *Henry VI*.

Finally, in the most gruesome crime yet, fat stage critic Meredith Merridew is force-fed his pet poodles and stuffed to death in a scene inspired by *Titus Andronicus*.

The sole survivor of the Critics Circle, Devlin, is captured by Edwina, who has been cooperating with her father's crazy plans all along. Devlin is taken to Lionheart's den, an abandoned theater, and forced to re-stage the Critics Circle Awards. If Devlin fails to name Lionheart the best actor of the year, he will meet the same fate as Gloucester in *King Lear*: blinded with hot knives!

Devlin refuses to overturn his choice, and angry Lionheart prepares to deliver retribution. The police arrive just in time, and soon the theater catches fire. In a terrible moment, Edwina dies at the hands of Lionheart's crazy audience, all homeless meth drinkers. As Devlin flees Lionheart's theater of blood, the mourning Lionheart takes his dead daughter in his arms and climbs to the roof. As the building burns, Lionheart plunges through the roof and lands in the theater far below, only to die amidst the flames.

COMMENTARY: Vincent Price handily steals the show in *Theatre of Blood*, a wicked and droll variation on the *Dr. Phibes* formula. This time, Price plays a "hammy" actor belittled by snobby critics. He takes bloody revenge, and in the process satirizes the world of theater, and quotes plenty of Shake-speare. It's all highly amusing, inventive stuff, and if this reviewer can indulge in a personal confession, he enjoyed *Theatre of Blood* more than either *Phibes* films. The film's knowing self-reference to the world of theater (and its critics) makes for a cutting and delightful horror film.

In *The Abominable Dr. Phibes*, Price's character killed his enemies by re-creating the 10 curses of the Pharaohs. In *Theater of Blood*, Edwin Lionheart stages the death of his opponents by re-framing the many works of William Shakespeare. Thus *Julius Caesar, Troilus and Cressida, Romeo and Juliet, Cymbeline, The Merchant of Venice, Titus Andronicus* and *Richard III* all get a horror re-vamp. These innovative reinterpretations and staging of the Bard's classic work might have snooty scholars spinning with dismay, but they are undeniably clever. Especially enjoyable is the ridiculous duel scene (set in a gymnasium) that quotes from *Romeo and Juliet*, but yet finds the zeal to include uneven bars, the balance beam, and a trampoline.

This scene, like most of the rest in the film, is done with a perfect sense of lightness. There may be deaths occurring, but *gosh, darnit*, it's all in good fun. This film represents the spirit the later *Elm Street* movies often went for, and missed.

No doubt that part of the reason the murders are so amusing in *Theatre of Blood* is that the victims are critics. This film has a wholly appropriate dislike of critics. First off, the film cleverly gives them names that epitomize their worst qualities. One is named Snipe, another Dickman, another Larding. These funny names reveal the nasty personalities of the murder victims. The film also notes of critics that they lack the "ability to create," and who would disagree with that assessment? Basically, *Theatre of Blood* sees critics as nasty, bitter, little people, and therefore the revenge conducted against them is venomously conceived, ferociously written and executed, and well-deserved.

One feels true sympathy for Price's character. Like many talents who perform or write, he keeps all of his bad reviews ... and remembers every word. That's one reason why critics probably should tread lightly, yet most often don't. There are people behind films, books, plays, et cetera, and those people can be fragile. It seems only appropriate that the act of "criticizing" should be punished when practiced so callously.

Ironically, in giving nasty critics their comeuppance, *Theatre of Blood* is also probably critic-proof. What bad can a critic say about it, really? It's funny, amusing, knowledgeable, and witty; the perfect self-reflexive horror film. In addition to its satirical qualities, the movie is filled with amusing moments. In one, the (not-so) great Shakespearean actor loses an award to a Brando-like method actor. In another, Vincent Price plays a gay hairdresser, and sports an afro. It sounds bizarre, but it is all part of this film's wacky tapestry.

Which brings the discussion, inevitably, to Vincent Price himself. Some horror fans haven't watched his work lately because they've been obsessed with slasher films or the like. Without getting on a soapbox or anything, they really ought to watch this man at work. He plays comedy flawlessly, yet also brings a tragic (one might say Shakespearean...) pathos to Lionheart. Though he is clearly insane, the audience never hates this character. He is pitiable, and to some degree at least, the audience sympathizes with his grievances. Price chews on every word, every line, as if he is having the time of his life, and he carries the film from start to finish. He is positively buoyant, lifting the humorous material to legitimately hilarious heights.

Theatre of Blood is a happy confection of blood, murder, and death, and the only reason it doesn't merit four stars is that this author would hate to support any anti-critic trend. He has to make a living, after all.

The Touch of Satan

Cast & Crew

CAST: Michael Berry (Jodie Thompson); Emby Mellay (Melissa Strickland); Lee Amber (Luther Strickland); Yvonne Winslow (Mary Strickland); Jeanne Gerson (Lucinda Strickland); Robert Easton (Keitel).

CREW: *Directed by:* Don Henderson. *Written by:* James E. McLarty. *Produced by:* George E. Carey. *Director of Photography:* Jordan S. Cronenweth. *Film Editor:* Dick Elliott. *M.P.A.A. Rating:* PG. *Running Time:* 90 minutes (approximate).

DETAILS: In this Dundee Production, a freewheeling wanderer (Bellay) befriends a beautiful girl (Mellay) only to discover her family hides a terrible secret: a murderous old witch who kills local farmers with a pitchfork. As the wanderer soon learns, witchcraft runs in the family. *The Giant Spider Invasion*'s (1975) Robert Easton has a cameo during a "burning at the stake"-style flashback.

The Vault of Horror

Cast & Crew

CAST: Tom Baker (Moore); Denholm Elliott (Dillant); Daniel Massey (Rogers); Anna Massey (Donna); Michael Craig (Maitland); Edward Judd (Alex); Curg Jurgens (Sebastian); Dawn Addams (Inez); Jasmina Hilton (Indian Girl); Glynis Johns (Eleanor);

CREW: *Directed by:* Roy Ward Baker. *Written by:* Milton Subotsky. *Director of Photography:* Denys Coop. *Film Editor:* Oswald Hafenrichter. *Produced by:* Max J. Rosenberg and Milton Subotsky. An Amicus Production, released by Cinerama. *M.P.A.A. Rating:* R. *Running Time:* 86 minutes.

DETAILS: This is the Amicus sequel to the successful *Tales from the Crypt* (1972). It features the stories "Midnight Mess" (about a vampire dining club ... with blood on tap), "Neat Job" (a revenge story about a married couple), "This Trick'll Kill You" (about a magician hoping to steal a colleague's magic trick), "Bargain in Death" (concerning a man who scams himself out of life), and "Drawn and Quartered" (which focuses on an artist who used voodoo to smite his enemies). Generally considered less successful artistically than its predecessor.

1974

Abby

Cast & Crew

CAST: Carol Speed (Abby Williams); William Marshall (Bishop Williams); Terry Carter (Reverend Emmett Williams); Austin Stoker (Cass Potter); Charles Kissinger (Dr. Hennings).

CREW: *Directed by:* William Girdler. *Written by:* William Girdler and Gordon Cornell Layne. *Produced by:* William Girdler, Gordon Cornell Layne, and Mike Henry. *Director of Photography:* William Asman. *Film Editors:* Henry Asman, Corky Ehlers. *Music:* Robert O'Ragland. *M.P.A.A. Rating:* R. *Running Time:* 89 minutes.

DETAILS: A terrific African-American cast sinks its teeth into this William Girdler blaxploitation spin on *The Exorcist.* Though not well reviewed when released, this is today considered a cult classic. Girdler regular Kissinger teams with Stoker (*Assault on Precinct 13* [1976]), *Blacula* star William Marshall, and a scenery-chewing Carol Speed to dramatize the tale of a bishop's daughter who becomes possessed by evil. If so inclined, one can actually read a great deal into this one. When possessed, Abby becomes a nymphomaniac, a bad girl. It's up to her stern father to set her straight. Demonic possession, adolescent rebellion, or more exploitation from the prolific Girdler? You decide.

Andy Warhol's Dracula (1974) * *

Critical Reception

"Innuendoes of kinky sex followed by disingenuous banalities are the familiar spices of *Andy Warhol's Dracula* … X-rated like its predecessor, *Dracula* is far less bloody … considerably sexier and more consistently amusing."— Charles Michener, *Newsweek*: "Down for the Count," February 24, 1975, page 83.

Cast & Crew

CAST: Joe Dallesandro (Mario); Udo Kier (Count Dracula); Arro Juerging (Anton); Aron Uvera, Maxime McKendr, Dominique Darel, Stefania Casini, Silvia Dionisio, Emi Califri, Vittorio De Sica.

CREW: *Photography:* Luigi Kuveiller. *Production Designer:* Enrico Job. *Music:* Claudi Gizzi. *Editing:* Franca Silvi, Jed Johnson. *Continuity:* Silvia Petroni. *Art Director:* Gianni Giovaghon. *Special Effects:* Carlo Rambaldi. *Producer:* Andrew Baunsberg. *Written and Directed by:* Paul Morrissey. *Production Manager:* Mara Blasetti. *Cameraman:* Ubaldo Terzano. *Wardrobe:* Bernito Persico. *Make-up:* Mario DeSalvio. *First Assistant Editor:* Loretta Mattioli. *Sound Mixer:* Carlo Palmieri. *Technical Consultant for Spacevision:* Robert V. Bernier. *First Production Assistant:* Vasio Mafera. *M.P.A.A. Rating:* X. *Running Time:* 96 minutes.

SYNOPSIS: In Romania, Count Dracula is dying. He needs the blood of virgins to survive, and so decides to move to Italy with his assistant, Anton, where there is apparently an abundance of the virtuous.

The vampire and his beard arrive in an Italian hotel, and learn that there is an aristocratic family nearby with four unwed daughters. Anton meets with the family and secures a room in the home for Dracula so he can interview the daughters as prospective brides. To help prepare for this opportunity, Dracula eats a loaf of bread drenched in the blood of a virgin who died in a road accident.

Dracula has an unpleasant surprise in store for him. Two of the daughters he plans to court are not virgins at all, but are being repeatedly laid by the hunky Communist farmhand, Mario. When Dracula arrives at the villa, he is introduced to the girls, unsuspecting. They are not particularly interested in him because he is so pale and weak, but the count nonetheless resolves to get his fill of them as soon as possible. He dines on one daughter, but becomes violently ill when he realizes she is not a virgin, and that her blood is contaminated.

Dracula then dines on daughter number two, with the same unpleasant result. Dracula finally resorts to feasting on Esmerelda, the eldest of the four daughters. She is a spinster but ... a virgin.

Meanwhile, the youngest daughter, barely fourteen, realizes that Dracula is a vampire, and that he intends to feed on her. Mario offers to relieve her of her virginity, the only way to make her unpalatable to the vampire. She gladly accepts his offer.

Mario and Dracula soon fight it out, the common man versus the vampire aristocrat. Anton is killed in a tussle with Esmerelda's mother, who also dies in the battle. Mario chops off Dracula's arms, rendering him impotent. Esmerelda attempts to defend her vampire lover, but Mario drives a stake through his heart. Seeing Dracula dead, Esmerelda impales herself on Dracula's death

spike, leaving Mario and the youngest of four daughters to carry on.

COMMENTARY: Here's a movie that unfolds like a dirty joke. What happened when the vampire went looking for a virgin to eat? Well, he met a family with four daughters. The first one wasn't a virgin. The second wasn't a virgin either. And so on, and so forth....

It's a ridiculous premise for a horror film, but director Morrissey is apparently all too aware that *Andy Warhol's Dracula* is a campy joke. The film doesn't take itself very seriously, but nor is it particularly amusing, except in apparently unintentional fashion. Most of all, there's an overriding sense of carelessness to the film. It looks and sounds thrown together, and indeed, some accounts of making of the film suggest the script was improvised day to day. It shows.

Udo Kier makes for an unusual Dracula, and for that matter, *Andy Warhol's Dracula* has some interesting ideas about the famous count. He can survive in sunlight and even touch a crucifix, but he needs the blood of virgins (or "wirgins," as Kier pronounces the word) to survive. This Dracula is not the creature of strength and power that moviegoers are used to, but one of impotence instead. He is wheeled about in a wheelchair, unable to move on his own two feet. He appears anemic, and is barely able to summon the strength to drain his victims.

More than that, Dracula seems none too interested in even going out to dine. In the bizarre opening, Anton informs Dracula that he must move to Italy to find some virgins, but Dracula is reluctant, a party-pooper. "I cannot leave my family down in the crypt," he begs off. Bizarre.

Even Dracula's death scene is symptomatic of the character's impotence. Mario chops his arms off, then his legs. The purportedly regal count is thus left flailing about with no usable limbs. He's a weakling, not a figure of fright or authority at all. At one disgusting point, Dracula is reduced to licking a virgin's blood up off the floor, after Dallesandro's Mario has made love to her.

Yet, oddly enough, there is a point to this depiction of Dracula. Much of the film points to the argument that the European aristocracy is weak, debauched, and dying out. Dracula represents that aristocracy. He has crippling ties to his family (he won't leave the tomb...) even though they are dead, and his once mighty power is weakened. He needs new, fresh blood to infuse his family line.

A stronger figure than Dracula is Mario, the farmhand. He is a Communist (with a sickle and hammer painted on his bedroom wall...), and continually makes comments about Communism and the evil of the aristocracy. Dracula may be of the "upper class," but he is "weak," and Mario is strong and vital by contrast. He slaps one of the family's sisters, then forces her to perform oral sex on him. Now *that*'s raw power! Representing the angry working man, the engine of the Communist model, Mario is powerful, lustful and everything the impotent Dracula is not. He cuts away the last vestiges of the upper class in Europe when he lops off Dracula's limbs.

The preceding paragraphs make it sound like there is actually a point to *Andy Warhol's Dracula*. There may be. But the film is still hilariously overplayed. Dallesandro speaks with a broad New York accent that is egregiously out of place in Italy. Kier is downright funny as Dracula, probably because the dialogue is rip-roaringly hysterical. "I'm sure they're very religious ... they

have a nice house," Dracula comments at one point. "The blood of these whores is killing me," he notes later, enunciating the film's most famous line. In fact, every time Dracula speaks, he says something that can be interpreted, without too much strain, as really funny.

Andy Warhol's Dracula is rated X, but not for violence, as one might expect of a horror film. Instead, this is a very sexual movie, replete with explicit couplings. Three daughters take off their shirts to reveal supple, perky breasts in an early scene. Later, Mario has sex with two daughters at once, and then the siblings proceed to have sex with one another. One sister orgasms when Dracula bites her, and then there is the oral sex, and, finally, the deflowering of a 14-year-old virgin. The women are quite beautiful, and Dallesandro is a glowering male presence who struts his way through the picture, so the movie's leaps into soft-core material are fun to watch. It is not hard to state that *Andy Warhol's Dracula* is better than just about any soft-core porn film that has aired on Cinemax (i.e. Skinemax...) in at least five years.

As a funny sexy romp with a theme about class distinctions and Communism, *Andy Warhol's Dracula* is certainly one of the odder vampire films to come out of the 1970s. The production values are slipshod, the filming and editing careless, and the performances outrageous, but this is a guilty pleasure. It's fascinating to watch because one is never sure if it is merely a bad film, or a truly inspired turkey.

Andy Warhol's Frankenstein (1974) ★ ½

Critical Reception

"In a muddy way, the movie attempts to instruct us about the universal insensitivity, living-deadness and the inability to be turned on by anything short of the grotesque. However, this *Frankenstein* drags as much as it camps ... it fails as a spoof and the result is only a coy binge in degradation."—Nora Sayre, *New York Times*, May 16, 1974, page 52.

"...a highly amusing film which never lives up to its ideas. Morrissey has a bizarre sense of how satirically to transpose a classic into the pop art subculture milieu but as a director he fails to maneuver the story's grotesque humor successfully."— Roy Frumkes, *Films in Review,* Volume XXV, Number 6, June-July 1974, page 375.

Cast & Crew

CAST: Joe Dallesandro (Farmer); Monique Van Vooren (Catherine Frankenstein); Udo Kier (Baron Frankenstein); Arro Juerging (Otto); Dalilia DiLazzaro, Srdjan Zelenovic, Nicolette Elmi, Liv Bosisio, Cristina Galoni, Carla Mancini, Marco Liofredi, Fiorella Masselli, Rosita Tarash, Imelda Marani.
CREW: *Photography:* Luigi Kuveiller. *Production Designer:* Enrico Job. *Music:* Claudi Gizzi. *Editing:* Franca Silvi, Jed Johnson. *Continuity:* Silvia Petroni. Art *Director:* Gianni Giovaghon. *Special Effects:* Carlo Rambaldi. *Producer:* Andrew Baunsberg. *Written and Directed by:* Paul Morrissey. *Production Manager:* Mara Blasetti. *Camerman:* Ubaldo Terzano. *Wardrobe:* Bernito Persico. *Make-up:* Mario DeSalvio. *First Assistant Editor:* Loretta Mattioli. *Sound Mixer:* Carlo Palmieri. *Technical Consultant for Spacevision:* Robert V. Bernier. *First Production Assistant:* Vasio Mafera. *M.P.A.A. Rating:* X. *Running Time:* 96 minutes.

P.O.V.

"...violence is what people want, so we're giving it to them. That's the secret of my success—just give the people what they want" (23).— Andy Warhol discusses his "horror" formula with the *New York Times.*

SYNOPSIS: Baron Frankenstein and his obsequious assistant, Otto, are in search of the perfect Serbian "nose" for their bizarre experiment in creating new life from pieces of corpses. Frankenstein's obsession with his work irritates his sister/wife, Catherine, who feels he is not devoting enough time to her or their two children. While out on a picnic with the children, the frustrated Mrs. Frankenstein befriends a rugged, charismatic peasant farmer who she previously caught fornicating in public on at least two occasions. Curious, she invites him to the castle.

At the same time, Frankenstein is assembling two new lives: a male and a female composed entirely of corpse parts. He seeks a man's head, specifically the head of a man who thinks only of pleasure. This is necessary, because Frankenstein wants to create a master race and to do so his two creations must mate. In search of a hedonist, Otto and Frankenstein proceed to a local bordello. Catherine's farmer and his stoic friend, Sascha, are there. Sascha is not partaking of the women, having no interest in sex. Otto and Frankenstein are unaware of this fact, and target Sascha as their perfect victim. After he leaves the bordello, they chop off Sascha's head, and steal it.

The next morning, the farmer awakens from a drunken stupor to find his best friend dead. This does not deter him from going to the Frankenstein castle and making love to Catherine. Afterwards, Catherine offers him the job of butler in the house.

In the laboratory, Frankenstein and Otto use electricity to reanimate their two creations. They bring these odd visitors to the dinner table, and the farmer recognizes Sascha's head. He becomes suspicious, and wants to see Frankenstein's lab. To this end, the children help him. Later, Frankenstein watches as Catherine and her new servant make passionate love in his bed.

But, when Frankenstein tries to get his man and woman to mate, the male is unresponsive ... just like Sascha had been in life. The farmer watches from the shadows, and swears to stop the baron's deranged work. As the farmer tries to free Sascha, Frankenstein confronts Catherine about her sexual dalliances. She tells him of the servant's plan to free Sascha in exchange for Sascha's sexual favors. Frankenstein and Otto capture the farmer and decide he has the right sexual instincts to be the brain of their new zombie.

Catherine instructs Sascha to make love to her, but he crushes her in his arms before the act is consummated. Feeling unappreciated, Otto decides to have sex with the resurrected female, but ends up killing her because he can't complete the act correctly. A furious Frankenstein kills Otto. Then the Sascha monster returns to the lab cradling Catherine's body. He kills his creator, Frankenstein, and then himself, leaving the farmer bound and incapable of escape. Unfortunately, the Frankenstein children decide it is time to take up their father's work...

———————

COMMENTARY: "To know death, Otto, you have to fuck life in the gall bladder," Baron Frankenstein informs his assistant in Paul Morrissey's dreadful *Andy Warhol's Frankenstein.* It's an outrageous line of dialogue in an outrageous, over-the-top film. As in *Andy Warhol's Dracula*, the real focus here is on sex, not horror. In fact, this film is an inversion of *Dracula*'s nutty plot. Instead of looking for virgin blood to "drink," this time Kier is looking for a lothario who can impregnate his latest monster, and thereby create a new race of undead.

A prime pleasure of both of these Warhol films is the absurd dialogue. Kier, Dallesandro, and the rest of the cast intone some of the craziest dialogue imaginable, and these flights of fancy make for a humorous film. Kier's accent is a running joke all its own. He pronounces the word "threshold" as "*trashold*," and the latter is probably a more accurate description of the movie. At another point, Kier gazes at his wife and says straight-faced, "You a sex maniac!" Not, "you are a sex maniac," but "you *a* sex maniac." Somehow, it's better that way. Kier's foreignness adds immeasurably to the off-kilter dialogue, and any viewer will realize he's not in Kansas, or Hollywood, anymore.

The situations are utterly ridiculous too. In the bizarre opening sequence of the film, Frankenstein searches for the "perfect nasum" for his monster, while arguing with the obsequious Otto about his unclean laboratory floor. It's a campy *Odd Couple*–cum–*Frankenstein* moment. Later, Frankenstein clips off Sascha's head with oversized hedge clippers, a bizarre choice for so precise a surgeon.

In perhaps the ultimate inanity of the film, Frankenstein makes love to a corpse. The viewer actually gets to see him do it, too. Kier hops up on the laboratory table and begins to pump the corpse. When he finishes the transaction, he politely asks Otto to help him get down. The payoff for that scene occurs when a jealous Otto attempts to perform the same sex act, but merely ends up making a gory mess out of the intercourse.

Then there's the riotous scene in which Otto and Frankenstein watch closely (a little too closely...) to see if their monster can sustain an erection. Admirers of Mary Shelley's novel will flinch at these tasteless updatings, but in at least one sense, it's a breath of fresh, bloody air. The staleness of so many other *Frankenstein* movies is certainly missing here; it's anything but stodgy. Sure the picture is amateurish and ridiculous in the extreme, but it has energy.

Unlike *Andy Warhol's Dracula*, *Andy Warhol's Frankenstein* does not appear to have a larger socio-political context. In the first film, it was the fall of the aristocracy (Dracula) before the hungry, sexually aggressive tide of Communism (Mario). Though this film also pits Kier and Dallesandro against each other, and again balances deviate (Kier) and normal (Dallesandro) sexual appetites, the larger background is missing. But who needs subtext in trash, anyway?

There's sex aplenty again in *Andy Warhol's Frankenstein*, but it is a less pleasant experience than in *Dracula* simply because there is also a leering tendency to focus on bloody, internal organs. In a film that advocates "fucking gall bladders," one can expect little else. Also, the film was originally designed to be viewed in the 3-D format, which means that all the gore pops right out at the audience. It is not a particularly pleasant experience.

What in the world is one to make of this, Andy Warhol's horror duo? They are important films because they represent a new way of looking at the old monsters, if nothing else. Frankenstein and Dracula had been done to death before the 1970s, and these new films have a really off-kilter perspective of these silver screen legends. Hardcore horror fans may not approve of the upgrade, but at least new ideas were being tried out. *Blac-*

ula offered an African-American take on Dracula. *Dracula AD 1972* brought the count into the 1970s. *The Legend of Seven Golden Vampires* mixed vampire lore with kung fu. And so on. The *Andy Warhol* horror couple is just another "new" take on these ghouls, and in keeping with the "new freedom" of the 1970s, the focus is on sex as much as horror.

Also, one must remember the sensitivities of Warhol the artist. In keeping with his work, these films are as much post-modern satires as they are literal narratives. That said, they aren't particularly well made or acted. But they're damn memorable.

The Beast Must Die

Cast & Crew

CAST: Peter Cushing (Dr. Lundgren); Marlene Clark (Caroline Newcliffe); Anton Diffring (Pavel); Charles Gray (Bennington).

CREW: *Directed by:* Paul Annett. *Written by:* James Blish and Michael Winder. *Produced by:* Milton Subotsky and Max Rosenberg. *Director of Photography:* Jack Hildyard. *Editor:* Peter Tanner. *Music:* Douglas Gamley. Amicus Pictures. *M.P.A.A. Rating:* PG. *Running Time:* 93 minutes.

DETAILS: This Amicus horror film took no chances. It was originally known as *Black*

Werewolf so as to tie in with *Blackenstein, Blacula, Abby* and other "black" horror films of the day. And, it featured the strange stylistic conceit of a voice-over narrator who asked audiences to "guess" the identity of the killer (monster). Other than that, the film digested, in equal parts, *The Most Dangerous Game, The Wolf Man,* and *Ten Little Indians.* Peter Cushing again headlines, this time as a man hunting werewolves. Hugely entertaining in a cheesy way.

Black Christmas (1974) ★ ★ ½

Critical Reception

"This moody depiction of the Christmas slayings ... is as murky as the script, which dotes largely on obscenities that are no more pointed than the violence, dull direction and pedestrian performances." — A.H. Weiler, *New York Times,* October 20, 1975, page 45.

Cast & Crew

CAST: Olivia Hussey (Jess Bradford); Keir Dullea (Peter Smythe); Margot Kidder (Barbara); Marian Waldman (Mrs. Mack); Andrea Martin (Phyl); James Edmond (Mr. Harrison); Douglas McGrath (Sergeant Nash); Art Hindle (Chris); Lynne Griffin (Clare Harrison); Michael Rapport (Patrick); John Saxon (Lt. Fuller); Les Carlson (Graham); Martha Gibson (Mrs. Quilfy); John Ratter (Laughing Detective); Robert Warner (Doctor); Syd Brown (Farmer); Jack Van Evera and Les Rubie (Search Party); Pam Barney (Jean); Marcia Diamond (Woman); Robert Hawkins (Wes); Dave Clement (Cogan); Julian Reed (Jennings); John Stoneham, Danny Gain and Tom Foreman (Cops).

CREW: Warner Brothers Presents a Film Funding Production, *Black Christmas. Music:* Chris Zittrer. *Director of Photography:* Reg Morris. *Screenplay:* Roy Moore. *Executive Producer:* Findlay Quinn. *Co-Producer:* Gerry Arbeid. *Produced and Directed by:* Bob Clark. *Associate Producer:* Richard Schouten. *Production Supervisor:* Dave Robertson. *Editor:* Stan Cole. *Sound Editor:* Ken Helley-Ray. *Art Director:* Karen Bromley. *Script Supervisor:* Sandra Ulosevich. *Assistant Producer:* Gary Goch. *Production Comptroller:* Barry Leyland. *First Assistant Director:* Tony Thatcher. *Second Assistant Director:* John Eckert. *Third Assistant Director:* Don Brough. *Production Assistant:* Melody Greene. *Camera Operator:* Bert Dunk. *Wardrobe:* Debi Weldon. *Hairdresser:* David Beecroft. *Make-up:* Bill Morgan. *Color by:* Quinn Labs. *Filmed in:* Panavision. *Distributed by:* Warner Brothers. *M.P.A.A. Rating:* R. *Running Time:* 98 minutes.

SYNOPSIS: At Christmas time in the town of Bedford, the sorority house of Pi Kappa Sigma at Six Belmont Place is terrorized by an obscene phone caller called the "Moaner." On this particular night, however, the phone stalker has gotten far more ambitious: he has scaled a wall, and found entrance to the house through an open window in the attic.

Unaware that a lunatic has entered their home, the girls of the sorority go about holiday business. Barbara is a heavy-drinking, sharp-tongued cynic whose abrasive personality hides the fact she has an empty family life. Beautiful Jess Bradford is dating a struggling, temperamental pianist named Peter, and has just learned that she is carrying his child. Phyl is the house "geek," and Clare Harrison is what Barbara describes as a "professional virgin." Running roughshod over this group of co-eds is Mrs. Mack, the alcoholic housemother who maintains her own suite in the house (including its own phone line).

Before long, the "Moaner" strikes. He lures Clare to her death by imitating the meows of the house cat, Claude. He strangles the poor girl with a plastic covering. After hiding the corpse in the attic, the Moaner calls the house phone, and Jess is terrified to hear many deranged voices, including those belonging to people named Agnes and Billy, shouting at her.

The next day, Clare's father arrives on campus and learns that his daughter is missing. Mr. Harrison goes to the police, who dismiss his story. When a thirteen-year-old girl is found dead in a nearby park, however, Lt. Fuller and the police realize there is real trouble and begin a search for Clare. Jess also warns Lt. Fuller that the sorority house has been receiving odd calls. Fuller determines to trace them and instructs Jess to stay on the line the next time the "Moaner" plays his game. Meanwhile, as the girls search for Clare, Mrs. Mack is murdered in the attic.

The night is filled with terror when the "Moaner" rings the sorority again, this time echoing in precise detail the words that Peter used during an argument with Jess about having an abortion. Jess comes to fear that her own boyfriend is the deranged killer, but she refuses to share her suspicions with Lt. Fuller. Unknown to Jess, the killer is already in the house again. This time, he kills Barbara as she sleeps, stabbing her repeatedly with a glass unicorn.

The next time the "Moaner" calls, the police trace is successful. Sergeant Nash informs Jess that the killer is calling from inside the house, from Mrs. Mack's separate line upstairs. Though ordered to get out of the house, Jess is curious to learn what has happened to her missing friend Phyl. Jess finds the answer in an upstairs bedroom: Phyl's corpse lies sprawled next to Barbara's. The Moaner strikes, pursuing Jess to the basement.

Jess locks herself in the basement, and is surprised when Peter breaks a window to gain entrance. Convinced he is the killer, Jess bludgeons Peter to death. The police arrive at the sorority house, and Lt. Fuller has come to the same conclusion: that Peter was the killer. Poor, traumatized Jess is sedated and left to sleep peacefully in her home until her folks arrive in a few hours.

Then, the phone rings again....

COMMENTARY: All the mechanisms of popular '70s slasher films appear in 1974's *Black Christmas*. That's rather shocking in and of itself since *Halloween* (1978) is often legitimately considered the beginning of the stalker/slasher '70s trend. Yet *Black Christmas* is centered around a holiday (you can guess which one...), it features a maniacal killer, it pits that killer against a group of attractive young people in an isolated setting, and in the end, the killer is not actually stopped, but kept alive ... for a sequel?

Additionally, the most convenient of 1970s conveniences, the telephone, plays a dramatic and important role in the "stalkings" of *Black Christmas*. This is a role that it would repeat in more well known examples of the genre such as *When a Stranger Calls* (1979) and *Scream* (1996). Even the P.O.V. first-person subjective "stalking" shots popularized by the flashy preamble of *Halloween* are in evidence in *Black Christmas* during critical moments. So, perhaps the movie deserves some credit for pointing audiences in the direction the genre would soon take. After *Halloween*, for instance, the floodgates of "stalker" films opened with everything from *Friday the 13th* to *He Knows You're Alone*, to *Mother's Day*, to *My Bloody Valentine*, to *April Fool's Day*. *Black Christ-*

mas is a pioneer of the format of that particular sub-genre.

But if one looks beyond the tools the film employs, *Black Christmas* is only so-so. There are many effective horror/attack sequences, some of them quite suspenseful, but the film ultimately reveals many of the same flaws as its less-than-satisfactory 1980s brethren. Remember, for instance, how the terror unfolded believably and quickly in *Halloween*, and how the Laurie Strode character responded to each of Michael's challenges in intelligent fashion. She was a believable human being, and when she was stalked, she responded in recognizable and ingenious human fashion.

Black Christmas does not afford its own *dramatis personae* that luxury. For instance, nobody in the whole film is interested in searching the attic. Not the girls and not the cops. Sure, the old housemother goes up there and is promptly murdered, but she has conveniently told everyone she is "going away" before this sojourn upstairs. Of course, nobody bothers to look for her body up there, and everyone just assumes she's already left town. How convenient, and how clichéd. One might think that if a killer had gained entrance into a house once, authorities would conduct a top to bottom search.

There's also a problem with the last portion of the film, the portion that sets up Peter as the (false) culprit. Misdirection is one thing, but it strains believability that Jess (Hussey) would kill her boyfriend without at least some kind of pretty solid confirmation that he is, in fact, the killer. Worse, after she murders Peter, the police sedate Jess and then leave her alone in the house! *At a crime scene!!!*

Again, the behavior doesn't ring true. When the phone blares again, revealing that the killer is still at large, the audience thus feels cheated. It wants to get to the same point of horror the movie does, but it wants that to happen in a believable, honest fashion. It is not likely the police would fail to search the sorority house, or that Jess would murder her boyfriend without knowing he was the murderer. It is even less likely that the police would leave a sedated college student alone at the scene of a bloody crime for the night. Horror fans are generally a very forgiving lot, and they look for gems where they can, but a movie that relies on plot holes and poor motivations tries their patience.

Despite the problems that make suspension of disbelief difficult for *Black Christmas*, the film is quite successful in other ways. For instance, the "Moaner" is a really creepy villain. His sick, oddball voice is frightening, and the things he says are downright horrid. "*You pig, you bitch, you pig … let me lick your #&$#*t,*" he says to one girl. That's pretty rough stuff, and pretty frightening too. The scenario works because we've all been plagued by crank callers, and some of us have even been plagued by crank callers while alone in our homes. That's a terrifying experience to have, and *Black Christmas* exploits it pretty well, though not nearly as powerfully as *When a Stranger Calls*.

The cast, consisting of Keir Dullea, Margot Kidder, and Olivia Hussey is also much stronger than this material requires. These are great performers, and one wonders why they are playing "victims" in a low-bud-get slasher picture of the "dead teenager" variety. Horror films are respectable all right, but some are more so than others. Usually, it is hungry unknowns (like Kevin Bacon in *Friday the 13th* or Jamie Lee Curtis in *Halloween*) who star in movies of this type, and then find mass acceptance because of well-conceived performances. It's a little disturbing to see established actors playing the common horror stereotypes: the virgin, the townee, the angry boyfriend, the alcoholic, et cetera. They deserve a better script. It could still be one in the horror genre, but it should be better than the one that was shot here.

Black Christmas is pretty good at what it does most of the time. The body of the film is fit, and many suspense and attack scenes are well orchestrated, but the picture's brain seems only half-engaged. And the ending is a huge cheat, no two ways about it. There are so many rotten slasher movies out there, and this was is somewhere in the upper middle class of that mostly undistinguished pack. It's no *Halloween*. It's no *Friday the 13th* either. It's good for a few jolts, a few shivers, and a peek into the future of the stalker film, but little else.

The Cars That Ate Paris

Cast & Crew

CAST: John Meillon (Mayor); Bruce Spence (Charlie); Kevin Miles (Midland); Rick Scully (George); Terry Canpilleri (Arthur); Danny Adcock (Policeman).

CREW: *Directed by:* Peter Weir. *Written by:* Peter Weir, Keith Gow, and Piers Davies. *Produced by:* Hal McElroy. *Director of Photography:* John McLean. *Film Editor:* Wayne LeClos. *Music:* Bruce Smeaton. *M.P.A.A. Rating:* PG. *Running Time:* 90 minutes.

DETAILS: Before *Picnic at Hanging Rock*, Peter Weir directed this intense story of an isolated Australian town that resorts to ambush and other atrocities to stay alive. The town youngsters drive souped-up, bizarre vehicles (from cannibalized cars), forecasting the *Mad Max* series. Tourists, beware!

The Dead Don't Die (1974) ✶ ✶ ✶

Cast & Crew

CAST: George Hamilton (Don Drake); Linda Cristal (Vera Lavelle); Joan Blondell (Mrs. Perditto); Ralph Meeker (Lt. Reardon); James McEachin (Specht); Reggie Nalder (Mr. Perditto); Ray Milland (Moss); Jerry Douglas (Ralph Drake); Milton Parsons (Funeral Home Receptionist); William O'Connell (Priest); Yvette Vickers (Miss Adrian); Brendon Dillon (Prison Chaplain); Russ Grieres (Prison Guard); Bill Smillie (Newspaperman).

CREW: *Director of Photography:* James Crabe. *Produced by:* Henry Colman. *Written by:* Robert Bloch. *Directed by:* Curtis Harrington. *Executive Producers:* Douglas S. Cramer, W.L. Baumes. *Music by:* Robert Prince. *Executive Production Manager:* Hal Polaire. *Film Editor:* Ronald J. Fagan. *Art Director:* Robert Kinoshita. *Casting:* Otto and Windsor Casting, Ltd. *Assistant Director:* Richard Moder. *Sound Engineer:* William Tremellen. *Music Editor:* Ken Hall. *Sound Editor:* Don Hall. *Property Master:* Gene Booth. *Set Decorator:* John Franco, Jr. *Costumes:* Oscar Rodriguez, Betsy Cox. *Executive Assistant:* Diana Arieto. *Title Design:* Phill Norman. *Special Effects:* A & A Special Effects. Filmed at 20th Century–Fox *M.P.A.A Rating:* Made for TV. *Running Time:* 75 minutes.

SYNOPSIS: On death row in 1934, a prisoner faces execution in the electric chair for the murder of his wife. He tells his brother, a lawyer named Don Drake, that he is innocent. He begs Don to find the real murderer. The execution is carried out, and then the interment follows at Maywood Cemetery. A woman in black attends the graveside service.

Determined to know the truth about his brother, Don pays a visit to Mr. Moss, the owner of the dance club where his brother's wife, Frances, was found dead. Don is unaware he is being followed by the lady in black. After the meeting with Moss, she introduces herself to him as Vera, and tells him to leave Chicago immediately for his own safety. Not long thereafter, Don is shocked to see his own brother, Ralph, staring at him from outside a window. Don goes to look for him, but he has vanished inside an antique store. Don fights with the owner, Perditto, who he thinks is hiding Ralph, and is knocked unconscious.

Don awakens the next afternoon, his wounds tended by Vera. She warns him that a dangerous man named Varek is responsible for the horrors he has witnessed. When Don demands that she take him to Varek, Vera leads him to a funeral home instead. There, they find the antique dealer, Perditto, dead. The corpse awakens and speaks to Don, informing him that the living dead are his children and that he, Varek, can manipulate bodies. The corpse rises from the coffin and pursues Don. He flees the building and reports the situation to the police. They investigate, and find nothing to corroborate his story. At the antique store, Perditto appears very much alive.

Don goes back to see Moss at the dance hall, and tells him what happened. Moss puts Drake up in his apartment while he looks into the crazy tale. At the cemetery that night, Don sees his brother, alive again. The lady in Black, Vera, then pays him a visit, warning that Varek has sent her to kill him. Oddly, she reveals that she belongs to Varek because she is already dead. In fact, Varek has revived her as a zombie to serve him. Varek is apparently a lord of the zombies, a sorcerer. He framed Vera in life for a crime she didn't commit, just like what happened to Ralph, and in death she is Varek's slave.

It is soon revealed that Varek controls Vera with a voodoo doll. If the doll is destroyed, then Vera will also die. In payment for her betrayal, Varek burns Vera's voodoo doll and kills her. A shattered Don then drives to Maywood cemetery with Moss to see if Ralph remains in his grave, or has risen as a zombie. An empty casket reveals that Vera's wild story was true. Drake is then attacked by zombies, but assisted by a black man, Specht, who warns him that Moss is actually Varek, the nefarious zombie master.

Specht and Don flee to Albert Storage to gather evidence of Varek's evil. Varek dispatches his zombies after them, and they kill Specht. Don is left on his own in the warehouse, where he finds more zombies in cold storage. One of them is Frances, Ralph's wife.

Varek arrives at the warehouse and reveals his plan. He will raise his zombie children and attempt world domination. His undead ghouls will man critical posts, and make him the most powerful man on Earth. After explaining this plan, Varek sends Ralph to kill Don, his own brother.

Don attempts to reason with his zombified brother, informing Ralph that Frances, Ralph's beloved wife, was also killed by Varek. Ralph turns on his master, and impales Varek on a meat hook. As Valek expires, so do his zombie servants.

When Don returns to the scene with police, Varek and the zombies have disappeared...

COMMENTARY: By rights, *The Dead Don't Die* shouldn't be included in this text, since it is devoted to theatrical horror features of the 1970s. Yet the rules were broken for *Duel*, a Steven Spielberg-directed TV movie that was released theatrically in Europe. And, the rules are bent slightly again to include *The Dead Don't Die*, another unique television movie.

The film is interesting and worthy of note for a number of reasons. In addition to a great horror pedigree (writer Robert Bloch and director Curtis Harrington), and an impressive B-movie cast (including Reggie Nalder, Ray Milland, and George Hamilton), *The Dead Don't Die* features a return to the old, pre–*Night of the Living Dead* conception of zombies. This is in direct contrast to most such films of the '70s, which adopted Romero's template of the undead for their productions (as seen in *Children Shouldn't Play with Dead Things* [1972], *Tombs of the Blind Dead* [1972], *Zombie* [1979], and others). So historically, *The Dead Don't Die* bucks a worldwide trend in zombie movies, and deserves some note for that. It was not until *The Serpent and the Rainbow* in 1987, that the original concept of zombies (as undead slaves of the living) was again featured prominently in film.

As Wade Davis's book *The Serpent and the Rainbow* defined it, a zombie (or zombi) was, as seen by the people of Haiti, is the "spirit of a dead man." Much of that book concerns how a strange native mix of chemicals caused people in Haiti to appear to die suddenly, and then rise as slaves without will. In the book, Davis encounters strange secret societies that utilize the zombie powder as a kind of punishment for those who have broken unspoken laws. When sold out by enemies or competitors, these so-called criminals are turned into zombies. Simply put, zombification (care of the chemical tetrodoxotin) was a method to control people.

This depiction of the zombie as mindless followers of a cabal or corrupt individual actually survived into early Hollywood. *White Zombie* (1932) starred Bela Lugosi as a zombie master in the West Indies who develops an army of the creatures. But in the late '60s the ghouls of *Night of the Living Dead* also became known as zombies. These critters were feral creatures not held under the authority or sway of any particular person or group. *The Dead Don't Die* reconsiders the zombies of Haiti and *White Zombie* by featuring, again, the story of a zombie master, this time Ray Milland.

What makes the film rather interesting is that it is all told within the venue of the 1930–40s detective film, or *film noir*. Don Drake is the intrepid sleuth, personally involved in a case. Vera Lavelle is the mysterious woman with a dark secret who also serves as a romantic distraction for Drake. And Moss/Varek is the evil man with the terrible plan. These are all "stock" detective genre characters, and even Nalder's character is familiar: the boss's nasty henchman.

Considering the subject manner, the

film is told much as it might have been in Hollywood's golden age. For instance, the stars of *The Dead Don't Die* appear in an "iris" with their names emblazoned underneath, in tried-and-true black-and-white movie fashion. That there is a central mystery to be solved also reflects the "private dick" films of that bygone era. Considering that later Hollywood productions such as *Angel Heart* (1987) and *Lord of Illusions* (1995) also tried to marry the detective *film noir* genre with out-and-out horror, *The Dead Don't Die* is historically valuable, a predecessor to what Hollywood imagined in later decades.

As a genre-blending, nostalgia-provoking film, *The Dead Don't Die* is really pretty good. It goes against the grain of history (by remembering the early definition of a "zombie"), and is directed with a simple hand that reflects the era it depicts. Where the film falters is in two areas. Don Drake (as portrayed by Hamilton) is not the best protagonist. He is led around on a leash (first by Vera, then by Moss), and does not register much surprise that someone can raise the dead and control them.

Likewise, Ray Milland plays the talking villain, a cliché defined by Roger Ebert. The talking villain appears in the James Bond films all the time, and occasionally in horror (as in 1970's *Scream and Scream Again*). Here, Milland thoughtfully explains his plan for world domination to the hero. He would have been better off just to keep his mouth shut, but some villains just never learn.

Frankenstein and the Monster from Hell

Cast & Crew

CAST: Peter Cushing (Baron Frankenstein); David Prowse (the Monster); Patrick Troughton (Body Snatcher); Shane Briant (Simon); Madeline Smith (Sarah).

CREW: *Directed by:* Terence Fisher. *Written by:* Anthony Hinds. *Produced by:* Roy Skeggs. *Director of Photography:* Brian Probyn. *Editor:* James Needs. *Music:* James Bernard. Hammer Studios. *M.P.A.A. Rating:* R. *Running Time:* 93 minutes.

DETAILS: Hammer's final Frankenstein film is weak business set at an insane asylum. This time, the mad doctor, Cushing again, is joined by a young and equally insane apprentice, Shane Briant. Together, they create a new monster, but get the same results as before…

The Ghoul (1974) ★ ★

Cast & Crew

CAST: Peter Cushing (Dr. Lawrence); John Hurt (Tom Rawling); Alexandra Bastedo (Angela); Gwen Watford (Ayush); Veronica Carlson (Daphne); Stewart Bevan (Billy); Ian McCulloch (Geoffrey); John D. Collins (Young Man); Dan Meaden (Policeman); Don Henderson (the Ghoul).

CREW: A Tyburn Film Production. *Director of Photography:* John Wilcox. *Art Director:* Jack Shampan. *Assistant Art Director:* Peter Williams. *Costumes Designed by:* Anthony Mendelson. *Costumes Executed by:* Behrens and Nathans of London. *Film Editor:* Henry Richardson. *Sound Editor:* Roy Baker. *Production Manager:* Ron Jackson. *Make-up Created by:* Roy Ashton. *Assistant Director:* Peter Saunders. *Continuity:* Pamela Davies. *Music Composed by:* Harry Robinson. *Music Supervision:* Philip Martell. *Recorded at:* Anvil Studios. *Screenplay by:* John Elder. *Produced by:* Kevin Francis. *Directed by:* Freddie Francis. *M.P.A.A. Rating:* R. *Running Time:* 90 minutes.

P.O.V.

"Ghoul: a person of revolting, inhuman tastes ... supposed in the East to haunt burial places and feed on the dead." — the opening card of *The Ghoul* (1974) defines its titular character.

SYNOPSIS: In London of the Roaring '20s, a bunch or rich folks play cruel, debauched jokes on one another at a party. Wealthy youngsters Daphne and Billy decide to race Angela and Geoffrey in their new motorcar, making for "land's end," the Atlantic coast.

The race becomes a competitive contest, but Daphne and Billy are unexpectedly sidelined when their car runs out of gas. After parking on the edge of a precipice overlooking the moors, Billy goes off in search of petrol. While he's away, an odd stranger named Tom Rawlings abducts Daphne. He warns her not to go near his master's house, but she escapes, and is invited inside the estate by the polite Mr. Lawrence, the owner.

Mr. Lawrence is former clergy, and he obligingly prepares a room for Daphne. In short order, Daphne meets the Indian housekeeper and learns that the lady of the house is deceased. Apparently, Mr. Lawrence used to live in India, and his late wife and his only son were corrupted by a holy man there ... someone that Lawrence describes only as "depraved." While Daphne naps, Mr. Lawrence sends his gardener, Tom, off to find Billy. Tom pushes Billy and his car off the cliff, killing him. He reports back that Billy has left and returned home.

Daphne starts to experience the odd feeling that Lawrence is keeping her in the house for some dark purpose. That night, a deformed stranger sneaks into Daphne's bedroom and brutally murders her with an Indian stabbing implement.

Elsewhere, Angela and Geoffrey identify Billy's body for the authorities and set about looking for the missing Daphne. They follow her trail to the moors, and Angela is abducted by Tom. While searching for Daphne and now Angela, Geoffrey arrives at the Lawrence estate and invites himself in. He meets Mr. Lawrence, who lies to him by claiming that Daphne took a bus back to London. He even tries to convince Geoffrey that Angela did likewise.

Geoffrey is not convinced, and questions Tom about the accuracy of these stories. Tom flees rather than answer, and Geoffrey chases him into an area of quicksand. Tom gets caught in the quicksand but Geoffrey offers to save him if he will tell him what really happened. Rather than sink in the quicksand, Tom reveals the truth. He also claims that there is an inhuman monster living in the Lawrence house — a monster that feeds on human beings.

Geoffrey returns to question Lawrence, and is promptly killed by the depraved thing living upstairs. This strange ghoul, Lawrence's son, plants a knife in Geoffrey's head.

At the same time, Tom attempts to rape Angela. She tries to escape, but is confronted by the ghoul. The ghoul kills Tom, but before it can murder Angela, Dr. Lawrence kills the filthy beast, his own son. As Angela flees the grounds, Lawrence puts a bullet in his own head, and ends the nightmare permanently.

COMMENTARY: *The Ghoul* is a tedious, slow-paced, "veddy British" thriller about a family "secret." It plays like an exploitation version of *Jane Eyre* or *Rebecca*, and suffers from inconsistent characters and motivations. The anti-climactic ending only serves to heighten the boredom factor.

The picture opens with a very stylized

preamble. The beautiful Daphne walks a long, dark hallway with candle in hand. Everything is filmed from a cockeyed angle, and there is a sense of expressionist film at work. A creepy voice calls out to her, and Daphne opens a closed door. Behind it, a drooling corpse is hanging in the middle of the room, swaying slowly...

It's a creepy, effective way to start a horror movie, and it yet has absolutely nothing to do with anything else in the film. The whole sequence is but a joke played by the decadent rich, a joke designed to see if Daphne will scream bloody murder when confronted by evil. It is very stylish, and very purposeless.

From that cryptic, if nicely Gothic, opening, the movie spends the next ten or so minutes embroiled in a car chase that establishes a few things about Daphne, ostensibly the film's lead character. She is haughty, pushy, forthright, and strong-willed. She didn't scream when faced with that corpse, and during the chase she even assumes control of the car's wheel. She is the "spoiled rich," and a very assertive personality. In fact, the film establishes Daphne's nature well. The audience gets to know her, and doesn't necessarily like her, but she's a tough cookie and kind of admirable in her toughness.

Yet, from the point Daphne is held captive by Tom, her character undergoes an about face. This aggressive, hell-on-wheels rich kid becomes, at the snap of the screenwriter's fingers, a shrinking violet. Suddenly she's a weak-willed prisoner who accepts the unlikely assurances of strangers on a variety of issues. This is a big-time switcheroo, and wholly inconsistent with everything that has already been depicted. Before long, Daphne dies as a result of her inaction, in a reiteration of the famous Janet Leigh trick, but her character has already been terribly compromised.

From Daphne's death forward, the film

is lugubriously paced, as John Hurt plays "psycho" and threatens the heroine-in-waiting, Angela. All the while, Cushing's Lawrence maintains his "haunting" secret upstairs. But even his character is inconsistent. He goes on record confirming that he hates the man who turned his son into a depraved maniac, yet he keeps the services of an Indian housekeeper who shares similar beliefs. Also, Lawrence, a former priest, imprisons Daphne so that his son might continue to live by those beliefs, and feed on her.

Finally, Lawrence changes his mind, and kills his son outright, claiming he should have done it years earlier. So is he a deceptive man? A willing accomplice to his son's evil? Why does he choose this moment (after years of helping his son...) to murder the ghoul? Why not kill him before Daphne died. Or before Geoffrey died? Or before Tom died? Clearly, Lawrence's decision to stop his depraved son is timed solely to provide the film a reasonable climax, not for any legitimate dramatic or character motivation.

The final revelation that Lawrence Jr. is something of a scarred monster is undercut by his appearance. He is a bald man wearing a bright yellow gown, and is not exactly fear inspiring. His make-up is bad too: his face is purple, while the rest of his complexion is pale white. The revelation of this inhuman "look" is not nearly enough of a jolt after all the build-up. But then again, nor is the insufficient ending that finds Cushing committing suicide, as Angela runs away, traumatized, but otherwise unharmed.

For long stretches of time in *The Ghoul*, nothing really happens. People talk, a secret is alluded to, and Hurt threatens to rape women, but never follows through. One might make the claim that the film is aiming for a steady, Gothic feel, with its familial secrets, its characterization of evil, and its (various) damsels in distress. But there's just not enough happening to keep the thin material afloat. It doesn't hang together.

House of Whipcord

Cast & Crew

CAST: Barbara Markham (Mrs. Wakehurst); Patrick Barr (Justice Bailey); Ray Brooks (Tony); Sheila Keith (Walker); Ivor Salter (Jack).

CREW: *Written, Produced and Directed by*: Peter Walker. *Music:* Stanley Myers. *Editor:* Matt McCarthy. *Director of Photography:* Peter Jessop. *M.P.A.A. Rating:* R. *Running Time:* 102 minutes.

DETAILS: Break out the whips! This is a tale of sadism, cruelty and revenge as "judge" Patrick Barr and a female colleague torture, brutalize, and whip women in the name of the law. Debauched.

It Lives by Night

Cast & Crew

CAST: Paul Carr (Dr. Kipley); Stewart Moss, Marianne McAndrew, Michael Pataki, Arthur Space, Robert Berk, Pat Delaney.

CREW: *Directed by:* Jerry Jameson. *Written and Produced by:* Lou Shaw. *Executive Producers:* Nicolas Jenna, Matthew Leonetti. *Special Effects by:* Howard Anderson Company. *Director of Photography:* Matthew Leonetti. *Film Editor:* Tom Stevens. *Music:* Artie Kane. *M.P.A.A Rating:* PG. *Running Time:* 90 minutes (approximate).

DETAILS: A bat expert (Moss) and his attention-starved wife (McAndrew), visit a cavern while on vacation, and hubbie is swiped by a disease-infected rat. Very soon, he is transforming into a rabid bat monster, despite the best efforts of Dr. Kipley (Carr).

The Legend of Seven Golden Vampires (1974) ★ ★ ★ ½

Cast & Crew

CAST: Peter Cushing (Van Helsing); David Chiang (Hsi Ching); Julie Ege (Vanessa Buren); Robin Stewart (Leyland Van Helsing); John Forbes-Robinson (Count Dracula); Shi Szu (Mai Kwai); Robert Hanna (British Consul); Chan Shen (Kah);James Ma (Hsi Ta); Liu Chia Yung (Hsi Kwei); Peng Ko An (Hai Sing); Chen Teh Loong (Hsi San); Wong Han Chan (Leung Hon).

CREW: *Director of Photography:* John Williams. *Editor:* Chris Barns. *Assistant Editor:* Larry Richardson. *Special Effects:* Les Bowie. *Martial Arts Sequences:* Kan Chia. *Assistant to Producers:* Christopher Garrison. *Screenplay:* Don Houghton. *Produced by:* Don Houghton, Vee-King Shaw. *Music by:* James Bernard. *Music Supervisor:* Philip Martell. *Directed by:* Roy

Ward Baker. A Hammer-Shaw Production made entirely in Hong Kong. *M.P.A.A. Rating:* Unrated. *Running Time:* 89 minutes.

SYNOPSIS: In Transylvania in the year 1804, Kah, the high priest (in Szechuan) of the golden vampires, resurrects the Prince of Darkness, seeking to restore his power base in China. Instead, Dracula steals Kah's "mortal coil," and inhabits his body.

One hundred years later, Professor Van Helsing is visiting the province of Chung King as an expert on the occult and vampirism. His lectures are met with skepticism by the Chinese locals, but for one man, Hsi Ching. In one symposium, Van Helsing recounts the legend of a farmer who fought the seven golden vampires to free his daughter of their demonic grip. The farmer killed one of the undead before being killed himself, but six are believed to survive.

To Hsi Ching, this is no legend or fairy tale: the story is about his village. To this day, the golden vampires, led by Dracula, steal the women of his community, and terrorize the inhabitants by night.

Van Helsing agrees to help Hsi Ching and his family — a band of agile warriors — defeat the vampires. Joining them on the long trek to the village is Van Helsing's son, Leyland, and a wealthy widower, Vanessa Buren. As they leave Chung King, Van Helsing's vampire-slaying squad is confronted by a local warlord's army, in revenge for a perceived slight from Leyland. Hsi Ching and his brothers (and sister!) defeat them easily in combat, and the trek continues. En route to the subjugated village, Van Helsing briefs his seven Chinese defenders in the ways of the vampire.

The vampires attack the approaching group by night, as they sleep in a cave. There is vicious, close-quarter combat, but Van Helsing's men are triumphant. Three vampires are killed in combat, leaving only three remaining ... plus the powerful leader, Dracula. Van Helsing and Hsi Ching make preparations for the final battle with evil at the Chinese castle of Dracula.

In the ensuing fight, Vanessa is bitten ... and transformed into a vampire. Hsi Ching, who has developed romantic feelings for her, is forced to kill her. When he is bitten as well, the courageous Hsi Ching commits suicide rather than become a servant of evil. Then Ching's sister is captured, and Leyland pursues her to the castle, and the ceremonial chamber where her blood is to be spilled.

Professor Van Helsing arrives in the nick of time, killing the last golden vampire and facing down Dracula ... who reveals his true face to the long-time nemesis. Van Helsing ends the affair with a stake aimed right at Dracula's heart.

COMMENTARY: All the vitality and energy that was missing from 1973's *The Satanic Rites of Dracula* has been infused into the *Legend of Seven Golden Vampires*, a kung-fu/vampire film with an excess of style, action and fun. Though Christopher Lee is missing from the film, Peter Cushing leads a talented cast in what amounts to a 90-minute celebration of acrobatic movement and exquisite violence. While also cashing in on the 1970s fascination with kung fu movies and Bruce Lee, *The Legend of Seven Golden Vampires* harks back to Kurosawa's *The Seven Samurai*. As in that classic film (later remade as *The Magnificent Seven*), a town is at risk, and a group of brave warriors must save it from exploitation. Only in this case, the warriors are lead by Van Helsing, and the bad guys are commanded by the Prince of Darkness.

Although it is a little sad to note that the Dracula franchise is now following film trends rather than inspiring them, the fun aspects of *The Legend of Seven Golden Vampires* outweigh the fact that the film is, essentially, an exploitation piece. The film is filled with the exaggerated chop-socky sound effects one has come to associate with Asian action cinema, and there is a lot of female nudity in the film too. Clearly, Hammer wasn't hedging any bets after the failure of *The Satanic Rites of Dracula*.

East meets west, and Kah (Chan Shen) meets Dracula (John Forbes-Robinson) in **The Legend of Seven Golden Vampires** (1974).

But, holding it all together (in a much more significant part than he had in the previous *Dracula* film) is that old friend Peter Cushing. He has a wonderful scene in this film in which he explains to his companions a simple feeling he is experiencing. He senses that something terrible, the lair of the vampire, may be around the next corner, and he is disturbed. As Cushing puts this feeling to words, he rivets the audience's attention with his voice and his inflection. He perfectly embodies the "veteran" who has faced evil before, and his "gut instincts" become the subject of the moment. It's a nice character moment, especially considering that Van Helsing was never as well developed as Cushing's Frankenstein. This film does much to rectify that wrong, making Van Helsing first a pariah for his beliefs and then a staunch advocate of Hsi Ching. Cushing has never been better.

Beyond Cushing's performance, the action scenes are pretty amazing. Every excuse imaginable is used to stage a fight, and these incredible dances of death are brilliantly orchestrated. In a few instances they appear a bit over-choreographed, but for the most part, they are rousing, and dynamic examples of kinetic movement and confrontation.

With spikier confrontations, a re-modeling of vampire conventions (with the Lord Buddha stepping in for the Christian crucifix), and compelling lead characters, not to mention fantastic battle sequences, *The Legend of Seven Golden Vampires* is one of the most enjoyable Hammer franchise films in some time. The film suffered from a limited release in the United States, and that's a shame, because its genre-blending nature was prophetic as well as successful. Both *The Matrix* (1999) and *Crouching Tiger, Hidden Dragon* (2000) dared to blend science fiction and fantasy with the martial arts, in much the same fascinating manner that *Golden Vampires* blends horror with the action. If re-released, or re-made today, this movie would be huge. It is a forerunner of the kind of action pieces now raking in hundreds of millions of dollars.

If there's any problem with the film at all, it is that the final battle seems easy. If the seven brothers can kill off the vampires so easily, why do they need Van Helsing to come along for the ride? Secondly, the final climax, Van Helsing vs. Dracula, is underwhelming after all the kung-fu gymnastics. Of course,

it would be hard to create a memorable or spectacular death for Dracula at this point in film history. He's been spiked, showered, electrocuted, iced, impaled and chased through a thorny thicket. His death in *Golden Vampires* is traditional: he gets run through the heart with a wooden spike. As Buffy might say, no muss, no fuss.

It's a shame this was the last film in Hammer's *Dracula* cycle, because it has ten times as much life as its predecessor, and is filled with enough action and fun for six horror films.

Seizure (1974) ✶ ✶ ½

Cast & Crew

CAST: Jonathan Frid (Edmund Blackstone); Martine Beswick (the Queen); Joe Sirola (Charlie); Christina Pickles (Nicole); Anne Meacham (Eunice); Roger De Koven (Serge); Troy Donahue (Mark); Mary Woronov (Mikki); Richard Cox (Gerald); Timothy Oasey (Jason); Henry Backer (Jackal); Lucy Bingham (Betsy); Herve Villechaize (the Spider); Alexis Kirk (Arris); Emil Meola (Gas Station Attendant); Timothy Rowse (Milkman); Aziz (Himself).

CREW: Cinerama Releasing and Euro-American Pictures Present *Seizure*. *Production Supervisor:* Jeffrey D. Kapelman. *First Assistant Director:* Timothy Rowse. *Second Assistant Director:* Emil Meola. *Camera Operator:* Daniel Arzouni. *First Assistant Camera:* Guy Bernadese. *Second Assistant Camera:* Johnny Bedroussian. *Grip:* Michel Lauzier. *Stills:* Herve Villechaize. *Electrician:* Jacques Rousseau. *Assistant Electrician:* Rejean Laramee. *Sound Recordist:* Martin Joyal. *Assistant Sound:* Larry Miller. *Sound Mixer:* Joe Grimaldi. *Sound Effects:* Ken Heeley-Ray. *Re-Recording:* Rejean Gigier. *Sound Editor:* Nobuko Oganesoff. *Assistant Editor:* Jacqueline Boucher. *Continuity:* Lise Venne. *Property Man:* James McCelmontt. *Property Mistress:* Michelle Marchand. *Makeup Supervisor/Special Effects:* Thomas Brumberger. *Wardrobe/Hair:* Linda Coleman. *Carpenter:* Gerard Legault. *Production Secretary:* Rigdon Reese. *Production Assistants:* Richard Morris, Lucy Bingham. *Edmund's Sketches:* Edward Mann. *Batick Paintings:* Judith Aranyi. *Director of Photography:* Roger Racine. *Art Director:* Najwa Stone. *Wardrobe and Jewelry Design:* Alexis Kirk. *Film Editors:* Nobuko Oganesoff, Oliver Stone. *Music:* Lee Gagnon. *Music Produced by:* Theme Variations (Montreal). *Executive Producers:* Harold Greenberg, Donald Johnston. *Original Screenplay:* Edward Mann, Oliver Stone. *Produced by:* Garrad L. Glenn, Jeffrey P. Kapelman. *Directed by:* Oliver Stone. Made on location at Val Morin Province of Quebec, Canada. *M.P.A.A. Rating:* R. *Running Time:* 90 minutes (approx).

SYNOPSIS: A frustrated writer, Edmund Blackstone, awakens from a nightmare and is deeply disturbed because he has had the same dream many times before. Meanwhile, his wife Nicole prepares their rural estate for a visit from some of Edmund's best friends. The wealthy and obnoxious Charlie, his sexy girlfriend Mikki, and Edmund's mentor Serge and wife Eunice are among the guests. Before the festivities around the lakeside house begin, Edmund's son, Jason, becomes upset when his dog, Aziz, disappears. Edmund later finds the pet dog hanged in the nearby woods.

The weekend party begins, but something more troubling than friends appear. Three specters, all straight from Edmund's imagination, materialize to terrorize the guests. There is the Queen of Evil, the very embodiment of the dark mother goddess (Kali) of the Hindu faith, a nasty (but diminutive) king from French history called the "Spider," and a black-skinned, mute executioner known as the "Jackal." These three villains soon terrorize Edmund's guests and family.

The Queen of Evil informs Edmund and his companions that only one of them will survive the night. She then sets them out on a series of tasks in which the loser is to be executed. Charlie dies of a heart attack after being forced to participate in a race. Eunice dies at the Spider's hand, consumed by her guilty feelings regarding an infidelity. Mikki is desperate to be the sole survivor and challenges Edmund in a knife fight. Edmund kills her instead.

Serge, an old philosopher, handles his death gracefully, and walks nobly to his own execution at the axe of the Jackal. Finally, Edmund must decide if he should give up his wife and son to ensure his own survival. Revealing himself to be a coward, Edmund chooses self over family, and lets Nicole and Jason be taken by the dark Queen.

Ultimately, however, Edmund's wife, Nicole, is a power of goodness, and she returns from the grave to save her son and punish Edmund for his choice. An ashamed Edmund flees his house, the Spider in hot pursuit. Just as he is being butchered by the dastardly dwarf, Edmund awakens sweaty in his bed and realizes he has had the same nightmare all over again. He breathes a sigh of relief ... and then is confronted with the dark Queen...

Sometime later, Nicole and Jason are shocked to discover that Edmund has died in his sleep from a seizure. He never woke up to enjoy his weekend with his friends...

COMMENTARY: Somewhere inside Oliver Stone's debut feature, *Seizure*, there's a great and meaningful horror movie yearning to find expression. Like an early *Jacob's Ladder* (1990), or contrarily, a latter-day *Occurrence at Owl Creek Bridge*, this film could have meaningfully concerned the death phantasm of a writer who has not yet made peace with his life. Unfortunately, characterization and plotting are so weak in the film that *Seizure* seems to change premises every twenty minutes, and ultimately fails to emerge as a cohesive (or coherent) piece of work.

A viewer can see so much provocative material in *Seizure*, and that's part of the problem: it's a film that seemingly has no idea just how good it could be. The premise is so rich and full of possibilities, yet the film itself is fairly empty and dull, given to long static dialogue scenes and confusing happenings. Judging by what is on screen, the film focuses on an imaginative but flawed man who dies in his sleep, the victim of a seizure. In those final instants of his life, he is confronted by his demons, his failings, and his true feelings for his loved ones. Thus each "player" in his death dream represents some facet of his personality, history and character; some facet that he either makes peace with, or fails to make peace with.

Serge, for instance, is Edmund's mentor: a wise, thoughtful writer who faces his death with dignity and perspective. These are all qualities Edmund wishes he too could possess.

Nicole, Edmund's wife, represents the best part of Blackstone: his goodness, his strength, his sense of loyalty even. While dying in his sleep, Edmund acknowledges that he is a coward and that his wife is infinitely better than he is.

Charlie, the money-grubbing friend, could be seen to stand in for Edmund's lust for material wealth and his financial success as a "commercial" writer of horror stories for children. And so it goes.

The three villains, the Jackal, the Spider, and the Queen, are Edmund's literary "creations" come back to taunt and challenge him, his personal demons given life in his suffering subconscious.

If *Seizure* had stuck to that interesting interpretation, it would have been a meaningful film about what it means to die, to face mortality, and to confront the totality of one's life. Instead, *Seizure* introduces too many characters (such as Betsy, the young maid and Gerald, the obnoxious house-guest), only to have them unceremoniously killed in none-too-exciting set pieces. Betsy doesn't seem to represent any particular "internal" battle for Blackstone, so her presence in his dream doesn't make sense.

Ditto for Mikki (Mary Woronov). While it's true that Mary Woronov is lovely, and a welcome addition to the cast, her part would have been so much richer if Mikki somehow related to an element of Edmund's life. Had she been his mistress instead of Charlie's, his embodiment of lust, infidelity, sexual yearning, then she would have fit in better with the thesis the film attempts to develop. Instead, she is just a woman who wants to survive, and betrays Edmund in the process.

Perhaps *Seizure*'s gravest problem is that it can't seem to stick to a single idea and run with it. It begins and ends with the clichéd "is it all a dream?" scenario and then moves into the familiar "haunted writer" territory in which a scribe's own creations terrorize him. Next, *Seizure* resembles a deranged "reality" TV show in which Edmund and his friends must compete for survival. They face challenges and hurdles (such as running around Blackstone's house five times in the pitch black of night). Instead of being voted off the island, however, the loser is killed. The Queen is the bizarre host of the proceedings, and though she doesn't declare the loser to be the "weakest link," she might as well. But again, after this challenge, the whole idea of murderous games is dropped in *Seizure*, overturned for something else of interest.

Part of the problem may also be Jonathan Frid's portrayal of the main character. A great horror icon, Frid brings almost no weight or humanity to Edmund. Ideally, Blackstone should be the center of the film, a force around which all the other characters orbit. Instead, he is a big black hole, a mystery that the audience never understands or even particularly likes. Though given to portentous declarations (such as "I'm scared of something in me"), the audience never identifies with Edmund, or comes to understand what makes him special or unique as a human being.

While watching *Seizure*, this author was reminded of *Don't Look Now*, and how that film played out like some terrible tragedy because Donald Sutherland and Julie Christie were so damned likable. When Sutherland's character died at the end of that film, there was a weight to the moment, a sense of something important lost. *Seizure* attempts to mimic Roeg's stygian; "my life flashed before my eyes" montage, but this time around it is a technique with no impact. We never like Edmund enough to mourn his loss. There's never that level of connection.

There's much to appreciate in *Seizure,* including the surreal, avante-garde feel of the piece as a whole. There are moments that are downright kinky, and there's even an *Alice in Wonderland* quality to the brutality and humor of the picture. But it's all kind of half-thought-out, and poorly executed. Oliver Stone is one of our greatest directors, and one can see in *Seizure* the seeds of that greatness, but little else.

Shriek of the Mutilated (1974) *

Cast & Crew

CAST: Alan Brock (Professor Ernst Prell); Jennifer Stock (Karen Hunter); Tawm Ellis (Dr. Karl Werner); Michael Harris (Keith Henshaw); Tom Grail (Spencer Ste. Claire); Darcy Brown (Lynn Kelly); Jack Neubeck (Tom Nash); Ivan Agar (Laughing Crow); Luci Brandt (April Ste. Claire); Marina Stefan (Party Hostess); Harriet McFaul (Girl at Party); Dwig Marfield (Station Attendant); Jimmy Silva (Policeman); Warren D'Oly-Rhind (Waiter).

CREW: An Ed Adlum and Mike Findlay Production. *Photographed by:* Robert Findlay. *Sound by:* R.B. Combs. *Edited by:* Mike Findlay. *Screenplay by:* Ed Adlum, Ed Kelleher. *Songs:* "Popcorn" *by:* Hot Butter; *and* "Love Shriek" *by:* Mark Pines and D.C. Joy. *Assistant Cameraman:* Ambrosio Bernal. *Art Direction:* John Zadrio. *Location Coordinator:* Joe Scarpinito. *Costumes:* Ortun. *Make-up:* Makum Kinsky. *Sound Mixing:* Magno Sound. *Production Manager:* Pat Triarch. *Continuity:* Kay Kressi. *Produced by:* Ed Adlum. *Directed by:* Mike Findlay. *M.P.A.A. Rating:* R. *Running Time:* 85 minutes.

SYNOPSIS: Professor Ernst Prell plans to take his university class to remote Boot Island, where they will search for the legendary yeti. On the night before the trip, Prell invites student Keith Henshaw to a "specialty" restaurant that serves an unusual dish called "gin sung."

Keith's girlfriend, Karen, is upset that Keith went out with the professor rather than her, and attends a college party instead. There, an unhinged fellow named Spencer reports that three students died on Prell's last field trip to Boot Island. He tells of a terrible monster and a godforsaken village where all Hell broke loose. Karen dismisses his story as the ramblings of a drunk, but when Spencer goes home that night, he kills his girlfriend, April. As she dies, she retaliates by electrocuting him in the bathtub.

The next day, Prell drives Karen, Keith, and two other students, Lynn and Tom, to Boot Island. There, they stay at the home of Prell's friend Dr. Karl Werner and his unusual manservant, the mute Laughing Crow. Werner reports that there is a ferocious white yeti in the area, and that Laughing Crow was once attacked by the creature. The students head out on an exploratory trip, and a yeti kills Tom. The next day, Lynn is killed by the same creature.

Karen begs to go home, but Keith and Prell are obsessed with capturing the beast. When two attempts to snare the yeti fail, Keith learns a secret: there is no yeti, only Werner in a hairy costume! Prell and Warner, along with Laughing Crow, are actually cannibals hoping to scare Karen to death so they can eat her body during a special meeting of the "Covenant," a society of cannibals! Worse, Keith learns that he has already partaken of human flesh in eating Prell's favorite dish, gin sung. A desperate Keith tries to rescue Karen before it is too late, but the trap is sprung.

COMMENTARY: *Shriek of the Mutilated* is a grade Z movie bordering on the amateurish. It is a low budget film featuring unknown actors and a deeply silly monster costume. The movie tries to be clever in its final twist, but by the time the so-called surprise has arrived, the audience has already given up because so few of the characters show any signs of intelligence.

The set-up is an interesting one. A university professor takes four students out to the remote woods to find the legendary yeti. Now, that one line description could also result in a brilliant horror film, as evidenced by *The Blair Witch Project*. But the twist here is that there is no yeti at all. Instead, the professor is a cannibal who wants to dine on all but one student, who he hopes to convert to his unusual eating habits. Even that plot could work, maybe, but this film is so badly edited, so lamely acted, so terribly written, that it becomes an exercise in viewing agony. It's the *Manos: The Hands of Fate* (1966) of the 1970s.

To list all the inanities in this film would be useless, but some are so extraordinary it would be unfair not to make mention of them. Near the film's opening, for instance, there is a swinging college party sequence set in a busy apartment. All the "hip" young people are excited because ... there's a popcorn machine (?!) at the get-together. Wow! Can you imagine the excitement that might generate? Somebody call the campus authorities, quick!

From that silly touch, the film digresses immediately into a scene of domestic despair as a suicidal student attacks his girlfriend, and she retaliates by electrocuting him. The scene begins with a slit throat and ends with a man fried in a bathtub. Delightful ... and completely unrelated to the main story at hand.

When the trip to Boot Island has finally begun, the movie's monster is revealed. It attacks Tom, or hops on Tom, more accurately. It is a big, white fluffy thing that looks like a bunny with shorn ears. Even though the monster is supposed to be "fake," part of Prell's ruse, this costume could fool absolutely no one. Not even for a second. The film attempts to cloak the beast by turning the film image "negative" whenever it appears on-screen, but even that can't do the trick.

Shriek of the Mutilated is shot with a deadpan earnestness, and it features an overly melodramatic score, both of which just make the bad monster suit appear that much more ridiculous. The dialogue is unintentionally funny too. In particularly, way too much is made of the monster's smell, his "rank, foul odor," and "fetid aroma." Sounds like my college roommate...

But seriously, why the obsession with the monster's smell, since it plays little part in the story? And if it isn't really a monster at all, in the final analysis, then where is the fetid aroma really coming from? Chew on that idea for a while!

Situational logic is also a stumbling block. Two people die horribly, and only then does a student suggest notifying the authorities. By that point, of course, the phone is dead...

And Keith must be the dumbest, most worthless boyfriend in the history of horror films. He doesn't believe anything Karen says, pays her no heed, and yet trusts implicitly everything his crazy professor tells him.

As for Professor Prell, his "twisted" plot is inane. For Karen to taste good, she has to be "scared" when she is eaten, so the last portion of the film involves scaring her to death with ... you guessed it ... the bad yeti costume. Good luck with that, Dr. Prell.

By the way, there are no shrieks in this film, and no one is actually mutilated. For a really amazing (and scary film) about cannibalism, look no further than *The Texas Chainsaw Massacre*, another low budget film on the subject. Its director, Tobe Hooper, got everything right. *Shriek of the Mutilated* should be so lucky.

The Terminal Man (1974) ✶ ✶ ✶

Cast & Crew

CAST: George Segal (Harry Benson); Joan Hackett (Dr. Janet Ross); Richard A. Dysart (Dr. John Ellis); Jill Clayburgh (Angela Black); Donald Moffat (Dr. Arthur McPherson); Matt Clark (Gerhard); Michael C. Gwynne (Dr. Robert Morris); Normann Burton (Detective Captain Anders); William Hansen (Dr. Ezra Manon); James Sikking (Ralph Friedman); Ian Wolfe (the Priest); Gene Borkan, Burke Byrnes (Benson's Guards); Jim Antonio (Richards);

Jordan Rhodes (Questioner #1); Dee Carroll (Night Nurse); Jason Wingreen (Instructor); Steve Kanaly (Edmonds) Al Checco (Farley); Fred Sadoff (Police Doctor); Jack Colvin (Detective); Lee De Broux (Reporter); Robert Elton (Anesthetist); Victor Argo (Orderly).

CREW: *Director of Photography:* Richard H. Kline. *Art Director:* Fred Harpman. *Film Editor:* Robert L. Wolfe. *Unit Production Manager:* Bruce Fowler, Jr. *Costume Designer:* Nino Novaresse. *Sound:* William Randall. *Camera Operator:* Albert Bettcher. *Set Decorator:* Marvin March. *Script Supervisor:* Margaret Tary. *Sound Editor:* Nicholas Stevenson. *Dubbing Mixer:* Hugh Strain. *First Assistant Director:* Dick Moden. *Second Assistant Director:* Leonard Smith, Jr., Robert Dijoux. *Make-up:* Leo Lotito, Jr., Fred Williams. *Hairdresser:* Sherry Wilson. *Casting:* Nessa Hyams. Goldberg Variation Number 25 by J. S. Bach *Played by:* Glenn Gould. *Associate Producer:* Michael Dryhurst. *Based Upon a Novel by:* Michael Crichton. *Screenplay by:* Mike Hodges. *Produced and Directed by:* Mike Hodges. *M.P.A.A Rating:* R. *Running Time:* 107 minutes.

SYNOPSIS: A peaceable man named Harry Benson has turned into a violent criminal as a result of a physical injury in an accident. Desperate to be cured of his condition, he is transported to a hospital and scheduled to undergo experimental brain surgery curbing his brutal tendencies. The doctors overseeing this revolutionary procedure think that a form of para-epilepsy makes Benson prone to fits of rage, and so implant in Benson's brain a tiny microcomputer to regulate the malfunction. This procedure is a problem for Benson, however, because he's a computer engineer who believes that machines will some day rule the world. Now, just such a machine is inside his head, controlling his very impulses!

The operation is successful, and the chip (powered by a mini-atomic pack) is inserted in Benson's head to prevent seizures, black outs and violent behavior. After the lengthy and complex surgery, Benson bonds with his psychiatrist, the lovely Janet Ross. Soon, they test his new chip together, and

successfully avert a seizure ... ending his violent fits. However, a snag is detected before long. Benson's brain starts to "enjoy" the chip's stimulation, getting a kind of "high" from the feeling, and begins to cause seizures so as to provoke the pleasurable response.

Before long, Benson escapes from the hospital and hitches a ride home with his girlfriend, Angela Black. The scientists grow fearful for Benson (and society at large) because in just a few hours his brain will be triggering constant stimulation of the violence-provoking seizures.

As the scientists scurry to find their lab rat, Benson's brain "activates." At precisely 3:02 A.M., he goes crazy, becoming an uncontrollable killing machine. He brutally murders Angela, and then goes on a rampage at the engineering plant where he helped to develop a new robot.

As the police close in on him, Benson murders a priest, and then shows up at Dr. Ross's house. Fearful of Harry, Ross stabs him with a kitchen knife, even as he begins seizing again. Ross finally escapes from Benson by locking herself away in her bathroom.

Harry flees to a local cemetery and falls into an open grave. There, the police catch up with him and shoot him dead from a circling helicopter. Undeterred, the scientists plan to repeat the procedure with another subject...

COMMENTARY: Like Stanley Kubrick's *A Clockwork Orange* (1971), *The Terminal Man* (based on the novel by Michael Crichton), worries about the day when civil authorities can deploy "modern" technology to treat society's most violent offenders ... and thereby control the individual rights of man. Unlike Kubrick's brutal opera, however, Mike Hodges' film essay heaps most of its scorn on overzealous, unemotional science (rather than the criminal justice system, police, parents, doctors, priests, callow youth, liberal intelligentsia and so on...).

Throughout *The Terminal Man*, the clever art direction (and Hodges' framing) reminds the audience that the lead character, Benson, is at the whim of unfeeling men who respect only their ability to "play God." Benson is thus lost (visually) amidst a world of stark, cold whiteness and unfamiliar, unemotional faces.

Hodges' most clear purpose in adapting Crichton's novel is to reveal how individual freedom and liberty (Benson's) suffers at the hands of a cold society determined to make its citizens "safe" at all costs. He makes this point in several cinematic ways. Firstly, the art direction provides a stunning white-on-white look for *The Terminal Man*. Ivory hospitals, white walls, and doctors in white uniforms dominate the proceedings. The white-on-white motif repeats so much that the film boasts a powerful antiseptic, almost overexposed feeling. If its theme is reminiscent of Kubrick's *A Clockwork Orange*, then *The Terminal Man*'s look evokes the perfectly structured universe of the same director's *2001: A Space Odyssey* (1968).

The motif of layered whites continues even into the latter portions of the film, when Benson leaves the hospital for the real world. Tellingly, from that point on he is garbed totally in ivory as well. This change in wardrobe seems to indicate that the dangerous Benson is now science's creation, white through and through — just like the world that gave him birth.

Furthermore, all of the violent scenes in the final portion of the film involve shadings of white as well. When Benson kills his girlfriend, Angela, crimson blood stains the purity of the white sheets on a waterbed. Later, blood also mars a bathroom's immaculate white tile. Even when Benson kills a priest, there is white suffusing the frame, indicating that Christ can't help Benson because science has already "possessed" him.

Finally, Benson ends up in a cemetery and is confronted with —*what else?* — a white tent and white chairs. Wherever he goes then, science follows him. It has changed him and made him a murderer, and even though he's escaped the hospital, resonances of that place (embodied in white) recur everywhere.

Science has re-made Benson in its own image, and he is a monster.

Importantly, the scientists of *The Terminal Man* seem to lack individual faces. They're often seen in long shots and groups, as a white mass (mob?) of humanity rather than as specific people with interesting personalities. They are thus depicted as distant and impersonal. Even when the doctors operate on Benson in the surgery theater, they are separated from him physically and emotionally, garbed in helmets and visors. These accouterments distance the men of science from the unholy work they do … and that work's subject: Benson. He is unimportant to them, except for what theories he can help them prove.

The extended surgery scene may be the best part in the film for getting across Hodges' point about "science gone awry." The sequence is quiet, lengthy, and intentionally rather dull, indicating the doctors don't realize they're involved in something of great moral and personal importance. To them, surgery is just routine; another day on the job. One doctor humorlessly recounts a stupid joke, and it is only indicative of how removed he is from the work he is doing (operating on a human brain…). There is no sense of decorum or respect for the patient during the surgery.

When science isn't represented as cold and unfeeling in *The Terminal Man*, it is instead revealed to be downright cruel. The operation on Benson resembles medieval torture, filled with arcane, painful-looking machinery and devices. As these tools cut deeply into his brain, Benson's head is held static in a painful vise, and later, a long metal probe is inserted into his brain tissue. It is a dehumanizing procedure, and one suspects that that is precisely the point Hodges is making again and again. The scientists don't feel human, and neither does their work.

The Terminal Man is an interesting and meaningful film, but not an inviting one. There's not a whole lot of human-sounding dialogue in the film, but again this facet of the drama buttresses Hodges' message.

Humans communicate through speech, and there's little of that here, just as there is little humanity. Most of what is spoken in the film is technical gobbledygook and jargon, again indicating that science operates on a different playing field than the rest of humanity. It's interesting that Crichton's other horror film of the '70s, *The Andromeda Strain* (1971), so obviously worshipped science, while this film takes the opposite stance and ridicules it. When one scientist describes, straight-faced and monotonously, how Benson will be outfitted with a mini-nuclear pack to power his microchip, the audience is tempted to laugh because the procedure sounds so over the top. It's a ridiculous idea to put a mini-nuclear reactor inside a human body. It's dangerous, silly, and it has nothing whatsoever to do with the Hippocratic oath. These doctors have lost touch with humanity so much that they don't even realize they are endangering their patient.

Ultimately, *The Terminal Man* fears the day that science and technology can determine and choose human responses to stimuli. It is fearful of that day because the men of science seem to have no care for or understanding of what they have wrought, and therefore take no responsibility for the results of their experiment. Had the film enunciated this through direct dialogue it would have been rather heavy-handed and preachy, and one has to admire Hodges for making a cold film that reflects its subject matter in such powerful visual terms. The frequent incidences of white and the depiction of the scientists as a faceless, humorless mob, all make the point better than dialogue ever could, even if the final result is a film totally lacking in joy and optimism.

The only truly heavy-handed touch in the film seems to be *The Terminal Man*'s recurring "signature shot": that of a black screen and an "iris" peep-hole with an eye looking through it at both an off-screen Benson (and by extension) the audience. This shot recurs several times, and seems to hammer home the point that science views the individual (and Benson in particular) as guinea pigs to be used on a whim. The shot is pretty and well composed, but the point is obvious without the repetition. The frequency of the shot makes the viewer feel as Benson must himself feel — manipulated and slightly out of control. That may have been the point. But Hodges has done his job so well generally in *The Terminal Man* that the audience already "gets it," even without the technique of putting the audience in Benson's shoes (or in this case, his prison).

The Texas Chainsaw Massacre (1974) ✶ ✶ ✶ ✶

Critical Reception

Despite a crippling low budget, it is even somewhat sophisticated, one of the few spawns of *Psycho* … whose makers actually seem to have learned something from the master of suspense."— John McCarty, *Psychos*, St. Martin's Press, 1986, page 133.

"…a vile little piece of sick crap … a film with literally nothing to recommend it: nothing but a hysterically paced, slapdash, imbecilic concoction of cannibalism, voodoo, astrology … and unrelenting sadistic violence as extreme and hideous as a complete lack of imagination can possibly make it."— Stephen Koch, *Harpers*: "Fashions in Pornography", November 1976, pages 108–111.

"…extremely well-acted and crafted for a low budget film…. Hooper … strives for terror … for realism … it perfectly reproduces our worst nightmare."— Danny Peary, *Cult Movies*, Delacorte Press, pages 347–350.

"A *reductio ad absurdum* of a horror movie … 'unrelenting' is a good word to use here…. And yet the movie could have been more harrowing. As it stands, there's surprisingly little blood-and-gore evident. Hooper's film has a weird sort of tact. The director trusts his title and his hardware: you don't see what the awful chainsaw does. You don't need to … the film is informed by a pristine viciousness."—Gordon Willis, *Horror and Science Fiction Films II*, page 393.

"A decidedly low-tech film with the human screaming getting its first real role since *King Kong* and *The Tingler*. What it lacks in polish it makes up for in its portrayal of 'mad evil'—the kind of inexplicable motivation that made Michael Myers and Bruce the Shark archetypes of the decade. The hitchhiker scene early in the film is one of the most unnerving, terrifying scenes in horror history, still powerful a generation later.—Bill Latham, *Mary's Monster*, Powys Books.

"This abattoir of a movie boasts sledgehammers, meat hooks and chainsaws, and the result, though not especially visceral, is noisy, relentless, and about as subtle as having your leg sawed off without anaesthetic…. Pernicious stuff."—Christ Petit, *Time Out Film Guide*, Seventh Edition, Penguin Books, 1999, page 900.

Cast & Crew

CAST: Marilyn Burns (Sally Hardesty); Allen Danziger (Jerry); Paul A. Partain (Franklin Hardesty); William Vail (Kirk); Teri McMinn (Pam); Edwin Neal (Hitchhiker); James Siedow (Old Man); Gunnar Hansen (Leatherface); John Dugan (Grandfather); Robert Courtin (Window Washer); William Creamer (Bearded Man); John Henry Faulk (Storyteller); Jerry Green (Cowboy); Ed Guinn (Cattle Truck Driver); Joe Bill Hogan (Drunk); Perry Lorenze (Pick-up Driver); John Larroquette (Narrator). **CREW:** A Vortex/Henkel/Hooper Production. A film by Tobe Hooper. *Editors:* Sallye Richardson, Larry Carroll. *Cinematographer:* Daniel Pearl. *Production Manager:* Ronald Bozman. *Executive Producer:* Jay Parsley. *Story and Screenplay:* Kim Henkel and Tobe Hooper. *Produced and Directed by:* Tobe Hooper. *Music Score:* Tobe Hooper and Wayne Bell. *Assistant Director:* Sallye Richardson. *Lighting:* Lynn Lochwood. *Assistant Cameraman:* Lou Perryman. *Location Sound Recorder:* Ted Alcolaou. *Post Production Sound/Boom Man:* Wayne Bell. *Art Director:* Robert A. Burns. *Titles and Opticals:* CFI. *Make-up:* Dorothy Pearl. *Camera Assistant:* J. Michael McClary. *Key Grip:* Linn Scherwitz. *Script Girl:* Mary Church. *Additional Photography:* Tobe Hooper. *Re-Recording:* Paul Harrison. *Grip:* Rod Ponton. *Stunt Driver:* Perry Lorenz. *Stunts:* Mary Church.

Associate Producer: Kim Henkel, Richard Saenz. *Production Assistants:* Ray Spaw, Robert Pustejovski, N. E. Parsley, Sally Nicolaou, Paulette Gochnour, Paula Eaton, Charlie Loring, Jerry Bellnoski, Jim Crow, David Spaw, George Baotz, Tom Foote. *M.P.A.A. Rating:* R. *Running Time:* 84 minutes.

SYNOPSIS: On a very hot day in August of 1973, young Sally Hardesty, her invalid brother Franklin, and three friends (Jerry, Pam and Kirk), drive out to rural Texas to check on the grave of Sally's grandfather. There has been a rash of grave desecrations in the area, and Sally is concerned that her grandfather's grave may have been disturbed. After determining that there has been no tampering, the group leaves the cemetery and drives off in their van.

Jerry's van passes a slaughterhouse on the road, one where Sally and Franklin's granddad used to sell cattle. The wheelchair-bound Franklin aggravates his friends by explaining, in nauseating detail, the methodology of slaughtering livestock. Not long after, the van stops to pick up a strange hitchhiker, an odd fellow with several nervous tics. Unaware that this guest is actually the local grave desecrator, the kids engage the weirdo in conversation. A former employee of the slaughterhouse, the hitchhiker lost his job when the organization updated the killing weapon from sledgehammer to mechanical bolt gun.

The hitchhiker grabs Franklin's knife and cuts himself for no reason, after snapping a picture of the group. Then he reveals a straight razor and asks to be taken to his house. The kids ask the stranger to leave, but the visitor grows angry and slices Franklin's arm with the rusty razor. Jerry and Kirk throw the strange hitchhiker out of the van and continue on their way.

Unsettled, they stop for gas at an out-of-the-way barbecue and gas station. To their dismay, the cook at the establishment informs them that the station has no gas, and a transport truck won't arrive for a day.

With little choice, Sally and her friends decide to find the old Hardesty place and hang out there for the night. They drive out to a dilapidated old home on the side of the road. They park in the overgrown front yard and explore the house, briefly noting that the strange hitchhiker left indecipherable symbols (written in his own blood) on the side of the van.

Pam and Kirk go to the old swimming hole behind the remote Hardesty place, and find it dried up. They explore a neighbor's property, thinking that they may have some spare gasoline. Pam and Kirk approach an old farmhouse. When they get no answer at the front door, Kirk opens the unlocked portal and goes inside. Pam waits outside, disturbed because she has found a human tooth on the porch.

Kirk searches the odd house for no more than a minute before a silver metal door to the kitchen slides open, and, without warning, a squealing, masked giant, Leatherface, attacks him. Leatherface smashes Kirk's head with a sledgehammer.

After a time, Pam follows Kirk into the house of horrors. One bedroom upstairs is decorated with furniture made from human and animal bones, and the way to the kitchen is decorated with animal skulls. Leatherface

chases Pam, and hangs her on a metal meathook in the kitchen. She's still alive and conscious when Leatherface goes to work with a chainsaw, butchering Kirk like a slab of beef.

Back at the Hardesty place, Jerry, Sally and Franklin wait for the others to return as dusk arrives. Jerry goes in search of his missing friends, leaving Franklin and Sally to quarrel about which of them last had possession of his missing knife. As sun sets, Kirk reaches the farmhouse and finds Pam's blanket there. He goes inside and finds Pam — still alive — in a freezer. Before Jerry can save her, Leatherface clubs and kills him too.

In the pitch of night, Sally and Franklin wait at the van. With no keys and no sign of their missing friends, they go in search of Jerry. Sally pushes Franklin and his heavy wheelchair through a thicket. There, they are confronted by Leatherface … who impales the crippled Franklin with the chainsaw. Sally runs for her life through the woods, chased by Leatherface. She finds the farmhouse and locks Leatherface outside, but the maniac cuts down the door. Then Sally meets two dead grandparents upstairs, perfectly positioned in easy chairs. She jumps out a window in horror and runs to the roadside barbecue stand. She seeks out the helpful proprietor, but Cook is one of Leatherface's clan and captures her. He returns her to the house, where the crazy hitchhiker is also waiting. Cook is especially upset because Leatherface has ruined the front door.

Sally is invited to a "special" dinner in which she is to be the main course. Sally is tied up and gagged as an elderly —*but not quite dead yet*— Grandpa attempts to bludgeon her with a sledgehammer. At the slaughterhouse, Grandpa used to be the best, but now he's past his prime, despite his family's support. Sally breaks free after Grandpa's fumbling and jumps through a first floor window. Bloodied but free, Sally runs for her life, making for the road beyond.

The hitchhiker and Leatherface pursue Sally, and the hitchhiker is run over by a passing truck. The truck driver pauses to

First he greets you, then he eats you: Leatherface (Gunnar Hansen) smiles for the camera in Tobe Hooper's *The Texas Chainsaw Massacre* (1974).

help Sally, but Leatherface attacks the truck's cab, forcing Sally and her would-be savior to run for their lives. Leatherface cuts himself in the leg with the chainsaw when the truck driver strikes him with a wrench.

Finally, a pick-up truck stops and rescues Sally. As she escapes, the psychotic Leatherface fades into the distance, twirling about insanely with his weapon of choice as the dawn comes...

COMMENTARY: *The Texas Chainsaw Massacre* is one of the craziest horror films ever made ... and no doubt one of the best. It is exciting, terrifying, and at times, quite funny. On the surface, it is representative of the 1970s "savage cinema," a film of such hardcore, raw power that the audience recoils from the film's bluntness. On a much deeper level, there is a method to director Tobe

Hooper's madness. Specifically, he exploits the language of film to foster the disturbing notion that man's existence, man's toils, means but little in the face of a vast, disordered, and cruel cosmos.

As the opening credits of *The Texas Chainsaw Massacre* roll, Hooper's camera focuses on close-ups of violent sunspots. The largest image in the frame is one of a red, boiling, almost "popping" sun. This fiery orb, randomly spitting fire and flame into space, is our first significant glimpse into Hooper's larger universe. Importantly, it is not a cosmos of serenity and peace, but one of chaos and eruption. The red shade of the sun speaks of a kind of anger, and that's a running theme in the film. The universe is disordered, anarchic, even cruel.

Rewardingly, the music on the soundtrack reinforces this notion, as it lacks melody of any sort. The music at this point in the film is all cymbal crashes and echoes, highly disordered and discordant. There is no melodic theme running through the music, no leitmotif, only a jumble of ugly sounds strung together in a row. Like the eruptions on the surface of the sun, the music reflects the absence of equilibrium, sanity, reason and order in the universe.

The first shot of the film proper (following the credits) is another image that reveals how the ordered universe has become topsy-turvy. An armadillo (road kill) lies upside down, its dead arms reaching up towards the sky, on a hot asphalt road. Again, the armadillo is overturned, upside down, and that position is a long-time signifier of death in the cinema. More to the point, an animal shouldn't die on the road (a symbol of man's intelligence, and his need to connect one place to another), but it *has* died there, because above man's sense of order (the road), has been imposed the chaos of the universe.

By the time Hooper's camera introduces the main characters, inhabiting their van on the side of a Texas road, he has meaningfully undercut another sense of order. Since the birth of the medium, movies have possessed a thing called *decorum*, a specific manner of viewing things, and a specific methodology in storytelling. Audiences may flock to see horror films, but audiences never expect to see truly unpleasant, unappetizing things. We have our lovely heroes and our hissable villains, our resolution and closure, and the defeat of evil. That's what is expected. Yet Hooper immediately undercuts that sense of decorum, and film structure too.

The first scene featuring the film's protagonists reveals the obnoxious Franklin perched in a wheelchair as he urinates on the side of the road. A truck roars by suddenly and the wind pushes this invalid down a hill, where he lands flat on his face, urine and all. On one hand, this is another overturning of order: the truck swoops in like a bird of prey and flips a human off his perch. More importantly, however, the idea implied by this sequence is that Hooper's movie will feature

no favorites, no bigger-than-life "stars," if you will, because that too would represent a kind of order—*cinematic* order. Imagine Jimmy Stewart in *Rear Window* facing such a humiliating situation. It just wouldn't happen. But here, it can happen, as Hooper makes plain in the staging. A cripple—usually handled in tender-footed fashion by PC Hollywood—takes an unceremonious spill, and the audience is shocked by such callous treatment. But the point is made: these little, foolish people are not characters in some remote drama. They are us, and they dwell in a universe where terrible things can and do happen, just as they happen in real life.

Compositions of order overturned dominate many frames of *The Texas Chainsaw Massacre*. Upon entering the Hardesty home, spiders are seen swarming in a corner of a ceiling. They have overrun their web, yet another symbol of order. Like the dead animal on the road, the image of another "road" (the web) is revealed to be scarred with chaos (teeming spiders). Later, Pam and Kirk go swimming, but instead of finding a water hole, they find only dry earth. Again, expectations are overturned; events seem random. That's very important to any reading of the film.

At other important points in The *Texas Chainsaw Massacre*, Hooper takes special pains to accentuate the vastness of the universe at large. This is critical because Hooper sees Sally and her friends in this film much as those very characters view the spiders or the cows in the slaughterhouse. They're little, meaningless creatures running around in their lives with a sort of tunnel vision, unable to see that they inhabit a much larger, and terribly frightening, domain. As human beings, we go to the bank, mow our lawns, eat our dinner, or do a hundred "normal" things, unaware that a tornado could be approaching, or that a serial killer could be roaming the neighborhood. We impose a false sense of order (and hence security) in our existence, but Tobe Hooper's m.o. is to strip that all away and reveal that nothing separates us from the cows or the spiders, or the ants. We're victims of a universe that unfolds randomly.

Take, for instance, an early shot in the film. Under the uncaring eye of the sun, Jerry's van picks up the hitchhiker in an extreme long shot. Under a giant sky, the hitchhiker and the van itself might as well be ants or cows, and to Hooper they are. Later, there's a beautifully composed tracking shot of Pam and Kirk as they approach the farmhouse where they meet their fate. The camera is positioned low, so the sun is visible all throughout the shot, glaring down on the oblivious characters. As Pam and Kirk move, so does the camera move with them, but, importantly, the sun remains positioned in its orbit ... unmoving. The ants are transitory, even our eye (the camera) is transitory, but the universe moves for no man. It is callous and unconcerned with the "ants" teeming on a tiny world.

Hooper repeats this tracking shot when Pam goes into the house later. Again, there is a lot of sky visible above her, as if it is a player, or at least observer, in the drama. These are instances in which Hooper makes novel use of the low angle shot. He is revealing not the strength of his protagonists (as the low angle is usually designed to depict). Instead, he is revealing the inherent hierarchy (or disorder) of the universe. High above his oblivious characters, stand outer space, suns, and galaxies. And those cosmic "entities" couldn't care less that five teens are about to meet their maker.

The film's dialogue reinforces many of these themes. Franklin's horoscope reads: "you will have a disturbing and unpredictable day." Sally reads her own horoscope, and it is equally frightening. "There are moments when we can't believe what is happening is really true. Pinch yourself and you'll find it is." The horoscope (and astrology in general) represents man's way of imposing order on the universe. Astrology charts the manner in which the planets (the universe at large...) affect man on a daily basis. But Hooper's point is not so much that astrology is real, it's that life is totally ran-

dom, and that on this horrible day, the horoscopes happen to be right. As tiny ants with tunnel vision, our actions, our mistakes, our choices, have unforeseen results, especially in a universe of chaos, eruptions and anger. You might wake up one morning, go on a trip, and have no inkling that you will die at the hands of a mad cannibal before the sun sets.

The manner of the death scenes and the structure of *The Texas Chainsaw Massacre* reinforce this sense of a random, purposeless existence in an existential universe. Take Kirk's death, for instance. There are no Hollywood illusions about it, no instances of heroism or near escape. It is merely brutal. He is clubbed with a sledgehammer and he goes down. His body spasms and jerks until Leatherface delivers a second blow, but then it's over. The whole death scene couldn't but last a few seconds. Again the equation is plain: Kirk is an animal being slaughtered by a cook, nothing more. His death is meaningless on any human scale.

As far as its structure is concerned, the film defies expectations. Pam, Kirk and Jerry all die in exactly the same fashion. They enter the farmhouse, are surprised by Leatherface, and are then killed. No additional information about the killer is learned in subsequent death scenes, no narrative progress is made, and there is no moving forward to the climax. These characters go to the farmhouse; they die. Thus the audience is denied the typical movie "structure" that teaches and informs it about the universe.

Ultimately, the very nature of Leatherface's villainy is a prominent part of Hooper's thesis about the universe too. Leatherface is a man who sees human beings as nothing but meat. He doesn't want to have sex with Sally, he doesn't want to know her as a "person," and he doesn't want her money. He simply desires to clobber her with a sledgehammer, cook her up, and eat her for supper. In this regard, Hooper's film might be viewed as a vegan anthem. Leatherface and his family see no difference between Sally, a rabbit, or a cow. To him, they're all merely ingredients. That's part of the crazy universe too: it doesn't care about predators, and it doesn't make distinctions. On this hot day in August, Sally Hardesty learns that she is no different from the cows in the slaughterhouse where her granddad once worked. Animal flesh is animal flesh, and meat is meat. If cows can be slaughtered and served up for dinner, so then, can Sally. It's highly disturbing, but *The Texas Chainsaw Massacre*, like no other film ever made, makes us sympathize with the cows, or the lambs, or any other animal that is slaughtered as food. Hooper's film makes us adopt the perspective of the slaughtered.

The Texas Chainsaw Massacre is a terrifying film because it surrounds the audience with a universe we dare not contemplate. The heavens don't care about us as "thinking" human beings. Each and every one of us will die one day, and yet the Earth will stay in its orbit. We can be hunted down, treated as cattle, and exposed to every atrocity imaginable, but the sky won't fall, or even protest such treatment. That's an important and terrifying realization because as human beings we all have "egos." We see the world through our own eyes, not the eyes of others. The universe, we think, revolves around our wants and needs. *The Texas Chainsaw Massacre*, by creating villains who see their fellow man as ingredients for barbecue, reminds us that our perception isn't accurate.

There's a strange equation to films like *The Texas Chainsaw Massacre*, and Tobe Hooper understands it. Insanity is so pronounced in a movie like this that the horror sometimes gives way to nervous laughter. At the same time that the Sawyer family is awful, it is distinctly funny. Sure, the family possesses values different from most, but the Sawyers also reveal universal elements of family life, and we want to laugh at that. Brothers don't always get along (just like Leatherface and the hitchhiker). Grandpa is past his prime, but encouraged by his progeny. The cook is upset by the price of electricity, and so forth. It's a twisted view of family, yet it is still a family. We laugh

because we recognize that, despite strange appetites, this family could be ours. After all, the Sawyers gather around the dinner table too — it's just that what they eat differentiates them from us. This is worthy of note too, that there's no superior force at work to end our lives (forces like vampires, aliens, or werewolves). No, the threat here on planet Earth is our own kindred. The values we hold dear aren't the values of others, and again, the universe has no comment on that.

The Texas Chainsaw Massacre hovers between unrelenting horror and nervous laughs and is possessed of more raw energy than a dozen low budget horror films. The cast is good, but it is Tobe Hooper's direction and his concentration on the facts of human life, the here and now of existential existence, that make the movie so incredible (and harrowing) a viewing experience. He has brilliantly created a universe without order and without hope. It is a universe where madmen roam freely, and the skies above just turn the other cheek. It's chilling.

LEGACY: *The Texas Chainsaw Massacre* (like *The Exorcist* before it), changed the nature of horror films while simultaneously meeting much controversy — and much animosity — when it was released. Nonetheless, it spawned a series of "mad" family films, including Wes Craven's similarly themed *The Hills Have Eyes* (1977). *Chainsaw* also launched the career of director Tobe Hooper, who went on to direct *Eaten Alive* (1976), *The Funhouse* (1981), *Poltergeist* (1982), *Lifeforce* (1985), *Invaders from Mars* (1986), *The Mangler* (1995), as well as the mini-series *Salem's Lot* (1978), the TV-movie *I'm Dangerous Tonight* (1990), and episodes of *Amazing Stories* (1985–87), *Freddy's Nightmares* (1988-89), *Tales from the Crypt* (1989–96), *Nowhere Man* (1995-1996), *Dark Skies* (1996-97), and *The Others* (2000).

As for Leatherface, his family reappeared in three sequels: the Hooper-directed *Texas Chainsaw Massacre 2* (1987), *Leather-*

face: The Texas Chainsaw Massacre 3 (1989), and *The Texas Chainsaw Massacre: The Next Generation* (1995), the last of which was directed by original scribe Kim Henkel and starred Matthew McConaughey and Rene Zellwegger.

Vampyres

Cast & Crew

CAST: Marianne Morris (Fran); Anulka Dziubinska (Miriam); Murray Brown (Ted); Brian Deacon (John); Sally Faulkner (Harriet).

CREW: *Directed by:* Jose Ramon Larraz. *Written by:* D. Daubeney. *Director of Photography:* Harry Waxman. *Editor:* Geoffrey Brown. Essay Films. *M.P.A.A. Rating:* R. *Running Time:* 84 minutes.

DETAILS: A sexually charged vampire thriller, with more emphasis on the sex than the thrills. The vampires are lesbians, and they feed on passersby at an old house. Strangely compelling.

1975

Beyond the Door (1975) ★ ½

Cast & Crew

NOTE: The Media edition of *Beyond the Door* features no opening credits, except a listing for Juliet Mills and Richard Johnson.

CAST: Juliet Mills (Jessica Barrett); Richard Johnson (Dimitri); Elizabeth Turner, David Colin, Jr.

CREW: Edward L. Montoro and Film Ventures International Present *Beyond the Door.* *Screenplay:* Richard Barrett. *Directed by:* Oliver Hellman. *Assistant Director, Second Unit:* Luciano Palermo. *Continuity:* Patrizia Zulini. *Assistant Cameramen:* Maurizio Maggi, Morio Bagnato. *Hairstylist:* Giancarlo De Honardis. *Sound Mixer:* Bruno Brunacei. *Boom Operator:* Adolfo Fabrizi. *Assistant to Art Director:* Giancarlo Stella. *Assistant Editor:* Bruno Sguelglia. *Dialogue Editor:* Christopher Cruise. *Sound Effects:* Roberto Arcangeli. Interiors were filmed at De Paolis Studios, Rome, Italy; exteriors were filmed in San Francisco, U.S.A. *M.P.A.A. Rating:* R. *Running Time:* 97 minutes.

SYNOPSIS: A decade ago, a bearded fellow named Dimitri would have died in a car crash, but the Devil granted him ten additional years of life on Earth. Now, as those ten years end, Dimitri is desperate for another extension. The Devil will oblige, if Dimitri functions as his go-between, and rips the baby out of Jessica Barrett's womb. Jessica, it seems, is Dimitri's former lover of many years earlier.

Unaware of the spectral events swirling about her, Jessica announces to Robert, her husband, that a third child is on the way ... even though she is on the pill. Robert is not especially pleased, since his two children, Ken and Gail, are in a particularly obnoxious "swearing" stage. Almost immediately into her unusual pregnancy, Jessica has bad feelings about the baby inside, fearing it will kill her. She is also troubled by bad dreams, and even imagines that sometimes she hears the Devil's laughter. Equally odd, the baby seems to be developing rapidly — three months of growth after only seven weeks!

As Jessica's behavior grows stranger during the pregnancy, demonic forces taunt Ken and Gail, and their dolls and toys come to life. Robert learns that his children are terrified, and fears that Jessica is possessed by the Devil. He seeks the help of Dimitri, who claims that Jessica is the "prey of a negative force." Dimitri also tells Robert that the child must be born at all costs. Robert is inclined to believe Dimitri, especially when Jessica's head spins around, and she spits up green vomit. Talking in multiple voices (including that of the Devil), Jessica also uses psychokinetic powers to torture Robert.

Dimitri intervenes when Jessica delivers her baby, but fails to fulfill his part of the evil bargain and lets the child live. The Devil kills Dimitri even as a strange mouthless child is born ... and then dies. The possession over, Jessica returns to normal. But little Kenny seems to be possessed now...

———————

COMMENTARY: An innocent woman is inexplicably possessed by an evil force, perhaps by the Devil himself. Medical science can't help, and the possessed female spits green vomit, and her head spins around completely. Finally, out of nowhere, a mysterious man arrives to help save the endangered soul, but there will be a crisis of faith and morality before anyone is saved. In the end, a final sacrifice resolves the terror....

No, the preceding description is not a synopsis of William Friedkin's landmark film *The Exorcist* (1973), it's the plot of an imitative Italian hack job called *Beyond the Door.*

"Oh God, I only wish I could forget the whole thing," a character solemnly intones early in the film, and this critic is inclined to agree with that assessment. With the exception of 1976's *Grizzly* (which studiously ripped off *Jaws*), there has rarely been a more derivative film than *Beyond the Door.* The director has apparently studied *The Exorcist* quite diligently, but has little clue how to generate the same level of emotional attachment to his film's characters.

For instance, both films center on a family in danger: the MacNeils in *The Exorcist*, the Barretts in *Beyond the Door.* In the former, a tender mother child-relationship was forged, and the audience saw evidence of strong family bonds. Viewers witnessed Regan and her mom visiting Washington monuments together and sharing a cute but believable rapport. When Regan's behavior changed and she turned into a violent, verbally abusive monster, the transformation was startling.

In the latter film, there is a running joke about how the Barrett children cuss like sailors (a symptom of possession in *The Exorcist...*) from the get-go. They use the word "asshole," implore one-another to "go stuff yourself," and even say "bullshit." These are not exactly charming kids, and the presence of foul-mouthed children instantly distances the audience rather than drawing it in. We're supposed to care about these little potty-mouths, but unlike Regan (and Linda Blair), the child performers have no charisma, and no character arc to travel. The final revelation, that one of the children is possessed, smacks more of a cheap, gimmicky ending than it does a tragic character development.

If the truth were told, this is a pretty weird family even before the demonic possession starts. Mr. Barrett charmingly refers to his unborn child as a "little bastard" (at least the children came by their vocabulary honestly...) and we don't connect with these actors in a meaningful way. It may be simply because their lines are dubbed in English (this is an Italian film, remember), and that tends to be an off-putting and humorous technique ... not at all conducive to empathy. We've been conditioned by generations of *Godzilla* films to see dubbing as inherently silly, and that "tradition" carries over to this mess.

And Richard Johnson, generally an admirable and solid performer, is also miscast in this film, coming across as ponderous, slow and barely conscious. He doesn't exactly seem like the charismatic, unforgettable lover Mills describes with so much enthusiasm. His fear of dying is revealed primarily through the Devil's voiceovers, not through Johnson's performance, and that's a serious weakness of the film, since that dread is Johnson's motivation, and the fear he must overcome. His sacrifice has little meaning (and even less emotional weight) because his fear of death is not suitably enunciated by the character himself. When he is "taken off" at the climax of the film (presumably to eternal damnation in Hell...) the moment should cause a lump in the throat. It doesn't.

And the special effects? They're quite good in spots, but are, inevitably, leftovers from *The Exorcist.* A head spinning here, a pile of green vomit there, some random objects flying about on their own ... this is all in conjunction with a possession, the same plot point informing *The Exorcist.*

American audiences thronged to this movie, and it was a huge hit, because they longed to relive the visceral experience of the Friedkin movie. In a sense then, *Beyond the Door* obliged. It is as much a special effects rerun as a new film.

Beyond the Door could have been an involving personal story, the tale of a husband who puts aside his jealousy for a wife's former lover so as to help her when she is possessed. There are hints of that human story throughout the film, but the movie just isn't smart enough to play up the human angle. Instead, it thrives on generic dialogue ("she's under a kind of arcane influence," Johnson explains cryptically at one point), and special effects set pieces. In addition, the film fails to exploit its San Francisco setting to the same degree that Georgetown was utilized in *The Exorcist.* All in all its an unpleasant film, and one has to wonder about all those poor souls who actually went to the theater and sat through this noxious variation on a great film. If *Beyond the Door* has any value, it is in remembering the period, circa 1974–76, when every new horror film (*Abby, To the Devil a Daughter, Beyond the Door, House of Exorcism, The Omen*) was seeking to cash in on *The Exorcist*'s blockbuster status.

Blood Waters of Dr. Z

Cast & Crew

CAST: Marshall Gracier (Dr. Leopold); Wade Popwell (the Monster); Paul Galloway (Sheriff Krantz); Gerald Cruse (Marine Biologist); Sanna Ringhaver (Agent Walsh); Dave Dickson (Stevens); Adrie Valliere (Deputy Sheriff).
CREW: *Written, Produced and Directed by:* Don Barton. *Original Story by:* Ron Kivett, Lee O'Larew. *Director of Photography:* Jack Mc-Gowan. *Electronic Music:* Jack Tamul. *Monster Costume:* Ron Kivett, Martin Fillyaw, Les Lan-caster. *M.P.A.A. Rating:* PG. *Running Time:* 90 minutes (approximate).

DETAILS: Filmed in Florida, this is the story of a deranged scientist who keeps a big tub in his lab. One day, the scientist injects himself with a special formula, strips down, swims with the fishes in the tub, and transforms himself into one of the cheesiest monsters in film history.

The Bug (a.k.a. *Bug*) (1975) ★ ★ ½

Critical Reception

"One has only sympathy for Bradford Dillman, who struggles embarrassingly with the impossible role of the scientist.... Most of the dialogue is laughable. Producer Castle and Thomas Page have adapted the latter's sci-fi novel, *The Hephaestus Plague* into a frequently boring, often confusing film which will disappoint even the most ardent sci-fi fans."— Michael Buckley, *Films in Review*, Volume XXVI, Number 8, October 1975, page 504.

"*Bug* is decidedly poisonous. It is not simply a scary picture, nor [*sic*] simply a violent one. It is a cruel picture ... sick, and literally sickening."— Richard Eder, *New York Times*, September 18, 1975, page 50.

"Tacky in parts ... and occasionally lacking in plot logic, it's nevertheless an imaginative little B thriller that manages to be genuinely suspenseful."— Geoff Andrew, *Time Out Film Guide*, Seventh Edition, Penguin Books, 1999, page 120.

Cast & Crew

CAST: Bradford Dillman (James Parmintir); Joanne Miles (Carrie Parmintir); Richard Gilliland (Gerald Metbaum); Jennie Smith Jackson (Norma Tucker); Alan Fudge (Mark Ross); Jesse Vint (Tom Tacker); Patty McCormack (Sylvia Ross); Brendan Dillon (Charlie); Fred Deans (Henry Tacker); James Green (Reverend Kern); Jim Payne (Kenny Tacker); Bard Stevens (Security Guard).

CREW: Distributed by Paramount Pictures. William Castle's Production of *The Bug*. *Art Director:* Jack Martin Smith. *Editor:* Allan Jacobs. *Assistant Director:* Jack Roe. *Insect Sequences:* Ken Middleham. *Wardrobe:* Ken Verhille. *Electronic Music:* Charles Fox. *Director of Photography:* Michel Hugo. *Based on the Novel by:* Thomas Page. *Screenplay:* William Castle and Thomas Page. *Produced by:* William Castle. *Directed by:* Jeannot Szwarc. *Make-up:* Tom Miller, Jr. *Set Decorator:* Reg Allen. *Hairdresser:* Judy Alexander. *Camera Operator:* Herb Pearl. *Special Effects:* Phil Cory. *Property Master:* Allan Gordon. *Casting:* Ramsay King. *Filmed in:* Panavision. *Color by:* Movielab. *Titles:* Modern Film Effects. *Script Supervisor:* Cynnie Troup. *M.P.A.A. Rating:* PG. *Running Time:* 100 minutes.

SYNOPSIS: The town of Riverside, California, is turned upside down by a terrible earthquake that not only destroys the town church but releases a plague of deadly cockroaches never before seen by man. A professor at a local university, Jim Parmintir, believes the insects may be millions of years old — the oldest species on Earth, in fact. These six-legged creatures have clawed legs, two body sections and a high metabolic rate. More interesting than those characteristics, the eyeless bugs have the capacity to make fire when they rub their dorsal, chitinous antennae together. This unusual ability causes havoc all over Riverside as cars explode, buildings burn, and fields go up in flames.

Parmintir soon realizes that the insects are relatively immobile because of the air pressure on Earth's surface. In effect, the insects have the bends. Despite this handicap, the critters are transported all across Riverside by man's own creations, specifically cars and pick-up trucks (to which they attach themselves...). Excited by the thought of a newly discovered species, Parmintir determines to breed the Riverside cockroaches with a more common variety of the species to see what unusual characteristics might carry over to the next generation.

Meanwhile, the bugs do more damage to the town. Among the many victims are a curious cat, a student's unsuspecting girlfriend, and eventually Parmintir's wife, Carrie. His wife's death sends Parmintir over the brink of sanity, and he sets up an impromptu science lab at an isolated house in the field where the bugs were first discovered. Parmintir carries out his plan to breed the insects, and the next generation is soon born. This new generation is more resistant to pressure, eats raw meat, has an incredible hive mind, and the capacity to learn language. Parmintir soon becomes a kind of God to these new, dangerously intelligent insects. One night, they break out of their container and start to suck blood from Parmintir's shirtless chest as he sleeps. Now, the bugs have a taste for humans.

Parmintir continues to lose his grip on both sanity and science as the bugs gain the upper hand. Another generation is born— this one with the ability to fly. One night, the fiery, winged insects attack Parmintir, and see to it that he falls deep into the hellish crevice from which they sprung. Then, the bugs return to the crevice, as if following their father to Hell. Another earthquake seals up the whole kit and caboodle (including the deranged Parmintir...) beneath the Earth.

COMMENTARY: What can be said of a film in which cockroaches pass explosive fire out of their rear ends?

Shot on location in the desert town of Riverside, California, *The Bug* is a low-budget collaboration of director Jeannot Szwarc, alumni of *Rod Serling's Night Gallery* (1970-73), and shlockmeister William Castle of *The Tingler* (1959), *The House on Haunted Hill* (1959), *Rosemary's Baby* (1968) and the TV series *Ghost Story* (1972). Both men have solid reputations in the horror field, and have done good work one many occasions, but *The Bug* (or *Bug* as it is most commonly

known) is not representative of either artist at his best.

Some elements of the story work fairly well, especially in the opening moments of the picture. As a priest sermonizes about fire and brimstone, and about a contemporary America filled with sin, suspicion and death, an earthquake rocks the establishment. It is as if God has spoken, and appropriately, the quake is of Biblical proportions, causing walls to crack and split, and floors to undulate. Like a plague from the Old Testament, or the hand of a wrathful God, this earthquake signals the arrival of God's vengeful hand: the monstrous bugs.

The religious metaphor is carried on for some time. The insects cause a bush to burn at one point (another Old Testament reference...), and later, Parmintir assumes the role of a pride-filled Prometheus, controlling and breeding the insects by his own whim and hubris. Eventually, of course, the bugs rebel against this pretender to deityhood, and destroy him for his trespasses. Disturbed by his own God complex, even Parmintir continually notes that he has "gone too far," and the message is clearly one that comes straight from the B movies of the 1950s: Do not tamper in God's domain. Period.

The Bug also concerns itself with Parmintir's belief that man can "talk" to the Earth and all the creatures on it. He thinks that this ability is an innate characteristic of mankind that has been lost over time, but again, this conceit is revealed as hubris. Such knowledge is apparently meant for the Creator alone, and Parmintir ultimately dies for seeking to go beyond man's purview. Though its point is somewhat anti knowledge, and definitely old fashioned, *Bug* adheres to its themes well, and the burning bush, the earthquake, and other tragedies portend a spiritual apocalypse. That's an interesting twist in the secular 70s.

The special effects are also quite good for a low-budget production. The insect photography is great, and so are the mechanical effects. When the winged roaches start flying about, they look pretty convincing. All the fire and earthquake effects are convincing too.

Yet the film goes wrong in the final half hour as Parmintir becomes an insane recluse. His descent from intrepid university professor to overreaching God-figure is not charted in a very satisfactory fashion. He grows a beard (symbolizing, apparently, his disaffection with human society), retreats to the woods, becomes a hermit, and goes absolutely bonkers. Bradford Dillman is a good actor, but his character's motivations are not clear. He is clearly "angry" that the bugs have killed his wife, but then becomes their protector and messiah, breeding new generations of the monsters. So, does he hate them, or does he love them? Is he mad at them for his wife's death, or is he their spiritual father, assuring their development and survival? The movie plays it both ways, with less-than-convincing results.

While watching this movie, the author thought of two other productions that successfully expanded on the ideas proposed in *Bug*. The first was the two-hour premiere of the new *The Outer Limits* anthology, entitled "The Sand Kings." In it, a professor (portrayed by Beau Bridges) became a God figure to a race of microscopic aliens. They demonstrated their intelligence by building a monument in sand to their "God"—a sculpture of his face. Just as the insects of *The Bug* spelled out words and sentences (such as "WE LIVE") for Parmintir, so do the aliens of *The Outer Limits* attempt to communicate with a creature who considers himself "above them."

The second production that recalls *Bug* is *Mimic*, an excellent 1997 horror film about an irresponsible scientist (Mira Sorvino) who breeds insects (playing God) to wipe out a plague in New York City. Unfortunately, the beasties adapt beyond science's understanding, and threaten mankind's prominence. In both situations, a scientist's "altering" of nature's plan nearly has catastrophic results.

Mimic and *The Outer Limits*, one must admit, are rather more adept in enunciating their themes than *The Bug*, but *The Bug* (based on the novel *The Hephaestus Plague*) is an earlier, perhaps prehistoric meditation on the same thoughts. It's a slow-paced, mildly entertaining film with some provocative moments. If the professor's mental disintegration had been carried off with a bit more aplomb, the film might have merited three stars. One thing's for sure: the bugs are great. Gassy, but great.

The Devil's Rain (1975) ⋆ ⋆

Critical Reception

> "The quality of writing, acting and directing give a general and routine witlessness to this movie.... The weave of black cloth used to blot out the eyes shows up clearly. The stuff leaking from the bodies is foamily chemical.... It is as horrible as watching an egg fry."—Richard Eder, *New York Times*, August 8, 1975, page 11.

Cast & Crew

CAST: Ernest Borgnine (Jonathan Corbis); Eddie Albert (Dr. Sam Richards); William Shatner (Mark Preston/Martin Fyffe); Keenan Wynn (Sheriff Owens); Tom Skerritt (Tom Preston); Joan Pratner (Julie Preston); Ida Lupino (Mrs. Preston); Woodrow Chambliss (John); John Travolta (Danny); Claudio Brook (Preacher); Lisa Todd (Lillith); George Sawaya

(Steve Preston); Erika Carlson (Aaronessa Fyffe); Tony Cortez (First Captor); Anton Lavey (High Priest); Diane Lavey (Priscilla Corbis); Robert Wallace (Matthew Corbis).

CREW: Bryanston Distributors Inc. Presents a Sandy Howard Production, *The Devil's Rain.* *Technical Advisor:* Anton Szandor Lavey, High Priest of the Church of Satan. *Associate Producer:* Gerald Hopman. *Production Assistant:* Ted Pravin. *First Assistant Director:* Mario Cisneros. *Production Designer:* Nikita Knatz. *Special Photographic Effects:* Film Effects of Hollywood, Linwood G. Dunn, Don W. Weed. *Videotape Production:* Sony International Corporation, Jaime H. Shandera, James A. Menorala. *Second Unit Director:* Rafael Portillo. *Art Director:* Jose Rodriguez Granada. *Camera Operator:* Felipe L. Mariscal. *Sound Mixer:* Manuel Topete. *Sound Effects Editor:* Gene Eliot. *Dialogue Editor:* Tony Garber. *Music Editor:* Milton Lustig. *Wardrobe:* Carol Wenger. *Set Decoration:* Carlos Granjean. *Assistant Film Editor:* Peter Berger. *Script Supervisor:* Ana Maria Quintana. *Production Coordinator:* Linda Sony. *Make-up:* The Burmans Studio. *Special Effects:* Cliff and Carol Wenger, Thoms Fisher, Frederico Farfan. *Title Backgrounds from Paintings by:* Hieronymus Bosch. *Photographed in:* TODD AO-35. *Locations by:* Cinemobile Systems. *In Charge of Production:* Terry Morse, Jr. *Casting:* Lea Stalmaster. *Music Composed and Conducted by:* Al De Lory. *Film Editor:* Michael Kahn. *Director of Photography:* Alex Phillips, Jr. *Written by:* Gabe Essoe, James Ashton, Gerald Hopman. *Produced by:* James V. Cullen, Michael S. Glick. *Directed by:* Robert Fuest. *M.P.A.A. Rating:* PG. *Running Time:* 86 minutes.

P.O.V.

"I wondered how they got the money to make it. The director was an English fellow who had a marvelous sense of humor. He and I were talking about things we could do with the script that would enrich it, make it more funny ... and tongue and cheek.... And halfway through it the producers had us re-shoot the stuff. They wanted a straight horror picture.... I knew it would be a disaster" (24).— Tom Skerritt reflects on his first horror feature, *The Devil's Rain* (1975).

SYNOPSIS: On a rainy night, Mark Preston returns home to his southwestern ranch to tell his mother that he was not able to find his missing father out in the raging storm. Then, a man appearing to be Mark's father, shows up at the homestead and warns that Corbis wants "his book" returned. After delivering this message, Mr. Preston's face promptly melts away....

Mark and his mother are convinced Corbis is trying to trick them, and that he is really holding Mr. Preston captive in a nearby ghost-town, Redstone. Mrs. Preston wants Mark to return the all-important book, which she keeps hidden in the floor board, but Mark refuses to give the devilish Corbis what he so deeply desires. Instead, Mark arms himself with a pistol, and determines to rescue his father. Mrs. Preston provides Mark with a magic amulet that prevents harm by Corbis.

When a truck pulls up outside the ranch, Mark checks it out, only to learn it is a diversion. He returns inside to find his mother abducted by Corbis. Now Mark has two people to rescue.

Mark drives to Redstone and meets Corbis there, who again demands the book. The two men confront one another, faith against faith. If Preston wins, he gets his parents back. If he loses, he hands over the book, and his eternal soul, to Corbis. The battle occurs in a church during a black mass, and Mark sees that his mother has been converted to evil, her eyes black pools. Mark attempts to escape, but is overpowered by Corbis's minions. When he loses the amulet, Mark is lost ... converted to evil like the rest of his family.

Elsewhere, Mark's brother, Tom, and his wife, Julie, conduct experiments in parapsychology with Dr. Sam Richards. During one ESP experiment, Julie has visions of the Corbis church, and realizes Mark is in danger. Julie, Tom and Sam head to Redstone to save Mark. They investigate the strange story of Corbis, and learn that in times past he was called Pilgrim Corbis, and his book was stolen. He believes it was someone in his flock who stole the book because the ledger names all those who have conspired with Satan. Without the book and its register of names, Corbis cannot lead his people to the kingdom of Satan, and his minions are doomed to everlasting limbo.

As it turns out, the thief was the wife of Martin Fyfe, a dead ringer for Mark Preston. Though she was burned at the stake, Corbis then swore to track the Fyfes (or the Prestons…) for all eternity until the book was once more in his possession.

After this strange vision, Tom heads off armed with a rifle to confront Corbis. Julie is captured by Mrs. Preston, now a servant of the devil. Tom infiltrates the coven to rescue his brother, Mark, but Mark is now an eyeless servant too, while Corbis has transformed into a horned demon.

Tom is outed at the mass as a blasphemer and he flees the ceremony, opening fire on Corbis's cloaked minions. Tom escapes and tells Dr. Richards about what has happened. He studies Corbis's book and realizes that these are the names of people who converted to Satanism 300 years earlier. If Tom turns over the book, their souls will be delivered to the Devil and doomed for eternity. Sam and Tom return to the church to rescue Julie, and they realize that Corbis is trapping all those souls in limbo in demonic crystal balls.

When Corbis steals the book from Tom, Sam threatens to destroy the crystal bottle containing the "Devil's Rain." The converted Mark gets his hands on the crystal dome himself, and seeking freedom, shatters it. An unearthly rain pours into the church, melting Corbis and all his followers. Tom and Sam free Julie and try to escape the wrath of Corbis, but the demon has one more trick up his sleeve. Unable to escape the scalding Devil's rain, Corbis jumps into Julie's body, imprisoning Julie's soul in limbo for all eternity…

COMMENTARY: Very few films can make the claim that the high priest of the Church of Satan was the production's technical advisor. Even fewer films would *want* to make that claim. That unsavory *The Devil's Rain* credit, which smacks of exploitation value more than it reflects the film's accuracy in depicting satanic rites, sets the tone of the movie. Like the rain that destroys its principals in the finale, the *Devil's Rain* is a goopy mess.

And this is a genuine surprise, since the director of *The Devil's Rain* is Robert Fuest, the same talent behind the riveting 1970 psycho-thriller *And Soon the Darkness*, and the sardonic *Phibes* films. He's a particularly clever director, but seems undone here by a story that never really comes together. An additional problem is that the film begins with a strong audience identification with one cast (Lupino and Shatner), and then switches to a new, more bland set (Skerritt, Albert and Pratner). Lupino and Shatner are sort of involving in their desperation, whereas Skerritt, Albert and Pratner have no idea what is going on, and therefore don't present much of a match for Borgnine's Corbis.

Albert is badly miscast in *The Devil's Rain*. He carries no psychic weight, no authority, as the "expert" in the occult/paranormal, Sam Richards. Maybe it's merely the echo of those years spent on *Green Acres*, but Albert is far too amiable for the audience to imagine him grappling with Satanists. This doesn't mean Albert is a bad actor, just that he is not used effectively in this film. In 1984, in the film *Dreamscape*, Albert portrayed a kindly Reagan-esque president plagued by nightmares of nuclear war, and his persona of decency and gentility worked splendidly in that environment. But it does not here, when he is meant to be a sharp-minded authority on the occult.

The Devil's Rain starts promisingly. The film displays a variety of Hieronymus Bosch paintings over the opening credits, and these disturbing images are edited to plaintive moaning on the soundtrack. These odd works of art depict inhuman, monstrous devils committing unspeakable acts upon men and women. The moaning becomes a discordant din, and the effect is one of discomfort. That sets the tone of tension, and the film opens with a thunderclap, and the shadow of a hand moving a cross a crucifix on the wall. The combination of the devilish art, the storm, and the religious icon lend the opening moments an expressionist feel in the best sense of that word.

From there, a man's face melts, deteriorating into a pile of goop before our very eyes. This is a startling effect, and quite effectively placed at the beginning of the film, because the audience is not prepared for it. Beginning *in medias res*, the film then proceeds with little explanation, as the concerned Shatner and Lupino discuss their frightening situation.

The opening sequence leads to a confrontation, faith against faith, between Borgnine's devil and Shatner's hero, and there is a frightening sequence as Shatner flees the church after he is tricked into removing his protective amulet. A "swarm" of Satanists descend on him, and it is kind of scary too. But once Shatner is out of the picture, the film never recovers the same momentum or interest.

Also, there's a gaffe in situational logic in the film. Only two people in the world know where Corbis's book is hidden: Mark Preston (Shatner) and his mother (Lupino). Yet, by a third of the way through the picture, both of these characters have been converted to evil, so there should be no further conflict. As enslaved disciples of Corbis, why do they simply not reveal the location of the book to their new master? The earlier battle of fates seems to establish that Corbis, as "Satan's minister on Earth," is more powerful than any human's will, so why does he not just demand of his converts that they reveal the location of the book? This question is never answered.

If the plot has flaws, it is not buttressed in any way by the special effects, which do not bear close scrutiny. The melting of Mr. Preston is an effective moment at the opening of the picture, but each subsequent melt-

ing becomes less impressive simply because it provides time and opportunity to examine the same effect again and again. By the time of the final "rain" that wipes out Borgnine's flock, it is clear that the melting flesh is merely hot wax. Thus the end of the movie is sloppy, mucky, yucky, and wholly ineffective. It looks like a sprinkler system has destroyed the denizens of a wax museum.

In another effects botch, it is clear on several occasions that the "black" eyes of Lupino and other Corbis disciples are actually made of stitched cloth, sewed in over the performers' real eye sockets. The "fake" eyes are incredibly obvious, yet Fuest obsesses on them in numerous close-ups.

The Devil's Rain has some interesting flourishes. The American Southwest, the primary setting of the film, has since become a favorite of horror directors, from *Near Dark* (1987) and *From Dusk Till Dawn* (1995) to *John Carpenter's Vampires* (1998). The ghost-town setting of the film is used to good effect here, even if it is never explained how (and when) Corbis and his people migrate from New England to the other side of the country.

Ernest Borgnine makes for a strong villain as Corbis, and there is a sense of terror underlying many moments of the film. A strong jolt comes when an eyeless, black-cloaked Lupino pops up in the back seat of Julie's car unexpectedly. But even these fine horror moments don't forge a very satisfying experience. The trick ending makes no sense, and since the audience has nothing invested in the movie's second string (Skerritt, Pratner and Albert), the final "possession" has but little impact. Fuest is a great director, and an important one to the genre, but this film is nothing to crow about. The plot structure robs the film of its most interesting characters early on, and the heavily scrutinized special effects only reveal them for what they are: special effects. *The Devil's Rain* is a sad punctuation for Fuest's 1970s horror career.

LEGACY: Today, *The Devil's Rain* is remembered primarily as John Travolta's first feature film. He plays one of Corbis's cloaked followers, and delivers the immortal line: "*Blasphemer!*" Other than that, he doesn't make much of an impression.

It is also interesting to note that *The Devil's Rain* "melting face" ending was later repeated lock, stock and barrel in the far superior Spielberg production *Raiders of the Lost Ark* (1981).

The Giant Spider Invasion

Cast & Crew

CAST: Steve Brodie (Dr. Vance); Barbara Hale (Dr. Jenny Langer); Robert Easton (Hester); Leslie Parrish (Ev); Alan Hale (Sheriff); Bill Williams (Dutch); Kevin Brodie (Perkins); Dianne Lee Hart (Terry); Paul Bentzen (Billy).
   CREW: *Directed by:* Bill Rebane. *Screenplay by:* Richard L. Huff and Robert Easton. *From an Original Story by:* Richard L. Huff. *Produced by:* Bill Rebane and Richard L. Huff. *Executive Producer:* William W. Gillett, Jr. *Director of Cinematography:* Jack Willoughby. *Film Editor:* Barbara Pokras. *M.P.A.A. Rating:* PG. *Running Time:* 90 minutes (approximate).

DETAILS: An infamous (notorious?) cult-classic, *The Giant Spider Invasion* concerns the chaos that ensues when a black hole (!?) opens up in rural Wisconsin and drops alien spider eggs across the countryside. Alan Hale (the Skipper of *Gilligan's Island*), is hilariously miscast as the town sheriff, and Robert Easton plays a reprobate redneck. Two past-their-prime scientists (Steve Brodie and Barbara Hale) team up to stop the carnivorous giant spider (a Volkswagen beetle disguised as an arachnid…) from destroying the town fair. This one must be seen to be believed.

In Search of Dracula

Cast & Crew

CAST: Christopher Lee (Narrator).
   CREW: *Produced and Directed by:* Calvin Floyd. *Written by:* Yvonne Floyd. *Photography:* Tony Forsberg. *Music:* Calvin Floyd. Independent International Pictures Releasing Corporation. *M.P.A.A. Rating:* PG. *Running Time:* 86 minutes.

DETAILS: This 1975 documentary, hosted by Christopher Lee, followed the legend of Dracula, and the life of Bram Stoker's inspiration, the notorious Vlad the Impaler. Replete with re-creations of Vlad's life (in which Lee played the count), this installment in a documentary film series was part of a '70s fad that also included such films as *In Search of Noah's Ark*, *In Search of Big Foot*, and *In Search of Historic Jesus*.

Jaws (1975) ★ ★ ★ ★

Critical Reception

"...a sensationally effective action picture — a scary thriller that works all the better because it's populated with characters that have been developed into human beings.... It's a film as frightening as *The Exorcist*, and yet it's a nicer kind of fright."— Roger Ebert, *Roger Ebert's Movie Home Companion* (1993 Edition), Andrews and McMeel, 1993, page 329.

"...eminently worth seeing for its second half: three men against a killer shark, but up to this point *Jaws* is often flawed by its busyness.... Agitated actors shout, argue, and trample heavily on one another's lines ... chilling high adventure, destined for box office statistics."— Marsha Magill, *Films in Review*, Volume XXVI, Number 7, September 1975, page 436.

"...the most efficient manipulation of mass emotion in the cinema since *Psycho*.... Several sequences have become suspense classics."— Neil Sinyard, *The Films of Steven Spielberg*, Bison Books Ltd., 1986, page 36.

"While primarily an adventure film, the opening scene of a young woman being attacked by Spielberg's great white shark is certainly as horrific as Hitchcock's famous shower scene, even with its none-too-subtle allusions to *Creature from the Black Lagoon*. While human beings have always been a reluctant part of the food chain, *Jaws* showed the actual process like no other film — stepping out of the cinema and actually influencing the culture (by keeping people out of the ocean for years to come)."— Bill Latham, *Mary's Monster*, Powys Books.

Cast & Crew

CAST: Roy Scheider (Chief Martin Brody); Robert Shaw (Quint); Richard Dreyfuss (Matt Hooper); Lorraine Gary (Ellen Brody); Murray Hamilton (Vaughn); Carl Gottlieb (Meadows); Jeffrey C. Kramer (Hendricks); Susan Backline (Chrissy); Jonathan Filley (Cassidy); Ted Grossman (Estuary Victim); Chris Rebellow (Michael Brody); Jay Mello (Sean Brody); Lee Fiero (Mrs. Kintner); Jeffrey Voorhees (Alex Kintner); Craig Kingsbury (Ben Gardner); Dr. Robert Nevin (Medical Examiner); Peter Benchley (Interviewer).

CREW: Universal Studios presents A Zanuck/Brown Production of *Jaws*. *Music:* John Williams. *Film Editor:* Verna Fields. *Director of Photography:* Bill Butler. *Screenplay:* Peter Benchley and Carl Gottlieb. *Based on a Novel by:* Peter Benchley. *Produced by:* Richard Zanuck and David Brown. *Directed by:* Steven Spielberg. *Production Design:* Joe Alves, Jr. *Special Effects:* Robert A. Mattey. *Production Executive:* William S. Gilmore, Jr. *Underwater Photography:* Rexford Metz. *Camera Operator:* Michael Chapman. *Sound:* John R. Canter, Robert Hoyt. *Unit Production Manager:* Jim Fargo. *First Assistant Director:* Tom Joyner. *Second Assistant Director:* Barbara Bass. *Script Supervisor:* Charlsie Bryant. *Location Casting:* Shari Rhodes. *Set Decorator:* John M. Dwyer. *Technical Advisor:* Manfred Zendar. *Cosmetics:* Cinamatique. *Live Shark Footage Filmed by:* Ron and Valerie Taylor. *M.P.A.A. Rating:* R. *Running Time:* 120 minutes.

SYNOPSIS: On Amity Island during summer, a girl named Chrissy goes for a swim after an all-night party and is promptly devoured by a great white shark.

The next morning, Amity's police chief, Brody, investigates the girl's disappearance. All too soon, her half-eaten corpse washes ashore, and the coroner rules the cause of death to be shark attack. Concerned for the safety of Amity's populace, Brody closes the beaches pending further investigation. The city elders, however, are worried about business since July 4th is fast approaching, and closing the beaches could destroy the island community's tourist-based economy. The mayor persuades Brody to cover up the truth about the shark attack, and the coroner recants his former findings, arguing now that Chrissy's death was the result of a boating accident. The beaches stay open.

A few days later, the great white shark glides inland again, and eats a little boy frolicking in the water. Amity is thrown into chaos as the boy's grief-stricken mother offers a reward for anybody who kills the shark that murdered her son. Brody closes the beach for 24 hours, and an oceanographic expert, Hooper, is summoned to town to help hunt the offending fish. Meanwhile, a seaman, the salty Quint, offers to kill the shark for $10,000, but Amity's Elders, still worried about money, won't ante up. Growing ever more worried, Brody researches sharks.

In another close call, the shark rips up a pier, going after a "roast" (i.e. bait) dangled by two local fishermen. Then Matt Hooper arrives, and promptly examines the remains of the shark victims even as Amity hunters take to the sea (most of them drunk...) in search of the predator. Hooper soon realizes that an abnormally large shark is on the prowl in the shallow waters near the island. When the locals kill a tiger shark and bring it inland, Hooper detects it has too small a bite radius to be their culprit.

Brody, who has a phobia about the water, and the more courageous Hooper take a boat out to sea to hunt the shark, but instead run across the wreckage of a fishing boat. All aboard are dead, the victims of a shark attack. Though Brody warns against it vehemently, the mayor of Amity orders the beaches "open" for the Independence Day weekend. July 4th comes, and the shark makes a deadly appearance, killing a boater and leaving Brody's youngest son, Michael, in shock, after a close encounter.

With few options remaining, the elders of Amity hire Quint to kill the shark. With Brody and Hooper serving as his crew, Quint ships out on his vessel, the *Orca*, to hunt the beast. Almost immediately, Quint and Hooper clash. As the days at sea pass, the crew of the *Orca* and the shark play a game of cat and mouse. The 3 ton, 25 foot long shark circles the ship, and Quint harpoons it. The *Orca* then tracks the shark for days.

One night during the hunt, Quint tells a story about his time aboard the U.S.S. *Indianapolis*. When the ship was torpedoed during World War II, 1100 men were forced to abandon ship ... and jump into the water. Sharks ate dozens of the sailors before a rescue ship arrived. Quint survived the experience, and has never forgotten it.

Before long, the shark returns, resisting all attempts to kill it. It nearly pulls the *Orca* underwater, and the ship starts to sink. Realizing he is facing a cleverer opponent than he estimated, Quint turns the ship for home, but the motor fails and the lower deck of the boat becomes submerged. In a last ditch effort to stop the shark, Hooper goes underwater in an anti-shark metal cage, armed with a hypodermic needle. His goal is to inject the fish with poison, but the plan requires close-quarters precision. Not surprisingly, the shark destroys the cage in short order, and the mission fails. Hooper's fate is left unknown as the shark mounts a new attack on the boat.

In the final battle, the shark eats Quint, and stalks Brody. Climbing a sinking crow's nest on the *Orca*, Brody confronts the shark. Armed with a rifle, he waits for the shark to swallow a canister of compressed air. Aiming carefully, Brody detonates the canister and blows the rapidly approaching predator to smithereens. Brody is relieved to discover Hooper still alive, and the survivors swim back to Amity...

———————————

COMMENTARY: Peter Benchley's best-selling novel *Jaws* is a horror tale for grown-ups. There are adulterous sexual affairs in the town of Amity, not to mention an unspoken societal rule about the roles of "outsiders" and "islanders." In the book, Brody is not a native of the town, and is looked down on for it. And, his wife has an affair with the visiting oceanographer, Hooper. By contrast, Steven Spielberg's film adaptation of *Jaws* is a horror tale for all ages, a streamlined entertainment that discards most of Benchley's adult character interplay and elements of "class warfare" in favor of a tense essay about man's greatest fears.

The movie has simplified the popular novel to a significant degree, but remains incredibly adroit in the manner by which it exploits heroic and mythological archetypes. The hero with the Achilles heel (Brody's fear of the ocean…), the old salt (Quint), the young buck who thinks he knows better (Hooper), and even the sea monster (the shark), all find new life under Spielberg's fresh-faced, enthusiastic approach to storytelling. Spielberg's *Jaws* is an offspring of Ernest Hemingway as much as it is of Peter Benchley.

The quality so remarkable about *Jaws*, even today, is that the scariest moments are those which suggest horror rather than depicting it outright. The late Robert Shaw (Quint) delivers one of the silver screen's great monologues near the end of *Jaws* when he shares the incredible true story of the U.S.S. *Indianapolis*. In 1945 (after delivering the atom bomb), the ship was sunk by a Japanese submarine. Eleven hundred men abandoned ship for the ocean. Within half an hour, the first shark arrived on the scene. The creatures dined on the sailors for more than a week. One hundred men died in the first day alone, and when rescue came, only 376 men (of 1100) were alive.

This story is so awful, so frightening that Spielberg knows he need do little to augment it but point his camera at a fine actor and let him attack the material. Since movies were once a communal experience (before home theaters and DVD players…), it is rewarding to watch *Jaws* with a large audience. When Quint commences his tale, the audience inevitably goes dead silent … hypnotized by his words, and the terrifying mental picture they conjure. It is to Spielberg's everlasting credit that he didn't take the easy way out, the way a more "typical" horror director might have. Specifically, he doesn't cut to a flashback actually showing the *Indianapolis* and its beleaguered men. Instead, the audience has the opportunity to imagine the encounter, and as has been proven many times, imagination can be far more frightening than visual depiction.

Spielberg builds scares throughout *Jaws* in this restrained fashion. He has an understanding that knowledge (as well as anecdotal information) is vital in the technique of building fear. A smart audience is a prepared audience. And a prepared audience is a worried one. Accordingly, *Jaws* is jam-packed with accurate and truly frightening information about sharks. In short order, the film reveals that most sharks attack humans within 10 feet of the shore, in less than 3 feet of water. It also provides further troubling information, about everything from shark territoriality and bite radius, to stomach contents. In one very difficult moment to watch, the film shows actual photographs of shark bite victims.

All of this information preps the audience for the confrontation to come. Viewers know what a shark can do, and know they should be scared. Spielberg provides them this information, then, like Hitchcock, ruthlessly manipulates them with it.

Of course, there's no way that a movie about shark attacks could avoid depicting the bloody encounters themselves. But, yet again, Spielberg is efficient, not showy, in laying out the blood and guts. Most of the time, the shark is not in the frame at all during the assaults. Instead, there are P.O.V. tracking shots from deep beneath the sea as a swimmer's legs or other bobbing body parts are seen swaying with a rippling ocean surface. Though legend has it that Bruce the shark perpetually malfunctioned, and that's why Spielberg didn't reveal more of his beast, the simple truth is that the horror scenes are more effective without the shark in full view. John Williams' pounding score coupled with subjective camera shots (from the shark's perspective), and the sight of swimmers jerking and being pulled under, are quite effective without resorting to close-ups of the monster's gnashing teeth. These moments leave enough to the imagination to be truly terrifying.

Conversely, the moments wherein the shark breaks the water to reveal its tooth-filled head are nothing less than adrenaline-inducing. Some people think the shark in this film looks phony. This reviewer wouldn't want to get close enough to be sure.

But, *Jaws* is much more than its accumulation of suggested (and actual) horror moments. Steven Spielberg understands how to create a sense of place, and Amity is a splendid locale to exploit. The habits of summer, the beach bum existence, the local annoyances, the local politics, and even scenes of Brody family life give the film that important quality of verisimilitude. Simply put, the film appears realistic rather than a "monster attack" fantasy of shlocky Hollywood. If Spielberg crosses the line into sentimentality anywhere (his only weakness as a filmmaker...), it is in depicting some of the father-son dynamics of the Brodys. The restraint he reveals in the film's horror is not to be found here, and a few of the family sequences, which call out for similar underplaying, are wrung for every bit of saccharine cutes the director can find. But, that is a small flaw in a very impressive film.

If one had to describe the subplot (and driving force) of *Jaws* in four words, it would be: "it's the economy, stupid." Much of the film revolves around the town elders, and their attempt to maintain a robust tourist economy despite the danger to life and limb posed by the hungry shark grazing in Amity's waters. The mayor initiates a cover-up and Brody is actually a conspirator, at least for a time. Basically, everybody in the town is terrified of losing money: that's the real monster in Amity, not the shark. The town scenes are shrill, contentious and highly effective. Spielberg not only plumbs the depths of the ocean, he delves deeply into the local bureaucracy to reveal how decisions are made purely on the basis of money.

The corruption of the town officials is surely a reflection of the Watergate scandal and the overriding '70s belief that government could not be trusted. It just plays out in the microcosm of Amity. Brody is a good man drawn into a conspiracy of silence, and the cover-up is eventually revealed ... but not before damage has been done. The Watergate analogy is probably lighter than some critics have suggested, but it is impossible to forget that *Jaws* has a political angle: the certain and understood knowledge that life and death decisions are made on the basis of how they affect one's pocketbook. What price is too high to pay for a profitable fourth of July weekend? So many horror films have repeated *Jaws*' "the beaches must stay closed" political debate that it has now become a standard trapping of the genre, seen in *Piranha* (1978), *Grizzly* (1976) and *Kingdom of the Spiders* (1977) to name just three.

Ultimately, the characteristics that make a film great go beyond any combination of acting, direction, photography, editing and music. It is a magic equation that some films get right, and some don't. *Jaws* is a classic and brilliant horror film because, in the final analysis, it works on a subconscious, mythological level. There is little doubt that the shark in the film is smarter than any animal has the right to be. It outthinks Hooper and Quint during the climactic battle, and is one tough critter. Throughout the film there is the very understated notion that the shark is a monster beyond biology. This shark, a creature that turns and attacks when threatened, is, like Michael Myers in the *Halloween* saga, a symbol of pure evil. It isn't just hunger that drives this monster. It seems to possess a personal desire to kill Quint, Brody and Hooper. This idea doesn't overpower the film, but it is there.

On a more basic level, viewers watching *Jaws* understand that the ocean is a realm of mystery they do not completely understand. In that sense, the shark has the home

Permission to come aboard? Bruce the Shark attacks the *Orca* during the climactic moments of *Jaws* (1975).

field advantage. It is comfortable, natural, and at a huge advantage, in the water. Meanwhile, man is awkward, out of place and endangered there. Beyond jolts, beyond "stinger" music, beyond well-written, evocative dialogue, *Jaws* is successful because it plays on the primeval fears of the "other," the creature we don't understand. That horror is doubled because the battle is waged in a territory that is also unfamiliar, dangerous, and to be feared.

Jaws is the perfect escapist entertainment, and any attempt to read too deeply into it wouldn't be fruitful. The film works because people are afraid of sharks, and because its characters are memorable ones. There is a male-bonding element to the picture with Brody and Hooper learning to love Quint, warts and all. And it is a beautiful film, with the last act set entirely on the deep blue sea. This sequence is breathtaking and

frightening, and the audience is reminded that the ocean is not only a dangerous world, but a lovely, seductive one as well. From its perfectly executed and pitched opening sequence (which sees Chrissy unexpectedly yanked down and eaten by the shark in the placid ocean waters...), *Jaws* is never anything less than slick entertainment. It has more jolts than most horror movies, is populated by interesting people, has a fantastic setting, and, most importantly, a great villain. But Spielberg's restraint and understanding of suspense is what keeps it all afloat.

LEGACY: *Jaws* overtook *The Exorcist* as the horror movie phenomenon of the '70s when it was released in 1975. Like *The Exorcist*, it received mixed reviews, but audiences were wowed. As a result of his work on the film,

Steven Spielberg became the most beloved and well-known director of the generation. After *Jaws*, Spielberg directed notable genre efforts including *Close Encounters of the Third Kind* (1978), *1941* (1979), *Raiders of the Lost Ark* (1981), *Indiana Jones and the Temple of Doom* (1984), *E.T.* (1982), *Indiana Jones and the Last Crusade* (1989), *Hook* (1991), *Jurassic Park* (1993), and *The Lost World* (1997).

As for *Jaws*, it became the tent pole of a long-lived Universal franchise that came to include *Jaws II* (1978), *Jaws 3D* (1983), and *Jaws: The Revenge* (1987). Perhaps more significantly, *Jaws* set off a second wave of "animal attacks" films, both in the water (*Orca* [1977], *Tentacles* [1977], *Tintorera—Tiger Shark* [1977], and *Devil Fish* [1984]) and out (*Grizzly* [1976]).

In 1999, sharks returned for big screen horror in the blockbuster *Deep Blue Sea*, a sort of *Jaws*-meets-*Jurassic Park*.

Legend of the Werewolf (1975) ✴ ✴ ✴

Cast & Crew

CAST: Peter Cushing (Professor Paul); Ron Moody (Zookeeper); Hugh Griffith (Maestro Pamponi); David Bailie (Boulon); Lynn Dalby (Christine); Stefan Gryffe (Max Gerard); Renee Houston (Chou-Chou); Norman Mitchell (Tiny); Mark Weavers (Young Etoile); Marjorie Yates (Madame Tellier); Roy Castle (Photographer); Elaine Baillie (Annabelle); John Harvey (Prefect); Patrick Holt (Dignitary); Hilary Labow (Zoe); Michael Ripper (Sewerman); David Rintoul (Etoile/the Werewolf); Pamela Green (Anne-Marie); Sue Bishop (Tania); James McManus (Emigré Husband); Jane Gussons (Emigré Wife).

CREW: A Tyburn Film Production, *Legend of the Werewolf*. *Director of Photography:* John Wilcox. *Art Director:* Jack Shampan. *Assistant Art Director:* Brian Ackland-Snow. *Film Editor:* Henry Richardson. *Sound Editor:* Roy Baker. *Production Manager:* Ron Jackson. *Special Photographic Effects:* Charles Staffell. *Assistant Director:* Peter Saunders. *Camera Operator:* Gerry Anstiss. *Continuity:* Pamela Davies. *Still Photographer:* Douglas Webb. *Sound Recordists:* John Bromnage, Ken Barker. *Production Assistant:* Lorraine Fennell. *Wardrobe Supervisor:* Mary Gibson. *Make-up:* Jimmy Evans, Graham Freeborn. *Hairstylist:* Stella Rivers. *Assistant Film Editor:* Roy Helmrigh. *Assistant Sound Editor:* Beverley Collings. *Construction Manager:* George Aill. *Properties:* Nick Rivers. *Grip:* George Beavis. *Gaffer:* John Tytner. *Music Composed by:* Harry Robinson. *Music Supervisor:* Phillip Martell. *Written by:* John Elder. *Produced by:* Kevin Francis. *Directed by:* Freddie Francis. *M.P.A.A. Rating:* PG. *Running Time:* 96 minutes.

SYNOPSIS: In central Europe in the 19th century, the legend arises of a human baby who is raised and cared for by a wolf pack. This legend has basis in fact, for it is the tale of young Etoile, a boy taken by wolves on Christmas Eve and raised wild.

Etoile returns to humanity when he is a toddler, performing as a circus attraction in the ramshackle traveling organization of Maestro Pamponi. Etoile travels with the circus for many years, and becomes a strapping, handsome adult. Then one night — when the moon is full — he turns into a werewolf and murders Pamponi's assistant, Tiny.

Etoile flees the circus and ends up in Paris. There, he seeks work at a local zoo, and is employed by the drunken caretaker. He also falls in love with Christine, a prostitute at the local brothel. Christine does not tell Etoile about her profession, fearing a parochial attitude. When Etoile finds out that his beloved girl is a prostitute, he tries to kill one of her clients, the prefect! The incident is forgotten in short order, since the prefect desires no publicity or scandal, but

Etoile's actions have humiliated Christine. When he asks her to marry him, she rejects him. As if in response, Etoile turns into a werewolf and goes on a killing rampage — murdering three of Christine's would-be clients.

The town coroner, the brilliant Professor Paul, suspects a loose wolf is responsible for the deaths in Paris, and visits the zoo to investigate. The trail of victims leads him to the brothel, and finally to Christine. Meanwhile, the prefect orders all wolves in the city destroyed. Etoile resists the idea, but is forced to kill his brethren in the zoo. That night, enraged again, Etoile becomes a wolf man and kills by (full) moonlight.

Professor Paul learns from a surviving victim that his attacker was neither wolf nor man, but a horrid combination of both. Equipped with books on the subject of lycanthropy, Paul sets out to capture the man-beast. He contacts Christine again, and realizes that Etoile is the monster he seeks. Paul determines that the werewolf is using the sewers beneath Paris to escape detection, and arms himself with silver bullets. He faces down Etoile, seeking to help him, but the police arrive and shatter the peace. Etoile is shot in the back. Dying, he flees to Christine and dies at her feet while the murderous authorities and the saddened Professor Paul look on.

COMMENTARY: By 1975, the werewolf film had been done to death. Yet Tyburn's *Legend of the Werewolf* is a good little unassuming film on the subject. Better than the company's previous effort (1974's *The Ghoul*), this story of a boy-turned-werewolf benefits from a gritty, interesting setting, and another stand-out performance by that perennial of '70s horror cinema, Peter Cushing.

Often, the setting of a film makes all the difference. *An American Werewolf in London* (1981) is a prime example of an old story redone in a fresh setting. *Legend of the Werewolf* demands attention by setting its story among the colorful underclass of 19th cen-

tury Paris. This is a world of drunks, orphans, prostitutes and scheming politicians, and the film does not shy away from an unromantic view of one of the world's most notoriously romantic cities. The heroine of the film is Christine, an orphan. She is so desperate for wealth that she has become a prostitute. She won't marry Etoile, not because her feelings don't support the idea of marriage, but because "he's got nothing." She desires a better life and will not settle for less, and the film is unflinching in its depiction of her as a desperate social climber.

In fact, the movie is filled with unsavory men and women. There's the brothel with an unscrupulous madam, the nasty showman who treats his living human attractions like cattle, and the drunken zoo-keeper. Then there's the scandal-plagued prefect, looking to preserve his reputation. With these examples in mind, the people of Paris are depicted as pretty terrible all the way around, and that's an interesting conceit. Etoile kills many of these thoroughly rotten human beings, but the audience's sympathy remains squarely with him. He does not like his lot in life, not only that he is a werewolf, but that he is exploited by men of all creeds, and kept apart from the woman he loves by the social construct of wealth. Etoile is the outsider not just because he is a monster, but because he is poor, and the movie is really about a man railing against his social class. Lycanthropy is just the tool that gives his protest teeth (or fangs.)

If there is a noble character in this film, it is (not surprisingly) Peter Cushing's coroner, Paul. As usual, Cushing is able to marshal audience identification with a minimum of fuss. Purely by his sparkling intelligence and sincerity, he comes across as sharp and insightful. Those qualities make him very different from the other denizens of Paris, and there's a bit of Van Helsing's sharp intellect in Cushing's depiction of this professional. About half way through *Legend of the Werewolf*, the film goes from being Etoile's personal story of revenge to a police procedural, and Cushing takes the lead role. In the best tradition of horror protagonists, Cushing shows compassion for his enemy, wishing to learn from it rather than simply destroying it. "You fools!" he shouts at the police, "Blundering idiots! Must you always kill?" Cushing's concern for his prey not only makes sense for a man of science, it reinforces the idea that the people of Paris are primitive, lustful people with base appetites that include, even, murder.

Legend of the Werewolf features some gory murders, great werewolf make-up, and plenty of red-hued "werewolf cam" tracking shots. And with Cushing leading the investigation, the film has a fine horror backbone. Yet on top of all the horror is the story of a boy raised in the wild, and unable to integrate into a human society that has set limits on people of his "breeding." Etoile is a pathetic character, but one who desires what we all desire: to love, and to, ultimately, amount to something. The very rules of Parisian life keep those things from Etoile, and when he strikes back, he is striking back not because he is a monster, but because society is.

Lisa and the Devil (released in America as *House of Exorcism* in 1975) * *

Critical Reception

"It's fairly incomprehensible in places, but quite moody, and has some interesting things to say about alienation and self-exploration. Bava's clever direction somewhat compensates for rather poor performances from the two leads."— Anthony Tomlinson, *Shivers* #30, June 1996, page 27.

Cast & Crew

CAST: Telly Savalas (Lehare); Elke Sommer (Lisa); Silva Koscina (Sophia); Alessio Orano (Maximilian). **WITH:** Gabriele Tinti, Kathy Leone, Eduardo Fajardo, Franz Von Treuberg, Espartaco Santoni, Alida Valli.
CREW: Alfred Leone Presents *Lisa and the Devil. Screenplay by:* Mario Bava and Alfred Leone. *Music by:* Carlo Savina. *Directed by:* Mario Bava. *Produced by:* Alfred Leone. *Director of Photography:* Cecilio Paniagua. *Film Editor:* Carlo Reali. *Production Manager:* Fausto Lupi. *Art Director:* Nedo Azzini. *Assistant Director:* Lamberto Bava. *Cameraman:* Emilio Varriano. *Assistant Camera:* Gianni Medica. *Make-up:* Franco Freda. *Hairdresser:* Gisa Favella. *Special Effects:* Franco Tocci. *Color:* Technicolor. A Leone International Film. *M.P.A.A. Rating:* R. *Running Time:* 90 minutes.

SYNOPSIS: A woman named Lisa visits a church and sees a fresco that depicts Satan carrying off the damned. Not long after, she spots a real-life, dead-ringer for Satan in a nearby antique store. When Lisa becomes lost, the satanic-looking man, a butler named Lehare, gives her directions. Mysteriously, Lehare seems to be carrying a corpse, or a mannequin, oddly mirroring the ghoulish work of art. Lisa thinks this odd, but not as odd as when she later runs into that corpse, apparently alive and well. His name is Carlos, and he claims to be Lisa's lover, though he calls her by the name "Elena." Baffled, Lisa pushes Carlos down a flight of stairs, killing him.

Attempting to escape the scene, Lisa hitches a ride with the wealthy Sophia, Sophia's husband, and her lover and chauffeur, George. They drive away, but that night their car breaks down at the palatial house where Lehare tends to an old blind woman and her son, Maximilian. Almost immediately, Maximilian calls Lisa "Elena," and tells her that things will be different "this time," that he will not let their love die. What follows is a bizarre night of horrors, as Lisa has encounter after encounter with Carlos, sometimes living, sometimes dead, and an unknown assailant murders the guests beginning with George. And, all through it all, Lehare seems to be enjoying himself.

When Francis and Sophia die, Lisa attempts to flee the house, learns that Carlos is actually Maximilian's stepfather, and that both men were in love with her Doppelgänger, Elena. Worse, Maximilian is apparently a murderous psychotic who has killed George and Sophia and who keeps Elena's corpse in his bed! Maximilian knocks Lisa out, and makes love to her while she is unconscious. Then he plans a strange wedding ceremony. When his mother objects, Maximilian kills her too. Then, the corpses seem to come to life, and Maximilian falls out a window to his death. Actually, it was Lehare, manipulating the corpses to add one more dead soul to his list.

Lisa awakens from her stupor and leaves the mansion. Neighborhood children see her, and are terrified. They think she's a ghost because no one has lived in the old house for a hundred years. Desperate to escape the nightmare, Lisa boards a plane. But, in midair, Lisa is terrified to see all the corpses of days past lined up in the passenger section. She seeks help from the pilot, but flying the plane … straight to Hell, apparently … is Lehare/Satan. Terrified, Lisa dies, and reverts to her true self: Elena.

COMMENTARY: Echoing the sentiments of viewers forced to endure this film, Elke Sommer breathlessly declares in *Lisa and the Devil* that she doesn't "want to spend the rest of her life in this nightmare." That's one line that a more self-aware film may have stu-

diously avoided, but *Lisa and the Devil* is a strange movie just as likely to state the obvious as it is to offer no explanation for a peculiar going-on. It's a truly baffling film, apparently the phantasm of a woman who is already dead (but doesn't realize it). Things happen (or don't happen) in the movie for little rhyme or reason, and the viewer is left in dire need of a scoring card. Who is that old woman mother to? Who killed whom? Who is really dead? Anyone seeking such answers is bound to walk away from *Lisa and the Devil* disappointed. It isn't linear.

On one hand, some critics might praise *Lisa and the Devil* for attempting to represent a nightmare on celluloid. The film does seem structured as a dream, and that is a daring way to create a movie, a fascinating strategy even. But it is also highly confounding. Nightmares are generally unpleasant experiences, not something most people care to endure. But, like a bizarre dream played out on the screen, *Lisa and the Devil* shares a funny understanding of time, blends identities with a vengeance, and is filled with symbols … some easily comprehensible and some not.

Any director worth his union card could have helmed a straightforward movie with these same ingredients: five guests in an old dark house; a man who may be the devil; a blind homeowner; a mysterious past; and a question of identity. Yet Bava blends these plot elements in a unique, if wholly oddball fashion. Some of the visuals remain striking to contemplate twenty years later: a corpse framed behind a wedding cake, Telly Savalas strong-arming corpses that may be dummies, and so forth. And, there's a strong sexual undercurrent to the story as well (culminating in a sick, if rather erotic, rape). Even the gothic touches (such as Lisa running in slow-motion photography through a Victorian garden) are welcome and unexpected. Yet, in the final analysis, a film is supposed to represent more than the sum of its parts. It should convey some meaning beyond mood. Bava's got the mood down pat, but not the plot, and that's a problem for this reviewer. Bava knows how he wants the audience to feel, he knows how to generate those feelings, but he isn't capable of putting them in a cohesive pattern in *Lisa and the Devil*. At least not as effectively as he did in *Hatchet for a Honeymoon* (1971), which also concerned a psychotic's obsession with the wedding bed.

Still, it should be noted that many fans and admirers of Bava's work consider *Lisa and the Devil* a masterpiece. The film was corrupted into *House of Exorcism* for the 1975 release (with Robert Alda as an exorcising priest...), but this viewer saw the re-mastered original and was, frankly, mystified. The film is beautiful in so many ways, a gorgeous tapestry on which to paint a depiction of terrifying dreams, but the film needs a bit more plot to go with the mood. There is a funny 1970s joke in the film, however. At one point, Telly Savalas offers Sommer a lollipop, referencing his popular *Kojak* persona. That's the only moment of fun in a very serious, very ponderous, and very confusing horror film.

Picnic at Hanging Rock (1975) ✶ ✶ ✶ ✶

Critical Reception

"...a diaphanous horror story, firmly situated in a time and place, shrewdly observed and knowingly acted.... Weir's movie is permeated with suppressed eroticism that never crudely surfaces. By lyric touches and the art of indirection he conveys the somewhat smelly radiance that emanates from the girlish admixture of innocent crush and diffused smut, which constitutes the eternal milieu of adolescents segregated from the other sex."— Vernon Young, *The Film Criticism of Vernon Young* (edited by Bert Cardullo), University Press of America, 1990, 288–289.

"...as a tantalizing puzzle, a tease, a suggestion of a forbidden answer just out of earshot, it works hypnotically and very nicely indeed...."— Roger Ebert, *Roger Ebert's Movie Home Companion* (1993 Edition), Andrews and McMeel, 1993, page 498.

"Peter Weir gives us a strong notion of what it is for these characters to be in an aboriginal and empty country populated by myths of ancient potency which are unknown to the present inhabitants.... [This film's] antecedents are in literature: not only in Henry James but also in the eighteenth century gothic writers.... One can afford to leave aside the occasional obscurantism and doominess of the surface of the film: its essence is thoughtful."— Penelope Gilliatt, *New Yorker*, April 23, 1979, page 122.

"Ultimately, the mystery is never solved, which is dramatically frustrating but thematically valid.... Weir's film is not about the solution of mysteries; it is about how the human mind copes with events that it cannot categorize according to known reality ... the film's strength is that it is not reducible to a single explanation, even a valid one; other explanations are equally valid ... the film is often mesmerizing."— Steve Biodrowski, *Cinefantastique*, Volume 30, #7/8: "Picnic at Hanging Rock; Mysteries Beyond Human Ken," October 1998, page 121.

Cast & Crew

CAST: Rachel Roberts (Mrs. Appleyard); Dominic Guard (Michael Fitzhubert); Helen Morse (Mlle de Portiers); Jacki Weaver (Minnie); Anne Lambert (Miranda); Karen Robson (Irma); Christine Schuler (Edith); Margaret Nelson (Sara); Jane Vallis (Marion); Vivean Gray (Miss McGraw); Kirsty Child (Miss Lumley); Frank Gunnell (Mr. Whitehead); Ingrid Mason (Rosamund); Jenny Lovell (Blanche); Janet Murray (Juliana); Wyn Roberts (Sgt. Bumper); Kay Taylor (Mrs. Bumpher); Garry McDonald (Constable Jones); Martin Vaughan (Ben Hussey); Jack Fegan (Doc MacKenzie); Peter Collingwood (Colonel Fitzhubert); Olga Dickie (Mrs. Fitzhubert); John Jarrett (Albert Camdall); With: Vivienne Granee, Angela Bengini, Melinda Cardwell, Annabel Powriek, Amanda White, Lindy O'Connell, Verity Smith, Deborah Mullins, Sue Jamieson, Bernadette Bengini, Barbara Lloyd.

CREW: A Janus Film Production. B.E.F. Film Distributors Pty. Ltd. with the South Australian Film Corporation and the Australian Film Commission Present a McElroy and McElroy Production. Produced in association with Patricia Lovell. Peter Weir's film of *Picnic at Hanging Rock. Screenplay:* Cliff Green. *From a Novel by:* Joan Lindsay. *Flute de Pan played by:* Gheorge Zamfir. *Additional Original Music:* Bruce Smeaton. *Art Director:* David Copping. *Director of Photography:* Russell Boyd. *Editor:* Max Lemon. *Executive Producer:* John Graves, Patricia Lovell. *Produced by:* Hal McElroy and Jim McElroy. *Directed by:* Peter Weir. *Camera Operator:* John Seale. *Nature Photographer:* David Sanderson. *Sound Recordist:* Don Connelly. *Dubbing Editor:* Greg Bell. *Artistic Advisor to Director:* Martin Sharp. *First Assistant Director:* Mark Egerton. *Second Assistant Director:* Kim Dalton. *Script Consultant:* Sidney Stebel. *Continuity:* Gilda Baracchi. *Casting:* M&L Casting Consultants. *Production Assistant:* Steve Knapman. *Wardrobe Designer:* Judy Dorsman. *Wardrobe Assistants:* Wendy Stites, Mandy Smith. *Make-up Supervisor:* Joe Perez. *Property Buyer and Set Dresser:* Graham Walker. *Property Master:* Monte Fieguth. *Assistant to Art Director:* Chris Webster. *Assistant to Art Department:* Neil Anguvin. *Titles and Opticals:* Optical and Graphic. *Assistant Film Editor:* Andre Fleurch. *Negative Matching:* Margaret Cardin. *Sound Mix:* United Sound. *Lab:* Colorfilm (Australia) Pty. Ltd. *Photographed in:* Eastmancolor. *Camera and Lenses:* Panavision. Made on location at Hanging Rock, Victoria, Stathalbyn and Clare, Marbury School, South Australia, and South Australia Film Corporation Studios. Picnic Productions Pty. Ltd, 1975. *M.P.A.A. Rating:* PG. *Running Time:* 120 minutes.

P.O.V.

"On Saturday the 14th of February 1900, a party of schoolgirls from Appleyard College picnicked at Hanging Rock near Mt. Macedon in the state of Victoria. During the afternoon several members of the party disappeared without a trace...." — opening card of Peter Weir's *Picnic at Hanging Rock* (1975).

"There's no documentary evidence whatsoever. We can't even determine whether the girls ever disappeared.... Of course, ever since the country was settled, there have been stories of people disappearing, to this very day. I think that quite likely (author Joan Lindsay) is referring to a true incident, not exactly as described.... I think people disappear for a variety of reasons.... I liked the idea of there being no solution, as there isn't to most things (25).— Peter Weir, describing the "true" nature of the story depicted in *Picnic at Hanging Rock*.

SYNOPSIS: On Valentine's Day, 1900, the girls at Appleyard College in remotest Australia prepare for an afternoon outdoors at scenic Hanging Rock. After a stern lecture from Miss Appleyard, the girls are on their way but for Sara Wayborn, who has been forced to remain at the school because she is behind in her work.

After a brief carriage ride, the girls and their caretakers, including the gruff Miss McGraw, examine the beautiful Hanging Rock, a volcanic upcropping of stone millions of years old. The beautiful Miranda decides to lead an expedition up the stone face, taking three other girls with her, including Irma, and the fat complainer, Edith. They climb steadily for a time, briefly watched by two attentive boys, but then grow tired. The four girls sleep for a time and then awaken mysteriously —*as if in a trance*— and continue up the high ridge of the mountain. Edith fails to join the others, spies a strange red cloud overhead, and races down to tell adults. On the way down, she sees Miss McGraw, who, for some reason, has removed her skirt, climbing the rock in a hypnotic state too.

At Appleyard College, it is 10:30 P.M., and no one has returned from the picnic. Then the group returns, minus Miranda, the two other girls, and Miss McGraw. Edith is in a state of shock, screaming bloody murder. The next morning, the local constable leads a search team on Hanging Rock, but the girls and McGraw have vanished. The two boys are briefly held under suspicion of foul play, and the police resort to using bloodhounds. Again, the search turns up nothing.

One of the boys, an English fellow named Michael, finds himself dreaming of Miranda. He returns to Hanging Rock, feels the lure of the mountain, and climbs to its peak. He too is overcome, but not before finding a scrap of a beautiful white dress, perhaps belonging to Miranda. Michael's friend, an Australian orphan, finds Michael and Irma, but Irma remembers nothing of what happened to her friends or teacher.

The story of the disappearances at Hanging Rock becomes world news, and parents rapidly withdraw their daughters from Appleyard College. Mrs. Appleyard seeks solace in the bottle, and is forced to expel Sara Wayborn when her guardian fails to pay for her tuition.

Time passes and the mystery of Hanging Rock deepens, haunting everyone in the area. On the day she is expelled, Sara commits suicide. Desperate and saddened, Mrs. Appleyard visits Hanging Rock. A day later, her dead body is found at the foot of the mountain. And the mystery continues...

COMMENTARY: Peter Weir's *Picnic at Hanging Rock* is the story of a mystery that deepens and grows until it becomes, for its participants and the audience alike, nothing less than an obsession. A horror film that plays like an art film, *Picnic at Hanging Rock* is the thoroughly unsettling story of a group of girls who climb a mountain ... and then disappear off the face of the Earth for all time.

Every mystery has its own unique taste. When the plane called *Stardust* disappeared in the skies of South America in the late 1940s, there were tantalizing and contradictory clues. The pilot sent a transmission with one word "*stendec*" just before the plane disappeared forever. That cryptic final message suggested the plane was only four minutes from landing, when in fact pieces of the plane were found over fifty miles away from the landing strip. What happened? What did these details mean? Today, there are some answers to these questions, but the details remain tantalizing, and sometimes contradictory. *Picnic at Hanging Rock* likewise constructs a clever story around a similarly bizarre disappearance, one in which the details are nothing less than mesmerizing.

Prime among these clues is the role of Miranda, a beautiful girl, who, for whatever reason, disappears on that ancient rock. The film opens with Miranda's enigmatic comment that she "won't be" at the school "much longer." Is this merely a reference to the fact that she is considering a transfer, or could something deeper be read into her remark? Is she, in fact, aware of what is to become of her on that strange rock? Later, she wonders aloud if "we as humans perform some function unknown to us." This comment likewise suggests a kind of special insight or knowledge. Whatever happened to Miranda on that picnic, awareness of it was dawning within her before she ever left the school.

Even the others note this strange sort of supernatural knowledge. Sarah, the friend Miranda leaves behind, notes that "Miranda knows things a lot of other people don't know. *Secrets*. She knew she wouldn't be coming back." This too is an indication of Miranda's special status as "different." But the question remains, how different? Could

Miranda's remarks have been innocuous ones, meaning nothing? Or are they critical to an understanding of what occurs at Hanging Rock? The film offers no respite from those questions, but one cannot help but ask them.

Miranda is the film's most interesting character, and Weir depicts her in sensual terms. She is often seen in loving slow-motion photography, and in fawning close-ups. We see her brushing her long silky hair, or removing a stocking with a delicate grace. She is an image of beauty, but innocence too. If awareness of her fate is dawning in Miranda, then so is knowledge of something else: an understanding of her powers as a woman. It is no secret that the boys of the film lust after Miranda (as does Sara...), and so the film revels in the moments when Miranda pauses to remove a black stocking (in close-up) or release her hand from the confining prison of white gloves. These scenes indicate that life itself may be obsessed with Miranda, that perhaps Hanging Rock shared the boys' lust for the girl and carried her off to have her for itself. Or did the boys' lust for the girls somehow result in their disappearance?

The rock itself is an important character in the film. It has existed for a million years (or as one girl claims "has been waiting a million years just for us..."). Weir stages several shots from the inner crevices of the rock, essentially shooting a P.O.V. from the stone mountain — as though the camera were gazing out on those who crawl across the rock's outer "skin," insects perhaps.

The rock is also representative, perhaps, of competing philosophies at work in the Australia of 1900. On one hand is the aborigine "pagan" religion that allows for magic, and on the other hand is the more restrained and refined tenets of Christianity (embodied by the Appleyard School). These two worlds clash at the rock, a geological marvel that has many secrets to tell ... yet remains silent. That the rock is otherworldly or at the least, mysterious, is also borne out in the film's dialogue and settings. One character on the picnic notes that her watch has stopped, and wonders if something magnetic is the cause. In another strange moment, one section of rock very much resembles a human face.

The preponderance of high angle views, looking down on the girls as they make their trek to the top of the mountain, also portend that something terrible will happen when they reach the apex. It is no surprise that when the girls first enter the park with the mountain, their horses rear and all the birds fly from the trees. Something strange and evil exists there, and the animals have detected the danger.

And what of eyewitness testimony that "a red cloud" descended on the girls before they disappeared? Is that merely the hallucination of a girl suffering heat stroke? Or is it representative of something more? And why was one woman (a teacher) found undressed on the mountain? Was she raped, attacked, or merely out of her mind, breaking out of the Appleyard atmosphere of repression? Like the details of the *Stardust* mystery, these are tantalizing questions about a story with no satisfactory answers. They could be debated forever.

Picnic at Hanging Rock is a brilliant film because it can support so many interpretations. The central mystery is compelling, and every new answer only raises more questions. Is Miranda responsible for her own disappearance? Is the great rock actually a living entity? Is this really just a conventional kidnapping, but one where we never meet the perpetrators? Or is it just a stupid accident? Have the girls merely fallen down a hole, never to be found? Who knows for sure?

One thing is certain, Peter Weir understands that a basic element of human life is uncertainty. In this existence we humans share, we don't always get the answers we want, for whatever reason. We don't always know why planes crash, or why loved ones should die suddenly of heart attacks ... even though they appear healthy. The point is the uncertainty: it's the essence of who we are.

Picnic at Hanging Rock is a meditation on that uncertainty. In this author's opinion, the horror film rises to its apex of quality when it plays on the fact that humans don't really control their universe. In *The Blair Witch Project*, the audience never saw the "witch," and was never even certain if there was such a creature. Instead, the film just offered tantalizing possibilities. That same could be written about the TV series *Space: 1999,* whose central thesis was that space was a realm of mystery, and that man was not yet knowledgeable enough to be certain about all of it laws and properties. *Picnic at Hanging Rock* is comparable to these productions because it sets up a mystery, offers some bizarre clues, but finally makes no determination on what "really happened."

A running theme throughout *Picnic at Hanging Rock* is not only the battle between Christianity and paganism, but between civilization and nature. The film opens with several shots of the mountainous rock, set to the flute of Pan. This wild music is mischievous and emotional, quite a contrast to the "refined" behavior of the girls, who live by rigid school schedules and societal rules (which dictate how they dress, how they wear their hair, how they frame their words, et cetera). When unleashed into the world of Pan, the world of unfettered nature, these "restricted" girls promptly disappear, a victim of nature's chaos.

Weir stages several shots of ants, spiders and other wildlife roaming nature, going about their business, and there seems to be a comparison to man. As the disappearance asserts, man knows no more about the true nature of his world than these creatures do. Next to the rock — an eternal — man is just as small as a lizard or a koala or a spider. The girls' ordered existence cannot compete with nature's raw power. Though *Picnic at Hanging Rock* features many beautiful shots (such as a swan gliding on a golden lake), these

shots only reinforce the lure: man believes nature is beautiful and harmless, but it may be malevolent. It may take three girls on a whim, and never return them.

Picnic at Hanging Rock is not a jolt 'em, blood-and-guts horror film by any definition. It represents a much more cerebral and sedate brand of terror, but one that stays with the viewer for a long time. It tells of an enigma that can never be solved, and how the loss of that doomed expedition shattered the civilized world around the rock. Unable to confront what has happened, Mrs. Appleyard becomes an alcoholic. The confrontation with nature has scared these people because they realize they have interfaced with something that can never adequately be explained or understood.

There are so many readings possible in this film. This author knows fans that insist the film is Lovecraftian because it suggests a dark reality co-existing with our own. This author wouldn't go that far, but it's interesting to contemplate. There is simply no evidence in the film of one answer or another, but the possibilities are endless. And that makes a fascinating and beautiful film about the human condition. In *Picnic at Hanging Rock,* Peter Weir has given the genre one of its most sensual and beautiful masterpieces, while not giving the horrific elements short shrift. This is a film that is haunting in the truest sense of the word and the mystery of Picnic Rock is one that lingers. One feels drawn to see the film again and again, to look for answers, to uncover clues, to impose order on a disordered world. In encouraging his viewers to take this hypnotic journey, Weir is, ironically, asking them to confront the deepest and most frightening aspects of human nature. Uncertainty is a bitch.

Race with the Devil (1975) ✶ ✶ ✶

Critical Reception

"...a ridiculous mish-mash of a movie for people who never grew up ... one would think that Mr. Fonda and Mr. Oates had better things to do, but perhaps not."— Vincent Canby, *New York Times*, July 10, 1975.

Cast & Crew

CAST: Peter Fonda (Roger); Warren Oates (Frank Stewart); Loretta Swit (Alice Stewart); Lara Parker (Kelly); R.G. Armstrong (Sheriff Taylor); Clay Tanner (Delbert); Carol Blodgett (Ethel Henderson); Phil Hoover (Mechanic); Ricci Ware (Himself); Paul A. Partoin (Cal Mathers); James N. Harrell (Gun Shop Owner); Karen Miller (Kay); Arkey Blue (Himself); Jack Starrett (Gas Station Attendant); Wes Bishop (Deputy Dave).

CREW: 20th Century–Fox Presents a Saber-Maslansky Production, *Race with the Devil*. *Production Supervisor:* Tony Wade. *Supervising Film Editor:* Allan Jacobs. *Music:* Leonard Rosenman. *Director of Photography:* Robert Jessup. *Producer:* Wes Bishop. *Executive Producer:* Paul Maslansky. *Written by:* Lee Frost and Wes Bishop. *Directed by:* Jack Starrett. *Unit Production Manager and Assistant Director:* Fred Brost. *Second Assistant Director:* Steve Lim. *Film Editor:* John Link. *Assistant Film Editor:* Michael Cipriano. *Production Mixer:* William Randall. *Re-Recording Mixer:* Don Bossman. *Script Supervisor:* Joyce King. *Property Master:* Mark Wade. *Wardrobe:* Nancy McArdle. *Make-up:* Dottie Pearl. *Stunt Coordinator:* Paul Knuckles. *Camera Operator:* George Billiet. *Special Effects:* Richard Helmer. *Main Title Design:* Jack Cole/N. Lee Lacy and Associates. *Filmed in:* Panavision *with Color by:* Deluxe. A Saber Maslansky Production. *M.P.A.A. Rating:* PG. *Running Time:* 88 minutes.

SYNOPSIS: Motorcycle designer Frank Stewart and professional bike racer Roger, along with their two wives (Alice and Kelly), embark on a vacation in a brand new, fully-equipped recreational vehicle. Frank is not thrilled that Ginger, Kelly's pet dog, has come along too, but he copes. After a bit of driving, the girls get tired and Frank, excited about the RV's self-sufficiency, takes them off-road into a wild, but beautiful region of Texas. The two men take their motorcycles off the back of the RV for a spin, while the girls walk Ginger. The foursome then spends the night in the woods, despite the dog's agitation about something out in the night.

As midnight comes, and Roger and Frank drink the night away, they see a bonfire near a lone, gnarled tree, far across a river. They hear chanting, and see cloaked figures dancing around a fire. They linger to spy on the strangers during a naked, ceremonial dance, and then see a virgin murdered in ritualistic fashion. Unfortunately, Frank and Roger are caught spying when Alice turns on the overpowering nightlights of the RV.

Roger and Frank pack up and flee in the RV with the girls, but the angry ritual-goers attack, jumping on the RV and smashing windows. Roger beats them back after a considerable battle.

The next morning, the vacationers go to the police. They meet Sheriff Taylor, who tells them they need to go back to the exact spot where the murder occurred. The girls remain in town while the men join the police and find remnants of the bonfire in daylight. Alice and Kelly find a threatening note pinned to a window on the RV. The hieroglyphs are indecipherable, so they go to a library to translate them. They soon come to realize that the boys witnessed a black mass.

Roger and Frank return, upset with the police for not doing anything substantive about the murder. They get their RV repaired by a local mechanic, drive a bit and then stop for the night in a campground. There, Kelly feels like the locals are watching them and tells Roger she wants to go home. They go out for dinner at a restaurant and meet up with the Hendersons, a couple staying at the same motor lodge.

When they return to the RV, they find Ginger dead ... hanged from the RV's side door. The vacationers flee the motor lodge and drive far away. After quite some time, the foursome discover that poisonous snakes have been planted all through the RV. Frank crashes the RV as the serpents attack, and Roger and Frank dispatch the snakes with great difficulty. At this point, Frank and Roger search the vehicle for any further dangers and lock up for the night.

The next morning, Roger buries Ginger as Frank repairs the vehicle. Their motorcycles are ruined. Worried, they go to a local store to purchase a shotgun and then resume their journey. Unfortunately, the Satanists are not about to give up. A group of vehicles attempt to crash into the RV on the highway, boxing the RV in and ramming into it with lethal force. Frank disables one car with a gunshot, but now the race is on. Trying to escape, Frank drives the RV into an accident zone — actually another ruse by the Satanists. A group of angry cultists jump onto the RV, boarding it while it is in motion. A battle royal occurs as Frank, Roger, Alice and Kelly repel the invaders.

The foursome survive the attack. They are only 82 miles from Amarillo and safety. They pull over while there's still light to tend to the RV's damage, but relief turns to horror as the vehicle is surrounded by a circle of flames and a coven of demon worshipers...

COMMENTARY: Fouled only by a cop-out, unjustified nihilistic ending, *Race with the Devil* is a souped-up horror vehicle in love with the idea of speed. The emphasis is clearly on the "race" aspect of the title (rather than the "Devil" portion), and that is just fine. For this is a movie that moves, generating audience adrenaline via speed, stunts, action and demolition. In toto *Race with the*

Devil is 90 hair-raising minutes of cars and motorcycles jumping, dodging, weaving, colliding, rolling and jockeying for superiority on the open road. The movie's visual *modus operandi* is perfectly in tune for such a purpose: the camera frequently adopts a low angle (granting perspective of the terrain ahead and behind) or is positioned on the racing vehicles themselves (thus capturing a feel of motion and distance). Director Jack Starrett manages these technical moves in masterful fashion, and his visual (and vehicular) prowess generates one of the best and most confident chase films this side of George Miller's incredible *The Road Warrior* (1982). Here, as in that classic, daredevil men leap (in mid race) from vehicle to speeding vehicle, automobiles tumble and explode, and jeopardized protagonists dangle and swing dangerously atop their chariots, clinging for life in rousing, exciting moments.

A demolition derby of near-perfect pitch and pace, *Race with the Devil* pauses between stunts long enough for Starrett to enunciate the deeper themes of the film, specifically the issue of self-sufficiency and what that term actually means in contemporary America. Much of the early portion of the film concerns itself exclusively with the sturdiness and "reliability" of Frank Stewart's new baby, his magnificent RV. This mega-vehicle comes fully loaded with a bathroom and shower, microwave oven, refrigerator, bar, color TV and stereo, thus providing all the luxuries of home while its riders are away on the road. Yet, importantly, none of these so-called luxuries or advances is particularly helpful to the hunted tourists, who find that being self-sufficient is isolating rather than comforting. They (erroneously) believe that any place they park is "home" because the RV represents a shelter, a sanctuary. Contrarily, however, their home on wheels merely targets them as different, and isolates them from the locals.

Instead of displaying caution, for instance, Roger and Frank blunder arrogantly into the secret (satanic!) practices of the locales. Were they not buttressed by a (false) confidence that they brought the safety of home with them, they may not have so blindly stumbled into danger. All the RV really does is provide an overblown feeling of security. This is especially dangerous when push comes to shove (as it inevitably does in horror films…), because the RV, no matter how comfortable, is just an assemblage of parts … parts that will need to be serviced or repaired. It is made up of flat tires, broken headlights and the like. And, because it is large and unwieldy, the RV is not only more difficult to navigate in road combat, it is slower moving than its opponent vehicles, which hound it across Texas like sharks attacking a whale. Self-sufficient? That is a delusion, as the movie points out, since Frank's vehicle still requires gas and a pavement on which to race, and most importantly, a driver who can responsibly handle the wheel.

Like Wes Craven's *The Hills Have Eyes* (1977), *Race with the Devil* reveals the folly of attempting to bring civilization to the wild. First, the wild does not appreciate the gesture, and secondly, modern luxuries (like RVs) provide only the impression of security, not the fact, and thus grant characters a false sense of confidence.

This material is played in compelling fashion, and the choice of Peter Fonda as the film's lead is especially thought-provoking. As Captain America in *Easy Rider* (1969), Fonda represented and spoke for the American counter-culture. The motorcycle reflected his character's transient, unstable, non-traditional life. There was room only for one (not a family!) on a motorcycle, and the choice of transport offered no modern amenities (not even air-conditioning…).

Yet scarcely a half-decade later, Peter Fonda returned to the silver screen piloting an RV, the very symbol of a fat, decadent American suburbia. This surprise trade-in seems representative of something worthy of mention: the maturation process of the 1960s hippie generation into the very thirtysomethings they had vowed not to trust. The aging hippies, like the generation before, were being reined in, seduced by the American middle-class dream of wealth, suburbia, hearth and home. This process was continued in the eighties with former hippies forsaking their earlier values, becoming yuppies instead.

Though it is debatable whether Fonda's presence intentionally reflects the theme, the casting works for the movie's ethos regardless. Fonda, manning an RV instead of a hog, must surely represent a powerful value shift in mainstream contemporary society. In the 1970s, the battles of the sixties were starting to be questioned, hippies were beginning families and buying homes for the first time, and making the very change seen here. Motorcycles were out; family cars were in. So either intentionally or unintentionally, *Race with the Devil* charts a generation's coming of age at the same time the movie expresses a lack of confidence in the same generation's new vehicle of choice. Does it represent a sell-out?

Race with the Devil also reflects the paranoia of a post–Watergate America. Fonda and his friends become mired in a satanic conspiracy stretching across Texas (it's always Texas, isn't it?). This cabal of evil claims members from librarians and policemen to the government itself. The point is probably twofold. On one hand, the conspiracy and fear that "everyone is against you" reflects the fear that our lives are not in our control and that a secret agenda may be working against our best interests. Another reading, perhaps more appropriate to the text of the film, relates again to that RV. When dwelling in self-sufficient luxury, there is no need to come out and meet your neighbor. Thus everyone you meet is a stranger to you … and under suspicion. In *Race with the Devil*, what is unknown is also frightening. The local yokels wearing the cowboy hats in that country-western bar seem menacing to us (as they do to the protagonists), because they look and sound different from us, and from our ivory tower (the RV), we have no experience or comfort with their ways or customs.

There is a great deal of unique, thoughtful material in *Race with the Devil,* particularly the briefly touched on notion that in an age without religious conviction, the occult will flourish. Still, much of the good will generated by the film is undercut by a hasty, ill-considered climax. The finale, in which the parked RV is surrounded by the Satanists in a ring of fire, looks suspiciously as though the production ran out of time or money (or both). As they realize they are trapped, the four protagonists (Swit, Parker, Fonda and Oates), are seen reacting to the (off-screen) threat in slow motion photography. The problem is that their responses do not seem to fit the particular moment in the film, and appear to be lifted from earlier tense moments in the picture. So, technically at least, the ending is weak.

Secondly, the ending feels wrong on narrative and emotional grounds. So many horror films of the 1970s end on a downnote, but this should not have been one of them. The film was artfully set up as a race between good and evil, and these four characters had done nothing wrong—not even bickered with one another à la *Night of the Living Dead*—to deserve such a rotten end. So *Race with the Devil* is a movie that nicely blends an interesting thesis about luxury and isolation with rampant paranoia and well-conceived action stunts. It seems a shame to end such an entertaining accomplishment on a tone of despair, and the downbeat ending retroactively casts a pall on the remainder of this effective thriller.

The Reincarnation of Peter Proud

Cast & Crew

CAST: Michael Sarrazin (Peter Proud); Jennifer O'Neill (Ann Curtis); Margot Kidder (Marcia Curtis); Cornelia Sharpe (Nora); Paul Hecht (Dr. Goodman); Tony Stephano (Jeff); Norman Burton (Dr. Spear).
CREW: *Directed by:* J. Lee Thompson. *Written by:* Max Ehrlich. *Director of Photography:* Victor J. Kemper. *Film Editor:* Michael Anderson. *Music:* Jerry Goldsmith. *Produced by:* Frank P. Rosenberg. A Cinerama Release, distributed by American International Pictures. *M.P.A.A. Rating:* R. *Running Time:* 104 minutes.

DETAILS: Previous lives and reincarnation are the subject matter of *The Reincarnation of Peter Proud.* The titular hero, a college professor, starts having disturbing dreams about events only foggily remembered. His quest takes him across the United States to a small town, where a horrible crime of passion was committed some thirty five years earlier.

Shivers (aka *They Came from Within; The Parasite Murders*) (1975) ✶ ✶ ✶

Critical Reception

"...a strong science-fiction/horror mixture with disgusting images never before witnessed.... Cronenberg's continuing theme is science gone mad for science's sake.... The writer/director explores that concept with exploitative glee. Nothing is too outrageous for Cronenberg to conceive and film."—Richard Meyers, SF 2, *Citadel Press*, 1984, page 31.

"It's apparent that someone connected with *They Came from Within* has an impertinent sense of humor even though the film is so tackily written and directed, so darkly photographed and the sound so dimly recorded that it's difficult to stay with it.—Vincent Canby, *New York Times*, July 7, 1976, page 46.

"The contrast between the clinical world of the Starliner complex and its casually promiscuous inhabitants turned into sex fiends by the rapidly spreading parasites is brilliantly captured by Cronenberg. The special effects ... are unusually shocking, not for their goriness in particular, but because they make visible and concrete the sense of uncleanness associated with the transmission of venereal disease."— Phil Hardy, *The Film Encyclopedia: Science Fiction*, 1984, page 320.

"Cult horror with only the gore to sustain it for anyone other than Cronenberg anoraks."—Howard Maxford, *The A to Z of Horror Films*, Indiana University Press, 1997, page 25.

Cast & Crew

CAST: Paul Hampton (Dr. Roger St. Luc); Joe Silver (Linsky); Lynn Lowry (Forsythe); Alan Migleovsky (Nicholas Tuder); Susan Petrie (Janine Tuder); Ronald Miodak (Merrick); Camille Cucharme (Mr. Guilbault); Wally Martin (Doorman); Charles Perley (Delivery Boy); Barry Baldero (Detective Heller); Harika Posnansko (Mrs. Guilbault); Vrasta Vrana (Kresimer Suibeh); Al Rosenman (Parkins); Julie Wildman (Miss Lewis); Edith Johnson (Olive); Joy Coghill (Mona Wheatley); Fred Doederieien (Emil Hobbes); Arthur Grosser (Mr. Wolfe); Dorothy Davis (Vi); Joan Blackman (Elevator Mother); Sonny Forbes (Garbage Room Man); Barbara Steele (Betts); Silvie Debois (Brenda Suiben); Kursten Bishoprio (Elevator Daughter); Nora Johnson (Laundry Woman); Cathy Graham (Annabelle); Robert Bremen (Boy); Ron Whitten (Bearded Man); Denis Payne (First Elevator Man); Kevin Fenlow (Second Elevator Man).

CREW: John Dunning and Andre Link present a DAL-Reitman production, *Shivers*. *Director of photography:* Robert Saad. *Special Make-up and Creatures by:* Joe Blasco. *Editor:* Patrick Dodd. *Sound Supervisor:* Dan Goldberg. *Production Manager:* Don Carmody. *Music Supervisor:* Ivan Reitman. *Executive Producer:* Alfred Parisier. *Producer:* Ivan Reitman. *Written and Directed by:* David Cronenberg. *Stunts:* Fournier Ereres. *Continuity:* Diane Boucher. *Production Assistant:* Stewart Harding, Cliff Rothman. *First Assistant Camera:* Rick Maguire, Yves Drapeau. *Assistant to Joe Blasco:* David Dittmer. *Make-up:* Suzanne Riou Garand. *Make-up Assistant:* Louisette Champagne. *Art Director:* Eric Giserman. *Art Assistant:* Rose Marie McSherry. *Sound Studios:* Microphonic Sound. *Lab:* Quebec Film Labs. *M.P.A.A. Rating:* R. *Running Time:* 100 minutes.

P.O.V.

"A lot of people pointed out a similarity between the parasite in *Alien* and the parasite in *Shivers*. I was disappointed in *Alien* … the parasite device isn't used in a metaphorical way…. In *Shivers*, the parasite stays inside the people and changes their behavior and their motives. It's used for … more than simple shock value" (26).— Director David Cronenberg comments on the similarities between his low-budget *Shivers* (1975) and mega-hit *Alien* (1979).

SYNOPSIS: Something strange is happening at the Star Liner Apartments, a housing complex of the future replete with all the amenities one could desire. In one apartment (#15), a middle-aged man murders a young girl, using a scalpel first to dissect her and then to search for something in her stomach. The murderer is Dr. Hobbs, and he kills himself after committing the atrocity.

The police investigate and Dr. St. Luc (resident physician at Star Liner Apts.) learns that Hobbs had a grant involving new organ-replacement experiments. Apparently, he was breeding parasites that would dissolve failing organs and then replace them, performing their functions as a perfect substitute. Dr. St. Luc suspects something has gone badly wrong with the experiment.

Meanwhile, Nick, a resident at the complex who had sex with the dead girl, comes home from work feeling sick. His wife, Janine, is concerned about him because of a fatty cyst he has developed. Nick won't go to see a specialist, so Janine sees Dr. St. Luc to report Nick's symptoms. At the same time, her husband has a seizure and throws up in the bathtub. A slimy organism slithers down the drain. Later, the grisly worm-like parasite attacks and kills a fat woman in the laundry room.

St. Luc investigates and learns that the dead girl was apparently quite promiscuous, having sex with a number of males at the apartment complex. All those men are now reporting lumps in their stomach, evidence of a sexually transmitted disease … or parasite. An associate of Dr. Hobbs' reports to St. Luc that his parasite is actually a combination of aphrodisiac and venereal disease, which has the effect of making people highly libidinous (so the parasite can spread…).

In one apartment, a parasite comes up a bathtub drain and slides between a female tenant's legs, entering her body through the exposed vagina. The parasitic infection spreads exponentially at Star Liner, turning people all over the campus into crazed rapists. One infected man tries to rape St. Luc's nurse, Forsythe, but she stabs him and escapes his advances. Meanwhile, Nick tries to force himself on Janine to spread the parasite, but Janine refuses. The parasite then evacuates through Nick's mouth.

Before long, the parasitic infection in the apartment complex has reached epidemic proportions. The phones are out, the hallways are dangerous and roving gangs of rapists, desperate to spread their infection, roam from apartment to apartment. Nurse Forsythe and Dr. St. Luc attempt to flee, but the parking garage doors are closed and all the exits are blocked. Before long, it becomes clear that Forsyth is now infected, and St. Luc knocks her out to prevent his own infection. Before long, St. Luc is hopelessly outnumbered. He attempts to escape via the pool room, but the night is filled with the infected. As St. Luc falls into the pool, he is surrounded by the zombies. He receives the kiss of infection from Forsythe.

The next morning, a line of cars drive out of Star Liner apartments, and the sexual predators seek new game in the city.

COMMENTARY: *Shivers* (or *They Came from Within*) is a fascinating variation on George Romero's influential *Night of the Living Dead* (1968). Like that film, *Shivers* features a closed-off setting and a mob of crazed villains (who are intent on devouring their prey). But where the two films differ is in focus. For Romero, his zombies are a method by which to debate the rise and fall of human society and the beginning of a new (anti-social) order. Director David Cronenberg reveals with *Shivers* (and in fact with his later film in the '70s, *Rabid*) that he is obsessed mostly with sex and the perceived fall-out of various sexual issues (such as infidelity, sexually transmitted diseases, pedophilia, and the like). *Shivers* concerns misguided science, man as the victim of his hormones, and a closed community in peril, but mostly it is about those things (including disease) that are carried along with the process of human sexual coupling.

Cronenberg opens the film with an advertisement for Star Liner Apartments, the setting for all the terror to come. This promotion reveals parking lots, fully equipped kitchens, heated Olympic-sized swimming pools, tennis courts, and golf courses. These apartments of the future also feature the trappings of a modern-day village including a delicatessen, a boutique, a dentist's office, and medical clinics. This advertisement for Star Liners saves Cronenberg the trouble of having to include all of the exposition in the text of the film. Instead, he gets it out of the way in a clever commercial, and establishes immediately how truly isolated and "self-sustaining" Star Liner is. This is important, because containment is a critical issue in the film.

From there, *Shivers* descends into a shocking series of vicious attacks. In one sequence an apparently crazed old man attacks a young, school-age girl. He strangles her, then throws her on a table, cuts her open, and pours acid in her open wound. Then he cuts his own throat. These violent, horrid images immediately, and rather thoroughly contrast with the "perfect world" envisioned by the preceding TV advertisement, revealing a harsh reality underneath the appearance of things.

Delightfully, Cronenberg is not interested in static interpretations of his symbols. His images represent different things at different points in the film. At the commencement of *Shivers*, the audience is horrified by the old man's brutal act against a

seemingly innocent child. But before long, Cronenberg has established that the "innocent" schoolgirl was actually a sexually promiscuous host to a terrible parasite, and that her murder … if unsavory … was necessary if infection of the community was to be prevented. Of course, it is already too late, and this is just the first of many deaths.

But even this sequence is but a prelude to the true horror of the film. The scientist (named Hobbes) has bred an organism, a parasite that is transmitted through sex. This worm-like monster (which resembles human fecal matter both in shape and shading…) goes from person to person, husband to wife, lover to lover, in rapid succession. This rapid-fire spread of the "disease" reveals how quickly an infection can be transmitted in a closed community, and one is reminded of a 1999 story about the 60 children in one American town who contracted syphilis after a few rounds of casual sex.

At work in *Shivers* is Cronenberg's fear of sexually transmitted diseases. The queasiness one feels about venereal disease, herpes, AIDS or any other "bug" is granted physical, visual form as this parasite, and Cronenberg unflinchingly reveals it passing from person to person, worming its way into new "partners."

Accordingly, the film's gross-out factor is quite high. In one nauseating moment, a man vomits over his apartment ledge, and a bloody lump (the parasite) is ejected, striking an old lady's umbrella with a watery splat some levels below. Barbara Steele, luxuriating in a bathtub, is caught unaware as a parasite travels up the drain into the tub and swims between her legs. As it penetrates her, the bath water turns bloody. It's all quite graphic, but purposeful. There are consequences to "random" sexual encounters, says *Shivers*, and with the parasite's fatal and bizarre consequences the film, sadly, forecasts the AIDS era (the 1980s) — when sexual encounters could literally prove lethal.

Clearly, *Shivers* fits into the "topical" horror of the 1970s. Just as *It's Alive* openly worried about how the new age of pollution,

X-rays, and nuclear power might change the human condition, *Shivers* asks its audience to contemplate what dangers may be hidden in the sexual act. Is there a dark side to the pleasure? Is "casual" sex dangerous, as well as immoral? In *Shivers*, sexual urges turn people into rapists, pervert morals, and spread sickness. In one harrowing sequence, a daughter watches as her mother is sexually assaulted in an elevator. Later the same child, now infected, seduces a guard, spreading the evil. Even innocence, corrupted by sex, can be infected.

The reason *Shivers* may not be a great film is that after the apartments has been overrun by the infected, the story stops, and the plot becomes a poor variation on *Night of the Living Dead*, with two heroes trying to escape from a mob of the "zombies." Up to that point, *Shivers* is thought-provoking, scary and original, so the retread plot is a disappointment. And, the protagonists are not terribly bright. A great deal of time in the finale seems spent without any sense of narrative purpose or objective. Doctor St. Luc and Nurse Forsyth go down to the basement, up to the apartments, over to a phone, down to the garage, and so on. They have legitimate reasons for all their actions, but in a film like this it should be a choice between hiding or fleeing. Instead, these two medical professionals buzz all over the Star Line complex, continually putting themselves in new dangers.

Much has been made of the fact that *Shivers* forecasts *Alien* (1979) by depicting a wormlike entity that jumps on people's faces, and then perverts them from within. That argument holds only so much water. The so-called "face hugger" of *Shivers* appears only once (jumping out of a laundry machine) and that act of attachment does not seem to typify the lifecycle of the sexual parasite. In *Alien*, the face hugger morphs into chest-burster, and then into a giant, malevolent humanoid organism. It is a distinct and separate cycle. There may be some surface similarities, but to say that *Alien* "copies" *Shivers* is an exaggeration. *Alien* also benefits from compelling, recognizable human characters, a factor *Shivers* may have benefited from. The story, its implications, and even its final turn, the spread of the infection beyond Star Liner, works beautifully, but the characters are never smart enough, or easy enough to identify with.

The Stepford Wives (1975) ✶ ✶ ✶ ✶

Critical Reception

"The best social horror movies achieve their effect by implication, and *The Stepford Wives*, by showing us only the surface of things and never troubling to explain exactly how these things are done, implies plenty."—Stephen King, *Danse Macabre*, a Berkley Book, 1981, page 168.

"...a well-made, entertaining movie. On a certain level the film works successfully, building up an effective mood of paranoia and tension ... but as science fiction ... it doesn't quite work."—John Brosnan, *Future Tense*, St. Martin's Press, 1978, page 230.

"Writer Goldman and director Forbes have done workmanlike jobs in pumping some life and even some entertainment into Levin's one-gimmick book, but they are somewhat at cross-purposes. Goldman sees an opportunity to satirize middle-class mores.... Forbes, on the other hand, sees an opportunity for serious suspense ... it aspires to be a woman's lib parable ... but it is too glibly on the side of the fashionable angels."—Richard Schickel, *Time*: "Women's Glib," March 3, 1975, page 6.

"…what happens … makes for an interesting satire and a horror story about the relations of men and women today, although … both male and female proponents won't find the film convincing…. But the film is entertaining, with some wildly funny moments … it's well-paced and has good acting."— Dorothy Somers, *Films in Review*, Volume XXVI, Number 4, April 1975, page 247.

Cast and Crew

CAST: Katharine Ross (Joanna); Paula Prentiss (Bobby); Peter Masterson (Walter); Nanette Newman (Carol); Tina Louise (Charmaine); Carol Bossen (Dr. Fancher); William Prince (Ike Mazzara); Carole Mallory (Kit Sanderson); Toni Reid (Marie Axhelm); Judith Baldwin (Mrs. Cornell); Barbara Rucker (Marie Ann Stavros); George Coe (Claude Axhelm); Franklin Cover (Ed Wimpiris); Robert Fields (Raymond Chandler); Michael Higgins (Mr. Cornell); Josef Somer (Ted Van Sant); Paula Trueman (Welcome Wagon Lady); Martha Greenhouse (Mrs. Kirgassa); Simon Deckard (David Markowe); Remak Ramsay (Mr. Atkinson); Mary Stuart Masterson (Kim); Ronny Sullivan (Amy); John Aprea (Young Cop); Matt Russo (Moving Man #1); Anthony Crup (Moving Man #2); Keith McMillan (Market Manager); Dee Wallace (Nettie the Maid); Tom Spratley (Doorman); Patrick O'Neal (Dale Coba).

CREW: Palomar Pictures International Presents *The Stepford Wives*. *Based on a Novel by:* Ira Levin. *Costume Designer:* Anna Hill Johnstone. *Film Editor:* Timothy Gee. *Production Design:* Gene Callahan. *Director of Photography:* Owen Roizman. *Music Composed and Conducted by:* Michael Small. *Associate Producer:* Roger M. Rothstein. *Executive Producer:* Gustave M. Berne. *Screenplay:* William Goldman. *Produced by:* Edgar J. Scherick. *Directed by:* Bryan Forbes. *Camera Operator:* Enrique Bravo. *Drawings by:* Don Bachardy. *Casting:* Juliet Taylor. *First Assistant Director:* Peter Scoppa. *Second Assistant Director:* Mike Haley. *Unit Manager:* Neil Machlis. *Titles:* Robert Ellis. *First Assistant Camera:* Tom Priestly. *Make-up Artist:* Andy Ciannella. *Hairdresser:* Romaine Greene. *Wardrobe:* George Newman, Peggy Farrell. *Script Supervisor:* B.J. Bjorkman. *Set Decorator:* Robert Drumheller. *Property Master:* Joseph M. Caracciolo. *Sound Mixer:* James Sabat. *Re-recording Mixer:* Dick Vorisek. *Assistant Editor:* Patrick McMahon. *Scenic Artist:* Stanley Cappiello. *Second Assistant Camera:* Gary Muller. *Sound Editor:* Janet Davidson. *Electronic Music Realized by:* Suzanne Ciani. *Locations by:* Cine Mobile Systems. *Color:* TVC. A Fadsin Cinema Association Production. *M.P.A.A. Rating:* R. *Running Time:* 120 minutes.

SYNOPSIS: The Eberharts move from the hustle and bustle of New York City to the sheltered village of Stepford. Walter Eberhart's wife, Joanna, is an amateur photographer, and none too thrilled about the move, partially because Walter didn't bother to consult her about it. Joanna comes to feel isolated in the big house in the country, and these feelings worsen when Walter joins a "men's only" association in Stepford.

At the local grocery story, the Eberharts witness a car accident in which a strange neighbor, Mrs. Van Sant, is jostled. After the incident, she starts behaving erratically: repeating stock phrases, and acting in almost mechanical fashion. Joanna takes note of the odd behavior, as well as the fact that the ambulance carts Ms. Van Sant in the opposite direction from the town hospital. Joanna's suspicions about Stepford grow when Walter returns from the Men's Club initiation in tears. He brushes off his behavior, and does not share with his wife what has upset him.

Soon, Joanna makes her first friend in Stepford, another transplanted city woman named Bobby. This friendship makes Joanna's transition easier, and she is even receptive when Walter invites members of his men's group over for a meeting late one night. One of the male guests is "Diz," Dale Coba, who used to work at Disneyland and now heads the Men's Association. The men seem to take a special interest in Joanna, and one gentleman even sketches her. After the party, Joanna fights with Walter about the men, who she thinks are humorless boors.

Then, there is a party at Diz's house, and Bobby and Joanna again run into Mrs. Van Sant, who is speaking in the same stock phrases as on the day of the accident. The next day, she goes around town apologizing for her behavior, claiming to be a recovering alcoholic. Her apology, driven by the men of the town, infuriates Joanna and spurs her to think about forming a women's lib group. Interestingly, none of the women in Stepford seem remotely interested in the idea. On the contrary, they are too busy baking, cleaning and raising children to worry about civil rights. Still, Bobby and Joanna enlist one local, the flamboyant Charmain. She is tired of the Men's Association too, and all too eager to stir up a bit of trouble. Joanna enlists other town women only after she refuses to help with a Men's Association "dialect" project.

Unfortunately, at the first meeting of the women's group, the Stepford wives are interested only in talking about how to more efficiently complete their housework. An increasingly suspicious Joanna takes a walk one night, and finds the mansion where the Men's Association meets. She is warned away from the property by a policeman. The next day, Joanna and Bobby meet with Charmain only to find she has suddenly changed. Where she was once an opinionated, assertive human being, she is now a loyal and dutiful servant who supports her husband without question, without thought even. This transformation disturbs Joanna and Bobby, and they begin to fear that something in the water is turning women into drones.

With the aid of Joanna's old boyfriend, a chemist, the water is tested ... and found to be fine. Desperate, Bobby determines to move out of Stepford before she is a victim of the plague that turns women into subservient sex objects. Joanna makes the same decision and begs Walter to move. He acquiesces, and promises to move from Stepford in August, just two months away.

Before long, Joanna loses another critical ally. She meets with Bobby only to learn that Bobby isn't Bobby anymore. She now wears make-up in the kitchen, serves as a maid to her husband, and is unwilling to leave Stepford. Panicked, Joanna asks Walter to move again, and then sees a psychologist about her fears. The psychologist is supportive and tells Joanna to leave Stepford as soon as possible if she feels endangered. Empowered, Joanna returns home to take her children from Walter, but he has sent them away. Worse, he has been drinking and is violent with Joanna when she refuses to go to bed.

While Walter is on the phone, talking in hushed tones, Joanna sneaks out into the rainy night to find her children. She seeks help from Bobby, and ends up stabbing her one-time friend with a kitchen knife. Amazingly, Bobby does not bleed. Instead, she starts to malfunction, as if some bizarre automaton. Still hoping to find her children, Joanna finds herself at the Men's Association mansion. She walks into a trap orchestrated by "Diz" Coba, a man who once designed "smart" animatronic robots for Disney attractions. He informs her that he has been waiting for her, and that her change will be "just perfect" for Walter and for her. Desperate not to meet the same fate as Charmaine and Bobby, Joanna runs for her life, and ends up confronting an exact replica of herself, a robot. There, at a make-up table, a robot duplicate of Joanna sits ready, with black, soulless eyes and abnormally enlarged breasts. Shocked, Joanna is killed by her "replacement."

Later, at a grocery store, Joanna, Bobby, Charmain and all the robot wives of Stepford enjoy their day out ... thinking only how they can best serve their men. Life goes on in Stepford, after a peculiar fashion.

COMMENTARY: It's a man's world. No matter how far the "equal rights" movement has come, that's a basic truth of our lives, even in the 21st century. Has there ever been a female president of the United States? A woman vice president? Do women receive an "equal day's pay" for an equal day's work? Unfortunately, the answer is no in all cases. In fact, even in 2001 some very powerful men believe they should be able to control a woman's reproductive choices, that they should have final say over what she does with her own biology, her own body. In the 1970s, the situation was, if anything, worse. The Equal Rights Amendment was torpedoed, and though advertisements shouted "you've come a long way, baby," that simply wasn't the case. The trend that occurred in the '70s, with the proliferation of the birth control pill and a more lax moral attitude about sexual liaisons, was actually self-serving for men. They got to have more intercourse with more women, with fewer consequences (such as pregnancy). If that was the "yardstick" for equality in America, then the definition was sadly lacking.

Out of this context of the "war between the sexes" comes *The Stepford Wives*, a socially minded horror film that sees (and ridicules) the male hierarchy that dominated (and dominates) the United States. The film is a sort of re-vamp of *Invasion of the Body Snatchers* (1956), with the casualty here being not the whole human race, but the female population of suburban America. They are secretly "changed," and their wills subverted by the Men's Association of the little town of Stepford. But *The Stepford Wives'* true strength is that it expertly fosters viewer sympathy with its lead character, Joanna. As played by Katharine Ross, Joanna is so likeable an individual that the viewer understands immediately what is at stake for her in Stepford. For her to conform to the "simple" roles of women in that town would be worse than death for her. It would be the loss of her identity, her individuality, and that is a horror that every human, male or female, understands implicitly.

Directed by Bryan Forbes, *The Stepford Wives* is actually a film essay about what it means to be part of an unspoken "underclass." This is Joanna's picture, and it is clear

that she is a second class citizen in her own country. The film opens with Joanna sitting alone near her apartment's window. The staging of the shot indicates her isolation and loneliness. She is being forced to move out of the city against her will, and the window separates her from the thriving world she wishes to be a part of. The image of a woman sitting alone in silence is one to meditate about. It is an insightful visual because it reveals that Joanna is upset and lonely, but also that she is thinking. She is pondering her situation in that shot, and that is a critical point to make. Joanna is a thinker, a contemplator, as the film takes special measures to remind us, and her intelligence will be lost if Stepford has its way.

From that opening, Joanna is forced to move to Stepford, where she finds herself knocking about alone in a vast, empty house. Her husband, Walter, treats her as a child, not allowing her to play a part in the family decisions. *He* decided to move. *He* decided on the particular house to buy. *He* joined the Men's Association. Like the men of Stepford, Walter sees himself as the ultimate authority in the family, the wise patriarch responsible for taking care of his wife and children. He doesn't see or understand that Joanna wants a hand in her own destiny. Joanna is trapped in a marriage to a man that doesn't share responsibility and decisions with her. She regrets the decision to marry him because she was once in love with a chemist. She believed Walter would become "Perry Mason," but he didn't.

Interestingly, the movie also bashes Joanna's former lover, Raymond Chandler. She loved him once, but he's an asshole now. The point is plain: a woman can't depend on a man to live up to the values and ideals he espouses. Ultimately, a man wants a woman to be a servant to his needs, and Joanna's independent voice cannot thrive in such a set-up.

Commendably, there's a deeper level to *The Stepford Wives*. Joanna is not defined, as women so often are in our society, by her desire to have children, to be a mother. To the contrary, Joanna has aspirations to be an artist. "I want to be remembered," she notes of her art. That puts her on "equal" territory with males. Don't men often note that they want accomplishments of their own, achievements outside of marriage and a family? That element is what makes Joanna special: she doesn't see herself as her society would. Children are not the end-all and be-all for her as a human being. The intellectual pursuit of art and photography, and the need for a professional legacy inform her character ... just as we would stereotypically expect them to do a man's. The film's success is that it makes plain and tangible Joanna's feelings of emptiness, and her desire to have the same things men automatically expect to get in this life.

In horror, terror is always much more effective when an identifiable human character is at the heart of the situation. *The Stepford Wives* is so splendid a film because its protagonist is not just a big blank mark in the middle of the action that is swept along by circumstances. She is an individual, a person, and that makes her ultimate fate (the removal of all that individuality) doubly terrifying.

The Stepford Wives must concern itself with more than Joanna, however, if it is to work as a "conspiracy" thriller, and fortunately, it does. The film has a wicked, but not far off, view of men. The Men's Association of Stepford re-programs all the women to serve husbands' needs. Men have simple needs: they want food, a clean house, and sex. Accordingly, all the women are "revised" to serve those basic desires. "I'll just die if I don't get this recipe," one Stepford wife, Mrs. Van Sant, repeats constantly, as if her husband's stomach is the most important thing in the world.

"Nobody's ever touched me the way you have, Frank," another Stepford wife moans as her husband makes love to her. "You're the king, Frank! You're the champion! You're the master!" she continues. This scene is not only funny, but it points out every man's fantasy: to be worshipped in bed. The Men's Association has arranged for that too.

Women have literally become sex slaves with no significant need beyond tending to the fragile egos of their husbands.

When people that Joanna knows start to change in Stepford, the *Invasion of the Body Snatchers* template comes into full play, but again the concept has been re-wired to accommodate sexual politics. People start to "change," and the "altered" women become the equivalent of the alien pods in *Body Snatchers*. One day Bobby's face and very figure are different. Her vocabulary is smaller, and she is nothing but a sexy house maid. Worse, she does not even realize that a change has occurred. She is a pod, a walking-talking imitation without a soul. It's a chilling premise, and the conspiracy and horror elements of *The Stepford Wives* are carried out brilliantly. There are some echoes of *Rosemary's Baby* since the horror involves a treacherous husband, a seemingly "paranoiac" wife, and a malevolent conspiracy.

The film even revives an old Gothic tradition by setting its headquarters of evil in a dark old mansion. There, Joanna comes face to face with a malevolent Doppelgänger. The setting and the situation (the "evil" double) reflect the anti-rational tenets of Gothic literature, and the "uncovering" of the town's dark secret also plays into that literary tradition.

Even in the horror, however, there is appropriate humor. Joanna's Doppelgänger is both terrifying (with black pools for eyes) and humorous because her breasts are much, much larger than those with which Katharine Ross has naturally been endowed. In other words, Walter wanted his "new" wife that way...

The final scene of *The Stepford Wives* is surreal, but terrifying in its implications. The women, including Joanna, are dressed to the hilt, strolling through a grocery store. They are serving men in their actions and appearance ... and utterly untroubled by their enslavement. This downbeat ending indicates that the male-controlled society is ultimately victorious, in life and in film. Eventually, you can't fight city hall, and the "change" overcomes you, for whatever reason. It may be societal pressure to conform, or it may be evil Doppelgänger robots.

The real terror of *The Stepford Wives* is best expressed in Joanna's fear mid-way through the picture when she realizes that her very soul, her identity, is truly at stake. She is aware that under the new regime she will cook and clean, but no longer be herself. She won't be a photographer any more, because that "hobby" is not as important to her husband as having a "maid" who cleans the house and calls him "the champion" in bed. Joanna understand that there are things that make us all special only to ourselves, and that those are the very things she will lose when "converted" into a Stepford wife. That's why the situation is universal beyond the male-female issue. Forbes was wise to make Joanna so interesting and strong a character. In her, the audience sees not just a woman, but humanity, and that makes the film's point about sex issues all the more powerful.

The Stepford Wives is a great horror film, and one of the best of the 1970s. It not only satirizes 1970s sexual politics, it does so with wit and scares. No doubt some conservative elements would see nothing wrong with the lives of the Stepford wives and would attack the film as liberal — but that's the point isn't it? One has to wonder if all the male critics who called the film poppycock were not willing to face their own role in furthering a male-dominated patriarchy. This film acknowledges uncomfortable truths for men, and it does so in a humorous, artful way. That should have been enough for crit-

ics, but the film was mostly dismissed as tongue in cheek during its release. Though humor is part of Forbes' arsenal in *The Stepford Wives,* the film is anything but tongue in cheek. But, as is appropriate, audiences had the last word about the film. Today, more than twenty-five years after it was released, the term "Stepford wife" is cultural shorthand, a part of America's modern lexicon. The film so powerfully made its point about sexual politics that, even if critics were unwilling to appreciate or laud it, the film nonetheless achieved immortality.

In the film, Joanna notes that she "wanted to be remembered" for what she achieved and what she stood for, not the clothes she wore or the children she bore. She'd be happy to know that *The Stepford Wives* has achieved that very legacy. It is a brilliantly visualized and conceived horror film, and so daring that it could only have been produced in the '70s.

LEGACY: Though followed by a series of inferior TV movies including *Return of the Stepford Wives* (1980) and *The Stepford Children* (1988), this film remains a horror landmark. It is a movie that has entered the pop culture lexicon with a vengeance. Everybody knows what it means to be from "Stepford," or a "Stepford wife," so the movie clearly captured (and still captures) the imagination of a nation. A 1997 horror film, *Disturbing Behavior,* delicately modified the Stepford formula, only this time with high school students. A remake of *The Stepford Wives* has been announced.